Cover

Christ's Entry into Jerusalem

"The next day the large crowd that had come to the feast heard that Jesus was coming to Jerusalem. So they took branches of palm trees and went out to meet him, crying out, 'Hosanna! Blessed is he who comes in the name of the Lord'" John 12:12–13a c. 1508–1509.

"Los luteranos entendemos que la razón para nuestra práctica está en aquello que creemos, enseñamos y confesamos. Por tanto no podemos pensar en cómo lidiar con el sufrimiento fuera de un ministerio en Palabra y Sacramentos. Fuera de Cristo, su propio sufrimiento vicario, perdón y compasión.

Hace tiempo que las iglesias luteranas necesitamos encontrar la motivación para servir al que sufre desde una confesionalidad genuina. Por lo que valoro muchísimo este libro, que asumió el desafío de compilar en un sólo volumen escritos sobre Misericordia desde Lutero hasta hoy.

Cuán bello y esperanzador es saber que la iglesia no olvida al ser humano que sufre en cuerpo y alma, centrados en la gracia de Cristo, con la que fuimos alcanzados. Para entender que una verdadera obra de misericordia es el resultado de la acción de Dios en el medio del caos del mundo."

— Rev. Cristian Rautenberg
President of the Confessional Lutheran Church of Chile

"Lutherans believe that the reason for our practice is in what we believe, teach and confess. Therefore, we cannot think how to deal with suffering outside of the ministry of Word and Sacrament — outside of Christ and His own vicarious suffering, forgiveness and compassion.

Lutherans need to find the motivation from a genuine confession to serve those who are suffering. I very much value this book, which took on the challenge of compiling, in a single volume, the writings on mercy from Luther until today.

How beautiful and encouraging it is to know that the church does not forget humans that suffer in body and spirit, centered in the grace of Christ, with which we are made. We understand that a true work of mercy is the result of God's action in the midst of the chaos of the world."

— English translation by Aaron Nielsen

"The Church is a mercy place because Jesus, who is the Merciful One, is there caring for the needs of His people through the hands of the Church. As one of the articles in this jewel of a book states, "The Church is a mercy place." Yet for too long, the importance of mercy has been misunderstood. This book clears up any misunderstandings and rightfully demonstrates that a church without mercy is a church without Jesus."

— Rev. Dr. Robert Bennett
Executive director of Luther Academy and international mission specialist/guest professor of Mission at Concordia Theological Seminary, Fort Wayne, Ind.

"Mercy is the love that flows from justification through faith by the gifts of Christ on the cross; it is expressed in the Christian life in a "free, willing and joyful way to serve others without reward perspective" (Luther). "Truly, I say to you, as you did it to one of the least of these my brothers, you did it to me," Christ says (Matt. 25:40).

Undoubtedly, *Mercy in Action* is the most important and relevant work in confessional Lutheran theology on mercy, bringing together the best Lutheran theologians of all time. This collection of essays supplies a great need for confessional Lutheran literature for theological education and the work of the Lutheran church in the world.

We celebrate Christ as a gift by His death on the cross and His mercy for the life of the world, and we celebrate Him as a work of mercy for God's people!"

— Rev. Sergio Fritzler
President of Concordia Seminary, Buenos Aires, Argentina

Mercy in Action:
Essays on Mercy, Human Care and Disaster Response

Mercy in Action:
Essays on Mercy, Human Care and Disaster Response

Compiled and Edited by Rev. Ross Edward Johnson
Introduction by Rev. Dr. Matthew C. Harrison

THE LUTHERAN CHURCH-MISSOURI SYNOD, SAINT LOUIS

Table of Contents

Contributors

DEACONESS SARA M. BIELBY graduated from Concordia Theological Seminary, Fort Wayne, Ind., in 2004 with a Master of Arts degree in Exegetical and Systematic Theology. She received her deaconess training from the Concordia University Chicago Deaconess Colloquy Program and also from Concordia Theological Seminary, where she was granted deaconess certification in 2005. She served as associate director of the Deaconess Program at Concordia Theological Seminary from 2004 to 2005. In 2006, she received a call to Immanuel Lutheran Church in Monroe, Mich., where she also serves students at University Lutheran Chapel on the campus of the University of Michigan in Ann Arbor.

THEODORE JULIUS BROHM (1808–1881) was born in Oberwinkel, Germany, near Saxony, and he studied in Leipzig. Brohm was the personal secretary to Martin Stephan and migrated with the Saxons to Perry County, Mo. He was a co-founder of Concordia College in Altenburg, which later moved to St. Louis and became Concordia Seminary. Brohm became close personal friends with C.F.W. Walther and served as vice-president of The Lutheran Church—Missouri Synod (LCMS) between 1851 and 1874.

MARTIN CHEMNITZ (1522–1586) is known as the "Second Martin." He was a prolific author, and is best known for writing the *Formula of Concord, Loci, The Two Natures in Christ, Examination of the Council of Trent* and *Enchiridion*.

REV. DR. ALBERT B. COLLVER III is director of Church Relations. He graduated from Concordia University, Ann Arbor, Mich., with a bachelor's degree and earned his M.Div., S.T.M. and Ph.D. in Systematic Theology from Concordia Seminary, St. Louis. After graduating with his Ph.D., he served in the parish and taught at Concordia University, Ann Arbor. From 2006 to September 2010, he served as executive pastoral assistant for LCMS World Relief and Human Care. In addition, he has taught at both Concordia Theological Seminary, Fort Wayne, Ind., and Concordia Seminary, St. Louis, and has written extensively. Collver has visited Lutheran churches in more than 50 countries and serves as the executive secretary for the International Lutheran Council.

REV. DR. CARL C. FICKENSCHER II is dean of Pastoral Education and Certification, director of the Specific Ministry Pastor (SMP) Program and professor of Pastoral Ministry and Missions at Concordia Theological Seminary, Fort Wayne, Ind. He has a bachelor's degree in Political Science and a Master of Business Administration, as well as a Master of Divinity degree from Concordia Theological Seminary. Fickenscher pursued his doctoral degree at Southwestern Baptist Theological Seminary, receiving a Ph.D. in Homiletics in 1996, making him the first man in the LCMS to hold a Ph.D. in this field. In addition, Fickenscher is editor of *Concordia Pulpit Resources*, the Synod's preaching journal published by Concordia Publishing House. He has published numerous articles, essays, sermons and curricular pieces, and he received an award from Concordia Historical Institute in 2012 for a series of articles on the preaching of C.F.W. Walther.

JOHANN GERHARD (1582–1637) is known as the "Archtheologian of Lutheranism" and was the most influential of the 17th-century theologians. Gerhard was, after Luther and Chemnitz, "the third after which there is no fourth." He is well known for his books *Loci Theologici* and *Meditationes Sacrae (Sacred Meditations)*. Some have said that *Sacred Meditations* is the greatest devotional literature ever produced.

ADOLF VON HARNACK (1851–1930) was a professor of Church History at Leipzig, Giessen, Marburg and Berlin. Well known for his 1900 lectures on "The Essence of Christianity," he published the three-volume set *History of Dogma* in 1885. Harnack reduced Christianity to "the fatherhood of God and the brotherhood of man." He rejected the atonement in favor of ethics. He believed that little of what the Gospels attribute to Jesus was actually spoken or done by Him but rather was invented by the disciples. However, as a historian, Harnack's *The Mission and Expansion of the Christian Church* is an excellent work on how the church combined missiology and *diakonia* in its corporate task.

REV. DR. MATTHEW C. HARRISON is the 13th person to serve as president of the 2.3-million-member Lutheran Church—Missouri Synod. As president, Harrison serves as the chief ecclesiastical officer of the LCMS, supervising the doctrine taught and practiced; representing the LCMS with its partner church bodies throughout the world; and overseeing all officers, executives and agencies of the LCMS.

Before becoming president, Harrison served for nine years as the executive director of LCMS World Relief and Human Care. During that time, LCMS World Relief and Human Care coordinated the $14 million LCMS response to Hurricane Katrina and the multimillion-dollar responses to the tsunami in Asia and the earthquake in Haiti; managed relationships with some 120 LCMS Recognized Service Organizations and other inter-Lutheran social-ministry organizations; worked in consultation with LCMS partner/sister churches to build capacity during numerous mercy outreach efforts; and managed LCMS pro-life efforts. Harrison has authored, edited and translated numerous articles and several books.

REV. ROSS EDWARD JOHNSON is director of Disaster Response for The Lutheran Church—Missouri Synod, a position he has held since 2013. Johnson is a graduate of Concordia Theological Seminary, Ft. Wayne, Ind. He spent three years in Latin America (2002–2005) with the LCMS mission board as a church planter and theological educator. From 2006 to 2013, he was a pastor at Redeemer Lutheran Church in Fairhope, Ala. In 2012, he deployed as a United States Army chaplain to Afghanistan. Johnson continues to serve as a Major in the United States Army Reserves. He has had book reviews and articles published in *Logia*, the *Journal of Lutheran Mission, The Lutheran Witness* and *Teachers Interaction*. He speaks nationally and internationally at pastors' conferences on disaster response, the theology of mercy, the theology of the cross, charity and ministry to those who suffer.

REV. DR. ARTHUR A. JUST JR. is professor and chairman of Exegetical Theology and director of Spanish Language Church Worker Formation at Concordia Theological Seminary, Fort Wayne, Ind. He is now working with churches and seminaries in Spain, Mexico and Argentina, as well as Spanish-speaking groups in the United States. He is the author of *The Ongoing Feast*; Concordia Publishing House's (CPH) *Concordia Commentary on the Gospel of Luke*; the Lukan volume of the *Ancient Christian Commentary on Scripture* for InterVarsity Press; a book from CPH for pastors, deaconesses and laypeople for the visitation of the sick and dying titled *Visitation*; and a book from CPH on the liturgy of the church titled *Heaven on Earth: The Gifts of Christ in the Divine Service*.

REV. DR. REED LESSING was on the faculty of Concordia Seminary, St. Louis, for 14 years. Now he serves as pastor of St. Michael Lutheran Church in Fort Wayne, Ind. Lessing has published articles and book reviews in the *Journal for the Study of the Old Testament, Catholic Biblical Quarterly, Concordia Journal* and *Concordia Theological Quarterly*. His books include *Interpreting Discontinuity: Isaiah's Tyre Oracle* (Eisenbrauns, 2004); *Jonah* (Concordia Publishing House, 2007); *Amos* (Concordia Publishing House, 2009); *Isaiah: Chapters 40-55* (Concordia Publishing House, 2011); *Prepare the Way of the Lord: An Introduction to the Old Testament* (co-authored with Andrew Steinmann, Concordia Publishing House, 2013); and *Isaiah: Chapters 56-66* (Concordia Publishing House, 2014).

WILHELM LÖHE (1808–1872) was educated in Nurnberg, Erlangen and Berlin and was pastor in Neuendettelsau. Löhe sent many missionaries to the United States and created a close relationship with The Lutheran Church—Missouri Synod. He was a prolific author and wrote on the subjects of mission, pastoral theology, history and liturgy. He started a deaconess home in Neuendettelsau in 1854 and was very active in starting institutions for human care.

Martin Luther (1483–1546) is known as "the father of Protestantism" and "the founder of Lutheranism." He was ordained a Roman Catholic priest in 1507 and served in the Augustinian tradition and taught at Wittenberg. Some of his best-known writings are his Small and Large Catechisms, German Bible, and commentaries on Genesis and Galatians. He also is known for his various *postils*, letters, treatises and tracts.

Rev. Michael Meyer, manager of Disaster Response for The Lutheran Church—Missouri Synod, graduated from Southern Methodist University, Dallas, Texas, with a Bachelor of Music in Performance in 2003 and from Concordia Theological Seminary, Fort Wayne, Ind., with a Master of Divinity in 2008. From 2008 until 2013, he served as a parish pastor in Denver, Colo. Since then, he has been serving in his current role in the LCMS Office of National Mission. In this role, Meyer assists with the church's response to natural and man-made disasters occurring domestically and internationally. In addition to on-site assessment, action planning and ongoing pastoral care for those who are suffering in the midst of disaster, he also regularly leads congregation preparedness training and Lutheran Early Response Team training throughout the 35 districts of the LCMS.

Rev. John T. Pless has served on the faculty of Concordia Theological Seminary, Fort Wayne, Ind., since 2000, teaching pastoral theology, theological ethics and catechetics. Prior to coming to the seminary, he served in campus ministry at Valparaiso University and the University of Minnesota. Pless is the author of numerous journal articles, chapters and books, including *Handling the Word of Truth* and *Martin Luther: Preacher of the Cross*. With LCMS President Rev. Dr. Matthew C. Harrison, he is co-editor of *Women Pastors? The Ordination of Women in Biblical Lutheran Perspective*. Beginning in 2009, he has served as visiting professor at Lutheran Theological Seminary in Pretoria, South Africa. He also is a fellow of the Luther Academy for Madagascar and serves as chairman of the Synod's Commission on Doctrinal Review. In addition, Pless is book review editor for *Logia* and a member of the editorial council for *Lutheran Quarterly*.

Rev. Dr. Jacob A.O. Preus III has served as executive vice-president for Mission Advancement at Bethesda Lutheran Communities; president of Concordia University, Irvine, Calif.; and dean of Faculty and professor of Systematic Theology at Concordia Seminary, St. Louis. Prior to that, he was a parish pastor in St. Louis, Mo., and Rancho Palos Verdes, Calif. Preus served as a chaplain in the U.S. Navy (Reserves) and was assigned to the 3rd Battalion, 24th Regiment of the U.S. Marine Corps during the First Gulf War.

C.F.W. WALTHER (1811–1887) graduated from the University of Leipzig in 1833 and was ordained in Braunsdorf, Germany, near Saxony. He emigrated to the U.S. in 1839 with Martin Stephan. Walther was the editor of *Lehre und Wehre*, and he was president of The Lutheran Church—Missouri Synod two different times (1847–1850 and 1864–1878). Two of his most well-known books are *Church and Ministry* and *Law and Gospel.*

REV. WILLIAM WEEDON is director of worship for The Lutheran Church— Missouri Synod and chaplain for the Synod's International Center. Prior to his current call, Weedon served parishes in North Carolina and southern Illinois for more than 25 years. He is an avid blogger, a follower of the Paleo diet and is hooked on reading the Church Fathers.

Preface

By Ross Edward Johnson

EAR BROTHERS AND SISTERS IN CHRIST:
Earthquakes. Floods. Tornadoes. Fires. Tsunamis. Typhoons. Disasters come in many different forms. They end lives and break bodies, destroy homes and devastate countries, cause suffering and dampen hope.

But thanks be to God, mercy comes in many different forms too! It is found in the comforting Word of Jesus Christ and in prayer, in hot meals and supplies, in relationships and in grants for rebuilding.

Our Lord's mercy, in all those different shapes and sizes, is at the very core of LCMS Disaster Response, the Synod's ministry that responds to immediate and long-term disaster-related needs. Always working in close proximity to Word and Sacrament, LCMS Disaster Response staff, districts and congregations labor together to respond and tend to the spiritual, physical and emotional needs of those who are suffering.

The essays you'll find within these pages are time-tested, Christ-focused pieces that outline why this kind of mercy is at the very core of who we are as Lutheran Christians. That's part of mercy work too: keeping our Lord's Word, sound theology and a faithful confession at the forefront of all the care we show to the suffering and the scared, the hurting and the embarrassed, the lonely and the desperate. It's what sets us apart from the Red Cross or FEMA. Our Lord's Word is enduring and lasting; it doesn't change. And it is all ours! We don't have a Lord who is far off; He draws near to us, in His Word and Sacraments, whether we are pastors or laity, deaconesses or teachers, grandparents or high schoolers.

Some of the documents found within this book may be familiar; they've previously been published by the former LCMS World Relief and Human Care. Some are quite old — Gerhard, Chemnitz and Luther — and have been translated by modern-day theologians. Others are new essays on important issues. The good news? Their emphasis on Christ's grace, forgiveness and peace in the midst of trial still holds true. In fact, the

9

themes of grace, love, forgiveness and mercy often seem as though they were written precisely for our time and culture! And perhaps, above all, they remind us that mercy, human care and genuine charity are all results of the Lord at work and that they are simply what we are about as Lutheran Christians.

God often allows amazing things to come out of tragic situations (Gen. 50:15–21). Job was eventually blessed after his time of tragedy (Job 42:10). We may not always directly see or understand the good that comes out of particular trials and tribulations, but we do know this: in times of tragedy, we trust in God's nature, that He is a loving and caring heavenly Father who is watching over each one of us. And thanks to the Church, and specifically to those involved in disaster response, in times of tragedy we also see God's mercy in action. God's mercy revealed to humanity is most clearly seen in the person of Jesus Christ who reminds us that we are reconciled to our heavenly Father and that there is nothing that can separate us from the love of God that is found in Christ Jesus (Rom. 8:38–39).

Do disasters come in many different forms? Certainly. But so does our Lord's mercy. It is my hope that by reading about and taking to heart the understanding of both found within these pages, you, too, will be encouraged to join LCMS Disaster Response in coming alongside those who need His love — His mercy! — the most.

YOURS IN CHRIST,

Rev. Ross Edward Johnson
DIRECTOR, LCMS DISASTER RESPONSE

Introduction

By Matthew C. Harrison

"Moved with pity, he stretched out his hand and touched him and said to him, 'I will; be clean'" (Mark 1:41).

Throughout Jesus' ministry, He had compassion on people with a variety of ailments, both physical and spiritual. The Greek word for "pity" or "compassion" is *splachna*, which refers to the bowels or the inner being of a person. *Splachna* refers to the deep ache and hurt that a person has for another person. Quite literally, your guts can hurt for another person.

Jesus used this sort of expression to describe the compassion that the Lord God feels for His people. Jesus has compassion on people on whom no one else will. Jesus has compassion on people who do not deserve to be shown compassion — including you and me. Jesus' mercy begins with the forgiveness of sins and extends to the entire person — body and soul. Jesus' compassion toward sinners — culminating with His suffering, death and resurrection — undoes the result of sin and death and will ultimately bring about the restoration of all creation in the new heaven and the new earth.

In the meantime, the Church and her redeemed show mercy and compassion to each other and to their neighbor. Christians show mercy to others because Christ has first loved them. The ancient pagans remarked of Christians, "See how they love one another." The acts of mercy Christians show to their neighbor are a powerful witness to the world about the love of Jesus. Those are the two messages you'll find within these pages and throughout these mercy-focused essays: that Christ loves us and that we, in turn, love one another, coming alongside those who are suffering and showing them mercy.

I love this book, and I love the pieces found within it. Some are contemporary, meant to discuss unique challenges we face today. Some were written by our Lutheran fathers in the faith centuries ago. I find it fascinating to see how the suffering they encountered is not so different from what we experience today. And maybe there is some comfort even in that: that we as pastors and laypeople care for one another in love just like the Christians in the Early Church or during the Reformation did. The content of these essays and the men who wrote them bear witness to the fact that our Lord is timeless, that the need for mercy never goes away and that Jesus Christ continues to respond in love, just as He always has.

This is also the basic message that I loved to share when I served as executive director of LCMS World Relief and Human Care. What was true for our Lutheran forefathers, true for the fledgling Lutheran Church in America, true for those of us who served in World Relief and Human Care is still true for us today. That's also the beauty of these essays — they remind us that *God really is good*, even in the midst of suffering, despite how things may feel or how they appear. And that's a message we can all rejoice in!

The people I met and the places I traveled in the course of my work with World Relief and Human Care changed me. But despite all the suffering I witnessed — the utter devastation of tsunamis, the horror of earthquakes, the hopelessness left by floods and fire — I came to understand in a very profound way that "God is able to make all grace abound to you, so that having all sufficiency in all things at all times, you may abound in every good work" (2 Cor. 9:8). This is one of my all-time favorite passages. Paul was writing to the Corinthians, encouraging them to complete their collection for the suffering church in Jerusalem. It reminds us that, in spite of a future that may appear uncertain to us, our future is never uncertain in Christ. It is precisely in our struggle, trial, want, need, pain, lack and sorrow that Christ does His very greatest and most profound work in us and through us.

Paul urged the comparatively wealthy Corinthians to give to the needy saints in Jerusalem, and he used the example of the relatively poor Macedonians to urge them on. Even though they were not well off, the Macedonians were generous. I take great comfort in knowing "God is able to make all grace abound." Having all grace (that is, the forgiveness of sins and every good and gracious gift to live), we have "all sufficiency in all things at all times." Paul writes precisely for times like these! And these gifts are given so "you may abound in every good work." The Lord blesses that we might be a blessing.

It is my prayer that this book on mercy will make these truths clear to you again and again, as you find within its pages the comfort and joy that is yours because of Jesus and His cross alone!

Sub cruce,

Rev. Dr. Matthew C. Harrison

President, The Lutheran Church—Missouri Synod

CHRIST AS THE MAN OF SORROWS
"He was despised and rejected by men; a man of sorrows, and acquainted with grief." Is. 53:3a c. 1511.

An Introduction to Disaster Response: Mercy in Action

By LCMS Disaster Response Staff

W HAT IS A DISASTER?

Generally, a *disaster* is an event beyond the control of the affected individuals that results in great harm, suffering, destruction and damage. Disasters disrupt personal and community life, involve a significant number of people, and cause physical, emotional, economic, social and/or spiritual crises. A disaster damages a community's ability to sustain life without outside assistance.

Natural disasters involve the forces of nature and creation — flood, windstorm, fires caused by lightning, tornado, earthquake, etc.

Human-caused disasters occur as a result of violent actions by individuals or groups against people and/or property. Human-caused disasters include such things as explosions, the collapse of a structure or the release of hazardous material.

atural Disasters
ood
indstorm
res caused by lightning
rnado
rthquake

uman-caused
isasters
xplosions
ollapse of a structure
n Attack

Presidentially-declared disasters impact 10,000 to 100,000 people or more. These major disasters require emergency relief efforts beyond the ability of local communities and churches to respond. A presidentially-declared disaster makes federal relief assistance available.

A *catastrophic disaster* event is presidentially declared and larger in scope. It involves a large number of deaths, injuries, extensive damage or destruction of facilities. Catastrophic disasters involve an overwhelming demand on state and local response resources and mechanisms. Federal relief is available.

Each disaster is different in magnitude and impact on the affected area. People react differently and local authorities are often hard-pressed to manage the impact of the disaster on the community.

While state and national relief efforts are being mobilized, the local church and schools have an opportunity to reach out and minister to those in need — whether they are Lutheran or non- Lutherans. The church's response to a disaster is a commitment and witness to the Gospel of Jesus Christ to assist those affected by the disaster.

What happens during a disaster? (Rescue)

A disaster may strike with or without warning. In the moments, hours and days surrounding a disaster, the concern is for safety and preservation of life.

Those affected by disaster seek temporary relief and assistance — often provided by agencies such as the American Red Cross and the Salvation Army. Local emergency management agencies are often strained to carry out their tasks. Respected community leaders, including clergy and other church leaders, help victims deal with the reality of danger and guide survivors to assistance.

What happens after a disaster? (Relief)

The relief process begins in the days following a disaster. Concerns for safety, security and sanitation remain high priorities. Federal Emergency Management Association (FEMA), local emergency management offices and the American Red Cross remain active with nongovernmental organizations (NGOs) and faith-based organizations beginning to participate.

The LCMS District Disaster Response Coordinator (DDRC) and District Disaster Response Team (DDRT) in your area will bring Lutheran ministry partners, local Lutheran leaders and community leaders together to share information and organize a systematic approach to a cooperative response to meeting the immediate and long-term needs of the community. Local congregations are already active at this stage offering basic life necessities like food, water and shelter.

Contact the American Red Cross for shelter information. At the same time, Lutheran congregations often work in conjunction with other local churches to help meet their community's needs for basic life necessities. Plans are implemented for the coordinated distribution of clothing, furniture, appliances and other donated items.

What happens in the long-term? (Recovery)

The long-term response to disaster focuses on the future. During the recovery phase, homes are being rebuilt and/or repaired. Unmet needs are assessed and met appropriately by both faith-based and community action committees.

Depending on the scope and scale of the disaster, recovery may take three to five years. During the recovery phase, outside support begins to diminish. Lutheran congregations play an essential role in sustaining the recovery in their communities. Organized and trained volunteers, including Lutheran Early Response Team (LERT) members, are engaged in the repair and rebuilding process and require support from local congregations.

LCMS DISASTER RESPONSE

The Lutheran Church—Missouri Synod's (LCMS) Disaster Response ministry responds to immediate and long-term needs following natural and man-made disasters, working through LCMS districts and congregations, international Lutheran churches and other partners. We build partners' capacity to respond with Christian care to the needs within the church and their communities with the following services:

> On-site assessment

> Emergency, relief and development grants

> Pastoral care for LCMS church workers and members

> Resources (volunteer coordination, donation and equipment management)

> Congregational preparedness and Lutheran Early Response Team (LERT) training

The last decade was an unprecedented time for LCMS Disaster Response efforts with multimillion-dollar responses to Superstorm Sandy, the tsunami in Japan, the earthquake in Haiti, and hundreds of other national and international disasters from Minot, N.D., to Leyte Island, Philippines. God calls us to be His hands reaching out to bring peace, relief and assistance to those who suffer the devastating effects of disasters.

The purpose of LERT taining is to be a resource to you during extraordinary times. In short order, it will attempt to answer why the church should respond to disasters. It also will offer suggestions as to how the church might respond. At the very least, it will serve as a discussion starter, a conversation piece that can guide and inform you as you minister to your congregation in times of great distress and to the community in which your members live and work.

LERT training is not intended to include every possible scenario nor is it intended to be a comprehensive and detailed "how to" manual. However, the hope is that it will give simple suggestions and examples of how the church can, in fact, be a church in the midst of disaster. The proclamation of the Word and the proper administration of the Sacraments according to Christ's command do not have to be set aside if a tornado strikes your community or church or if a gunman horrifically attacks the neighborhood school. In fact, if the church is to show mercy in the midst of disaster at all, it can only be in close proximity to Word and Sacrament — otherwise it is neither mercy nor the work of the church but only the actions of a group of well-meaning individuals. May it not be so among us.

Mercy is a hallmark of the church. Throughout history, Christians have been known by the world around them as a generous people, as a people whose good works are motivated by their faith in God, Who has prepared those works for His people (Eph.

4:20). Disasters, while terrible, are a time when the church can take a moment to truly care for the greatest treasures of this world — people.

THE BASIS FOR THE CHURCH'S RESPONSE

The church's response to disaster is found first and foremost in Christ and His love for us.

"By this we know love that [Christ] laid down his life for us, and we ought to lay down our lives for the brothers. But if anyone has the world's goods and sees his brother in need, yet closes his heart against him, how does God's love abide in him? Little children, let us not love in word or talk but in deed and in truth" (1 John 3:16-18).

True love and service begin with Christ. We too begin by focusing on Christ and what He has revealed to us about Christian care. Not only does He forgive us all our sins and give us new life in Him, but He also encourages us to live by faith, responding boldly in His name with the gifts He has given us.

"So then, as we have opportunity, let us do good to everyone, and especially to those who are of the household of faith" (Gal. 6:10).

DISASTER RESPONSE COLLABORATION BETWEEN LCMS DISTRICTS AND THE SYNOD

Overview

When LCMS Disaster Response works with each district in disaster preparedness and response, resources can be directed from across the LCMS to the places where they are most needed. This collaboration provides for reliable information sharing and helps to build capacity between districts and congregations, providing a more comprehensive response to disasters across the board. By intentionally working together, the needs of professional church workers, congregations and communities can be met quickly and appropriately.

As a result, districts can remain in closer contact with their congregations, as well as those in other districts who have specific needs. Through LCMS Disaster Response, districts are quickly informed of where the latest disaster is and what help is needed. This enables the LCMS Office of National Mission to have closer ties with each district, allowing for faster response in times of disaster. These ties also open doors for other mercy projects in which districts may have an interest. Some examples include opening a child-care center, operating a food pantry, organizing a mission trip and becoming involved with any of the other program areas of the LCMS, such as Life Ministry or Veterans of the Cross.

For a district to tackle disaster preparedness and response alone would require a great deal of time, effort and money. The LCMS provides DDRCs and DDRTs with essential training in preparedness and response plus on-site consultations and advice as detailed here.

Working together allows districts and the LCMS to meet more needs and to meet them more effectively. The duplication of efforts is lessened as we work together. This means our ability to respond quickly and effectively grows ever stronger.

LCMS Disaster Response also can help access the capacity of other national and international Lutheran organizations including Lutheran Women's Missionary League, Lutheran Hour Ministries and Lutheran World Relief and Recognized Service Organizations such as Orphan Grain Train and Lutheran Church Charities.

In addition, LCMS Disaster Response maintains contact with governmental organizations and NGOs as well as other faith-based organizations.

The distinct role of LCMS Disaster Response is to work directly with districts, professional church workers and congregations to enhance their ministry to their own members and the local community. This is done by implementing a comprehensive disaster response plan that uses trained DDRCs and DDRTs. The theology of the cross, which forms the basis for our care, is an integral part of this disaster response training. In this way, collaborative ministry is very complementary and addresses the needs of individual congregations, professional church workers and entire communities.

Collaboration in this way is fully dependent upon voluntary congregational participation and training. It places LCMS Disaster Response in a supportive and facilitative role, allowing the local congregation to be a hallmark of mercy in its community.

While state and national relief efforts are being mobilized, the local congregation and the district have an opportunity to reach out with Christ's mercy to those in need — whether they are Lutherans or non Lutherans, Christian or non Christian.

The church's response to a disaster is a commitment and witness to the Gospel of Jesus Christ to assist those affected by the disaster by providing immediate relief and long-term recovery assistance.

Christian Care in Times of Disaster

In His great compassion, the Triune God does not separate the care of body and soul. Rather, He sees and cares for people wholly — as created beings that consist of both body and soul. Therefore, LCMS Disaster Response seeks to practice Christian care — whole-person care founded in Christ at all times and especially in times of disaster.

Understanding body and soul independently may be common in western thought[1] but this understanding does not reflect the scriptural understanding of human

---

[1] Platonism, one of the major influences on western thought, stands behind this dualism. Gnosticism and a number of other heresies are characterized by such dualism, resulting in much Christian literature addressing the fallacies and harm involved in such understanding.

beings, in whom body and soul are united. Christ Himself sees and cares for people in every aspect, as does the church — His body. The Apostles' Creed, along with the Small Catechism's explanations of its three articles, creates a firm foundation for whole-person, Christian care.[2] Whole-person grace and mercy pervade the creed — Christians confessing belief in "God the Father Almighty," affirming faith in the Father, who "has given me my body and soul, eyes, ears, and all members, my reason and all my senses, and still takes care of them."[3] They confess a unity of spirit and flesh in the Son of God Himself, "conceived by the Holy Spirit, born of the Virgin Mary."[4] Christians also confess in the creed that the Holy Spirit is not an abstract being but works through the hearing of God's Word in this world, even as His work in and through the church brings about "the resurrection of the body."[5] It is the union of body and soul not their separation that is characteristic of the Christian faith. This unity of body and soul is therefore foundational for Christian care.

It is precisely this, our Lord's gracious care for both body and soul, that we see in the ministry of Christ and the apostles. The incarnate Son of God, Preacher of the Good News, was simultaneously the Healer of the sick,[6] the Feeder of the hungry.[7] The Light of the world did not overlook the darkened eyes of the blind.[8] Similarly the apostles ensured the care of the poor.[9]

With their understanding of the church as the Body of Christ, the early Christians could not ignore the physical needs of the members of this body.[10] In fact, consistent with the Old Testament, Christians also offer care to those outside the church, reflecting the Lord's mercy on all people and all creation.[11]

---

[2] As a summary of the Bible, the *Small Catechism* consistently addresses the entire person. This Christian care statement will focus on its second chief part, the Apostles' Creed. Not only do all the commandments have application in body and soul, but all six of the chief parts highlight what God has done for us and our very bodies and souls. All references here will be to the *Small Catechism in the Lutheran Service Book* (Concordia Publishing House, St. Louis, 2006, Pages 321-330) and in *The Book of Concord: The Confessions of the Evangelical Lutheran Church* (Robert Kolb and Timothy J. Wengert, editors, Fortress Press, Minneapolis, 2000, Pages 345-367).

[3] *Lutheran Service Book*, Page 322; and *The Book of Concord*, Page 354.

[4] Ibid.

[5] John 6:63, 68; and Rom. 8:11, 10:17.

[6] Jesus healed the sick throughout His ministry (Matt. 4:23–25, 8:14–16, 9:35–38, 14:14, 14:34–36; Mark 1:34, 6:53–56; and Luke 4:40), reflecting the care of the Father (Ps. 41 is one example.). His apostles did likewise (Matt. 10:8; Mark 6:13; Luke 10:9; and Acts 3:1–10, 5:16, 28:8).

[7] Jesus feeds the hungry physically and spiritually (Matt. 15:32–39; Mark 8:1–10; Luke 6:21; and John 6) as His followers did also (Matt. 25:35 and Rom. 12:20).

[8] John 8–9. Jesus is the light of the world (John 8:12, 1:4–5) in all ways. After the final resurrection, the glory of God will give light so that the city of God has no need of sun or moon to shine (Rev. 21:23)!

[9] See Luke 6:1–7; Rom. 15:26; 2 Cor. 9:1–15; Gal. 2:10; and James 2:2–6, 14–26.

[10] Acts 6:1–7 is an excellent example of the church's corporate work of mercy and Phil. 2:1–18 focuses on the Christ-centric nature of the Christian's work and interaction in this world. Sometimes overlooked is the large role the collection for Jerusalem plays throughout Acts. This is a huge, ongoing, international effort for mutual support and interaction within the church body.

[11] See Reed Lessing's excellent essay, "Mercy in the Old Testament," (Mercy Insight series, LCMS).

Practically speaking, "What does this mean?" How does this unity of body and soul translate into real life? LCMS Disaster Response happily provides an answer to this familiar question.[12] During disaster, first and foremost, Christian care seeks to meet the basic needs of those affected — providing food, water, clothing and shelter. This first line of care reflects the First Article of the creed, where God is the giver of "clothing and shoes, food and drink, house and home," family, property and "all that I have."[13] Because every person, regardless of race, color, creed or confession is a precious creation of God, for whom He cares, LCMS Disaster Response provides disaster victims with what they need "to support this body and life."[14] Beyond these fundamental human needs, Christian care candidly acknowledges the fact that we live in a less than perfect — and sometimes miserably inexplicable — world. Disaster and catastrophe only affirm this fact. Only Scripture reveals the full effect of the fall into sin and only Scripture reveals to us God's response and eternal rescue.

Christians can be uniquely responsive in the face of catastrophe to the questions, doubts, misgivings and fears of those facing the fragility and mortality of human life. Disaster, like all reminders of sin, calls all of us to daily repentance. It can be tempting to search for specific sins or people to blame, but Christian care brings the message of Jesus' salvation for the entire world and offers hope in spite of such guilt, doubt and fear.

Christ already bore the sins of the world and God is still working His gracious will for the world through the humble suffering, perseverance and reign of Christ. The world is groaning and we groan too as we wait for Christ's return and the final resurrection.[15] In Christ, we see that suffering can serve God and, indeed, Christ's suffering reveals God. God has hidden Himself in Christ's suffering and death on the cross.

This theology of the cross holds that Christ is the only mediator who effected reconciliation between God and man. In doing so, God's wrath is completely removed because of, and only in, Christ's sacrifice on the cross. Lutheran theology is set opposite the popular theology of glory, which seeks to know God directly in His evident, divine power, wisdom and glory. The theology of glory expects earthly goods and comfort as rewards and sees every disaster or loss as a personal judgment and punishment. In times of disaster, those who hold to the theology of glory must try to earn earthly comfort for themselves. They are without the comfort of Jesus' promises and assurances.

They are without the external comforts of God's Word as they try desperately to find their own solutions apart from God's abundant mercy in Christ. The theology of glory

---

[12] This repeated question from the *Small Catechism*, our handbook of the Christian faith, reminds us to hear God's Word, trust His Word and apply this Word to our lives.

[13] *Lutheran Service Book*, Page 322; and *The Book of Concord*, Page 354.

[14] Ibid.

[15] Rom. 8:22–23. For further reading, see Gerhard Uhlhorn's book, *Christian Charity in the Ancient Church* (Charles Scribner's Sons, New York, 1883) and Norman Nagel's essay, "The Twelve and the Seven in Acts 6 and the Needy" (LCMS, Mercy Insights series).

is built on man's perspective and expectations, making God to look like man as seen in man's own attributes and perceived good works. Christian care, however, points all of us away from ourselves and toward the love God has for each of us. God does not act according to man's natural expectations. His goodness and mercy exceed all human need or desire, as seen in the solid revelation of Christ in Scripture.

Christian care offers open ears. Often those suffering from disaster have a very real need to have someone with whom to talk. An ideal approach with those traumatized by disaster reflects the Christian caregiver's readiness and willingness to listen. This compassionate listening affirms that the world is indeed broken and sometimes incomprehensible. There are not always answers to give but in Christ, Christians are free to say, "I am sorry, I don't know." At the same time, Christian care also brings a well-spoken word, based on Christ and the Gospel, at the proper time. For Jesus Christ, no stranger to suffering, died and rose that He might overcome death, grant life freely and abundantly, and bring all who believe in Him to everlasting life,[16] "that I may be His own and live under Him in His kingdom and serve Him in everlasting righteousness, innocence, and blessedness, just as He is risen from the dead, lives, and reigns to all eternity."[17]

The firm hope of the Christian is in the life, death and resurrection of Jesus, a hope which sustains us even in the wake of disaster. Sin, death, guilt and pain are serious and very real, so Jesus took them on Himself. He knew pain, betrayal, suffering, torture and the extent of disaster in this world, but Jesus' suffering and salvation reach further with more power than even the worst disaster or tragedy.

The Second Article confirms Christ's work on our behalf and encourages ongoing Christian care for all people. Only Christians can offer the comfort and assurance that Christ's salvation brings, as physical care is offered in close proximity to Word and Sacrament ministry, built on Christ's mercy for body and soul. The church offers God's Word, Baptism and the Lord's Supper and connects us to Jesus, His death and His life,[18] encouraging the ongoing cycle of sharing God's mercy with the world. Christians, when asked, cannot but speak of this hope, which is in them![19]

The question might be raised: Does this mean that Christian volunteers "target" victims of disaster for evangelism? Certainly not. The aftermath of a catastrophe is no place for misguided, opportunistic or manipulative evangelism! In Luther's explanation of the Third Article, we are reminded that it is the Holy Spirit who calls (by the Gospel), gathers, enlightens and sanctifies the whole Christian church on earth.

---

[16] See John 5:24, 10:10; Rom. 5, 6:10–13, 6:23, 8; 2 Cor. 4:10–12; Phil. 1:20; 2 Tim. 1:10; Heb. 2:15; and Rev. 2:10.

[17] *Lutheran Service Book*, Page 323; and *The Book of Concord*, Page 355.

[18] See John 5:24, 6:63, 6:68; 1 Cor. 10:16; Rom. 6:4; Eph. 4:3–6; Col. 2:12; and 1 Peter 1:23, 3:21.

[19] Col. 4:6 and 1 Peter 3:15.

The Holy Spirit works when and where He pleases to bring the lost to faith even in the midst of disaster.[20]

Christian care points to the true comfort of Christ and away from the despair of disaster. It points to Christ and His church. And it does not manipulate or take advantage of the weak. Christ provides His Spirit, working through the Word and the church, to guide our speech and interactions. Lutheran workers and volunteers are freed by the Gospel to help those in need, speaking honestly as baptized children of God. LCMS Disaster Response reaches into the community by working with and through districts and congregations, through partner churches and through other Lutheran entities as existing points of contact within communities affected by disasters. In this way, we come into contact with individuals in need and can readily point disaster victims to local congregations, confident that they will receive further long-term assistance and ongoing care, which treats those in need as whole persons with the love and mercy of Christ Jesus, our Lord.

A Ministry of Presence

Christ's presence after His resurrection demonstrates the power He has to console and comfort the needy. Christ's powerful presence is the pre-eminent paradigm for our ministry of mercy, which can dispel the darkness of fear and uncertainty of the future (John 20:19–20).

It was the power of Christ's presence that moved His disciples from the tragedy of death to the triumph of life. That same power is realized today in the ministry of the church through those who stand in His stead to transcend the critical events that affect people's lives. Our Lutheran presence is a clear testimony of the Gospel, not just in deed, but also in Word — the Word of Christ's forgiveness and eternal love.

Lutheran accompaniment

In Lutheran accompaniment, members of the local congregation join together to provide mercy to those in need whether near or far, regardless of race, creed, culture or religion. Congregation, community and world! Faith, family and friends!

Lutheran accompaniment allows us to work through the means of grace that God provides for His ministry of mercy — Word and Sacraments, working through the church, pastors, teachers and other professional church workers.

Caring through Christ

The deep human needs and psychological scars left after a disaster require care beyond the restoration of physical needs. Putting lives back together requires real care, hope and love. Counseling, understanding and direction are needed to enable persons, especially children, to cope with grief expressed as anger, guilt, loneliness and turmoil.

---

[20] John 3:5–8.

We give care through effective listening. William J. McKay, author of "Beginnings: A Christ Care Group Experience Group Member Guide" by Stephen Ministries, offers these points in a session entitled, "Listening as an Act of Love." "Listening means paying attention to the other person — real attention, the kind that drops everything else and ignores distractions to focus on what the other person is saying and feeling," it says.

McKay continues to define the task of listening by highlighting six important facts:

1. Listening is hard work. Your full attention and focus are on the persons peaking.

2. Listening is an important way to show care. Giving your time and effort says to the other person that they are valuable to you.

3. Listen to more than just words. Notice facial expressions, body language and tone of voice.

4. Listening involves talking, too. Say just enough to demonstrate attention and encourage the other person.

5. Listening also involves a response, such as asking appropriate questions. Ask open-ended and clarifying questions. The goal of listening is to draw out the other person, not to find solutions or smooth over a problem.

6. Listen with patience and care to help the other discover solutions to problems.

Respond with love and compassion

Most of those affected by disaster have experienced various levels of loss: property, keepsakes, memories and/or life. They often will be grieving.

This is important and normal for them to work through; however, it is also important for you to recognize what is happening and how to respond.

Not everyone grieves in the same way.

People suffering loss are particularly open to hearing and accepting the Gospel through the care of those living it out. As members and ministry groups from your congregation serve victims, they are sharing Christ. The church may take the initiative in reaching out to those who are in denial or depression. Some will be unable to seek assistance.

ANGEL APPEARING TO JOACHIM

The despondent Joachim went into the wilderness where an angel appeared before him announcing that his wife would bear a daughter. The angel continued, "And your daughter will someday bear a son and she will give him the name of Jesus, and he will save his people from their sins." c. 1505

THEOLOGY FOR MERCY

By Matthew C. Harrison

$\mathcal{L}$ove, care and concern for those in need (diakonic mercy/love) are actions motivated by the Gospel, when faith (*fides qua creditur*/the faith by which we believe) apprehends the righteousness of Christ and His merits (Augsburg Confession IV, VI) unto eternal life. The Gospel thus laid hold of produces love. Love seeks and serves the neighbor.

Love for the neighbor, while an action mandated by the law of God, is a reflection of the very being of the Triune God, Father, Son and Holy Spirit (1 John 4:7). This love finds its source and motivation in the deep Gospel matrix and totality of the true faith (*fides quae creditur*/ the faith which is believed). Thus:

- **Diakonic love has its source in the Holy Trinity.** The Son is begotten of the Father from eternity. The Holy Spirit proceeds from the Father and the Son. Such begetting and procession are Trinitarian acts of love expressing the communality of God. In these acts the Triune God, from eternity, and in time, has found humankind as the object of divine love and mercy (John 3:16; Luke 6:36; 1 John 3:16–17; James 3:17). Diakonic love reflects the very being of God.

- **Diakonic love is born of the incarnation and humiliation of Christ.** In Christ the eternal God became man. Such identity occurred that Christ might have mercy upon His "brothers" (Heb. 2:17). Christian service of the neighbor finds its source, motivation and example in Christ's incarnate, redeeming, atoning, active love (Phil. 2:1–11).

- **God "desires all people to be saved and to come to the knowledge of the truth"** (1 Tim. 2:4). A biblically and confessionally faithful theology of mercy clearly confesses that "the Father has decreed from eternity that whomever He would save He would save through Christ, as Christ Himself says, 'No one comes to the Father except through me' (John 14:6), and again, 'I am the door. If anyone enters by me, he will be saved' (John 10:9)" (Solid Declaration XI, 66). This fundamental

27

truth of the Bible, that there is no salvation outside of faith in Christ and His merits, animates the church's work for those in need. If this is not so, such work becomes merely secular, and may be performed by any entity in society.

• **The Gospel gifts bring forgiveness, and beget merciful living.** Lives that have received mercy (grace!) cannot but be merciful toward the neighbor (love!). Thus the merciful washing of Baptism (Rom. 6:1ff) produces merciful living (Rom. 7:4–6). In absolution, the merciful word of the Gospel begets merciful speaking and living (Matt. 18:21ff.). In the Supper, Christ gives Himself for us, that we might give ourselves to our neighbor (1 Cor. 10:15–17; 1 Cor. 12:12ff, 26). "Repentance ought to produce good fruits … the greatest possible generosity to the poor" (Apol. 12.174).

• **Christ's mandate and example of love for the whole person remains our supreme example for life in this world and for care of the needy, body and soul.** Christ's Palestinian ministry combined proclamation of forgiveness and acts of mercy, care and healing (Luke 5:17–26). Christ likewise sent forth the apostles to proclaim the Good News and to heal (Luke 9:2ff.). Christ mandated that His Gospel of forgiveness be preached to all (Matthew 28; Mark 16) and that "all nations" be baptized for the forgiveness of sins. Christ also left His church a feast of His body and blood unto forgiveness, life and salvation. In describing the events of the last day, Christ noted the importance of mercy in the life of the church ("As you did it to one of the least of these My brothers …" [Matt. 25:40].

• **The church has a corporate life of mercy.** There is absolute support in the New Testament for acts of mercy, love and kindness done by individuals within the realm of individual vocation. Moreover, the Old and New Testaments clearly bear witness to a "corporate life of mercy" of the people of God. Indeed, "corporate" comes from "corpus" (body; i.e. *hoc est corpus meum*). Through the body of Christ (incarnate and sacramental; Rom. 6; 1 Cor. 11–12) the body of Christ (mystical) is created. Thus "if one member suffers, all suffer together" (1 Cor. 12:26). Acts 6 and the creation of the proto-diakonic office and St. Paul's collection for the poor (Acts 11:29; 2 Cor. 8–9) in Jerusalem clearly bear witness to the church's corporate life of mercy based upon these theological foundations.

• **The Lutheran Confessions explicitly and repeatedly state that the work of diakonic love (alms, charity, works of love) is an assumed reality in the church's corporate life.** See Treatise 80–82; Apology IV.192f.; Apology XXVII.5ff. Moreover, the Smalcald Articles explicitly state that "works of love" (*operum caritatis*) are, along with "doctrine, faith, sacraments, [and] prayer," an area in which the church and its bishops (pastors) are "joined in unity" (Smalcald Articles, II.IV.9).

• **The vocation to mercy is addressed to the church at all levels.** The vocation to diakonic love and mercy is as broad as the need of the neighbor (Luther). While the call to love the needy applies to Christian individuals as such (love your neighbor as yourself), the call to diakonic mercy is particularly addressed to Christians as a corporate community (church!), whether local or synodical, even national or international (1 Cor. 16:1–4; Acts 11:28; Rom. 15:26; 2 Cor. 8:1–15; Acts 24:17).

• **Within the church, there is a multiplicity of diakonic vocations.** Within these communities individuals serve in diakonic vocations (pastoral concern for the needy, chaplain/spiritual care, deacon, deaconess, parish nurse, medical disciplines, the host of administrative and managerial vocations, etc.). These diakonic vocations are flexible in form and determined by need (Acts 6). Within an ecclesial setting, their common goal is the integration of proclamation of the Gospel, faith, worship and care for those in need. The range of the legitimate disciplines of human care (First Article gifts!) may be used in the church's diakonic life to the extent that such disciplines/tools do not contradict the Gospel, and the doctrine of Holy Scripture. "Christ's kingdom is spiritual … At the same time it permits us to make outward use of legitimate political ordinances of whatever nation in which we live, just as it permits us to make use of medicine or architecture or food, drink and air" (Apol. XVI.2).

• **The Church's work of mercy extends beyond its own borders.** In the New and Old Testaments, we see a priority of concern for those in need within the orthodox fellowship of faith in Christ. But just as the Gospel itself reaches beyond the church and is intended for all, love for the neighbor cannot and must not be limited only to those in the fellowship of the orthodox Lutheran faith. In following the apostolic mandate to "do good to all, especially those of the household of faith" the church's diakonic work will persistently address the need of those within its midst. The church's diakonic life will also reach beyond its borders according to the intensity of need confronted and level of resources provided by God (1 Cor. 9:10–11; Gal. 6:10). The church's missionary work will be a persistent arena for the expression of diakonic love and mercy. Diakonic love will often function as "pre-evangelism," and rightly so, so long as word (Gospel) and deed (love) continue to mark the missionary church's life at every stage. Strengthening and reaching out in love to Lutheran partner churches will be a priority. Reaching beyond these borders in love according to the intensity of need and opportunity (particularly in times of disaster) and in partnership with others is entirely appropriate, so long as motivations and expectations of the parties involved is clear. These matters are governed by theological/ethical integrity and evangelical freedom.

• **The church will cooperate with others in meeting human need.** *Cooperation in externals* has long been an expression describing the church's legitimate ability to cooperate with other entities (whether churches, societies, Lutheran, Christian or not) in meeting some human need. To cooperate in externals means to work toward common goals in endeavors, which do not necessitate, require or necessarily imply church fellowship (*communio in sacris*) or involve joint proclamation of the Gospel

29

and administration of the Sacraments (worship). Such cooperative endeavors are entered upon often for practical reasons (e.g., lack of critical resources). But such endeavors are also often an expression of the belief (when entered into with other Christian entities) of the catholicity of the church (See Formula of Concord, Preface; Tappert, p. 11), as well as an expression of love for fellow Christians. Through such endeavors, the LCMS will often have opportunity to insist on theological integrity and the truth of God's word, and thereby make a positive contribution to ecumenical activities. Such endeavors may range from providing resources for a simple community food bank to the highly complex ecclesial and civil realities involved in operating a jointly Recognized Service Organizations (RSO). Such endeavors must recognize legitimate doctrinal differences and provide for the requisite integrity of its partners.

- **The Lutheran doctrine of the two kingdoms grants broad freedom for the church to engage and be active in its community.** The church has a role in its community (local, national, international) by virtue of the fact that congregations and national churches are actually "corporate citizens" of their respective communities. As such, congregations, churches and Synod as a whole engage the community as corporate citizens of God's "left-hand kingdom," working toward worthy civic goals (good citizenship, just laws and society, protection of the weak, housing, etc.). "Legitimate civil ordinances are good creations of God and divine ordinances in which a Christian may safely take part" (Apol. XVI.1). As such a corporate citizen, the church has civic and political capital. In addition to encouraging its members to be responsible citizens, the church may from time to time speak with a collective voice on issues of great significance to society, particularly where the basic value of human life is diminished (e.g., abortion, racial injustice). "Public redress, which is made through the office of the judge, is not forbidden but is commanded and is a work of God according to Paul in Romans 13 ... public redress includes judicial decisions" (Apol. XVI.7). There have been times in the life of the church when it was the sole guardian and provider for the needy. In our day, the rise of the modern welfare state has shifted that (monetary) responsibility in large measure to the civil realm. But there is a large intersection of civil and churchly endeavor at just this point. Thus the church's response to these issues is always mutating and nuanced. In these matters the church must spend its capital wisely and sparingly. It must avoid both quietism and political activism. The former shuns the ethical demand of love for the neighbor (ignoring for instance, the ethical urgency of the Old Testament minor prophets), the latter may obscure the church's fundamental and perpetual task as bearer of the Word of salvation to sinners in need of Christ. Where the church loses sight of this proclamation of the Gospel, it thereby loses the very motivation for diakonic work (the Gospel)!

CHRIST AMONG THE DOCTORS IN THE TEMPLE
The twelve-year-old child sits among the doctors, while to the left his frantic parents look on in amazement. c. 1503

MERCY IN ACTION

BY ROSS EDWARD JOHNSON

I
t's important to realize that contrary to what popular culture says, people are not spiritually good or deserving of God's favor in and of themselves. In fact, the Bible constantly reminds us that we are sinners even after conversion (see Rom. 7: 13–23). The Bible says, "For all have sinned and fall short of the glory of God" (Rom. 3:23). The Bible also says, "For the wages of sin is death" (Rom. 6:23). We confess in the Divine Service that we "justly deserve" God's "temporal and eternal punishment" (LSB 184).

There will always be aspects of our all-knowing, all-powerful and all-loving God that we as humans will never understand. We should not assume that God doesn't care, and we should not demand that God explain His actions to us. Rather, we should trust in His love even if we don't understand what is happening to us or around us. It is because of God's love for you that He is at work redeeming you and saving you from yourself. This love is clearly evident in God sending His Son to die on the cross to pay for your sin, so that one day you will be rescued from this world of tragedy and live in the perfection of heaven.

In times of trouble, instead of trying to speculate about God's nature or demand that God do our will, we should repent. In Luke 13, Pilate slaughters the pious Galileans. It was an evil action against undeserving people. Yet Jesus in Luke 13:3 told the people to repent, saying, "Unless you repent, you will all likewise perish."

Jesus did not justify or explain Himself or why evil was happening; rather He told them to repent. Repentance is humbling, and it moves you from being self-centered to trusting in God's goodness and mercy. It turns you as a sinful person away from your pride to reliance on your almighty and all-loving God who does not always give you explanations except "I am who I am" (Ex. 3:14), "For my thoughts are not your thoughts, neither are your ways my ways, declares the Lord" (Is. 55:8) and, as St. Paul explains, "Will what is molded say to its molder, 'Why have you made me like this?'" (Rom. 9:20).

33

Why does God allow suffering?

Suffering is a result of sin and the fall. God never wanted Adam and Eve to fall into sin. God explicitly warned them about the eating of the tree and the consequences if they did. However, they chose to sin against God, and ultimately sin and brokenness entered the world. As soon as humanity fell into sin, your loving God began His work of redemption (see Gen. 3:15). From the fall until the final day, there will be suffering and sin. However, your loving God is actively rescuing you from sin, death and the devil in ways that you do not realize.

It is always best to put our faith in what is revealed to us about God: that He loves us, He died for us and He rescues us from brokenness and sin. Everything that is necessary for us to know about God and salvation is clearly revealed in Holy Scripture.

If something bad happens to me, is God punishing me for my sin?

When something bad happens to you, it is not necessarily related to a particular sin that you have committed. However, it is always because we live in a sinful and broken world (Genesis 2–3). In this world, our bodies betray us, and we get sick and die. In this broken world, other people also betray us and cause us a great deal of problems and misfortune. Often times, we endure personal agony because of the sinful choices that we ourselves make (see Psalm 51). And at times, we are spiritually attacked by the devil and his demons, who like to harass people and cause misery and misfortune (see Job).

What do I do when I feel like my life is falling apart?

1) Prayer is always good when you feel overwhelmed by the world.

2) Attend the Divine Service where you receive the ongoing forgiveness of sins and you are reminded that Christ is bodily present with you in a special way.

3) Consider talking to your pastor to get wise Christian advice when you are overwhelmed.

4) Consider talking to a pastor for private confession and absolution (see 1 John 1:9).

5) Use your suffering as a reminder that you live in a broken world and that Christ promises to suffer right along with you.

6) Place your hope in Christ and the resurrection and not in this world or in sinful people who will disappoint you.

Can anything good come out of bad things?

God often allows amazing things to come out of tragic situations (see Gen. 50: 15–21). Job was eventually blessed after his time of tragedy (Job 42:10). However, there is no promise that you will always directly see or understand the good that comes out of particular trials and tribulations. In times of tragedy, it is important to trust in God's nature, that He is a loving and caring heavenly Father who is watching over you. In times of tragedy, we see God's mercy in action. God's mercy revealed to humanity is most clearly seen in the person of Jesus Christ who reminds us that we are reconciled to our heavenly Father and that there is nothing that can separate us from the love of God that is found in Christ Jesus (Rom. 8:38–39).

LAST JUDGMENT
"And Jesus said, 'I am, and you will see the Son of Man seated at the right hand of Power, and coming with the clouds of heaven.'" Mark 14:62 c. 1510

Being Active in Mercy

by Matthew C. Harrison

The contents of this essay were presented at the International Disaster Conference held at Concordia Theological Seminary, Fort Wayne, Ind., in September 2014. The conference provided a forum for international Lutheran church leaders to consider both the theology of mercy and the practical implications for implementing it in their churches.

My first call was out of Concordia Theological Seminary in 1991, and it was to a small Iowa community called Westgate, St. Peter's Lutheran Church. As I was there, I served for about four years, and the church was rather vibrant and active. When I left, we had 440 members in a town of 200 and a lot more milk-cows — several thousand of those.

The ministry went well there. It was a strong church and a very tight knit community, but challenges that had plagued urban America were clearly also plaguing rural America, such as methamphetamine. I had members who were involved in meth trade. We had inactive members who were active pot smokers and messing with other drugs. We had an alcoholism epidemic in the community. We had youth alcohol abuse all over the place. We had single parent households, rural welfare — all these things now plague rural America virtually everywhere.

In the course of my time there, I began to think, you know, I wonder if there isn't something else that we, as a corporate community, as a church, ought to be doing in a community like that. I was nagged by this idea, even as I ended up leaving. I just didn't have my finger on resources to refer to, and theologically, I was struggling with exactly what it might mean for the church. I had been taught rather strongly that the Church is involved in the preaching of the Gospel and the administration of the Sacraments, and really, being involved in care for the body was somehow the domain of the liberals.

I was called to Zion Lutheran Church, Fort Wayne, to a very unique situation. It was, at the time, the poorest census track in the state of Indiana, and that's pretty poor when you consider Gary over by Chicago. All around Zion — a beautiful gothic structure built in 1893 and an anchor for the neighborhood for a century — the neighborhood had gone through a number of changes. When I was there, it was mostly a black neighborhood, and within a block and a half of the church, there were 45 vacant, dilapidated buildings. So, I began looking at that problem, and I told my assistant pastor, Paul Kaiser, "Why don't you take care of the shut-ins? I'll do the senior pastor stuff and also take a look at this neighborhood and see if we can't do something about it."

I think, initially, there were several reasons for doing so. One was that the people from the rest of the community don't like to come down to the black section of town. There were a lot of racial tensions in this town. Fort Wayne had been a very Southern town during the Civil War. If you read E.G. Zealor's autobiography — that's the son of Vilhelm Zealor who was the vice president of the Synod in the 1860s and 70s — he talks about an effigy of Lincoln on a parade float being hauled through town with derisive language on it and then being lit on fire and thrown into the river with everybody celebrating. So, this town, like St. Louis, which you have unfortunately seen as of late, has its racial tensions.

So, I felt inspired to do something that would take down barriers from people coming into go to church at Zion while also looking at the community around the church. I realized that the dilapidation was in largest measure caused by rental properties. In other words, there were many homeowners in the neighborhood who kept up their homes and worked hard to do so, but others who lived outside the community would rent their homes to people who would be allowed to run their homes down to nothing. Finally, windows would be smashed out, and then the homeless or somebody with mental illness would occupy the place. There were homes that I went in that were just 100 yards from Zion that were filled five-feet deep with everything you could collect free at every Goodwill center — clothing and everything else you can imagine, like drug paraphernalia, pornography, etc. A story I have often told is that I went around one house north of the church that was dilapidated, and with the help of a lawyer in town, I bought it. I was just going around buying property right and left, making deals for old houses and vacant lots.

Zion became pretty well known in the community and greatly appreciated in the immediate community. We had many, many different challenges and problems. I was convinced that there had to be some better theological rationale for not only that kind of effort, but for the church as a corporate body taking a stand and an active stance toward people in need and other issues happening in communities. In that particular case, at Zion, I became convinced that the church was a corporation. Every one of our congregations in America is registered with the state, so we can have the proper tax benefits, and we are Zion Evangelical Lutheran Church, Inc. That means, as a corporation of people, our congregations, indeed our districts and the body itself, are all corporate citizens of their respective communities. So, if your neighborhood is in atrophy, you will take action in your community. You will if your neighborhood is going to participate actively. If you see some injustice going on in your community, you will, as a citizen of your community who has a responsibility, indeed as a Christian citizen, act. You will not be quiet. Just where to act and where not to act, that's always a challenge to discern, and we are criticized sometimes for acting in some places and not acting in others. Fundamentally, as corporate citizens, the church must act in its community.

It was only after leaving Fort Wayne that I began to think about some kind of theological rationale for what became a catchword for the theological rationale for mercy. I was called to St. Louis to be the executive for the Missouri Synod's LCMS World Relief and Human Care departments. That encompassed disaster response and the whole realm of mercy activities, including relationships with social ministry agencies.

I remember when I got the call to St. Louis, I began to look at the theological issues involved, and working with the Board for Human Care, I suggested that we try to lay out some kind of theological rationale for mercy. As I began to study the issue more and more, I realized that right within my own tradition there was a lot of "ammo." I saw parts of text and older text that I had never noticed before. I went on a journey through Paul's collection for Jerusalem and became convinced that the collection for Jerusalem drives Paul's entire third missionary journey. He is consumed with this for almost a decade. He ends up taking money to Jerusalem to distribute to the poor as a gift from the Gentile churches. It's kind of an eschatological realization of the kingdom in some fashion, as he actually goes to Jerusalem with the money to deliver the gifts, and he ends up getting in trouble because he did so — imprisoned, shipped off to Rome and finally beheaded. All the words we use for stewardship and giving money — God loves a cheerful giver; the gift is acceptable according to what a person has, not according to what a person does; 1 Corinthians 8-9, where Paul is urging the Corinthian Christians who are cosmopolitan and rather wealthy to give money — I discovered in Paul's words for money that they represent aid to Christians. Paul calls that money a *liturgia*. He calls it a liturgy, a public service. He also calls it a *diakonia*, a service, a ministry. He calls it a *koinonia*, a fellowship, a partaking. He even calls it a *charis*, a grace. So, all of a sudden, I realize St. Paul is using the most powerful words in the New Testament to talk about aid to the needy. Then I began to think, "Well, gee, this has really been missing among us. Why, why have we nothing to say on this?"

Then, other sudden classic texts began to pop out, like Walther's *Pastoral Theology*. Here, Walther says the official duties of the pastoral office are to care also for the poor, the weak, the needy and the orphaned. The congregation is even obligated to ensure that the impoverished, if they don't have enough money for a funeral, are buried properly. Why had all this slipped away from so many of our congregations, indeed our whole Church? There are many other such texts. Luther says in the 1519 Sermon on the Sacrament, that at the Sacrament, you come to the altar, you kneel and you lay your burdens upon Christ and the gathered community. When you leave the altar, you take up the burdens of the others at that same altar.

If you look at Dr. Walther's famous *The Proper Form of the Christian Congregation* — the *Die Rechte Gestalt* it is called — there are page after page of the congregation and the pastor's responsibility to see that people in need are cared for. I think in the wake of the welfare state in America since World War II, the realm of care of people shifted from local communities, churches especially, to the government. Churchly institutions, one after another, became intensely secularized until they were either sold, or in many cases, separated from the churches altogether.

So, we began working with the Board for Human Care to have a theological rationale for what resulted in a theology for mercy. It was my conviction that pastors, especially many younger pastors, would not be averse to the church being active in mercy, if in fact there was a decent attempt at a theological basis. I think that proved to be correct.

Diaconic love has its source in the Holy Trinity. The Son is begotten of the Father from eternity. The Holy Spirit proceeds from the Father and the Son. Such begetting and procession are trinitarian acts of love, expressing the commonality of God, as in Luke 6:36: "Be ye merciful, as your Father in heaven is merciful." Diaconic love reflects the very being of God. If you're going to say, "Forget it. I don't have any responsibility toward my neighbor," you are not breaking the law only, you are denying who God is. Diaconic love is born of the incarnation and humiliation of Christ. In Christ, the eternal God became man. Such identity occurred that Christ might have mercy upon His brothers — like them in every way, except sin. Christian service of the neighbor finds its source, motivation, and example in Christ's incarnate, redeeming, atoning, active love. Christ is born for us, becomes incarnate for us, and Luther says, "We, as it were, become incarnate for our neighbor in need."

God would have all come to the knowledge of the truth and be saved (1 Tim. 2:4). A biblically and confessionally faithful theology of mercy clearly confesses that the Father has decreed from eternity that whomever He would save, He would save through Christ, as Christ Himself says, "No one comes to the Father except through me" (John 14:6), and again, "I am the door. If anyone enters by me, he will be saved" (John 10:9).

What is the essence of being a Lutheran Christian in mercy? Christ! What does Christ do? He speaks Law and Gospel. He speaks consolation. He speaks His Word. He makes promises, and He acts in love. What do we do as Christians? We speak. We speak of Christ. We can't help but speak of Christ. The fundamental truth of the Bible that there is no salvation outside faith in Christ and His merits animate the Church's work for those in need. If this is not so, such work becomes merely secular and may be performed by any entity in society.

The Gospel gives forgiveness and begets merciful living. Lives that receive mercy and grace cannot but be lovingly merciful toward the neighbor. The merciful washing of Baptism in Romans 6 produces the merciful living in Rom. 7:4–6. I noticed when Paul taught about the Sacraments or the Gospel, the consequence was also always a life of mercy and service. In absolution, the merciful Word of the Gospel begets merciful speaking and living.

Repentance ought to produce good fruits, the greatest possible generosity to the poor (Apology 12, 174). When we refuse to address the needs within the community as people of God and particularly as the Church of God, we are not merely breaking the Law, but we are also denying the Sacraments. We are denying what we are made in Baptism. We're denying what Christ's body and blood is for us. Christ's mandate and example of love for the whole person remains our supreme example for life in this world and for care of the needy body and soul.

The Lutheran Confessions explicitly and repeatedly state that the work of diaconic love (charity, works of love) is an assumed reality in the Church's corporate life (see Treatise 80–82, Apology 4 and Apology 7). Moreover, the Smalcald Articles explicitly state that works of love are along with, doctrine, faith, Sacraments and prayer, areas that the Church and its bishops are joined in unity. This scene does not dominate our confessions. There is no doubt about that, but it certainly is there.

The call to mercy is particularly addressed to Christians as a corporate community, church, whether local or synod, even national or international. Within these communities, individuals serve in diaconic vocations, pastoral concern for the needy, chaplain, spiritual care, deacon, deaconess, parish nurse, medical disciplines, disaster care and a host of administrative and managerial vocations. These diaconic vocations are flexible in form and determined by need. Within an ecclesial setting, their common goal is the integration of proclamation of the Gospel, faith, worship and care for those in need. The range of the legitimate disciplines of human care may be used in the Church's diaconic life to the extent that such discipline tools do not contradict the Gospel and the doctrine of Holy Scripture.

So, the Apology says, "Christ's kingdom is spiritual." At the same time, it permits us to make outward use of legitimate political ordinances of whatever nation in which we live, just as it permits us to make use of medicine or architecture or food, drink or air. The Church's work of mercy extends beyond its own borders. In the New and Old Testaments, we see a priority of concern for those within the Orthodox fellowship of faith, but add, "Do good also to those outside the kingdom of God, especially to those inside, but also to those outside the house of God." [Gal. 6:8-10]

About 10 or 11 years ago, there was a small tornado that hit south of St. Louis, and it hit a small community there, and we have a church there. The high school was leveled. There were no deaths, but there was a lot of loss and a lot of people adversely affected. Up until this time, the only thing the Missouri Synod had done for disaster for congregations was to work through Lutheran Disaster Response [in Chicago] and send dollars for disbursement among social ministry organizations. The social ministry organizations act as government partners and also do ongoing care for people, case management and get people back on their feet over time. We had not addressed our own congregations in any significant way, our own immediate need.

In fact, the rules of Lutheran Disaster Response precluded assisting congregations in anything, any damage to churches, or anything like that.

Out of this came a so-called Congregation Model of LCMS Disaster Response, and we discovered that what happened was when you go to help a family, you call the family first, and you check with the pastor. Then we go, and our disaster responders then say,

> "Okay, here is what we are going to do. We have some people here that are going to take care of your wife, and we got you some interim housing taken care of, and now we're going to make sure that you come along. Here, we are going to visit your congregation elders first. We will pull them together and start developing a plan. Because the whole community will respond, it will be important for you to be in the middle of that as part of your community to serve. There is probably a niche for you to serve, and I think your niche might well be a staging ground for immediate repairs on something. We can house the volunteers in a large part of your property, if we bring in the proper equipment. By the way, we have a mobile food unit that we funded, and we can bring that down and make sure we have it all set up. And we'll start cooking meals for all the volunteers that are coming in."

So you see, what is initial concern for our own is a concern also to increase their local capacity immediately and care for those well beyond their own borders.

Next the Church will cooperate with others in meeting human need. "Cooperation in externals" has long been an expression describing the Church's legitimate ability to cooperate with other Christians, whether churches, societies, Lutheran or Christians, in meeting human need. To cooperate in externals means to work toward common goals and endeavors which do not necessitate, require or necessarily imply church fellowship or involve joint proclamation of the Gospel in administration of the Sacraments. Such cooperative endeavors are entered for practical reasons, such as, lack of critical resources for instance, but such endeavors are also often an expression of the belief that when entered to with other Christian entities of the catholicity of the Church. You know, the Formula of Concord very carefully distinguishes between hard-necked false teachers and Christians who find themselves in denominations other than Lutheran, and it is very charitable to them. As well as an expression of love for fellow Christians, through such endeavors the LCMS will often have opportunities to insist on theological integrity and the truth of God's word and everyone makes a positive contribution to activities.

So then, the Lutheran doctrine of the two kingdoms grants broad freedom for the Church to engage and be active in its community. The Church has a role in its community, local, national and international, by virtue of the fact that the congregations in national churches are actually corporate citizens of their respected communities. As such, congregations, churches and synods as a whole engage the community as corporate citizens of God's left hand kingdom, working toward worthy civic goals, good citizenship, just laws in society, protection of the weak, housing, etc. Legitimate civil ordinances are good creations of God and divine ordinances in which a Christian may safely take part. As such, a corporate citizen, the church has civic and political capital. In addition to engaging its members to be responsible citizens, the Church may from time to time speak with a collective voice on issues of great significance to society, particularly where the basic value of human life is diminished.

Public redress, which is made through the office of the judge is not forbidden, but is commanded and is a work of God, according to Paul in Romans 13. Public redress includes judicial decisions. Luther, in his writing on temporal authority, to what extent it should be obeyed, says that Christians should not take recourse against government in any way, shape or form. Fortunately, the Confessions did not agree with Luther here and said that Christians indeed may make use of legitimate civil ordinances like juries and trials and judges. There have been times of necessity, and so we have acted on numerous religious freedom cases. The Missouri Synod files briefs for numerous cases around the country which are from time to time referenced by U.S. Supreme Court judges in their opinions. We have also famously been involved very directly in religious freedom cases, and those cases will continue to be upon us with intensity.

There have been times in the life of the Church when it was the sole guardian and provider for the needy. In our day, the rise of the modern welfare state has shifted that monetary responsibility in large measure to the civic, civil realm. There is a large intersection of civil and churchly endeavor at just this point. Thus, the Church's response to these issues is always mutating and nuanced. In these matters, the church must spend its capital wisely and sparingly. They must avoid both quietism and political activism. The former shuns the ethical demand of love for the neighbor, ignoring for instance the ethical urgency of the Old Testament Minor Prophets. The latter may obscure the Church's fundamental and perceptual task as bearer of the Word to sinners in need of Christ. Where the Church loses sight of this proclamation of the Gospel, it thereby loses the very motivation for diaconic work, the Gospel itself. Thus, the Church must not speak when it *may* do so; the Church must speak only when it *must* do so — easier said than done.

PREPARATION FOR BURIAL
"So they took the body of Jesus and bound it in linen cloths with the spices, as is the burial custom of the Jews." John 19:40. c. 1509–1510

Answering the "Why" Question: Martin Luther on Human Suffering and God's Mercy

BY JOHN T. PLESS

The contents of this essay were presented at the International Disaster Conference held at Concordia Theological Seminary, Fort Wayne, Ind., in September 2014. The conference provided a forum for international Lutheran church leaders to consider both the theology of mercy and the practical implications for implementing it in their churches.

HY?

The 13th anniversary of 9/11 and a string of events within the last decade — including tsunamis; Hurricane Katrina; earthquakes in Haiti, Chile and Japan; flooding in the Philippines; mindless shootings in a Connecticut school; tornadoes in the American Midwest; grisly persecution of Christians in Syria and the Ebola epidemic in West Africa — are compounded with countless personal tragedies that press people to ask the ancient question, "Why is there suffering?" More existentially put, "What did I do to deserve this?"

These are questions raised to Christians, and before them we cannot remain silent. In venturing into this territory, we do well to heed the counsel of D. Z. Philips:

> Philosophizing about the problem of evil has become common place. Theories, theodices abound, all seeking either to render unintelligible, or to justify, God's ways to human beings. Such writing should be done in fear: fear that in our philosophizing, we will betray the evils people have suffered, and, in that way, sin against them. Betrayal occurs every time explanations and justifications of evil which are simplistic, insensitive, incredible or obscene. Greater damage is often done to religion by those who think of themselves as its philosophical friends than by those who present themselves as religion's detractors and despisers. Nowhere is this damage more than in evidence, in my opinion, than in philosophical discussions of the problem of evil.[1]

Martin Luther was not a stranger to suffering and affliction.[2] It is the thesis of this paper that the Reformer does have a good bit to teach us both about what we are

---

[1] D. Z. Philips, *The Problem of Evil & the Problem of God* (Minneapolis: Fortress Press, 2005), xi. Also see Thomas G. Long, *What Shall We Say? Evil, Suffering, and the Crisis of Faith* (Grand Rapids: Eerdmans, 2011).

[2] Here see the fine study by Ronald K. Rittgers, *The Reformation of Suffering: Pastoral Theology and Lay Piety in Late Medieval and Early Modern Germany* (Oxford: Oxford University Press, 2012), 84–124 and John T. Pless, Martin Luther: *Preacher of the Cross-A Study of Luther's Pastoral Theology* (Saint Louis: Concordia Publishing House, 2013).

authorized by the Word of God to say and how we, who live under the cross of Jesus Christ, respond to those who suffer in this world. But I would like to come to Luther by first attending to alternative responses.

Theodicy: Justification of God or Man?

In 1981, Rabbi Harold Kushner wrote a best-selling book *When Bad Things Happen to Good People.*[3] The book is an anguish-laden attempt of the rabbi to come to terms with a painful illness that claimed the life of his young son. Struggling with issues of God's providence and mercy, creation and chaos, the rabbi can finally only conclude that those who suffer must "forgive God." Believing that God's intentions might be good but His power is limited seems to be a better solution than calling into question His goodness. Thomas G. Long sensitively examines but finds wanting the approach of Rabbi Kushner, noting:

> Process theologians like Kushner want to draw an emphatic picture of God, but they end up producing merely a pathetic one, a God one might find endearing, but not worthy of worship. Here is God in the midst of chaos, whispering, pleading, trying to persuade a balky world to be better, to be less trivial and more aesthetically pleasing, but the results are less impressive.[4]

In addressing the question of evil and suffering, three things must be held together: (1) God's merciful love, (2) His omnipotence and (3) the far-reaching consequences of human sin in and on creation. Kushner seeks to rescue God's reputation as a God of love by sacrificing His omnipotence.

If a Lutheran were to do a re-write of Kushner's book, it would have a different title: *When Good Things Happen to Bad People.* In the Divine Service, we confess that "We justly deserve" God's "present and eternal punishment," but times of calamity call into question whether we really believe it. In defiance or moaning resignation, we cry out "Why me?" as though God had to explain Himself.[5] In this role reversal, God becomes the defendant and man the judge.

Theodicy is a term coined from two Greek words *theos* (God) and *dike* (judgment) literally meaning a judgment of or justification of God. The term became the title of a book by G. W. Leibnitz (1646–1716) in which he argued optimistically that this is the best of all possible worlds. After the destructive All Saints Day earthquake of 1755 killed thousands in Lisbon, his argument was ridiculed, but the term would remain. Its use would indicate something of a reversal. Werner Elert writes that, "We try to ensnare God in our moral categories, and we do it with the best of intentions, because

---

[3] See Harold Kushner, *When Bad Things Happen to Good People* (New York: Avon, 1981).

[4] Long, *What Shall We Say? Evil, Suffering, and the Crisis of Faith,* 75.

[5] In fact, Gerhard Forde writes, "The attempt to make God answerable to the likes of us — that is the original sin itself." Gerhard Forde, *The Captivation of the Will: Luther versus Erasmus on Freedom and Bondage* (Grand Rapids: Eerdmans, 2005), 64.

we wish to rationalize our assertion that he is just and kind."[6] But as Elert goes on to explain, there is a reversal going on. The Creator, who is the judge, now becomes the defendant, while the creature now becomes judge over the Creator. Rather than God justifying man, man now attempts to justify God.

Recent attempts at theodicy often attempt to excuse God. After the tsunami, one North American clergyman when interviewed on a national television broadcast claimed "that God had nothing to do with it." In a futile effort to protect the Lord God from anything that might cause human beings to fear Him, this cleric tried to extract God from the picture altogether! The attempt falters, leaving a God who is remodeled according to human imagination. This is hardly the God known by Job and Jonah in the Old Testament.

Others would suggest that God is not the cause of suffering, but He merely allows it. If God is almighty, then it is of little comfort to assert that this all-powerful God allowed evil when He could have stopped it. To this argument, Oswald Bayer responds:

> The first attempt is an effort to soften or give up completely on the concept of omnipotence. It is thus often said that God does not cause evil, but simply lets it happen. But such talk about the bland 'permitting' (*permissio*) of evil is too harmless. It assumes the possibility of a power vacuum or even that there is an independent power that is in opposition. At the very least, it assumes that the human being has the power to stand up against God.[7]

But God is not impotent. He is "God the Father Almighty maker of heaven and earth" as we confess in the creed. Attempts to get God off the hook, to defend Him by limiting or weakening His omnipotence end up with an idol.

Listening to Jesus

Rather than try to construct a philosophical theodicy that would assign human beings the impossible task of justifying God, we do better to listen to Jesus, as He responds to the "why" question in Luke 13:1–9. Whether it is Pilate's slaughter of the pious as he mingles their blood with the blood of sacrificial animals, the engineering failure of the Tower of Siloam or more contemporary examples of seemingly unjust suffering, such stories prompt us also to inquire of God, "Why?" Yet the words of Jesus pre-empt the question with a stark warning: "Unless you repent, you will all likewise perish" (Luke 13:3).

Jesus does not offer a philosophical explanation for the religious massacre in the temple or the random toppling of Siloam's tower upon the heads of 18 innocent bystanders. The Lord wastes no time with theoretical distinctions between the

---

[6] Werner Elert, *The Christian Ethos*. Trans. Carl J. Schindler (Philadelphia: Fortress Press, 1957): 156.

[7] Oswald Bayer, *Martin Luther's Theology: A Contemporary Interpretation*. Trans. Thomas H. Trapp (Grand Rapids: Eerdmans, 2008): 206–207. Also see Oswald Bayer, "God's Omnipotence" *Lutheran Quarterly* (Spring 2009): 85–102.

malicious banality of the butchery done by the human will of Pilate and catastrophic collapse of stone and mortar. Jesus' words will not let us go there. His words call for repentance, not speculation.[8]

Repentance lets go of the silly questions that we would use to hold on to life on our own terms, to try to protect ourselves against the God who kills and makes alive. The theologian Oswald Bayer observes that the world is forensically structured, arranged in such a way as to demand justification. We find evidence of this, Bayer says, in the way we defend our own words and deeds.[9] What happens when we are confronted with wrongdoing? We attempt to justify our behavior. It is a rerun of Eden: "The woman whom you gave to be with me, she gave me fruit of the tree, and I ate" (Gen. 3:12). Adam blames Eve. But behind his accusation of Eve is the accusation of his Creator. To repent is to die to self-justification and turn to the God who justifies the ungodly by faith alone. He is the God who takes no pleasure in the death of the wicked but instead has sent forth His own Son to pour out His blood in atonement for the world's sin, to be crushed by the weight of God's wrath that in His righteousness sinners might not perish but have life in His name.

Speculation or faith: God in hiding or God revealed?

Speculation, it seems, is more comfortable than repentance and less risky, we imagine, than faith in a God who kills and makes alive. But speculation cannot penetrate God in His absolute hiddenness; it ultimately yields no answers. In providing pastoral care to folk vexed by questions concerning predestination, Luther directs us away from God in His hiddenness. This is precisely where the "why" questions lead. Instead, Luther points to God's mercy revealed in the manger and the cross, coming at God from below. The table talk recorded by Caspar Heydenreich, Feb. 18, 1542, sets forth Luther's response to those who use the doctrine of election for speculation rather than faith. Luther warns against an "epicurean" approach that is nothing more than fatalism. Such a fatalistic approach casts aside the Passion of Christ and the Sacraments. It is the work of the devil to make us unbelieving and doubtful. It would be foolish of God to give us His Son and the Scriptures if he wished us to be uncertain or doubtful of salvation.

God is truthful, and His truth gives us certainty. A distinction must be made, Luther asserts, between the knowledge of God and the despair of God. We know nothing of the unrevealed God, the hidden God. God blocks the path here. "We must confess

---

[8] Gerhard Forde asserts "I heard a rabbi in one of the memorial ceremonies for the destruction of the two World Trade Towers declaim that nothing or no one could convince us that God somehow willed the terrible tragedy with all its attendant suffering and loss of life. But the problem is that such declamations, alas, do not hold. When all is said and done, the pain and sorrow and mourning continue ... All such declamations accomplish is to throttle the preaching of the gospel. They substitute lame explanations and shallow comfort where there should be proclamation." Gerhard Forde, *The Captivation of the Will* (Grand Rapids: Eerdmans, 2005), 44–45.

[9] Oswald Bayer, *Living by Faith: Justification and Sanctification* (Grand Rapids: Eerdmans, 2003): 1–8.

that what is beyond our comprehension is nothing for us to bother about."[10] We are to stick with the revealed God. "He who inquires into the majesty of God shall be crushed by it."[11] God gives us His Son so that we may know that we are saved. Hence we are "to begin at the bottom with the incarnate Son and with your terrible original sin."[12] We are to stick with Baptism and the preaching of God's Word.

Turning to his own experience, Luther recalls the consolation he received from Staupitz when vexed by the question of election. Staupitz directed him to the wounds of Christ wherein we have the mercy of God revealed; God is surely there for us. The example of Adam and Eve is a warning against every attempt to find God apart from His Word, for such an endeavor is more than spiritually frustrated; it ends in unbelief, for God wraps Himself in His promises of mercy and grace, and He will not let sinners access Himself in places other than His Gospel:

> Without the Word there is neither faith nor understanding. This is the invisible God. The path is blocked here. Such was the answer which the apostles received when they asked Christ when he would restore the kingdom to Israel, for Christ said, 'It is not for you to know.' Here God desires to be inscrutable and to remain incomprehensible.[13]

Apart from the baby of Bethlehem who goes on to suffer and die as the man of Calvary, God remains an evasive presence whose ways are inexplicable and whose power is condemnation.

No comfort is to be found in the "hidden God" (*deus absconditus*) but only in the "revealed God" (*deus revelatus*) that is in Christ.[14] Hence, theology and pastoral care begin below at manger and cross and not above in the majesty that terrifies.

> Paul ... desires to teach Christian theology, which does not begin above in the utmost heights, but below in the profoundest depths ... If you are concerned with your salvation, forget all ideas of law, all philosophical doctrines, and hasten to the crib and his mother's bosom and see him, an infant, a growing child, a dying man. Then you will be able to escape all fear and errors. This vision will keep you on the right way. He (Luther) says the same in the briefest possible formula: "To seek God outside of Jesus is the devil."[15]

---

[10] Theodore Tappert, ed., *Luther: Letters of Spiritual Counsel* (Vancouver: Regent College Publishing, nd), 132.

[11] Tappert, 132.

[12] Ibid.

[13] Ibid.

[14] On God's hiddenness, see the excellent treatment by Steven Paulson, "Luther's Doctrine of God" in *The Oxford Handbook of Martin Luther's Theology*, ed. Robert Kolb, Irene Dingel, L'ubomir Batka (Oxford: Oxford University Press, 2014), 187–200.

[15] Gerhard Ebeling, *Luther: An Introduction to his Thought*, trans. R.A. Wilson (Philadelphia: Fortress, 1972), 235.

We are given only to hear the "preached God," the Deus *revelatus* as Luther puts it in *The Bondage of the Will*:

> The God who is preached and revealed to us, who gives himself to us and is worshipped by us, differs from the unpreached, unrevealed, not given, not worshipped God … The preached God purifies us from sin and death, so that we become holy. He sends his son to heal us. The God hidden in his majesty, however, does not weep bitterly over death and does not abolish it, rather this hidden God effects life, death, and everything in between. As such he has not become restrained in his Word; rather he has reserved for himself freedom above everything else.[16]

Divine mercy in word and deed

Unexplainable tragedies bring pain and chaos. God leaves the wound open to use the words of Bayer.[17] We cry out to God in lamentation in the face of events that defy our capacities for understanding. But the anguished lament ascends from the crucible of faith, not unbelief. It is a confession of trust in the God who works all things for the good of those who are called (Rom. 8:28). Living in repentance and faith, we are freed from the inward turn of speculation that seeks to investigate the hidden God and instead we trust in the kindness and mercy of God revealed in Christ Jesus. With such a freedom we are liberated to rely on God's promises and turn our attention to works of mercy to bring compassion and relief to those who suffer in this sinful world.

What is the nature and shape of this mercy? Mercy is the Lord's compassionate action toward sinful human beings in that He does not leave us alone with our sin, forsaking us to death and condemnation, but instead rescues us by His death and resurrection to live with Him. Jesus Himself is the source of God's mercy for humanity. The Lord puts that mercy into action in His preaching and miracles which all point to His death and resurrection which reconcile us to His Father.

Mercy, Bayer reminds us, is not self-evident in this world.[18] We do not see it in nature. We do not see mercy in the way of life in the world where the consequences of sin are all too evident. Mercy is what God does (See Ex. 34:6; Ps.103:2–4; Luke 1:46–55;

---

[16] Cited from LW 33:319 by Notger Slenczka, "God and Evil: Martin Luther's Teaching on Temporal Authority and the Two Realms" *Lutheran Quarterly* XXVI (Spring 2012), 19-20. Commenting on this Luther text, Slenczka says "The way God works in the rubble of history might as well be called fate; either way, no person will ever understand the motives and intentions of the force which drives history" (20). In history the works of God remain "opaque" (21) as they are hidden to human beings. Compare with Werner Elert's discussion of "fate" in *An Outline of Christian Doctrine*, trans. Charles M. Jacobs (Philadelphia: The United Lutheran Publication House, 1927), 33–36.

[17] Oswald Bayer, "Poetological Doctrine of the Trinity" Lutheran Quarterly (Spring 2001), 56. Also see Oswald Bayer, "Toward a Theology of Lament" in *Caritas et Reformatio: Essays on Church and Society in Honor of Carter Lindberg*. Edited by David M. Whitford (St. Louis: Concordia Publishing House, 2002): 211–220. Also see Bernd Janowski, *Arguing with God: A Theological Anthropology of the Psalms*, trans. Armin Siedlecki (Louisville: Westminster/John Knox, 2013).

[18] "Mercy is not self-evident. It cannot become an existential or epistemological principle. On the contrary mercy is actually something won and is something that, emerging, happens unpredictably. And so this justifying God is not simply and in principle merciful, so also is sinful man not simply and in principle on the receiving end of God's mercy." Oswald Bayer, "Mercy From the Heart" *Logia* XIX (Eastertide 2010), 30.

Luke 1:68–79; Eph. 2:4–7; Titus 3:4–8; 1 Peter 1:3; 1 Peter 2:10, etc.) Mercy is not something we earn or deserve; it is a gift. That is why we speak of God's mercy in an "ethic of gift."[19] Who we are and what we do is established by what we have been given. Think of the explanation of the First Article of the Creed in *Luther's Small Catechism*, where the Reformer confesses that God the Father Almighty has

> "made me and all creatures ... given me my body and soul, eyes, ears and all my members, my reason and all my senses, and still takes care of them. He also gives me clothing and shoes, food and drink, house and home, wife and children, and all that I have. He richly and daily provides me with all that I need to support this body and life. He defends me against all danger and guards and protects me from all evil. All this He does only out of fatherly, divine goodness and **mercy**, without any merit or worthiness in me. For all this it is my duty to thank and praise, serve and obey Him."

We show mercy because we have received mercy from the Triune God – Father, Son and Holy Spirit. The triune God, in His mercy, has created, redeemed and sanctified us in body and soul. God's mercy is proclaimed and enacted. Francis of Assisi is often quoted as saying, "Preach the Gospel; use words if necessary." If Saint Francis said it, he was wrong. The Gospel requires words for it is through Jesus' words – words that are spirit and life – that faith is created and sustained. A wordless "ministry of presence" is quite presumptuous! We are to proclaim the deeds of Him who called us out of darkness into His marvelous light (1 Peter 2:9–10), and this is nothing less than preaching the Word of the cross. In the face of inexplicable suffering, we proclaim the promise that there is no condemnation for those in Christ Jesus (Rom. 8:1) and that even in these events, God is at work for the good of His children even though we cannot understand how this is so.

The mercy that we proclaim and confess is also demonstrated as God uses us as "masks" from behind which He works to deliver mercy to those who suffer. One particularly potent example of this in Luther is his 1527 letter to the Breslau pastor John Hess on whether Christians may flee in times on plague. Just a few months before, in the summer of 1527, the plague struck Wittenberg. The university was relocated to Jena where it would remain until the following April. Even though the elector ordered Luther and his family to leave Wittenberg in August, he refused to do so. Instead, he continued lecturing on 1 John to the students who elected to remain in the town. Along with Bugenhagen and others, Luther would minister to the sick, dying and grieving. Luther referred to his home as a hospital. At the end of December after the epidemic had abated, Luther described his situation as hanging on to Christ by a thread even as Satan had bound him with an anchor chain and pulled him into the depths.[20] It was against this backdrop that Luther answered Pastor Hess's inquiry.

---

[19] See Oswald Bayer, "The Ethics of Gift" *Lutheran Quarterly* XXIV (Winter 2010), 275–287.

[20] See Martin Brecht, *Martin Luther: Shaping and Defining the Reformation* 1521–1532,trans. James L. Schaaf (Minneapolis: Fortress Press, 1990), 209.

Luther provides an answer from the context of Christian freedom as it is to be applied within one's calling, where both the offices of faith and love are exercised. Faith trusts in God's providential care in the face of danger, recognizing that one's life is in God's hands whether one stays or leaves. Believers are to commend themselves into God's keeping whatever course of action they may take. So Luther writes:

> If anyone is bound to remain in peril of death in order to serve his neighbor, let him commit himself to God's keeping and say: 'Lord, I am in thy hands. Thou hast obligated me to serve here. Thy will be done, for I am thy poor creature. Thou canst slay or preserve me here as well as if I were duty bound to suffer fire, water, thirst, or some other danger.' On the other hand, if anyone is not bound to serve his neighbor and is in a position to flee, let him also commit himself to God's keeping and say: 'Dear God, I am weak and afraid; I am therefore fleeing from this evil and am doing all that I can to defend myself against it. Nevertheless, I am in thy hands, whether in this or some other evil that may befall me. Thy will be done. My flight will not save me, for evils and misfortunes will assail me everywhere and the devil, who is a murderer from the beginning and tries to commit murder and cause misfortune everywhere, does not sleep or take a holiday.'[21]

Noting that some insist that the believer must not flee a deadly epidemic but accept the affliction as God's judgment enduring whatever fate may come in patience and unswerving faith, while other believers think it acceptable to leave if not bound by other obligations, Luther cautions that neither alternative is the grounds for inflicting the conscience of those who come to opposing conclusions. Those who are strong in faith may indeed wait the pestilence out, but they are not to bind those whose faith is weak to their opinion. "Let him who is strong in faith stay, but let him not condemn those who flee."[22]

However, one may not flee an infected place if his calling to serve the neighbor is jeopardized. In cases where one's office — that of a pastor, governmental official or medical worker, for example — obligates him to serve the suffering neighbor, then there is no question in Luther's mind. He must stay even at the risk of his health and life in order to discharge duty to the neighbor. Drawing on Christ's words in John's Gospel (10:11–12) about the hireling who forsakes the flock when the thief comes, Luther concludes that faithful shepherds will not forsake those committed to their care in order to save their own lives. Here, Luther observes that there are two ways of fleeing death. One is to act contrary to God's Word or to recant one's confession of faith in order to preserve one's own life. The other ungodly way of escaping death is to abandon the neighbor in order to save one's self.

---

[21] Tappert, 236.

[22] Ibid., 235.

This does not mean for Luther that the instinct to preserve one's life is intrinsically wrong. He notes examples of Old Testament patriarchs and prophets who fled from death without abandoning their offices. Further, Luther suggests that if an adequate ministry is provided, not all pastors need remain in a time of crisis. Luther recalls the example of the apostle Paul in Damascus (see Acts 19:30) who slips out of the city to escape persecution. Given the fact that other ministers remained in Damascus to provide spiritual care for the Christians there, Paul was not himself bound to remain and face unnecessary danger. In a matter-of-fact manner, Luther offers the counsel that:

> In time of death one is especially in need of the ministry which can strengthen and comfort one's conscience with God's Word and Sacrament in order to overcome death with faith. However, where enough preachers are available and they come to agreement among themselves that some of their number should move away because there is no necessity for their remaining in such danger, I do not count it a sin because an adequate ministry is provided, and, if need be, these would be ready and willing to stay.[23]

Luther does not call for impulsive heroism when the neighbor's well-being is not at stake: "The instinct to flee death and save one's life is implanted by God and is not forbidden, provided it is not opposed to God and the neighbor."[24] However, to neglect the well-being of the neighbor in body or soul is sin. Not only pastors but those who hold secular offices needed to protect the common good are bound to stay at their posts. Drawing on God's institution of governing authorities (Rom. 13:6) and parenthood (1 Tim. 5:8), Luther notes that these responsibilities override personal comfort and safety: "No one may forsake his neighbor when he is in trouble. Everybody is under obligation to help and support his neighbor as would himself like to be helped."[25] Having recently lectured to his university students on I John, Luther cites 1 John 1:14–17 where the apostle teaches that failure to love amounts to murder to instruct his readers as to what is at stake here. The Fifth Commandment binds us to care for the neighbor, helping and supporting him in every physical need. "Godliness," Luther says, is "nothing but divine service, and divine service is service to one's neighbor."[26] Christ hides behind the mask of the sick and needy to receive this service from us. To run away from an infected neighbor is to run away from Christ Himself.

Luther's letter to Pastor Hess gives expression to the place of faith and love in relationship to vocation. Faith that trusts in Christ alone is driven neither by foolish impulsiveness nor cowardice but by the confidence that living or dying, our lives are in the Lord's hands. The language of Luther's morning and evening prayers is

---

[23] Tappert, 232.

[24] Tappert, 233.

[25] Tappert, 233.

[26] Tappert, 239. For a helpful discussion of Luther's understanding of the positive demand of the fifth commandment, See Albrecht Peters, *Commentary on Luther's Catechisms: Ten Commandments*, 226–232.

expressed in the realization that God gives His holy angels charge over us. They watch over us in times of danger and protect us in ways that exceed our imagination. Love will risk all things — even life itself — to do good to the neighbor in need.

Praying for Mercy

In the face of suffering, we are bold to proclaim the mercy of God in the cross of Christ Jesus, to enact this mercy in our calling to serve the neighbor in need, but also to pray. The Lord's Prayer, to use the words of Georg Vicedom, is a prayer that spans the world so in one sense the whole of this prayer is prayed out of the crucible of suffering, but it is in particular the Seventh Petition that Luther accents when it comes to the Christian's supplication in the face of evil.

Luther, in the Large Catechism, sees the Seventh Petition as directed against Satan "who obstructs everything for which we ask: God's name or honor, God's kingdom and will, our daily bread, a good and cheerful conscience etc." In this petition where we summarize the Lord's Prayer, he tutors believers to call upon the heavenly Father for "rescue from every evil of body and soul," to use the language of the Small Catechism. Luther expands this in the Large Catechism:

> This petition includes all the evil that may befall us under the devil's kingdom: poverty, disgrace, death, and, in short all the tragic misery and heartache, of which there is so incalculably much on earth. For the devil is not only a liar but a murderer as well, he incessantly seeks our life and vents his anger by causing accidents and injury to our bodies. He crushes some and drives others to injury; some he drowns in water, and many he hounds to suicide or other dreadful catastrophes (LC III:115, K/W, 455).[27]

The recognition of the presence of evil and the inevitability of suffering, Luther says, drives us to pray this petition that Jesus has given us.

God has a love-hate relationship with afflictions. "God both loves and hates our afflictions. He loves them when they provoke us to prayer. He hates them when we are driven to despair by them."[28] Luther then goes on to specific biblical references to drive home this point. Coupling Ps. 50:23 ("The one who offers thanksgiving as his sacrifice glorifies me") and Ps.51:17 ("The sacrifices of God are a broken spirit and a contrite heart"), Luther seeks to demonstrate that even in the brokenness of affliction, the believer renders his life to God in the confidence that the Lord will remain true to His Word and not cast off those who hope in His mercy. Luther does not attempt to trivialize the pain, nor does he offer stoic-like advice to endure detached from the

---

[27] Here see Albrecht Peters: "While the devil appeared in the Sixth Petition as a lying and seductive tempter, he now approaches as the destroyer of all the living, as the 'murderer' from the beginning onward. He ultimately stands behind the diversity of evil. Against him all the individual petitions of the Lord's Prayer are directed" – Albrecht Peters, *Commentary on Luther's Catechisms*, trans. Daniel Thies (Saint Louis: Concordia Publishing House, 2011), 2004.

[28] Tappert, 87.

reality of one's situation. Instead, the broken heart is offered up to God knowing that "the Lord hears the gentle sighs of the afflicted."[29]

Two Governments and God's Mercy

Another aspect of Luther's response to evil and suffering is seen in his understanding of the two kingdoms or the two governments.[30] Both of these governments or realms are under lordship of the triune God but he is working with different means and toward different ends. Through the government of His right hand, God is establishing an eternal kingdom through the preaching of the Gospel for the forgiveness of sins. Through the government of the left hand, God is not bestowing salvation, but working to curb evil, to do damage control so that this old creation does not completely collapse into chaos. Evil itself does persist in this old world, and it will not be done away with until Christ Jesus returns and brings about the new heaven and earth (see Is. 65:17–25; 2 Peter 3:13; Rev. 21:1–25). In the meantime, He uses various callings or stations in life within the government of His left hand to curb evil both through the punishment of evil doers (Rom. 13) and caring bodily for those who suffer the effects of evil. Here think of physicians, nurses, rescue workers and the like. These offices are rightly confessed as good works of God, instruments through which God does His work of limiting the effects of evil in a fallen world that awaits its final redemption at the Day of the Lord.

Luther's pastoral response to suffering is multifaceted and rich with evangelical insight. Unlike those who attempt to pry into heaven in search of an answer to the "Why?" question, Luther points to the "Who?" and "What then?" The God who is Lord over wind and wave, who kills and makes alive, is none other than the baby who rests on Mary's lap and hangs on a Roman cross. In Him, we know the good and gracious will of God to save sinners by forgiving them their sins. He is the God who is for us in every way, and on the Last Day, He will raise the dead and give eternal life to all believers in Christ. In the meantime, He calls us by the Gospel to walk by faith, not sight, trusting in His promises. As we wait for that final day, we are not idle. The mercy we have received turns our lives toward those in need of mercy. Indeed, hidden in their suffering is the Lord Himself. To care for them is to care for Christ.

---

[29] Ibid.

[30] The literature on the two governments or two kingdoms is extensive. The treatments by Gerhard Ebeling are particularly helpful. See "The Necessity of the Doctrine of the Two Kingdoms" in Gerhard Ebeling, *Word and Faith*, trans. James W. Leitch (Philadelphia: Fortress Press, 1963), 386–406 and "The Kingdom of Christ and the Kingdom of the World" in Gerhard Ebeling, *Luther: An Introduction to His Thought*, trans. R. A. Wilson (Philadelphia: Fortress Press, 1970), 175–191. Also see James Nestingen, "The Two Kingdom's Distinction: An Analysis and Suggestion" *Word & World* 19(Summer 1999), 268–275. For the purposes of this paper, the article by Notger Slenczka, "God and Evil: Martin Luther's Teaching on Temporal Authority and the Two Realms" *Lutheran Quarterly* XXVI (Spring 2012), 1–25 is especially significant.

Refusal of Joachim's Offering
According to the Golden Legend, Mary's father, Joachim, was a priest whose offering was refused because he and his wife Anna (who were both well along in years) were childless. c. 1504

by Reed Lessing

INTRODUCTION

Today there was a global tragedy of epic proportions. Today 35,000 people died. All of the victims were children. But worst of all, this disaster will happen again and again and again. Every day in our world 35,000 poverty-stricken children die of malnutrition and starvation.[1] But this is only one of numerous challenges that face a church that seeks to witness to the Gospel through acts of mercy. Other pressing horrific issues include people who suffer due to AIDS, unjust laws, forced childhood slavery and prostitution, and the list could go on and on. Too often texts like Deut 15:11, "there will never cease to be poor in the land" (cf. also Matt. 26:11; Mark 14:7; John 12:8) are improperly understood to be expressions of fatalism; as though poverty is part of the natural order of the world and therefore there is nothing anyone can do about it. Certainly the New Testament instructs the church to respond to the broken and helpless people in the world (e.g., Acts 4:32-37; 2 Cor. 8-9; Gal. 6:10). But what about the Old Testament? Does it have anything to say to the church as she seeks to address world relief and human care?

Yes, it does. What follows is an overview of what the Old Testament teaches in regards to acts of mercy. After a look at the Hebrew word *racham*, often translated "mercy," a general investigation of what the Pentateuch teaches about mercy will provide the foundation for a more focused study of mercy in the book of Amos. The study then concludes by offering several suggestions on how the Old Testament is able to motivate and inform Jesus' call to "be merciful, even as your Father is merciful" (Luke 6:36).

Mercy (*Racham*) in the Old Testament

As a noun, *racham* denotes "grace" or "mercy" and is almost always associated in one way or another with Yahweh. He is often described as being great in mercy (e.g., 2 Sam. 24:14 -1 Chron. 21:13; Dan. 9:18; Neh. 9:19). *Racham* sometimes appears with

---

[1] As noted in Readings in *Christian Ethics*, vol. 2, eds. David Clark and Robert Rakestraw (Grand Rapids: Baker, 1996), 339.

the verb "to give" (e.g., 1 Kings 8:50; Jer. 42:12), in which case it is always traced back to Yahweh. In poetic texts *racham* is often parallel with *hesed*, or "loyal covenant faithfulness" (e.g., Ps. 40:11; Lam. 3:22), which indicates that *racham* is never just an emotion — it is always oriented toward a specific action that displays covenantal faithfulness. The adjective from the root *racham* is *rachum*, and it modifies Yahweh exclusively. It is frequently paired in poetic texts with "gracious" (*hanun*), e.g., Ex. 34:6: Yahweh is a "God merciful (*rachum*) and gracious (*hanun*), slow to anger, and abounding in steadfast love (*hesed*) and faithfulness" (cf. Neh. 9:17; Ps. 86:15, 103:8, 145:8; Joel 2:13). Every human act of *racham* in the Old Testament is derived from Yahweh. He is the source of all mercy.

The beliefs of Israel's neighbors in Canaan, Mesopotamia, and Egypt show no such understanding of their deities. The mythologies composed by these pagan people present gods and goddesses who are violent, inaccessible, dominating, and capricious. The characteristics of care and compassion are strikingly absent from these texts.[2] Mercy and compassion are unique to Yahweh, the God of Israel.

Also unique is Israel's belief that people are created in the image of God (Gen. 1:26-27). Israel's ancient Near Eastern neighbors believed in myths portraying people as afterthoughts with no other purpose than to serve the gods and keep them comfortable. In contrast, Israel held to a high view of humanity, whose purpose is to procreate and care for the world (Gen. 1:28). Being made in God's image is analogous, in the ancient Near East, to a governing sovereign who cannot be present everywhere in the realm, but who erects statues of himself as witnesses and reminders of who the real sovereign is. By analog, the invisible God has placed human beings in creation so that, upon seeing the human creature, other creatures are reminded of Yahweh's rule (cf. Ps. 8:5). To value people is to value Yahweh.

Yahweh places infinite value on each person, even if he or she is outcast and disenfranchised. For example, in Gen. 11:30 Sarai is described as being "barren" (*aqarah*). It was through this socially ostracized old woman and her husband Abram that all the families of the earth would be blessed (Gen. 12:3). This narrative is paradigmatic in that it demonstrates how Yahweh has a deep affection and affinity with people who have *nothing*. In fact, the barrenness of Israel's three matriarchs, Sarah, Rebekah (Gen. 25:31), and Rachel (Gen. 29:31), highlight the important fact that Yahweh "chose what is foolish in the world to shame the wise; God chose what is weak in the world to shame the strong; God chose what is low and despised in the world, even things that are not" (1 Cor. 1:27-28; cf. also Is. 54:1; Luke 1:7).

Because of His mercy granted to the patriarchs and their wives, Yahweh remembered His covenant with the slaves in Egypt who had nothing. He came down to rescue

---

[2] Studies addressing the characteristics of these deities and their resulting anthropologies include Jean Bottéro, *Religion in Ancient Mesopotamia*, translated by Teresa Lavender Fagan (Chicago: University of Chicago Press, 2001); John Day, *Yahweh and the Gods and Goddesses of Canaan* (Sheffield: Sheffield Academic Press, 2000); and John Davis, *Moses and the Gods of Egypt* (Winona Lake: BMH Books, 1996).

them (Ex. 3:6-7), while at the same time inflicting judgment upon the gods of Egypt (Ex. 12:12), whose mythologies encouraged the slavery and marginalization of others (Ex. 1:8-22). After the exodus, the Old Testament teaches that any system that impoverishes people will be placed under Yahweh's judgment. He hears the cry of the oppressed (Ex. 2:23). He feels their pain (Ex. 3:7).

By means of the plagues, culminating in the slaughter of the first-born and the Passover, Yahweh had bound the strong man and plundered his house (cf. Matt. 12:29). The Red Sea crossing sealed Israel's deliverance and was a type of baptism (cf. 1 Cor. 10:2). Yahweh had furnished water, quail, and manna (Ex. 15:22-17:7; cf. John 6:32-33). He defended them against their enemies (Ex. 17:8-16; cf. 1 Cor. 15:56-57). God's work constituted the foundation on which his covenant with Israel was built. By the time Israel reached Sinai in Exodus 19, they had a long list of experiences indicating that Yahweh's mercy had followed them all the days of their lives (cf. Ps. 23:6).

These events highlight a key structural element in the Pentateuch which is the inter-weaving of law and narrative. The law does not stand as an external code but is integrated with Israel's ongoing story. In Exodus, for example, readers move from story (ch. 19) to law (20:1-17) to story (20:18-21) to law (20:22-23:22) to story (ch. 24) to law (chps. 25-31) to story (chps. 32-34). The following interpretive implications for understanding acts of mercy are highlighted by this integration of genres:

1. Mercy is seen not as a response to the law as law, but as a response to the great acts of Yahweh's salvation;

2. The narrative shows that the law is given to those already redeemed; acts of mercy are not a means to achieve salvation;

3. The shape that the law takes in Israel's life is defined by the shape of the narrative action of Yahweh;

4. The motivation for following the law is drawn from Israel's experience with Yahweh rather than from abstract ethical arguments or divine imperatives.

These ideas are best illustrated in the preamble to the covenant at Sinai, which begins with the salvation-work of Yahweh: "I am the Lord *your* God, who brought you out of the land of Egypt, out of the house of slavery" (Ex. 20:2). This individualized address from Yahweh, your God, lifts up the importance of internal motivation within a relationship rather than heteronomous imposition ("obey because God said so"). Yahweh's saving relationship with Israel provided the motivation for each person delivered from Egypt to live lives of mercy. What Horace Hummel writes of the Ten Commandments pertains to the rest of the Book of the Covenant (Ex. 20:22-23:19):

> It is of utmost importance to underscore the fact that grammatically the Decalogue is in *indicative*, not imperative form. (The negative is *lo'*, not *'al*.)

These are statements of what the believer who has experienced God's grace *will* voluntarily do … They represent the perimeters or boundaries of God's kingship, beyond which the believer will not stray, but *within* which He [*sic*] is essentially free to respond joyfully and voluntarily, as illustrated by the rest of the "laws" or "codes" of the Old Testament.[3]

In reference to the Book of the Covenant, whose stipulations expand on the Decalogue by treating more specific acts of mercy, Hummel asserts, "We could partly describe them as illustrations or examples of faithful response to redemption."[4] This code is introduced and concluded with the First Commandment (Ex. 20:22-26; 23:20-23). There are also interspersed throughout the section brief reiterations of the basic injunction not to acknowledge any other god but Yahweh (e.g., Exodus. 22:19; 22:28; 23:13). Israel's relationship with Yahweh encloses, as it were, every human relationship. Israel loved people because Yahweh first loved Israel (cf. Deut. 7:7; 1 John 4:19).

Continuing the narrative, in Ex. 25:1-9 Yahweh states to Moses, "And let them [the Israelites] make me a sanctuary, that I may dwell in their midst." The sanctuary will bring heaven to earth, allowing Yahweh to take up residency with the people. The Israelites diligently built the sanctuary, or tabernacle (Exodus 35-39), and God descended the mountain and dwelt among His people full of grace and truth (cf. John 1:14). At the tabernacle — and later at the temple — Yahweh delivered His means of grace by means of blood sacrifices (cf. Lev. 1-7) and priestly Torah instruction. These gifts, along with the exodus redemption, continually empowered Israel to be merciful to others.

In the Pentateuch, the theme of Yahweh's care for the powerless is not only in the Book of the Covenant (e.g., Ex. 22:21-24; 22:25; 23:3, 6, 9, 10-11), but also in the Holiness Code (e.g., Lev. 19:9-10, 15, 32; 25:35-38), and in Deuteronomy (e.g., 14:28-29; 15:7-11; 26:12-15). Julian Morgenstern has collected and arranged the passages in the Pentateuch into these four categories:

1. Commandments dealing with human relations and implying social responsibility; Lev. 19:14, 16-18, 32, 35-36; Deut. 19:14; 22:8; 25:13-15.

2. Commandments providing specifically for the protection of the poor and the weak; Ex. 22:20-26; 23:3, 6, 9; Lev. 19:9-10, 13b, 33; Deut. 15:2; 23:16, 20-21, 25, 26; 24:10-15, 17-22.

3. Commandments dealing with the administration of justice; Ex. 23:1-3, 6-8; Lev. 19:11-13a, 15; Deut. 16:19-20; 24:16.

4. Commandments enjoining consideration for animals; Ex. 23:4-5; Deut. 22:1-4, 6-71, 10; 25:4.[5]

---

[3] Horace D. Hummel, *The Word Becoming Flesh* (St. Louis: Concordia, 1979), 74; emphasis his.

[4] Hummel, *The Word Becoming Flesh*, 75.

[5] Julian Morgenstern, "The Book of the Covenant, Part IV," *HUCA* 5 (1962): 59-105, 61.

Morgenstern's distinctions are useful categories and serve to illustrate the different kinds of mercy that were to be practiced in the Old Testament. The activities in the first category have to do not so much with acts of mercy as they do with what might be called basic honesty and integrity (e.g., honest weights and measures, Lev. 19:35-36). Morgenstern's third group concentrates on justice specifically in the courts, but is applicable to every branch of civil administration, while the last category has as its focus the treatment of both animals and their owners.

The applicability of the second group of passages to the present study is more direct, but even then the directions are expressed in broad terms like, "You shall not wrong a sojourner or oppress him … You shall not mistreat any widow or fatherless child" (Ex. 22:21a, 22), while the provisions for gleaning (Lev. 19:9-10; Deut. 24:19-22) illustrate how mercy was to be exercised toward those who might be primes targets for mistreatment. Mercy consists not of the extraordinary, but of the ordinary. The pentateuchal legislation as it applies to matters of mercy deals primarily not in detailed casuistry but in the enunciation of broad principles. And yet Jeffries Hamilton is correct when he concludes that one of the features of "social justice in Deuteronomy" — which is closely connected if not synonymous with mercy — is "that doing social justice is not an abstraction but is something which can be detailed."[6]

One detailed and specific pentateuchal text that enjoins mercy upon Israel is the jubilee year. Every fiftieth year Yahweh commanded Israel to restructure her assets. This served as a reminder to the nation that all property and land belonged to Him; they were an exodus people who must never return to a system of slavery (Lev. 25:42). The jubilee aimed to dismantle social and economic inequality by releasing each member from debt (Lev. 25:35-42), returning forfeited land to its original owners (vv. 12, 25-28), and freeing slaves (vv. 47-55).

Of course the Pentateuch is not alone in directing and empowering Israel to be merciful to others. The theme is frequent in the Psalter (e.g., 72:2-4, 12-14; 82:3-4; 107:41; 113:7; 132:15; 146:7) and in Proverbs (e.g., 14:21, 31; 19:17; 21:13; 22:9, 22-23; 23:10-11; 29:7, 14; 31:9, 20). At the core of the Old Testament is the teaching that Yahweh's act of mercy in delivering Israel out of Egypt is the springboard for all acts of mercy.

Old Testament Mercy in a Specific Case — Amos

The Old Testament prophets add still another dimension to the practice of mercy. They join their voices with the Pentateuch, Proverbs, and Psalms in exhorting Israel to have compassion for people on the margins. For example, Is. 10:1-4 directs a woe-saying against those who oppress widows, orphans, and the poor. The widow has no husband, the orphan no parent, and the poor have no money to give them access to the basic necessities of life. Jeremiah (e.g., 5:28; 7:6), Ezekiel (e.g., 16:49; 18:12), and

---

[6] Jeffries M. Hamilton, *Social Justice and Deuteronomy: The Case of Deuteronomy* 15 (Atlanta: Scholars Press, 1992), 139.

Zechariah (e.g., 7:10) likewise express Yahweh's concern for marginalized people. The cause of the helpless is the cause of Yahweh.

However, it would be a misreading of prophetic texts to interpret them as if they cared only about justice and mercy and little or nothing about Israel's liturgical life. Unfortunately, passages like Is. 1:10-20 and Hos. 6:6 are often understood as promoting acts of mercy in place of worship. But such texts need to be interpreted as examples of "both/and" rather than "either/or" exhortations. For example, a proper reading of Hos. 6:6 is that Yahweh desires *both* mercy and sacrifice, the knowledge of God *as well as* whole burnt offerings.

Perhaps the strongest voice for *both* mercy *and* a vibrant liturgical life in Israel's prophetic corpus is that of Amos. This statement might come as a shock to those acquainted with this prophet. Why, isn't Amos a "fire and brimstone" preacher who delights in telling people that they are going to be obliterated by God? And in 5:21-24 doesn't the prophet relegate external forms of worship to a second class status? Indeed, a quick reading of the book might convince someone that Amos is a "turn or burn" zealot, who travels north from Tekoa, dumps Yahweh's wrath at Bethel, and dismisses Israel's liturgical life. But nothing could be further from the truth.

Amos is a great advocate for mercy. This belief is depicted in the prophet's two-fold plea, "How can Jacob stand because he is so small?" (cf. 7:5). Amos is interceding, not for the "notable men of the foremost nation" (Amos 6:1), but for the masses who are described throughout the book as the righteous and needy people being oppressed by the systemic sin that kept them down and lifted the rich up. "Little Jacob" denotes all of the "small people" throughout the book who are the prime objects of Yahweh's mercy. To know this about Amos is to understand that throughout the rest of the book his disturbing oracles against Israel, Judah, and the nations are not spoken with sadistic glee. Like Jesus after him, Amos looked at the multitudes who were harassed and helpless, sheep without a shepherd — and he had compassion upon them (cf. Matt. 9:36).

Throughout his book Amos mentions the same group of "small people" by means of several different referents. A listing is as follows:

1. The "needy" (*evyonim*) 2:6; 4:1; 5:12; 8:4, 6
2. The "poor" (*dalim*) 2:7; 4:1; 5:11; 8:6
3. The "oppressed" (*anavim*) 2:7; 8:4
4. The "righteous" (*tsedakim*) 2:6; 5:12

God's compassion for the lowly is also expressed in the New Testament. Mary sings about it (Luke 1:46-55), Jesus preaches about it (Luke 4:18-21), and the disciples model it (Acts 4:32-37; 6:1-6). At the final judgment in Matt. 25:31-46 Jesus reflects his compassion for the stranger, the naked, the prisoner, and the hungry.

Representative of the group of "small" people in Amos are "the afflicted ones" (*anavim*]) (e.g., Amos 2:7; 8:4). The noun is synonymous with hardship, torment, pain, and despair. It denotes the darkness of human experience, the shadow side of life. Many texts employing *anavim* demand Yahweh's intervention. An often-used idiom is, "Yahweh saw the oppression of ... " (e.g., Gen. 29:32; 1 Sam. 1:11; Ps. 119:153). Oppression is always a misery that affects Yahweh. The *anavim* enjoy Yahweh's special protection (e.g., Is. 11:4; 26:6; 61:1; Zeph. 3:12). The Septuagint translates *anavim* in Amos 2:7 with *tapeinon* ("humble"), while in 8:4 the word *ptochous* ("poor") is used. In the NT, *ptochous* takes on the accent of humble ones (e.g., Matt. 5:3; 11:5; Luke 4:18). Paul places priority on the lowly as well (1 Cor. 1:26-28) and maintains that Christ became poor so that the baptized might become rich in grace (2 Cor. 8:9). It is for this reason that Jesus announces that He comes "to proclaim good news to the poor" (Luke 4:18; cf. James 2:5). Like Jesus, Paul was eager to "remember the poor" (Gal. 2:10).

In the book of Amos the *anavim*, along with the "needy," "poor," and "righteous," were being abused sexually (2:7b), fiscally (2:8; 5:11), judicially (5:10), spiritually (2:12), and vocationally (2:7; 4:1; 5:11). There was no justice or righteousness for these people, who were on the edges of Israelite society, because the nation's leadership was rotten at its core (e.g., 2:6-8; 4:1-5; 7:10-17). The elite denied their core identity as Yahweh's people; the once-oppressed in Egypt had become the oppressors of their own countrymen.

Israel's sins against the needy are a greater abomination to Yahweh than are the sins of the nations (cf. Amos 1:3-2:3). The nations mistreated unknown foreigners, whereas Israel's leaders were guilty of oppressing members of their own brotherhood. Rebelling against Yahweh's clear command (cf. e.g., Ex. 21:2-11; Lev 25:35-43; Deut. 15:7-18; 24:15), Israel's leaders were oblivious to the needs of the poor, and to oppress the poor was an indication that they did not fear Yahweh (Lev. 25:43).

But it would be a misreading of Amos to believe that he idealized the poor or their poverty. The poor were not righteous because they had been denied their rights, but rather because *Yahweh had reckoned their faith as righteousness* (Gen. 15:6; Hab. 2:4; Rom. 3:19-31). Responding to their gift of a righteous standing before Yahweh, these poor people were faithful to their covenantal calling and the rich were not.

The purpose of Amos' advocacy for the poor is not to put them on a pedestal, but to point out that Israel's leaders will have to face judgment because of their treatment of these people. Amos did not advocate class warfare; the righteous poor will be vindicated by Yahweh and Yahweh alone. The prophet's oracles call for conversion, not revolution.

At the heart of the book of Amos is the prophet's admonition toward Israel's leadership to practice justice (*mishpat*) and righteousness (*tsedekah*). These two words are paired together in Amos 5:7, 24, and 6:12, as well as in almost eighty other texts in the Old Testament. *Mishpat* and *tsedekah* were to mark Israel off as different from the rest of the nations (e.g., Deut. 4:8). The charter of Israel's existence was fair and just ethical action in every realm of life. And just as Israel was called upon to be merciful because Yahweh was merciful, so the nation was to practice justice and righteousness because first and foremost *mishpat* and *tsedekah* are attributes of Yahweh (cf. Jer. 9:24). In fact all Old Testament ethics are an expression of Yahweh's character and originate in Him.

The word pair "justice and righteousness" does not occur in pentateuchal legal texts. However, Abraham is described by Yahweh as someone who does "righteousness and justice" (Gen. 18:19). The words appear in wisdom texts, e.g. Prov. 16:8, 21:3. Wisdom may even say of herself, "I walk in the way of righteousness (tsedekah), in the paths of justice (mishpat)." Wisdom is summed up using this word pair (e.g., Prov. 1:3; 2:9).

Mishpat denotes decisions, judgments, and laws, while *tsedekah* is the underlying principle and relationship that finds expression in *mishpat*. Put another way, *tsedekah* is the basis for a person's relationship with Yahweh and *mishpat* is an expression of that relationship. Marginalized people in society receive *mishpat* when they are housed, fed, clothed, and incorporated into the economic fabric of the community. *Mishpat* begins with Yahweh's declaration of *tsedekah* to all who believe. This passive gift of *tsedekah* that comes through faith in Yahweh's mercy empowers active *mishpat* that seeks a more just and humane world.

In Amos 5:21-24 it appears as though the prophet categorically rejects Israel's worship. But like Hos. 6:6, the main problem wasn't Israel's worship, but Israel's conduct *outside* of worship. Amos does not offer the people advice to make their festivals more meaningful like "a few less sacrifices here, a few more songs there." The only remedy is consistent moral and ethical action. If *mishpat* and *tsedekah* are not present, "religious life, with all its ritual accoutrements, becomes a sham."[7]

In Amos 5:24 the prophet pictures *mishpat* and *tsedekah* as a surging, churning and cleansing stream. They do not entail merely theological or theoretical ideas. Justice and righteousness are "self-giving and neighbor-regarding."[8] But in following other gods (cf. Amos 2:7; 5:26; 8:14), Israel's leaders adopted systems of belief and behavior that were opposed to Yahweh's command to "love your neighbor as yourself" (Lev. 19:18). The elite worshipped fertility gods and goddesses, whose stories contained violence, oppression, injustice, and sexual license. Their action reflected these narratives rather than the narrative of redemption from Egypt and the inheritance of the Promised Land. Jer. 2:5 and 2 Kings 17:15 indicate that the object of worship

---

[7] Shalom Paul, Amos (Minneapolis: Augsburg/Fortress, 1991), 192; cf. J.A. Motyer, who writes that the people were "praying on their knees in the temple and preying on their neighbors everywhere else" (*The Message of Amos* [Downers Grove, IL: Inter-Varsity Press, 1974], 132).

[8] Robert Benne. *Reasonable Ethics: A Christian Approach to Social, Economic, and Political Concerns* (St. Louis: Concordia, 2005), 62.

becomes the pattern for life; "they went far from me, and went after worthlessness, and became worthless."[9]

At the heart of Amos 5:24 is a water metaphor. "But let justice (*mishpat*) roll like the waters, and righteousness (*tsedekah*) like a never-failing wadi." "Waters" and "never-failing wadi" complement each other in that the meaning of "waters" is made clearer by the following reference to a wadi that is never-failing, perennial, steady flowing, permanent; that is, it is supported by a wellspring or underground reservoir.

What is this additional source of water? Yahweh is Israel's only source of life (cf. Amos 5:4, 6, and 14). His declaration of righteousness to all who believe (cf. Gen. 15:6) provides the wellspring to live a life characterized by mishpat and tsedekah. Israel did not trust Yahweh's provision of righteousness, so their intermittent, occasional, and sporadic ethical and moral conduct is like a wadi that only flows when it rains. Worshipers attended to the liturgical festivals, but justice and righteousness failed to flow out into the irrigation channels of daily life and relationships.

The torrential flow of a year-round wadi emphasizes power, permanence, and dependability. Most wadis flow with water in the rainy season, but when water is needed most, in the arid season, they become "a dry and weary land where there is no water" (Ps. 63:1). Apart from trusting Yahweh's gift of righteousness, justice and righteousness in Israel were dehydrated, dry, and dead.[10]

Climactically, Jesus provides the free gift of living water that delivers His love *to* the baptized. His surging love then moves through them out into the world (cf. John 7:38-39). Baptismal cleansing and new life (cf. Titus 3:4-7; John 3:5) is made possible because of Christ's sacrificial death upon the cross. Water flowed from His riven side (John 19:34) to heal and cleanse all sinners. Sacramentally, this same water flows into the baptismal font to forgive filth, quench thirst, and defeat death. Apart from the baptized life freely imparted by Jesus, justice and righteousness will never cascade as a river of mercy.

Amos indicates as much. In 9:11 he envisions the day when Yahweh will raise "David's fallen booth." The restoration of the Davidic era implies that justice and righteousness will abound in Israel. Justice and righteousness marked the Davidic era (cf. 2 Sam. 8:15) and were to be the defining marks of every Israelite king (cf. Ps. 72:1).

Justice and righteousness, so central to Amos, will only be accomplished by the restoration of the Davidic line fulfilled in Jesus the Christ (e.g., Matt. 15:22; 20:31; Rom. 1:3). This is in harmony with the rest of the prophetic corpus. For example,

---

[9] Douglas Stuart notes that in behaving this way the Israelites were being consistent with the practices of the Canaanites. "Canaanite cultic religion allowed people to be personally immoral and unethical; they could still be right with the gods if they merely supported the cult enthusiastically" (*Hosea-Jonah* [Waco: Word, 1987], 355).

[10] Hans W. Wolff writes: "That which Israel has perverted into wormwood and poison (5:7; 6:12) was meant to effect blessing and prosperity among the people, just as the streams and rivers of a land bring the gift of fertility and life" (*Joel and Amos* [Philadelphia: Fortress, 1977], 264).

Jeremiah promises a "Righteous Branch," a Davidic leader who "shall execute justice and righteousness in the land" (23:5); He will be called "Yahweh is our righteousness" (23:6). Isaiah 11 begins with the image of the shoot from Jesse, given before in Is. 6:13. The use of "Jesse" rather than "David" in v. 1 and again in v. 10 indicates that this new king is not only of the lineage of David, but indeed a new David (Jer. 30:9; Ezek. 34:23-24; Hos. 3:5). The Messiah coming from the house of David is also affirmed elsewhere (Is. 16:5; 55:4-5; Jer. 23:5; 33:15; Ezek. 34:23-25; Zech. 12:7-12; 13:1). Matthew's genealogy (1:6, 17), Luke's birth narrative (2:4), and Paul's sermon in Acts 13:22-23 confirm that this promise of a Messiah is fulfilled in Jesus. According to Is. 52:13-53:12, the way in which the Messiah will bring forth His righteous rule and justice (Is. 9:2-7; 11:11-16) is through His humble suffering and death. Christ's death and resurrection achieved a righteous standing for all believers. Those who are declared righteous by faith (e.g., 2 Cor. 5:21) are also empowered to live lives of justice and mercy (e.g., Rom. 12).

Conclusions

Jesus gave His disciples one mandate: to make disciples from among all the nations (Matt. 28:18-20). The Great Commission, however, does not mean the Church must remain passive in its engagement with a myriad of earthly issues that continue to face people.[11]

It is unfortunate, however, that many Christians believe the word "spiritual" means otherworldly piety. They have been taught that a "spiritual" person is one whose inner eyes are cast heavenward in prayer and contemplation, focusing on the joys of the life to come. To be "spiritual" implies that one is life-denying; it suggests communing with one's heavenly Creator by focusing upon the invisible realities and eternal mysteries of God's holiness. To live "spiritually" is often thought of in terms of passive detachment from this world, a transcending of the self to a higher, more sublime world. A "spiritual" person is really consumed with one agenda: "to win souls for Jesus." All other activity is inferior and lacking in priority.

But the Old Testament in general, and Amos in particular, challenges the Church to renounce this type of dualism where spiritual issues are divorced from social issues, as if the latter were of no spiritual significance, and as if God had no better vision to offer the world. "The vertical dimension of faith — our confidence in the justifying grace of God in Christ — is accompanied by horizontal effects."[12]

Jesus not only offers the free gift of life *after* death; He also empowers the baptized for life *before* death. And this life is to intercede and assist orphans, widows, the diseased, the disenfranchised, all of the "small people" (cf. Amos 7:2, 5) for whom our Lord was so concerned during His earthly ministry (i.e., Mark 10:46-52 — blind Bartimaeus;

---

[11] The famous advocate for the social gospel, Walter Rauschenbusch, gave this analysis of Lutheranism: "Thus far Lutheranism has buried its ten talents in a tablecloth of dogmatic theory and kept its people from that share in the social awakening which is their duty and right" (*Christianizing the Social Order* [New York: Macmillan, 1912], 125).

[12] Benne, *Reasonable Ethics*, 06.

Matt. 15:22-28 — the Canaanite woman's sick daughter; Luke 8:41-56 — Jairuis' deceased daughter and the woman with the flow of blood).

Of course, assisting the poor, working toward fairer wages, lobbying for a more humane way to address immigration, and so on, are not in any way salvatory. Society cannot be governed by the Gospel, and salvation will never be accomplished by means of political achievement. Although Amos takes up the cause of human need and destitution throughout his book, he never proposes concrete ways to eliminate poverty. Nor does he address issues of responsibility in terms of government or the private sector. However, Amos does make it clear that acting unjustly toward marginalized people is a *theological* issue. Material and economic poverty is an outrage that is not in accord with God's will. Yahweh hears the cries of people who are enslaved in economic systems that create intense suffering. Andersen and Freedman write: "The issue of right behavior to one's neighbors is the ultimate test of true religion, if not its actual essence and substance. It is not a substitute for theology but its necessary adjunct."[13] Martin Luther famously puts it this way:

> Faith is a living, daring confidence in God's grace, so sure and certain that the believer would stake his life on it a thousand times. This knowledge of and confidence in God's grace makes men glad and bold and happy in dealing with God and with all creatures. And this is the work which the Holy Spirit performs in faith. Because of it, and without compulsion, a person is ready and glad to do good to everyone, to serve everyone, to suffer everything, out of love and praise to God who has shown him this grace. Thus it is impossible to separate works from faith, quite as impossible as to separate heat and light from fire.[14]

Christians are resident aliens (Phil. 3:20; 1 Peter 1:1, 2:11). Solving political and social issues brings only provisional order and peace. The Church must be involved in public life. This, however, is penultimate; giving the gifts of the Gospel and Sacraments is *ultimate*. The danger may be that the Church involves itself in the latest issue rather than the eternal issue.

Although the Church has no divine mandate to address politics and economics in any specific way, it may, however, seek to catechize and empower its laity so that they faithfully speak to current issues in the four orders where God has placed them: marriage and family, work, public life, and church.[15] Preferring this indirect way of making public impact, Lutheran pastors are called upon to educate and equip their

---

[13] Francis Andersen and David Noel Freedman, *Amos* (New York: Doubleday, 1989), 92; cf. James 1:27.

[14] "The Preface to the Epistle of St. Paul to the Romans," *Luther's Works* American edition 35:370-71.

[15] For example, in Rom. 13:8-14 the apostle instructs how the baptized are called upon to live in the public sphere.

laity to engage the world ethically in their respective vocations.[16] Benne calls this "the ethics of character."[17]

As the Church heeds Amos' call to channel Yahweh's justice and righteousness into the world, dangers are at least three-fold: (1) expect too much and offer the world a false hope; (2) deny the true mission, the proclamation of the Gospel and administration of the Sacraments; and/or (3) simplistically apply biblical texts to complex issues. However, "the Lutheran vision leads to a nonutopian view of history that is not cynical."[18]

The Church works for relative victories while it prays for the final coming of the kingdom of God, when "David's fallen booth" (Amos 9:11) will be completely restored when the Son of Man comes again. By anticipating another kingdom from another place, the Church, through its preaching, liturgy, and catechesis, undercuts the morally ambiguous kingdom of this world and its pretentious estimation of itself. The Church best confronts injustice in the world by being different than, but not separate from, the world. As the Church awaits the Second Coming of her Lord, the baptized are called upon to intercede and live for "Jacob who is so small," and to marshal resources in order to lovingly address human need.

---

[16] Benne writes: "Affecting people catechetically and sacramentally affirming their identity in Christ is arguably the most fundamental and potentially the most effective way the church affects economic life" (*Reasonable Ethics*, 195).

[17] Benne, *Reasonable Ethics*, 197.

[18] Benne, *Reasonable Ethics*, 79.

PENTECOST
"When the day of Pentecost arrived, they were all together in one place … And they were all filled with the Holy Spirit and began to speak in other tongues as the Spirit gave them utterance." Acts 2:1, 4 c. 1510

THE GOSPEL OF LOVE AND CHARITY[1]

"I was hungry and you gave me food, I was thirsty and you gave me drink, I was a stranger and you welcomed me, I was naked and you clothed me, I was sick and you visited me, I was in prison and you came to me … . As you did it to one of the least of these my brothers, you did it to me."

These words of Jesus have shone so brilliantly for many generations in his church, and exerted so powerful an influence, that one may further describe the Christian preaching as *the preaching of love and charity*. From this standpoint, in fact, the proclamation of the Savior and of healing would seem to be merely subordinate, inasmuch as the words "I was sick and you visited me" form but one link in the larger chain.

Among the extant words and parables of Jesus, those which inculcate love and charity are especially numerous, and with them we must rank many a story on his life.[2] Yet, apart altogether from the number of such sayings, it is plain that whenever he had in view the relations of mankind, the gist of his preaching was to enforce brotherliness and ministering love, and the surest part of the impression he left behind him was that in his own life and labours he displayed both of these very qualities. "You have one teacher, and you are all brothers"; "Whoever would be first among you must be slave of all. For even the Son of Man came not to be served but to serve, and to give his life as a ransom for many." It is in this sense that we are to understand the commandment to love one's neighbour. How unqualified it is becomes evident from

---

[1] In his work, *Die christliche Liebestätigkeit in der alten Kirche* (1st ed., 1882; Eng. Trans., *Christian Charity in the Ancient Church*, Edinburgh), Uhlhorn presents a sketch which is thorough, but unfair to paganism. The Greeks and Romans also were acquainted with philanthropy.

[2] One recalls particularly the parable of the good Samaritan, with its new definition of "neighbour," and also the parable of the lost son; among the stories, that of the rich young man. The gospel of the Hebrews tells the latter incident with special impressiveness. "Then said the Lord to him, How canst thou say, 'I have kept the law and the prophets,' when it is written in the law, 'Thou shalt love thy neighbour as thyself'? And look, many of thy brethren, sons of Abraham, are lying in dirt and dying of hunger, while thy house is full of many possessions, and never a gift comes from them.'"

the saying, "Love your enemies and pray for those who persecute you,[3] so that you may be sons of your Father who is in heaven. For he makes his sun rise on the evil and on the good, and sends rain on the just and on the unjust."

"Blessed are the merciful" — that is the keynote of all that Jesus proclaimed, and as this merciful spirit is to extend from great things to trifles, from the inward to the outward, the saying which does not pass over even a cup of cold water (Matt. x. 42) lies side by side with that other comprehensive saying, "Forgive us our debts, as we also have forgiven our debtors." Brotherliness is love on a footing of equality; ministering love means to *give and to forgive*, and no limit is to be recognized. Besides, *ministering love is the practical expression of love to God.*

While Jesus himself was exhibiting this love, and making it a life and a power, his disciples were learning the highest and holiest thing that can be learned in all religion, namely, to believe in the love of God. To them the Being who had made heaven and earth was "the Father of mercies and God of all comfort," — a point on which there is no longer any dubiety in the testimony of the apostolic and post-apostolic ages. Now, for the first time, that testimony rose among men, which cannot ever be surpassed, the testimony that *God is love.* The first great statement of the new religion, into which the fourth evangelist condensed its central principle, was based entirely and exclusively on love: "We love because he first loved us," "God so loved the world," "A new commandment I give to you, that you love one another." And the greatest, strongest, deepest thing Paul ever wrote is the hymn commencing with the words: "If I speak in the tongues of men and of angels, but have not love, I am a noisy gong or a clanging cymbal." The new language on the lips of Christians was the language of love.

But it was more than a language, it was a thing of power and action. The Christians really considered themselves brothers and sisters, and their actions corresponded to this belief. On this point we possess two unexceptionable testimonies from pagan writers. Says Lucian of the Christians: "Their original lawgiver had taught them that they were all brethren, one of another. ... They become incredibly alert when anything of this kind occurs, that affects their common interests. On such occasions no expense is grudged." And Tertullian (*Apolog.*, xxxix.) observes: "It is our care for the helpless, our practice of loving kindness, that brands us in the eyes of many of our opponents. 'Only look,' they say, 'look how they love one another!' (they themselves being given to mutual hatred). 'Look how they are prepared to die for one another!' (they themselves being readier to kill each other)."[4] Thus had this saying became a fact: "By this all people will know that you are my disciples, if you have love for one another."

---

[3] The saying "Fast for them that persecute you" is also traditional (Didache, i).

[4] Also Caecilius (in *Minuc.* Felix, ix): "They recognise each other by means of secret marks and signs, and love one another almost before they are acquainted."

The gospel thus became a social message. The preaching which laid hold of the outer man, detaching him from the world, and uniting him to his God, was also a preaching of solidarity and brotherliness. The gospel, it has been truly said, is at bottom both individualistic and socialistic. Its tendency towards mutual association, so far from being an accidental phenomenon in its history, is inherent in its character. It spiritualizes the irresistible impulse which draws one man to another, and it raises the social connection of human beings from the sphere of a convention to that of a moral obligation. In this way it serves to heighten the worth of man, and essays to recast contemporary society, to transform the socialism which involves a conflict of interests into the socialism which rests upon the consciousness of a spiritual unity and a common goal. This was ever present to the mind of the great apostle to the Gentiles. In his little churches, where each person bore his neighbour's burden, Paul's spirit already saw the dawning of a new humanity, and in the epistle to the Ephesians he has voiced this feeling with a thrill of exultation. Far in the background of these churches — i.e., when they were what they were meant to be — like some unsubstantial semblance, lay the division between Jew and Gentile, Greek and barbarian, great and small, rich and poor. For a new humanity had now appeared, and the apostle viewed it as Christ's body, in which every member served the rest and each was indispensable in his own place. Looking at these churches, with all their troubles and infirmities, he anticipated, in his exalted moments of enthusiasm, what was the development of many centuries.[5]

We cannot undertake to collect from the literature of the first three centuries all the passages where love and charity are enjoined. This would lead us too far afield, although we should come across much valuable material in making such a survey. We would notice the reiteration of the summons to unconditional giving, which occurs among the sayings of Jesus, whilst on the contrary we would be astonished to find that passages enforcing the law of love are not more numerous, and that they are so frequently overshadowed by ascetic counsels; we would also take umbrage at the spirit of a number of passages in which the undisguised desire of being rewarded for benevolence stands out in bold relief.[6] Still, this craving for reward is not in every case

---

[5] Warnings against unmercifulness, and censures of this temper, must have begun, of course, at quite an early period; see the epistle of James (iv.-v.) and several sections in the "Shepherd" of Hermas.

[6] All these points are illustrated throughout the literature, from the Didache and Hermas downwards. For unconditional giving, see Did. I. 5 f.: παντι τῷ αἰτοῦντί σε δίδου καί μὴ ἀπαίτει · πᾶσι γὰρ θέλει δίδοσθαι ὁ πατερ ἐκ τῶν ἰδίων χαρισμάτων. Μακαριος ὁ διδοὺς κατὰ τὴν ἐντολήν · ἀθῷος γάρ ἐστιν · οὐαὶ τῷ λαμβάνοντι · εἰ μὲν γάρ χρείαν ἔχων λαμβάνει τις, αθῷος ἔσται · ὁ δὲ μὴ χρείαν ἔχων δώσει δίκην, ἵνα τί ἔλαβε καὶ εἰς τί · ἐν συνοχῇ δὲ γενόμενος ἐξελεύσεται ἐκεῖθεν μέκρις οὗ ἀποδῷ τὸν ἔσχατον κοδράντην ("Give to everyone who asks of thee, and ask not back again; for the Father desireth gifts to be given to all men from his own bounties. Blessed is he who gives according to the commandment, for he is guiltless. But woe to him who receives; for if a man receives who is in need, he shall be guiltless, but if he is not in need he shall give satisfaction as to why and wherefore he received, and being confined he shall be examined upon his deeds, and shall not come out till he has paid the uttermost farthing"). The counsel of unconditional giving, which is frequently repeated, is closely bound up with the question of earthly possessions in the early church, and consequently with the question of asceticism. Theoretically, from the very outset, there was to be neither property nor wealth at all; such things belong to the world which Christians were to renounce. Consequently, to

immoral, and no conclusion can be drawn from the number of times when it occurs. The important thing is to determine what actually took place within the sphere of Christian charity and active love, and this we shall endeavour to ascertain.

Three passages may be brought forward to show the general activities which were afoot.

In the official writing sent by the Roman to the Corinthian church *c.* 96 A.D., there is a description of the first-rate condition of the latter up till a short time previously (1 Clem., i., ii.), a description which furnishes the pattern of what a Christian church should be, and the approximate realization of this ideal at Corinth. "Who that had stayed with you did not approve your most virtuous and steadfast faith? Who did not admire your sober and forbearing Christian piety? Who did not proclaim the splendid style of your *hospitality?* Who did not congratulate you on your perfect and assured knowledge? For you did everything *without respect of persons;* you walked by the ordinances of God, submitting to your rulers and rendering due honour to your senior men. Young persons also you charged to have a modest and grave mind; women you instructed to discharge all their tasks with a blameless, grave, and pure conscience, and to cherish a proper affection for their husbands, teaching them further to look after their households decorously, with perfect discretion. You were all lowly in mind, free from vainglory, yielding rather than claiming submission, *more ready to give than to take;* content with the supplies provided by God and holding by them, you carefully laid up His words in your hearts, and His sufferings were ever

---

devote one's means to other people was a proceeding which demanded a fresh point of view; to part with one's property was the authorised and most meritorious course of action, nor did it matter, in the first instance, who was the recipient. In practical life, however, things were very different, and this was constantly the result of the very theory just mentioned, since it never gave up the voluntary principle (even the attempt at communism in Jerusalem, if there even was such an attempt, did not exclude the voluntary principle). It was by means of this principle that Christian love maintained its power. In practical life, complete renunciation of the world was achieved only by a few; these were the saints and heroes. Other people were in precisely the same position, with the same feelings and concern, as serious, devoted Catholics at the present day; they were actuated by motives of asceticism and of love alike. It is needless, therefore, to depict this state of matters in closer detail. The extreme standpoint is represented by Hermas, *Sim.*, I. (see above, pp. 97 f.).

A great deal has been written upon early Christian "communism," but nothing of the kind ever existed in the great Gentile church – for we need not take any account of an isolated phenomenon like the semi-pagan sect of the Carpocratians and their communism. Monastic "communism" is only called such by a misuse of the term, and, besides, it is irrelevant to our present subject. Even on the soil of Jewish Christianity, no communism flourished, for the example of the Essenes was never followed. Uhlhorn remarks truly (*op. cit.*, p. 68; Eng. trans., 74) that "we cannot more radically misconceive the so-called 'communism' of early Christianity than by conceiving it as an institution similar to those which existed among the Essenes and the Therapeutae. It is far more correct to represent the state of things as an absence of all institutions whatsoever." Directions not infrequently occur (e.g., Barn., xix. 8; Tert., *Apol.*, xxxix.) which have a communistic ring, but they are not to be taken in a communistic sense. The common formula ouvk evrei/j i;dia ei=nai ("thou shalt not say these things are thine own") simply enjoins liberality, forbidding a man to use his means merely for his own advantage.

I have already remarked that, upon the whole, the voluntary principle was never abandoned in the matter of Christian giving and the scale of gifts. This statement, however, admits of one qualification. While the West, so far as I can judge, knew nothing as yet of the law of first-fruits and tithes throughout our epoch (for Cyprian, de Unit., xxvi., is not to be understood as implying the law of tithes), in some quarters of the East the law of first-fruits was taken over at a very early period (see *Didache*, xiii.). From the Didache it passed, as an apostolic regulation, into all the Oriental apostolic constitutions. Origen, however, does not appear to regard it yet as a law of the church, though even he admits the legitimacy of it (*in Num. Hom.*, xi. I ; *in Jos. Nav. Hom.*, xvii.).

present to your minds. Thus a profound and unsullied peace was bestowed on all, with *an insatiable craving for beneficence.* ... Day and night you agonized for all the brotherhood, that *by means of compassion and care* the number of God's elect might be saved. You were sincere, guileless, and void of malice among yourselves. Every sedition and every schism was an abomination to you. *You lamented the transgressions of your neighbours and judged their shortcomings to be your own. You never rued an act of kindness, but were ready for every good work.*"

Then Justin concludes the description of Christian worship in his *Apology* (c. lxvii.) thus: "Those who are well-to-do and willing, give as they choose, each as he himself purposes; the collection is then deposited with the president, who succours orphans, widows, those who are in want owing to sickness or any other cause, those who are in prison, and strangers who are on a journey."

Finally, Tertullian (*Apolog.*, xxxix.) observes: "Even if there does exist a sort of common fund, it is not made up of fees, as though we contracted for our worship. Each of us puts in a small amount one day a month, or whenever he pleases; but only if he pleases and if he is able, for there is no compulsion in the matter, everyone contributing of his own free will. These monies are, as it were, the deposits of piety. They are expended upon no banquets or drinking-bouts or thankless eating-houses, but on feeding and burying poor people, on behalf of boys and girls who have neither parents nor money, in support of old folk unable now to go about, as well as for people who are shipwrecked, or who may be in the mines or exiled in islands or in prison — so long as their distress is for the sake of God's fellowship — themselves the nurslings of their confession."

In what follows we shall discuss, so far as may be relevant to our immediate purpose:

1. Alms in general, and their connection with the cultus and officials of the church.

2. The support of teachers and officials.

3. The support of widows and orphans.

4. The support of the sick, the infirm, and the disabled.

5. The care of prisoners and people languishing in the mines.

6. The care of poor people needing burial, and of the dead in general.

7. The care of slaves.

8. The care of those visited by great calamities.

9. The churches furnishing work, and insisting upon work.

10. The care of brethren on a journey (hospitality), and of churches in poverty or any peril.

1. Alms in general and in connection with the cultus.

Liberality was steadily enjoined upon Christians; indeed, the headquarters of this virtue were to lie within the household, and its proof was to be shown in daily life. From the apostolic counsels down to Cyprian's great work *de Opere et Eleemosynis*, there stretches one long line of injunctions, in the course of which ever-increasing stress is laid upon the importance of alms to the religious position of the donor, and upon the prospect of a future recompense. These points are already prominent in Hermas, and in 2 Clem. we are told that "almsgiving is good as a repentance from sin; fasting is better than prayer, but almsgiving is better than either" (Καλὸν ἐλεημοσύνη ὡς μετάνοια ἁμαρτίας, κρείσσων νηστεία προσευχῆς, ἐλεημοσύνη δὲ ἀμφοτέρων). Cyprian develops alms[7] into a formal means of grace, the only one indeed which remains to a Christian after baptism; in fact he goes still further, representing alms as a spectacle which the Christian offers to God.[8]

It is not our business to follow up this aspect of almsgiving, or to discuss the amount of injury thus inflicted on a practice which was meant to flow from a pure love to men. The point is that a great deal, a very great deal, of alms was given away privately throughout the Christian churches.[9] As we have already seen, this was well known to the heathen world.[10]

---

[7] *De Op. et Eleem.*, i.: "Nam cum dominus adveniens sanasset illa quae Adam portaverat vulnera et venena serpentis antiqui curasset, legem dedit sano et pracepit ne ultra jam peccaret, ne quid peccanti gravius eveniret. Coartati eramus et in angustum innocentiae praescriptione conclusi, nec haberet quid fragilitatis humanae infirmitas atque imbecillitas faceret; nisi *iterum* pietas divina subveniens justitiae et misericordiae operibus ostensis viam quandam tuendae salutis aperiret ut sordes postmodum, quascumque contrahimus, *eleemosynis* abluamus" ("For when the Lord had at his advent cured the wounds which Adam brought, and healed the poison of the old serpent, he gave a law to the sound man and bade him sin no more, lest a worse thing should befall the sinner. We were restrained and bound by the commandment of innocence. Nor would human weakness and impotence have any resource left to it, unless the divine mercy should *once more* come to our aid, by pointing out works of righteousness and mercy, and thus opening a way to obtain salvation, so that by means of *alms* we may wash off any stains subsequently contracted".)

[8] *Op. cit.*, xxi.: "Quale munus cuius editio deo spectante celebratur! Si in gentilium munere grande et gloriosum videtur proconsules vel imperatores habere presentes, et apparatus ac sumptus apud munerarios maior est ut possint placere maioribus – quanto inlustrior muneris et maior est gloria deum et Christum spectatores habere, quanto istic et apparatus uberior et sumptus largior exhibendus est, ubi ad spectaculum conveniunt caelorum virtutes, conveniunt angeli omnes, ubi munerario non quadriga vel consulatus petitur sed vita aeterna praestatur, nec captatur inanis et temporarius favor vulgi sed perpetuum praemium regni caelestis accipitur" ("What a gift is it which is set forth for praise in the sight of God! If, when the Gentiles offer gifts, it seems a great and glorious thing to have proconsuls or emperors present, and if their better classes make greater preparations and display in order to please the authorities — how much more illustrious and splendid is the glory of having God and Christ as the spectators of a gift! How much more lavish should be the preparation, how much more liberal the outlay, in such a case, when the powers of heaven muster to the spectacle, when all the angels gather, when the donor seeks no chariot or consulship, but life eternal is the boon; when no fleeting and fickle popularity is craved for, but the lasting reward of the kingdom of heaven is received!").`

[9] The pagan in Macarius Magnes (iii. 5) declares that several Christian women had become beggars by their lavish donations. "Not in the far past, but only yesterday, Christians read Matt. xix. 21 to prominent women and persuaded them to share all their possessions and goods among the poor, to reduce themselves to beggary, to ask charity, and then to sink from independence into unseemly pauperism, reducing themselves from their former good position to a woebegone condition, and being finally obliged to knock at the doors of those who were better off."

[10] With Clement of Alexandria, the motive of love to men is steadily kept in the front rank; cp. *Paed.*, iii., and in particular the fine saying in iii. 7. 39: Καθάπερ τῶν φρεάτων ὅσα πέφυκεν βρύειν ἀπαντλούμενα εἰς τὸ ἀρχαῖον ἀναπιδύει μέτρον, οὕτως ἡ μετάδοσις, ἀγαθὴ φιλανθρωπίας ὑπάρχουσα πηγή, κοινωνοῦσα τοῖς διψῶσι ποτοῦ αὐξεται πάλιν καὶ πίμπλαται ("Even as such wells as spring up rise to their former level even after they

But so far from being satisfied with private almsgiving,[11] early Christianity instituted, apparently from the first, a church fund (Tertullian's *arca*), and associated charity very closely with the cultus and officials of the church. From the ample materials at our disposal, the following outline may be sketched: Every Sunday (cp. already 1 Cor. xvi. 2), or once a month (Tertullian), or whenever one chose, gifts in money or kind (*stips*) were brought to the service and entrusted to the president, by whom they were laid on the Lord's table and so consecrated to God.[12] Hence the recipient obtained them from the hand of God. "'Tis God's grace and philanthropy that support you," wrote bishop Cornelius (Eus., *H.E.*, vi. 43). The president decided who were to be the recipients, and how much was to be allocated to each, a business in which he had the advice of the deacons, who were expected to be as familiar as possible with the circumstances of each member, and who had the further task of distributing the various donations, partly at the close of worship, partly in the homes of the indigent. In addition to the regular voluntary assessments — for, as the principle of liberty of choice was strictly maintained, we cannot otherwise describe these offerings — there were also extraordinary gifts, such as the present of 200,000 sesterces brought by Marcion when, as a Christian from Asia, he entered the Roman church about the year 139.[13]

Among these methods of maintenance we must also include the love-feasts, or agapae, with which the Lord's Supper was originally associated, but which persisted into a later age. The idea of the love-feast was that the poor got food and drink, since a common meal, to which each contributed as he was able, would unite rich and poor alike. Abuses naturally had to be corrected at an early stage (cp. 1 Cor. xi. 18 f.), and the whole affair (which was hardly a copy of the pagan feasts at the Thiasoi) never seems to have acquired any particular importance upon the whole.[14]

---

have been drained, so that kindly spring of love to men, the bestowal of gifts, imparts its drink to the thirsty, and is again increased and replenished"). Cyprian (in *de Unit.*, xxvi.) complains of a lack of benevolence: "Largitas operationis infracta est ... nunc de patrimonio nec decimas damus et cum vendere jubeat dominus, emimus potius et augemus" ("Liberality in benevolence is impaired ... we do not now give even the tithe of our patrimony away. The Lord bids us sell, but we prefer to buy and lay up").

[11] One recommendation very frequently made, was to stint oneself by means of fasting in order to give alms. In this way, even the poor could afford something. See Hermas, Sim., v. ; Aristides, Apol., xv. ("And if anyone among them is poor or needy, and they have no food to spare, they fast for two or three days, that they may meet the poor man's need of sustenance"); Apost. Constit., v. 1, etc. The habit also prevailed in pre-Christian ages. Otherwise, whenever the question is raised, how alms are to be provided, one is pointed to work; in fact, this is almost the only point at which work is taken into consideration at all within the sphere of the religious estimate. See Eph. iv. 28 ("Let him that stole, steal no more, but rather work with his hands at honest work, so that he may have something to give the needy"); and Barn. xix. 10: διὰ χειρῶν σοθ ἐργάσῃ εἰς λύτρον ἁμαρτιων σου [the reference being to alms]. Cp. my short study (in the "Evange-lisch-Sozial" Magazine, 1905, pp. 48 f.) on "The Primitive Christian Conception of the Worth of Labour."

[12] The relation of *stips* and *oblationes* is a question which has not been cleared up yet, and need not be raised here.

[13] See on this point Book IV. Chap. I. (I). The money was returned.

[14] Cp. also Jude ver. 12; Tert., Apol., xxxix. ; de Ieiun., xvii. ; Clem., Paed., ii. 1. We need not enter into the controversies over the *agapae*:; cp. Keating's *The Agape and the Eucharist* (1901), Batiffol's *Etudes d'hist. et de theol. positive* (1902), pp. 279 f., and Funk on "L' Agape" (*Rev. d' hist. ecclesiastique*, t. iv. 1, 1903). In later days the feasts served to satisfy the poor at the graves of the martyrs. Constantine justified this practice of feasts in honour of the dead against objections

From the very first, the president appears to have had practically an absolute control over the donations;[15] but the deacons had also to handle them as executive agents. The responsibility was heavy, as was the temptation to avarice and dishonesty; hence the repeated counsel, that bishops (and deacons) were to be ἀφιλάργυροι, "no lovers of money." It was not until a later age that certain principles came to be laid down with regard to the distribution of donations as a whole, from which no divergence was permissible.

This system of organized charity in the churches worked side by side with private benevolence — as is quite evident from the letters and writings of Cyprian. But it was inevitable that the former should gradually handicap the latter, since it wore a superior lustre of religious sacredness, and therefore, people were convinced, was more acceptable to God. Yet, in special cases, private liberality was still appealed to. One splendid instance is cited by Cyprian (*Epist.* lxii), who describes how the Carthaginian churches speedily raised 100,000 sesterces (between £850 and £1000).[16]

In 250 A.D. the Roman church had to support about 100 clergy and 1500 poor persons. Taking the yearly cost of supporting one man at £7, 10s. (which was approximately the upkeep of one slave), we get an annual sum *of* £12,000. If, however (like Uhlhorn, *op. cit.*, p. 153; Eng. trans., p. 159), we allow sixty Roman bushels of wheat per head a year at 7s. 6d., we get a total of about £4300. It is safe to say, then, that about 250 A.D. the Roman church had to expend from half a million to a million sesterces (*i.e.*, from £5000 to £10,000) by way of relief.

The demands made upon the church funds were heavy, as will appear in the course of the following classification and discussion.

2. The support of teachers and officials.

The Pauline principle[17] that the rule about "The laborer deserves his wages" applied also to missionaries and teachers, was observed without break or hesitation throughout the Christian churches. The conclusion drawn was that teachers could lay claim to a plain livelihood, and that this claim must always have precedence of any other demand upon the funds. When a church had chosen permanent officials

---

which were apparently current; cp. his address to the council (xii.), where he dwells expressly on their charitable uses: ta. sumpo,sia (for the martyrs, at their graves) τὰ συμπόσια πρὸς ἔλεον καὶ ἀνάκτησιν τῶν δεομένων ποιούμενα καὶ πρὸσ βοήθειαν τῶν ἐκπεςόντων. ἅπερ ἄν τις φορτικὰ εἶναι νομίδῃ, οὐ κατὰ τὴν θείαν καὶ μακαρίαν διδασκαλίαν φρονεῖ

("These feasts are held for the purpose of helping and restoring the needy, and in aid of the outcast. Anyone who thinks them burdensome, does not judge them by the divine and blessed rule of life").

[15] On the traces of an exception to this rule in the *Apostolic Constitutions*, see *Texte u. Untersuch.*, ii. 5, pp. 12 f., 58.

[16] For special collections ordered by the bishop, see Tertull., *de Jejun.* xiii., and Clem., *Hom.*, iii. 71: ὑπότε χρεία τινὸς πόρυο πρὸς τὸ ἀναγκαῖον γένοιτο, ἅμα οἱ πάντες συμβάλλεσθε ("Whenever any funds are needed, club together, all of you").

[17] Paul even describes the principle as a direction of Jesus himself; see 1 Cor. ix. 14: ὁ κύριος διέτεξεν τοῖς τὸ εὐαγγέλιον καταγγέλλουσιν ἐκ τοῦ εὐγγενλίου ζῆν

for itself, these also assumed the right of being allowed to claim a livelihood, but only so far as their official duties made inroads upon their civil occupations.[18] Here, too, the bishop had discretionary power; he could appropriate and hand over to the presbyters and deacons whatever he thought suitable and fair, but he was bound to provide the teachers (i.e. missionaries and prophets) with enough to live on day by day. Obviously, this could not fail to give rise to abuses. From the Didache and Lucian we learn that such abuses did arise, and that privileges were misemployed.[19]

3. The support of widows and orphans.[20]

Wherever the early Christian records mention poor persons who require support, widows and orphans are invariably in the foreground. This corresponds, on the one hand, with the special distress of their position in the ancient world, and on the other hand with the ethical injunctions which had passed over into Christianity from Judaism. As it was, widows and orphans formed the poor κατ' ἐξοχὴν The church had them always with her. "The Roman church," wrote bishop Cornelius, "supports 1500 widows and poor persons" (Eus. *H.E.* vi. 43). Only widows, we note, are mentioned side by side with the general category of recipients of relief. Inside the churches, widows had a special title of honour, viz., "God's altar,"[21] and even Lucian the pagan was aware that Christians attended first and foremost to orphans and widows (*Peregrin,* xii). The true worship, James had already urged (i.

---

[18] The circumstances are not quite clear; still, enough is visible to corroborate what has been said above. Church officials were not, in the first instance, obliged to abandon their civil calling, and so far as that provided them with a livelihood they had no claim upon the church's funds. But in the course of time it became more and more difficult, in the larger churches, to combine civil employment with ecclesiastical office. There is one very instructive account in the Clementine Homilies (iii. 71) which indicates that some people were sceptical upon the duty of supporting the bishop and clergy. The author writes: Ζακχαῖος [the bishop] μόνιν ὑμῖν ὅλος ἑαυτὸν ἀσχολεῖν ἀποδεδωκώς, κοιλίαν ἔχων καὶ ἑαυτῶν μὴ εὐσχολῶν, πῶς δύναται τὴν ἀναγκαίαν πορίδειν τροφήν; οὐχὶ δὲ εὐλογόν ἐστιν πάντας ὑμᾶς τοῦ ζῆν αὐτοῦ πρόνοιαν ποιεῖν, οὐκ ἀναμένοντας αὐτὸν ὑμᾶς αἰτεῖν, τοῦτο γὰρ πρόσαιτοῦντός ἐστιν · μᾶλλον δὲ τεθνήξεται λιμῷ ἢ τοῦτο ποιεῖν ὑποσταίη · πῶς δὴ καὶ ὑμεῖς οὐ δίκην ὑφέξετε, μὴ λογισάμενοι ὅτι "ἄξιός ἐστιν ὁ ἐργάτης τοῦ μισθοῦ αὐτοῦ"; καί μὴ λεγέτω τις · Οὐκοῦν ὁ δωρεὰν παρασχεθεὶς λόγος πωλεῖται; μὴ γένοιτο · εἴ τις γὰρ ἔκων πόθεν ζῆν λάβοι, οὗτος πωλεῖ τὸν λόγον – εἰ δὲ μὴ ἔχων τοῦ ζῆν χάριν λαμβάνει τροφήν, ὡς καὶ ὁ κύριος ἔλαβεν ἔν τε δείπνοις καὶ φίλοις, οὐδὲν ἔχων ὁ εἰς αὖθις πάντα ἔχων, οὐκ ἁμαρτάνει. ἀκολούθως οὖν τιμᾶτε [by an honorarium] πρεσβυτέρους κατηχητάς, διακόνους χρησίμους, χήρας εὖ βεβιωκυίας, ὀρφανοὺς ὡσ ἐκκλησίας τέκνα ("Zacchaeus alone has devoted himself wholly to your interests; he needs food, and yet has no time to provide for himself; how then is he to get the requisitive provisions for a livelihood? Is it not reasonable that you should all provide for his support? Do not wait for him to ask you – asking is a beggar's role, and he would rather die than stoop to that. Shall not you also incur punishment for failing to consider that 'the labourer is worthy of his hire'? Let no one say, 'Then is the word which was given freely, to be sold?' God forbid. If any man has means and yet accepts any help, *he* sells the word. But there is no sin in a man without means accepting support in order to live — as the Lord also accepted gifts at supper and among his friends, he who had nothing though he was the Lord of all things. Honour, then, in appropriate fashion the elder catechists, useful deacons, respectable widows, and orphans as children of the church"). A fixed monthly salary, such as that assigned by the church of Theodotus to her bishop Natalis, was felt to be obnoxious. (Cp. the primitive story in Eus., *H.E.*, v. 28).

[19] Details will be found below, in the chapter [Book III. Chap. I.] on the mission-agents.

[20] In the liturgy, widows and orphans are also placed immediately after the servants of the church.

[21] See Polycarp, *ad Phil.,* iv. ; Terl., *ad Uxor.,* i. 7 ; pseudo-Ignat., Tars., 9; and *Apos. Constit.,* ii. 26 (where the term is applied also to orphans; cp. iv. 3). I shall not discuss the institution of widows, already visible in the first epistle to Timothy, which also tended to promote their interests. The special attention devoted to widows was also meant to check the undesirable step of re-marriage.

27), is to visit widows and orphans in their distress, and Hermas (*Mand,* viii. 10) opens his catalogue of virtues with the words: χήραις ὑπηρετεῖν, ὀρφανοὺς καὶ ὑστερημένους ἐπισκέπτεσθαι ("to serve widows and visit the forlorn and orphans").[22] It is beyond question that the early church made an important contribution to the amelioration of social conditions among the lower classes by her support of widows.[23] We need not dwell on the fact, illustrated as early as the epistles to Timothy, that abuses crept into this department. Such abuses are constantly liable to occur wherever human beings are relieved, in whole or in part, of the duty of caring for themselves.[24]

4. The support of the sick, the infirm, the poor, and the disabled.

Mention has already been made of the cure of sick people; but where a cure was impossible the church was bound to support the patient by consolation (for they were remembered in the prayers of the church from the very first; cp. 1 Clem. lix. 4), visitation,[25] and charitable gifts (usually in kind). Next to the sick came those in trouble (ἐν θλίψει) and people sick in soul (κάμνοντες τῇ ψθχῇ, Herm., *Mand.*, viii. 10) as a rule, then the helpless and disabled (Tertullian singles out expressly *senes domestici*), finally the poor in general. To quote passages would be superfluous, for the duty is repeatedly inculcated; besides, concrete examples are fairly plentiful, although our records only mention such cases incidentally and quite accidentally.[26] Deacons,

---

[22] *In Vis.,* II, 4. 3, it is remarkable also how prominent are widows and orphans. See Aristides, *Apol.,* xv.: "They do not avert their attention from widows, and they deliver orphans from anyone who oppresses them." Instances of orphans being adopted into private families are not wanting. Origen, for example, was adopted by a Christian woman (Eus., *H.E.,* vi. 2); cp. *Acta Perpet.* et Felic., xv.; *Apost. Const.,* iv. 1. Lactantius (*Instit.,* vi. 12) adduces yet another special argument for the duty of supporting widows and orphans: "God commands them to be cared for, in order that no one may be hindered from going to his death for righteousness' sake on the plea of regard for his dear children, but that he may promptly and boldly encounter death, knowing that his beloved ones are left in God's care and will never lack protection."

[23] See, further, Herm., *Simil.* i., v. 3, ix. 26-27, x. 4; Polyc., *Epist.* vi. 1; Barn., xx. 2; *Ignat.,* Smyrn., vi. (a propos of heretics: "They care not for love, or for the widow, or for the orphan, or for the afflicted, or for the prisoner or ransomed, or for the hungry or thirsty" – περὶ ἀγάπης οὐ μέλει αὐτοις, οὐ περὶ χήρας, οὐ περὶ ὀρφανοῦ, οὐ περὶ θλιβομένου, οὐ περὶ δεδεμένου ἢ λελυμένου, ἢ περὶ πεινῶντος ἢ διψῶντος(ad Polyc., iv.; Justin's Apol., I. lxvii.; Clem., Ep. ad Jacob. 8 τοῖς μὲν ὀρφανοῖς ποιοῦντες τὰ γονέων, ταῖς δὲ χήραις τὰ ἀνδρῶν ("acting the part of parents to orphans and of husbands to widows"); Tert., *ad Uxor.,* i.7-8; *Apost. Constit.* (Bks. III., IV.); and pseudo-Clem., *de Virgin.,* i. 12 ("pulchrum et utile est visitare pupillos et viduas, imprimis pauperes qui multos habent liberos"). For the indignation roused by the heartlessness of many pagan ladies, who were abandoned to luxury, read the caustic remark of Clement (*Paedag.,* iii. 4. 30): παιδίον δὲ οὐδὲ προσίενται ὀρφανὸν αἱ τοὺς ψιττακοὺς καὶ τοὺς χαραδριοὺς ἐκτρέφουσαι ("They bring up parrots and curlews, but will not take in the orphan child").

[24] Scandalmongering, avarice, drunkenness, and arrogance had all to be dealt with in the case of widows who were being maintained by the church. It even happened that some widows put out to usury the funds they had thus received (cp. *Didasc. Apost.,* xv.; *Texte u. Unters.,* xxv. 2. pp. 78, 274 f.) But there were also highly gifted widows. In fact (cp. *Apost Constit.*), it was considered that true widows who persevered in prayer received revelations.

[25] See Tert., *ad Uxor.,* ii. 4, on the difficult position of a Christian woman whose husband was a pagan: "Who would be willing to let his wife go though street after street to other men's houses, and indeed to the poorest cottages, in order to visit brethren?"

[26] Naturally, neither private nor, for the matter of that, church charity was to step in where a family was able to support some helpless member; but it is evident, from the sharp remonstrance in 1 Tim. v. 8, that there were attempts made to evade this duty ("If anyone does not provide for his own people, and especially for his own household, he has renounced the faith and is worse than an infidel").

"widows," and deaconesses (though the last-named were apparently confined to the East) were set apart for this work. It is said of deacons in the *Apostolic Constitutions* (see *Texte u. Unters.*, ii. 5. 8 f.): "They are to be doers of good works, exercising a general supervision day and night, neither scorning the poor nor respecting the person of the rich; they must ascertain who are in distress and not exclude them from a share in the church funds, compelling also the well-to-do to put money aside for good works." Of "widows" it is remarked, in the same passage, that they should render aid to women afflicted by disease, and the trait of φιλόπτωχος (a lover of the poor) is expected among the other qualities of a bishop.[27] In an old legend dating from the Decian persecution, there is a story of the deacon Laurentius in Rome, who, when desired to hand over the treasures of the church, indicated the poor as its only treasures. This was audacious, but it was not incorrect; from the very first, any possessions of the church were steadily characterized as poor-funds, and this remained true during the early centuries.[28] The excellence of the church's charitable system, the deep impression made by it, and the numbers that it won over to the faith, find their best voucher in the action of Julian the Apostate, who attempted an exact reproduction of it in that artificial creation of his, the pagan State-church, in order to deprive the Christians of this very weapon. The imitation, of course, had no success.[29]

Julian attests not only the excellence of the church's system of relief, but its extension to non-Christians. He wrote to Arsacius (Sozom. v. 16): "These godless Galileans feed not only their own poor but ours; our poor lack our care." This testimony is all the more weighty inasmuch as our Christian sources yield no satisfactory data on this point. Cp., however, under (8), and Paul's injunction in Gal. vi. 10: "Let us do good *to all*, especially to those who belong to the household of the faith." "True charity," says Tertullian (*Apol.*, xlii), "disburses more money in the streets than your religion in the temples." The church-funds were indeed for the use of the brethren alone, but private beneficence did not restrict itself to the household of faith. In a great calamity, as we learn from reliable evidence (see below), Christians did extend their aid to non-Christians, even exciting the admiration of the latter.

5. Care for prisoners and for people languishing in the mines.

The third point in the catalogue of virtues given by Hermas is: ἐξ ἀναγκῶν λυτροῦσθαι τοὺς δούλους τοῦ θεοῦ ("Redeem the servants of God from their bonds"). Prisoners might be innocent for various reasons, but above all there were people incarcerated for their faith or imprisoned for debt, and both classes had to be reached by charity. In the first instance, they had to be visited and consoled, and

---

[27] *Apost. Constit.*, in *Texte u. Unters.*, ii. 5. 8 f. In the *Vita Polycarpi* (Pionius) traits of this bishop are described which remind us of St Francis. On the female diaconate, see Uhlhorn (*op. cit.*, 159-171; Eng. trans., 165 f.).

[28] It was not possible, of course, to relieve all distress, and Tertullian (*de Idolat.*, xxiii.) mentions Christians who had to borrow money from pagans. This does not seem to have been quite a rare occurrence.

[29] We may certainly conclude that a register was kept of those who had to be maintained. This very fact, however, was a moral support to poor people, for it made them sure that they were not being neglected.

their plight alleviated by gifts of food.[30] Visiting prisoners was the regular work of the deacons, who had thus to run frequent risks; but ordinary Christians were also expected to discharge this duty. If the prisoners had been arrested for their faith, and if they were rather distinguished teachers, there was no hardship in obeying the command; in fact, many moved heaven and earth to get access to prisoners,[31] since it was considered that there was something sanctifying about intercourse with a confessor. In order to gain admission they would even go the length of bribing the gaolers,[32] and thus manage to smuggle in decent meals and crave a blessing from the saints. The records of the martyrs are full of such tales. Even Lucian knew of the practice, and pointed out the improprieties to which it gave rise. Christian records, particularly those of a later date,[33] corroborate this, and as early as the Montanist controversy it was a burning question whether or no any prominent confessor was really an impostor, if, after being imprisoned for misdemeanours, he made out as if he had been imprisoned on account of the Christian faith. Such abuses, however, were inevitable, and upon the whole their number was not large. The keepers, secretly impressed by the behaviour of the Christians, often consented of their own accord to let them communicate with their friends (*Acta Perpet.*, ix.: "Pudens miles optio, prae-positus carceris, nos magnificare coepit, intelligens magnam virtutem esse in nobis; qui multos ad nos admittebat, ut et nos et illi invicem refrigeraremus" ("Pudens, a military subordinate in charge of the prison, began to have a high opinion of us, since he recognized there was some great power of God in us. He let many people in to see us, that we and they might refresh one another").

If any Christian brethren were sentenced to the mines, they were still looked after, even there.[34] Their names were carefully noted; attempts were made to keep in touch

---

[30] Heb. x. 34, τοῖς δεσμίοις συνεπαθήσατε; Clem. Rom., lix. 4 (in the church's prayer), λύτρωσαι τοὺς δεσμίους ἡμῶν; (the duty of caring peri. περὶ δεδεμένου ἢ λελυμένου); Clem., Ep. ad Jacob., 9 (τοῖς ἐν φυλακαῖς ἐπιφαινόμενοι ὡς δύνασθε βοηθεῖτε) ; Arist., Apol., xv. ("And if they hear that anyone of their number is imprisoned or in distress for the sake of their Christ's name, they all render aid in his necessity, and if he can be redeemed, they set him free"). Of the young Origen we are told (Eus., H.E., vi. 3) that "not only was he at the side of the holy martyrs in their imprisonment, and until their final condemnation, but when they were led to death he boldly accompanied them into danger." Cp. Tert., ad Mart., i. f. (both the church and charitable individuals supplied prisoners with food), Acta Pass. Perpet., iii.; Petri Alex., Ep. c. 2 (Lagarde's Reliq. jur. eccles. p. 64, 14 f.), c. II (ibid., p. 70, I f.), c. 12 (ibid., p. 70, 20 f.).

[31] Thekla, in the Acta Theclae, is one instance, and there are many others; e.g., in Tertull., ad Uxor., ii. 4.

[32] As in Thekla's case; see also Lucian's Peregr., xii., and the Epist. Lugd., in Euseb., H.E., v. I. 61.

[33] Cp. Lucian, Peregr., xii., xiii., xvi. ("costly meals"). Tertullian, at the close of his life, when he was filled with bitter hatred towards the Catholic church, wrote thus in de Jejun., xii. : "Plainly it is your way to furnish restaurants for dubious martyrs in the gaols, lest they miss their wonted fare and so grow weary of their life, taking umbrage at the novel discipline of abstinence! One of your recent martyrs (no Christian he!) was by no means reduced to this hard regime. For after you had stuffed him during a considerable period, availing yourselves of the facilities of free custody, and after he had disported himself in all sorts of baths (as if these were better than the bath of baptism), and in all resorts of pleasure in high life (as if these were the secret retreats of the church), and with all the seductive pursuits of such a life (preferable, forsooth, to life eternal) — and all this, I believe, just in order to prevent any craving for death — then on the last day, the day of his trial, you gave him in broad daylight some medicated wine (in order to stupefy him against the torture)!"

[34] Cp. Dionysius of Corinth (in Eus., H.E., iv. 23), who pays a brilliant testimony to the Roman church in this connection.

with them; efforts were concocted to procure their release,[35] and brethren were sent to ease their lot, to edify and to encourage them.[36] The care shown by Christians for prisoners was so notorious that (according to Eusebius, *H.E.*, v. 8) Licinius, the last emperor before Constantine who persecuted the Christians, passed a law to the effect that "no one was to show kindness to sufferers in prison by supplying them with food, and that no one was to show mercy to those who were starving in prison." "In addition to this," Eusebius proceeds to relate, "a penalty was attached, to the effect that those who showed compassion were to share the fate of the objects of their charity, and that those who were humane to the unfortunate were to be flung into bonds and imprisonment and endure the same suffering as the others." This law, which was directly aimed at Christians, shows, more clearly than anything else could do, the care lavished by Christians upon their captive brethren, although much may have crept in in connection with this which the State could not tolerate.

But they did more than try to merely alleviate the lot of prisoners. Their aim was to get them ransomed. Instances of this cannot have been altogether rare, but unfortunately it is difficult for us to form any judgment on this matter, since in a number of instances, when a ransom is spoken of, we cannot be sure whether prisoners or slaves are meant. Ransoming captives, at any rate, was regarded as a work which was specially noble and well-pleasing to God, but it never appears to have been undertaken by any church. To the last it remained a monopoly of private generosity, and along this line individuals displayed a spirit of real heroism.[37]

---

[35] Cp. the story told by Hippolytus (*Philos.*, ix. 12) of the Roman bishop Victor, who kept a list of all Christians sentenced to the mines in Sardinia, and actually procured their liberty through the intercession of Marcia to the Emperor Commodus.

[36] Some extremely beautiful examples of this occur in the treatise of Eusebius upon the Palestinian martyrs during the Diocletian persecution. The Christians of Egypt went to the most remote mines, even to Cilicia, to encourage and edify their brethren who were condemned to hard labour in these places. In the mines at Phaeno a regular church was organized. Cp. also *Apost. Constit.*, v. 1: εἴ τις Χριστιανὸς διὰ τὸ ὄνομα τοῦ χριστοῦ...κατακριθῇ ὑπὸ ἀσεβῶν εἰς...μέταλλον, μὴ παρίδητε αὐτόν, ἀλλ' ἐκ τοῦ κόπου καὶ τοῦ ἱδρῶντος ὑμῶν πέμψατε αὐτῷ εἰς διατροφὴν αὐτοῦ καὶ εἰς μισθοδοσίαν τῶν στρατιωτῶν ("If any Christian is condemned for Christ's sake ... to the mines by the ungodly, do not overlook him, but from the proceeds of your toil and sweat send him something to support himself and to reward the soldiers").

[37] Herm., *Sim.*, I. : ἀντὶ ἀργῶν ἀγοράζετε ψυχὰς θλιβομένας, καθά τις δυνατός ἐστιν ("Instead of fields buy souls in trouble, as each of you is able"); *Sim.*, X. v. 2 f. ; *Clem. Rom.*, lv. 2:ἐπιστάμεθα πολλοὺς ἐν ἡμῖν παραδεδωκότας ἑαυτοὺς εἰς δεσμά, ὅπως ἑτέρους λυτρώσονται · πολλοὶ ἑαυτοὺς ἐξέδωκαν εἰς δουλείαν, καὶ λαβόντες τὰσ τιμὰς αὐτῶν ἑτέρους ἐψώμισαν ("We know that many of our own number have given themselves up to be captives, in order to ransom others; many have sold themselves to slavery, and with the price of their own bodies they have fed others") *Apost. Constit.*, iv. 9: τὰ ἐκ τοῦ δικαίου κόπου ἀθτοιζόμενα χρήματα διατάσσετε διακονοῦντες εἰς ἀγορασμοὺς τῶν ἁγίων ῥυόμενοι δούλους καὶ αἰχμαλώτους, δεσμίους, ἐπηρεαζομένους, ἥκοντας ἐκ καταδίκης, κ.τ.λ. ("All monies accruing from honest labour do ye appoint and apportion to the redeeming of the saints, ransoming thereby slaves and captives, prisoners, people who are sore abused or condemned by tyrants," etc.), cp. v. 1-2. In *Idolol.*, xxiii., Tertullian refers to release from imprisonment for debt, or to the efforts made by charitable brethren to prevent such imprisonment. When the Numidian robbers carried off the local Christians, the Carthaginian church soon gathered the sum of 100,000 sesterces as ransom-money, and declared it was ready to give still ampler aid (Cypr., *Ep.* lxii.). When the Goths captured the Christians in Cappadocia about the year 255, the Roman church sent contributions in aid of their ransom (Basil., *Ep. ad Dam.* lxx.). See below (10) for both of these cases. The ransoming of captives continued even in later days to be reckoned a work of special merit. Le Blant has published a number of Gallic inscriptions dating from the fourth and fifth centuries, in which the dead person is commended because "he ransomed prisoners."

6. Care of poor people requiring burial, and of the dead in general.

We may begin here with the words of Julian, in his letter to Arsacius (*Soz.*, v. 15): "This godlessness (*i.e.*, Christianity) is mainly furthered by its philanthropy towards strangers and its careful attention to the bestowal of the dead." Tertullian declares (see p. 153) that the burial of poor brethren was performed at the expense of the common fund, and Aristides (*Apol.*, xv.) corroborates this, although with him it takes the form of private charity. "Whenever," says Aristides, "one of their poor passes from the world, one of them looks after him and sees to his burial, according to his means." We know the great importance attached to an honourable burial in those days, and the pain felt at the prospect of having to forego this privilege. In this respect the Christian church was meeting a sentiment which even its opponents felt to be a human duty. Christians, no doubt, were expected to feel themselves superior to any earthly ignominy, but even they felt it was a ghastly thing not to be buried decently. The deacons were specially charged with the task of seeing that everyone was properly interred (*Const. Ap.*, iii. 7),[38] and in certain cases they did not restrict themselves to the limits of the brotherhood. "We cannot bear," says Lactantius (*Instit.*, vi. 12), "that the image and workmanship of God should be exposed as a prey to wild beasts and birds, but we restore it to the earth from which it was taken,[39] and do this office of relatives even to the body of a person whom we do not know, since in their room humanity must step in."[40] At this point also we must include the care of the dead after burial. These were still regarded in part as destitute and fit to be supported. Oblations were presented in their name and for the welfare of their souls, which served as actual

---

[38] A certain degree of luxury was even allowed to Christians; cp. Tertull., *Apol.*, xlii. : "If the Arabians complain of us [for giving them no custom], let the Sabeans be sure that the richer and more expensive of their wares are used as largely in burying Christians as in fumigating the gods." Another element in a proper burial was that a person should lie among his companions in the faith. Anyone who buried his people beside non-Christians needlessly, incurred severe blame. Yet about the middle of the third century we find a Spanish bishop burying his children among the heathen; cp. Cyprian, Ep. lxvii. 6: "Martialis [episcopus] praeter gentiliam turpia et lutulenta conviva in collegio diu frequentata filios in eodem collegio exterarum gentium more apud profana sepulcra deposuit et alienigenis consepelivit" ("Martialis himself frequented for long the shameful and filthy banquets of the heathen in their college, and placed his sons in the same college, after the custom of foreign nations, amid profane sepulchres, burying them along with strangers"). Christian graves have been found now and then in Jewish cemeteries.

[39] Christians were therefore opposed to cremation, and tried to gather even the fragments of their brethren who had been martyred in the flames. The belief of the "simplices" about the resurrection of the body wavered a little in view of the burning of the body, but the theologians always silenced any doubts, though even they held that burning was a piece of wickedness. Cp. *Epist. Lugd.* (Eus., *H. E.*, v. 1, towards the close; Tert., *de Anima*, li.: "Nec ignibus funerandum aiunt (i.e., some pagans), parcentes superfluo animae (i.e., because particles of the soul still clung to the body). Alia est autem ratio pietatis istius (*i.e.*, of Christianity), non reliquiis animae adulatrix, sed crudelitatis etiam corporis nomine aversatrix, quod et ipsum homo non mereatur poenali exitu impendi"; Tert., *de Resurr.*, i: "Ego magis ridebo vulgus, tum quoque, cum ipsos defunctos atrocissime exurit, quos postmodom gulisossime nutrit. ... O pietatem de crudelitate ludentem!" ("I have greater derision for the crowd, particularly when it inhumanely burns its dead, only to pamper them afterwards with luxurious indulgence. ... Out upon the piety which mocks its victims with cruelty!"). The reasons which seem to have led Christians from the first to repudiate cremation have not been preserved. We can only surmise what they were.

[40] The question of the relation between the churches and the collegia tenuiorum (collegia funeraticia) may be left aside. Besides, during the past decade it has passed more and more out of notice. No real light has been thrown by such guilds upon the position of the churches, however convincing may be the inference that the rights obtained by these collegia may have been for a time available to Christians as well. Cp. Neumann, *Röm. Staat und Kirchc*, i. 102 f.

intercessions on their behalf. This primitive custom was undoubtedly of immense significance to the living; it comforted many an anxious relative, and added greatly to the attractive power of Christianity.[41]

7. Care for slaves.

It is a mistake to suppose that any "slave question" occupied the early church. The primitive Christians looked on slavery with neither a more friendly nor a more hostile eye than they did upon the State and legal ties.[42] They never dreamt of working for the abolition of the State, nor did it ever occur to them to abolish slavery for humane or other reasons — not even amongst themselves. The New Testament epistles already assume that Christian masters have slaves (not merely that pagan masters have Christian slaves), and they give no directions for any change in this relationship. On the contrary, slaves are earnestly admonished to be faithful and obedient.[43]

Still, it would not be true to assert that primitive Christianity was indifferent to slaves and their condition. On the contrary, the church did turn her attention to them, and effected some change in their condition. This follows from such considerations as these:

(a) Converted slaves, male or female, were regarded in the full sense of the term as brothers and sisters from the standpoint of religion. Compared to this, their position in the world was reckoned a matter of indifference.[44]

(b) They shared the rights of church members to the fullest extent. Slaves could even become clergymen, and in fact bishops.[45]

---

[41] Tertullian is our first witness for this custom. It did not spring up independently of pagan influence, though it may have at least *one* root within the Christian cultus itself. Tertullian attacked the common pagan feasts of the dead and the custom of bringing food to the graves; but this rooted itself as early as the third century, and was never dislodged.

[42] The Didache (iv. 11) even bids slaves obey their (Christian) masters ὡς τύπῳ θεοῦ ("as a type of God").

[43] The passages in Paul's epistles are well known; see also 1 Peter. In his letter to Philemon, Paul neither expects nor asks the release of the slave Onesimus. The only possible sense of 1 Cor. vii. 20 f. ἕκαστος ἐν τῇ κλήσι ᾗ ἐκλήθη, ἐν ταύτῃ μενέτω · δοῦλος ἐκλήθης; μή σοι μελέτω · ἀλλ' εἰ καὶ δύνασαι ἐλεύθερος γενέσθαι, μᾶλλον χρῆσαι is that the apostle counsels slaves not even to avail themselves of the chance of freedom. Any alteration of their position would divert their minds to the things of earth — such seems to be the writer's meaning. It is far from certain whether we may infer from this passage that Christian slaves begged from Christian masters the chance of freedom more often than their pagan fellows. Christian slave-owners often appear in the literature of the second and third centuries. Cp. Athenag., *Suppl.*, xxxv.; *Acta Perpetuæ*; etc.

[44] Paul is followed on this point by others; e.g., Tatian, *Orat.*, xi.; Tertull., *de Corona*, xiii.; and Lactantius, *Instit.*, v. 16, where, in reply to the opponents who cry out, "You too have masters and slaves! Where then is your so-called equality?" the answer is given, "Alia causa nulla est cur nobis invicem fratrum nomen impertiamus nisi quia pares esse nos credimus. Nam cum omnia humana non corpore sed spiritu metiamur, tametsi corporum sit diversa condicio, nobis tamen servi non sunt, sed eos et habemus et dicimus spiritu fratres, religione conservos" ("Our sole reason for giving one another the name of brother is because we believe we are equals. For since all human objects are measured by us after the spirit and not after the body, although there is a diversity of condition among human bodies, yet slaves are not slaves to us; we deem and term them brothers after the spirit, and fellow-servants in religion"). De Rossi (*Boll. di Arch. Christ.*, 1866, p. 24) remarks on the fact that the title "slave" never occurs in the sepulchral inscriptions of Christianity. Whether this is accidental or intentional, is a question which I must leave undecided. On the duty of Christian masters to instruct their slaves in Christianity, cp. Arist., *Apol.*, xv. : "Slaves, male and female, are instructed so that they become Christians, on account of the love felt for them by their masters; and when this takes place, they call them brethren without any distinction whatsoever."

[45] The Roman presbyter or bishop, Pius, the brother of Hermas, must have belonged to the class of slaves. Callistus, the

(c) As personalities (in the moral sense) they were to be just as highly esteemed as freemen. The sex of female slaves had to be respected, nor was their modesty to be outraged. The same virtues were expected from slaves as from freemen, and consequently their virtues earned the same honour.[46]

(d) Masters and mistresses were strictly charged to treat all their slaves humanely,[47] but, on the other hand, to remember that Christian slaves were their own brethren.[48] Christian slaves, for their part, were told not to disdain their Christian masters, *i.e.*, they were not to regard themselves as their equals.[49]

Roman bishop, was originally a slave. Cp. the eightieth canon of Elvira: "Prohibendum ut liberti, quorum patroni in saeculo fuerint, ad clerum non promoveantur" ("It is forbidden to hinder freemen from being advanced to the rank of clergy, whose owners may be still alive").

[46] Ample material on this point is to be found in the Acts of the Martyrs. Reference may be made in especial to Blandina, the Lyons martyr, and to Felicitas in the Acts of Perpetua. Not a few slaves rank among "the holy martyrs" of the church. Unless it had been set down, who would imagine that Blandina was a slave — Blandina, who is held in high honour by the church, and whose character has such noble traits? In Euseb., *Mart. Pal.* (*Texte u. Unters.*, xxiv. 2. p. 78), we read: "Porphyry passed for a slave of Pamphilus, but in love to God and in amazing confession of his faith he was a brother, nay more, a beloved son, to Pamphilus, and was like his teacher in all things." — Cp., however, the penitential ordinance appointed for those astute Christian masters who had forced their Christian slaves to offer sacrifice during the Diocletian persecution (canons 6 and 7 of Peter Alex., in Routh's *Reliq.* Sacr., iv. 29 f.). The masters are to do penance for three years καὶ ὡς ὑποκρινάμενοι καὶ ὡς καταναγκάσαντες τοὺς ὁμοδούλους θῦσαι, ἄτε δὴ παρακούσαντες τοῦ ἀποστόλου τὰ αὐτὰ θέλοντος ποιεῖν τοὺς δεσπότας τοῖς δούλοις, ἀνιέντας τὴν ἀπειλήν, εἰδότας, φησίν, ὅτι καὶ ὑμῶν καὶ αὐτῶν ὁ κύριός ἐστιν ἐν οὐρανοῖς, καὶ προσωπολὴ ψια παρ' αὐτῷ οὐκ ἔστιν (Eph. vi. 9; then follows Col. iii. 11) ...σκοπεῖν ὀφειλοῦσιν ὃ κατειργάσαντο θελήσαντες τὴν ψυχὴν ἑαυτῶν σῶσαι, οἱ τοὺς συνδούλους ἡμῶν ἑλκύσαντες ἐπι εἰδωλολατρείαν δυναμένους καὶ αὐτοὺς ἐκφυγεῖν, εἰ τὸ δίκαιον καὶ τὴν ἰσότητα ἦσαν αὐτοῖς παρασχόντες, ὡς πάλιν ὁ ἀπόστολος λέγει (Col. iv. 1) ("for having played the hypocrite and for having compelled their fellow-servants to sacrifice — in disobedience to the apostle, who enjoins masters and servants to do the same things, and to forbear threatening, knowing, saith he, that you and they have a Lord in heaven, with whom there is no respect of persons. ... They ought to consider this compulsion of theirs, due to their desire to save their own lives, by which they drag our fellow-servants into idolatry, when they could themselves avoid it — that is, if masters treated them justly and equitably, as the apostle once more observes"). Only a single year's penance was imposed on slaves thus seduced. Tertullian, on the contrary (*de Idol.*, xvii.), shows that the same courage and loyalty was expected from Christian slaves and freedmen as from the highly born. The former were not to hand the wine or join in any formula when they attended their pagan lords at sacrifice. Otherwise they were guilty of idolatry. For attempts on the part of pagan masters to seduce their slaves from the faith, cp. *Acta Pionii*, ix., etc.

[47] A beautiful instance of the esteem and position enjoyed by a Christian female slave in a Christian home, is afforded by Augustine in his description of the old domestic ("famula decrepita") belonging to his maternal grandfather's house, who had nursed his grandfather as a child ("sicut dorso grandiuscularum puellarum parvuli portari solent" = as little children are often carried on the backs of older girls); *i.e.*, she was active as early as the year 300 A.D. "On account of her age and her excellent character, she was highly respected by the heads of that Christian home. Hence the charge of her master's daughters [i.e., including Monica] was given her, and she fulfilled her duty thoroughly [better than the mother did]. When necessary, she was strict in restraining the girls with a holy firmness, and in teaching them with a sober judgment" ("Propter senectam ac mores optimas in domo christiana satis a dominis honorabatur; unde etiam curam filiarum dominicarum commissam diligenter gerebat, et erat in eis coercendis, cum opus esset, sancta severitate vehemens atque in docendis sobria prudentia," *Confess.*, ix. 8. 17). The basis of Augustine's own piety rested on this slave!

[48] A long series of testimonies, from the Lyons epistle onwards, witnesses to the fact that Christian masters had heathen slaves. Denunciations of their Christian masters by such slaves, and calumnies against Christian worship, cannot have been altogether uncommon.

[49] As early as 1 Tim. vi. 1 f. It proves that Christianity must have been in many cases "misunderstood" by Christian slaves.

(e) To set a slave free was looked upon, probably from the very beginning, as a praiseworthy action;[50] otherwise, no Christian slave could have had any claim to be emancipated. Although the primitive church did not admit any such claim on their part, least of all any claim of this kind on the funds of the church, there were cases in which slaves had their ransom paid for out of such funds.[51] The church never condemned the rights of masters over slaves as sinful; it simply saw in them a natural relationship. In this sphere the source of reform lay, not in Christianity, but in general considerations derived from moral philosophy and in economic necessities.

From one of the canons of the Council of Elvira (*c.* 300 A.D.), as well as from other minor sources, we learn that even in the Christian church, during the third century in particular, cases unfortunately did occur in which slaves were treated with revolting harshness and barbarity.[52] In general, one has to recollect that even as early as the second century a diminution of the great slave-establishment can be detected — a diminution which, on economic grounds, continued during the third century. The liberation of slaves was frequently a necessity; it must not be regarded, as a rule, in the light of an act prompted by compassion or brotherly feeling.

8. Care for people visited by great calamities.

As early as Hebrews x. 32 f. a church is commended for having nobly stood the test of a great persecution and calamity, thanks to sympathy and solicitous care. From that time onward, we frequently come across counsels to Christian brethren to show themselves specially active and devoted in any emergencies of distress; not counsels merely, but also actual proofs that they bore fruit. We shall not, at present, go into cases in which churches lent aid to sister churches, even at a considerable distance;

---

[50] Authentic illustrations of this are not available, of course.

[51] From the epistle of Ignatius to Polycarp (iv.) two inferences may be drawn: (1) that slaves were ransomed with money taken from the church collections, and (2) that no *claim* to this favour was admitted. Δούλους καὶ δούλας μὴ ὑπερηφάνει · ἀλλὰ μηδὲ αὐτοὶ φυσιούσθωσαν [Christian slaves could easily lose their feelings of deference towards Christian owners], ἀλλ' εἰς δόξαν θεοῦ πλέον δουλευέτωσαν, ἵνα κρείττονος ἐλευθερίας ἀπο θεοῦ τύχωσιν· μὴ ἐράτωσαν ἀπὸ τοῦ κοινοῦ ἐλευθεροῦσθαι, ἵνα μὴ δοῦλοι εὑπεθῶσιν ἐπιθυμίας ("Despise not male or female slaves. Yet let not these again be puffed up, but let them be all the better servants to the glory of God, that they may obtain a better freedom from God. Let them not crave to be freed at the public cost, lest they be found to be slaves of lust").

[52] Canon v.: "Si qua femina furore zeli accensa flagris verberaverit ancillam suam, ita ut intra tertium diem animam cum cruciatu. effundat," etc. ("If any mistress, in a fit of passion, scourges her handmaid, so that the latter expires within three days," etc.). Canon xli. also treats of masters and slaves. We do not require to discuss the dispensation given by Callistus, bishop of Rome, to matrons for entering into sexual relations with slaves, as the object of this dispensation was to meet the case of high-born ladies who were bent on marriage, and not to admit that slaves had equal rights. Hippol. *Philos.*, ix. 12: καὶ γυναιξὶν ἐπέτρεψεν, εἰ ἀνάνδροι εἶεν καὶ ἡλικίᾳ ἢ ἑαυτῶν ἀξίαν μὴ βούλοιντο καταιρεῖν διὰ τὸ νομίμως γαμηθῆναι, ἐκεῖν ἕνα ὃν ἂν αἱρήσωνται, σύγκοιτον, εἴτε οἰκέτην, εἴτε ἐλεύθερον, καὶ τοῦτον κρίνειν ἀντὶ ἀνδρὸς μὴ νόμῳ γεγαμημένην ("He even permitted women, if unmarried and inflamed with a passion unworthy of their age, or unwilling to forfeit their position for the sake of a legal marriage, to have anyone they liked as a bedfellow, either slave or free, and to reckon him their husband although he was not legally married to them").

these fall to be noticed under section 10. But some examples referring to calamities within a church itself may be set down at this stage of our discussion.

When the plague raged in Alexandria (about 259 A.D.), bishop Dionysius wrote (Euseb., *H.E.*, vii. 22): "The most of our brethren did not spare themselves, so great was their brotherly affection. They held fast to each other, visited the sick without fear, ministered to them assiduously, and served them for the sake of Christ. Right gladly did they perish with them. ... Indeed many did die, after caring for the sick and giving health to others, transplanting the death of others, as it were, into themselves. In this way the noblest of our brethren died, including some presbyters and deacons and people of the highest reputation. ... Quite the reverse was it with the heathen. They abandoned those who began to sicken, fled from their dearest friends, threw out the sick when half dead into the streets, and let the dead lie unburied."

A similar tale is related by Cyprian of the plague at Carthage. He exclaims to the pagan *Demetrianus (x.)*: "*Pestem et luem criminaris, cum peste ipsa et lue vel detecta sint vel aucta crimina singulorum, dum nec infirmis exhibetur misericordia et defunctis avaritia inhiat ac rapina. Idem ad pietatis obsequium timidi,[53] ad impia lucra temerarii, fugientes morientium funera et adpetentes spolia mortuorum*" ("You blame plague and disease, when plague and disease either swell or disclose the crimes of individuals, no mercy being shown to the weak, and avarice and rapine gaping greedily for the dead. The same people are sluggish in the discharge of the duties of affection, who rashly seek impious gains; they shun the deathbeds of the dying, but make for the spoils of the dead"). Cyprian's advice is seen in his treatise *de Mortalitate.* His conduct, and the way he inspired other Christians by his example, are narrated by his biographer Pontianus (*Vita*, ix. f.):

> "*Adgregatam primo in loco plebem de misericordiae bonis instruit. Docet divinae lectionis exemplis ... tunc deinde subiungit non esse mirabile, si nostros tantum debito caritatis obsequio foveremus; cum enim perfectum posse fieri, qui plus aliquid publicano vel ethnico fecerit, qui malum bono vincens et divinae clementiae instar exercens inimicos quoque dilexerit. ... Quid Christiana plebs faceret, cui de fide nomen est? distributa sunt ergo continuo pro qualitate hominum atque ordinum ministeria [organized charity, then]. Multi qui paupertatis beneficio sumptus exhibere non poterant, plus sumptibus exhibebant, compensantes proprio labore mercedem divitiis omnibus cariorem ... fiebat itaque exuberantium operum largitate, quod bonum est ad omnes, non ad solos domesticos fidei*" ("The people being assembled together, he first of all urges on them the benefits of mercy. By means of examples drawn from the sacred lessons, he teaches them. ... Then he proceeds to add that there is nothing remarkable in cherishing merely our own people with the

---

[53] Cp. Cyprian, *per Pont.*, ix.: "Jacebant interim tota civitate vicatim non jam corpora, sed cadavera plurimorum" ("Meanwhile all over the city lay, not bodies now, but the carcasses of many").

due attentions of love, but that one might become perfect who should do something more than heathen men or publicans, one who, overcoming evil with good, and practising a merciful kindness like to that of God, should love his enemies as well. … What should a Christian people do, a people whose very name was derived from faith? The contributions are always distributed then according to the degree of the men and of their respective ranks. Many who, on the score of poverty, could not make any show of wealth, showed far more than wealth, as they made up by personal labour an offering dearer than all the riches in the world. Thus the good done was done to all men, and not merely to the household of faith, so richly did the good works overflow").

We hear exactly the same story of practical sympathy and self-denying love displayed by Christians even to outsiders, in the great plague which occurred during the reign of Maximinus Daza (Eus., *H.E.*, ix. 8): "Then did they show themselves to the heathen in the clearest light. For the Christians were the only people who amid such terrible ills showed their fellow-feeling and humanity by their actions. Day by day some would busy themselves with attending to the dead and burying them (for there were numbers to whom no one else paid any heed); *others gathered in one spot all who were afflicted by hunger throughout the whole city, and gave bread to them all.* When this became known, people glorified the Christians' God, and, convinced by the very facts, confessed the Christians alone were truly pious and religious."

It may be inferred with certainty, as Eusebius himself avows, that cases of this kind made a deep impression upon those who were not Christians, and that they gave a powerful impetus to the propaganda.

9. The churches furnishing work and insisting upon work.
Christianity at the outset spread chiefly among people who had to work hard. The new religion did not teach its votaries "the dignity of labour," or "the noble pleasure invariably afforded by work." What it inculcated was just the *duty* of work.[54] "If anyone is not willing to work, let him not eat" (2 Thess. iii. 10). Over and again it was enunciated that the duty of providing for others was conditioned by their incapacity for work. The brethren had soon to face the fact that some of their numbers were falling into restless and lazy habits, as well as the sadder fact that these very people were selfishly trying to trade upon the charity of their neighbours. This was so notorious that even in the brief compass of the Didache there is a note of precautions which are to be taken to checkmate such attempts, while in Lucian's description of

---

[54] At the same time there was a quiet undercurrent of feeling expressed by the maxim that absolute devotion to religion was a higher plane of life — "The heavenly Father who feeds the ravens and clothes the lilies will provide for us." Apostles and prophets (with the heroes of asceticism, of course, from the very outset) did not require to work. The idea was that their activity in preaching demanded their entire life and occupied all their time.

the Christians he singles out, as one of their characteristic traits, a readiness to let cunning impostors take advantage of their brotherly love.[55]

Christianity cannot be charged at any rate with the desire of promoting mendicancy or with underestimating the duty of work.[56] Even the charge of being "*infructuosi in negotiis*", (of no use in practical affairs) was repudiated by Tertullian.

"How so?" he asks. "How can that be when such people dwell beside you, sharing your way of life, your dress, your habits, and the same needs of life? We are no Brahmins or Indian gymnosophists, dwelling in woods and exiled from life. ... We stay beside you in this world, making use of the forum, the provision-market, the bath, the booth, the workshop, the inn, the weekly market, and all other places of commerce. We sail with you, fight at your side, till the soil with you, and traffic with you; we likewise join our technical skill to that of others, and make our works public property for your use" (*Apol.* xlii.).[57] Even clerics were not exempted from making a livelihood,[58] and admirable sayings on the need of labour occur in Clement of Alexandria as well as in other writers. We have already observed (pp. 155 f.) that one incentive to work was found in the consideration that money could thus be gained for the purpose of supporting other people, and this idea was by no means thrown out at random. Its frequent repetition, from the epistle to the Ephesians onwards, shows that people recognized in it a powerful motive for the industrious life. It was also declared in simple and stirring language that the labourer was worthy of his hire, and a fearful judgment was prophesied for those who defrauded workmen of their wages (see especially Jas. v. 4 f.). It is indeed surprising that work was spoken of in such a sensible way, and that the duty of work was inculcated so earnestly, in a society which was so liable to fanaticism and indolence.

But we have not yet alluded to what was the really noticeable feature in this connection. We have already come across several passages which would lead us to infer that, together with the recognition that every Christian brother had the right to a bare provision for livelihood, the early Christian church also admitted its obligation to secure this minimum either by furnishing him with work or else by maintaining

---

[55] The pseudo-Clementine *de Virgin.*, i, 11, contains a sharp warning against the "*otiosi*," or lazy folk, who chatter about religion instead of attending to their business.

[56] Cp. 2 Thess. iii. 6: παραγγέλλομεν ὑμῖν ἐν ὀνόματι τοῦ κυρίου I.X. στέλλεσθαι ὑμᾶς ἀπὸ παντὸς ἀδελφοῦ ἀτάκτως περιπατοῦντος cp. ver. 12.

[57] Tertullian at this point is suppressing his personal views; he speaks from the standpoint of the majority of Christians. In reality, as we see from the treatise *de Idololatria*, he was convinced that there was hardly a single occupation or business in which any Christian could engage without soiling his conscience with idolatry.

[58] The earliest restrictions on this point occur in the canons of the Synod of Elvira (canon xix.). They are very guarded. "Episcopi, presbyteres et diacones de locis suis [this is the one point of the prohibition] negotiandi causa non discedant ... sane ad victum sibi conquirendum aut filium, aut libertum, aut mercenarium, aut amicum, aut quemlibet mittant; et si voluerint negotiari, intra provinciam negotientur" ("Let no bishop or presbyter or deacon leave his place for the purpose of trading ... he can, of course, send his son, or his freedman, or his hired servant, or a friend, or anyone else, to procure provisions; but if he wishes to transact business, he must confine himself to his own sphere").

him. Thus we read in the pseudo-Clementine homilies (cp. *Clem.*, viii.): "For those able to work, provide work; and to those incapable of work, be charitable."[59] Cyprian also (*Ep.* ii.) assumes that if the church forbids some teacher of dramatic art to practise his profession, it must look after him, or, in the event of his being unable to do anything else, provide him with the necessaries of life.[60] We were not aware, however, if this was really felt to be a duty by the church at large, till the discovery of the Didache. This threw quite a fresh light on the situation. In the Didache (xii.) it is ordained that no brother who is able to work is to be maintained by any church for more than two or three days. The church accordingly had the right of getting rid of such brethren. But the reverse side of this right was a duty. "If any brother has a trade, let him follow that trade and earn the bread he eats. If he has no trade, exercise your discretion in *arranging for him to live among you as a Christian, but not in idleness.* If he will not do this (*i.e.,* engage in the work with which you furnish him), he is trafficking with Christ (χριστέμπορος). Beware of men like that." It is beyond question, therefore, that a Christian brother could demand work from the church, and that the church had to furnish him with work. What bound the members together, then, was not merely the duty of supporting one another — that was simply the *ultima ratio*; it was the fact that they formed a guild of workers, in the sense that the churches had to provide work for a brother whenever he required it. This fact seems to me of great importance, from the social standpoint. The churches were also labour unions. The case attested by Cyprian proves that there is far more here than a merely rhetorical maxim. The Church did prove in this way a refuge for people in distress who were prepared to work. Its attractive power was consequently intensified, and from the economic standpoint we must attach very high value to a union which provided work for those who were able to work, and at the same time kept hunger from those who were unfit for any labour.

---

[59] Παρέχοντες μετὰ πάσης εὐφροσύνης τὰς τροφάς...τοῖς ἀτέχνοις διὰ τῶν ἐπιτεδευμάτον ἐννούμενοι τὰς προφάσεις τῆς ἀναγκαίας τροφῆς · τεχνίτῃ ἔργον, ἀνδρανεῖ ἔλεοϲj ("Providing supplies with all kindliness ... furnishing those who have no occupation with employment, and thus with the necessary means of livelihood. To the artificer, work; to the incapable, alms").

[60] "Si paenurian talis et necessitatem paupertatis obtendit, potest inter ceteros qui ecclesiae alimentis sustinentur huius quoque necessitatis adiuvari, si tamen contentus sit frugalioribus et innocentibus cibis nec putet salario se esse redi¬mendum, ut a peccatis cesset" ("Should such a person allege penury and the necessities of poverty, his wants may also be met among those of the other people who are maintained by the church's aliment — provided always that he is satisfied with plain and frugal fare. Nor is he to imagine he must be redeemed by means of an allowance of money, in order to cease from sins").

10. Care for brethren on a journey (hospitality) and for churches in poverty or peril.[61]

The diaconate went outside the circle of the individual church when it deliberately extended its labours to include the relief of *strangers, i.e.*, in the first instance of Christian brethren on their travels. In our oldest account of Christian worship on Sunday (Justin, *Apol.*, I. lxvii.; see above, p. 153), strangers on their travels are included in the list of those who receive support from the church-collections. This form of charity was thus considered part of the church's business, instead of merely being left to the goodwill of individuals; though people had recourse in many ways to the private method, while the virtue of hospitality was repeatedly inculcated on the faithful.[62] In the first epistle of Clement to the Corinthian church, it is particularly noted, among the distinguishing virtues of the church, that anyone who had stayed

---

[61] I have based this section on a study of my own which appeared in the *Monatsschrift f. Diakonie umd innere Mission* (Dec. 1879, Jan. 1880); but, as the relations of the individual church with Christendom in general fail to be noticed in this section, I have thought it appropriate to treat the subject in greater detail. The ideal background of all this enterprise and activity may be seen in Tertullian's remark (*de Praescr.*, xx.): "Omnes ecclesiae una; probant unitatem ecclesiarum communicatio pacis et appellatio fraternitatis et contesseratio hospitalitatis" ("All churches are one, and the unity of the churches is shown by their peaceful intercommunion, the title of brethren, and the bond of hospitality").

[62] Rom. xii. 13, "Contribute to the needs of the saints and seek to show hospitality."; 1 Pet. iv. 9, "Show hospitality to one another without grumbling"; Heb. vi. 10, xiii. 2, "Do not neglect to show hospitality to strangers, for thereby some have entertained angels unawares." Individuals are frequently commended by Paul to the hospitality of the church; *e.g.*, Rom. xvi. 1 f., "welcome her in the Lord in a way *worthy of the saints.*" See also 3 John 5-8. In the "Shepherd" of Hermas (*Mand.*, viii. 10) hospitality is distinctly mentioned in the catalogue of virtues, with this remarkable comment: ἐν γὰρ τῇ φιλοξενίᾳ εὑρίσκεται ἀγαθοποίησίς ποτε ("for benevolence from time to time is found in hospitality"), while in Sim., viii. 10. 3, praise is assigned to those Christians who εἰς τοὺς οἴκους αὐτῶν ἡδέως ὑπεδέξαντο τοὺς δούλους τοῦ θεοῦ ("gladly welcomed God's servants into their houses"). Aristides, in his *Apology* (xv.), says that if Christians "see any stranger, they take him under their roof and rejoice over him as over a very brother" ξένον ἐαν ἴδωσιν, ὑπὸ στέγην εἰσάγουσι καὶ χαίρουσιν ἐπ' αὐτῷ ὡς ἐπὶ ἀδελφῷ ἀληθινῷ. The exercise of hospitality by private individuals towards Christian brethren is assumed by Tertullian to be a duty which no one dare evade; for, in writing to his wife (*ad Uxor.*, ii. 4), he warns her against marrying a heathen, should he (Tertullian) predecease her, on the ground that no Christian brother would get a spiritual reception in an alien household. But hospitality was inculcated especially upon officials of the church, such as elders (bishops) and deacons, who practised this virtue in the name of the church at large; cp. 1 Tim. iii. 2, Tit. i. 8 (1 Tim. v. 10). In Hermas (*Sim.*, ix. 27. 2) hospitable bishops form a special class among the saints, since "they gladly received God's servants into their houses at all times, and without hypocrisy." In the Didache a comparatively large amount of space is taken up with directions regarding the care of travellers, and Cyprian's interest in strangers is attested by his seventh letter, written to his clergy at Carthage from his place of retreat during the Decian persecution. He writes: "I beg you will attend carefully to the widows, and sick people, and all the poor. You may also pay the expenses of any strangers who may be in need, out of my own portion which I left with my fellow-presbyter Rogatianus. In case it should be all used, I hereby forward by the hands of Naricus the acolyte another sum of money, so that the sufferers may be dealt with more promptly and liberally" ("Viduarum et infirmorum et omnium pauperum curam peto diligenter habeatis, sed et peregrinis si qui indigentes fuerint sumptus suggeratis de quantitate mea propria quam apud Rogatianum compresbyterum nostrum dimisi. Quae quantitas ne forte iam erogata sit, misi eidem per Naricum acoluthum aliam portionem, ut largius et promptius circa laborantes fiat operatio"). Cp. also *Apost. Const.*, iii. 3 (p. 98, 9 f., ed. Lagarde), and *Ep. Clem. ad Jacob.* (p. 9, 10 f., ed. Lagarde): τοὺς ξένους μετὰ πάσης προθυμίας εἰς τοὺς ἑαυτῶν οἴκους λαμβάνετε ("Receive strangers into your homes with all readiness"). In his satire on the death of Peregrinus (xvi.), Lucian describes how his hero, on becoming a Christian, was amply provided for on his travels: "Peregrinus thus started out for the second time, and betook himself to travelling; he had an ample allowance from the Christians, who constituted themselves his bodyguard, so that he lived in clover. Thus for some time he provided for himself in this fashion." From the pseudo-Clementine epistle *de Virginitate* one also learns to appreciate the appeal and exercise of hospitality. Finally, Julian (*Ep. ad Arsac.*) emphasises ἡ περὶ τοὺς ξενους φιλανθρωπία,a among Christians, and wishes that his own party would imitate it (see above, p. 162).

there praised their splendid sense of hospitality.[63] But during the early centuries of Christianity it was the Roman church more than any other which was distinguished by the generosity with which it practised this virtue. In one document from the reign of Marcus Aurelius, a letter of Dionysius the bishop of Corinth to the Roman church, it is acknowledged that the latter has maintained its *primitive* custom of showing kindness to *foreign* brethren. "Your worthy bishop Soter has not merely kept up this practice, but even extended it, by aiding the saints with rich supplies, which he sends from time to time, and also by addressing blessed words of comfort to brethren coming up to Rome, like a loving father to his children" (Eus., *H.E.*, iv. 23. 10). We shall return to this later on; meanwhile it may be pointed out, in this connection, that the Roman church owed its rapid rise to supremacy in Western Christendom, not simply to its geographical position within the capital of the empire, or to the fact of its having been the seat of apostolic activity throughout the West, but also to the fact that it recognized the special obligation of caring for Christians in general, which fell to it as the church of the imperial capital. A living interest in the collective church of Christ throbbed with peculiar intensity throughout the Roman church, as we shall see, from the very outset, and the practice of hospitality was one of its manifesttions. At a time when Christianity was still a homeless religion, the occasional travels of the brethren were frequently the means of bringing churches together which otherwise would have had no common tie; while in an age when Christian captives were being dragged off, and banished to distant spots throughout the empire, and when brethren in distress sought shelter and solace, the practical proof of hospitality must have been specially telling. As early as the second century one bishop of Asia Minor even wrote a book upon this virtue.[64] So highly was it prized within the churches that it was put next to faith as the genuine proof of faith. "For the sake of his faith and hospitality, Abraham had a son given him in his old age." "For his hospitality and piety was Lot saved from Sodom." "For the sake of her faith and hospitality was Rahab saved." Such are the examples of which, in these very words, the Roman church reminds her sister at Corinth.[65] Nor was this exercise of hospitality merely an aid in passing. The obligation of work imposed by the Christian church has been already mentioned (cp. pp. 173 f.); if any visitors wished to settle down, they had to take up some work, as is plain from the very provision made for such cases. Along roads running through waste country hospices were erected. The earliest case of this occurs in the *Acta Archelai*[66] (fourth century).

---

[63] 1 Clem.i. 2: τίς γὰρ παρεπιδημήσας πρὸς ὑμᾶς...τὸ μεγαλοπρεπὲς τῆς φιλοξενίας ὑμῶν ἦθος οὐκ ἐκήρυξεν ("What person who has sojourned among you ... has not proclaimed your splendid, hospitable disposition?"); cp. above, p. 152.

[64] Melito of Sardes, according to Eusebius (*H.E.*, iv. 26. 2).

[65] 1 Clem. x. 7, xi. 1, xii. 1.

[66] Ch. iv. : "Si quando veluti peregrinans ad hospitium pervenisset, quae quidem diversoria hospitalissimus Marcellus instruxerat."

It was easy to take advantage of a spirit so obliging and unsparing (*e.g.*, the case of Proteus Peregrinus, and especially the churches' sad experience of so-called prophets and teachers). Heretics could creep in, and so could loafers or impostors. We note, accordingly, that definite precautions were taken against these at quite an early period. The new arrival is to be tested to see whether or not he is a Christian (cp. 2 and 3 John; Did., xii.). In the case of an itinerant prophet, his words are to be compared with his actions. No brother is to remain idle in any place for more than two days, or three at the very most; after that, he must either leave or labour (Did., xii). Later on, any brother on a journey was required to bring with him a passport from his church at home. Things must have come to a sad pass when (as the Didache informs us) it was decreed that any visitor must be adjudged a false prophet without further ado, if during an ecstasy he ordered a meal and then partook of it, or if in an ecstasy he asked for money. Many a traveller, however, who desired to settle down, did not come with empty hands; such persons did not ask, they gave. Thus we know (see above) that when Marcion came from Pontus and joined the Roman church, he contributed 200,000 sesterces to its funds (Tert., *de Praescr.*, xxx.). Still, such cases were the exception; as a rule, visitors were in need of assistance.

Care lavished on brethren on a journey blossomed naturally into a sympathy and care for any distant churches in poverty or peril. The keen interest shown in a guest could not cease when he left the threshold of one's house or passed beyond the city gates. And more than this, the guest occupied the position of a representative to any church at which he arrived; he was a messenger to them from some distant circle of brethren who were probably entire strangers and were yet related to them. His account of the distress and suffering of his own church, or of its growth and spiritual gifts, was no foreign news. The primitive churches were sensible that their faith and calling bound them closely together in this world; they felt, as the apostle enjoined, that "if one member suffers, all suffer together; if one member is honored, all rejoice together" (1 Cor. xii. 26). And there is no doubt whatever that the consciousness of this was most vigorous and vital in the very ages during which no external bond as yet united the various churches, the latter standing side by side in almost entire independence of each other. These were the ages when the primitive article of the common symbol, "I believe in one holy church," was really nothing more than an *article of faith*. And of course the effect of the inward ties was all the stronger when people were participating in a common faith which found expression ere long in a brief and vigorous confession, or practising the same love and patience and Christian discipline, or turning their hopes in common to that glorious consummation of Christ's kingdom of which they had each received the earnest and the pledge. These common possessions stimulated brotherly love; they made strangers friends, and brought the distant near. "By secret signs and marks they manage to recognize one another, loving each other almost before they are acquainted"; such is the description of Christians given by the pagan Caecilius (*Min. Felix,* ix. 3). Changes afterwards took place; but this vital sense of belonging to *one brotherhood* never wholly disappeared.

In the great prayers of thanksgiving and supplication offered every Sabbath by the churches, there was a fixed place assigned to intercession for the whole of Christendom throughout the earth. Before very long this kindled the consciousness that every individual member belonged to the holy unity of Christendom, just as it also kept them mindful of the services which they owed to the general body. In the epistles and documents of primitive Christianity, wherever the church-prayers emerge their oecumenical character becomes clear and conspicuous.[67] Special means of intercourse were provided by epistles, circular letters, collections of epistles, the transmission of acts or of official records, or by travellers and special messengers. When matters of importance were at stake, the bishops themselves went forth to settle controversial questions or to arrange a common basis of agreement. It is not our business in these pages to describe all this varied intercourse. We shall confine ourselves to the task of gathering and explaining those passages in which one church comes to the aid of another in any case of need.

Poverty, sickness, persecution, and suffering of all kinds formed one class of troubles which demanded constant help on the part of churches that were better off; while, in a different direction, assistance was required in those internal crises of doctrine and of conduct which might threaten a church and in fact endanger its very existence. Along both of these lines the brotherly love of the churches had to prove its reality.

The first case of one church supporting another occurs at the very beginning of the apostolic age. In Acts xi. 27 ff. we read that Agabus in Antioch foretold a famine. On the news of this, the young church at Antioch made a collection on behalf of the poor brethren in Judea, and dispatched the proceeds to them by the hands of Barnabas and Paul. It was a Gentile Christian church which was the first, so far as we are aware, to help a sister church in her distress. Shortly after this, the brotherly love felt by young Christian communities drawn from pagans in Asia and Europe is reported to have approved itself on a still wider scale. Even after the famine had passed, the mother church at Jerusalem continued poor. Why, we do not know. An explanation has been sought in the early attempt by which that church is said to have introduced a voluntary community of goods; it was the failure of this attempt, we are to believe, that left the local church impoverished. This is merely a vague conjecture. Nevertheless, the poverty at Jerusalem remains a fact. At the critical conference in Jerusalem, when the three pillar-apostles definitely recognized Paul's mission to the Gentiles, the latter pledged himself to remember the poor saints at Jerusalem in distant lands; and the epistles to the Galatians, the Corinthians, and the Romans, show how widely and faithfully the apostle discharged this obligation. His position in this matter was by no means easy. He had made himself responsible for a collection

---

[67] Cp. 1 Clem. lix. 2 f. with my notes *ad loc.* Polyc., *Phil.,* xii. 2 f.

whose value depended entirely on the *voluntary* devotion of the churches which he founded. But he was sure he could rely on them, and in this he did not deceive himself. Paul's churches made his concerns their own, and money for the brethren far away at Jerusalem was collected in Galatia, Macedonia, and Achaia. Even when the apostle had to endure the prospect of all his work in Corinth being endangered by a severe local crisis, he did not fail to remember the business of the collection along with more important matters. The local arrangements for it had almost come to a standstill by the time he wrote, and the aim of his vigorous, affectionate, and graceful words of counsel to the church is to revive the zeal which had been allowed to cool amid their party quarrels (2 Cor. viii. 9). Not long afterwards he is able to tell the Romans that "For Macedonia and Achaia *have been pleased* to make some contribution for the poor among the saints at Jerusalem. For they were pleased to do it, and indeed they owe it to them. For if the Gentiles have come to share in their spiritual blessings, they ought also to be of service to them in material blessings" (Rom. xv. 26 f.). In this collection Paul saw a real duty of charity which rested on the Gentile churches, and one has only to realize the circumstances under which the money was gathered in order to understand the meaning it possessed for the donors themselves. As yet, there was no coming or going between the Gentile and the Judean Christians, though the former had to admit that the latter were one with themselves as brethren and as members of a single church. The churches in Asia and Europe were imitators of the churches of God in Judea (1 Thess. ii. 14), yet they had no fellowship in worship, life, or customs. This collection formed, therefore, the one visible expression of that brotherly unity which otherwise was rooted merely in their common faith. This was what lent it a significance of its own. For a considerable period this devotion of the Gentile Christians to their distressed brethren in Jerusalem was the sole manifestation, even in visible shape, of the consciousness that all Christians shared an inner fellowship. We do not know how long the contributions were kept up. The great catastrophes which occurred in Palestine after 65 A.D. had a disastrous effect at any rate upon the relations between Gentile Christians and their brethren in Jerusalem and Palestine.[68] — Forty years later the age of persecutions burst upon the churches, though no general persecution occurred until the middle of the third century. When some churches were in distress, their possessions seized[69] and their existence imperilled, the others could not feel happy in their own undisturbed position. Succour of their persecuted brethren seemed to them a duty, and it was a duty from which they did not shrink. Justin (*loc. cit.*) tells us that the maintenance

---

[68] The meaning of Heb. vi. 10 is uncertain. I may observe at this point that more than three centuries later Jerome employed this Pauline collection as an argument to enforce the duty of all Christians throughout the Roman empire to support the monastic settlements at the sacred sites of Jerusalem and Bethlehem. In his treatise against Vigilantius (xiii.), who had opposed the squandering of money to maintain monks in Judea, Jerome argues from 2 Cor. viii., etc., without more ado, as a scriptural warrant for such collections.

[69] Even by the time of Domitian, Christian churches were liable to poverty, owing to the authorities seizing their goods; cp. Heb. x. 34 (if the epistle belongs to this period), and Eus., *H.E.*, iii. 17.

of imprisoned Christians was one of the regular objects to which the church collections were devoted, a piece of information which is corroborated and enlarged by the statement of Tertullian, that those who languished in the mines or were exiled to desert islands or lay in prison all received monies from the church.[70] Neither statement explains if it was only members of the particular church in question who were thus supported. This, however, is inherently improbable, and there are express statements to the contrary, including one from a pagan source. Dionysius of Corinth (Eus., *H.E.*, iv. 23. 10) writes thus to the Roman Christians about the year 170: "From the very first you have had this practice of aiding *all* the brethren in various ways and of sending contributions to *many* churches in *every* city, thus in one case relieving the poverty of the needy, or in another providing for brethren in the mines. By these gifts, which you have sent from the very first, you Romans keep up the hereditary customs of the Romans, a practice your bishop Soter has not merely maintained but even extended." A hundred years later Dionysius, the bishop of Alexandria, in writing to Stephen the bishop of Rome, has occasion to mention the churches in Syria and Arabia. Whereupon he remarks in passing, "To them you send help regularly, and you have just written them another letter" (Eus., *H.E.*, vii. 5. 2). Basil the Great informs us that under bishop Dionysius (259-269 A.D.) the Roman church sent money to Cappadocia to purchase the freedom of some Christian captives from the barbarians, an act of kindness which was still remembered with gratitude in Cappadocia at the close of the fourth century.[71] Thus Corinth, Syria, Arabia, and Cappadocia, all of them churches in the East, unite in testifying to the praise of the church at Rome; and we can understand, from the language of Dionysius of Corinth, how Ignatius could describe that church as the προκαθημένη τῆς ἀγάπης ("the leader of love."[72] Nor were other churches and their bishops behindhand in the matter. Similar stories are told of the church at Carthage and its bishop Cyprian. From a number of letters written shortly before his execution, it is quite clear that Cyprian sent money to provide for the Christians who then lay captive in Numidia (*Ep.* lxxvi.-lxxix.), and elsewhere in his correspondence there is similar evidence of his care for stranger Christians and foreign churches. The most memorable of his letters, in this respect, is that addressed to the bishops of Numidia in 253 A.D. The latter had informed him that wild hordes of robbers had invaded the country and carried off many Christians of both sexes into captivity. Whereupon Cyprian instituted a collection on their behalf and forwarded the proceeds to the bishops along with the following letter (*Ep.* lxii.). It is the most elaborate and important document from the first three centuries bearing upon the support extended to one church by another, and for that reason we may find space for it at this point.

---

[70] Tert., *Apol.*, xxxix. : "Si qui in metallis et si qui in insulis, vel in custodiis, dumtaxat ex causa dei sectae, alumni suae confessionis fiunt" (cp. p. 153).

[71] Basil, *Ep. ad Damasum Papam* (lxx).

[72] Ign., *ad Rom.*, proemium. Cp. Zahn, *ad loc.*: "In caritatis operibus semper primum locum sibi vindicavit ecclesia Romana" ("The Roman church always justified her primacy in works of charity").

Cyprian to Januarius, Maximus, Proculus, Victor, Modianus, Nemesianus, Nampulus, and Honoratus, the brethren: greeting.

With sore anguish of soul and many a tear have I read the letter which in your loving solicitude you addressed to me, dear brethren, with regard to the imprisonment of our brothers and sisters. Who would not feel anguish over such misfortunes? Who would not make his brother's grief his own? For, says the apostle Paul: Should one member suffer, all the others suffer along with it; and should one member rejoice, the others rejoice with it also. And in another place he says: Who is weak, and I am not weak? We must therefore consider the present imprisonment of our brethren as our imprisonment, reckoning the grief of those in peril as our grief. We form a single body in our union, and we ought to be stirred and strengthened by religious duty as well as by love to redeem our members the brethren.

For as the apostle Paul once more declares: Know ye not that ye are God's temple and that the Holy Spirit dwelleth in you? Though love failed to stir us to succour the brethren, we must in this case consider that it is temples of God who are imprisoned, nor dare we by our procrastination and neglect of fellow-feeling allow temples of God to remain imprisoned for any length of time, but must put forth all our energies, and with all speed manage by mutual service to deserve the grace of Christ our Lord, our Judge, our God. For since the apostle Paul says: So many of you as are baptized into Christ have put on Christ, we must see Christ in our imprisoned brethren, redeeming from the peril of imprisonment him who redeemed us from the peril of death. He who took us from the jaws of the devil, who bought us with his blood upon the cross, who now abides and dwells in us, he is now to be redeemed by us for a sum of money from the hands of the barbarians. … Will not the feeling of humanity and the sense of united love incline each father among you to look upon those prisoners as his sons, every husband to feel, with anguish for the marital tie, that his wife languishes in that imprisonment?" Then, after an account of the special dangers incurred by the consecrated "virgins" — "our church, having weighed and sorrowfully examined all those matters in accordance with your letter, has gathered donations for the brethren speedily, freely, and liberally; for while, according to its powers of faith, it is ever ready for any work of God, it has been raised to a special pitch of charity on this occasion by the thought of all this suffering. For since the Lord says in his gospel: I was sick and ye visited me, with what ampler reward for our alms will he now say: I was in prison and ye redeemed me? And since again he says: I was in prison and ye visited me, how much better will it be for us on the day of judgment, when we are to receive the Lord's reward, to hear him say: I was in the dungeon of imprisonment, in bonds and fetters among the barbarians, and ye rescued me from that prison of slavery! Finally, we thank you heartily for summoning us to share your trouble and your noble and necessary act of love, and for offering us a rich harvest-field wherein to scatter the seeds of our hope, in the expectation of reaping a very plentiful harvest from this heavenly and helpful action. We transmit to you a sum of a hundred thousand sesterces [close upon £1000] collected and contributed by our clergy and people here in the church over which by God's mercy we preside; this you will dispense in the proper quarter at your own discretion.

In conclusion, we trust that nothing like this will occur in future, but that, guarded by the power of God, our brethren may henceforth be quit of all such perils. Still, should the like occur again, for a test of love and faith, do not hesitate to write of it to us; be sure and certain that while our own church and the whole of the church pray fervently that this may not recur, they will gladly and generously contribute even if it does take place once more. In order that you may remember in prayer our brethren and sisters who have taken so prompt and liberal a share in this needful act of love, praying that they may be ever quick to aid, and in order also that by way of return you may present them in your prayers and sacrifices, I add herewith the names of all. Further, I have subjoined the names of my colleagues (the bishops) and fellow-priests, who like myself were present and made such contributions as they could afford in their own name and in the name of their people; I have also noted and forwarded their small sums along with our own total. It is your duty — faith and love alike require it — to remember all these in your prayers and supplications.

Dearest brethren, we wish you unbroken prosperity in the Lord. Remember us.

Plainly the Carthaginian church is conscious here of having done something out of the common. But it is intensely conscious also of having thus discharged a *duty* of Christian love, and the religious basis of the duty is laid down in exemplary fashion. It is also obvious that so liberal a grant could not be taken from the proceeds of the ordinary church-collections.

Yet another example of Cyprian's care for a foreign church is extant. In the case (cp. above, p. 175) already mentioned of the teacher of the histrionic art who is to give up his profession and be supported by the church, if he has no other means of livelihood, Cyprian (*Ep.* ii.) writes that the man may come to Carthage and find maintenance in the local church if his own church is too poor to feed him.[73]

---

[73] "Si illic ecclesia non sufficit ut laborantibus praestat alimenta, poterit se ad nos transferre (*i.e.*, to Carthage), et hic quod sibi ad victum atque ad vestitum necessarium fuerit accipere" ("If the local church is not able to support those who labour, let it send them on to us to get the needful food and clothing").

Lucian's satire on the death of Peregrinus, in the days of Marcus Aurelius, is a further witness to the alert and energetic temper of the interest taken in churches at the outbreak of persecution or during a period of persecution. The governor of Syria had ordered the arrest of this character, who is discribed by Lucian as a nefarious impostor. Lucian then describes the honour paid him, during his imprisonment, by Christians, and proceeds as follows: "In fact, people actually came from several Asiatic townships, sent by Christians, in the name of their churches, to render aid, to conduct the defence, and to encourage the man. They become incredibly alert when anything of this kind occurs that affects their common interests. On such occasions no expense is grudged. Thus they pour out on Peregrinus, at this time, sums of money which were by no means trifling, and he drew from this source a considerable income."[74] What Lucian relates in this passage cannot, therefore, have been an infrequent occurrence. Brethren arrived from afar in the name of their churches, not merely to bring donations for the support of prisoners, but also to visit them in prison, and to encourage them by evidences of love; they actually endeavoured to stand beside them in the hour of trial. The seven epistles of Ignatius form, as it were, a commentary upon these observations of the pagan writer. In them we find the keen sympathy shown by the churches of Asia Minor as well as by the Roman church in the fortunes of a bishop upon whom they had never set eyes before: we also get a vivid sense of their care for the church at Antioch, which was now orphaned. Ignatius is being taken from Antioch to Rome in order to fight with beasts at the capital, and meanwhile the persecution of Christians at Antioch proceeds apace. On reaching Smyrna, he is greeted by deputies from the churches of Ephesus, Magnesia, and Tralles. After several days' intercourse, he entrusts them with letters to their respective churches, in which, among other things, he warmly commends to the brethren of Asia Minor his own forlorn church. "Pray for the church in Syria," he writes to the Ephesians. "Remember the church in Syria when you pray," he writes to the Trallians; "I am not worthy to belong to it, since I am the least of its members." And in the letter to the Magnesians he repeats this request, comparing the church at Antioch to a field scorched by the fiery heat of persecution, which needs some refreshing dew: the love of the brethren is to revive it.[75] At the same time we find him turning to the Romans also. There appears to have been some brother from Ephesus who was ready to convey a letter to the Roman church, but Ignatius assumes they will learn of his fortunes before the letter reaches them. What he fears is, lest they should exert their influence at court on his behalf, or rob him of his coveted martyrdom by appealing to the Emperor. The whole of the letter is written with the

---

[74] It may be observed at this point that there were no *general collections* in the early church, like those maintained by the Jews in the Imperial age. The organization of the churches would not tend greatly to promote any such under¬takings, since Christians had no headquarters such as the Jews possessed in Palestine.
Eph. xxii. 2; Trall., xiii. 1; Magn., xiv.

[75] *Eph.* xxii. 2; *Trall.*, xiii. 1; *Magn.*, xiv.

object of blocking the Roman church upon this line of action.[76] But all that concerns us here is the fact that a stranger bishop from abroad could assume that the Roman church would interest itself in him, whether he was thinking of a legal appeal or of the Roman Christians moving in his favour along some special channels open to themselves. A few days afterwards Ignatius found himself at Troas, accompanied by the Ephesian deacon Burrhus, and provided with contributions from the church of Smyrna.[77] Thence he writes to the churches of Philadelphia and Smyrna, with both of which he had become acquainted during the course of his journey, as well as to Polycarp, the bishop of Smyrna. Messengers from Antioch reached him at Troas with news of the cessation of the persecution at the former city, and with the information that some churches in the vicinity of Antioch had already despatched bishops or presbyters and deacons to congratulate the local church (*Philad.*, x. 2). Whereupon, persuaded that the church of Antioch had been delivered from its persecution through the prayers of the churches in Asia Minor, Ignatius urges the latter also to send envoys to Antioch in order to unite with that church in thanking God for the deliverance. "Since I am informed," he writes to the Philadelphians (x. 1 f.), "that, in answer to your prayers and love in Jesus Christ, the church of Antioch is now at peace, it befits you, as a church of God, to send a deacon as your delegate with a message of God for that church, so that he may congratulate the assembled church and glorify the Name. Blessed in Jesus Christ is he who shall be counted worthy of such a mission; and ye shall yourselves be glorified. Now it is not impossible for you to do this for the name of God, if only you have the desire." The same counsel is given to Smyrna. The church there is also to send a messenger with a pastoral letter to the church of Antioch (*Smyrn.*, xi.). The unexpected sudden-ness of his departure from Troas prevented Ignatius from addressing the same request to the other churches of Asia Minor. He therefore begs Polycarp not only himself to despatch a messenger with all speed (*Polyc.*, vii. 2), but to write in his name to the other churches and ask them to share the general joy of the Antiochene Christians either by messenger or by letter (*Polyc.*, viii. 1). A few weeks later the church at Philippi wrote to Polycarp that it also had made the acquaintance of Ignatius during that interval; it requested the bishop of Smyrna, therefore, to forward its letter to the church of Antioch whenever he sent his own messenger. Polycarp undertakes to do so. In fact, he even holds out the prospect of conveying the letter himself. As desired by them, he also transmits to them such letters of Ignatius as had come to hand, and asks for reliable information upon the fate of Ignatius and his companions.[78]

---

[76] Even here Ignatius remembers to commend the church at Antioch to the church of Rome (ix.): "Remember in your prayers the Syrian church, which has God for its shepherd now instead of me. Jesus Christ alone shall be its over¬seer (bishop) — he and your love together."

[77] *Philad.*, xi. 2; *Smyrn.*, xii. 1

[78] Polyc., ad *Phil.*, xiii.

101

Such, in outline, is the situation as we find it in the seven letters of Ignatius and in Polycarp's epistle to the Philippians. What a wealth of intercourse there is between the churches! What public spirit! What brotherly care for one another! Financial support retires into the background here. The foreground of the picture is filled by proofs of that personal cooperation by means of which whole churches, or again churches and their bishops, could lend mutual aid to one another, consoling and strengthening each other, and sharing their sorrows and their joys. Here we step into a whole world of sympathy and love.

From other sources we also learn that after weathering a persecution the churches would send a detailed report of it to other churches. Two considerable documents of this kind are still extant. One is the letter addressed by the church of Smyrna to the church of Philomelium and to all Christian churches, after the persecution which took place under Antonius Pius. The other is the letter of the churches in Gaul to those in Asia Minor and Phrygia, after the close of the bloody persecution under Marcus Aurelius.[79] In both letters the persecution is described in great detail, while in the former the death of bishop Polycarp is specially dwelt on, since the glorious end of a bishop who was well known in the East and West alike had to be announced to all Christendom. The events which transpired in Gaul had a special claim upon the sympathy of the Asiatic brethren, for at least a couple of the latter, Attalus of Pergamum and Alexander, a Phrygian, had suffered a glorious martyrdom in the Gallic persecution. The churches also took advantage of the opportunity to communicate to the brethren certain notable experiences of their own during the period of persecution, as well as any truths which they had verified. Thus the Smyrniote church speaks very decidedly against the practice of people delivering themselves up and craving for martyrdom. It gives one melancholy instance of this error (*Mart. Polyc.*, iv.). The churches of Gaul, for their part (in Eus., *H.E.*, v. 2), put in a warning against excessive harshness in the treatment of penitent apostates. They are able also to describe the tender compassion shown by their own confessors. It was otherwise with the church of Rome. She exhorted the church of Carthage to stand fast and firm during the Decian persecution,[80] and at a subsequent period conferred with it upon its mode of dealing with apostates.[81] Here a special case was under discussion. Cyprian, the bishop of Carthage, had fled during the persecution; nevertheless, he had continued to superintend his church from his retreat, since he could say with quite a good conscience that he was bound to look after his own people. The Romans,

---

[79] It is preserved, though not in an entirely complete form, by Eusebius (*H.E.*, v. 1 f.). The Smyrniote letter also occurs in an abbreviated form in Eusebius (iv. 15); the complete form, however, is also extant in a special type of text, both in Greek and Latin.

[80] Ep. viii. in Cyprian's correspondence (ed. Hartel).

[81] Cp. my study (in the volume dedicated to Weizsäcker, 1892) on "The letters of the Roman clergy from the age of the papal vacancy in 250 A.D." There is also an interesting remark of Dionysius of Alexandria in a letter addressed to Germanus which Eusebius has preserved (*H.E.*, VII. xi. 3). Dionysius tells how "one of the brethren who were present from Rome accompanied" him to his examination before AEmilianus the governor (during the Valerian persecution).

who had not been at first informed of the special circumstances of the case, evidently viewed the bishop's flight with serious misgiving; they thought themselves obliged to write and encourage the local church. The fact was, no greater disaster could befall a church in a period of distress than the loss of its clergy or bishop by death or dereliction of duty. In his treatise on "Flight during a Persecution," Tertullian relates how deacons, presbyters, and bishops frequently ran away at the outbreak of a persecution, on the plea of Matt. x. 23: "When they persecute you in one town, flee to the next." The result was that the church either collapsed or fell a prey to heretics.[82] The more dependent the church became upon its clergy, the more serious were the consequences to the church of any failure or even of any change in the ranks of the latter. This was well understood by the ardent persecutors of the church in the third century, by Maximin I., by Decius, by Valerian, and by Diocletian. Even a Cyprian could not retain control of his church from a place of retreat! He had to witness it undergoing shocks of disastrous force. It was for this very reason that the sister churches gave practical proof of their sympathy in such crises, partly by sending letters of comfort during the trial, as the Romans did, partly by addressing congratulations to the church when the trial had been passed. In his church history Eusebius furnishes us with selections from the ample correspondence of Dionysius, bishop of Corinth, and one of these letters, addressed to the church of Athens, is relevant to our present purpose. Eusebius writes as follows (*H.E.*, IV. xxiii. 2 f.): "The epistle exhorts them to the faith and life of the gospel, which Dionysius accuses them of undervaluing. Indeed, he almost says they have fallen away from the faith since the martyrdom of Publius, their bishop, which had occurred during the persecution in those days. He also mentions Quadratus, who was appointed bishop after the martyrdom of Publius, and testifies that by the zeal of Quadratus they were gathered together again and had new zeal imparted to their faith." The persecution which raged in Antioch during the reign of Septimius Severus claimed as its victim the local bishop of that day, one Serapion. His death must have exposed the church to great peril, for when the episcopate was happily filled up again, the bishop of Cappadocia wrote a letter of his own from prison to congratulate the church of Antioch, in the following terms: "The Lord has lightened and smoothed my bonds in this time of captivity, by letting me hear that, through the providence of God, the bishopric of your holy church has been undertaken by Asclepiades, whose services to the faith qualify him thoroughly for such a position" (Eus., *H.E.*, VI. xi. 5).

---

[82] "Sed cum ipsi auctores, id est ipsi diaconi et presbyteri et episcopi fugiunt, quomodo laicus intellegere potuerit, qua ratione dictum: Fugite de civitate in civitatem? (Tales) dispersum gregem faciunt et in praedam esse omnibus bestiis agri, dum non est pastor illis. Quod nunquam magis fit, quam cum in persecutione destituitur ecclesia a clero" ("But when the very authorities themselves — deacons, I mean, and presbyters and bishops — take to flight, how can a layman see the real meaning of the saying, 'Flee from city to city'? Such shepherds scatter the flock and leave it a prey to every wild beast of the field, by depriving it of a shepherd. And this is specially the case when a church is forsaken by the clergy during persecution"). — *De Fuga*, xi.

Hitherto we have been gleaning from the scanty remains of the primitive Christian literature whatever bore upon the material support extended by one church to another, or upon the mutual assistance forthcoming in a time of persecution. But whenever persecutions brought about internal crisis and perils in a church, as was not infrequently the case, the sympathetic interest of the church extended to this sphere of need as well, and attempts were made to meet the situation. Such cases now fall to be considered — cases in which it was not poverty or persecution, but internal abuses and internal dangers, pure and simple, which drew a word of comfort or of counsel from a sister church or from its bishop.

In this connection we possess one document dating from the very earliest period, viz., the close of the first century, which deserves especial notice. It is the so-called first epistle of Clement, really an official letter sent by the Roman church to the Corinthian.[83] Within the pale of the latter church a crisis had arisen, whose consequences were extremely serious. All we know, of course, is what the majority of the church thought of the crisis, but according to their account certain newcomers, of an ambitious and conceited temper, had repudiated the existing authorities and led a number of the younger members of the church astray.[84] Their intention was to displace the presbyters and deacons, and in general to abolish the growing authority of the officials (xl.-xlviii.). A sharp struggle ensued, in which even the women took some part.[85] Faith, love, and brotherly feeling were already threatened with extinction (i.-iii.). The scandal became notorious throughout Christendom, and indeed there was a danger of the heathen becoming acquainted with the quarrel, of the name of Christ being blasphemed, and of the church's security being imperiled.[86] The Roman Church stepped in. It had not been asked by the Corinthian church to interfere in the matter; on the contrary, it spoke out of its own accord.[87] And it did so with an affection and solicitude equal to its candour and dignity. It felt bound, for conscience' sake, to give a serious and brotherly admonition, conscious that God's voice spoke through its words for peace,[88] and at the same time for the strict maintenance of respect towards the authority of the officials (cp. xl. f.). Withal it never forgets that its place is merely to point out the right road to the Corinthians, not to lay commands upon them;[89] over and again it expresses most admirably its firm confidence that the church knows the will of God and will bethink itself once more of the right course.[90] It even clings to the hope that the very agitators will mend their ways (cp. liv.). But

---

[83] Cp. the inscription.

[84] Cp. i. 1, iii. 3, xxxix. 1, xlvii, 6, etc.

[85] This is probable, from i. 3, xxi. 6.

[86] Cp. xlvii. 7, i. 1.

[87] i. 1, xlvii. 6-7.

[88] Cp. lix. 1, lvi. 1, lxiii. 2.

[89] Cp. especially lviii. 2: δέξασθε τὴν συμβουλὴν ἡμῶν ("accept our counsel").

[90] Cp. xl. 1, xlv. 2 f., liii. 1, lxii. 3.

in the name of God it asks that a speedy end be put to the scandal. The transmission of the epistle is entrusted to the most honoured men within its membership. "They shall be witnesses between us and you." And we have done this that you may know we have had and still have every concern for your speedy restoration to peace" (lxiii. 3). The epistle concludes by saying that the Corinthians are to send back the envoys to Rome as soon as possible in joy and peace, so that the Romans may be able to hear of concord regained with as little delay as possible and to rejoice speedily on that account (lxv. 1). There is nothing in early Christian literature to compare with this elaborate and effective piece of writing, lit up with all the brotherly affection and the public spirit of the church. But similar cases are not infrequent. The church at Philippi, for example, sent a letter across the sea to the aged Polycarp at Smyrna, informing him of a sad affair which had occurred in their own midst. One of their presbyters, named Valens, had been convicted of embezzling the funds of the church. In his reply, which is still extant, Polycarp treats this melancholy piece of news (Polyc., *ad Phil.*, xi.). He does not interfere with the jurisdiction of the church, but he exhorts and counsels the Philippians. They are to take warning from this case and avoid avarice themselves. Should the presbyter and his wife repent, the church is not to treat them as enemies, but as ailing and erring members, so that the whole body may be saved. The bishop lets it be seen that the church's treatment of the case does not appear to him to have been entirely correct. He exhorts them to moderate their passion and to be gentle. But, at same time, in so doing he is perfectly conscious of the length to which he may venture to go in opposing an outside church. When Ignatius, bishop of Antioch, is being conveyed across Asia Minor, he takes the opportunity of writing brief letters to encourage the local churches in any perils to which they may be exposed. He warns them against the machinations of heretics, exhorts them to obey the clergy, urges a prudent concord and firm unity, and in quite a thorough fashion gives special counsels for any emergency. At the opening of the second century a Roman Christian, the brother of the bishop, desires to lay down the *via media* of proper order and discipline at any crisis in the church, as he himself had found that *via*, between the extremes of laxity and rigour. His aim is directed not merely to the Roman church but to Christendom in general (to the "foreign cities"); he wishes all to learn the counsels which he claims to have personally received from the Holy Spirit through the church (Herm., *Vis.*, ii. 4). In the days of Marcus Aurelius it was bishop Dionysius of Corinth in particular who sought (no doubt in his church's name as well as in his own) by means of an extensive correspondence to confirm the faith of such churches, even at a great distance, as were in any peril. Two of his letters, those to the Athenians and the Romans, we have already noticed, but Eusebius gives us the contents of several similar writings, which he calls "catholic" epistles. Probably these were meant to be circulated throughout the churches, though they were collected at an early date and also (as the bishop himself is forced indignantly to relate) were interpolated. One letter to the church at Sparta contains an exposition of orthodox doctrine with an admonition to peace and unity. In the epistle to the church of Nicomedia in Bithynia he combats the heresy of Marcion. "He also wrote a letter to the church in Gortyna, together with the other churches in Crete, praising their bishop Philip for the testimony borne to the great piety and steadfastness of his church, and warning them to guard against the aberrations of heretics. He also wrote to the church of Amastris, together with the other churches in Pontus. … Here he adds explanations of some passages from Holy Scripture, and mentions Palmas, their bishop, by name. He gives them long advice, too, upon marriage and chastity, enjoining them also to welcome again into their number all who come back after any lapse whatsoever, be it vice or heresy. There is also in his collection of letters another addressed to the Cnosians (in Crete), in which he exhorts Pinytus, the bishop of the local church, not to lay too heavy and sore a burden on the brethren in the matter of continence, but to consider the weakness of the majority" (Eus., *H.E.*, iv. 23). Such is the variety of contents in these letters. Dionysius seems to have spoken his mind on every question which agitated the churches of his day, nor was any church too remote for him to evince his interest in its inner fortunes.

After the close of the second century a significant change came over these relationships, as the institution of synods began to be adopted. The free and unconventional communications which passed between the churches (or their bishops) yielded to an intercourse conducted upon fixed and regular lines. A new procedure had already come into vogue with the Montanist and Quartodeciman controversies, and this was afterwards developed more highly still in the great Christological controversies and in the dispute with Novatian. Doubtless we still continue to hear of cases in which individual churches or their bishops displayed special interest in other churches at a distance, nor was there any cessation of *voluntary* sympathy with the weal and woe of any sister church. But this gave place more than ever both to an interest in the position taken up by the church at large in view of individual and particular movements, and also to the support of the provincial churches.[91] Keen interest was shown in the attitude taken up by the churches throughout the empire (or their bishops) upon any critical question. On such matters harmony could be arranged, but otherwise the provincial churches began to form groups of their own. Still, for all this, fresh methods emerged in the course of the third century by which one church supported or rallied another, and these included the custom of inviting the honoured teachers of one church to deliver addresses in another, or of securing them, when controversies had arisen, to pronounce an opinion, to instruct the parties, and to give a judgment in the matter. Instances of this are to be found, for example, in the career of the great theologian Origen.[92] Even in the fourth and fifth centuries, the material support of poor churches from foreign sources had not ceased; Socrates, in his church history (vii. 25), notes one very brilliant example of the practice.

---

[91] Instances of this occur, *e.g.*, in the correspondence of Cyprian and of Dionysius of Alexandria.

[92] Cp. Eus., *H.E.*, vi. 19. 15; 33. 2; 37: 32. 2.

Crucifixion
"… He said, 'It is finished,' and he bowed his head and gave up his spirit." John 19:30b. c. 1509

THE CHURCH IS A MERCY PLACE!

BY MATTHEW C. HARRISON

"'m goin' t'die! I'm goin' t'die!" Zion lives its life-giving life in Christ in the heart of what was Fort Wayne's most troubled neighborhood. But even this congregation, so used to seeing the unveiled sins of humanity (more easily concealed in suburbia!), was more than a little shocked at what it beheld. Attendance was high. Expectation was joyous yet solemn. The Sanctus had just been belted out as the massive pipe organ shook the plaster of the old ornate Gothic sanctuary. From behind the altar I had seen him come in, move to the lectern side, sit, then move to the front of the pulpit side. The Lord's Prayer ended, he rose, faced the congregation and began blowing kisses, shouting, "I'm goin' t'die!" Behind the altar, arms outstretched, facing the congregation, I moved only my index finger (as frantically as one digit can be moved!), directing four rather perplexed ushers to deal with the poor man. They moved closer. He wobbled. Wide, intoxicated eyes peered at them with fear. His large body became tense, ready to fight or flee as he listed backward, cornered. Not wanting a scene, the ushers paused and looked helplessly back to me. "Now what, Pastor?" I read in their eyes.

Complexities are common at the rough edge of the church's life (the mercy edge!) as it is confronted by real physical and spiritual need. It has always been so.

Jesus faced these complexities, misunderstandings and challenges. Yet He never failed to proclaim His Gospel of forgiveness and bear witness to himself as the Divine Savior by works of mercy. The crowds pursued Him for bread, not the bread of life, yet He did not cease to deliver both (John 6). The apostolic church faced similar challenges. Was the church's task Word and Sacrament or caring for the needy? In affirming the essential nature of the church's "marks" (Gospel and sacrament) that tell us surely where the church is present, we dare not miss the fact that love and mercy toward the needy mark the church's corporate life. If not, it risks denial of the very Gospel and sacraments that constitute it. The apostles ordained the seven to "wait tables" (i.e., bread to the widows) that they might not "give up preaching the Word" (Acts 6:2). However, we dare never forget (at the very risk of the "destruction of the Church," says Sasse) that the apostles established a churchly office to care for the needy in its midst, and for those who came to it from without with spiritual and physical need (Gal. 6:10). From Jesus to the apostolic church to the Missouri Synod (see Walther's *"Proper Form of Christian Congregation"* on caring for the poor), it has always been so. But why?

"Missions! That's it! We care in order to evangelize the needy! Find the need, meet it and grow the church!" I don't know about you, but I'm not happy at all with this idea. It's very pragmatic, very American, but not particularly Lutheran. Don't get me wrong. I'm fully convinced that the Bible teaches that eternal life is only through faith in Christ and His cross, and so evangelism is an essential part of the church's life (Matt. 28:19). But it smacks of bait and switch to me. Jesus proclaimed the Gospel and cared for the needy because that's who He is as mercy incarnate. Mercy responds to human need and suffering, whether spiritual or physical. The church doesn't reach out to those in need with some whiz bang program because it's guaranteed to fill pews. Proclaiming Jesus and loving the neighbor has to do with who and what the church is as the body of Christ. Where proclamation of the Gospel or acts of love and mercy are missing, the church's life is not what Christ intended it to be. Mere social gospel substitutes our work for Christ's. Proclamation absent love renders us a mere "clanging cymbal" (1 Corinthians 13).

Why should the church show mercy to the needy? "Simple! It's Christ's command! Love your neighbor as yourself!" This is certainly true. I don't want to minimize the importance of God's Law in guiding us as His church. And yet, not only is the law not the proper motivation for Christian acts of mercy, but the church shows mercy to the needy for reasons deeper than mere command. The church has a mandate for mercy. A mandate (comes from *mandatum*) is a given thing. The church performs acts of mercy because this is what it's given to be: a mercy place! The saints in Matthew 25 aren't even aware of how they served Christ by serving the needy! They did these things because they were a people of mercy. Loehe (so tremendously influential in the founding of Synod, institutions of mercy, the deaconess movement, etc.) expressed this beautifully: "God's mercy (*Barmherzigkeit*) is divine love meeting need. When divine mercy meets human sin, that mercy becomes the grace of forgiveness. When divine love meets human suffering, it becomes merciful care and healing."

Why should the church care for those in need? "I'm still not convinced it should. The church should be about preaching and the administration of the sacraments, period." Well, you would certainly agree that each individual has the mandate to be merciful to others within his/her vocation ("Here consider your station in life"). Rendering love to the neighbor is in large measure the content of the priesthood of the baptized ("Present your bodies as a living sacrifice ... the one who does acts of mercy, with cheerfulness" Rom. 12: 1, 8b). So that you begin to see mercy as the church's corporate task, consider St. Paul's collection for the needy church in Jerusalem (1 Cor.

16:1ff; Acts 11:28; 2 Cor. 8:1–15; 9:12–14; and Acts 24:7). Individuals provide gifts. These gifts are collected by congregations, and even by whole "national churches" (Macedonia). More than that, they are delivered to the church in Jerusalem by none other than the Apostle Paul. This "churchly" life of mercy is expressed by Luther in the Smalcald Articles: "The church cannot be better ruled and preserved than if we all live under one head, Christ ... and keep diligently together in unity of teaching, faith, sacraments, prayers, and works of love" (S.A. II.4.9.). That says it all.

Luther, in fact, left us stirring descriptions of the church as a mercy place and of its gospel-driven motivation to be merciful. The Reformer often speaks of Christ's incarnation and sacrificial death as our motivation to be merciful to the needy (including the non-believer!). He wrote to the Duke of Saxony who was ill:

> *Our Lord and Savior Jesus has left us a commandment which applies equally to all Christians, namely, that we are to render the works of mercy (Luke 6:36) to those who are afflicted, and that we visit the sick, try to free the captives, and do similar things for our neighbor so that the evils of the present may be somewhat lessened. Our Lord Jesus Christ himself gave us the brightest example of this commandment when, because of his infinite love for the race of men, he descended from the bosom of the Father into our misery and our prison, that is, into our flesh and our most wretched life, and took upon himself the penalty for our sins so that we might be saved. And while we have the duty to visit and console all who are afflicted with sickness, we are especially obligated to those of the household of faith* ("Fourteen Consolations," LW 42:122).

His comments in "The Blessed Sacrament of the Holy and True Body of Christ" of 1519 (LW 35) are a must read in order to understand the church's work of mercy as part of the church's corporate life. Luther offers an antidote for a individualistic "Jesus and me" piety regarding the Lord's Supper:

> *There your heart must go out in love and devotion and learn that this sacrament is a sacrament of love, and that love and service are given you and you again must render love and service to Christ and His needy ones. You must feel with sorrow all the dishonor done to Christ in His holy Word, all the misery of Christendom, all the unjust suffering of the innocent, with which the world is everywhere filled to overflowing; you must fight, work, pray, and if you cannot do more, have heartfelt sympathy* (LW 35:54).

"You must fight, work, pray." There are no words more apt for describing the church's challenge to be a mercy place today. It is often very difficult for a parish to understand its life as one that receives Christ's gifts at altar, font and pulpit, then moves out to the world "in fervent love for all." There has never been a more complex era for Lutheran institutions of mercy, which sorely need and want to be reconnected with congregations. We as the LCMS have opportunities the world over to share Christ's mercy in word and deed — and so very much good is taking place (at the Synod level: Disaster Response! Institutional Chaplaincy! Housing! Life Ministry! Health Ministry! etc.). But as with all measurable things, there is so very much more that can be done, such tremendous need to re-think and re-commit to what it means to be Lutheran and merciful, as institutions of care, and as congregations, districts and Synod. There is need for us to revisit and recommit to what it means for us to be Lutheran as we cooperate in externals with other Christians. We must not sacrifice our clear confessional and biblical Lutheran convictions even as we recognize the breadth of one, holy, catholic and apostolic church. Where shall we find the wherewithal for the tasks at hand in this complex world?

"What do we do now, Pastor?" The ushers' eyes were pleading. The entire congregation was frozen, silent. I left the altar. Soon I had extended my arm around his shoulders. "Friend, we are really glad that you are here with us. Let me help you." His tension eased as I literally folded him into the green, Trinity season chasuble I was wearing. It was ample enough to cover us both. Not a snicker, not a smirk marked the faces of the silent observers as we made our way to the rear of the sanctuary. I handed him to others and returned to altar. The "sacrament of love" commenced. After the service, I sought him out. He had slipped away. I never saw him again. Somehow he knew we were a "mercy place" yet to this day I have a nagging visceral disquiet about him. We failed him.

Yet much more ample than that chasuble that covered an unworthy servant of Christ — and a poor soul trapped by sin, death and devil — is Holy Baptism. How shall we deal with our consciences disquieted by our failures at mercy? Where shall we find the strength of faith and fortitude as the church to be ever more what Christ has made us and called us to be: a mercy place? How shall we face the complexities of remaining faithful to our beautiful Lutheran confession in today's vexing world? Luther, no Christ himself, has an answer:

> "We must hold boldly and fearlessly to our baptism, and hold it up against all sins and terrors of conscience, and humbly say, 'I know full well that I have not a single work which is pure, but I am baptized, and through my baptism God, Who cannot lie, has bound Himself in a covenant with me, not to count my sin against me, but to slay it and blot it out.'" ("Treatise on Baptism," LW, Phila. Ed., 1:63).

O Lord Christ, Fount of everlasting compassion, grant Your church on earth grace according to Your promise, that it may be the channel of your mercy to all those in need, body and soul. And may Your merciful washing ever more beget in us merciful living.

Lord, have mercy.
Christ, have mercy.
Lord, have mercy.

ADORATION OF THE MAGI
c. 1511

THE VOCATION OF EVERY CHRISTIAN: LIFE IN CHRIST AS A HOLY CALLING

BY JACOB A.O. PREUS

INTRODUCTION

What does it mean to be a Christian? There are, perhaps, many ways to answer that question. We could say something like, "Being a Christian means believing in Jesus or accepting him as our Savior," or "Being a Christian means seeking and doing God's will in our lives," or, "Being a Christian means loving God and our neighbors." All of these have value and capture at least a part of what it means to be a Christian. But, is there not a better way to capture the essence of what it means to be a Christian, without making it sound like it all depends on us or what we do?

Christian Life as a Calling

One way of speaking about what it means to be a Christian is to think of the Christian life as a calling: We are called by the Gospel to faith in Christ and through and from that Gospel we are called to a life of love and service. Now, to think of our lives in Christ in terms of a holy calling means that we should think of our lives as having, you might say, a certain directionality or movement. The Christian life is never static; it is never going nowhere. And this is because the Word through which God calls His children, that Gospel Word, is a transformational Word. It does not leave us unchanged, indeed, it cannot, for it is a Word saturated with and energized by the living Spirit of God. It is dynamic. It is a living Word, which, as Isaiah says, "goes out … it shall not return to me empty, but it shall accomplish" (Is. 55:11) what the Lord intends.

In this respect, the Word of the Gospel (as the Word of God in general) is unlike human words. Human words, powerful though they may be, are merely descriptive. They describe; they give names to things that already exist. God's Word, on the other hand, is not merely descriptive, it is performative, it performs, it does what it says. It brings things into being that are not. God uses His Word to create *ex nihilo*, out of nothing. He simply speaks things into being. So, the Word of God is not static. Rather, it is vibrant, active, productive; alive with the power and Spirit of the God who is alive and who through His Word gives life.

So, the Gospel Word has an impulse about it, a thrust, you might say. It "goes forth." It gathers and it sends. It draws and disperses. It draws Christ's own to Him, by His Word, and gathers them around His Word. And it sends His own out into the world, dispersing them, with His Word on their lips and His love in their hearts. There is a two-fold thrust, therefore, about the Gospel — inward and outward, gathering and sending, drawing and dispersing; a two-fold calling.

A. THE CALL INTO CHRIST BY THE GOSPEL (BAPTISM)

Each Christian has a two-fold calling. First, the call of the Gospel draws us to Christ. The Holy Spirit gathers us by the Word of Christ. Through the Word of the Gospel, principally through Baptism, God gathers those who are His own. He brings them into His sheepfold, calling them by name and making them His beloved. Luther captured this well in his explanation to the Third Article of the Apostles' Creed, where he said that the Holy Spirit "calls, gathers, enlightens and sanctifies the whole Christian church on earth." The Gospel call involves an ingathering of God's children whereby He draws them to Himself.

And this Word affects every aspect of our lives in Christ and in His Spirit. Although sin lingers in the believer throughout his or her entire earthly life, and, at times, seems to get the upper hand, what the Gospel brings about is, as Paul says, "A new creation. The old has passed away" (2 Cor. 5:17). The Gospel has that kind of trans-forming power: to bring to life what was dead. Through the Gospel in Baptism, the believer is incorporated into Christ: "We were buried therefore with him by baptism into death, in order that, just as Christ was raised from the dead by the glory of the Father, we too might walk in newness of life," Paul writes to the Romans (Rom. 6:4).

Thus, in a very real sense, we begin to shed our own individual identity. The Bible says this in a lot of interesting ways. We become conformed to Christ (Rom. 12:3) and are given his mind (Phil. 2:5). In Christ we become members of a body (Eph. 5:30; 1 Cor. 12:12ff), we are incorporated into Him. We live in Him, He lives in us, as Paul says in Galatians, "I have been crucified with Christ. It is no longer I who live, but Christ who lives in me" (Gal. 2:20). So, in a unique and mysterious way, the Gospel calls us in, it draws us into Christ, to live in Him through faith and to undergo a real transformation. There is no part of us that is unaffected by this transforming Word; no part that we can reserve as our own; nothing that we would wish to continue in the old way, to hold back from that new thing Christ engenders in us. For, "we are [God's] workmanship, created in Christ Jesus ... " (Eph. 2:10).

B. THE CALL OUT TO THE NEIGHBOR BY CHRISTIAN VOCATION

But the Gospel also has an outward thrust; it sends us out into the world, to proclaim God's love in Christ and to live His love. It impels us, freely, to action, to charity. Now,

I have to speak carefully here. Of course, the Gospel does not command anything of us; the Gospel is not about us at all. It is about Christ, what He has done, what He does. But the Gospel has what we often call motivational power, the power to motivate us to response. In this sense, the Gospel is a call, a sending, outward into the world, into our various vocations or careers or stations in life, there to live out the implications of the Gospel. It is in the world, at work, at school, at home, where Christians manifest the "fruit" or the "implications" of the Gospel. God has not given the treasure of the Gospel for the church to hoard and protect within the safe confines of its sanctuaries. He has given it to be given. Those whom He calls, He sends. He sends them into all the world with the words of His love on their lips and His works on their hands so that, as they have been transformed by the power of God's Word, they may likewise transform their realities through word and deed. Thus, there is an outward impulse of the Gospel whereby through telling and acting, those whom God has drawn draw others. They go out so that others might come in.

I am not speaking here of the special call into the Ministry of Word and Sacraments in the church. Rather, I am talking about a call, a vocation, which every single Christian has. It is a two-fold call, in fact. First, the call of the Gospel through Baptism or the proclamation of the Word into Christ to live in Him through faith, and the resulting call, or sending, out into the world to reflect the love Christ has shown by loving others.

The Outward Orientation of the Christian (Inside-out People)

So, if one can say it this way, and this is the way Luther says it is, "a Christian doesn't live in himself. If he lives in himself, he is not a Christian."[1] Christians, that is those who live in Christ through faith, are "outwardly referenced" people; they are "inside-out people." That's what Christians are, they are "inside-out" people. You see, there are just these two ways for a Christian to live — in faith and in love, these two.

That's what Luther said about the Christian. He said, "In faith he ascends above himself to God and in love he descends beneath himself to the neighbor. The Christian always lives outside of himself — he lives in God and in his neighbor. If he lives inside himself, he is not a Christian."[1] You see, to live inside oneself, that's the old way. That's to live in and for yourself. That's the old way, which has passed away. Now a new way has come — living inside-out.

A. IN GOD THROUGH FAITH IN CHRIST

The Christian lives in God through faith. You know, faith is the only appropriate response to a God who deals with people graciously. It is God's way, the way of the Gospel, to give freely, without any consideration of our merit or worthiness. That's the way God saves; solely on account of Christ, not on account of our works; "by works of

---

[1] Luther, M. (1999). Career of the Reformer I, vol. 31, Luther's Works, ed. J. J. Pelikan, H. C. Oswald & H. T. Lehmann (Philadelphia: Fortress Press), 371.

the law no human being will be justified in his sight," Paul wrote (Rom. 3:20). In fact, what's wrong with dragging the business of human righteousness into the question of how we get saved is precisely that it denies the graciousness of God towards sinners on account of Christ. Good works make a claim upon God, and in doing so, they destroy the gratuitous nature of our salvation.

Rather, God saves solely because of His favorable disposition towards us on account of Christ. The theological word we use to describe how it is that we come into possession of the favor of God apart from our own merits or worthiness is *faith*. Faith is, thus, a purely passive attitude whereby God is the Giver and we are the receivers of His favor. To intrude our so-called good works into the picture, which are really not all that good when all is said and done, is to commit, at best, an irrelevancy. Faith alone is the only response to a God who graciously bestows His favor upon us on account of the works of another; on account of Christ.

That we are justified by faith, apart from works of the law, gives us tremendous freedom. It frees us from the need to justify ourselves. That's already been done. Everything has already been done. Christ did it all, and there is nothing left for us to do. There are no finishing touches for us to complete. Our justification before God is as complete as it can be, for God Himself did it. It is finished. Our role is simply to receive it, simply to be given to. God's role is to give. And so He does. He gives us everything: Baptism, Absolution, Lord's Supper, preaching of the Gospel — everything. So, the Christian lives in God alone through faith.

B. IN THE NEIGHBOR THROUGH LOVE
Before God we are only passive and receptive. But before our fellow human beings, we are only active and giving. We live in the neighbor through love. Good works have nothing to do with our relationship of faith with God, but they have everything to do with our relationship of love with our fellow human beings. Our good works are irrelevant and even shameful before the perfection of Christ, but they are not only relevant, they are absolutely necessary before the needs of our neighbor. Thus, the Christian pours himself out and herself out in love for others and gives unstintingly in good works for the neighbor.

So, bringing forth a second freedom, the freedom to be in action, in our lives wherever we are called to live them out, what God has declared us to be through faith. Faith in love. No longer bound to store up our good works for ourselves, we are free simply to give them away to others. God doesn't need our good works. He has the perfect works of Jesus Christ and is fully satisfied with them. And we don't need our good works, either. We have everything that Christ died on the cross to give us. God doesn't need our good works, nor do we. So we are free to give them away to our brothers and sisters in Christ who need them, and sometimes desperately.

Gustaf Wingren beautifully summarizes the teaching of Luther in his 1535 *Commentary on Galatians* about how the Christian lives in and for the neighbor:

> There is nothing more delightful and lovable on earth than one's neighbor. Love does not think about doing works, it finds joy in people; and when something good is done for others, that does not appear to love as works but simply as gifts which flow naturally from love. Love never does something because it has to. It is permitted to act. And earth with its trees and grass is the site of man's vocation. He who has the Holy Spirit knows it by the fact, among others, that in faith and gladness he fulfills his vocation. He rejoices in his labor.[2]

So, as Christians we rejoice in our labor, even as we live in our neighbor.

The Vocation of a Christian

This is the theological foundation for the teaching on the vocation of a Christian. The Christian has a two-fold calling, or vocation, both of which involve our living outside of ourselves. The first is the call to live in God through faith in Christ. That comes through the Gospel in one of its forms, Baptism, evangelism, the Word about Christ, etc. The second is the call to live in the neighbor through love. That comes from, it flows out from, the Gospel. In the first call, our good works are **nothing**. In the second, they are **everything**. So, we live out the implications of the Gospel call through our vocation as Christians.

A. CHRISTIAN VOCATION AND GOD

One of the things that is so impressive about this teaching is its radicality. It is radical in the sense that it penetrates to the *radix*, to the root of what it means to be a Christian. This Gospel Word is a radical word, it brings about a transformation which is complete and profound. The Christianity of a Christian is not something that can be applied like a mantle or a veneer over the world. Rather it is something that transforms a person's entire existence so that he or she lives all of life, even and especially in what many judge to be the trivial everyday things, as a holy calling and appointment from God. And one's vocational connection to God is essential, and incarnational. It is actually God working through the vocation of a Christian.

Luther's teaching on vocation grows largely out of his rich and robust concept of creation, which is peculiarly concrete and vital. There is a direct connection between God's work in creation, or His ongoing creative work in divine providence,[3] and His work through the various offices he has created for human beings to occupy. Luther generally speaks of three offices or estates within which every person is located

---

[2] Gustaf Wingren, *Luther on Vocation* (Philadelphia: Muhlenberg Press, 1957), 43-44. As the reader will note, I am heavily indebted to Wingren's excellent work in this article.

[3] Ibid., 17.

according to his or her calling. At times Luther calls these estates economies, hier-archies or governments. Two are earthly, one is spiritual. The political economy encompasses all the relationships having to do with common life together in society, such as ruler or ruled. The domestic economy includes all domestic relationships such as father, mother, son, daughter, etc. The spiritual estate is the spiritual authority wielded by the pastor through the Word of God in the church.[4] The offices may differ; mother, farmer, magistrate, teacher, pastor, but the purpose is always the same: it is a "participation in God's own care for human beings."[5]

So vocation belongs to this world, to the created order; it is directed towards the neighbor, not to God. Yet, through fulfilling his vocation, man is "an instrument in the hand of God who thus carries on his [i.e. God's] creative work."[6] In this connection, Luther uses the at-first strange, but ultimately very helpful concept of "God's masks." The good things that a Christian does on earth are God's creation and are directed towards the neighbor. Before God the good is not ours but God's. Only before the neighbor does the good done appear as coming from the one who does it. Thus, Luther refers to the Christian as a "mask" of God. It is actually God acting, but only behind ("in, with and under"?) the actions of the Christian.[7] God is hidden behind the "mask" of the neighbor. Thus, the connection between the ongoing creative work of God in the world and the vocation of a Christian is essential and intimate. And it is quite incarnational in the sense that God's love and activity are "enfleshed" in the love and activity of those who through faith live in Him. In a remarkable passage, Luther says

> Through this work in man's offices, God's creative work goes forward, and that creative work is love, a profusion of good gifts. With persons as his "hands" or "coworkers," God gives his gifts through the earthly vocations, toward man's life on earth ... Thus love comes from God, flowing down to human beings on earth through all vocations ...[8]

Luther says that an estate instituted by God is a "channel for God's love to the world and his care of human beings."[9] God's own love, he says, "reaches out to others through Christians as channels."[10] Thus, God's love becomes concrete and actualized through the Christians. This is how you can tell if what you are doing is a good work

---

[4] See ibid., 23-37.

[5] Ibid., 9.

[6] Ibid., 16.

[7] Ibid., 18-19. This notion of "masks" is an exceedingly rich concept, which Luther even applies to all created things. For example, he says that natural occurrences such as "storms and thunder, or sun, or rich harvests are also God's masks, behind which his wrath and his love are hid." See ibid., 137 ff.

[8] Ibid., 27.

[9] Ibid., 125.

[10] Ibid., 126. Luther also calls man "a tool in God's hand." See ibid., 137.

or not. First of all, it must be discernible to others; "What love is must show itself in relation to time and place,"[11] he writes. That is, it may not be merely internal or interior. Secondly, it must be solely for the neighbor, "If you find yourself in a work by which you accomplish something good for God, or the holy, or yourself, but not for your neighbor alone," he says, "then you should know that that work is not a good work."[12] So, a good work may not be merely "spiritual," that is, it must be tangible and for the neighbor.

B. CHRISTIAN VOCATION AND FAITH

Luther's lively interpretation of the biblical teaching that faith is "the conviction of things not seen" (Heb. 11:1) is an important part of his teaching on vocation. Luther taught that we are brought in touch with the way things really are only by the Word of God, which often contradicts the evidence of our senses. God's Word is definitive. It defines our lives. Our immediate apprehension of reality cannot be trusted because of our limitations and our sinfulness. This means that, if we really want to know how things are with us, we cannot trust our perception of things. Instead we must by faith listen to the Word of God. Only by faith do we know our real condition. And only by faith may we see our good works as the good works of God Himself. Only by faith may we see Christ in our neighbor.

Faith is necessary, first of all, in order to distinguish between God and His masks. Luther writes,

> He who does not have faith and, through faith, access to the heavenly kingdom, knows only different masks. He knows only the earth, where God appears solely as hidden behind his many masks: parents, rulers, neighbors, wives, children, etc. Without faith, a man cannot distinguish between God and his masks.[13]

Without faith, therefore, God is eternally hidden and cannot be known as the one who is intimately involved with His creation. Only faith sees God in, or behind, all created things, particularly behind the good works of Christians.

Faith is necessary, secondly, in order to see our humble works as the divinely good works of God Himself that they are. Their goodness can only be seen by faith. Luther writes,

> Thus a Christian finds himself called to drab and lowly tasks, which seem less remarkable than monastic life, mortifications, and other distractions from our vocations. For him who heeds his vocation, sanctification is hidden

---

[11] Ibid., 120.

[12] Ibid.

[13] Ibid., 140.

in offensively ordinary tasks, with the result that it is hardly noticed at all that he is a Christian. But faith looks on simple duties as tasks to which vocation summons the man; and by the Spirit he becomes aware that all those "poor, dull and despised works" are adorned with the favor of God "as with costliest gold and precious stones."[14]

Heeding one's vocation enables a Christian to view his or her tasks, no matter how humble, as a high and holy calling from God. Is one's vocation to be a mother and to tend to the care of children and home? It is an exalted calling from God Himself. Is one's vocation to be teacher, a truck driver, a civil servant? All are raised up and are given the name "divine," and are honored by God by the fact that through these estates He Himself does His loving and preserving work in the world.

Finally, faith enables the Christian to see the positive outcome God will bring about through our actions, even when all the evidence seems to indicate otherwise. Luther writes: "Faith trusts that the mandate of a man's vocation leads to something good; behind all stations and offices stands the Creator, who is none other than the God of the gospel."[15] By faith we are given to see that "all things work together for good" (Romans 8:28) even when we are faced with arduous and thankless tasks and even when we cannot see the good outcome of our love. This is by no means rationale for fatalism and inactivity among Christians. Quite the contrary, it is an encouragement which should spur Christians on to spend themselves in good works and in service to all who need it, regardless of the likelihood of a positive outcome. Christian vocation is not merely a strategy for changing society, although it may at times involve that. To view it as merely that, however, would be far too limiting. What is happening as Christians live out their vocations in the Lord is far more than that they are bringing about a more just and equitable society, as desirable and necessary as that may be. What is happening is that God, who is at work through the lives and actions of Christians, bringing about His good and gracious will.

C. CHRISTIAN VOCATION AND THE CROSS OF CHRIST

Luther's theology of the cross plays a central role in his theology of vocation. Simply put, the Christian is incorporated into Christ, His cross and His resurrection. Luther explicitly links vocation with the cross. He says that our vocation is necessary for a full incorporation into Christ's cross. This means that living out one's vocation may at times appear to be a rather difficult way to go. Christian life is lived under the cross, it is a life of service and suffering, just as the life of Christ was. Luther makes an analogy between the two natures of Christ and the dual nature of Christian vocation, as God's works in the works of men. Wingren says,

---

[14] Ibid., 73.

[15] Ibid., 211.

Thus a Christian finds himself called to drab and lowly tasks, which seem less remarkable than monastic life, mortifications, and other distractions from our vocations. For him who heeds his vocation, sanctification is hidden in offensively ordinary tasks, with the result that it is hardly noticed at all that he is a Christian. But faith looks on simple duties as tasks to which vocation summons the man; and by the Spirit he becomes aware that all those "poor, dull and despised works" are adorned with the favor of God "as with costliest gold and precious stones."[16]

What a beautiful way to say it! "Cross-marked vocation." From the roughness of earthly life there opens up a vista of life and freedom in the coming kingdom, and only one way leads to it — subjection to the cross here.[17] In fact, Christ's suffering and cross give meaning and purpose to our vocation, particularly when our obedience to it involves us in suffering. Wingren beautifully expresses this in the following way, "A striking gladness rests upon the very hardships that underlie [Luther's] words. In these simple difficulties on earth there is fellowship with God's son, who was [also] mocked and buffeted."[18] In what we suffer because of our vocation, we are blessed to see the sufferings and cross of Christ, and to participate in them. Likewise, others are also given to see the Christ in those who live, serve, and suffer according to His vocation.

Another aspect of Luther's teaching as it relates to the cross is that to fulfill our vocation is certainly a risky business. The primary risk is that we may scatter our good works also upon the unjust and those who are undeserving. Luther treats this danger colorfully, using the metaphor of the sun and the rain,

> Despite their sighing, the sun and the rain nevertheless obey God, who is unstinting love and scatters his gifts upon an ungrateful world. Likewise the Creator is heeded by flowers, berries, trees, and singing birds; they bestow their gifts on any who pass by, even though it be the world's worst cheat or knave. "It is written on all leaves and on every blade of grass; no bird, no fruit, no berry, no kernel of grain is too small to show this and to say, 'For whom do I bear my delicious fruit or berry? For the worst rogues and rascals on earth!'" This is the pattern for Christian love, which must be willing to be misused, and to be "a lost love."[19]

Accordingly, Christian love may be "lost" or "wasted" on those who do not deserve it. Our love may be abused or put to evil purposes. It may be returned to us in the form of hatred or scorn. Many certainly will take advantage of us. This is not an excuse for

---

[16] Ibid., 73.

[17] Ibid., 58.

[18] Ibid.

[19] Ibid., 170-171. Luther uses the German phrase *die verloren Liebe* to characterize the kind of love God has for the sinful and undeserving world. It is a "lost love" poured out in unstinting measure upon all, even those who ultimately reject it.

naiveté in the performance of our good works. But such is the pattern of Christian love. It is given as God has given His love in Christ; fully, without reserve and without the expectation of reward.

Perhaps the most remarkable aspect of Christian vocation as participation in the cross of Christ, and the most mysterious, is that it is a gift. Just as the Gospel call to live in Christ through faith and the consequent vocation to live in the neighbor through love are gifts, likewise the cross of Christ is a gift. According to Luther, "The cross is not to be chosen by us; it is laid upon us by God, i.e. the cross comes to us uninvoked in our vocation."[20] It is a profound mystery, perhaps the central mystery of Christian life, that Christians are enabled to see the crosses they bear as gifts of God's grace. At least, it is essential to the Christian's calling, and the cross marks our vocation as inextricably bound up with Christ and with our life in Him.

Conclusion: Our Cross-marked Identitiy

Throughout this discussion of the Christian's vocation we have been moving toward an inescapable conclusion that forms the climax of Luther's teaching on the subject. The Christian's faith and life are inextricably bound up with Christ. We live in Him through faith. He lives in us through love. As we are called outside of ourselves, we begin to lose our old identity and take on a new one, marked by the suffering Servant — a "cross-marked identity." We take on the identity of the One in whom we live. Luther said, in a bold and risky statement, that Christians are "little Christs" to the neighbor. We now know, having looked briefly at his teaching on vocation, what he meant. Now we live as Christ lived. He lived not for Himself, but for others. So, when I live in Him, I live not for myself, but for you.

---

[20] Ibid., 53.

VISITATION
Mary visits Elizabeth after learning that she also is expecting in her old age. c. 1503

by Arthur A. Just Jr. and Sara M. Bielby

Serving Christ by Serving Our Neighbor: Theological and Historical Perspectives on Lutheran Deaconesses

Lutheran deaconesses serve Christ by serving their neighbor. They receive their office of service from the very person of Jesus Himself who came "not to be served but to serve, and to give his life as a ransom for many" (Matt. 20:28). Jesus tells His disciples, after breaking bread with them on the night in which He was betrayed, that "I am among you as the one who serves" (Luke 22:27). All Christians are called to this service, but deaconesses embody this life of *diakonia* as called laborers in Christ's church to demonstrate in their lives and actions the mercy and compassion of Christ. The motto of Lutheran deaconesses says it best: "What is my want? I want to serve. Whom do I want to serve? The Lord in His suffering ones and His poor."[1]

In a church body that does not ordain women, deaconesses provide women with an opportunity to serve in the church that reflects who they are as women. A deaconess brings a uniquely feminine care, perceiving need and responding with gentle helpfulness, expressing the compassion of Christ in a tender, nurturing way. She serves by using her skills and theological training to embody Christ's incarnational care in the midst of suffering. A deaconess serves alongside a pastor, attending to those in need and dwelling with them. She points them to the pastor and the means of grace where Christ comes to them in His body to join them to Himself for eternity.

Congregations that are served by male pastors are able to care for the needs of God's people in an essentially masculine way. Without the presence of women serving as deaconesses alongside the pastors, a feminine care is often absent from a congregation's service to her members. Just as a family needs both a father and mother to nurture and teach the children, so also will congregations be blessed by having

---

[1] This motto was created by Wilhelm Loehe for his deaconesses in Germany.

a pastor and a deaconess serving together, representing the care that is uniquely characteristic of both their offices and their genders.

Through the deaconess programs in our church, we are now able to offer women a rigorous program of theological study. This provides them with the foundation for a charitable life as they live and breathe the Gospel as servants of Christ in the midst of His people. Concordia Theological Seminary, Fort Wayne, was founded in 1846 to share the Gospel of Christ as biblically and historically confessed by the Lutheran Church. One of its founders, Pastor Wilhelm Loehe of Neuendettelsau, Germany, was committed to the training of deaconesses for service in the church through acts of mercy and charity.

The Mercy of Jesus: The Theological Foundation for the Office of Deaconess

Even though it is not possible to establish the office of deaconess from the New Testament, the theological rationale and foundation for the office is clearly affirmed in the person and work of Jesus and in the teaching of St. Paul. For both Jesus and Paul, the Gospel must be embodied, that is, the love of God that entered our world in His only Son continues now through us by the Spirit of the Son who comes to us in the waters of our Baptism (Gal. 4:3–5). Christ, by His Spirit, brings us into communion with Him and His life that knows no end. His life is now our life. He lives through us, and His love continues in the world through us, through our mouths and hands (Gal. 2:20–21).

Our life in Christ is founded on this remarkable reality: that in this present evil age, Christ dwells among us as Emmanuel and has rescued us by giving Himself up for our sins (Gal. 1:4). Our sins are evidence that this world had been infected with a virus from which we cannot escape. Things are very wrong. Everyone can see it, especially in those people who suffer physical, emotional and spiritual pain from the consequences of sin — those broken by violence and tragedy, by sickness and death — the very ones deaconesses are called to serve. Only God is able make right what has gone wrong in this world. He does it by sending His Son from heaven into our world to show us His mercy through miracles of healing the sick and raising the dead. The ultimate miracle that healed the whole creation was that He loved us so much that He was willing to bear all our burdens, even to the point of death, a death through which He brings in the new creation. When He rose from the dead on the third day, He showed us what we will one day become and already are now: bodies washed clean and made holy, healed eternally from sin's dread disease. In Jesus' resurrected body, we see ourselves, Jesus in us and we in Him. Heaven and earth are embodied in Jesus and now in us. His mercy for a fallen creation is now present in the creation through our acts of mercy as we bear witness to Him in all we say and do.

It is the mercy of Jesus Christ that is at the heart of the theological foundation for the role of the deaconess. Jesus calls us to a life of charity when He tells us to "Be merciful, even as your Father is merciful" (Luke 6:36). In the Early Church, the office of deaconess existed as a vocation for women in consecrated service of Christ and His church, providing acts of mercy through various tasks that served the neediest in the church's midst. They served Christ by serving "the least of these my brethren" (Matt. 25:40), providing the hungry with food, the thirsty with drink, welcoming strangers into the community of saints, clothing the naked and visiting the sick and those who are in prison (Matt. 25:35–36). "Be merciful, even as your Father is merciful" echoes the Old Testament creedal description of God as "gracious and merciful, slow to anger and abounding in steadfast love" (Ps.103:8). Still today, this theological foundation has not changed. Deaconesses continue to carry out the mercy that God in Christ shows to us.

The Service of Women to Jesus

Many people are unaware that it was through the loving service and financial means of women on behalf of Jesus and the apostles that enabled Him to engage in a three-year ministry of teaching and performing miracles. Luke reports the news that some women put forth their possessions and their time in caring for Jesus and the Twelve ("were serving them" [Luke 8:3]). Thus they helped make it possible by providing the human care necessary for Jesus to travel about with His disciples, who themselves served through the Word and healing they brought. Those named in Luke 8 appear again prominently as witnesses of Jesus' death and resurrection. They watch the crucifixion from a distance as they mourn for their Lord (23:49); they come to the tomb early in the morning to finish anointing His body (23:55–56a); they are the first witnesses of the resurrection and the first evangelists as they report the passion and resurrection facts to the 11 apostles (24:1–12). These women who were with Jesus since early in His ministry and through the three days of His passion and resurrection will be key members of the emerging church in Acts (see Acts 1:14). They will be essential links in the "'chain of evidence' for the Christian claims about Jesus,"[2] helping to transform the 11 and others who were "eyewitnesses from the beginning" into "ministers of the Word" (Luke 1:2).

According to the theology of the cross (or the "Great Reversal"), to serve is to be great in God's kingdom. Of the eight occurrences of *diakonia*, "service," in Luke, the first three are of women who serve Jesus: Peter's mother-in-law (4:39), these women (8:3) and Martha (10:40). In serving, they are following Jesus' own ministry as one of service; by becoming the "least," they are among the "greatest" (Luke 22:24–27). The women's service to Jesus is of great import, particularly in the context of the attitude prevailing in Judaism of Jesus' day regarding the exclusion of women in religious matters. In the kingdom He brings, the Spirit is poured out on His male servants and His female servants alike (Acts 2:18). Whoever does the will of God, which is to

---

[2] L. T. Johnson. *The Gospel of Luke.* Sacra Pagina. (Collegeville: Liturgical Press, 1991), 383.

believe in Him, is His brother and sister and mother, for they "hear the word of God and do it" (Luke 8:21).[3]

A Corporate Office of Mercy

The diaconal role of women is rightly identified in the context of the life of the church. The church's activities fall into three categories. *Leitourgia*, or Divine service, is the foundational activity of the church where God is serving us with His gifts of forgiveness, life and salvation through the bodily presence of Christ in Word and Sacrament. *Marturia*, or public witness, is our response to the gifts as we confess to God and to the world that which He works in us, namely, our faith. *Diakonia*, or service, is Christ in us in the midst of the world as we act out the love, mercy, grace and charity God gives to us in Christ amongst one another as He satisfies the needs of our neighbor through us.

These three activities take place in each one of us as we are members in the Body of Christ. This incarnational reality of God's presence in us is also true among us, thus these activities are located corporately in the church. *Leitourgia* takes place regularly in the public worship service at font, pulpit and altar, as Christ comes to us and as we come into communion with Him. In the Divine Service, we do not serve ourselves inwardly by turning in upon ourselves, but rather Christ serves us through the office of the public ministry as the pastor stands in the stead and by the command of Christ. Through the pastor, Christ speaks His Word and serves His Bride, the church, at His table. *Marturia* occurs both as an act of worship, in the Creed of the church, in hymns and prayers, as well as proceeding from the church into the highways and byways as we bear witness to the hope that is in us. *Diakonia* flows from the altar where we are served and takes place outside the doors of the worship service, finding expression wherever suffering and sin afflict and infect our lives.

While pastors carry on the work of the apostles among us, deacons and deaconesses are offices created in Christian freedom to ensure that this work of practical, human serving of need is completed. It was in the midst of a particular need that individuals were first consecrated and set apart by the church to administer its care. In Acts 6, the diaconal office is first seen when seven men were appointed to administer the care of the physical need of widows. Those chosen were "full of the Spirit and wisdom" and given the responsibility of acting on behalf of the church. The work they were given was crucial and necessary to the existence of the church as it lived out its daily life. In the same way that justification and sanctification cannot be separated, faith must live by expressing itself as love in action. God's desire and will to extend compassion to both body and soul must be expressed corporately by the church. As the church grew, it continued to appoint and consecrate individuals for tasks on its behalf. One

---

[3] These paragraphs on the ministry of women with Jesus are adapted from A. A. Just Jr., *Concordia Commentary: Luke 1:1–9:50 and Luke 9:51–24:53*. (St. Louis: Concordia Publishing House), 1996 and 1997.

example is Phoebe, who met the needs of the saints in the particular, located church at Cenchreae in a different way, a need that was best met by a woman.

Phoebe: The First Deaconess?

No one really knows for sure what Paul meant when he referred to Phoebe as a deaconess in his letter to the Roman Christians. He calls her "our sister Phoebe, a deaconess (*diakonos*) of the church at Cenchreae" (Rom. 16:1). Most scholars believe that what we today know as the office of deaconess did not exist in the New Testament era, although Phoebe's loving service became the foundation for the order of deaconesses in the early church. St. John Chrysostom, a patron of deaconesses, said this about Paul's reference to Phoebe: "Note how many ways Paul dignifies Phoebe. He mentions her before all the rest and even calls her his sister. It is no small thing to be called the sister of Paul! Moreover, he has mentioned her rank as deaconess as well."[4]

Phoebe was a "*prostasis*" or protectress (Rom. 16:2), indicating that she was a person of means and influence in the community that she could lend to saints, both in the public forum and in her own home. She expressed the gift of hospitality, hosting apostles and saints who were about the ministry of the Word in much the same manner as the women in Luke did for Jesus. She probably opened her home for the gathering of the church and was entrusted by Paul as an assister and helper, traveling to deliver his letter to the church at Rome.

Regardless of the status of development of churchly offices in New Testament times, Phoebe expressed the service that marks the diaconal office. She is an inspiration for all women who have chosen to serve their Lord as deaconesses. She served others, especially the apostles and saints, because her Lord first served her by giving up His life for her. The name Phoebe comes from the word "*phoibe*," which is translated "radiant." Phoebe's service is commended by Paul since she clearly cast a bright beam of light through her presence in the church.

A Brief History Beyond the New Testament

The first secular mention of women ministering to the church is found in the second century in a letter of Pliny the Younger, a governor in the Roman empire, to Emperor Trajan, requesting guidance in the matter of persecution of the captured Christians. He writes:

> I judged it so much the more necessary to extract the real truth, with the assistance of torture, from two female slaves, who were styled deaconesses: but I could discover nothing more than depraved and excessive superstition.[5]

---

[4] Cited from J. Chrysostom, *Homilies on Romans 30* in the *Ancient Christian Commentary on Scripture: Romans,* edited by G. Bray (Downers Grove: Intervarsity Press, 1998), 369.

[5] William Weinrich. *Readings in Early Church History.* (Fort Wayne: CTS Press).

This Roman governor testifies that very early on, women who received the gifts of Christ in the church's *leitourgia* shared both the activities of *marturia* and *diakonia* in appointed roles of service on behalf of the church.

The roles of deacons and deaconesses were not exactly parallel. Both deacons and deaconesses were responsible for the care of individuals in need. From the beginning, however, deacons performed liturgical duties and assisted in the public worship. Deaconesses never performed liturgical duties, but rather functioned as leaders and keepers among the women of the assembly, primarily as caretakers of the suffering and the poor who were in need of human care. They also served as supporters and advisors of women catechumens in applying the teaching of the bishop to matters of feminine propriety. They assisted in the baptism of women, visited the sick, took care of the believing women in the homes of unbelievers and ministered to those who were unable to worship with the faithful.

Formal affirmation of the role of the deaconess is found in the *Didascalia*, dated in the early to mid-third century. The chapter entitled "On the Institution of Deacons and Deaconesses" states:

> The ministry of deaconesses is necessary for you for many reasons. The fact is that deaconesses are necessary for the houses of pagans where Christian women are also living. Deaconesses can go there and visit those who are ill, serve them in whatever their needs might be and bathe those who have begun to recover from their illness ... There should be enough so that everyone is known and everyone succored. Thus, old women whose strength has declined and brothers and sisters who are ill should be able to enjoy from the deacons the service they properly need.[6]

The stated purpose of the diaconal offices as instituted in the Early Church is the same purpose of deaconesses today: to serve so that "everyone is known and everyone succored." Even the most marginal received honor and worth in God's eyes, becoming known to the community through deaconesses who embodied Christ's mercy as they reached out to give help in time of need.

The third through the seventh centuries are known as the "Golden Age of Deaconesses." Deplorable social conditions, coupled with the urgent response of the church to care for those in need, caused the number and work of deaconesses to multiply. St. John Chrysostom both appointed deaconesses and was assisted by them in his service to the saints. Perhaps the most well-known of the deaconesses of his era was Olympias, a beautiful young widow of means who lived in Constantinople in the fourth century, where she built a hospital and orphanage and devoted herself to serving the poor and needy. Her noble character and servant heart has been an inspiration to deaconesses to this day.

---

[6] Aime Georges Martimort. *Deaconesses: An Historical Study.* (San Francisco: Ignatius Press, 1986), 38–39.

The presence of deaconesses in the church declined with the approach of the Middle Ages. This was largely due to the fact that the theological foundation of incarnational care from which deaconesses sprung gave way to asceticism, causing the feminine churchly vocation of service to decline and retreat into the cloistered life. While the Reformation reclaimed this theological foundation, it was not until the early 19th century that the deaconess vocation again experienced a resurgence in the Lutheran church under the guidance and separate efforts of both Wilhelm Loehe and Theodore Fliedner.

Both pastors Loehe and Fliedner were instrumental in planting of deaconesses in the United States. Such efforts were received and carried on by pastors in this country, leading to the establishment of the first Missouri Synod Lutheran deaconess training school in Fort Wayne during the early 1900s. Today, there are more than 270 rostered deaconesses in the LCMS who stand in continuity with Phoebe, Olympias and all deaconesses who have served their Lord by serving their neighbor.

Standing alongside the pastor, who dispenses Christ's gifts as a steward of the mysteries, deaconesses bind up the brokenhearted and the distressed. They go out from the door of the church and bring in Christ's lost and broken lambs into His sheepfold where the Pastor feeds these lambs by bringing them into communion with Christ as He comes to them in Word and Sacrament. Throughout our church today, watch for deaconesses to declare humbly through their *diakonia*: "What is my want? I want to serve. Whom do I want to serve? The Lord in His suffering ones and His poor."

CHRIST BEFORE CAIAPHAS
"Then those who had seized Jesus led him to Caiaphas the high priest, where the scribes and the elders had gathered." Matt. 26:57 c. 1508–1509

134

Giving Thanks in Times of Adversity and Strife

BY WILLIAM WEEDON

The contents of this essay were presented at the International Disaster Conference held at Concordia Theological Seminary, Fort Wayne, Ind., in September 2014. The conference provided a forum for international Lutheran church leaders to consider both the theology of mercy and the practical implications for implementing it in their churches.

"It is indeed right and salutary that we should at *all* times, and in *all* places, give thanks to you holy Lord, almighty Father, everlasting God, through Jesus Christ, our Lord." At all times, in all places.

Really? When the tornado or the typhoon has swept through and obliterated houses, businesses, church, lives? When plague snatches children from their parents' arms? And parents from their children? And neighbor begins to look at neighbor in fear and suspicion? When war arises and sweeps over an area and brings what war always brings: rape, pillaging, torture and bloodshed? When the earth trembles beneath your feet and houses topple, roads lay in pieces and even water is hard to come by? When fire sweeps out of the mountains and consumes houses and lives? When weeping and sorrow become your daily bread, such are really times and places for thanksgiving? Really?

Really! The words tumble off our lips, week in and week out, and we seldom think how radical they are, how the whole Church of Jesus Christ is solidly grounded in the age to come. That's what you are. That's what the Church of Jesus Christ is. It's a colony from the future. We are a people who belong to an age that is truly coming and that all will finally see, but that now is hidden and often hidden deeply beneath suffering. The Church of Jesus Christ has stood for these 20 centuries before high altar or lowly table, and she has sung out her praise and her thanks to God, the Father, for the gift of His son, Jesus Christ. Come hell or high water, the Church gives thanks for the new life of Baptism, for the gift of the Savior's body and blood, for our forgiveness and eternal life. People loved by God, these are gifts that are stable. They are secure. They cannot be shaken when everything else in your life wobbles and falls to the ground. The Church goes on speaking and singing and proclaiming out into the world these unshakable promises of Christ. Through war and bloodshed, through tempest and plague, through persecution and death, she goes on raising to heaven a song of thanks and praise for Jesus Christ, who overcame death from the grave and who opened the kingdom of heaven to all believers.

135

The Church is paradise restored. Have you ever thought about how Isaiah describes what Eden really was? Look at these words: "The Lord comforts Zion. He comforts all her waste places and nature wilderness like Eden, her desert like the garden of the Lord." Now, do you know your Hebrew parallelism? What's it then to be like Eden, like the garden of the Lord? Look! Joy and gladness will be found in her thanksgiving, in the voice of a song. She sings out the Lord's comfort for Zion, for a suffering people, a comfort that reaches the waste places, all the places where her life has become wilderness and desolation. She has the power to change things, and she changes them by singing. She changes them by singing praise and thanksgiving to God. She makes the desert bloom as she trumpets the promises of God.

So, let's look at this in Lutheran history. What does it look like in operation? Let's look at a small town in Westphalia, Germany, in 1597 called Unna and observe a tragedy in the making and its pastor's response. The pastor's name was Nicolai. He saw his congregation decimated by plague. Think about this in your life — 300 funerals in his congregation in the month of July alone! And it didn't stop. By the time the plague ran its course in January1598, a course of seven months, more than 1000 lives were lost. I suppose he could have fled the plague, but then again he had Luther's words. Luther wrote in his little document on whether you could flee the plague. He says, "Those who are engaged in a spiritual ministry such as preachers and pastors must likewise remain steadfast before the peril of death. We have a plain command from Christ, the good shepherd lays down his life for the sheep, but the hireling sees the wolf coming and flees."

When people are dying, they need a spiritual ministry that strengthens and comforts their consciences by Word and Sacrament, and in faith, overcomes death. So, Nicolai wasn't about to flee; he stayed put, and he preached and he kept on baptizing because children still were born. He kept on administering the Sacrament every Sunday, and he prayed for his congregation over and over again. He visited the sick and the dying constantly, and he buried some more. And what do you think he also did? He decides to write a book!

The name of the book is *Freudenspiegel* (Mirror of Joy), meaning the joy of eternal life. It's a great book. Here are the opening words:

> As often as I call to mind, the surpassing comfort of the promise of eternal life in our heavenly home, my heart bursts out with joy, and my soul rejoices in God my Savior. Oh, think of it, there we believing Christians will behold with joyful eyes, the almighty King of glory, our only Redeemer and Savior, Jesus Christ, who for us trampled the ancient serpent. There, we will gather with the holy patriarchs, prophets, and apostles, and there we will see again with overflowing joy those we loved on earth, father, mother, brothers, and sisters, husband and wife, children, and all our acquaintances who have blessedly fallen asleep in the Lord and have gone before us in the true faith.

There, God will wipe away all tears from our eyes, and he will transform our morning into dancing. He will clothe us with joy so that our hearts rejoice for all eternity, and this awesome joy no one can ever take from us. There we will enter into the heavenly Jerusalem, the city of the living God. We will be brought into the company of many thousands of angels and to the assembly of the first born who are written in heaven, and in that place, joy will simply overwhelm us as we contemplate the awesome gifts that our God has bestowed on us. To think that heaven should be ours, that everything which Christ has is now our imperishable heavenly treasure. God Himself will be our very great reward, our temple, our light, and our awe. Why would we trade all the world's perishable splendor, honor, joy, and glory for what God has in store for us? Our future is that we will see and laugh together with the holy angels. Indeed, the entire heavenly host will call us blessed because we believed in Jesus Christ and trusted His unfailing word even today.

That's just the opening of the book! It goes on like that, page after page, joy after joy, my personal favorite is the middle of the book. He is just talking about Adam and Eve and paradise, and he is like, "How did they know that they were naked?" This one just blows me away. He said, "Well, they knew that they were naked because their bodies stopped shining." Because of sin, all of us had fallen short of the glory of God, and our bodies no longer shined the way God meant them to and the way they will in the Resurrection. I've never thought about Genesis the same way again. Anyway, it's a great book, but that's just the beginning, and yet you can see it puts a smile on your face, thanksgiving in your heart. And guess what else it does? It puts a song on your lips.

Nicolai also wrote a few songs. One is known as the queen of the Lutheran chorales, a spiritual bride-song of the soul who believes in Jesus Christ, our heavenly bridegroom, based on Psalm 45, a song of the bride of Christ to, to her beloved bridegroom. He wrote a second hymn that's the midnight call of the wise virgins who greet the bridegroom, "*O Morning Star, How Fair and Bright.*"

4 Almighty Father, in Your Son!
  You loved us when not yet begun
    Was this old earth's foundation!
  Your Son has ransomed us in love
  To live in Him here and above:
    This is Your great salvation.
      Alleluia!
    Christ the living,
    To us giving
      Life forever,
  Keeps us Yours and fails us never!

5 O let the harps break forth in sound!
  Our joy be all with music crowned,
    Our voices gladly blending!
  For Christ goes with us all the way —
  Today, tomorrow, ev'ry day!
    His love is never ending!
      Sing out! Ring out!
    Jubilation!
    Exultation!
      Tell the story!
  Great is He, the King of Glory!
          [LSB 395: 4,5]

Do you see what he did? He took the promises, and he wrapped them up in music, and he gave them to his people, so they could take them in hand and throw them at death and throw them at fear, so that they could rejoice in God and give thanks to the Father in all circumstances. Let's do the other one, too. Last verse of this one.

6 What joy to know, when life is past,
  The Lord we love is first and last,
    The end and the beginning!
  He will one day, oh, glorious grace,
  Transport us to that happy place
    Beyond all tears and sinning!
      Amen! Amen!
    Come, Lord Jesus!
    Crown of gladness!
      We are yearning
  For the day of Your returning!
          [LSB 395: 6]

In the face of unspeakable tragedy, to families where mothers had lost sons, and daughters their fathers, and sisters their brothers, and brothers their sisters, and husbands their wives, with absolutely no family left untouched by the horror of death, square in the midst of unspeakable tragedy, faithful Pastor Nicolai wrote and sang the hope of heaven into the hearts of his people. It's the fulfillment of "in at all times and in all places." Is it any wonder that these two pieces became known as the king and queen of the two chorales? They just are amazing for what they give us. I think that it is high treason for a Lutheran, for any Christian, to be deprived of the comfort and the joy of such great hymns, and they abound. Those are just two, but in Reformation hymns, they shine at its finest. They sing of Christ and belief in the comfort of Christ

138

against the darkness. They hold tight to the joy of what will be when Christ renews all things. They proclaim Christ is your Christ, and Christ will come again, and they add the promise, "And He did it all for you!"

So, they do what the prefaced Communion summons us to do. They become the vehicles for giving thanks to God, even in times of tragedy and loss. These songs are like David's stones aimed at Goliath's head. So, they really capture what St. Paul sang about: "Whom shall separate us from the love of Christ? You think trouble is going to do it? Tribulation? Distress? Persecution? What about not having anything to eat? Or not having any clothes? Or danger? As it written, for your sake, we are being killed all day long. We are counted like sheep to be slaughtered. No, in all these things, we are more than conquerors through Him who loves us. I'm sure that neither death nor life, nor angels, nor rulers, nor things present or things to come, nor fires, nor death, nor anything in all creation is ever going to be able to separate us from the love of God in Christ Jesus, our Lord."

So, there was another one. His name was Paul Gerhardt. He is known as "the man sifted in Satan's sieve." Well, he happened to be a good preacher. So, all the good confessional Lutherans hated him because he kind of showed them up. He didn't like to argue and fight. The real hard-nosed people thought he wasn't hard-nosed enough, and he was unyieldingly Lutheran. When the prince said, "You are going to stop preaching that doctrine of the Lutheran Lord's Supper, or you are going to lose your job, buddy," he said, "So fire me." The prince did.

After losing four of his five children and his wife, Gerhardt had only one son left, and he had been restored to the ministry of the Church for just about two years when he was approaching his 70s. In his 70th year, he decided to write a will. He didn't have anything to give his son, no earthly goods at all, except for some pieces of advice. I'm not going to actually give you the pieces of advice, but listen, listen to the opening of this man's will:

> After reaching the 70th year of my life and truly having a joyful hope in my loving and gracious God that in a short time he will deliver me from this world and lead me into a much better life than I've had so far on this earth, I thank God ahead of time for all the kindness and faithfulness He has given me and demonstrated, even from my mother's womb, in body and soul, everything until this hour. I pray from the bottom of my heart that He would grant me when my last hour comes a happy departure and take my soul into His fatherly hand. Give my body a gentle rest on the earth until He returns on the wonderful judgment day, and then I will be with all my family whom have died and with those who will die in the future, and I will awaken to see my precious Lord Jesus in whom I believe even though I have never seen Him. I will see Him then, face to face.

Are you shocked then to learn that a man who could write that at the end of such a miserable ministry would be key in leading us to sing in thanksgiving to God at all times and in all places? Of course not. Here is another one. It's not as popular as the two that we just did, but I want you to sing it with me again, and I need you up here again to go verse by verse with us here. It's a beautiful little tune too. Think of that life that I just described to you, and then think of these words ["*Why Should Cross and Trial Grieve Me*"]*:

1 *Why should cross and trial grieve me?*
   Christ is near
   With His cheer;
   Never will He leave me.
   Who can rob me of the heaven
   That God's Son
   For me won
   When His life was given?

2 *When life's troubles rise to meet me,*
   Though their weight
   May be great,
   They will not defeat me.
   God, my loving Savior, sends them;
   He who knows
   All my woes
   Knows how best to end them.
   Think of this verse:

3 *God gives me my days of gladness,*
   And I will
   Trust Him still
   When He send me sadness.
   God is good; His love attends me
   Day by day,
   Come what may,
   Guides me and defends me.

4 *From God's joy can nothing sever,*
   For I am
   His dear lamb,
   He, my Shepherd ever.
   I am His because He gave me
   His own blood
   For my good,
   By His death to save me.

5 *Now in Christ, death cannot slay me,*
   Though it might,
   Day and night,
   Trouble may dismay me.
   Christ has made my death a portal
   From the strife
   Of this life
   To His joy immortal!
                        [LSB 756]

*LSB #756 *Why Should Cross and Trial Grieve Me*, text (sts. 4-5) ©2004 Stephen P. Starke, admin. By CPH. Used with permission under license number 15:9-4. *cph.org.*

Do you notice the theme of joy again? This is a hymn written by a man who had lost so much, who had suffered so much, but all he could think to do is sing praise to God in his time of suffering, in his hour of disaster. I could point you to so many more in our hymn book, old and new. The hymn *"In Thee Is Gladness."** This is the joy of the Lord as your strength.

In Thee is gladness	*Since He is ours,*
Amid all sadness,	*We fear no powers,*
Jesus, sunshine of my heart.	*Not of earth nor sin nor death.*
By Thee are given	*He sees and blesses*
The gifts of heaven,	*In worst distresses;*
Thou the true Redeemer art.	*He can change them with a breath.*
Our souls Thou wakest,	*Wherefore the story*
Our bonds Thou breakest;	*Tell of His glory*
Who trusts Thee surely	*With hearts and voices;*
Has built securely;	*All heav'n rejoices*
He stands forever: Alleluia!	*In Him forever: Alleluia!*
Our hearts are pining	*We shout for gladness,*
To see Thy shining,	*Triumph o'er sadness,*
Dying or living	*Love Him and praise Him*
To Thee are cleaving;	*And still shall raise Him*
Naught can us sever: Alleluia!	*Glad hymns forever: Alleluia!*

[LSB 818]

Do you notice that theme? "And we'll raise Him glad hymns forever?" That's what heaven's all about. When you get there, that's what it's going to be: singing the praises of the land forever, in joy and gladness. Right now, the Church on earth gives a foretaste, a teasing taste of that blessedness of that heaven itself. That is the very gift of the Church's worship in times of disaster. She shouts for gladness. She triumphs over sadness, loving and praising and still raising our wonderful triune God. She can do this because of the one before whom she stands and for whom she sings. He is no stranger to suffering. He knows what it is to be a refugee in a foreign land, hunted down. He knows what it is to go without food and of hunger. He knows what it is to be homeless. He knows what it is to be so tired that you just can't put one more foot in front of the other. He knows what it is to have friends die and to cry beside their bodies. He knows, in His own flesh, the hatred of those who think that they offer God's service by dishing out torture and violence. He knows it all, and through it all, His love did not fail. His love remains strong and secure and firm through it all. So, He has a life that does not end, and that is where He reaches us, and that is what the

*Public domain.

gift of the Church is, a gift of a love so strong that no hatred thrown its way is going to be able to overcome it, a joy so big, and the forgiveness of sin and gift of eternal life that nothing that is tossed our way will be able to destroy it.

We have seen a few examples from standard Lutheran hymnody, but a few years ago, one of my close friends, Rev. Randy Asbury, went to Sudan and visited with Lutherans there who many times suffered greatly from their Muslim neighbors, and he learned there a song they sing as they face intense persecution. I wish I could sing it for you. I can't. Look at the English words though:

Come and see. Come and see. Hallelujah!
Nothing can defeat our God. Hallelujah!
Nothing can defeat God.
Come and see. Love is filled. Hallelujah!
Nothing can defeat God. Hallelujah! Nothing can defeat God.
Though you don't have food? Hallelujah!
Nothing can defeat God. Hallelujah! Nothing can defeat God.
Though you don't have your mother? Hallelujah!
Nothing can defeat God. Hallelujah! Nothing can defeat God.
Though you don't have your father? Hallelujah!
Nothing can defeat God. Hallelujah! Nothing can defeat God.
Though you don't have your son? Hallelujah!
Nothing can defeat God. Hallelujah! Nothing can defeat God.

This is the Church. She goes on singing and offering praise and thanksgiving to the Father of our Lord, Jesus Christ, in one unbroken sacrifice of praise. This is the big point I hope you get: When things are going pretty good for you in your life, that's the time for you to practice the praise, the hymns, the songs, so that you can continue to sing them when tragedy strikes, whether it's a big communal tragedy like you all are here to talk about, the horrible mess that we just heard of in Lebanon and Syria, or whether it's the doctor walking back in to your room and having a look on his face so that he doesn't really need to say anything else. All of liturgy and hymn to God is practice. The real moment will come that we are all rehearsing for, because what we want to do as the people of God is to march our way through the gate of death singing its defeat, singing sin's forgiveness, singing Christ's victory in life that has no end. We want to look its horror and its stink right in the face, and as the Church of God, announce and declare, "You have not won. You have won nothing at all. We are baptized. We live on promises stronger than you." So, spend the time when things are not falling apart, singing and teaching yourself and others the songs that will sustain you when everything begins to fall apart.

Will you pardon me if I throw one more at you? It's an old German hymn. Luther's musician, Johann Walter, wrote the hymn. It's got a lively tune written by Pistorius. Pistorius is really important, because he had to live through a bit of the ups and downs of 30 Years War. What happens to your worship when you don't have musicians? Your music gets simple, but it doesn't stop singing. The joy doesn't stop. You may not have all the orchestra up there to make the beautiful sound that you are accustomed to, but you still sing, and you still bless God. *"The Bridegroom Soon Will Call Us,"** this is a real treasure of a hymn.

1 The Bridegroom soon will call us,

"Come to the wedding feast."
May slumber not befall us
Nor watchfulness decrease.
May all our lamps be burning
With oil enough and more
That we, with Him returning,
May find an open door!
[LSB 514:1]

It's a dance, and look, the joy keeps unfolding verse by verse. Next verse:

2 There shall we see in glory
Our dear Redeemer's face;
The long awaited story
Of heav'nly joy takes place:
The patriarchs shall meet us,
The prophets' holy band;
Apostles, martyrs greet us
In that celestial land.
[LSB 514:2]

The Church is never alone. In the Church, it's always together. That's why I dislike the hymn "I Come to the Garden Alone." Nonsense! No one comes to the garden alone! You come to the garden with all of God's people! And so when you're welcomed home, you're not alone. The patriarchs are there. Abraham, Isaac, Jacob, Joseph. He's there to throw your arms around. Joseph! The story of Joseph, right? Disaster after disaster! How can God possibly bring good out of this? Sitting in prison, wondering, "Has God forgotten me?" And then the exaltation, and it all comes out and paints such a picture of Jesus. He's there waiting to meet you, to put those arms around you and say, "See, it comes out good in the end! You meant it for evil. God meant it for good for the saving of many lives, lives to this day."

*LSB #514 The Bridegroom Soon Will Call Us, text (st.1)©1982 CPH. Used with permission under license number 15:9-4. cph.org.

3 There God shall from all evil
  Forever make us free,
  From sin and from the devil,
  From all adversity,
  From sickness, pain, and sadness,
  From troubles, cares, and fears,
  And grant us heav'nly gladness
  And wipe away our tears.
            [LSB 514:3]

And it has to end in music because that's where it is.

4 In that fair home shall never
  Be silent music's voice;
  With hearts and lips forever
  We shall in God rejoice,
  While angel hosts are raising
  With saints from great to least
  A mighty hymn for praising
  The Giver of the feast
            [LSB 514:4]

At all times and in all places, giving thanks to God through Jesus Christ, our Lord. That's what the Church does at times of disaster, and in times peace, she prepares us to face the moments of calamity and the joys of our sin's forgiveness and in the certainty of death's defeat, and in the joy of eternal life. That's it.

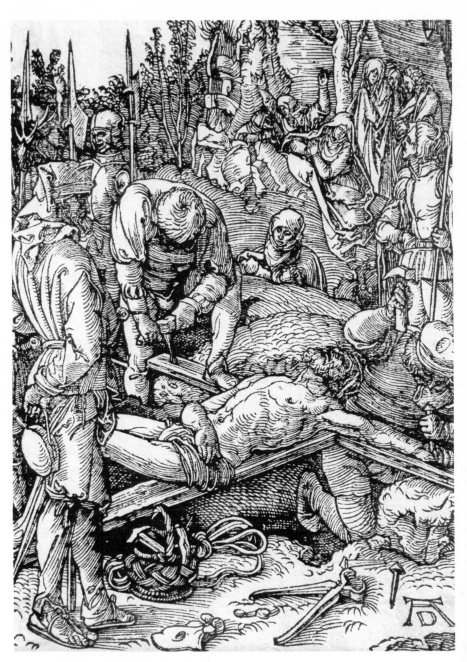

CHRIST NAILED TO THE CROSS
"And when they came to the place that is called The Skull, there they crucified him." Luke 23:33a. c. 1509

Sharing the Gospel in Time of Suffering

by Carl C. Fickenscher II

The contents of this essay were presented at the International Disaster Conference held at Concordia Theological Seminary, Fort Wayne, Ind., in September 2014. The conference provided a forum for international Lutheran church leaders to consider both the theology of mercy and the practical implications for implementing it in their churches.

'*I*n the spring of 2005, just a few months after the devastating tsunami in the Indian Ocean, Dec. 26, 2004, I had the — I think I can call it — the pleasure or the joy (while it was mixed with a lot that wasn't joy or pleasure at all) of touring, along with Synod President Harrison (who at the time was executive director of LCMS World Relief and Human Care), those places in India and Indonesia that were hit very hard. Our mission was certainly not to fix things by any means. We clearly understood that we were there to listen and to learn, and it was a learning experience if ever there could be one! It was a listening experience. In the process, many images were exceedingly memorable and painfully so.

And to me, the most memorable, and in a way the most painful, image actually was one day when we went to a fishing village in southern India, near the southern tip of India, and we visited a particular parish there. We arrived in the village, and the first thing we were shown was essentially the vacant lot next to the Roman Catholic parish house, which had become a cemetery for 380 members of this parish. It had been a vacant lot, but now it was filled with the graves of members of this relatively small Catholic congregation in this fishing village. We then went in and visited with the local parish priest, a man in his thirties who had been there for just three or four years.

But that had included the very significant Sunday morning about five months before. Obviously some time had passed, and that was a chance for him to have some perspective, but in his sharing with us, it was still very clear that he was emotionally and perhaps even spiritually *very* empty. Feeling the trauma to his parish — and imagine 380 funerals in a very short period of time and the kind of toll that took! — as we sat with him in his office (he was behind his desk and we were around the desk in front of him and asking questions), frankly, it was a matter of sensitivity. It couldn't be like doing an interview. It was very clear that he was having difficulty, even five months later, talking to us at all, though he was very gracious to invite us to be there. The words came so painfully, so slowly.

He said when the tsunami happened, it was a Sunday morning. A week went by before Sunday worship services again. The following Sunday he did not feel up to addressing the disaster in the sermon. In fact, he said it was more than a month before he felt he could address it in a sermon at all. And even now as he described it, he described feeling very empty in addressing the question, even from God's Word. So traumatic! Such a stressful event for him, he felt it was! And we understand that. Well, we actually can't begin to understand that, but we imagine. He had a difficult time finding anything that he felt God's Word would say to this situation. That's really the question I'd like to begin with: Does God's Word really give us anything to say in these times of suffering?

We know the answer is going to be yes. But we can imagine that in some moments, in some situations, it's difficult to find what God's Word says. It's also true that God's Word gives us a lot of cautions about some things not to say.

It's interesting: When you think about the Scriptures in light of situations like this, it's not quite as easy as we might think to find passages that really apply. You know that the Bible unquestionably does talk about all kinds of disasters. It talks about all kinds of crises. It talks about huge kind of cataclysms — like there was a really big flood once, and it wiped out a whole lot of people! And there have been plagues — ten of them in one shot once, and other plagues like in Jerusalem in the days of David when thousands were killed. And there've been wars that have ravaged God's people, and there's been fire sent down from heaven at dramatic moments when it would wipe out 50 soldiers once and 50 soldiers again and 50 soldiers a third time. Countless other such disasters occur in Holy Scripture. So you'd think the Bible would have answers for almost any crisis situation.

The interesting thing, though, is that as we begin to unpack those particular narratives, those historic events described in Scripture that describe these kinds of situations, the truth is, most of them don't fit all that well into the kinds of situations that we've been talking about. If you stop to think about that, I think it's really true. Those situations in Scripture, for the most part, are different from the situations we address in one of several ways. Sometimes in Scripture there's a clear explanation about God doing something as a direct punishment for some kind of sin. God sends the Babylonians to carry Judah off into captivity, and we know why. God sends a flood, and we know why. There's direct, clear punishment involved. On the other hand, for us, as we deal with disasters today, there's usually a total absence of explanation.

You think about the situation with Job. Although Job never gets an explanation, we've got one. We know there's that heavenly dialogue ahead of time that Job is unaware of even at the end of the book. In the Bible, we usually get some kind of explanation or some clear word that a disaster is a direct punishment for sin. In our day, we don't get that explanation. Of course, there are lots of other disasters or near-disasters in Scripture where God, as Christ Himself during His ministry, delivers people right there on the spot from starvation or from illness or from some other kind of suffering. But we usually don't see that happen in the disasters we face today.

Some Law for the preacher to hear

With most of the crisis situations we address, we don't get a clear word if it is a punishment for sin nor do we get any other kind of explanation. And we aren't seeing Jesus enter the scene and still the storm. So when you stop to think, it is probably not as easy as we might presume to find within the Bible ready, easy answers for suffering. Of course, the Bible has lots to say about these situations, but it's not as obvious as one might think.

This leads us to some important cautions. We'll identify these as "don'ts." This is "some Law for the preacher to hear." We'll also look at Gospel that the preacher absolutely *does* have to proclaim. But for now, let's talk about some cautions, some "don'ts," the six of them are wake-up calls in terms of God's Word in what it doesn't say or tells us not to say in times of responding to suffering. Some of these are fairly obvious. In our theology, they're fairly clear, but they're not so obvious to everybody else.

1. Don't presume to read God's mind.

This of course is the matter of the *Deus absconditus* (the hidden will of God). Perhaps some of you here from the United States remember, in August 2012, Hurricane Isaac was coming out of the Caribbean and looked as if it was going to hit the mainland of the U.S. somewhere. Eventually it did. But it looked initially as if it was headed for Florida, and then it turned away and actually hit New Orleans, the same basic landing spot as Hurricane Katrina a number of years earlier. Pat Robertson — a televangelist in the United States, a non-denominational, evangelical Christian — decided he figured out what God had in mind. Guess what it was: the Republican National Convention was about to begin in Florida, and Pat Robertson decided that God had protected the Republicans. "Rejoice!" Or clear your throat and wonder if Pat Robertson was going where he might not have been wise to go. It's just possible that wasn't really what God had in mind.

Sometimes when we're addressing crises, we can fall into a similar fallacy. Job is the classic example here. God doesn't explain Himself to Job. God did tell us in chapters 1 and 2 what was going on. But then there's the lengthy dialogue between Job and his friends in chapter 3 all the way through chapter 37, and there's one speculation after another after another after another about what's on God's mind. Job's friends, they've got an answer. Job isn't too sure, and eventually Job loses that "patience of Job" and is ready to take God to task when God shows up finally in chapter 38.

Remember what God does in chapters 38 through chapter 42. What he *doesn't* do is say, "Hey, Job, you've been good about this. You've hung tough through all of this, and you've finally reached the breaking point. Well, back in chapters 1 and chapter

2, see, there was this dialogue where the devil came before the sons of God and said, 'You know this guy Job. The only reason he's faithful to you is because you're making things so nice for him. If things get tough for him, he'll curse you to your face and die.' " We, the readers, know that part of the story, and I almost wish God had told the poor guy. But He doesn't. In fact, what God says there from the whirlwind in chapter 38 and following is simply to say, essentially, "Where were you when I laid the foundations of the earth, when I told the waves, thus far no farther?" Bottom line: "You're not getting that information out of me even now, Job." What God does tell Job is vastly more wonderful. But God doesn't give Job His explanation for what's been going on. And that's an important caution. We mustn't presume to read God's mind and try to explain why disasters have happened when God doesn't tell us.

2. Don't assign guilt where God's Word doesn't.

This even sounds like an awful thing to do, and again, our theology warns us wisely against it. But it's not universal to recognize this as an error, not only among non-denominational evangelical Christians, but also among many of our own Lutheran members. I remember very vividly in my own experience in my last congregation one of my dear members, who served many years on the board of elders, had an automobile accident, and he was quite sure that he must be guilty of some particular sin that had caused his accident. He didn't know what the sin might be, but he was pretty sure that there must be something he had done that was the reason God caused this accident. The accident was very serious. He did survive, but it was very serious indeed.

Consider Hurricane Katrina, the other recent New Orleans hurricane, in August 2005. In the minds of some people, there was a clear explanation for why the hurricane happened. According to some, it was because of New Orleans' reputation as one of America's "sin cities." For them, this had to be the reason Hurricane Katrina devastated New Orleans. We remember, of course, John chapter 9, where the disciples, like most of the Jews in Jesus' day, had that same line of thinking: The man is born blind; we know one of two things happened. Either he sinned before he was born, or his parents were guilty of some kind of sin before he was born. One or the other caused God to zap him with blindness from birth.

But Jesus says that's not it. Again, Jesus doesn't give us the full explanation. He does tell us in this instance that it's going to be an opportunity for Christ Himself to give glory to God by working a wonderful miracle, which, again, we wish he'd do every time there's a disaster. But the point here is that the disciples weren't to see this man's blindness as God punishing him for some particular sin. In the same way, it's not for us to imagine that New Orleans is guiltier of sin than somewhere else, say, Houston, Texas, that Houston is spared and New Orleans is struck. When disasters or suffering strike, we mustn't presume to assign guilt where God's Word doesn't.

3. Don't assume the victims are innocent either.

Some of you may remember that after the 9/11 tragedy, there was a widely circulated cartoon with the Twin Towers, that iconic view, and above it a cloud of three thousand souls going up to heaven. The implication was they were all innocents killed by terrorists, so people picture them innocently received into heaven. We'd like to think that everyone who dies in a tragedy automatically goes to heaven. That would be a cushion that would seem to make everything turn out better. But, of course, we know this is not the case. Remember in Luke chapter 13 the whole tower of Siloam thing? We can assume that those killed when that tower fell were innocent victims, and yet Jesus says, "Unless you repent, you will all likewise perish" (Luke 13:5). That wasn't specifically identifying those eighteen as *particularly* sinful, but it was recognizing that they, we, all, are anything but innocent. We are all sinful, not of a particular sin to which we could assign guilt for causing a disaster, but neither are we without sinful involvement in this fallen world. When disaster strikes, we mustn't speak as if those who died are automatically received into heaven, as if they were all innocent and holy and deserving of heaven.

4. Don't forget that "disaster" is whatever disaster is to the sufferer.

A Doctor of Ministry graduate from our seminary a few years ago, Pastor Mark Nuckols, a very well-decorated U.S. Army chaplain, was called to his current parish in Austin, Texas, and it was a very short time thereafter when he was called up to deploy to Iraq. While deployed, he saw traumatic scenes one would expect a chaplain to see and minister to in war. Mark actually had two deployments to Iraq; another one just a couple of years later. He said that in his second return from deployment, he was a wiser pastor than he had been after the first deployment, because he learned something. The first time when he came back, he would be sitting in his office, and he would have church members come to him with issues that were very important to them. They would say, "Pastor, I just lost my job," or "Pastor, my son is having trouble in his high school." And Pastor Nuckols confesses that that first time back, his reaction was, "Get a life! Guys are losing their lives where I just was. I was ministering to people who'd seen their friends blown apart. What's the big problem? What's the crisis? What's the disaster?" Pastor Nuckols realized later that suffering is relative to the sufferer. A seemingly lesser issue to him was a disaster to the one suffering it. It was a very big deal to the church member going through it. It was a situation for which his pastoral care really needed to be every bit as sensitive as it had been eight thousand miles away a month earlier. In fact, the second time back from deployment he was very appreciative of one of the projects of our Synod, Project Barnabas, that enables chaplains returning from deployment to have a decompressing time while his congregation remains covered by another pastor filling in.

This need to be sensitive to whatever seems to be a disaster to the person suffering it is very real. We certainly realize that there are crises that might objectively be measured as huge, and others we wouldn't call crises at all. But we remember what

Jesus says about the smallest things, like a cup of water given because someone is His disciple (Matt. 10:42). You see, Jesus cares about a person who's parched with thirst. To Jesus, that's a really big deal. So as we care for those who are facing small disasters, it's important that we not forget that it *is* a real disaster, if they see it as such.

5. Don't promise what God doesn't promise.

A number of years ago, there were two tragic events within a couple months of each other: Payne Stewart, a professional golfer here in the United States and a Christian who had been wonderfully outspoken in his Christian faith, died while piloting a private plane. He was all alone in the sky, and for whatever reason, he crashed and was killed. Not long after, a player in the National Football League was involved in a car accident. This man also professed to be an evangelical Christian. (I won't give his name, because this might make him sound as if he isn't sincere.) He claimed as he was heading off the road toward a tree, he just threw up his hands — took them off the steering wheel — and said, "Jesus, take over!" He survived with just a few scratches. Later, this football player was speaking about the experience — and this may have been intended to be a testimony to the trust we can have in the Lord — he said God had saved him because he was a Christian. A reporter then asked him, "What about Payne Stewart? He was a Christian, too, and he died in his plane crash." The football player said, "Well, if he had just turned it over to the Lord, he wouldn't have." The reporter asked, "Do you know that he didn't turn it over to the Lord?" And the player said, "I bet he didn't, because he died."

This football player, I'm sure well-meaning, was saying that if you're trusting in the Lord, everything is going to be fine. If you're trusting in the Lord, no automobile accident, no plane crash will hurt you. Hurricanes won't get you. Earthquakes won't get you. That's trying to promise something that God definitely does not promise. And there are countless ways this is described in Scripture, including the promise Jesus does make to His disciples that you're going to bear crosses and that some of those things are going to be pretty big disasters. There's also the example in Habakkuk, one of the suffering passages that is kind of intriguing. You do have the situation there where God's people are going to suffer, and we know in this case as well that God's people stand under condemnation; that's a problem in Judah already. But then Habakkuk raises the concern that "While it's true our people here — your people, Lord — are sinning, the fact is that the Chaldeans are worse. So how come they're going to get the upper hand and innocent people among the people of Judah are going to die?" We don't know why, but it is true that many of God's faithful people also died when the Chaldeans destroyed Jerusalem. God doesn't promise that His people will never suffer. Don't promise what God doesn't promise. That's the "prosperity gospel," and it's misleading.

6. But don't settle for proclaiming less than God promises.

Now, God promises that by faith in Christ Jesus we're going to be in heaven. You're going to get to go to heaven. It's impossible to imagine a greater promise. And without question that is the promise that is the answer for believers in Christ who we know have perished in a disaster, loved ones who we know are believers in Christ and have now died. There's the ultimate answer: they get to go to heaven. But the fact is we don't need to proclaim the Gospel to believers in Christ who have died. They don't need it anymore. We are called to proclaim the comfort of the Gospel to those who are grieving, mourning over lost ones, wondering what the next steps in life for them will be. Whether it's a congregation in Pilger, Neb., that doesn't have a church building now; whether it's a family in New Orleans who doesn't have a home now; whether it's someone who's lost his or her job; or whatever the particular loss may be, those are the people we're addressing. And while "you get to go to heaven by faith in Christ" is the greatest promise that we get to apply again and again and one that always, always has relevance, because the ultimate future does impact our present, this isn't the only thing God promises. Don't promise less than what God promises. Be bold to proclaim every promise that God gives. And some of them go beyond "you get to go to heaven someday."

Gospel for the preacher to proclaim

All that Law we've been given is for us as preachers or as people who are sharing God's Word privately with their friends in crisis situations — those who are the speakers. Those are the "don'ts" — serious cautions to consider. But there's also Gospel for us to speak, Gospel that people are comforted to hear when we proclaim it even in the most difficult times of suffering, which brings us to our very important "do's."

In order to be Gospel — and this is crucial — what we say has to be *one particular thing*. At times of suffering, times of crisis, disasters, when it is really difficult to know what to say, a lot of things are said and spoken that may not be Gospel. They may be helpful, practical, sympathetic and gentle and, therefore, have value. But we're talking about sharing the Gospel in times of suffering. And Gospel is more than just a nice touch on the hand. It's more than just figuring out how we're going to rebuild the town that's been destroyed by a tornado. Gospel is something a lot more specific than that.

St. Paul gives us some very helpful counsel on what that is. In fact, Paul is really very clear on what we say any time we seek to proclaim. **"For I decided to know nothing among you except Jesus Christ and Him crucified" (1 Cor. 2:2).** That's an amazing thing for him to be saying. Paul had spent a year-and-a-half in Corinth, a very lengthy stop, one of the longest of his whole missionary experience, and all that time he was there, he really only talked about one thing: Jesus Christ and Him crucified. In the book of 1 Corinthians, Paul addresses such diverse issues as meat sacrifices, adultery, misunderstandings of the resurrection, schisms and so many others. Yet Paul says here at the beginning of the book that it's all Jesus Christ and Him crucified. It's all the cross of Christ.

We've got no problem with that when we're telling people they get to go to heaven someday, because there's no other way to heaven except by what Jesus did on the cross. The challenge is that many times in facing a disaster we're really addressing needs that could be understood as First Article needs. New Orleans has been devastated by a hurricane, and your house and business are gone. Your church and your home in Pilger, Neb., have been leveled by a tornado. Where do we go from here? You've lost a loved one to death in a disaster, and you're comforted that *she* is in heaven, but what do *I* do now in life? What's tomorrow going to be all about here in *my* life, here on earth? This includes those smaller "disasters" that Pastor Nuckols initially dismissed, too, doesn't it? It involves members who lost their jobs, members whose son is having trouble in school, so many of those kinds of situations. Those, too, are needs that we call First Article needs.

God's care and access to His throne of grace — we always have that, and it isn't just God caring for us when we die so that we get to go to heaven as did a loved one who died. God's care is when you don't have any idea how you're going to provide clothing and shoes, meat and drink, to your kids when your severance package is used up. Access to the throne of grace isn't just "Let me in! Let me in! Let me in to heaven!" when I die. It's "Lord, I'm at the end of my rope for sure, and I have no earthly idea how this is going to work out. But You've invited me to bring this before you, and You've promised to hear. And You will hear because of Jesus' death on the cross," because of nothing but Jesus Christ and Him crucified.

That's all there is; that's all we preach. But think of all that that means! And so you see, the *Deus absconditus* (hidden will of God) isn't really a matter of "Will God take care of me?" or "You know why God didn't take care of me." There is much we don't know. In what ways, in what's happening now, is God taking perfect care of me? I don't know; that's hidden from me. Or, this care that God's taking of me now ... how is this good? I don't know; that's hidden. But that's a different set of questions altogether. It's a different set of questions for which we won't get the answers this side of heaven. But in each of those questions, unlike the others, in each of those questions, what is intact is God caring for us in the very best way because Jesus Christ and His death on the cross have reconciled us to God.

In our discussion with the Roman Catholic parish priest in India, we did ask him, "More than a month after the tsunami, when you did address it in a sermon, what did you say?" He said, "Fear not. I am with you." It might have taken a month to say the words, but he couldn't have done better. "I am with you:" this is the peace with God in reconciliation. This is the *shalom*, the total condition of well-being that comes when sin has been removed by Jesus' death on the cross. Many things we might say are anything but comforting, but the cross of Christ fully understood with all its ramifications always gives us a word of comfort to share.

ADORATION OF THE KINGS

The Wiseman followed the star to the Bethlehem house where the child and his parents reside. A Mohammedan is beckoned also to come worship, depicting the Epiphany as the "Gentiles' Christmas." c. 1502

A translation of the essay "Intentional Care of the Poor and the Sick Is Essential for the Well-being of a Christian Congregation"

BY THEODORE JULIUS BROHM

TRANSLATED BY MATTHEW C. HARRISON

INTENTIONAL CARE OF THE POOR AND THE SICK IS ESSENTIAL FOR THE WELL-BEING OF A CHRISTIAN CONGREGATION

What a lovely and moving picture St. Luke paints of the faith and love of the first Christian community in Jerusalem! "They remained constant in the apostles' teaching and in the fellowship, in the breaking of bread and in prayer. But all who had become believers were together and held all things in common. They sold their goods and possessions and divided them among all according to need. The multitude of the believers was of one mind and spirit. And none said of his possessions that they were his, rather they belonged to all in common. And there was no one among them in need. For as many as had land or houses sold them and brought the money and laid it at the feet of the apostles and each was given what he needed" (Acts 2:42-45; 4:34-35).

What an astounding change had taken place among these people. Just a few days and weeks previous they were blasphemers and murderers of the Lord, standing with the crowd and shouting: Away with him! Crucify him! They had been proud, quarrelsome, envious, undisciplined men, slaves to all kinds of sinful lust. But the preaching of the Gospel, by the working of the Holy Spirit upon their hearts, had made of them believing disciples and worshippers of the Lord Jesus. They were humble, chaste, full of love, and henceforth gave all their possessions in order to serve their poor brethren. What a powerful, living, life-changing, blessed word must the Gospel be, that it brought about such a powerful, blessed turn of events! Indeed, it is the power of God unto salvation for all who believe it [Rom. 1:16-17].

This sharing of possessions was indeed an entirely unique and extraordinary appearance in the life of the Jerusalem Christians. It was neither mandated nor recommended by the apostles. Nor was it precisely imitated by other Christian communities, such as Antioch, Corinth, or Thessalonica. It was nothing less than a precious good work of self-sacrificing, self-denying love for the poor by those who had means. In this sense it is a bright shining example of the mother for all her daughters throughout the world. Even if this particular form of love was not prescriptive of precisely how other Christian communities would exercise love, the significant thing is the very love expressed in a way that had such impact. There is, in fact, a sharing of possessions, which for all Christians every place at every time is not merely suggested, but is mandated. It is an inevitable fruit of the faith and an essential mark of the Christian life. This is the sharing of possessions of which the prophet speaks: "Is it not to share your bread with the hungry and bring the homeless poor into your house; when you see the naked, to cover him, and not to hide yourself from your own flesh?" (Is. 58:7). Or as John the Baptizer commanded: "Whoever has two tunics is to share with him who has none, and whoever has food is to do likewise" (Luke 3:11). Or of which Christ said: "Give to everyone who begs from you" (Luke 6:30). The sharing of possessions in Jerusalem was a temporary appearance of that sharing of possessions which remains for all times, namely love. What it possesses as its own it does not use for its own honor and comfort. It is rather concerned to make use of it for the alleviation and reduction of the need of the neighbor. As soon as the Gospel is effective in the heart of a man, where faith and love are planted in the heart by the Gospel, there a man does not say: "This land, this house, this business, this property is mine and I'll do with it as I please." He says rather, "This all belongs to God and my neighbor. I am only the guardian and steward of my possessions. My Lord has given me way too much to use. I am like an official given pay which exceeds his needs and those of his family. The proper and necessary use of my possessions is for my neighbor whom God places before me in his stead: the poor, the widow and the orphan, the persecuted, the sick, the churches and schools. This sharing of possessions, which is certainly not given us as a matter of personal discretion, is expressly mandated by God, but does not demand from us a surrender of our ownership of things. It does not demand a monkish or fanatical oath of perpetual poverty, nor some sort of renunciation of the use of our possessions which are entrusted to each of us. Nor does it present to us a specific tax, like the O.T. tithe that was placed upon the people of Israel. It is completely free, bound to no law, but only to love. Still, I must assert that the law of love is by no means fulfilled through sharing a spare scrap from the excess of wealth, which a person feels in his money bag as little as a bucket of water taken from the ocean. On the contrary, love will have sacrifice, sacrifice, sacrifice.

If the sharing of possessions as I have described it were in full sway, it would happen that all the difference between the rich and the poor — the disparity between them — would be something other than it now is in the world. There would scarcely be millionaires who year after year pile up money with no end, and just as few poor people plagued by the pangs of hunger. Without this sharing of possessions the rich man would fatten himself from the sweat of his debtors. Without this canal of generosity his purse and money chest would swell and he would smother in his own fat. The wealth of the middle class would not be sucked dry by the taking of interest by the rich, and the kind hand of the rich would happily grant and give to those without means, and the poor, what their need requires.

Now what Christ applies to every individual, true faith's fruit and proof — namely love, active, self-sacrificing, self-denying love — also applies to an entire community of Christians. If the preaching of Christ has occurred with power within that community, if it has begun to grow deep roots, it will also be the case within the community as a whole that this love more and more will come into evidence. Works of love will no longer be those of individual members of the community; rather the community as a whole will take part in them.

So that love will ever have opportunity to demonstrate itself and act, God according to his marvelous wisdom has mixed together rich and poor in the world. And so it happens, not by accident, that in Christian communities there are always the poor, widows, orphans and the ill. It is true, these needy ones appear to a congregation to be a great burden, and indeed are often viewed and treated as a burden. In truth however, they are no burden, but much rather a gift. They are a field in which a congregation can prepare a bountiful harvest. Indeed, it is in the form of the poor, the widows, the orphans and the sick that Christ clothes Himself. He approaches the community in order to be fed, clothed, and cared for, and He does this so that He might place upon that community on the last day a glorious crown. Oh! If only a Christian community would recognize this, it would not complain about the number of its poor and sick. That community would thank Christ that He has considered it worthy for Him to dwell within its friendly protection in the form of the poor.

How praiseworthy and lovely is what we know of the charitableness of the first Christians. They were not satisfied that their own poor did not suffer want, they also assisted other congregations. For instance, at the time of Caesar Claudius there was a great inflation of prices throughout the world, and it was decided by the disciples at Antioch that each, as much as he could, would send an offering to the brothers who were in Judea. They in fact did so, and sent it to the elders by the hand of Barnabas and Saul (Acts 11:28-30). Paul boasted of the community in Macedonia. "For they gave according to their means, as I can testify, and beyond their means, of their own accord, begging us earnestly for the favor of taking part in the relief of the saints" (2 Cor. 8:3-4). And through the example of the community in Macedonia the communities of believers in Achaia were also stirred up to take part in the collection for the poor saints in Jerusalem (Rom. 15:26).

The fire of love did not dwindle in post-apostolic times either. With great fidelity each community tended to its poor, sick and imprisoned. Each Sunday, after the divine service, every member willingly brought generous contributions from which the needs of those suffering were met, and moreover, individuals took pains to provide assistance as needed. It was particularly the business of the Christian housewife to look after the protection of the poor and sick. The love of the first Christians was not limited to the narrow circle of their neighboring vicinity. When other Christian communities needed assistance, they hastened to gather funds and the proceeds were always generous. They also demonstrated their love to non-Christians. At Carthage in Africa a terrible plague broke out which daily claimed countless people. The non-Christians were overwhelmed by the numbers, and in their dismay they neglected to bury the dead. Cyprian, the bishop of the community of believers at Carthage, a man full of burning love for his Lord (he himself suffered martyrdom in 258), bid his parish come together, and he lectured them on mercy. He demonstrated to his people that if they did no more than the non-Christians and tax collectors, who only took care of their own, they were not worthy of the name Christian. For it was their duty also to love their enemies. And Cyprian did not speak in vain. A holy zeal of love was enflamed within all of them. The Christians divided themselves into groups in order to render effective assistance in the emergency. The wealthy gave generously. The poor gave what they had, namely the work of their hands. The non-Christians who were ill who had been abandoned by their own, found comfort and consolation. Bodies were buried. Streets were cleaned. No one considered the danger in which he placed his life, and the non-Christians looked on in amazement at the effects of the love of God in Christ. They also had a salutary opportunity to compare these works of love with their own selfishness and lack of humanity.

The horrors of the plague were followed by the terrors of war. The province of Numidia, near Carthage, was laid waste by an unexpected invasion of barbarians. Among others, many Christians were taken captive. Eight Numidian bishops communicated the horrendous circumstances to Bishop Cyprian. What he felt and did in response is demonstrated best by his own answer. "With deep sorrow," he wrote, "and with tears, dear brothers, we have read your letter regarding the imprisonment of our brothers and sisters. The apostle says, 'If one member suffers, so all suffer.' Therefore we view your imprisonment as our own. The same apostle also says, 'Do you not know that you are God's temple and the Spirit of God dwells in you all?' How shall we allow the temple of God to remain imprisoned? We thank you that you have made us partakers of your travails and have shown us fruitful fields upon which we can sow the seeds of our hope unto a rich harvest. We send to you 100,000 sesterces (nearly $4000 [1860 dollars]) as the result of a collection held among us for the cost of freeing our imprisoned brothers. The Lord protect you from similar unfortunate events, but should it please Him to take you captive, waste no time in reporting to us and be assured that we will willingly help you with our prayers and our money." From the Christian community in Rome through the duration of three years it was reported that they cared for more than 1,500 poor, widows and sick. Such examples of Christian mercy spread a refreshing fragrance through the Christianity of all times, and are a voice saying to us, "Go and do likewise."

If all hearts were full of such faith and such love, the care of the poor and the sick would be an easy business. Everyone — man and woman, young man and young woman — would compete with each other and, unasked, seek out need in homes and at the beds of the ill. When the individual Christian suffers, so suffers also an entire community of Christians, and [it suffers] precisely where there is all form of infirmity of life. One person is thoughtless and pays no attention and does not notice the need, until he is made particularly aware of it. Another is particularly slothful in his willingness to sacrifice for others, and needs admonishment. Furthermore there are, in the nature of this earthly life, certain hindrances. Many are not permitted by their earthly vocation to care with their own hands for those suffering. Human shortsightedness means many needs, namely of the mentally handicapped and the needs of the poor who are too ashamed to come forward, remain hidden. Indeed, the larger a Christian community is, the more imminent the danger of overlooking those in need of assistance. In general, individual assistance can never accomplish that which is possible with unified power. In the very mother and model community of believers in Jerusalem there arose the injustice that the widows of the Greeks were being overlooked in the daily distribution of bread by the apostles. The result was a grumbling of the Greeks against the Hebrews. What did the apostles do? They did not deny that out of human weakness a mistake had taken place. They desired to remedy the problem, and counseled the community to choose, for this need, seven men of good reputation, full of the Holy Spirit and wisdom, so they could continue unhindered in prayer and the office of the word. This counsel pleased the entire community and without delay was put into action, as we read in Acts 6:1-6.

The entire apostolic church followed this example. From the epistles of St. Paul we see how, next to the office of bishop or elder, there was also an office of minister or deacon, and in I Tim. 3:8-13 the apostle gives recommendations on what characteristics these ministers must have. Indeed, there was also in the apostolic church an office of female servant or deaconess. Phoebe is mentioned in Romans 16:1. She was in the service of the community at Cenchrea in the neighborhood of Corinth. Her ministry consisted in the care for the poor and the sick among the women. Widows were called to this task who, according to the apostle, were to be at least sixty years old (I Tim. 5:9). Also in the post-apostolic era we find the office of the deacons maintained and indeed with such a precise imitation of the Jerusalem model that the number of deacons serving a bishop was maintained at seven. There was a change, however, in that the circle of their official duties expanded somewhat, and certain clerical responsibilities were assigned to them, such as assisting the bishop. Also the office of the women and the deaconesses continued, and traces of it are found into the 5th and 6th centuries. Princesses and empresses were not ashamed of the office, or to be called "deaconess." The names of Placilla, the wife of Emperor Theodosius the Great, and of

161

Radegundis, the wife of the king of the Franks, Glothar, have been preserved for us. As deaconesses, they gave of themselves in an extraordinary way to care for the sick. Along with the offices of deacon and deaconess, there was also a particular office for men who cared for the sick in the church. They occupied a difficult and life-threatening office. With the final rise of the monastic movement and papaldom, the care of the poor and the sick as a ministry of the community gradually became extinct and withdrew to the cloister.

It is not necessary to continue to describe the model of apostolic and post-apostolic times. The matter of Christian love demands that Christian communities aim for similar institutions, so that mercy may be demonstrated consequentially, effectively, and by all. And though we may not make exact use of the sevenfold almoners of the Jerusalem congregation, yet they teach us that concern for the poor and the sick may not be left to chance. Indeed, according to necessity, a definite number of men — whether larger or smaller — should be tasked to this end, who, in the name of the entire congregation, assure the needy of equitable and sufficient help.

There are two concerns which stand in the way of an ordered care of the poor and the sick. One concern is that a definite order is not compatible with the ready free will of mercy. There is a concern that, by such an effort, the spirit of charity will gradually be pressed under compulsion into certain external forms. Finally, it is believed, the spirit of willing love must have to diminish. But this prejudice will fade as soon as one is convinced that such external forms and orders in no way limit love. They much rather provoke, bring forth, make effective, and direct it to the greatest possible good. If there really were such an inner dissonance between order and the free exercise of charity, as is feared, then by all means the first of the two would have to recede. But the essence of order does not alienate such love. Thus it is certainly only a misuse of the order, contrary to the nature of the Gospel, which has been asserted against an ordered exercise of charity. We do well to guard against mixing willingness with arbitrariness. Love, as free as it is, is still not arbitrary. The Lord indeed wants willing givers, but He still wants givers! He leaves it to the judgment of the individual Christian where, when, how, in what measure, and under which circumstances he demonstrates love. But He does not leave it to him as a matter of indifference whether or not he demonstrates love at all. A free, willing love and an ordered love can stand in the most beautiful harmony. This is demonstrated most clearly by the beautifully described establishment of the office of almsgiving in Jerusalem [Acts 6]. A second prejudice is the concern that, through an ordered care of the poor, the individual, personal act of love of the individual Christian is too limited and paralyzed. But this is not the case when it is otherwise correctly conducted. Certainly the guilt lay not in the order, but in the lack of love, when through that order love should become lazy or indolent. The order only exists to assist where the assistance of the individual is not sufficient for the need. Love is like a caring house mother who orders her affairs in the best manner so that every member of the house knows what he is obliged to do. Yes, she is diligent about the affairs of the house, and she takes hold of matters where the need demands.

Indeed, the smaller a Christian community is, the less order is needed. Every member knows the other. When a need occurs, everybody knows about it. The personal willingness to act charitably has plenty of room to work. Indeed the preacher of the small congregation (who above all others is obliged to see that the poor are cared for) can oversee and carry out this care himself. If there are orphans at hand, they, in a manner most convenient, will be brought into God-fearing families, and a new home can be prepared for them. And the care of the sick presents little difficulty if only others' hearts are filled with brotherly love. It becomes more difficult the larger the congregation is. Larger congregations require an ordered way to care for the sick and assist the poor. Thus at the time of the Reformation, all cities of Germany which fell to the Gospel quickly considered how to establish such care. The cloisters, which up to then had only been the refuge of the lazy, were disbanded, turned into schools or hospitals, and their income dedicated to the service of God and the poor. The beginnings were made by the little city of Leisnig in Saxony. Scarcely had the first rays of the Gospel shone upon this city when the citizens united with the neighboring nobility, chose from their midst ten men, and put together an order of the common chest, formed in part from the available income of the cloister and in part from the freely-given contributions of a fund which was designated for this purpose. In 1523 Luther provided this order of the common chest with a foreword, hoping as he wrote that this order would become an example followed by other communities. And his hope was not mistaken. The example of Leisnig was followed by the evangelical cities of all German lands, and they established well-equipped homes for the poor and the sick. While in the papal cities and lands the custom of begging remained as before, the evangelicals could boast that no beggars were to be seen in their streets. A very intriguing history was recounted for us of the first establishment of the care of the poor in Breslau. Johan Hess, the first Lutheran preacher in Breslau (d. 1547), could no longer accept how beggars, crippled, and mentally ill people lay on the streets and in front of all the churches in Breslau. He began to publicly admonish the governing authorities from the pulpit. But from it came no establishment of means to care for the poor in the community. Then Hess quit preaching. This had a significant effect upon the magistrate and the congregation, because he very much enjoyed preaching and they knew it. Finally they resolved to ask him why he stopped preaching. The answer was this: "My Lord Jesus lay in His members at the doors of all the churches. I can not simply step over Him. If He is not cared for, neither will I preach." These words had a very significant influence. Places to care for the poor were prepared. Illegitimate beggars were dismissed, and in one day, 500 persons were brought to newly established hospitals. Thus there arose gradually in all the cities and villages of Lutheran Germany a well-ordered and equipped way of caring for the poor and the sick, as we now see it everywhere.

The Lutheran communities of America must however go without a very significant advantage of the communities of Germany. There entire city communities — both church and government — were communities of one faith, with the exception of cities in which the governance of the city was divided between Catholics and Lutherans. Here there are only Lutheran communities which make up a small portion of the population. There the public institutions of charity benefited from what pious organizations of earlier centuries had established. Here they can only be maintained by the modest gifts of the [Lutheran] members of the community. Indeed, the greater the difficulties which stand in our way, the greater zeal should consume us to overcome them. There is scarcely a congregation within our synod in which something is not done for the care of the poor and the sick. In some older and larger congregations it is already taking place in well-known fashion. I know of one congregation in which over 700 dollars a year is directed for care of the poor. The young men and women have united to take over the nightly care of the sick, and through a special society a hospital is sustained. In another Lutheran community of a large city, in order to more easily oversee the care of the poor, the city has been divided into various districts, and each of four elders appeals each month to every congregational member for alms for the poor chest. The church council has to determine whether and how much assistance in each individual case of need is necessary. In another congregation, money for the poor is obtained through public collections, from which house payments, money for fuel, doctors and the cost of medicines, clothing, etc., can be had. In individual cases of need extraordinary collections are taken. A very important paper on the question: "What is the state of charity in the congregations?" is found in the report of the Eastern District of our Synod from the year 1859.

It is not my intention to lay out a proposal for an order for care of the poor, only that these lines should aim at this part of Christian love being ever more carefully tended and cultivated. This is so that these matters may be more carefully considered, and that the care of the poor could be ever more joyously brought to reality.

I conclude by putting a few questions to our congregations, preachers and elders:

1. What have we done thus far and what remains to be done in order as a collective whole, as a community, to demonstrate our faith active in love? What could and should happen in order to make our current methods of caring for the poor more effective, useful and consequential?

2. Is it a self-evident matter for us that the widows and orphans of a congregation which are to be supported also include the widows and orphans of their deceased pastor or school teacher?

3. Do we let our love also flow to strangers who are poor but who do not belong to our congregation, as did the above mentioned community at Carthage?

4. Would it not be for a larger and wealthier city congregation a very praiseworthy work to establish an orphanage in order to provide the countless forlorn, wild, despised orphans a place of refuge and to prepare for the church a school start?

5. Where do we allow our brothers and sisters to be buried? Do we begrudge their mortal remains a little space with the graves of pious Christians, so that they have rest at their side?

Finally, I leave for your consideration a word of Luther which he speaks in the Church Postil on St. Stephen's Day: "In this history you first of all see how a Christian community should be formed. Here you see a proper picture of a spiritual regimen, which the apostles here exercise. They take care of souls, and go about preaching and praying. They also see that the body is cared for, and set up certain men who dole out material goods. Thus, the Christian regimen cares for people in both body and soul, that no one suffer any need, as Luke says, 'and all are richly fed and well cared-for in both body and soul.' [Acts 4] That is a right fine picture and example. And it would be very good, if there were the people for it, that a city such as this one [Wittenberg] be divided into four or five sections, and each section be given a preacher and a specific deacon, who would care for that section with preaching, and distribute the goods, visit sick people, and see to it that no one suffer need. However, we do not have the people for this; therefore I trust it won't happen until our Lord God makes more Christians."

ANNUNCIATION
The angel Gabriel brings news to Mary that she will bear a son who will be the Christ. c. 1500–1502

THE CHURCH'S ROLE OF MERCY IN THE COMMUNITY

BY MATTHEW C. HARRISON
CONCORDIA THEOLOGICAL SEMINARY, FORT WAYNE, MAY 2002

*P*resident Wenthe, honored members of the President's Action Committee, dear fathers, brothers and sisters in Christ,

Introduction

In his *Praktische Theologie*, the great 19th century Luther scholar Theodosius Harnack complained that *"diakonia* was not of interest as a constituent part of ecclesiology, but was seen only as an expression of Christian groups and societies alongside the church. *Diakonia* was described as the life-expression of a particular Christian piety active in associations and institutions."[1]

The theological tradition Harnack complains about is alive and well among us today. We note, for instance, two significant points about the great dogmatics text of Franz Pieper, who along with Sasse and Elert, ranks as one of the greatest confessional Lutheran theologians of the 20th century. A cursory perusal finds not a word in Pieper's section on ecclesiology about the church having any collective role of mercy in the church or world. And second, we note that the locus on sanctification is directed entirely toward the Christian individual. Please correct me if I am wrong, but Pieper would appear to know of no collective role for the church as such as a bearer of the work of mercy, or *diakonia*, and certainly no such idea of *diakonia* as a "constituent part of ecclesiology." Pieper, of course, stands in one venerable tradition of Lutheran theology in this regard. By *"diakonia"* we mean the act of loving service to the needy by the church as such. It is by and large what we in the English-speaking world have, unfortunately, termed "social ministry" (a term I am now prone to avoid for reasons I hope will become evident, not the least of which is its close association with the heresy of the "social gospel").

The question: Has the church as church any mandate for *diakonia* as such? Has the church any role in the world in these last days beyond the proclamation of the Gospel

---

[1] Thus Carter Lindberg's description of Harnack's position in "Luther's Concept of Offering" in *Dialogue*, Fall 1996, vol. 35, no. 4, p. 252.

and the distribution of the sacraments? Are acts of mercy and *diakonia* simply the expression of individual Christian piety, even when done collectively by Christians? Is *diakonia*, or mercy over against the needy, simply a matter of individual Christian ethics? Is corporate, churchly *diakonia* an adiophoron? Does the church as such have any role over against government on behalf of the needy?

I for one believe, on the basis of the New Testament, that it is high time for us (especially us who hold to the inerrant word of God as sole source and norm for faith, and who dare yet today to confess the entire Book of Concord with an unqualified "*quia*," and who rejoice in the fact that the confessional Lutheran church is a church firmly in the western liturgical tradition, and who believe that the Lutheran Church is a evangelistic and missionary church), to answer these questions.

Fundamental to my own wrestling with these questions has been Luther's theology of "offering" which, as Lindberg points out, "bridges worship and social ethics, and it reminds us that both worship and social ethics are communal."[2] Says Luther, "Through the interchange of [Christ's] blessings and our misfortunes, we become one loaf, one bread, one body, one drink, and have all things in common."[3] "This fellowship is twofold: on the one hand we partake of Christ and all saints, on the other hand we permit all Christians to be partakers of us, in whatever way they and we are able."[4] In attacking and abolishing the sacrifice of the mass, Luther got law and Gospel right at the heart of the church's life, and fundamentally changed the trajectory of worship and the church's life. In the sacrament, Christ is the one who sits at table to serve, not to be served. "The inhaling of the offering of Christ in the sacrament leads to the exhaling of the distributing gifts in the community."[5] Lindberg aptly points out that unfortunately our American

> individualistic mindset tends to read the sequence of proclamation, faith, love and works in terms of individualistic ethics. The corporative character of the double faceted community with Christ and the communion of saints, so emphasized by Luther, is thus lost.[6]

Luther in fact, appealed to the very corporate nature of the sacrament, and its consequent, concern for the needy, while noting that in the early church the offering consisted of the elements for the communion, and the additional goods were distributed to the poor (can there be a more corporate, churchly and intentional form of diaconia?). States Luther:

---

[2] Lindberg, p. 251.

[3] LW 35:58, quoted by Lindberg, p. 252.

[4] LW 35:67, Lindberg, p. 252.

[5] Lindberg, p. 252.

[6] Lindberg, p. 253.

We have a vestige of this [practice] in the little word "collect" in the mass, which means a general collection, just as a common fund is gathered to be given to the poor. [Then] Christians cared for one another, supported one another, sympathized with one another, bore one another's burdens and affliction. This has all disappeared, and now there remain only the many masses and the many who receive this sacrament without in the least understanding or practicing what it signifies.[7]

Diakonia of the Church as Church

Does the church have a role of mercy in the community? I believe it does. Is *diakonia* a fundamental part of the church's mission in this world? I believe it is. In fact, I'm convinced, on the basis of the New Testament, that there is a threefold reality in the life of the church as church. All three hang inseparably together. The church must be about proclamation of the Gospel of Christ (*martyria*). In fact, to the extent that any mission of the church ceases this proclamation of the vicarious atonement of Christ and salvation by grace through faith, or alters this definition of the Gospel, it ceases to be Christian. Second, the church must be on about worship (*leitourgia*). Proclamation produces faith in Christ, and draws the faithful into the full sacramental life of the church. Wherever the church would have a "mission" or endeavor that is not clearly flowing from, to and connected with altar, font and pulpit, that mission is sectarian at best, and non-Christian at its worst. Third, wherever the church breathes in the blessed Gospel and sacraments, it cannot but exhale mercy and love toward the neighbor (*diakonia*). *Diakonia* is as much a part of the church's life as good works are a part of the life of faith. This applies to Christians both individually and collectively. Wherever these three realities of the church's life are not functioning in balance, there is a truncation of the church's life, and a diminution of its mission.

After surveying the landscape of our own Lutheran Church—Missouri Synod, from a unique if bureaucratic vantage, I'm convinced our churchly life is suffering this truncation. Among those dear Christians most involved in the life of our so-called "social ministry organizations," 120 of which are officially recognized by the LCMS, there is a tremendous need to re-think what it means to be confessionally Lutheran today in such circumstances and endeavors. Quite often, for a number of reasons, not least of which is the relationship of these institutions to federal and state government, and to the ELCA, *diakonia* is thriving, but there is far less intentionality regarding *martyria* and *leitourgia*. Among those traditionally NOT involved in such institutions and endeavors (parish, district or synodical) there is a strong emphasis upon *martyria* (after all, the whole experience of the LCMS in the '70s was an attempt to re-assert the possibility of certain dogma for the sake of Gospel proclamation). In such circles, common to those present here there is also great and necessary emphasis upon *leitourgia*. However, there has been and is an ambivalence toward or even a reaction

---

[7] LW 35:57, Lindberg, p. 253.

against *diakonia*. And this threatens to reduce such proclamation and liturgy to the realm of the "clanging cymbal" (1 Corinthians 13). It is also the case then, that those in the church who have tended to be most intensely interested in and conservers of orthodox dogma for proclamation, and of an orthodox liturgical life, have all but abandoned the diakonic/institutional life of the church. The CEOs of Lutheran institutions who have had theological training or are ordained are disappearing. The clergy with credentials for chaplaincy are both declining in number and aging. And this is occurring just when our theological institutions are most capable of producing graduates who can distinguish between trendy, less enduring therapeutic, and more classical models of chaplaincy as *Seelsorge*. And more than ever, our students should have the tools to use first article gifts of sociology and psychology in clearly delineated service to the blessed *Seelsorge* of gospel and sacraments.

And make no mistake; this abandonment of *diakonia* on the institutional level has enormous consequences. Our recognized institutions make up roughly one-third of Lutheran Services of America, recently recognized by The Not-for-Profit Times as the largest not-for-profit umbrella in America, with a combined budget of nearly $7 billion dollars (only 80 percent of the institutions reporting). These institutions serve millions, including tens if not hundreds of thousands of LCMS members. LSA has the world's largest adoption network. One of every three not-for-profit nursing home beds in this country is in a Lutheran institution. Right now, more than ever, we need pastoral theologians to lead the way to create Lutheran institutions and agencies for *diakonia*, set from the start on the firm foundation of the Lutheran Confessions. We need orthodox clergy who are engaged in *diakonic* work, or encouraging their parishes to be in the business of *diakonia*, thereby gaining experience and credibility for service to larger institutions, via called or volunteer positions. But where is such vision? Where are such men? Where is the vision for *diakonia* in its proper relationship to proclamation and worship as the mission of the church? Where are clergy with multiple discipline training? It is time for those most interested in *martyria* and *leitourgia* to turn also to *diakonia*, both in theoretical study and practical endeavor.

What then is the mandate (implicit and explicit) for the church's role of mercy in the world?

Loehe presents a very intriguing and unifying definition of mercy. God's love exists as an expression of His very being (1 John 4:7). Love (agape) is an act of the will of God without respect to the worthiness/unworthiness of the recipient (Rom. 11:32). Mercy is love responding to need. Where divine love meets sin, mercy exists as grace in Christ. Where divine love meets bodily suffering and need, that love becomes mercy and care for those suffering. According to Loehe, care and concern for spiritual and physical need are born of the same divine love in Christ.[8] They cannot be separated in the life of the church (Matt. 25:31ff.; 1 Cor. 13:1; James 2:14ff.; Gal. 6:7ff.; 1 John 3:10ff.).

---

[8] See Von der Barmherzigkiet in Wilhelm Loehe, *Gesammelte Werke*, Neuendettelsau (Freimund 1962), vol. IV, pp. 468ff.

1 John 4:7 — Beloved, let us love one another, for love is from God, and whoever loves has been born of God and knows God.

Rom. 11:32 — For God has consigned all to disobedience, that he may have mercy on all.

Matt. 25:31ff. — ... as you did it to one of the least of these my brothers, you did it to me ...

1 Cor. 13:1 — If I speak in the tongues of men and of angels, but have not love, I am a noisy gong or a clanging cymbal.

James 2:14ff. — What good is it, my brothers, if someone says he has faith but does not have works? Can that faith save him? If a brother or sister is poorly clothed and lacking in daily food, and one of you says to them, "Go in peace, be warmed and filled," without giving them the things needed for the body, what good is that?

Gal. 6:7ff. — Whatever one sows, that will he also reap ... Let us not grow weary of doing good, for in due season we will reap, if we do not give up. So then, as we have opportunity, let us do good to everyone, and especially to those who are of the household of faith.

1 John 3:10ff. — By this it is evident who are the children of God, and who are the children of the devil: whoever does not practice righteousness is not of God, nor is the one who does not love his brother.

The Manifold Mandate for Mercy

I use the word "mandate" here for a specific reason. A mandate is something that is "given" or literally "handed over" (*mandatum*). It is much more gift language than law language. We might simply reduce the cause of the church's diakonic life to the command: Love your neighbor as yourself. But such a reduction does not reflect the fullness of the biblical witness on the topic. Much less does this mere law-approach to the problem provide the full New Testament rationale, and more importantly, Gospel motivation for the church's life of mercy. What follows then, is an attempt to mine the fuller biblical and doctrinal matrix, which encompasses and propels the church's life of mercy. For it is my conviction that mercy is deeply rooted in and inseparably connected to the full dogmatic content of the faith.

1. Diakonic mercy has its source in the Holy Trinity. In Christ, a restless divine love was sent forth to find its object, a world in need of mercy (John 3:16). Likewise, that divine love, dwelling in hearts by faith, cannot but express itself in mercy toward those in need (Luke 6:36; 1 John 3:17-18; 1 John 4:7-8; Rom. 12:1, 8; Jude 21-22). Thus the mercy, which marks the church's life, has its source in the Holy Trinity, and those who know and believe in Father, Son and Holy Spirit, are merciful (Matt. 18:21ff., note v. 33; James 3:17).

1 John 4:7-8 — Anyone who does not love does not know God, because God is love.

John 3:16 — For God so loved the world, that he gave ...

Luke 6:36 — Be merciful, even as your Father is merciful.

1 John 3:17-18 — If anyone has the world's goods and sees his brother in need, yet closes his heart against him, how does God's love abide in him? Little children, let us not love in word or talk but in deed and in truth.

Rom. 12:1, 8 — I appeal to you therefore, brothers, by the mercies of God, to present your bodies as a living sacrifice, holy and acceptable to God, which is your spiritual worship.

Jude 21-22 — Keep yourselves in the love of God, waiting for the mercy of our Lord Jesus Christ that leads to eternal life. And have mercy on those who doubt.

Matt. 18:21ff., v. 33 — Should not you have had mercy on your fellow servant, as I had mercy on you?

James 3:17 — But the wisdom from above is ... full of mercy.

2. Diakonic mercy is born of the incarnation of Christ. In Christ, God became one with and identified totally with sinful humanity. The New Testament states that such identity was necessary that Christ might have mercy upon His "brothers" (Heb. 2:17). Having the mind of Christ, the church is called to identify with and humbly serve the needy (Matthew 25:31ff.; Philemon 2). The overwhelming majority of New Testament passages dealing with mercy for the needy direct the church to care for fellow-believers. Therefore, this must remain a central focus of the church. Nevertheless, just as divine love in the very incarnation of Christ, the atonement, and the continued proclamation of the Gospel, is directed to and seeks all, so the church's mandate for mercy knows only the bounds of "opportunity" and resources (2 Cor. 9:10-12; Gal. 6:10).

Heb. 2:17 — Therefore he had to be made like his brothers in every respect, so that he might become a merciful and faithful high priest in the service of God, to make propitiation for the sins of the people.

Matt. 25:31 — ... When did we see you hungry ... thirsty ... sick or in prison ... ? (Note the collective nature of *diakonia*, damnation and salvation.)

Philemon 2 — [To all the saints in Christ Jesus who are at Philippi, with the overseers and deacons ... 1.1] So if there is any encouragement in Christ ... complete my joy by being of the same mind, having the same love, being in full accord and of one mind. Do nothing from selfish ambition or conceit, but in humility count others more significant than yourselves. Let each of you look not only to his own interests, but also to the interests of others. Have this mind among yourselves, which is yours in Christ Jesus …

Gal. 6:10 — As we have *opportunity*, let us do good to everyone …

2 Cor. 9:10-12 — He who supplies seed to the sower and bread for food will supply and multiply your seed for sowing and increase the harvest of your righteousness. *You will be enriched in every way to be generous* in every way, which through us will produce thanksgiving to God. For the ministry of this service is not only supplying the needs of the saints but is also overflowing in many thanksgivings to God.

3. Diakonic mercy is born of the universal atonement (Rom. 11:32; 12:1). The universal condition of mankind apart from Christ, and the universality of Christ's atoning death demonstrate the equal value of each and every human life to God and thus to His church (Rom. 3:23; Rom. 5:12ff.). And the benefits of the universal atonement, accessed in Holy Baptism (Rom. 6:1ff.), bring forth a life released from self-centeredness and for service (Rom. 7:6). The universality of the need for and benefits of the atonement have direct ramifications for the nature of the church as a merciful corporate community, in which individual and diverse gifts are exercised for the good of the body (Rom. 12:4ff.).

Rom. 11:32; 12:1 — For God has consigned all to disobedience, that he may have mercy on all … I appeal to you therefore, brothers, by the mercies of God, to present your bodies as a living sacrifice, holy and acceptable to God, which is your spiritual worship.

Rom. 3:23 — All have sinned and fall short.

Rom. 5:12ff. — Therefore, just as sin came into the world through one man, and death through sin … Therefore, as one trespass led to condemnation for all men, so one act of righteousness leads to justification and life for all men.

Rom. 6:1ff. — We know that our old self was crucified with him … that we would no longer be enslaved to sin. Present yourselves to God as those who have been brought from death to life, and your members to God as instruments for righteousness.

Rom. 7:6 — But now we are released from the law … so that we serve in the new way of the Spirit.

Rom. 12:4ff. — For as in one body we have many members, and the members do not all have the same function, so we, though many, are one body in Christ, and individually members one of another. Having gifts that differ ... let us use them: if service, in our serving (*diakonia!*) ...

4. Christ's Palestinian ministry ever combined proclamation of forgiveness with acts of mercy, care and healing for those in need. Wherever Christ was present to disperse the gifts of the kingdom, He did so in word and deed (Luke 5:17-26; Luke 9:2-17; John 6).

Luke 5:17-26 — "Which is easier, to say, 'Your sins are forgiven you,' or to say, 'Rise and walk'? But that you may know that the Son of Man has authority on earth to forgive sins ... I say to you, rise."

Luke 9:2-17 — He sent them [the twelve] out to proclaim the kingdom of God and to heal the sick.

John 6 — [Feeding the five thousand] Jesus then took the loaves, and when he had given thanks, he distributed them to those who were seated.

5. The apostolic church continued Christ's concern for the whole person and care for the needy (Acts 6:1-7). In fact, we see in Acts that a portion of the task of the apostolic office was care and concern for the physical needs of widows. The office of "deacon" was born as ministry to the needy. In faithfulness to the New Testament we will encourage and promote such "diakonic" offices today wherever possible and appropriate (deacon, deaconess, parish nurse). There can be hardly any more convincing evidence than the ordination of the deacons that diakonic tasks were and ought remain "churchly" and corporate, and not merely in the realm of individual ethics (Acts 4:34-35; Acts 11:29-30).

Acts 6:1-7 (Note the daily distribution.)

Acts 4:34-35 — There was not a needy person among them, for as many as were owners of lands or houses sold them and brought the proceeds of what was sold and laid it at the apostles' feet, and it was distributed to each as any had need. [Note: churchly collection and distribution]

Acts 11:29-30 — So the disciples [collectively] determined, every one according to his ability [individually], to send relief to the brothers [church] living in Judea. And they did so, sending it [collective, singular] to the elders [a churchly office for churchly distribution] by the hand of Barnabas and Saul [apostles and evangelists].

6. *Diakonia* is born of New Testament sacramentology; consequently it flows from the sacramental/liturgical life of the church. Lives that have received mercy cannot but be merciful (James 2:13f.; James 3:17). In Baptism a merciful washing begets merciful living (Rom. 6:1-4; 7:4-6). In confession and absolution the merciful word of the Gospel begets merciful speaking and living (Matthew 18:21ff). In the Supper Christ gives himself totally for us, that we might give ourselves totally to our neighbor (1 Cor. 10:15-17; 1 Cor. 12:12ff; 26). "No, we must on our part make others' evil our own, if we desire Christ and His saints to make our evil their own; then will the fellowship be complete and justice be done to the sacrament. For the sacrament has no blessing and significance unless love grows daily and so changes a man that he is made one with all others" (Luther: *Sermon on the Blessed Sacrament*, 1519).

James 2:14ff. — What good is it, my brothers, if someone says he has faith but does not have works? Can that faith save him? If a brother or sister is poorly clothed and lacking in daily food, and one of you says to them, "Go in peace, be warmed and filled," without giving them the things needed for the body, what good is that? James 3:17 — But the wisdom from above is … full of mercy.

Rom. 6:1-4; 7:4-6 — We … died to sin … Do you not know that all of us who have been baptized into Christ Jesus were baptized into his death? … Likewise, my brothers, you also have died to the law through the body of Christ, so that you may belong to another, to him who has been raised from the dead, in order that we may bear fruit for God … But now we are released from the law, having died to that which held us captive, so that we serve [*diakonia!*] in the new way of the Spirit and not in the old way of the written code.

Matt. 18:21ff. — You wicked servant! [he said.] I forgave you all that debt because you pleaded with me. And should not you have had mercy on your fellow servant, as I had mercy on you?

1 Cor. 10:15-17 — Because there is one bread, we who are many are one body, for we all partake of the one bread.

1 Cor. 12:12ff. — For in one Spirit we were all baptized into one body — Jews or Greeks, slaves or free — and all were made to drink of one Spirit. For the body does not consist of one member but of many … If one member suffers, all suffer together; if one member is honored, all rejoice together.

7. The vocation to mercy is as broad as the need of the neighbor (Matt. 25:31ff), and applies to Christians as individuals (Micah 6:6-8; Matt. 9:12-13; Matt. 5:7; Lk. 10:37; Acts 10:2; 4; Acts 9:36; 2 Tim. 1:16) and to the church as a whole, whether local or synodical (1 Cor. 16:1-4; Acts 11:28ff.; Rom. 15:26; 2 Cor. 8:1-15; Acts 24:17). The work of mercy is also an expression of churchly unity (2 Cor. 9:12-15). "Therefore the church cannot be better ruled and preserved than if we all live under one head, Christ, and all the bishops — equal according to the office (although they may be unequal in their gifts) keep diligently together in unity of teaching, faith, sacraments, prayers, and works of love, etc." (Smalcald Art.II.4.9).

Matt. 25:31ff. When did we see you hungry ... thirsty ... naked?

Micah 6:8 — What does the LORD require of you but to do justice, and to love kindness, and to walk humbly with your God? [though this is addressed to Israel collectively]

Matt. 9:12-13 — Those who are well have no need of a physician, but those who are sick. Go and learn what this means, "I desire mercy, and not sacrifice." For I came not to call the righteous, but sinners.

Luke 10:37 — He said, "The one who showed him mercy." And Jesus said to him, "You go, and do likewise."

Acts 10:2; 4 — [Cornelius was] a devout man who feared God with all his household, gave alms generously to the people, and prayed continually to God ... And he stared at him in terror and said, "What is it, Lord?" And he said to him, "Your prayers and your alms have ascended as a memorial before God."

Acts 9:36 — Now there was in Joppa a disciple named Tabitha, which, translated, means Dorcas. She was full of good works and acts of charity.

2 Tim. 1:16 — May the Lord grant mercy to the household of Onesiphorus, for he often refreshed me and was not ashamed of my chains ...

1 Cor. 16:1-4 — Now concerning the collection for the saints: as I directed the churches of Galatia, so you also are to do. On the first day of every week, each of you is to put something aside and store it up, as he may prosper, so that there will be no collecting when I come. And when I arrive, I will send those whom you accredit by letter to carry your gift to Jerusalem. If it seems advisable that I should go also, they will accompany me.

Acts 11:28ff. — So the disciples determined, every one according to his ability, to send relief to the brothers living in Judea. And they did so, sending it to the elders by the hand of Barnabas and Saul.

Rom. 15:26 — For Macedonia and Achaia have been pleased to make some contribution for the poor among the saints at Jerusalem.

2 Cor. 8:1-15 — We want you to know, brothers, about the grace of God that has been given among the churches of Macedonia, for in a severe test of affliction, their abundance of joy and their extreme poverty have overflowed in a wealth of generosity on their part ... Your abundance at the present time should supply their need, so that their abundance may supply your need.

Acts 24:17 — Now after several years I came to bring alms to my nation and to present offerings.

2 Cor. 9:12-15 — For the ministry of this service is not only supplying the needs of the saints but is also overflowing in many thanksgivings to God. By their approval of this service, they will glorify God because of your submission that comes from your confession of the gospel of Christ, and the generosity of your contribution for them and for all others, while they long for you and pray for you, because of the surpassing grace of God upon you. Thanks be to God for his inexpressible gift!

8. The "royal priesthood" of the baptized exists for mercy (Rom. 12:1ff). We concur with Paul Althaus:

The priesthood means: We stand before God, pray for others, intercede with and sacrifice ourselves to God and proclaim the Word to one another. Luther never understands the priesthood of all believers merely in the "Protestant" sense of the Christian's freedom to stand in a direct relationship to God without a human mediator. Rather he constantly emphasizes the Christian's evangelical authority to come before God on behalf of the brethren and also of the world. The universal priesthood expresses not religious individualism but its exact opposite, the reality of the congregation as community (*The Theology of Martin Luther*, Philadelphia: Fortress Press, 1966, p. 314).

Rom. 12:1ff. I appeal to you therefore, brothers, by the mercies of God, to present your bodies as a living sacrifice, holy and acceptable to God, which is your spiritual worship ... The one who does acts of mercy, [let him do it] with cheerfulness.

9. People exist created by God as body and soul. This unity — though temporarily interrupted as a result of temporal death — will continue in a physical eternity, after the resurrection on the last day. Christ came as a man, body and soul, to redeem all, body and soul. The church's concern is therefore for the whole person. The proclamation of the Gospel of forgiveness by grace through faith is accompanied by Christian concern for physical and psychological need as well as spiritual need. If it is not, it is a ministration, which is less than the intent of Christ at best, and Gnostic (denial of the unity of body and soul) at its worst. The concern and care for physical need is accompanied by proclamation of the Gospel and a concern for incorporation into the church's life, or it is merely secular at best, and may deprive of eternal life at its worst. Proclamation of the Gospel and mercy for the needy belong together like faith and love.

10. The church exists to proclaim the Gospel and to administer the means of grace. These are its sine qua non mandate and source of existence. These only, as the unimpeachable guarantees of the church's presence, are its sole "marks" (A.C. VII). These central, permanent and dominant marks are not, however, its sole tasks. Jesus said of His preaching of the Gospel, "For that is why I came out" (Mark 1:38). Then the text states immediately, "And he went throughout all Galilee, preaching in their synagogues and *casting out demons*" (Mark 1:39). (Can we think of a more intensely spiritual/physical ailment?) Then states Luke's Gospel, "A man full of leprosy ... begged him, 'Lord, If you will, you can make me clean'" (Luke 5:12). Christ's miracles bore witness to His person. They also pointed to a fully healed eschatological future. So today, mercy in the life of the church bears witness to Christ's gospel, and its eschatological ramifications. "The proclamation of the gospel produces faith in those who receive the gospel. They call upon God .... They do good works on account of the glory of Christ. In this way the name of the Lord becomes great among the nations" (Ap. XXIV.32).

According to the New Testament, three things belong together in the church's sacred task of mercy:

1. Proclamation (*Martyria*) of the Gospel of forgiveness by grace, through faith in Christ's cross. (Acts 6:1-7. Note: the "ministry of the word" is the priority for the apostles.)

2. Worship (*Leitourgia*), which first receives Christ's gift of forgiveness, then sings his praises (Acts 2:42).

3. Merciful service (*diakonia*) of the neighbor, especially those in need.

(Acts 6:1-7. Caring for the needy was administered by the apostles. That responsibility was kept by the apostolic church, but transferred to the diakonic office created for this purpose, not merely relegated to the realm of private piety.)

I am convinced that there is an overwhelming explicit and implicit mandate for mercy as a corporate churchly task, inherent in biblical Lutheran theology. Perhaps you have noted that I have not mentioned much of the church's missiological task. Though I do think much could be said on this also with respect to *diakonia*, in fact, I wonder if our missiological efforts are a poor reflection of those of the early church, at least in part, because we have failed to keep these three (proclamation/worship/ *diakonia*) in unity. After the "deacons" are ordained (Acts 6:7) the text states, "So the word of God spread. The number of disciples in Jerusalem increased rapidly, and a large number of priests became obedient to the faith." I have not talked about "missions" and *diakonia* as some remedy for our domestic missional doldrums. That is because then I would be talking about us, about our doing, about another program, as opposed to "being" what our merciful God has made us in Christ.

The great strength of this magnificent institution is in being. This seminary has taught us what it means to be Christ's, to be confessionally Lutheran, to be sacramental, to be Christological, to be liturgical, to be biblical, to be called to an office, to have a vocation. The single greatest influence upon my theological life was moving from Kurt Marquart's classroom on dogma to Kramer chapel where the dogma, the doctrine lived and lives in its sacramental verities at altar and pulpit. And so I don't ask you to train anyone to do an additional task, to add another "job" to the agenda. What you have done and done magnificently is to teach the church and its clergy the centrality of *martyria* and *leitourgia*. Now, I plead with you to turn your attention to the task of a theology of mercy, and to begin to teach us what it means to be merciful in the life of the church that we may fulfill our vocation to mercy in this world, and in so being, be ever more what Christ in his mercy has called us and made us to be — a people of mercy.

Kyrie eleison, Christe eleison, Kyrie eleison.

CLEANSING THE TEMPLE
"And Jesus entered the temple and drove out all who sold and bought in the temple." Matt. 21:12a c.
1508–1509

Works of Mercy and Church Unity
Does Service Unify and Doctrine Divide?

by Albert B. Collver III

BACKGROUND

While it is somewhat prevalent to blame divisions in the church on the Reformation[1] in the sixteenth century or the rise of denominationalism[2] in the nineteenth and twentieth centuries, the fact is people have been divided over Jesus ever since he ministered on earth.[3] This division over Jesus even has entered into the church. Saint Paul warned the Corinthians, the Galatians, and the Romans about divisions.[4] Jude says that those who cause divisions are worldly people and devoid of the Spirit.[5] From the time of the Apostles, the church faced both heresy and schisms. "The church has always from its beginning suffered such divisions."[6] Knowing that his church would face heresy and division, Jesus prayed that his church might be "one."[7] In the Nicene Creed, the church confesses, "And we believe in one holy Christian and apostolic church." Yet this one holy Christian church is not seen with the eye, but is believed by faith. The eye sees the Christian church divided into several major

---

[1] Werner Elert, *Eucharist and Church Fellowship in the First Four Centuries*, trans. Norman E. Nagel (Saint Louis: Concordia Publishing House, 1966), 43. "Hans Asmussen, speaking for many, sees their origin in the 'confessional churches' which arose from the Reformation. 'The division at the Lord's Table as we have it today has a history of four hundred years.' According to the context of this statement it is clear that in his view such divisions first arose 400 years ago."

[2] Ronald E. Osborn, "Role of the Denomination: An Essay in Ecclesiology," *Encounter* 22, no. 2 (1961): 160. "Parallel denominational structures, their true nature hidden as well as revealed by their designation as churches, emerged with the grant of religious toleration in the generous world-view of the Enlightenment. Since then denominationalism has increased and multiplied, not only in the United States, where it is seen in extreme form, but throughout the Christian world wherever freedom prevails."

[3] John 7:43, "So there was a division among the people over him." (ESV)

[4] Romans 16:17; 1 Corinthians 11:18; Galatians 5:20.

[5] Jude 19.

[6] Elert, *Eucharist and Church Fellowship in the First Four Centuries*, 44.

[7] John 17:22.

181

confessional families and 9,000 denominations[8] with some estimates reaching 20,000 to 30,000. Herein, lies the problem. The church that can be seen is fractured and that fracture causes offense both to the world and to those in the church.

"The question of the one church of God," wrote Hermann Sasse, "arose on the mission field as a necessary question in light of the division of churches. It was a practical necessity born of the multiplicity of denominations carrying on mission work, and a necessity of the faith which had arisen as a result of the work."[9] The divisions of the Christian church hindered missionary activity. "Non-Christians often reacted to missionary efforts with the feeling that, before asking them to convert, the missionaries ought to agree among themselves what Christianity is."[10] Not only did the divisions in the Christian church cause scandal but also it seemed to be a waste of resources. What sense did it make to have three or four, let alone ten different denominations send missionaries to a given country? More often than not it was the missionaries themselves asking these questions and not the church bodies in Europe or America.[11] In the case of Africa, major missionary activity took place in the eighteenth and the nineteenth centuries, and during the twentieth century, there were many different denominations in Africa.[12] It is from the mission field where the question of Christian unity was asked in the late nineteenth and early twentieth centuries.[13]

In 1910, the World Missionary Conference of Edinburgh was held to address how the gospel could be proclaimed to the whole world.[14] For all intents and purposes, the ecumenical movement was born from this gathering of missionary societies, although before this there were some efforts to cooperate across denominational lines in the

---

[8] "World Christian Database," Christian Denominations, August 8, 2009, *worldchristiandatabase.org/wcd/about/denominations.asp*.

[9] Hermann Sasse, "The Question of the Church's Unity on the fission Field," in *The Lonely Way*, vol. 2 (SaintLouis: Concordia Publishing House, 2002), 182.

[10] Avery Robert Dulles, "Saving Ecumenism from Itself," *First Things*, no. 178 (2007): 24.

[11] James Good, "Kikuyu 1913: A Cradle of Ecumenism," *AFER* 25, no. 2 (1983): 86-89. "The beginnings of ecumenism in this century were, of course, motivated by something other than the unselfish desire for Christian reunion. The missionaries of the colonial era simply found themselves with more territory than they could handle, and the only viable arrangement was to parcel it out among themselves."

[12] Setri Nyomi, "Christian World Communions in Africa: Their Impact in Overcoming Denominationalism," *Ecumenical Review* 53, no. 3 (2001): 333.

[13] Sasse, "The Question of the Church's Unity on the fission Field," 180. "It is no accident that in our century the mission field was the place from which the question of the unity of the church was raised, and indeed the first in the form of the call to unify Christianity. Since the days of the apostles, the mission field has always been the place where the church and that which is not church, divine truth and demonic lies, encounter each other and separate. It is also the place where the deepest questions of the Christian faith first arise and where the last judgments in the history of the church are rendered."

[14] Brian Stanley, "Defining the Boundaries of Christendom: The Two Worlds of the World Missionary Conference, 1910," *International Bulletin of Missionary Research* 30, no. 4 (2006): 181.

area of Christian education, particularly for Sunday school.[15] From the movement came the World Conference on Faith and Order in the 1920s and eventually the World Council of Churches in the late 1940s. One of the outcomes of the 1910 Edinburgh meeting was that Protestants would not proselytize Roman Catholics and the Orthodox;[16] they were considered "Christian" and not in need of missionary work. It should be noted that many of the denominations that participated in the Edinburgh conference were spiritual descendents and offshoots of the Anglican Church such as the Episcopalians, Presbyterians, Baptists, Methodists, etc. Many of these groups had a similar theological heritage and foundation in the Reformed tradition. From a certain perspective, these groups were not so much divided by fundamental doctrinal differences as they were by practice and church government. This recognition may help to explain some of the initial growth of the ecumenical movement. Many of the denominational developments from the Old World and America did not seem applicable on the mission field. The time was also ripe for such a development as the ecumenical movement was a child whose mother was Pietism and whose father was the Enlightenment.[17]

Doctrine Divides But Service Unites

Out of the ecumenical movement came the phrase, "Doctrine divides, but service unites."[18] It has been a rallying cry in ecumenical circles at least since 1925.[19] When the attempt to pool missionary resources for the preaching of the gospel was hindered

---

[15] Forrest L. Knapp, *Church Cooperation: Dead-End Street or Highway to Unity* (Garden City, New York: Doubleday & Company, Inc., 1966), 169. "In Christian education we have one of the oldest fields of cooperation across denominational lines." Ibid., 170. "The insistent need of all Sunday schools for lesson materials led to a decision in the 1872 International Sunday School Convention (United States and Canada) to appoint a committee to prepare uniform lessons. After a struggle with the difficult task, the committee produced results, and the cooperative preparation of Uniform Lesson Outlines continues to this day, now under the Division of Christian Education of the National Council of Churches."

[16] Stanley, "Defining the Boundaries of Christendom," 176. "Edinburgh 1910 implicitly declared Protestant proselytism of Roman Catholics and, rather less clearly, of Orthodox and Oriental Christians to be no valid part of Christian mission."

[17] Carter Lindberg, "Luther's Critique of the Ecumenical Assumption That Doctrine Divides but Service Unites," *Journal of Ecumenical Studies* 27, no. 4 (1990): 694. "These endeavors are rooted in pietism and the Enlightenment, not the Reformation." See also Sasse, "The Question of the Church's Unity on the fission field," 188. "The modern Protestant world mission effort is a child of Pietism, and it cannot deny its origin. But Pietism has never had any understanding of dogmatic questions, and thus neither any understanding for the unique significance of pure doctrine."

[18] The phrase is attributed to Dr. Hermann Kapler (1867-1941), president of the Federation of German Evangelical Churches (1925-1933).

[19] Ruth Rouse and Stephen Charles Neill, eds., *A History of the Ecumenical Movement, 1517-1948*, vol. 1, 2nd ed with revised bibliography. (Philadelphia: The Westminister Press, 1968), 540. "At Halsingborg, the International Committee had before it the suggestion, made by the General Secretary of Faith and Order, that Life and Work might be interested in holding its conference in Washington in 1925, just after the first World Conference which Faith and Order was planning to hold in that city in May of that year. After thorough consideration, the International Committee arrived at the conclusion that it would be better to keep the two conferences separate. The goal of the Faith and Order movement was relatively distant, whereas the Christian churches should be able 'without difficulty' to unite at once in an effort to apply Christian principles to burning social and international problems. The answer of the Committee quoted Dr. Kapler: 'Doctrine divides, but service unites.' The Life and Work movement, it said, was aiming at common service; such common service in the field of practical problems might well help to break down walls and prejudices between church bodies, and create a spirit of brotherhood which would make it easier to realize also the aims of the Faith and Order movement."

by the confessional stances of some churches, the ecumenical movement turned to *diakonia* as a means of unity. If doctrine or theology might prevent two different denominations from sharing a missionary or preacher, what theological or doctrinal objection could be raised to different denominations sharing resources in order to dig a well or to establish a medical clinic? If the unity of the church could not be seen in preaching and teaching, perhaps it could be seen in *diakonia* — in works of service and mercy.[20] The world would see the church working together on projects involving human care rather than being divided. The cooperating together in matters external to doctrine made a good and positive witness.

Several factors contributed to the phase "doctrine divides but service unites" arising in the mid-1920s. Pietism from the eighteenth century contributed to it. The Enlightenment and the events of the nineteenth century made contributions to it. Both of these movements fed into the ecumenical movement with the effect of de-emphasizing orthodoxy, that is, doctrine, while emphasizing orthopraxis, this is, deeds.[21] The end of World War I also created a desire for churches to work beyond their traditional confessional lines. Other events in the twentieth century such as World War II, the civil rights movement, socialism, church denomination unions, etc., affected how "doctrine divides but service unites" developed. An examination of the assertion that "doctrine divides but service unites" is a mere snapshot of a given period of its development over the past century. Nevertheless, there are certain common themes that remain throughout its development.

In the late 1950s and early 1960s, an important development was the division of evangelism into three components: *kerygma, koinonia,* and *diakonia.* Sometimes *kerygma* — the proclamation of a gospel for the whole world, *koinonia* — the welcoming of all into the new covenant, and *diakonia* — Christian service are described as "forms of communication."[22] The three together are the church's mission to the world. This way of speaking about the mission of the church and *diakonia* emerged as socialism and secular and government humanitarian efforts were on the rise. Those who promoted the notion that "doctrine divides but service unites" pondered the question of the way in which humanitarian aid given by church differs

---

[20] Stephen Cranford, "Aid and the Unity of the Church," *Mid-Stream* XVIII, no. 2 (1979): 157. "Too often the world sees only a divided church; inter-church aid is one way, however, of demonstrating visibly the essential unity which is God's gift to his church."

[21] Lindberg, "Luther's critique," 680. "The idea that ecclesial unity is rooted in ethics arose in pietism. It was Gottfried Arnold (1666-1714) who forcefully advanced the claim that the mark of true Christianity is piety (orthopraxis), not doctrine (orthodoxy)."

[22] Theodore Wedel, "Evangelism's Threefold Witness: Kerygma, Koinonia, Diakonia," *Ecumenical Review* 9, no. 3 (1957): 239. "The kerygma proclaiming a gospel for the whole world, the koinonia welcoming all into the new-covenant-life, and then a demonstration of the power of the Spirit in diakonia (Christian service)-only when the 'people of the mission' utilize the full orb of these three forms of communication as an inseparable triad can the church witness rightly to itself and to its Lord. This triad has never been disrupted by internal rivalry except when the church has lost its sense of mission to the world."

from that of government and secular agencies? In a certain sense, if churches are cooperating with each other in matters apart from doctrine and external to the sacred things, the humanitarian efforts of the church are not clearly distinguishable from that of secular and government agencies. This recognition led to the recognition that "Christianity has no monopoly of humanitarian service to mankind" and that "secular loyalties" might be a stronger motive to serve than the "Christian conscience."[23]

Humanitarian work, once the domain primarily of the church, became the domain of the secular world and government. Some even imagined the day when secular entities and governments, inspired in part by socialism, would do most if not all of the humanitarian work in the world. Theodore Wedel wrote, "Christian *diakonia* will, accordingly, have to accustom itself to the presence in our modern world of this rival religion of brotherhood without God."[24] Increasingly, as the world became concerned with issues such as racism, justice, and liberation of the oppressed, so did the church as both pursued similar humanitarian aid and service. During the 1960s and 1970s these concerns, which arose in the secular world, were "theologized," creating a "theological" rational for *diakonia* work and service in the church. In the absence of a biblical, creedal, and confessional theology, a humanistic theology, that is, anthropology, would fill the vacuum.

Some thought that the increasing presence of governmental and secular agencies in humanitarian work would only increase *koinonia* (fellowship) between church bodies in works of *diakonia* (service). As denominational specific agencies were subsumed by the state, as Christian hospitals and orphanages gave way to state supported and/or run hospitals and orphanages, the role of the lay church member was seen as even more important. A Christian doctor working in a state run hospital will seek the companionship and fellowship of other Christians, even those who are not a part of his confessional or denominational heritage, as he carries out his Christian witness. In this way, it was thought that lay people, rather than clergy, would promote the *koinonia* between church bodies.[25]

The thought that the laity would play a greater role or perhaps even the greatest role in church unity was not entirely new in the ecumenical movement. Since the earliest days of the ecumenical movement, a contingency thought that church unity had

---

[23] Ibid., 235. "Christianity has no monopoly of humanitarian service to mankind. Indeed, puzzling paradox though it may be, if the concept of 'welfare' is equated with that of 'salvation,' the Church's diakonia may soon find itself outdistanced by its secular rivals. Even the motive for service to the needy may, when judged by external standards of sacrificial devotion to a cause, appear stronger under secular loyalties than that which animates the Christian conscience."

[24] Ibid., 236.

[25] Ibid., 237. "The Christian doctor in a state-supported hospital, or the Christian teacher in a secular school, is called upon to be a lay evangelist in a more difficult environment than that which lay specialists encountered in the era of protected diakonia. He will escape the prison of loneliness only as he finds strength for his ministry in the fellowship of his brethren in Christ. Thus under the threat of failure to witness at all the connection between diakonia and koinonia will be rediscovered."

been hindered since the time of the Reformation by the clergy who unnecessarily divided the church by rigidly holding to non-essential and divisive doctrines. It is not surprising that a lay movement went through the entire church during this time. As service and humanitarian aid increasingly became associated with the mission of the church, the role of the laity as missionaries becomes more prominent. In the first decade of the twenty-first century, in many church bodies, lay missionaries vastly out numbered professional missionaries or clergy missionaries. There seems to be no reduction in this trend.

For our purposes, the theological rationale for the increased role of the laity given by any particular church body is not of primary importance. Theological principles or a new biblical understanding of the laity was not the primary impetus in this movement. The focus in this movement is on orthopraxis not orthodoxy. The focus is on getting what is necessary done and developing the rationale after the fact. In some ways, it seems as if the ecumenical movement was seeking how to address issues raised from the doctrine of the two kingdoms and Christian vocation-to use Lutheran categories. In this sense, perhaps, the churches of the Augsburg Confession, rather than ignoring the ecumenical movement or being drawn into its presuppositions, might have done better to speak clearly on the doctrines of the two kingdoms and vocation.

During the 1960s and 1970s, the understanding that doctrine divided while service united shifted once again. Works of service were seen as a theology in and of themselves. The lack of cooperation in works of service was seen as the source or origin of heresies, schisms, and divisions within the church.[26] Nikos Nissiotis wrote, "The greatest sin of the people of God is that they have neglected to perceive the theological, vertical dimension of *diakonia* in the ecclesiological, horizontal one."[27] In other words, the failure of the church to cooperate in works of service indicates a theological problem in *koinonia* (fellowship). There are really only two alternatives: either 1) *diakonia* (works of service) is not doctrinal, in which case there is little to distinguish the humanitarian work of churches from that of government and secular agencies, or 2) *diakonia* has a doctrinal component related to ecclesiology and church fellowship. Many in the church were not willing to give *diakonia* wholesale to the secular realm. *Diakonia* must be redefined not as a good moral act or as the expression of compassion but as the "overflowing of the grace which binds and moves their inner life as a total fellowship."[28] Thus, *diakonia* attached to a

---

[26] Nikos A. Nissiotis, "The Ecclesiological Significance of Inter-Church Diakonia," *Ecumenical Review* 13, no. 2 (1961): 195. "Among the main reasons for the church heresies, schisms and divisions is the lack of this inner power of mutual service, of mutual inter-dependent existence."

[27] Ibid.

[28] Ibid., 191. "This diakonia is neither a good moral act springing from the good will of a regenerated Christian nor an expression of compassion for the misery of man outside the church. The care of the churches for the world is not a vehicle for showing compassion for the suffering or the weak or the uneducated man. The help of the churches offered to the world is not of a humanistic nature. The churches are not primarily philanthropic institutions. The act of the diakonia of the

doctrine of ecclesiology and *koinonia* would become one of the primary vehicles by which to obtain visible unity of the church on earth.[29] This line of thought leads to the conclusion, "This greatest sin has been in the past, and still is, to hasten to offer service to the world without practicing *diakonia* between the separate churches. It is our calling now to restore church unity through a practical, existential, living process of sharing each other's life beyond any confessional barriers."[30]

By the late 1970s, the ecumenical movement had come full circle. Initially, it was said that doctrine divided but service united. Jürgen Moltmann wrote in "Fifty Years of Faith and Order," "... fifty years ago in the early days of the ecumenical rapprochement it was said 'Doctrine divides-service unites' ... Today the situation is almost completely reversed. Now, after many years of patient, painstaking work it would be true to say 'Theology unites-praxis divides.' Controversy in the ecumenical movement no longer centers on the filioque, but concerns instead the Programme to Combat Racism. The problem now is not the theological understanding of the eucharist and of ministry, but the practical recognition of ministries and common celebration. After fifty years of concerted theological effort we now have to say quite openly to Christians and church authorities that there are no longer any doctrinal differences which justify the divisions of our churches ... "[31] As the ecumenical movement seemingly overcame doctrinal differences,[32] the visible unity still did not appear. As the focus intensified on *diakonia*, controversy actually increased among some churches[33] in part because churches feared cooperation would endanger their own institutional interests.[34] In the course of the ecumenical movement, *diakonia* went from a uniting force devoid of doctrine to a divisive force linked to a *koinonia* doctrine. Therefore, works of service (*diakonia*), in fact, are doctrinal. Works of service both unite and divide.

With Moltmann's statement that "theology unites-praxis divides" and the failure of churches to unite on the basis of service, the ecumenical movement in the late

---

churches is *ecclesiale* namely it is the overflowing of the grace which binds and moves their inner life as a total fellowship."

[29] Richard Dickinson, "Diakonia in the Ecumenical Movement," In *History of The Ecumenical Movement* vol. 3, 1968-2000 (Geneva: WCC Publications), 413. "This conscious linking of diakonia and koinonia signals a significant evolution in ecumenical thinking."

[30] Nissiotis, "The Ecclesiological Significance" 197.

[31] Michael Kinnamon and Brian Cope, eds., *The Ecumenical Movement: An Anthology of Key Texts and Voices* (Grand Rapids: Eerdmans, 1997), 210.

[32] Raymond Hickey, "Ecumenism Beneath the Cross in Africa," *AFER* 26, no. 3 (1984): 155. "The rigid barriers which had been erected — and frequently reinforced! — between Christians for over four hundred years were now seen to be tumbling in a planned and orderly manner."

[33] Dickinson, "Diakonia in the ecumenical movement," 419. "Leslie Cooke's wry warning in 1966 could not have been more apt. He observed that the more involved in real development-as distinguished from relief-the churches were, the more controversial and sometimes unpopular their diaconal witness would become."

[34] Knapp, *Church Cooperation*, 174-175. "Too often local churches and denominations have discovered reasons for only limited cooperation. When their own institutional interests have been endangered, they have tended to draw back. The strength and continued existence of denominational life has been allowed to have primary place."

1970s in some ways was in a period of crisis. Despite the ecumenical movement's reconciled diversity and convergence-statements on creeds, sacraments, and justification, churches remained divided. Carter Lindberg asked the question whether, "there are fundamental differences between the churches that have to do with ethics."[35] Some in the Orthodox Church identified the cause of the crisis in the WCC as a false assumption, "that all its member churches were able to agree together in giving a universal Christian answers to the questions arising at any given time."[36] In order to promote "solidarity in *diakonia*," some in the Orthodox Church proposed that the answer be sought in the liturgy.[37] Orthodox and Roman Catholic authors suggested the eucharist could be the bridge between the liturgy and *diakonia* by suggesting "an interpersonal relationship, not only between the community and God but also between the community and all present or absent members of the church."[38]

In essence, the linking of the liturgy to *diakonia* via the eucharist stated that communion with God produces communion between human beings. From this approach, the WCC concluded, "Service, *diakonia* and the eucharist belong together; by sharing through bread and wine Christ's body, we become his body, we are made into share- people, are empowered to share with others our own lives, our gifts."[39] Whatever inspiration the liturgy and eucharist provided *diakonia* service, within a church body, the eucharistic vision was an empty formula for producing a unity through *diakonic* service "as long as the churches themselves have no real eucharistic community with each other."[40] In other words, the eucharist promotes *diakonic* service but churches need to have communion fellowship with each other. Once again, the lack of common participation in the eucharist prevents church unity and common *diakonia* service.[41]

Ultimately, the lesson the ecumenical movement learned from the Orthodox and Roman Catholic churches about the connection between the eucharist and *diakonia* is that of "sharing." "The language of sharing is even more basic than any of our theological or ecclesiological concepts, for it is the people's language in an elementary sense. All people know what sharing means, whether from experience or longing hope, and they know that fullness of life is only found in sharing life with one another. 'Sharing'

---

[35] Lindberg, 680.

[36] Alexandros K. Papaderos, "Liturgical diakonia: Biblical and Theological View of Diakonia," *Mid-Stream* 18, no. 2 (1979): 137.

[37] Ibid., 138. "But I believe we can use this term 'liturgical' to show why and in what sense every Christian diakonia to the world, to culture, to politics, to human beings must be a liturgical diakonia."

[38] Cesare Giraudo, "The Eucharist as Diakonia: From the Service of Cult to the Service of Charity," In *Liturgy in A Postmodern World*, ed. Keith Pecklers (New York: Continuum), 119.

[39] Martin Robra, "Theological and Biblical Reflection on Diakonia: A Survey of Discussion within the World Council of Churches," *Ecumenical Review* 46, no. 3 (1994): 282.

[40] Ibid., 283.

41 Good, "Kikuyu 1913," 88. "But there is one major exception, and it remains a stumbling-block: common participation in the eucharist today, for many Christians, as big a crime as it was in Kikuyu in 1913."

is thus a fundamental symbol of life."[42] Thus, God's sharing of himself in Jesus Christ allows the church to share with each other and with the world. The language of sharing is remarkably similar to that used in ecumenical statements about the Lord's Supper in that the gift of the supper is Christ sharing himself.

A Preliminary Excursus on Cooperatio in Externis (cooperation in externals)

The principle *cooperatio in externis* is most commonly defined as cooperation between or the working together of a church with another church that do not have doctrinal agreement or fellowship in matters not related to the preaching and teaching of the faith or the administration of the sacraments.[43] This principle seems to have developed from the interaction between the ecumenical movement's focus on *diakonia* disconnected from doctrine and the efforts to unite various Lutheran groups in America. While there may not be a direct cause and effect link or proof of direct influence between the efforts of the ecumenical movement to practice *diakonia* apart from doctrine and the union discussions between various Lutheran groups in America, there is a similarity of thought between the two efforts. It also seems the ecumenical movement's conversation about "doctrine divides, but service unites" influenced the further development of the cooperation in externals principle. It seems appropriate to discuss briefly cooperation in externals in light of the discussion on service uniting the church.

Although some have reported discovering *cooperatio in externis* in the Lutheran dogmaticatians, our preliminary research was unable to locate the term using the index to Baier's Compendium. Nor have we located the term in the Francis Pieper's Christian Dogmatics. Although our research into the origin of the term, *cooperatio in externis* has not been exhaustive, the term, at least as a technical term (and dare we suggest the concept) did not come into widespread usage until the end of the nineteenth century and the beginning of the twentieth century. The earliest reference we found to the term *cooperatio in externis* was located in a Roman Catholic work on moral theology.[44] In this work, the term *cooperatio in externis* is used to distinguish the cooperation of individuals in a moral transgression from a moral transgression committed by a sole individual.[45] The context of this usage is different from what has

---

[42] Robra, "Theological and Biblical Reflection" 285.

[43] Kurt E. Marquart, "The Issue of Church Fellowship and Unionism in the Missouri Synod and Its Associated Churches," *Logia* XII, no. 1 (2003): 20. "Church fellowship has always been understood as *communio in sacris* (communion in sacred things) as distinct from mere *cooperatio in externis* (cooperation in externals)."

[44] Iosepho D'Annibale, *Summula Theologiae Moralis* (Rome: Ex Typographia Polyglotta, 1896).

[45] Ibid., 161. "*Cooperatio in externis dumtaxat transgressionibus locum habet; externa autem legis transgressio constat intentione et opere externo: qui est particeps utriusque, correus seu cooperator jormalis; qui operis tantum, cooperator materialis dici solet.*" "Cooperation only takes place in external transgressions. An external transgression of the law consists in intention and external work. Whoever [or whatever] is a participant in both [is usually called] co-guilty or a formal cooperator. Whoever [or whatever] [is a participant in] the work alone is usually called a material cooperator." (Translation by Rev. Benjamin Mayes, Ph.D.)

become more commonplace among some Lutherans, but it does indicate, that cooperation occurs between individuals in works external to an individual. People are not able to cooperate in a work occurring within the mind of an individual. By extension, one can understand how the term *cooperatio in externis* could be used to describe works external to the *communio in sacris* (communion in sacred things). Our preliminary research has not uncovered evidence that Lutherans were reading this Roman Catholic work on moral theology but it is certainly a possibility.

An early appearance of the concept and words but not the exact phrase "cooperation in externals" among American Lutherans is found in the "Declaration of Principles Concerning the Church and Its External Relationships," adopted at the Second Convention of the United Lutheran Church in America[46] at Washington, D.C., October 26, 1920.[47] The purpose of this document was to "define the attitude of The United Lutheran Church in America toward cooperative movements, both within and without the Lutheran Church, toward organizations, tendencies, and movement, some of them within and some of them without the organized church."[48] The document states that there can be "complete cooperation and organic union" with church bodies calling themselves Evangelical Lutheran and who subscribe to the Confessions.[49] While this may not be the same doctrinal standard used by some confessional Lutheran churches for pulpit and altar fellowship, it is important to note that this document distinguishes those who call themselves Lutheran from general Protestant churches and from non- church groups. Since Protestant church groups are not Lutheran, separate ministers, pulpits, fonts, and altars must be kept and not shared.[50] Thus, The United Lutheran Church in America could not have *communio in sacris* with the Protestant church.

"In view of the many proposals for cooperation of the Protestant churches in various departments of practical activity and in view of the many organizations already formed," the document offers some guidelines for carrying out cooperative work.[51] As long as cooperation in "works of serving love" between The United Lutheran Church

---

[46] Erwin L. Lueker, ed., *Christian Cyclopedia* (Saint Louis: Concordia Publishing House, 1975). "The United Lutheran Church in America. Organized in a convention November 14-18, 1918, New York City, by merger of General Council of the Ev. Lutheran Church in North America, The General Synod of the Ev. Lutheran Church in the USA, and The United Synod of the Ev. Lutheran Church in the South; ceased to exist 1962 with the formation of the Lutheran Church in America."

[47] "Declaration of Principles Concerning the Church and Its External Relationships," *Concordia Theological Monthly* VI, no. 1 (1935): 46-53.

[48] Ibid., 46.

[49] Ibid., 49.

[50] Ibid., 50. "That until a more complete unity of confessions is attained than now exists, The United Lutheran Church in America is bound in duty and in conscience to maintain its separate identity as a witness to the truth which it knows; and its members, its ministers, its pulpits, its fonts, and its altars must testify only to that truth."

[51] Ibid.

in America and various Protestant churches or service organizations did not "involve the surrender of our interpretation of the Gospel, the denial of conviction, or the suppression of our testimony to what we hold to be the truth," such cooperation was possible.[52] However, The United Lutheran Church in America rejected the possibility of cooperation in external matters if the basic tenets of the Christian faith were rejected, such as a rejection of the Holy Scriptures, the Trinity, the universality of sin, etc. Nor was cooperation in external matters possible if the church's confession of the truth was limited in any way. Nor could cooperation be possible with movements or organizations whose purposes lie outside the proper sphere of church activity. An example given of an activity outside of the proper sphere of the church was that of law enforcement.[53] For our discussion here, there are two crucial points: 1) cooperation in external matters in this document is defined more narrowly than it is by many who speak of cooperation in externals today, and 2) the seminary journal, Concordia Theological Monthly, of the Missouri Synod reprinted without comment this declaration of The United Lutheran Church in America in 1935 "in view of recent developments in the American Lutheran Church."[54]

Six years after the *Concordia Theological Monthly* published The United Lutheran Church's *Declaration*, President Behnken of the Missouri Synod issued a statement, "You realize, of course, that Missouri has been cooperating in externals in matters which do not involve pulpit, altar, and prayer fellowship. Such cooperation must not be interpreted as a step towards fellowship or a method of bringing about fellowship among Lutherans."[55] President Behnken did state that such cooperation in externals did not include "joint work in missions, in Christian education, in student welfare work, or in joint services celebrating great events."[56] President Behnken's statement represents the first official statement by the Missouri Synod on cooperation in externals and was one component of Wisconsin Synod's breaking of fellowship with the Missouri Synod some years later.

---

[52] Ibid.

[53] Ibid., 52.

[54] Ibid., 53.

[55] John Behnken, "Fellowship Among Lutherans: Address to the American Lutheran Conference," *Quartalschrijt* 44, no. 1 (1941): 68. President Behnken's entire statement: "Today efforts are being put forth toward fellowship via cooperation. Cooperative efforts have been proclaimed and heralded as harbingers of Lutheran fellowship and Lutheran union. Let me speak very frankly. If such cooperation involves joint work in missions, in Christian education, in student welfare work, in joint services celebrating great events, then cooperation is just another name for pulpit, altar and prayer fellowship. Without doctrinal agreement this spells compromise. It means yielding in doctrinal positions. Such fellowship will not stand in the light of Scripture. You realize, of course, that Missouri has been cooperating in externals in matters which do not involve pulpit, altar and prayer fellowship. Such cooperation must not be interpreted as a step towards fellowship or a method of bringing about fellowship among Lutherans. Fellowship among Lutherans is possible and biblical only where there is agreement in biblical doctrine and scriptural practice. Where such agreement has been reached, pulpit, altar and prayer fellowship will necessarily follow."

[56] Ibid.

Two years after President Behnken's statement on "cooperation in externals," Theodore Graebner wrote, "We are living in an age which calls for a re-thinking, a new thinking-through all of our principles of church work, not in order to revise them, but in order to obtain a clear understanding of their application to new issues and new conditions."[57] Graebner helped bring acceptance to the concept of "cooperation in externals" within the Missouri Synod. The fruit of his work was seen in 1965, when the Missouri Synod in convention adopted the concept of "cooperation in externals."[58] According to one author on social ministry in the Lutheran tradition, the Missouri Synod church leaders invented "cooperation in externals" to get around the denomination's conservative theology on church fellowship which prohibited cooperation in inter-Lutheran efforts, in military chaplaincy, and praying with other Christians.[59] This view may represent the position some had in the Missouri Synod. Many in the Missouri Synod simply accepted "cooperation in externals" uncritically. The principle of cooperation in externals led to the creation of the Department of Social Welfare in the Missouri Synod.[60]

On the one hand, the Missouri Synod's position on cooperation in externals provided the church with a freedom in how it interacts with the world. On the other hand, it also allowed some to define "externals" so broadly and "fellowship" so narrowly that nearly any cooperation that did not involve preaching, worship, or prayer was permissible. If the extreme of no cooperation in external matters without full doctrinal agreement was not helpful to the church, neither is the other extreme that all so-called "external matters" are permissible. A more nuanced and critically thoughtful approach is required lest the sacred things are violated.

---

[57] Theodore Graebner and Paul E. Kretzmann, *Toward Lutheran Union: A Scriptural and Historical Approach* (SaintLouis: Concordia Publishing House, 1943), 231.

[58] Commission on Theology and Church Relations, "Theology of Fellowship," 1965. See Part III.C.4, pg 28.

[59] Foster R. McCurley, ed., *Social Ministry in the Lutheran Tradition* (Minneapolis: Fortress Press, 2008), 101-102. "Inter-Lutheran efforts for social ministry work and military chaplaincies were characterized as 'cooperation in externals' by the Lutheran Church—Missouri Synod leaders as a way of getting around the denomination's conservative theology and refusal even to pray with other Lutherans. John W. Behnken, the synod's president, wrote a policy statement in 1941 declaring that his church could not cooperate 'in any form in the dissemination of the gospel.' Any cooperation had to be confined to 'externals,' such as relief to orphaned missionaries and work among soldiers and sailors. Still others contended that the term suggested that social ministry was an external matter to Christian faith and the life of the church. Not so, Missouri Synod welfare leader Henry F. Wind insisted in 1943. Social ministry is a sign of the presence of the grace of God and a necessary fruit that grows out of faith."

[60] Lueker, *Christian Cyclopedia*. "H.F. Wind was appointed Executive Secretary of the Department of Social Welfare in 1953. 'Cooperation in externals' led to establishment of Lutheran welfare councils, federations, and associations in New York City, Chicago, Ohio, Washington state, and elsewhere. The Armed Services Commission (called Armed Forces Commission beginning in 1965) cooperated with the National Lutheran Council in maintaining service centers for military personnel." The Department of Social Welfare in the Missouri Synod was the forerunner to the "Human Care" component in LCMS World Relief and Human Care.

Conclusion

"The venerable ecumenical slogan 'doctrine divides, but service unites' no longer seems valid."[61] Even those within the ecumenical movement recognize that *diakonia* without agreement in doctrine, a common philosophy or worldview, or a common ethic is incapable of producing visible unity of the church on earth. Without a common foundation and agreement in doctrine, *diakonia* (works of service and mercy) become nearly indistinguishable from humanitarian aid provided by government or other secular and non-religious organizations. Without agreement on "ethics" or "Christian ethos" (to speak in Lutheran categories), various church bodies are incapable of agreeing on common works of service. For instance, if one church body holds that homosexual unions or marriages are ethically acceptable and another church body does not, how can these two church bodies cooperate in placing children through an adoption agency? Ultimately, a common ethic or Christian ethos comes from theology and doctrine. In a certain sense, the ecumenical movement has done the church a favor by disproving its own mantra that "doctrine divides but service unites" over the past century. Whether or not the ecumenical movement wishes to recognize the fact, it has demonstrated that service without agreement in doctrine will not ultimately provide unity to the church.

It is no accident of history or coincidence that Lutheran churches in America coined the phrase "cooperation in externals" around the same time that the ecumenical movement proclaimed, "doctrine divides, but service unites."[62] As churches of different confessions and denominations began to cooperate in social and humanitarian projects around the world, Lutherans did not want to be left behind. At the same time, Lutherans, especially Confessional Lutherans, recognized that the lack of doctrinal agreement and fellowship prevented certain types of cooperation. The formulation of "cooperation in externals" was an attempt to delineate a realm where Lutheran churches could cooperate with other Christians and even with non-religious humanitarian organizations. In a certain sense, "cooperation in externals" is an attempt to address what it means for the church to exist in two realms or two kingdoms and to define the role of Christian vocation in the world.[63] "Externals" are matters not connected to the sacred, that is, the pulpit, the altar, and the font. In theory, such a definition of "externals" is rather broad and all encompassing. However, the further removed the parties who wish to cooperate are from a common ethical and philosophical framework, the more likely that the so-called "externals" will touch upon the sacred.[64]

---

[61] Lindberg, 680.

[62] Sasse, "The Question of the Church's Unity," 180. "It belongs to the unfathomable mysteries of the history of the church that it experiences mighty movements, independent from all national and confessional boundaries, which pass through all of Christianity and transform it both inwardly and outwardly."

[63] We might have done much better to address these questions in terms of the doctrine of the two kingdoms and the doctrine of Christian vocation rather than in terms of "cooperation in externals."

[64] For example, if a group of different denominations band together for a legal brief in order to promote religious freedom, the common ethic or philosophical framework is not a union of religious belief but rather the legal principle that religions

A re-examination of the principle of "cooperation in externals" is in order for the inter-Lutheran community because many Lutheran church bodies have inherited the principle from The Lutheran Church—Missouri Synod without critical or thoughtful evaluation. In the current pluralistic age, it is perhaps more important now than previously to consider what "externals" can be cooperated in without compromising confession. As more church bodies within the Lutheran World Federation ordain or consider the ordination of women and homosexuals, confessional Lutheran church bodies need to consider if they can cooperate in so-called externals. Or does such cooperation end up compromising their confession, or even worse, open the door for such practices to enter their church?

As many in the ecumenical movement recognized, large amounts of money are involved in humanitarian work.[65] Confessional church bodies need to question themselves whether the tithes and donations of their church members given to serve the neighbor out of love for Christ, can be given to church bodies and organizations that promote women's ordination, homosexual unions and marriages, homosexual adoption, abortion, euthanasia, and so on. Many inter-Lutheran and inter-denominational organizations intentionally limit or forbid the proclamation of the gospel in proximity to the giving out of humanitarian aid. Careful thought needs to be given to whether cooperation with church bodies, groups, and organizations that promote an "ethos" different from that of historic Christianity can be done without compromising confession. It seems that such cooperation without compromise will become increasingly difficult. Such a reconsideration of cooperation in externals also may alter some arrangements in the mission field. Working alone for the sake of the confession of faith is not some- thing to be criticized and in fact may be very commendable.

Ultimately, Christian works of mercy (*diakonia*) flow out of the gifts that Christ has given his church. Christ's love for humankind expressed in his suffering, death, and resurrection along with his forgiving gifts of absolution, baptism, communion, and preaching give the Christian a heart to love his neighbor, whoever that may be. Ultimately, it is the common confession of faith and the recognition that we are part of Christ's body because he has put his holy name upon us in baptism and has made us a part of his body by giving us his body and blood in Holy Communion. Doctrine and service are connected. Service disconnected from the sacred things does not remain Christian for long. Doctrine without works of service to the neighbor is a dead faith.[66] We need to reclaim the connection between doctrine and service, faith and works, and the connection of *diakonia* in close proximity to the Lord's altar. As Hermann Sasse wrote, "There is no unity of Christianity without deep and serious

---

have the right to practice unencumbered by the State or other hindrances.

[65] Cranford, "Aid and the Unity of the Church," 156. "It is simply that the major obstacle to church unity in many places in the world is not theological or doctrinal — it's money."

[66] James 2:17

wrestling over the truth, without the seriousness which, in dialogue of confession with confession, glosses over no difficulty."[67] Without doctrine and truth, works of service cease to be Christian. If such service is not Christian, the church needs to ask why it has engaged in such activity.

---

[67] Sasse, "The Question of the Church's Unity," 194.

DESCENT FROM THE CROSS
"Pilate was surprised to hear that he should have already died … And when he learned from the centurion that he was dead, he granted the corpse to Joseph." Mark 15:44a, 45. c. 1509–1510

Fight, Work, Pray!

The Blessed Sacrament of the Holy and True Body of Christ, and the Brotherhoods

BY MARTIN LUTHER, 1519

TRANSLATED BY JEREMIAH J. SCHINDEL
REVISED BY E. THEODORE BACHMANN
INTRODUCTION BY E. THEODORE BACHMANN

INTRODUCTION

This last treatise in Luther's trilogy of 1519 on the sacraments[1] is his first extended statement on the Lord's Supper. He addressed it specifically to laymen[2] and dedicated it to Margaret, duchess of Brunswick. He also made it double-pronged in that he contrasted the spiritual reality of the communion with the corrupt practices of certain fraternal groups; this accounts for the bifocal title.

Luther structures this treatise according to the three parts of the sacrament: the outward sign (paragraphs 1–3, but cf. 14–16), the inward significance (4–16), and the living faith (17–22). He then appends his critique of the brotherhoods.

His proposal that the laity should receive both of the elements was promptly attacked by Duke George of Saxony when he read one of the first copies just before Christmas, 1519. By December 27 he was complaining to the Elector Frederick of Saxony, and soon forwarded his protests also to the Saxon bishops of Meissen and Merseburg. Later Pope Leo X echoed this protest in the bull of June 15, 1520, which condemned forty-one of Luther's alleged errors.

Here, as yet, Luther raised no such controversial issues as the sacrifice of the mass or the mode of the Real Presence. In fact there is a strong suggestion that he probably still accepted the doctrine of transubstantiation. The main thing is that here he offered a practical interpretation of what the body of Christ means in the life of those who would seek to die as well as to live like Christians.

---

[1] See pp. 5, 25.

[2] The subtitle read, *"Fur die Leyen."* WA 2, 739.

Footnote page references refer to LUTHER'S WORKS VOL. 35.

Ecclesiastically, Luther admitted, a person can be excommunicated and thus deprived of the formal ministrations of the papal hierarchy. But what Luther is here talking about is a fellowship that goes deeper and rises higher than human designs. Therefore Luther could later show uncommon confidence in burning the bull of Leo X; no such device, he believed, could ever separate him from the communion of saints.[3]

The third part was theologically the crux of the treatise. The nature of faith, Luther points out, is all too often misunderstood, particularly because of the confusing terminology employed by the scholastic theologians. In trying to guarantee the objective reality of the sacrament, the scholastics had called its celebration an *opus operatum*, a faithless work. Luther, on the contrary, contended for the sacrament as an *opus operantis*, a working faith.

This led him to the practical problems of Christian living. Between the sacraments on the one hand, and an upright moral and ethical life on the other, Luther saw a profound connection. The brotherhoods or fraternal associations provided a kind of case study for Luther's sacramentally sensitive theological ethics. Societies or sodalities of laymen organized for charitable and devotional purposes; they also filled a social need among the workers in the various trades and occupations from which they drew their membership. Luther looked upon them as centers of group selfishness, spiritual pride, and immoral conduct, far removed from the opposite pole of the communion of saints.

The following translation, based on one made originally by Jeremiah J. Schindel,[4] is from the original printing by Johann Grünenberg, *Eyn Sermon von dem Hochwirdigen Sacrament, des heyligen waren Leychnams Christi. Und von den Bruderschafften,* that appeared in Wittenberg some time before December 24, 1519, and has been reproduced with annotations from later texts in *WA* 2, (738) 742–758. By 1525 a total of fourteen editions had come out in German, and in 1524 a translation in Latin.

---

[3] Cf. *A Treatise Concerning the Ban* (1520). PE 2, (35) 37–54.
[4] *PE* 2, (7) 9–31.

THE BLESSED SACRAMENT OF THE HOLY AND TRUE BODY OF CHRIST, AND THE BROTHERHOODS

1. The holy sacrament of the altar, or of the holy and true body[1] of Christ, also has three parts[2] which it is necessary for us to know. The first is the sacrament, or sign. The second is the significance of this sacrament. The third is the faith required with each of the first two. These three parts must be found in every sacrament. The sacrament must be external and visible, having some material form or appearance. The significance must be internal and spiritual, within the spirit of the person. Faith must make both of them together operative and useful.

2. The sacrament, or external sign, consists in the form or appearance of bread and wine, just as baptism has water as its *sign*; only the bread and wine must be used in eating and drinking, just as the water of baptism is used by immersion or pouring. For the sacrament, or sign, must be received, or at least desired, if it is to work a blessing. Of course at present both kinds are not given to the people daily, as in former times.[3] But this is not necessary since the priesthood partakes of it daily in sight of the people. It is enough that the people desire it daily and at present receive one kind, as the Christian Church ordains and provides.[4]

3. For my part, however, I would consider it a good thing if the church should again decree[5] in a general council that all persons be given both kinds, like the priests. Not because one kind is insufficient, since indeed the desire of faith is alone sufficient, as St. Augustine says, "Why do you prepare stomach and teeth? Only believe, and you have already partaken of the sacrament."[6] But it would be fitting and fine that the form, or sign, of the sacrament be given not in part only, but in its entirety, just as I said of baptism: it would be more fitting to immerse in the water than to pour with it, for the sake of the completeness and perfection of the sign.[7] For this sacrament [of the Body of Christ], as we shall see, signifies the complete union and the undivided fellowship of the saints; and this is poorly and unfittingly indicated by [distributing]

---

[1] *Waren Leychnams* is the actual body which was given into death. *MA*³, Er 2, 540, n. 382, 2.

[2] Cf. *The Sacrament of Penance*, in this volume, p. 11, and *The Holy and Blessed Sacrament of Baptism*, in this volume, pp. 29–30.

[3] The custom of giving only the bread but not the wine to the laity was enacted into canon law by the Council of Constance which burned an earlier advocate of both kinds, John Huss, as a heretic, even though the council itself admitted the custom's divergence from the institution of Jesus and the practice of the early church. Denzinger, *The Sources of Catholic Dogma*, No. 626.

[4] Later Luther continued to allow for the voluntary use of one kind, but he soon expressed himself more forthrightly on the propriety of both kinds and the wickedness of forbidding both kinds. Cf. *A Treatise on the New Testament, that is, the Holy Mass*, in this volume, pp. 106–107. LW 36, 19–28.

[5] The Council of Basel had concluded the *Compactata* of Prague (November 30, 1433), which reversed the decision of Constance to the extent of allowing the followers of Huss to administer the sacrament in both kinds. Cf. LW 36 27, and 13.

[6] *Sermo* 112, cap. 5. Migne 38, 645.

[7] Cf. p. 29.

only one part of the sacrament. Nor is there as great a danger in the use of the cup as is supposed,[8] since the people seldom go to this sacrament. Besides, Christ was well aware of all future dangers, and yet he saw fit to institute both kinds for the use of all his Christians.

4. The *significance* or effect of this sacrament is fellowship of all the saints. From this it derives its common name *synaxis* [Greek] or *communio* [Latin], that is, fellowship. And the Latin *communicare* [commune or communicate], or as we say in German, *zum sacrament gehen* [go to the sacrament], means to take part in this fellowship. Hence it is that Christ and all saints are one spiritual body,[9] just as the inhabitants of a city are one community and body, each citizen being a member of the other and of the entire city. All the saints, therefore, are members of Christ and of the church, which is a spiritual and eternal city of God.[10] And whoever is taken into this city is said to be received into the community of saints and to be incorporated into Christ's spiritual body and made a member of him. On the other hand *excommunicare* [excommunicate] means to put out of the community and to sever a member from this body; and that is called in our language "putting one under the ban"— though a distinction [is to be made in this regard] as I shall show in the following treatise, concerning the ban.[11]

To receive this sacrament in bread and wine, then, is nothing else than to receive a sure sign of this fellowship and incorporation with Christ and all saints. It is as if a citizen were given a sign, a document, or some other token to assure him that he is a citizen of the city, a member of that particular community. St. Paul says this very thing in I Corinthians 10[:17], "Because there is one bread, we who are many are one body, for we all partake of the one bread."

5. This fellowship consists in this, that all the spiritual possessions of Christ and his saints[12] are shared with and become the common property of him who receives this sacrament. Again, all sufferings and sins also become common property; and thus love engenders love in return and [mutual love] unites. To carry out our homely

---

[8] The danger, readily conceded by pious laity who trembled at the thought of it, was that a drop of the consecrated wine might fall to the floor. Since the bread was regarded as the more important anyway — and could be placed in the mouth of the communicant without his even having to touch it — it seemed possible, by dispensing with reception of the wine, to avoid the danger of desecrating the sacrament. Cf. Albert Hauek (ed.), *Realencyklopädie für protestantische Theologie und Kirche* (3rd ed., 24 vols.; Leipzig: Hinrichs, 1896–1913), XII, 721.

[9] Cf. Rom. 12:5; I Cor. 12:5.

[10] Cf. Is. 60:14; Heb. 12:22; Rev. 3:12.

[11] See *A Treatise Concerning the Ban* (1520) (PE 2, 35–54), where Luther distinguishes between the external ban (excommunication) which excludes from the church's sacramental fellowship and the internal ban (sin and unbelief) which excludes from the fellowship with Christ. Cf. in this volume, p. 144.

[12] As early as 1515–1516 in his lectures on Romans [12:13] Luther distinguished between the contemporary understanding of "saints" as those who "are blessed and participating in glory" and the biblical understanding of "saints" as "all those who believe in Christ." WA 56, 469; MA3, Er 2, 398. This second sense is implicit in his use of the term here and throughout this treatise.

figure, it is like a city where every citizen shares with all the others the city's name, honor, freedom, trade, customs, usages, help, support, protection, and the like, while at the same time he shares all the dangers of fire and flood, enemies and death, losses, taxes, and the like. For he who would share in the profits must also share in the costs,[13] and ever recompense love with love.[14] Here we see that whoever injures one citizen injures an entire city and all its citizens; whoever benefits one [citizen] deserves favor and thanks from all the others. So also in our natural body, as St. Paul says in I Corinthians 12[:25–26], where he gives this sacrament a spiritual explanation, "The members ... have the same care for one another. 26 If one member suffers, all suffer together; if one member is honored, all rejoice together." This is obvious: if anyone's foot hurts him, yes, even the little toe, the eye at once looks at it, the fingers grasp it, the face puckers, the whole body bends over to it, and all are concerned with this small member; again, once it is cared for all the other members are benefited. This comparison must be noted well if one wishes to understand this sacrament, for Scripture uses it for the sake of the unlearned.

6. In this sacrament, therefore, man is given through the priest a sure sign from God himself that he is thus united with Christ and his saints and has all things in common [with them], that Christ's sufferings and life are his own, together with the lives and sufferings of all the saints. Therefore whoever does injury to [the believer], does injury to Christ and all the saints, as he says through the prophet [Zech. 2:8], "He who touches you touches the apple of [my] eye." On the other hand whoever does him a kindness does it to Christ and all his saints; as he says in Matthew 25[:40], "As you did it to one of the least of these my brothers, you did it to me." Again, man must be willing to share all the burdens and misfortunes of Christ and his saints, the cost as well as the profit. Let us consider more fully these two [sides of the fellowship].

7. Now adversity assails us in more than one form. There is, in the first place, the sin that remains in our flesh after baptism: the inclination to anger, hatred, pride, unchastity, and so forth. This sin assails us as long as we live.[15] Here we not only need the help of the community [of saints] and of Christ, in order that they might with us fight this sin, but it is also necessary that Christ and his saints intercede for us before God, so that this sin may not be charged to our account by God's strict judgment. Therefore in order to strengthen and encourage us against this same sin, God gives us this sacrament, as much as to say, "Look, many kinds of sin are assailing you; take this sign by which I give you my pledge that this sin is assailing not only you but also

---

[13] Cf. the English aphorism, "What's none of my profit shall be none of my peril" (Vincent Stuckey Lean, *Lean's Collectanea* [Bristol: Arrowsmith, 1904], IV, 178) with its German equivalents in Karl F. Wander (ed.), *Deutsches Sprichwörter-Lexikon* (5 vols.; Leipzig: Brockhaus, 1867–1880), I, 1557, "*Geniessen,*" Nos. 3, 4, 10, 14.

[14] Cf. the English aphorism, "Love is love's reward" (*Lean's Collectanea*, IV, 39), with its German equivalents in Wander (ed.), *Sprichwörter-Lexikon*, III, 136ff., "*Liebe,*" Nos. 146, 386, 388, 635, 661, and especially No. 410 which also cites the English, "Love can neither be bought nor sold, its only price is love."

[15] Cf. pp. 30–34.

my Son, Christ, and all his saints in heaven and on earth. Therefore take heart and be bold. You are not fighting alone. Great help and support are all around you." King David speaks thus of this bread, "Bread to strengthen man's heart" [Ps. 104:15]. And the Scriptures in numerous places ascribe to this sacrament the property of strengthening, as in Acts 9[:18–19] [where it is written] of St. Paul, he "was baptized; and taking food, he was strengthened."

In the second place the evil spirit assails us unceasingly with many sins and afflictions. In the third place the world, full of wickedness, entices and persecutes us and is altogether bad. Finally our own guilty conscience assails us with our past sins; and there is the fear of death and the pains of hell. All of these afflictions make us weary and weak, unless we seek strength in this fellowship, where strength is to be found.

8. Whoever is in despair, distressed by a sin-stricken conscience or terrified by death or carrying some other burden upon his heart, if he would be rid of them all, let him go joyfully to the sacrament of the altar and lay down his woe in the midst of the community [of saints] and seek help from the entire company of the spiritual body — just as a citizen whose property has suffered damage or misfortune at the hands of his enemies makes complaint to his town council and fellow citizens and asks them for help. The immeasurable grace and mercy of God are given us in this sacrament to the end that we might put from us all misery and tribulation [*anfechtung*] and lay it upon the community [of saints], and especially on Christ. Then we may with joy find strength and comfort, and say, "Though I am a sinner and have fallen, though this or that misfortune has befallen me, nevertheless I will go to the sacrament to receive a sign from God that I have on my side Christ's righteousness, life, and sufferings, with all holy angels and the blessed in heaven and all pious men on earth. If I die, I am not alone in death; if I suffer, they suffer with me. [I know that] all my misfortune is shared with Christ and the saints, because I have a sure sign of their love toward me." See, this is the benefit to be derived from this sacrament; this is the use we should make of it. Then the heart cannot but rejoice and be strengthened.

9. When you have partaken of this sacrament, therefore, or desire to partake of it, you must in turn share the misfortunes of the fellowship, as has been said. But what are these? Christ in heaven and the angels, together with the saints, have no misfortunes, except when injury is done to the truth and to the Word of God. Indeed, as we have said, every bane and blessing of all the saints on earth affects them. Here your heart must go out in love and learn that this is a sacrament of love. As love and support are given you, you in turn must render love and support to Christ in his needy ones. You must feel with sorrow all the dishonor done to Christ in his holy Word, all the misery of Christendom, all the unjust suffering of the innocent, with which the world is everywhere filled to overflowing. You must fight, work, pray, and — if you cannot do more — have heartfelt sympathy. See, this is what it means to bear in your turn the misfortune and adversity of Christ and his saints. Here the saying of Paul is fulfilled,

"Bear one another's burdens, and so fulfil the law of Christ" [Gal. 6:2]. See, as you uphold all of them, so they all in turn uphold you; and all things are in common, both good and evil. Then all things become easy, and the evil spirit cannot stand up against this fellowship.

When Christ instituted the sacrament, he said, "This is my body which is given for you, this is my blood which is poured out for you. As often as you do this, remember me."[16] It is as if he were saying, "I am the Head, I will be the first to give himself for you. I will make your suffering and misfortune my own and will bear it for you, so that you in your turn may do the same for me and for one another, allowing all things to be common property, in me, and with me. And I leave you this sacrament as a sure token of all this, in order that you may not forget me, but daily call to mind and admonish one another by means of what I did and am still doing for you, in order that you may be strengthened, and also bear one another in the same way."

10. This is also a reason, indeed the chief reason, why this sacrament is received many times, while baptism is received but once. Baptism is the taking up or entering upon a new life,[17] in the course of which boundless adversities assail us, with sins and sufferings, both our own and those of others. There is the devil, the world, and our own flesh and conscience, as I have said. They never cease to hound us and oppress us. Therefore we need the strength, support, and help of Christ and of his saints. These are pledged to us here, as in a sure sign, by which we are made one with them — incorporated into them — and all our woe is laid down in the midst of the community [of saints].

For this reason it even happens that this holy sacrament is of little or no benefit to those who have no misfortune or anxiety, or who do not sense their adversity. For it is given only to those who need strength and comfort, who have timid hearts and terrified consciences, and who are assailed by sin, or have even fallen into sin. How could it do anything for untroubled and secure spirits, who neither need nor desire it? For the Mother of God[18] says, "He has filled the hungry [Luke 1:53], and comforts them that are distressed."

11. In order that the disciples, therefore, might by all means be worthy and well prepared for this sacrament, Christ first made them sorrowful, held before them his departure and death, by which they became exceedingly troubled. And then he greatly terrified them when he said that one of them would betray him. When they were thus full of sorrow and anxiety, disturbed by sorrow and the sin of betrayal, then

---

[16] Cf. p. 82, n. 5.

[17] Cf. p. 30.

[18] Luther often called the Virgin Mary by this term of veneration which was common in Western Christendom. Cf. his discussion of the name in *The Magnificat* (1521). LW 21, 326–327.

they were worthy, and he gave them his holy body[19] to strengthen them.[20] By which he teaches us that this sacrament is strength and comfort for those who are troubled and distressed by sin and evil. St. Augustine says the same thing, "This food demands only hungry souls, and is shunned by none so greatly as by a sated soul which does not need it."[21] Thus the Jews were required to eat the Passover with bitter herbs, standing and in haste [Ex. 12:8, 11]; this too signifies that this sacrament demands souls that are desirous, needy, and sorrowful. Now if one will make the afflictions of Christ and of all Christians his own, defend the truth, oppose unrighteousness, and help bear the needs of the innocent and the sufferings of all Christians, then he will find affliction and adversity enough, over and above that which his evil nature, the world, the devil, and sin daily inflict upon him. And it is even God's will and purpose to set so many hounds upon us and oppress us, and everywhere to prepare bitter herbs for us, so that we may long for this strength and take delight in the holy sacrament, and thus be worthy (that is, desirous) of it.

12. It is Christ's will, then, that we partake of it frequently, in order that we may remember him and exercise ourselves in this fellowship according to his example. For if his example were no longer kept before us, the fellowship also would soon be forgotten. So we at present see to our sorrow that many masses are held and yet the Christian fellowship which should be preached, practiced, and kept before us by Christ's example has virtually perished. So much so that we hardly know any more what purpose this sacrament serves or how it should be used. Indeed with our masses we frequently destroy this fellowship and pervert everything. This is the fault of the preachers who do not preach the gospel or the sacraments, but their humanly devised fables about the many works [of satisfaction][22] to be done and the ways to live aright.

But in times past this sacrament was so properly used, and the people were taught to understand this fellowship so well, that they even gathered food and material goods in the church, and there — as St. Paul writes in I Corinthians 11[23] — distributed among those who were in need. We have a vestige of this [practice] in the little word "collect" in the mass,[24] which means a general collection, just as a common fund is gathered to be given to the poor. Those were the days too when so many became martyrs and saints. There were fewer masses, but much strength and blessing resulted from the masses; Christians cared for one another, supported one another, sympathized with one another, bore one another's burdens and affliction. This has all

---

[19] *Leychnam*; cf. p. 49, n. 1.

[20] Following Matt. 26:20–25 and Mark 14:17–21, Luther places the announcement of the betrayal prior to the institution of the Lord's Supper.

[21] Cf. Augustine's commentary on Ps. 22:26 (Vulgate 21:27) in Migne 36, 178.

[22] Cf. pp. 12–18.

[23] I Cor. 11:21, 33; cf. Acts 2:44–46.

[24] Cf. p. 95.

disappeared, and now there remain only the many masses and the many who receive this sacrament without in the least understanding or practicing what it signifies.

13. There are those, indeed, who would gladly share in the profits but not in the costs. That is, they like to hear that in this sacrament the help, fellowship, and support of all the saints are promised and given to them. But they are unwilling in their turn to belong also to this fellowship. They will not help the poor, put up with sinners, care for the sorrowing, suffer with the suffering, intercede for others, defend the truth, and at the risk of [their own] life, property, and honor seek the betterment of the church and of all Christians. They are unwilling because they fear the world. They do not want to have to suffer disfavor, harm, shame, or death, although it is God's will that they be thus driven — for the sake of the truth and of their neighbors — to desire the great grace and strength of this sacrament. They are self-seeking persons, whom this sacrament does not benefit. Just as we could not put up with a citizen who wanted to be helped, protected, and made free by the community, and yet in his turn would do nothing for it nor serve it, no, we on our part must make the evil of others our own, if we desire Christ and his saints to make our evil their own. Then will the fellowship be complete, and justice be done to the sacrament. For the sacrament has no blessing and significance unless love grows daily and so changes a person that he is made one with all others.

14. To signify this fellowship, God has appointed such signs of this sacrament as in every way serve this purpose and by their very form stimulate and motivate us to this fellowship. For just as the bread is made out of many grains ground and mixed together, and out of the bodies of many grains there comes the body of one bread,[25] in which each grain loses its form and body and takes upon itself the common body of the bread; and just as the drops of wine, in losing their own form, become the body of one common wine and drink — so it is and should be with us, if we use this sacrament properly. Christ with all saints, by his love, takes upon himself our form [Phil. 2:7], fights with us against sin, death, and all evil. This enkindles in us such love that we take on his form, rely upon his righteousness, life, and blessedness. And through the interchange of his blessings and our misfortunes, we become one loaf, one bread, one body, one drink, and have all things in common. O this is a great sacrament,[26] says St. Paul, that Christ and the church are one flesh and bone. Again through this same love, we are to be changed and to make the infirmities of all other Christians our own; we are to take upon ourselves their form and their necessity,

---

[25] The figure is very ancient, going back at least into the second century as attested by a document unknown to Luther, *The Didache* 9:4, "As this piece [of bread] was scattered over the hills [the reference is likely to the sowing of wheat on the hillsides of Judea] and then was brought together and made one, so let your church be brought together from the ends of the earth into your kingdom." Cyril C. Richardson (trans., ed.), *Early Christian Fathers* ("The Library of Christian Classics," Vol. I [Philadelphia: Westminster Press, 1953]), p. 175.

[26] In the Vulgate of St. Jerome, the Greek word *mysterion* (mystery) in Eph. 5:32 is translated *sacramentum*. Cf. Luther's later discussion of the term in LW 36, 93–95.

and all the good that is within our power we are to make theirs, that they may profit from it. That is real fellowship, and that is the true significance of this sacrament. In this way we are changed into one another and are made into a community by love. Without love there can be no such change.

15. Christ appointed these two forms of bread and wine, rather than any other, as a further indication of the very union and fellowship which is in this sacrament. For there is no more intimate, deep, and indivisible union than the union of the food with him who is fed. For the food enters into and is assimilated by his very nature, and becomes one substance with the person who is fed. Other unions, achieved by such things as nails, glue, cords, and the like, do not make one indivisible substance of the objects joined together. Thus in the sacrament we too become united with Christ, and are made one body with all the saints, so that Christ cares for us and acts in our behalf. As if he were what we are, he makes whatever concerns us to concern him as well, and even more than it does us. In turn we so care for Christ, as if we were what he is, which indeed we shall finally be — we shall be conformed to his likeness. As St. John says, "We know that when he appears we shall be like him" [I John 3:2]. So deep and complete is the fellowship of Christ and all the saints with us. Thus our sins assail him, while his righteousness protects us. For the union makes all things common, until at last Christ completely destroys sin in us and makes us like himself, at the Last Day. Likewise by the same love we are to be united with our neighbors, we in them and they in us.

16. Besides all this, Christ did not institute these two forms solitary and alone, but he gave his true natural flesh in the bread, and his natural true blood in the wine, that he might give a really perfect sacrament or sign. For just as the bread is changed[27] into his true natural body[28] and the wine into his natural true blood, so truly are we also drawn and changed into the spiritual body, that is, into the fellowship of Christ and all saints and by this sacrament put into possession of all the virtues and mercies of Christ and his saints, as was said above[29] of a citizen who is taken and incorporated into the protection and freedom of the city and the entire community. For this reason he instituted not simply the one form, but two separate forms — his flesh under the bread, his blood under the wine — to indicate that not only his life and good works, which are indicated by his flesh and which he accomplished in his flesh, but also his passion and martyrdom, which are indicated by his blood and in which he poured out his blood, are all our own. And we, being drawn into them, may use and profit from them.

---

[27] *Vorwandelt.* While this term and the imagery involving change are associated with the doctrine of transubstantiation, it is clear that, through rejecting all scholastic speculation concerning substance (see p. 63), Luther is already beginning to call into question that very doctrine which within a year he was to condemn as "the second captivity of the sacrament" (LW 36, 28–35). Cf. Charles E. Hay (trans.) Reinhold Seeberg's *History of Doctrines* (Grand Rapids: Baker, 1952), II, 286, n. 1, "Literally, transubstantiation is here retained, but really Luther is only concerned to hold fast the idea that the body is 'in' the bread."

[28] *Leychnam*; cf. p. 49, n. 1.

[29] See pp. 50–55.

17. So it is clear from all this that this holy sacrament is nothing else than a divine sign, in which are pledged, granted, and imparted Christ and all saints together with all their works, sufferings, merits, mercies, and possessions, for the comfort and strengthening of all who are in anxiety and sorrow, persecuted by the devil, sins, the world, the flesh, and every evil. And to receive the sacrament is nothing else than to desire all this and firmly to believe that it is done.

Here, now, follows the third part of the sacrament,[30] that is, the *faith* on which everything depends. For it is not enough to know what the sacrament is and signifies. It is not enough that you know it is a fellowship and a gracious exchange or blending of our sin and suffering with the righteousness of Christ and his saints. You must also desire it and firmly believe that you have received it. Here the devil and our own nature wage their fiercest fight, so that faith may by no means stand firm. There are those who practice their arts and subtleties by trying [to fathom] what becomes of the bread when it is changed into Christ's flesh and of the wine when it is changed into his blood and how the whole Christ, his flesh and blood, can be encompassed in so small a portion of bread and wine. It does not matter if you do not see[31] it. It is enough to know that it is a divine sign in which Christ's flesh and blood are truly present. The how and the where, we leave to him.[32]

18. See to it that here you exercise and strengthen your faith, so that when you are sorrowful or when your sins press you and you go to the sacrament or hear mass, you do so with a hearty desire for this sacrament and for what it signifies. Then do not doubt that you have what the sacrament signifies, that is, be certain that Christ and all his saints are coming to you with all their virtues, sufferings, and mercies, to live, work, suffer, and die with you, and that they desire to be wholly yours, having all things in common with you. If you will exercise and strengthen this faith, then you will experience what a rich, joyous, and bountiful wedding feast your God has prepared for you upon the altar. Then you will understand what the great feast of King Ahasuerus signifies [Esther 1:5]; and you will see what that wedding feast is for which God slew his oxen and fat calves, as it is written in the gospel [Matt. 22:2–4]. Then your heart will become truly free and confident, strong and courageous against all enemies [Ps. 23:5]. For who will fear any calamity if he is sure that Christ and all his saints are with him and have all things, evil or good, in common with him? So we read in Acts 2[:46] that the disciples of Christ broke this bread and ate with great gladness of heart. Since, then, this work is so great that the smallness of our souls

---

[30] The three parts are listed on p. 49.

[31] *Suchist*, literally "seek." WA 2, 750, n. 1 and MA3 1, 390, 17 both suggest that *siehest* may have been intended. There need not have been a typographical error here, however. The Indogermanic antecedent of *suchen* in meaning was close to the Latin *sagio*, to perceive. Luther may have been using the term with its early connotations, in the sense of tracing a thing down or ferreting it out until you fathom or grasp it. Cf. Jacob Grimm and Wilhelm Grimm (eds.), *Deutsches Wörterbuch* (16 vols.; Leipzig: Hirzel, 1854–1954), X, 835.

[32] See *The Babylonian Captivity of the Church*. LW 36, 32–35.

would not dare to desire it, to say nothing of hoping for it or expecting it, therefore it is necessary and profitable to go often to the sacrament, or at least in the daily mass to exercise and strengthen this faith on which the whole thing depends and for the sake of which it was instituted. For if you doubt, you do God the greatest dishonor and make him out to be a faithless liar; if you cannot believe, then pray for faith, as was said earlier in the other treatise.[33]

19. See to it also that you give yourself to everyone in fellowship and by no means exclude anyone in hatred or anger. For this sacrament of fellowship, love, and unity cannot tolerate discord and disunity. You must take to heart the infirmities and needs of others, as if they were your own. Then offer to others your strength, as if it were their own, just as Christ does for you in the sacrament. This is what it means to be changed into one another through love, out of many particles to become one bread and drink, to lose one's own form and take on that which is common to all.[34]

For this reason slanderers and those who wickedly judge and despise others cannot but receive death in the sacrament, as St. Paul writes in I Corinthians 11[:29]. For they do not do unto their neighbor what they seek from Christ, and what the sacrament indicates. They begrudge others anything good; they have no sympathy for them; they do not care for others as they themselves desire to be cared for by Christ. And then they fall into such blindness that they do not know what else to do in this sacrament except to fear and honor Christ there present[35] with their own prayers and devotion. When they have done this, they think they have done their whole duty. But Christ has given his holy body for this purpose, that the thing signified by the sacrament — the fellowship, the change wrought by love — may be put into practice. And Christ values his spiritual body, which is the fellowship of his saints, more than his own natural body. To him it is more important, especially in this sacrament, that faith in the fellowship with him and with his saints may be properly exercised and become strong in us; and that we, in keeping with it, may properly exercise our fellowship with one another. This purpose of Christ the blind worshipers do not perceive. In their devoutness they go on daily saying and hearing mass, but they remain every day the same; indeed every day they become worse but do not perceive it.

Therefore take heed. It is more needful that you discern the spiritual than the natural body of Christ; and faith in the spiritual body is more necessary than faith in the natural body. For the natural without the spiritual profits us nothing in this sacrament; a change must occur [in the communicant] and be exercised through love.

---

[33] Cf. *The Sacrament of Penance* (1519). pp. 3–22.

[34] See pp. 59–60.

[35] *Kegenwertig*, i.e., present in the consecrated host.

20. There are many who regardless of this change of love and faith rely upon the fact that the mass or the sacrament is, as they say, *opus gratum opere operato*,[36] that is, a work which of itself pleases God, even though they who perform it do not please him. From this they conclude that however unworthily masses are said, it is nonetheless a good thing to have many masses, since harm comes [only] to those who say or use them unworthily. I grant everyone [the right to] his opinion, but such fables do not please me. For, [if you desire] to speak in these terms, there is no creature or work that does not of itself please God, as is written in Genesis 1[:31], "God saw all his works and they pleased him." What is the result if bread, wine, gold, and all good things are misused, even though of themselves they are pleasing to God? Why, the consequence of that is condemnation. So also here: the more precious the sacrament, the greater the harm which comes upon the whole community [of saints] from its misuse. For it was not instituted for its own sake, that it might please God, but for our sake, that we might use it right, exercise our faith by it, and through it become pleasing to God. If it is merely an *opus operatum*,[37] it works only harm everywhere; it must become an *opus operantis*.[38] Just as bread and wine, no matter how much they may please God in and of themselves, work only harm if they are not used, so it is not enough that the sacrament be merely completed (that is, *opus operatum*); it must also be used in faith (that is, *opus operantis*). And we must take care lest with such dangerous interpretations the sacrament's power and virtue be lost on us, and faith perish utterly through the false security of the [outwardly] completed sacrament.

All this comes from the fact that they pay more attention in this sacrament to Christ's natural body than to the fellowship, the spiritual body. Christ on the cross was also a completed work which was well pleasing to God. But to this day the Jews have found it a stumbling block because they did not construe it as a work that is made use of in faith. See to it, then, that for you the sacrament is an *opus operantis*, that is, a work that is made use of, that is well pleasing to God not because of what it is in itself but because of your faith and your good use of it. The Word of God too is of itself pleasing to God, but it is harmful to me unless in me it also pleases God. In short, such expressions as *opus operatum* and *opus operantis* are vain words of men,[39] more of a

---

[36] Literally, a work (that is) acceptable by (virtue of) the work (having been) performed.

[37] *Opus operatum* is an action that is done, completed, finished, considered as such without reference to the doer of it.

[38] *Opus operantis* is an action considered with reference to the doer of it, the action of the one acting.

[39] *Opus operatum* and *opus operantis* were terms used generally in discussion of the difference between the sacraments of the old law and those of the new. The latter, according to Alexander of Hales (d. 1245), are in their own right signs and causes of invisible grace, and hence superior to the former which were merely signs but *not causes*. "Otherwise," added Thomas Aquinas (d. 1274), "they would have obviated the necessity of Christ's passion (Gal. 2:21)." Thus the sacraments of the Old Testament *signified* the passion of Christ and its effects; but they had no *power* to justify — their effect depended rather on the faith they were able to stimulate in the believer. The sacraments of the New Testament, on the other hand, in and of themselves effectively impart grace *ex opere operato*, i.e., simply through the use of them, apart from any act of the soul. Thomas, however, still presupposed faith; not as the *cause* of the sacrament's effect to be sure, but as the *receptivity* for the sacrament's effect. Bonaventura (d. 1274) also included faith as a factor in the justification of the New Testament sacraments, only he regarded it as something supplementary to the *opus operatum*, the external action in and of itself, to

hindrance than a help. And who could tell of all the abominable abuses and misbeliefs which daily multiply about this blessed sacrament, some of which are so spiritual and holy that they might almost lead an angel astray?

Briefly, whoever would understand the abuses need only keep before him the aforesaid use and faith of this sacrament; namely, that there must be a sorrowing, hungry soul, who desires heartily the love, help, and support of the entire community — of Christ and of all Christendom — and who does not doubt that in faith [all these desires] are obtained, and who thereupon makes himself one with everyone. Whoever does not take this as his point of departure for arranging and ordering his hearing or reading of masses and his receiving of the sacrament is in error and does not use this sacrament to his salvation. It is for this reason also that the world is overrun with pestilences, wars, and other horrible plagues,[40] because with our many masses we only bring down upon us greater disfavor.

21. We see now how necessary this sacrament is for those who must face death, or other dangers of body and soul, that they not be left in them alone but be strengthened in the fellowship of Christ and all saints. This is why Christ instituted it and gave it to his disciples in the hour of their extreme need and peril. Since we then are all daily surrounded by all kinds of danger, and must at last die, we should humbly and heartily give thanks with all our powers to the God of all mercy for giving us such a gracious sign, by which — if we hold fast to it in faith — he leads and draws us through death and every danger unto himself, unto Christ and all saints.

Therefore it is also profitable and necessary that the love and fellowship of Christ and all saints be hidden, invisible, and spiritual, and that only a bodily, visible, and outward sign of it be given to us. For if this love, fellowship, and support were apparent to all, like the transient fellowship of men, we would not be strengthened

---

which the justifying grace and its effect were inseparably attached.

From this reduction of faith to something *supplementary*, it was only a step to the elimination of it as something altogether *expendable*. The step was taken by Duns Scotus (d. 1308) and Gabriel Biel (d. 1495) when they defined the subjective condition for the sacrament's effecting a blessing no longer in terms of a positive disposition, but in terms of the negative absence of any impediment. Reception of the sacrament in and of itself invariably imparts grace so long as man does not "interpose an obstacle," such as positive disbelief or mortal sin. Thus the scholastics all agreed that the sacraments impart grace *ex opere operato*. They differed as to whether faith was necessary for the *reception* of that grace. According to Duns Scotus and Gabriel Biel the necessity of faith is expressly denied and a purely passive receptivity is held to be sufficient. Intended originally to affirm that the power and effect of the sacrament are caused not by any disposition on man's part but solely by God and the sufferings of Christ, the concept *ex opere operato* thus came ultimately to mean that the proper disposition on the part of the recipient need not be one of positive faith but of merely negative passivity. It was this latest, fullest, and perhaps logical development of the scholastic view that Luther is attacking. F. Kattenbusch in Hauck (ed.), *Realencyklopädie*, XVII, 363–365.

The concept of the *opus operatum* also proved useful for guaranteeing the validity of the sacrament irrespective of the personal worthiness of the celebrating priest (see p. 102 and LW 36, 47, 55). Ultimately Luther's solution lay not in the preference for *operantis* over *operatum* but in the rejection of the *opus* altogether. The sacrament is not a good work or sacrifice on the part of man, but a testament or promise on the part of God, to be received by man in faith — not an *officium* but a *beneficium* (see p. 93 and LW 36, 35–57).

[40] Cf. I Cor. 11:30.

or trained by it to desire or put our trust in the things that are unseen and eternal [II Cor. 4:18]. Instead we would be trained to put our trust only in things that are transient and seen, and would become so accustomed to them as to be unwilling to let them go; we would not follow God, except so far as visible and tangible things led us. We would thereby be prevented from ever coming to God. For everything that is bound to time and sense must fall away, and we must learn to do without them, if we are to come to God.

For this reason the mass and this sacrament are a sign by which we train and accustom ourselves to let go of all visible love, help, and comfort, and to trust in the invisible love, help, and support of Christ and his saints. For death takes away all the things that are seen and separates us from men and transient things. To meet it, we must, therefore, have the help of the things that are unseen and eternal. And these are indicated to us in the sacrament and sign, to which we cling by faith until we finally attain to them also with sight and senses.

Thus the sacrament is for us a ford, a bridge, a door, a ship, and a stretcher, by which and in which we pass from this world into eternal life. Therefore everything depends on faith. He who does not believe is like the man who is supposed to cross the sea, but who is so timid that he does not trust the ship; and so he must remain and never be saved, because he will not embark and cross over. This is the fruit of our dependence on the senses and of our untrained faith, which shrinks from the passage across the Jordan of death; and the devil too has a gruesome hand in it.

22. This was signified long ago in Joshua 3[:14–17]. After the children of Israel had gone dry-shod through the Red Sea [Ex. 14:21–22] — in which [event] baptism was typified — they went through the Jordan also in like manner. But the priests stood with the ark in the Jordan, and the water below them was cut off, while the water above them rose up like a mountain — in which [event] this sacrament is typified. The priests hold and carry the ark in the Jordan when, in the hour of our death or peril, they preach and administer to us this sacrament, the fellowship of Christ and all saints. If we then believe, the waters below us depart; that is, the things that are seen and transient do nothing but flee from us. The waters above us, however, well up high; that is, the horrible torments of the other world, which we envision at the hour of death, terrify us as if they would overwhelm us. If, however, we pay no attention to them, and walk over with a firm faith, then we shall enter dry-shod and unharmed into eternal life.

We have, therefore, two principal sacraments in the church, baptism and the bread. Baptism leads us into a new life on earth; the bread guides us through death into eternal life. And the two are signified by the Red Sea and the Jordan, and by the two lands, one beyond and one on this side of the Jordan. This is why our Lord said at the Last Supper, "I shall not drink again of this wine until I drink it new with you in my

Father's kingdom" [Matt. 26:29]. So entirely is this sacrament intended and instituted for a strengthening against death and an entrance into eternal life.

In conclusion, the blessing of this sacrament is fellowship and love, by which we are strengthened against death and all evil. This fellowship is twofold: on the one hand we partake of Christ and all saints; on the other hand we permit all Christians to be partakers of us, in whatever way they and we are able. Thus by means of this sacrament, all self-seeking love is rooted out and gives place to that which seeks the common good of all; and through the change wrought by love there is one bread, one drink, one body, one community. This is the true unity of Christian brethren. Let us see, therefore, how the neat-looking brotherhoods, of which there are now so many, compare and square with this.

The Brotherhoods[41]

1. First let us consider the evil practices of the brotherhoods. One of these is their gluttony and drunkenness. After one or more masses are held,[42] the rest of the day and night, and other days besides, are given over to the devil; they do only what displeases God. Such mad reveling has been introduced by the evil spirit, and he calls it a brotherhood, whereas it is more a debauch and an altogether pagan, yes, a swinish way of life. It would be far better to have no brotherhoods in the world at all than to countenance such misconduct. Temporal lords and cities should unite with the clergy in abolishing it. For by it God, the saints, and all Christians are greatly dishonored; and the divine services and feast days are made into a laughingstock for the devil. Saints' days are supposed to be kept and hallowed by good works. And the brotherhood is also supposed to be a special convocation of good works; instead it has become a collecting of money for beer. What have the names of Our Lady,[43] St.

---

[41] Originally made up of monks and monasteries, later primarily of laymen, these sodalities ("fraternities," "confraternities") were associations for devotional purposes. Members were obligated to the recitation of certain prayers and the attendance upon certain masses at stipulated times. Each member was believed to participate — and, most important of all, even after death — in the benefits accruing from these "good works" of all the other members. In the case of most of the sodalities, membership (for which the fees ranged from one to twenty gulden) entitled the member to the enjoyment of certain indulgences. In 1520 little Wittenberg boasted of twenty such fraternities; Hamburg had more than one hundred. In 1519 Degenhard Peffinger of Wittenberg was a member of eight such fraternities in his home city and through their cartel relationships derived benefits from twenty-seven more in other places. The brotherhood of St. Peter in Salzburg was united in fellowship with eighty other fraternities. Hauck (ed.), *Realencyklopädie*, III, 434–437; Karl Benrath (ed.), *An den christlichen Adel deutscher Nation, von D. Martin Luther* (Halle: Verein für Reformationsgeschichte, 1884), pp. 106–107.

[42] A brotherhood usually came together monthly — often weekly — as well as on the day of its particular saint and on festival days of its related monastic order, ostensibly for pious exercises but in reality for feasting and debauchery which had long been a source of concern to the civil and ecclesiastical authorities as well as to the Reformers. Henry C. Lea, *A History of Auricular Confession and Indulgences* (Philadelphia: Lea, 1896), III, 474–476.

[43] The Carmelites were possibly the first to form sodalities with the specific purpose of devotion to the Virgin Mary, having organized in the fourteenth century the "Confraternity of Our Lady of Mount Carmel." Jackson (ed.), *The New Schaff-Herzog Encyclopedia of Religious Knowledge*, III, 226.

Anne,[44] St. Sebastian,[45] or other saints to do with your brotherhoods, in which you have nothing but gluttony, drunkenness, useless squandering of money, howling, yelling, chattering, dancing, and wasting of time? If a sow were made the patron saint of such a brotherhood she would not consent. Why then do they afflict the dear saints so miserably by taking their names in vain in such shameful practices and sins, and by dishonoring and blaspheming with such evil practices the brotherhoods named after these saints? Woe unto them who do this, and [unto them who] permit it!

2. If men desire to maintain a brotherhood, they should gather provisions and feed and serve a tableful or two of poor people, for the sake of God. The day before they should fast,[46] and on the feast day remain sober, passing the time in prayer and other good works. Then God and his saints would be truly honored; there would be improvement too, and a good example would be given to others. Or they should gather the money which they intend to squander for drink, and collect it into a common treasury, each craft for itself. Then in cases of hardship, needy fellow workmen might be helped to get started, and be lent money, or a young couple of the same craft might be fitted out respectably from this common treasury. These would be works of true brotherhood; they would make God and his saints look with favor upon the brotherhoods, of which they would then gladly be the patrons. But where men are unwilling to do this, where they insist on following the old ways of simulated brotherhood, I admonish that they not do it on the saints' days, nor in the name of the saints or of the brotherhood. Let them take some other weekday and leave the names of the saints and of their brotherhoods alone, lest the saints one day punish it. Although there is no day which is not dishonored by such doings, at least the festivals and the names of the saints should be spared. For such brotherhoods call themselves brotherhoods of the saints while they do the work of the devil.

3. There is another evil feature of the brotherhoods, and it is of a spiritual nature. That is the false opinion they have that their brotherhood is to be a benefit to no one but themselves, those who are members on the roll or who contribute. This damnably wicked opinion is an even worse evil than the first, and it is one of the reasons why God has brought it about that with their gluttony, drunkenness, and the like the brotherhoods are becoming such a mockery and blasphemy of God. For in them men learn to seek their own good, to love themselves, to be faithful only to one another, to despise others, to think themselves better than others, and to presume to stand higher before God than others. And so perishes the communion of saints, Christian love, and the true brotherhood which is established in the holy sacrament, while selfish love grows in them. That is, by means of these many external brotherhoods devoted

---

[44] According to tradition, St. Anne was the mother of the Holy Virgin; sodalities to her honor and bearing her name spread, as Kolde says, "like an epidemic" after the fourteenth century. Hauck (ed.), *Realencyklopädie*, III, 437.

[45] St. Sebastian was martyred on January 20 (year unknown) in Rome under Diocletian, who was emperor in 284–305. *Schaff-Herzog*, X, 320.

[46] Cf. pp. 39–40.

to works they oppose and destroy the one, inner, spiritual, essential brotherhood common to all saints.

When God sees this perverted state of affairs, he perverts it still more, as is written in Psalm 18[:26], "With the perverse thou wilt be perverted."[47] So God brings it to pass that they make themselves and their brotherhoods a mockery and a disgrace. And he casts them out of the common brotherhood of saints — which they have opposed and with which they do not make common cause — and into their own brotherhood of gluttony, drunkenness, and unchastity; so that they, who have neither sought nor thought of anything more than their own, may find their own. Then, too, God blinds them so that they do not recognize it as an abomination and disgrace, but adorn their misconduct with the names of saints, as though they were doing the right thing. Beyond this, God lets some fall into so deep an abyss that they boast publicly and say that whoever is in their brotherhood cannot be condemned; just as if baptism and the sacrament, instituted by God himself, were of less value and more uncertain than that which they have concocted out of their blinded heads. Thus will God dishonor and blind those who, with their crazed conduct and the swinish practices of their brotherhoods, mock and blaspheme his feasts, his name, and his saints, to the detriment of that common Christian brotherhood which flowed from the wounds of Christ.

4. Therefore for the correct understanding and use of the brotherhoods, one must learn to distinguish correctly between brotherhoods. The first is the divine, the heavenly, the noblest, which surpasses all others as gold surpasses copper or lead — this being the fellowship of all saints, of which we spoke above.[48] In this we are all brothers and sisters, so closely united that a closer relationship cannot be conceived. For here we have one baptism, one Christ, one sacrament, one food, one gospel, one faith, one Spirit, one spiritual body [Eph. 4:4–5], and each person is a member of the other [Rom. 12:5]. No other brotherhood is so close and strong. For natural brothers are, to be sure, of one flesh and blood, one heritage and home; yet they must separate and join themselves to the blood and heritage of others [in marriage]. The organized brotherhoods have one roll, one mass, one kind of good works, one festival day, one fee; and, as things are now, their common beer, common gluttony, and common drunkenness. But none of these penetrates so deeply as to produce one spirit, for that is done by Christ's brotherhood alone. For this reason, too, the greater, broader, and more comprehensive it is, the better it is.

Now all other brotherhoods should be so conducted as to keep this first and noblest brotherhood constantly before their eyes and regard it alone as great. With all their works they should be seeking nothing for themselves; they should rather do them for God's sake, entreating God that he keep and prosper this Christian fellowship and brotherhood from day to day. Thus when a brotherhood is formed, they should let it

---

[47] This rendering is according to the Douay Version, which is based on the Vulgate from which Luther is quoting.

[48] See pp. 50–67.

be seen that the members are a jump ahead of others in rendering Christendom some special service with their prayers, fastings, alms, and good works, and [that they do this] not in order to seek selfish profit or reward, or to exclude others, but to serve as the free servants of the whole community of Christians.

If men had such a correct conception, God would in return also restore good order, so that the brotherhoods might not be brought to shame by debauchery. Then blessing would follow: a general fund could be gathered, whereby material aid too could be given to other persons. Then the spiritual and material works[49] of the brotherhoods would be done in their proper order. And whoever does not want to follow this [proper] order in his brotherhood, I advise him to let the brotherhood go, and get out of it; it will [only] do him harm in body and soul.

But suppose you say, "If I do not get something special out of the brotherhood, of what use is it to me?" I answer: True, if you are seeking something special [for yourself], of what use indeed is the brotherhood, or the sisterhood either? But if by it you serve the community and other men, as is customarily the nature of love [to do], you will have your reward for this love without any desire or search on your part. If, however, you consider the service and reward of love too small, this is evidence that yours is a perverted brotherhood. Love serves freely and without charge, which is why God in return also gives to it every blessing, freely and without charge. Since, then, everything must be done in love, if it is to please God at all, the brotherhood too must be a brotherhood in love. It is the nature of that which is done in love, however, not to seek its own,[50] or its own profit, but to seek that of others, and above all that of the community [of saints].

5. To return once more to the sacrament, since the Christian fellowship is at present in a bad way, such as it has never been before, and is daily growing worse, especially among those in high places, and since all places are full of sin and shame, you should be concerned not about how many masses are said, or how often the sacrament is celebrated — for this will make things worse rather than better — but about how much you and others increase in that which the sacrament signifies[51] and in the faith[52] which it demands. For therein alone lies improvement. And the more you find yourself being incorporated into the fellowship of Christ and his saints, the better it is with you. [It is good] if you find that you are becoming strong in the confidence of Christ and his dear saints, so that you are certain that they love you and stand by you in all the trials of life and of death; and that you, in turn, take to heart the shortcomings and lapses of all Christians and of the entire community [of saints] [as these occur] in any individual Christian, so that your love goes out to each one

---

[49] *Merck* (in WA 2, 757, l. 7) in all likelihood was intended to be *werck*; cf. WA 21, 161, l. 8.

[50] I Cor. 13:5 (KJV); cf. I Cor. 10:24.

[51] Cf. p. 49 and pp. 50–62.

[52] Cf. p. 49 and pp. 62–67.

and you desire to help everyone, hate no one, suffer with all, and pray for all. See, as the work of the sacrament proceeds aright, you will come many times to weep, lament, and mourn over the wretched condition of Christendom today. If, however, you find no such confidence in Christ and his saints, and the needs of Christendom and of every single neighbor do not trouble or move you, then beware of all other good works, by which you think you are godly and will be saved. They are surely nothing but hypocrisy, sham, and deceit, for they are without love and fellowship; and without these nothing is good. To sum it all up: *Plenitudo legis est dilectio*, "Love is the fulfilling of the law" [Rom. 13:10]. Amen.

[Postscript][53]

There are some who have unnecessarily rejected this treatise because I said in the third paragraph:[54] I should consider it a good thing if a Christian council were to decree that both kinds be given to everyone. They have opened their mouth so wide that they are saying, "This is an error and it is offensive." God in heaven have mercy! That we should live to see the day when Christ — the noble Lord and God — is publicly insulted and blasphemed by his own people, who rebuke his order as an error! It would have been enough had they allowed it to remain a permissive order and not turned it into a command. Then, at least, it would not be forbidden or regarded as an error. Yet I beg them to look carefully at the second and third paragraphs,[55] in which I have stated clearly that one kind is sufficient. I have experienced too that my writings are being rejected only by those who have not read them and who do not intend to do so. To such men I send my greetings and inform them that I am paying no attention to their blind and frivolous criticism; as long as God grants me life, I do not intend to tolerate it, that they so brazenly condemn and blaspheme my Lord Christ as an erring, offensive, and revolutionary teacher — they can act accordingly.

---

[53] This paragraph is found only in two of the Wittenberg printings, the so-called Editions C (*WA* 2, 739) and N (*WA* 9, 791), the only two which profess to having been corrected by Luther himself.

[54] See p. 50.

[55] See pp. 49–50.

LAST SUPPER

"When it was evening, he reclined at table with the twelve. And as they were eating, he said, 'Truly, I say to you, one of you will betray me.'" Matt. 26:20–21 c. 1508–1509

All Become One Cake

by Martin Luther

Sermon on Maundy Thursday[1]

You dear people have often heard before how one is to be prepared at this time to receive the blessed Sacrament of the body and blood of Christ. But because this day is ordered to the end that we receive the Sacrament, we are compelled once again to speak of it, so long as there is need to do so. For I am certain that there are some here who are still in need of instruction. But I maintain, however, that it cannot be better comprehended and understood than if the misuse of the Sacrament is compared with the proper and Christian use, which Christ instituted.

First, up to now, it has been taught that one should be confident and firmly believe that under the bread is the true body and under the wine the true blood of Christ. This is the first part, which has been asserted above all else. When this point had been drilled into the people, it was believed that the matter of the Sacrament had been very well preached. Then people were asked if they desired the Sacrament, and if so, then it was freely given to them with no further questions.

That was it, regarding the two parts of the Sacrament: a person believed [Christ's body and blood are present] and desired the Sacrament. On just why a person should desire it or what more belongs to the matter, no one agreed. Nor has it been recognized that the devil and all non-Christians have such "faith." A person is quite ready to say that he believes this article of faith. For I can believe that Christ is risen from the dead, likewise that He passed through the stone placed at the entrance to the grave and that He made no opening by which to leave the tomb. And I can also believe that He passed through closed doors, that when He did so He did not break or destroy

---

[1] The sermon, here in English translation for the first time, is taken from WA Schriften, Teil 1, Band 12, pp. 472ff.

anything. I can believe that wood and His body occupied one and the same space, and yet true flesh and blood were there. And so I can indeed also believe that in the bread and wine are the body and blood of Christ.

But it is still quite an insignificant thing should a person let it go at that and only believe what he has understood up to this point, thinking he has got it all down pat. Such faith and desire are not at all sufficient for the Sacrament. All those who know nothing more of the Sacrament, and don't have a higher faith and desire for it, should not receive it. For giving the Holy Sacrament to these people is not much different from shoving it down a pig's throat. It is a mockery and a dishonor of the Sacrament, therefore, to think that you will become something else or not die. I will let it happen once more this year that anyone come [to the Sacrament] according to his own devotion. But after that we must mandate that one allow no one to go to the Sacrament unless he be asked beforehand and it be found out how his heart stands, whether he also knows what it is and why he goes.

It will have to suffice for us yet once more to look through our fingers and let the old misuse go. But so that the Sacrament may be further urged in the world, we must now get to the heart of the matter and improve what needs improvement.

So one should proceed in this matter as one deals with a child or someone else who needs to be instructed. When he is brought to the Sacrament of Baptism, it is not enough that he believes that this is Baptism and a Sacrament instituted by God. Nor is it enough that one press him about whether or not he wants to be baptized, what sin he has committed recently, etc. But first he is asked, "Do you forsake the devil and all his works and ways?" There the one who baptizes presses him to find out whether he has and understands a genuine faith, what he seeks, and why he is present, and to what end he is going to use the Sacrament [of Baptism]. Much more so then shall one hear whether he is such a vessel [prepared to receive the Sacrament], so that he understands that one does not shove the body and blood of Christ into the mouth of an unclean beast. For those who go with only that kind of faith, reflect no further on it, simply take the Sacrament, view it as a work and then think that this suffices. And they receive the Sacrament merely because it is instituted and in use, and one ought do it. It is like asking someone why he allows himself to be baptized and he answers, "I don't know. It was instituted, so I'll do it too. I think it's a good work."

Now, a person cannot slander and disgrace the blessed Sacrament in any worse fashion than by viewing it merely as a good work. You see, a good work is something I can do for someone else, and so it is my work. The Sacrament is not mine; it is God's work. In the Sacrament I only allow myself to be served and to receive God's good gifts. Therefore, as far distant as God's works are from my works, so one must also separate and hold this Sacrament as God's work from our work. So it is now evident that it is a great affront to the Sacrament and blasphemy against God when you maintain that it is not God's work.

One should ask when someone wants to come to the Sacrament, "First, what is this Sacrament?" There he should answer, "The Sacrament is the word that Christ spoke at the supper, 'Take and eat. This is My body, which is given for you. This is My blood that is poured out for you, for the forgiveness of sin.' Accordingly, He has established along with the words, that bread and wine, under which are His flesh and blood [Fleysch und blut], are the sign and seal that the words are true."

Then he should ask further, "What is the benefit of these words that Christ there speaks and upon which he hangs a sign?" Answer, "They are beneficial to this end that I should believe them, not that I therein should do a good work, but that my faith and heart trust them and not doubt that it is also as the words sound." How do these words sound? Thus, "This is My body which is given for you," which words He says to all who receive this Sacrament. Therefore, you must cling to the same word in faith and thus say, "For this reason I come, and desire the Sacrament, that I believe that His body is given for me, His blood poured out for me, so that thereby my faith be strengthened. For this reason will I receive this sign." Whoever cannot do or believe this should not be present for the Sacrament. For where such faith is not in the heart, all is lost.

Now do you see how far different that faith is from this faith? For if you merely believe that the Sacrament is the flesh and blood of Christ, what good is that to you and what use is it for you? The devil also believes this, but what good is it for him? Here you don't do anything more than a work and taste nothing more than the monstrance in which it is placed or a cloth upon which is laid. For you are not a vessel that is made so that the Sacrament be displayed in you as though you were a monstrance.

But when faith, which grabs hold of the word, comes and says, "Christ has spoken the word, and I believe that it is true. I'll die trusting that word, and I am certain and sure that He is there, that He is given to me and is mine. Thus I receive what is His, as though it were my own good, which God has freely given me," that is very powerful and quite different from that faith that believes He gives you nothing. This [genuine] faith, however, gives you and brings to you all the treasure of which the word speaks, as you believe. Therefore I wanted to say this to you and to spare you this [misuse of the Sacrament]. But from this point on it is necessary to give no one the Sacrament unless it is known how he believes, and that He is such a vessel that can lay hold of it and that he knows how to declare what he believes.

It is also very necessary to do this for another reason: the Sacrament was externally instituted that one confess and testify to the faith and that he do so publicly before the world. Before God it is enough in this matter that we believe the Gospel. Now, however, He wants us on earth to serve others and confess the faith, which we have in the heart. We do this with certain signs, which are Baptism and this Sacrament. With the mouth we must confess the Gospel and then claim the Sacrament as a testimony that we are Christians. Furthermore, I am certain for my person that I have a gracious God and I have also done enough before the world [to confess this fact]. Now, if you do not [make this confession], what do you make of the Sacrament? What will you do when you face death and the cross? What will you do when death comes and you must die, and the devil afflicts you? If you then say, "Yes, I believe that I have received the Sacrament. I believe that it is the true flesh and blood of Christ," the devil will retort, "Yes. I believe that too!" Thus your faith does not help you at all. The devil has conquered you and will march you off to a place where you can never be helped.

Rather you should say, therefore, "Behold! You tyrant, devil and death! I have received the Sacrament in which my Lord Christ, through His word, speaks to me and consoles me. He tells me that His body and blood are mine! I believe not only as much as you do, that it is His flesh and blood. I also believe that everything that the words say and carry is a gift to me. Therefore, I set this faith against you and all misfortune. I stand fast upon the words that will not lie to me, for they are God's word and testimony." When you die you will be propped up, and at that moment neither I, nor any man will be able to help you, even if all priests should stand next to you with the Sacrament. That is what was done until now. They made and intended of the Sacrament nothing but a work. Indeed! As though that would help!

We read in the Books of the Kings in 1 Kings 4 [1 Sam. 4:3] where the children of Israel fought against the Philistines and they were killed and put to flight. The elders of Israel said to the people, "The reason God has allowed us to be defeated is because we do not have the ark of the Lord with us."[2]

Was the ark still there? There God was, as in the Sacrament. Why then would he not help them? This is the reason. They, too, had made a work out of it. They relied upon that work and did not have faith. Therefore, God punished them and they were more horribly struck down than before. We do the same, proceeding without faith, relying only upon the work that we have received the Sacrament. So also when the devil comes to strike us he will slay us much worse than before.

To be sure, I know that this misuse, unfortunately, has a deep hold. Therefore, we must drive home this matter with resolution, so that we remove this error, and strike with terror those who think that it is enough that one believe that in the Sacrament the body and blood of Christ are there. It is true, the food is indeed there, but you eat and partake of it not. For you partake when you believe that it is a gift for you, as we have said. Christ does not say, "Behold! There it is! There it lies!" He rather says, "Take it. I shall be yours." He is not in the Sacrament merely so that we may lay hold of Him. He is there so that we make use of what is His. Thus there is then no correct use but that you believe that the body is given for you and the blood is poured out for you. And so you have it as you believe. Now if your conscience deceives you and says,

---

[2] Luther cites the text from memory and, according to the sense of the passage, not word for word.

"You have sinned thus and so! If only you were free [of this guilt]!" then go back to the Sacrament and say, "I have sinned. But the body [of Christ] has not sinned, and is guiltless. The body is there given for me and the blood is shed for me for the forgiveness of sin. This I believe, and to prove it I will receive the Sacrament." When you do this your sin is taken away, and no misfortune can harm you any longer. For who can do anything to me now? Every mouth must be stopped and rendered dumb despite the devil and all misfortune. I am now one cake with Christ, so that no suffering can assail me again. I have won.

Now this is necessary for each and every Christian to know, so that he, too, can recount it and know when he is asked, why he receives the Sacrament. Therefore, I say it once more so that you may be warned about this matter if you still desire to go. I will allow it, and bear your weakness. But henceforth it shall not remain so. He who desires to receive the Sacrament will be asked beforehand what the Sacrament is and what he seeks there, so that he can answer as we have demonstrated above. First, that the word of Christ and the sign of the body and blood of Christ is the Sacrament. Second, that he therein seek to strengthen his faith and console his conscience so that we come out of ourselves and to Christ. Thus you must be prepared in this matter so that you know how you shall make use of the Sacrament. If you cannot do this, then you shall not be given the Sacrament.

Along with this see to it that you do not feign a false faith when you at the same time believe that there Christ is given to you and is yours, and that this faith is merely a human thought that is your own doing. If this is the case, do not partake of this Sacrament. For it must be a faith, which God produces. You must know and perceive that God works such faith in you, that you believe, without doubt, that it is true, that this word and sign is given you, and you are so brave as to think that you would die for this Sacrament. And if you still flounder and doubt, kneel down and plead that God grant you his grace so that you thus drive away such doubts and come to upright faith. There you will see how few Christians there are who would then gladly go to the Sacrament. However, if you could set it up and bring it about, I would desire that those who believe could also find a place to gather. I would already have loved to do this, but it has not been possible. For it has not been preached or emphasized enough. And Christ also preached to all, as did the apostles after Him, so that all have heard, believers and unbelievers, and whoever caught hold of it caught hold of it. We must also do the same. But one shall not cast the Sacrament among the people in a heap as the pope has done. When I preach the Gospel, I do not know if it hits home. Here, however, I maintain that it has been believed by those who come to the Sacrament. I must not cast it in doubt, rather be certain that the one to whom I give the Sacrament has understood the Gospel and truly believes. It is similar to Baptism where if I should baptize one as also the one who receives it shall not doubt it. But one should not cast the Sacrament among the people in a mob as the pope has done. When I preach the Gospel I do not know whom it strikes. Here, however, I maintain that it has indeed struck the one who comes to the Sacrament. I must not cast this in doubt. I should be certain that the one to whom I give the Sacrament has been grabbed by the Gospel and believes aright, as when I baptize someone I should not doubt the one who receives the Baptism.

Thus you now have the correct and Christian use for the reception of the Sacrament. Furthermore, we shall speak of the fruit, which follows when one uses the Sacrament aright. The Holy Sacrament produces two things: one is that it makes us brothers and fellow heirs of the Lord Christ, such that it makes us one cake with Him; the other that we also become common and one with all other people upon earth and also all become one cake. These two benefits Paul emphasized in 1Corinthians 10. We should all know this passage along with those words by which Christ instituted the Sacrament. Thus Saint Paul said, "We are all one bread and one drink, for we all participate in one bread and drink." Likewise in the same passage, he says, "Is it not so that the bread that we break is the distribution or participation of the body of Christ? And the cup of blessing which we bless, is it not the participation of the blood of Christ?" These words should be in full use and well-known in Christendom, since so much depends upon them.

When we eat the bread, he says, we all have one food. You have that which I have, and it makes no difference that you are man or woman. In that which we all have in common in the Sacrament, we all receive what Christ has and is. When I believe that His body and blood is mine, I have the Lord Christ whole and complete. Thus He makes my heart joyous and confident since I leave nothing to my own piety, but depend upon the innocent blood and the pure body that I receive there.

Now what does Christ have and what does He bring about? His body and blood are without sin, full of grace — yes, the corporal dwelling of the divine majesty. In short, everything God has is Christ's. The benefits here become altogether mine, and because of this I have a sign and seal, or assurance, that such great and unspeakable benefits are mine when I receive the flesh and blood of Christ. Therefore, in the Sacrament, no sin is removed because of my work, as the poor, stupid people have been deluded. Sin is removed there because I truly believe that the body and blood are given for me. Therefore, I am certain and sure that Christ graciously gives me all good things that He has and all His strength and power. Thus He gives His wisdom, truth and goodliness, and takes away all my sins. His eternal life gobbles up death for me. Through His strength and power, I defeat the devil. In the Sacrament then a Christian man becomes an heir of eternal life and of all good things and an heir over all things, for which he can do nothing himself.

Such great benefits you cannot obtain by means of any work, though you conducted a thousand masses every day. Christ is such a high person, who gives Himself for you, that it is impossible that sin, death, hell and devil can remain for Him. Much less could you suppress the high majesty. Where His flesh and blood are, there He will certainly have one eye open and not let that flesh and blood be trampled underfoot. Therefore, since you have His flesh and blood, thus you have all the power that God Himself has. That is, we become one cake with the Lord Christ; we walk in the fellowship of His benefits and He in the fellowship of our misfortune. For here are thrown together His godliness and my sin, my weakness and His strength, and thus all is held in common. What is mine becomes His. What is His, I also have. This is a high unspeakable grace, over which the heart must become joyous and courageous.

Now if you are one cake with Christ, what more do you want? You now have incomparably more than your heart desires and you sit in paradise. This is what should have been emphasized when the Sacrament was treated. But it had gone so far under that one heard not a word about it. When one wanted to emphasize what the fruit of the Sacrament is, it was taught that a person who heard one mass a day would suffer no evil that day. Thus they connected it to external fortune and misfortune. And they did even more. They covered and hid the word so that no one in Christendom should hear or read it, and they claimed that the words in the mass are the holiest words. Who but the wretched devil in hell had spoken and brought it about that the words one should say and emphasize more than any other in Christianity, and should be better known than any other words, were covered and hidden?[3] That means the devil ruled Christendom! Lord have mercy.

That is the first fruit of the Sacrament. The second is that we become one bread with one another, as Paul says, and one drink. These are extraordinary words, and they come in such a way that they are difficult to comprehend. That is entirely the reason that the Sacrament is turned into a work. How then does it happen that we all are one bread and partake of one another? It happens in this way: When I receive the Sacrament, I partake twice. Externally I partake of the Sacrament; inwardly, however, and spiritually I receive all the benefits of Christ as though I ate physical bread that strengthens the body inwardly. Again, when I receive the Sacrament Christ takes me and devours me and gobbles me up together with my sins. I partake of His righteousness such that His godliness swallows up my sin and misery so that I have nothing but righteousness.

It is the same also among us. We all become one cake and partake of each other. You know that when a person bakes bread all the grain is thoroughly ground. Thus each kernel becomes flour with all the others, and thus all are mixed together so that in one sack full of flour the grain is so mixed and thrown together that each becomes the flour of the other. No kernel retains its form. Each gives to the other its flour and each loses its own body. Thus many small kernels of grain become one loaf of bread, just as in the same way when one makes wine, each grape mixes its juice with that of the others and each forsakes is form. From all comes one drink. Thus it should also be

---

[3] Luther's complaint here refers to the contemporary practice of the celebrant whispering the "verba" or Words of Institution during the mass, such that they were inaudible to the laity.

with us. I give myself for the common good and serve you and you make use of what is mine of which you are in need. Thus I am your food, just as you make use of bread when you are hungry that in turn your body may help and give strength to the one who is hungry. Therefore, when I help and serve you in all need, I am your bread. On the other hand, if you are also a Christian, you in your turn act in the same way that you, with everything you have, serve me. For me, all comes together for good, and I partake of the same as food or drink. If it happens that I am a sinner and you by God's grace are pious, you strengthen me and you share your piety with me, pray for me, intercede before God for me and cast all of it upon yourself. You swallow up my sin with your godliness just as Christ has done for us. Thus you partake of me, and I in turn partake of you.

There behold how unbelievably great a thing it is regarding that Sacrament when one uses it in the right way, that a man must therein be delivered from death when he correctly perceives it for the great [thing that it is]. Reason can not conceive of it. Is it not great that the high Majesty steps forth for me and gives Himself to me for mine own, thereupon that all saints step forth for me and stand, take upon themselves what is mine and have concern for me, serve and help me? Thus God places us in the fellowship of Christ and all His chosen; there we have a great consolation where we forsake ourselves. If I am a sinner, thus Christ stands there and says, "The sinner is mine whom I grab hold of with My holy fingers. Who will grumble about that?" Thus my sin falls away, and I partake of His righteousness. Thus we Christians also do with each other, take upon ourselves that of another, so that one person bears the sin and failings of another and serves the other with his piety. This we don't understand, and if we likewise often hear and understand it, we don't believe it. And so we retreat ever more and experience no fruit or improvement.

These are the benefits of the blessed Sacrament, and that is the proper Christian use that consists briefly in this, that we conclude that a person understand the words that belong to the Sacrament, and then go to the Sacrament and confess that he is a Christian. Then one can take note and see whether those who receive the Sacrament demonstrate the fruit, which follows there from, and have demonstrated love. Where they will not act thus, one may exclude them from the community [gemein]; so that it may again come into vogue that one know who the true Christians are.

That is enough on this occasion regarding the reception of the Sacrament. Now we also want to say a little something about confession and briefly conclude. In confession there is also a word spoken by which the priest in God's stead absolves you. This word should not be despised. We do not desire to force anyone to recount all his sins, yet no one should go to the Sacrament if he despises confession. But we have often enough preached about that. When you wish to make confession, pay much more attention to your future life than the past, and do not do what has been done up to now. A person has gone to confession because it was commanded once each year. And consciences had been so plagued because a person had to recount every detail with all the circumstances. Only by recounting when, how and where, was it thought the confession was made, while there was no concern how one would improve the future life. Therefore it should be turned around and directed completely to the future. For it is soon forgiven that you have sinned in the past. You must see how you are beginning another life, that you are disgusted with your former life, and be satisfied with that.

See to it that you think about this matter in this way. If not, it does not help you if you go to confession every day of your life. When you return and go to confession, it is to the end that you allow yourself be absolved and now think about leading a different life. Now you must say that your sin is taken away and God is pleased with you. The pope commanded and made a law of it that one must go to confession once a year at Easter when one goes to the Sacrament. A person confessed everything that had been done the entire year. Thus from now it shall remain free. Those who are prepared to live a new life may make confession when they desire. Some have thought sorrow over sin, and the beginning of a different life are within our power and free will. So they have forced [confession] with laws, forced the people to confession, so that they have had to lie and say they are sorry for their sin when it is not true. They see this as comprehending confession.

The other part, which is also heard on this matter, is that you with true faith believe the absolution and not doubt that the word spoken to the one making confession is spoken by God Himself. For God has thus humbled Himself such that He places His holy divine word in the mouth of men. This is so that we should absolutely not doubt that God Himself says it. Therefore we should also accept it as though God spoke it Himself. He has done it to you for your good. For you might not be able to bear it, if He Himself were to speak with you. Wouldn't you run to the end of the world if you heard that God Himself speaks there? This is what you have right at home in front of your door. Why can't you see it? And it is just as certain as your own front door, yes still more certain. For here I have His promise; there I do not. Therefore prepare yourself thus to this end, that you believe and contemplate leading a different life. Otherwise it would be better for you to stay away from confession and the Sacrament. This will suffice for now.

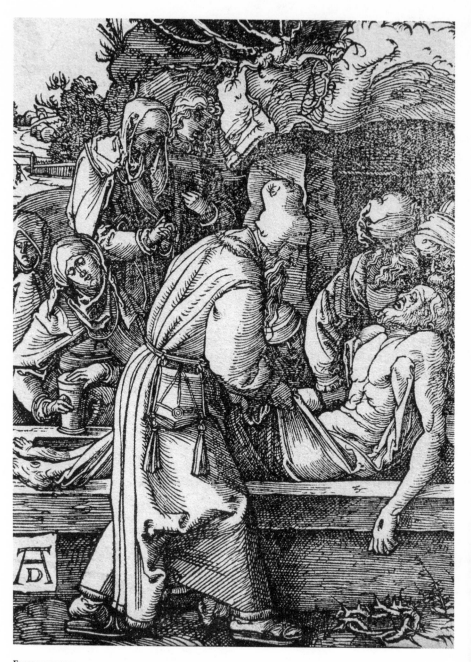

Entombment
"And laid it in his own new tomb, which he had cut in the rock ..." Matt. 27:60a c. 1509–1510

THE PASTOR'S RESPONSIBILITY TO CARE FOR THE PHYSICAL NEEDS OF MEMBERS OF HIS CONGREGATION

Although a preacher above all has concern for the spiritual needs of the members of his congregation, concern for the physical well-being, particularly the needs of the poor, the sick, widows, orphans, the infirm, the destitute, the aged, etc., are within the scope of the duties of his office. Gal. 2:9-10; Acts 6:1ff., 11:30, 12:25, 24:17; Rom. 12:8,13; James 1:27; I Tim. 5:10; I Thess. 4:11-12.

Note 1

Here in this country this is a very important point. Like a horrible cancer, the secret societies are devouring the body of the church. Thousands upon thousands are joining these organizations initially only so that they are assured of some help at a time of need, illness or other necessity. But the result is that they are finally completely estranged from the church and they conclude that their secret society is a better bearer of the true religion than the church, because it is an active religion. The basic reason for this is unbelief — lack of Christian knowledge and a more discerning knowledge. But at the same time a chief cause is that the Christian congregations do not do what they are obliged to do, in the minds of those who are their members, who find themselves in physical need. People recognize that even if they are members of a Christian congregation, they are still left in need, sickness and other necessity. Thus, unawakened as they may be, they decide to join a society which provides them the prospects of some assistance in time of physical need. This brings unspeakable dishonor upon the church and the Word of God.

"Concerning the Exercise of the Duty of a Congregation to Care for Its Members Also in Earthly Needs" is chapter three, part four from *The Form of a Christian Congregation* © 1963, 1991 CPH. Used with permission.

The apostle wrote to the Christians in Thessalonica, "Aspire to live quietly, and to mind your own affairs, and to work with your hands, as we instructed you, so that you may walk properly before outsiders and be dependent on no one" (1 Thess. 4:11-12). Thus the word of God desires that Christians shall act in such a way that they do not face situations in which they must seek the generosity of "those who are outside." Hedinger remarks on the words, "That you be dependent upon no one": "[Neither be dependent upon] the people themselves, or their possessions and assistance. Paul desires that they should work for themselves in blessing so that they need not look to the godless for a handout. That would be to their disgrace, an offence to their faith, and a misleading of their souls through the interaction." But it is clear, if Christians want to work and eat of their own bread, but are not able, and it is necessary for them to rely upon the kindness of unbelievers, then they don't bear the guilt for giving offense to the world, or the dishonor which thereby comes to the Gospel.

The zeal of congregations against the secret societies is completely pharisaic if it is not tied with sufficient concern for their poor and suffering. A Christian congregation can not simply claim that there are state funds for the poor and homes for them, which they also support. No Christian congregation should allow their poor to be cared for in this way. The state should much more see that it need not forcibly impose taxes for the poor in order to maintain poor Christians, but only for those who have been forsaken by all the world. Christian congregations should view it as a disgrace to see their poor cared for by the secular state. In the so-called state churches, in which a confusion of the church and the state existed, it was a different matter. There the state institutions for the poor were essentially those of the church. Here, where church and state are strictly separated, the church should not allow its sole care for its poor to be taken away. If God already called upon the church of the old covenant that: "There will be no poor among you" (Deut. 15:4), how much more does this apply to the church of the New Testament! If it dishonors God, if Christians among Christians have to go about as beggars because they are not provided with the necessities of life, so that Christ in them must go begging, what an insult must it be to the name *Christian*, if Christians close their hearts to their brothers, and they are forced to go begging from the loveless world!

Seidel writes:

> That the care for the poor from the first times of the church was entrusted to the preaching office, and that the same office had the administration and oversight of the poor houses and hospitals, there is absolutely no doubt, when we consider that in the Justinian Code invariably the "poor" and "homes for the poor" are dealt with under the title, "Regarding the Bishops and Clerics." At the time of the Reformation it was thus the case, as is right, that care for the poor was among the episcopal rights of the territorial lord, and by these lords it was handed over to the spiritual jurisdictions. But

these jurisdictions created the order that the preacher and the government authorities of every place gathered money for the poor and other benevolent institutions, through certain elders (*Vorsteher*) designated for that task. It was to be administered in such a form that the matters of the poor were never to be mixed with the common matters of state. And the supervision of all *Pia Corpora* were retained by the superintendents and the consistories. (*Pastoral Theology* I, 11; para. 1, p. 197 f.)

Luther writes further, regarding the history of the establishment of a particular office of almoner (*Almosenpfleger-Amts*) in the apostolic congregations at Jerusalem (Acts 6:1 ff.): "In this history you see first of all how a Christian community (*Gemeine*) should be formed. There you see a proper picture of a spiritual government (*Regiment*), which the apostles here exercise. They look after the souls, and go about preaching and praying. They also bring it about that the body is cared for, and set up certain men who dole out the goods, as you have heard. Thus the Christian government (*Regiment*) is concerned both with body and soul, that no one has any need, and all are richly fed and well cared for in both body and soul" (*Church Postil* XI, 2754 ff.).

Note 2

That the concern for the poor belongs to the particular official responsibilities of the preacher is clear especially from Gal. 2:9-1 and Acts 6:1 ff. As often, therefore, as our old theologians enumerate the official functions of a preacher, they also bring forth care for the poor among those functions. Thus, for instance, Johann Gerhard: "There are in general seven duties or tasks of the minister of the Church, to which the rest can be easily reckoned: 1. the proclamation of the word of God; 2. the administration of the sacraments; 3. the intercession for the flock entrusted to them; 4. an honorable life; 5. the administration of church discipline; 6. the maintenance of church rites; 7. the care for the poor and the visitation of the sick" (*Loc. Th. De Minister.* Ecclesiasti. Para 265). On this remarkable passage of Gal. 2:9-10 Luther remarks: "If a faithful shepherd or one who cares for souls is concerned above all with the preaching of the Gospel to his little flock, then he should be concerned with nothing else so much as that the poor also may be nourished and preserved. For it never fails that where a church or community of God is, there must certainly also be poor people, who are commonly only the real disciples or followers of the Gospel, as Christ himself testifies in Matt. 11:5. For the poor will have the Gospel preached to them; and I Cor. 1:27-28: 'What is foolishness before the world' etc. For evil people and the devil persecute the church and the community of God and make many poor people, who are afterwards so destitute that no one will care for them or give them a thing" (VIII, 1762).

Hartmann writes:

As in a flock, the sheep suffering need require greater and more ample help from their shepherd (Ezek. 34:4); thus in the parishes, suffering persons who are impoverished, particularly if they are ill, widows, orphans and those destitute of all help and oppressed by others, expect with full right the particular aid and care of their pastors. For although Christian love demands this duty also from others, still the pastor is more responsible than all others to express fatherly care for the suffering persons. He may not object that it suffices that they receive assistance from the administrators of the poor chest. He must pay heed to the soul and conscience of the poor so that they not fall away from the Gospel, withdraw to another place, or envy those who are wealthier, on account of lack of the necessities to sustain life. Therefore the pastor must, according to the example of St. Paul, also frequently urge the congregation to collect funds for the poor, Gal. 2:10. And as Paul directs the Corinthians to the example of the Galatians, so the custom of the one congregation kindles the other, since by nature we are not inclined to do something which is not done elsewhere. Here the zeal of love of many others destroys sluggishness ... Above all the pastor must diligently investigate which among those of his flock are suffering, and who deserve to be mercifully cared for ... To this end the pastor must have an up to date list of the poor, kept by himself and the officers [of the church], noting if someone has fallen ill or otherwise been impoverished by increase in the cost of those things necessary for life, or through other unfortunate circumstances, in order to assist these people from the congregation's poor chest and out of their own means. Then he shall see to it that the officers divide the proceeds, given as free gifts, from which the poor are cared for. They are collected on Sunday in the divine service, on festival days, or at funerals. The carefully gathered and collected alms are divided with such wisdom and fidelity that they, so much as possible, leave no one in need, nor here do anything from party love or hate, or also from selfishness (if perchance the poor have served the pastor in some way). Therefore the pastor must in times of famine, or when out of other causes more difficult times transpire, admonish his flock, in these times, to likewise think of the poor and vigorously care for them. And therewith the pastor must guard his attachment and preferences over against all, and he must, with reciprocal consensus and council of the presbyterium, exercise this part of his office, and at the proper time provide an account of what has been done. When the pastor and the almoner, while completely convinced of their own honorable administration, are unjustly [accused] by many poor, to whom one can never give enough, or also by any other people are wrongly defamed, they must pay no attention, nor in their zeal of office cede anything. Rather much more think, as it is stated in the saying, "He who builds by a road has many masters." (*Pastoral*. Ev. III, 54 p. 1023 ff.)

Note 3

The preacher should see to it in his congregation, especially if it is a large congregation, that the concerns of the poor be ordered and that there be established, for the proper administration of the same, definite almoners according to the example of the congregation at Jerusalem, Acts 6:1ff, and that they are supplied with appropriate instructions. Luther wrote in the text already cited, "This is a right fine picture and example, and would indeed be good to begin if there were people to do it, that a city such that this one be divided into four or five sections, and each section be given a preacher and some deacons who would take care of each section with preaching and the distribution of goods, visit the sick people, and see to it that no one suffer need. But we don't have the people to do it; therefore I trust it won't happen until our Lord God makes Christians" (XI, 2755). Regarding the churchly offices alongside the office of the Word we shall later have express opportunity to treat them.

Note 4

Regarding the persons who are to be assisted and supported by the congregation, and regarding the character of the support, we share the following witnesses. Already in the year 1520 Luther wrote in "Regarding the Improvement of the Christian Estate":

> 21. One of the greatest necessities is the abolition of all begging throughout Christendom. Nobody ought to go begging among Christians. It would even be a very simple matter to make a law to the effect that every city should look after its own poor, if only we had the courage and the intention to do so. No beggar from outside should be allowed into the city whether he might call himself pilgrim or mendicant monk. Every city should support its own poor, [In our circumstances in the free church, for "every city" we would say "each and every congregation." Walther] and if it was too small, the people in the surrounding villages should also be urged to contribute, since in any case they have to feed so many vagabonds and evil rogues who call themselves mendicants. In this way, too, it could be known who was really poor, and who was not.
>
> There would have to be an overseer or warden who knows all the poor, and informs the city council or the clergy what they needed, or some other better arrangement might be made.
>
> To be sure, some think that if these proposals were adopted the poor would not be so well provided for, that fewer great stone houses and monasteries would be built, and fewer so well furnished. I can well believe all this. But none of it is necessary. He who has chosen poverty ought not to be rich. If he wants to be rich, let him put his hand to the plow and seek his fortune from the land. It is enough if the poor are decently cared for so that they do not die of hunger or cold. It is not fitting that one man should live in idleness on another's labor, or be rich and live comfortably at the cost of

another's hardship, as it is according to the present perverted custom. St. Paul says, "Whoever will not work shall not eat" [II Thess. 3:10]. God has not decreed that any man shall live off another man's property, save only the clergy who preach and have a parish to care for, and these should, as St. Paul says in I Corinthians 9[:14], on account of their spiritual labor. And also as Christ says to the apostles, "Every laborer is worthy of his wage" [Luke 10:7]. (X,367f)

Furthermore, Porta writes:

If it is asked to whom or which people one should especially give aid, you have plenty of doctrine and instruction in Holy Scripture. For in Deuteronomy chapter 15 it says, 'If thy brother is in any need in any of the cities of your land, which the Lord thy God will give to you.' Here it shall be well noted that God, the Lord, said through Moses, 'When there is a poor person in your city and in your land, so shall you open your hand and give him what he needs.' Therefore the church also sings, 'Open up thy gentle hand to the poor in the land.' For thereby he specifically commends to us the poor who are among us, such as the ill, the feeble, or those who cannot earn enough to feed themselves because of their age; or when paupers and impoverished tradesmen and workers are present, who have not caused their circumstances because of drunkenness, voraciousness, gambling or mischievousness, or perhaps have fallen into harm or been victim of an accident, especially through misfortune, even if they at the same time work, but cannot advance and therefore have to suffer need. Likewise, poor widows, orphans, poor but diligent students, who have a good testimony from their preceptor — one should give to these first of all. (*Pastorale Lutheri*. Cramer p. 1082f.).

Indeed, each individual Christian should demonstrate his kind readiness toward everyone, also toward the stranger (including those of a different belief); but first of all he should do this, that he thereby do good "especially to those of the household of the faith." Second, it is to be considered that the poor chest of the congregation is established not so much for the assistance of the poor in general, as it is for the poor of the congregation. Therefore out of the same, only these are to be assisted. [According to Deyling there appeared in 1715 a princely/electoral mandate which, at the threat of a 10 Thaler penalty, forbade preachers from providing testimony and letters of recommendation for itinerant beggars (*Institut. Prud. Pastoral.* p. 714).] In any case it is incorrect and a very cheap kind of mercy to a man who seeks assistance, without evaluation of hasty claims of conversion.

Regarding the distinction to be made between the worthy and the unworthy recipient of alms, Hartmann treats it (pp. 1062-34) in a thorough and express manner, and writes, "Where there is a distinction among the poor, particularly among those who are begging, wisdom is absolutely necessary so that one not strengthen the unworthy in their wickedness. However, because we cannot know a person's heart, one has to be careful not to treat a person as unworthy who is in fact worthy of assistance. Therefore it is better to give to the unworthy than to deny help to someone who is actually worthy. Even if a person is not worthy, he may still be needy."

Note 5

Regarding the sick, it is the preacher's duty to see to it that these people, if they are poor, are not only provided with the necessary means to sustain them, but that to them are provided also the necessary medical treatment, care, assistance and nursing. In certain circumstances also he will procure, for those who don't have the means, particular people for assistance, nursing, care during the night, etc. In the apostolic times there appeared to be established in many larger congregations a particular office for the care of the sick. Regarding the words, "He who shows mercy, let him do so with cheerfulness," Calov writes, "Here the text is speaking about the office which has to do with the ill and those in need. Those who show mercy are those who are entrusted with the care for the sick, the weak, and the afflicted. In general, this now could be understood as those who demonstrate this mercy privately. But as those who are designated and bound to such work through an office, thus the text here is concerned properly with such churchly offices for which also pious widows were used, I Tim. 5:9; Acts 6:1." (*Bibl. Illust. Ad* l.c.) Where there is not an office for care for the needy, there it is required of every Christian member of the congregation, by virtue of his membership, in cases which arise, to take over the functions of this office or to see to it that these functions are taken over by someone in his place.

THE FORM OF A CHRISTIAN CONGREGATION

CHAPTER III

PART FOUR

Concerning the Exercise of the Duty of a Congregation to Care for Its Members Also in Earthly Needs

In the first place, the congregation should do everything in its power to see to it that its pastor has food, clothing, and a home for himself and his family. (This should include a room where he may be undisturbed in conference with those entrusted to his care.) (Matt. 10:9, 10: Acquire no gold or silver or copper for your belts, no bag for your journey, or two tunics or sandals or a staff, for the laborer deserves his food.") Moreover, that the pastor has sufficient means to exercise hospitality (1 Tim. 3:2: "An overseer must be above reproach, the husband of one wife, sober-minded, self-controlled, respectable,hospitable, able to teach"; cf. Titus 1:8); that the pastor may live solely of the Gospel (1 Cor. 9:14: "Even so hath the Lord ordained that they which preach the Gospel should live of the Gospel"); finally, that he may give attendance to reading, practice fellowship, and need not entangle himself with the affairs of this life [Luther, "of support"] (1 Tim. 4: 13: "Devote yourself to the public reading of Scripture"; 2 Tim. 2:3, 4: "Share in suffering as a good soldier of Christ Jesus. No soldier gets entangled in civilian pursuits"; Ecclus. 38:25, 26: "How can he get wisdom that holdeth the plough and that glorieth in the goad, and driveth oxen and is occupied in their labors, and whose talk is of bullocks? He giveth his mind to make furrows and is diligent to give the kine fodder.") In its scope this applies also to the teachers of the children (*Einfaeltigen*).

Note. Concerning this matter Sebastian Schwan has collected an anthology of testimonies from the writings of Luther and Runge, in which we read, among other things: "It is not good to speak, preach, or write much about this subject. But what are we to do about it? Should we be altogether silent about the doctrine of the support and salary of ministers and let it lie buried? That would mean that we despise the truth and the office of the ministry, especially since this doctrine has to do with the Third Commandment. Also, if the ministry and office of pastors did not receive financial support, many would be deterred from it, and from this the church of God would suffer great harm. But if we speak of this and say something in church and school about the support of ministers, then we get the good-for-nothing crowd excited and meet with many godless people who hate, envy, and attack the pastor because of this very thing; they would rather rob and steal with Heliodorus, Julian, and Phocas than dedicate anything to the glory of God with Constantine, who founded many religious establishments ... But both the Old Testament and the New Testament bear witness that it is the will of God the Lord that His servants who conduct divine worship be honorably and well provided for. In the Old Testament the priests were well supported and richly provided for. In the New Testament this is repeated; for the great Shepherd and Bishop of our souls, our Lord Jesus Christ, Himself tells us (Matt. 10:10): 'The workman is worthy of his meat.'

"Concerning these words Martin Luther writes: 'Here we must note that to the ministers of the Word food and clothing are due because of the divine command. Today those sin grievously who indeed pretend to be Christians, but give the ministers of the church nothing; indeed, who steal and take from them what has been donated by others to be given to them, as our peasants, noblemen, citizens, and others are doing. These rascals will have to give an account to Him who says here that the laborer is worthy of his hire, for they take away from him his hire of which he is worthy and which he has earned.' Again, bear in mind also that our Lord Christ demands that the ministers of the Word are to receive not only food and drink but also money and pay so that they may procure for themselves other necessities; for they, too, must have clothing and whatever else they need. In the epistles of St. Paul this matter is often repeated and inculcated, [namely] that they [the Christians] are to treat well, adequately pay and support, and richly provide for those who labor in the divine Word. Though many whom I will not name ... do not regard it as labor what faithful ministers do by studying, praying, writing, preaching, visiting the sick, accompanying those imprisoned, which often forces them to give up their life or at times to be in extreme peril of death. This matter is emphasized so strongly in the writings of St. Paul and repeated so persistently that Dr. Martin Luther himself at first was surprised why it was that he [the apostle] was so serious in urging this matter.

"For so he comments on the passage of St. Paul, Gal. 6:6 ff.: 'I recall the time when I was very much surprised that St. Paul commanded Christian congregations so earnestly to support their teachers and ministers. For I noticed that in the papacy everybody contributed richly and gave with both hands to erect churches and monasteries, as also that the priests were cared for extremely well with interest and income. From this it followed that the wealth and possessions of the bishops and priests increased and multiplied so greatly that they occupied almost the whole of Christendom so far as the best cities and lands were concerned. So I thought that it was hardly necessary for St. Paul to issue any commands concerning this matter, since the priests were given more than enough of all things and were, so to speak, deluged with gifts. On the contrary, I thought that it would have been more necessary to keep the people from this excessive giving than further to urge them to contribute. For I saw that with their overmuch giving they accomplished nothing more than that they gradually made the priests more avaricious. But since I now see why formerly the priests were rewarded so abundantly while now the poor pastors and ministers have hardly enough bread to satisfy their hunger, I no longer wonder. Formerly when nothing was preached but error and falsehood, the devotion of the people was so great and their giving so excessive that St. Peter's patrimony, that is, his inheritance (he himself says in Acts 3:6: 'Silver and gold have I none' — how then did he [the pope] get it?) and the treasures of the church were so increased that the pope became the emperor and the cardinals and bishops the kings and rulers of the world. But after the light of the holy Gospel has again risen at this time, the faithful and devout ministers are about as rich as Christ and His disciples were.'

"These and other things Luther writes, and he finally concludes with the earnest words: 'It is impossible that true Christians can permit their pastors to be in need and suffer want. But when they not only allow this but also laugh about it, rejoice when they fare badly, and fail to give them what is coming to them, or when they give by coercion and do it grudgingly and with the gift wish them every kind of evil, it is certain that they are worse than the heathen and Turks.' Hence this New Testament passage concerning the support of Christian teachers and ministers is fundamental (Gal. 6:6,7): 'Let him that is taught in the Word communicate unto him that teacheth in all good things. Be not deceived; God is not mocked.' Here we must also consider 1 Tim. 5:17, 18 and 1 Cor. 9: 14. This exhaustive and earnest instruction of St. Paul is directed against the foolishness and avarice of those who want to withhold what they owe to Christian ministers. We may also note how powerfully St. Paul defends his instruction concerning the proper support of Christian pastors and ministers (including the schoolmasters), and [how] he proves it from the command and institution of God in the Old and the New Testament, from the natural law, and from the reason and judgment of every right-minded person, which we call sound reason; and [how] he finally confirms it from [the principle of] universal justice, all of which serves to demonstrate how very necessary and just it is that the Christian church and congregation should well support its ministers of the Word.

"However, what and how much should be given to the servants of the church, its teachers and ministers, for their support, cannot be legally prescribed and determined except by the principle of justice and love. It is reasonable to give to the ministers of Christ as much as is right, necessary, fair, and in accord with Christian love and justice. For as there is a difference of gifts, calling or state, and labor, as God the Lord Himself has distinguished the persons of the ministers according to a certain measure and order, so it is not unfair that a certain order should be fixed and a proper distinction be made with regard to their pay, salary, and support. But the law of love prescribes that everyone should be given as much as he needs for his own adequate support and that of his dependents, especially of his household. This should be done in order that such a servant of Christ may not become impatient and negligent in his calling, office, and work on account of want and poverty in his household, or on account of starvation, or because he can hardly clothe, support, and rear his children; or in order that in his distress he may not seek and obtain his support by other means or be forced to entangle himself in secular work, business, and the like. And since there are different opportunities at different times and places, and the problem of food and support for a family becomes more complex from day to day, it is only fair that the pious elders of the churches should keep this in mind and be directed by these matters to determine and grant the support of Christian teachers and ministers according to such circumstances." (*Dedekennus, Thesaurus.* II, 827-830)

Concerning the teachers in [Christian] schools Porta writes in his *Pastorale Lutheri:* "It is necessary, where the government fails in this, to support schoolmasters and schoolteachers from the common treasury in an adequate way. For schools are the beautiful, precious streams of the holy city of God, as the sacred [psalmist] David calls them (Ps. 46:4), and from them the whole welfare of government must flow and proceed. Where the schools must be staffed with inexperienced and untrained persons because of inadequate pay and support, and these often come and go, the children are neglected, and from this results such harm that it can never be repaired with money or good. Therefore it is only fair that we should spend more on the schools than, alas, we [actually] do, to our great havoc and harm. Besides the schools for boys, Christian congregations should also have lady teachers for girls, who are also to be supported from the common treasury, especially for the sake of children of poor parents who are unable to pay tuition" (pp. 1119 f.).

What is meant by food and clothing Luther explains in his *Admonition to Pastors to Preach Against Usury*. He writes: "'Having food and raiment, let us be therewith content' (1 Tim. 6: 8). That is addressed to all Christians, both rich and poor. And the reason is stated in v. 7: 'For we brought nothing into this world, and it is certain we can carry nothing out.' A prince has for his [own] person food and clothing, and more than that he cannot use for himself; the rest he must leave behind [when he dies], like any citizen, peasant, and beggar … His house, castle, land, clothing, and what else there may be, is his clothing. His meat, drink, wine, and beer are his food. For food here does not mean horse fodder, nor is clothing a pigsty or sack, but everyone's necessity, according to his station, including all goods." (X, 1055; SL X, 884 f.)

The congregation shall also provide food, clothing, habitation, and all other necessities for the poor, widows, orphans, aged, and invalids, which these themselves cannot procure and [for which] they have no relatives who first of all owe them these things. (2 Thess. 3:11, 12: "For we hear that some among you walk in idleness, not busy at work, but busybodies. Now such persons we command and encourage in the Lord Jesus Christ to do their work quietly and to earn their own living." 1 Tim. 5:16: "If any believing woman has relatives who are widows, let her care for them. Let the church not be burdened, so that it may care for those who are truly widows." Cf. 1 John 3:17; Matt. 25:35,36,40,42,43,45; James 1:27.) The congregation shall also care for those who suffer distress through special calamities like fire, famine, scarcity, robbery, and so forth. (2 Cor. 8:13,14: "For I do not mean that others should be eased and you burdened, but that as a matter of fairness your abundance at the present time should supply their need, so that their abundance may supply your need, that there may be fairness." Rom. 12:15: "Rejoice with those who rejoice, weep with those who weep." 1 Cor. 12:26: "If one member suffers, all suffer together; if one member is honored, all rejoice together.") [This should be done] in order that no brother or sister may be tempted, to the disgrace of the Gospel, to seek the help of those who are without or even to join secret societies which advertise mutual assistance. (1 Thess. 4:11,12: "and to aspire to live quietly, and to mind your own affairs, and to work with your hands, as we instructed you, so that you may walk properly before outsiders and be dependent on no one.") For this purpose the congregation shall appoint special almoners. (Acts 6:1-7)

Note 1. Compare the testimonies of Luther under paragraph 8. Luther writes in his monograph *Concerning the Improvement of the Christian State*, 1520: "It is perhaps one of the most pressing needs that all begging for alms should be abolished in all Christendom, for among Christians no one ought to go begging. Nor would it be difficult to establish a law about this matter if only we had the courage and earnest intention to do so; for every town could take care of its own poor and refuse to admit any strange beggars, no matter what they would call themselves, hermits of the woods or mendicant friars. Every town could support its own poor, and if it should be too small, it could ask the neighboring villages and the [country] folk to contribute. As it is, they must support many tramps and vagabonds who appear as beggars. Then people could know who is truly poor and who is not. But there must be a manager or administrator who would know all the poor and what they need and tell this to the council or the pastor, or in what other way this matter might be adjusted ... I agree very strongly with what some say, [namely] that in this way the poor would not be provided for so well and that not such large stone houses and monasteries would be built and richly endowed. Nor is that necessary. He who pretends to be poor should not be rich. But if he wants to be rich, let him put his hand to the plow and let him dig it out of the ground himself.

"It is sufficient that the poor be provided for adequately so that they need not die of hunger or freeze to death. It is not right that one should be idle at the expense of another's labor, or that one should be rich and fare well while the other lives in poverty, as it now happens in our perverse world. For St. Paul says, 2 Thess. 3:10: 'If any would not work, neither should he eat.' God has appointed no one to live from the possessions of others except only the preaching and ruling ministers because of their spiritual work (as St. Paul says, 1 Cor. 9:14). Just so Christ says, Luke 10:7: 'The laborer is worthy of his hire.'" (X, 367 f.; SL X, 326 f.)

Also Porta writes in his "Instruction for Ministers": "If the question is put to whom or to what people you should chiefly give, you will find enough information and instruction in Holy Scripture. We read in Deut. 15:7: 'If there be among you a poor man of one of thy brethren within any of thy gates in thy land, which the Lord, thy God, giveth thee, thou shalt not harden thine heart,' and so forth. Here we may note that God the Lord tells Moses that if anyone is poor in your town or your land, you should open your hand and give to him. Therefore also the church sings, 'Open your helping hand to the poor in your land,' and so on. For by these words He wishes to commend to our care especially the poor among us, the sick and invalid, or those who because of their advanced age or feebleness cannot earn their bread, or who are without a home. For instance, unsuccessful craftsmen or laborers who have not maliciously wasted their goods by drunkenness, gluttony, gambling, or in any other evil way; or such as suffered injury and harm through some particular calamity, so that they cannot succeed even though they work, and therefore suffer want. The same is true of poor widows, orphans, and indigent but diligent students who come with a good report from their teachers. All these should be given support." (*Pastorale Lutheri* [ed. Cramer], pp. 1082 f.)

Later Porta writes: "To these belong also those who for a long time have served faithfully in the holy ministry and who now, because of old age and infirmity, can no longer minister. These we are in duty bound to support, as God the Lord Himself commanded that after the age of fifty years the Levites were to be free from service and should no longer serve, but minister with their brethren (that is, as tried and experienced persons they should serve them with good counsel) in the tabernacle of the congregation, but should not do service (Num. 8:24-26). If, then, in the Old Testament the aged Levites were relieved from their service, but kept with the others and supported, why should not we Christians show the same kindness to the aged emeriti, our pastors and ministers, who deserve this well? It certainly would be great and atrocious ingratitude to disown them in their old age and let them starve like old horses or dogs, as this happens now and then with great offense" (Ibid., p. 1119).

With regard to the survivors of a minister the Church Order of Lower Saxony declares: "It is therefore Christian, proper, and just that after the death of poor pastors their indigent, mourning, and pitiable widows with their forsaken, greatly distressed, and fatherless children should have roof and shelter. Surely God's unceasing punishments would not fail to follow if in this matter Christian provision were not made. Therefore, moved by gracious and fatherly will and love, which we owe to God, His holy Word, the sacraments, the ministry, and the pastors and their survivors, we command and order that every town and parish in the whole princely dominion should build, at a suitable place, with plenty yard and garden space, a home in which such a poor, distressed surviving widow of a minister may be domiciled free of charge during her whole widowhood with her forsaken children, and also that she should enjoy the common protection, pasture, fodder, and necessary fuel which the others have. Such homes, besides the other buildings of the church, should be carefully kept in good condition, in towns and villages alike, by the church officials and church members.

"In addition there should also be supplied to such greatly distressed, pitiable widows, besides homes, some of the fair annual rentals of the pastor's fields and meadows, or of the land of the church or of the chapel, so that they may all the better provide their household with bread. Nor is the pastor [in charge] to deny them any of this, especially since his own widow and orphaned children are also to receive and enjoy such support. But as long as there are no [pastors'] widows, the officials of the church shall lease the home and devote the income to the improvement of the church and other [parish] buildings. But should there be two widows, the younger shall meanwhile stay at other people's homes, but without charge to her, and after the death of the older move into the home for widows. Furthermore, such widows, after the death of their husbands, shall receive and enjoy without curtailment for a whole year during their mourning the parsonage and the whole year's salary, while the neighboring ministers, during this period of grace, administer the office and supply the place of the departed" (*Dedekennus, Thesaurus.* II, 833 f.).

Note 2. A testimony from earlier times against joining secret societies by our church members is found in the order of the consistory of Hanover addressed to the superintendents in 1745. We read, among other things: "We herewith give you to understand that a certain minister in these lands has dared to join the so-called Freemasons. It does not become a minister to do anything, even though it were an adiaphoron, which causes offense or becomes a stumbling block to the congregation entrusted to him or also to others. Therefore, because of Holy Scripture and his conscience, he is in duty bound to omit such things. Much less does he have the right to join a society whose laws and statutes he does not know and understand beforehand, obligating himself by an oath or otherwise binding his conscience. It may be pretended that such a society has for its foremost objective a *vinculum caritatis* (a bond of love), but Christians in Holy Scripture have so strong a *vinculum caritatis* that they need no other. Hence the action of this minister is not only seriously rebuked, but he is also commanded to separate himself from this society and to renounce its customary ceremonies" (*Acta hist.-eccles.*, IX, 404 f.).

A congregation shall see to it that its members in their sickness are not without the necessary help, daily and nightly nursing, and comfort. (Matt. 25:36: "I was sick and you visited me." Cf. v.43. 1 Tim. 5:10: "If she … has caref for the afflicted.")

Note. The duty of nursing the sick Porta places especially upon those who are supported by the congregation. He writes: "If a male or female citizen in town desires to take care of a sick brother or sister (in a charitable institution), whether during an epidemic or at another time, this should not be denied to anyone who is able to do so. But if anyone refuses to do it, he should be reproved with due earnestness by the elders" (Pastorale Lutheri, p. 1128).

A congregation shall see to it that every member, even the poorest, be given a decent, honorable, and Christian burial. (Matt. 14:12: "And his [John's] disciples came and took the body and buried it." Acts 8:2: "Devout men buried Stephen and made great lamentation over him." Jer. 22:18, 19: "Therefore thus says the Lord concerning Jehoiakim the son of Josiah, king of Judah: They shall not lament for him, saying, 'Ah, my brother!' or 'Ah, sister!' They shall not lament for him, saying, 'Ah, lord!' or 'Ah, his majesty!' With the burial of a donkey he shall be buried, dragged and dumped beyond the gates of Jerusalem." Tobit 1:18: "And if the king Sennacherib had slain any … I [Tobit] buried them.")

Note. Ludwig Hartmann writes about this: "Also the poor are to be given a [Christian] burial, for it is shameful to bury the departed poor without the sacred ceremonies. Therefore those shall be buried without charge who have not left sufficient [funds] so that they can be buried at their own expense. Many indeed are offended when they see that the poor are buried without song and prayer" (*Pastorale evang.*, p. 1334).

Christ before Herod

"And when he learned that he belonged to Herod's jurisdiction, he sent him over to Herod, who was himself in Jerusalem at that time." Luke 23:7 c. 1509

On Mercy

Six Chapters for Everyone

by Wilhelm Löhe

FORWARD

The following text is not motivated by the request of others, but by the desire of the editor to do the house of deaconesses at Neuendettelsau a little favor. It seemed to him that prospective servants of mercy should themselves primarily receive instruction on mercy. Because of this, he initially gave them instruction in the form of dictation meant to be copied by the students by hand and later interpreted by a teacher. However, because a deaconess's time for studying is limited, the dictation turned out to be too long for copying.

Someone tried to solve the problem by publishing portions of the dictation in the deaconesses' journal at Neuendettelsau. However, it became clear that the space available in the journal was limited as well and that the dictation would have to be torn into too many parts. Some people suggested that the text be published separately to reserve the space in the journal for other things. Those who made the suggestion thought the text's content was applicable to a wider audience, even though one chapter out of seven, though by no means the longest, was solely addressed to prospective deaconesses. A publisher was found, and the whole matter was settled when it was decided that the origin and purpose of the text could be explained in the foreword, as it is actually done here.

There are many people who can read and write something better about mercy; they, of course, will not find the following text necessary to read. However, there are also those who find other books on the same topic too long and difficult or who find this text more accessible and understandable in their particular circumstances. Perhaps those people will welcome this book. If after reading this they are stimulated to study the works of mercy themselves, then the publication has served its purpose.

I do not have to make any preliminary comments regarding this little book other than that I will gladly accept it if someone wants to make me aware of mistakes in my writing. May God grant this booklet His blessing. Let it serve others as much as it pleases Him and do no damage.

Neuendettelsau, 28 June 1860

Wilhelm Löhe

First Chapter

What Is Mercy?

1. Mercy is goodness, goodness is love, and, therefore, mercy is love. Mercy is goodness and love but in a specific relationship, namely, in relation to the unfortunate and wretched. Love is manifold. When it is directed to God on high, it becomes devotion and adoration. When it is directed over the whole earth to other redeemed brothers, it becomes goodness, affability, and friendliness. But when it enters areas filled with misery and brings with it consolation, relief, and help, then it becomes mercy. May the God who is love grant us manifold love and awaken in us a sense of and a will for mercy at the beginning of this inquiry.

2. The Old Testament uses five different words that mean "mercy" and the New Testament uses three. But these words are distinct in the sense that they point to the different stages of mercy's existence from the first inner impulses of mercy to its external practice. Other languages, too, have many words that mean the same thing, but rarely do the words so clearly and markedly point to various expressions that are used in the Old and New Testaments. Usually all of these expressions are translated in the same way into German, because the German language does not have distinct expressions for the different stages and forms of mercy. But there are some things that are understandably lost in the translation, which the text in the original languages reveals to the diligent reader.

3. One could ask whether mercy has been from eternity or whether it slowly came into being over time. The answer for the question is not difficult. Insofar as mercy is love and goodness, it is certainly from eternity. Insofar as it is a relation of love and mercy to misery, it cannot be older than misery itself. And because one always has to see love and mercy together, it is fitting to say that mercy came into being like misery, that is, in time, but that it lasts in eternity even when there will be no more misery. Eternal love cannot forget the misery of the creature, even when it is taken care of. There is no doubt that misery would return if mercy would not keep watch at the gates of heaven.

4. What is mercy? Is it a mere impulse? Is it a state? Is it a doing? Those are three questions in one. A possible answer is this: mercy is love toward the wretched, and it comes into being with misery. As we saw, it does not even cease to exist with

misery. But if it does not end with misery, does it cease before misery itself ends? Is it, therefore, something that lasts or is even a state of being? Whenever love meets misery, mercy is awakened. However, because misery is continually present in God's eyes, mercy cannot be an impulse, but it has to be a continuous inner movement of God, who created the world and who did not cease to love it although it fell. Mercy is, therefore, a state, that is, a state of continuous transfer of divine love to the wretched. But is it thinkable that God's love toward the broken is given to them without physical deeds? Can anybody stop the waters of grace, which want to come down from heaven, so that they would not flood the languishing earth? As the inner impulses of mercy are without number, so also are the deeds of mercy without number. Therefore, mercy is a state that does not suddenly cease after coming into being, but it is an endless impulse of God's heart toward the lost world, an endless row of God's gifts given to sinners. Thus all three questions are answered in the affirmative. If anyone wants to contradict, let him contradict, but it is more profitable that your mercy become like God's.

5. Mercy is only one thing, but its relations are without number, and in every relation it appears in a different form. This is why one can say that mercy is manifold. Misery, however, comes in just one form. And the greatest misery that there is, the origin and source of all other misery, is sin. It is difficult for mercy to relate to sin because they are so opposite. But in the end, mercy wrestles with justice and holiness and comes into a cleansing fire, and it emerges with a new name. From then on it is not called mercy anymore but grace.

Grace is mercy in its relation to sin and the sinner. After winning the victory for the salvation of the sinner and, as Scripture says, rejoicing against judgment (James 2:13), all other relations become easy for mercy. Once it has dealt with the sin itself, it only has to deal with the consequences of sin.

The consequences of sin are both bodily and spiritual, and we all know there is much bodily and spiritual misery. There is poverty in the bodily realm as well as nakedness, sickness, disease, age, and death. They are all vast, expansive areas in which mercy reigns as queen according to the will of the Lord, which is rich in activity, continually moving, and overflowing in good works. There is much misery in the spiritual realm as well. There is ignorance and error, lust, passion, outrage, and crime. Along with this, spiritual death and a hardening of hearts are constantly lurking around the corner. Oh, what expansive areas and lands Queen Mercy must not simply conquer, but also, according to the orders of her almighty Bridegroom, occupy and rule with the powers of the world to come!

We can see then that mercy is great, and just as a person has and is given many names during his lifetime, so mercy also is given many names according to her appearances. Under all of her forms is hidden a loving essence toward the wretched, a characteristic that is manifested in many different forms. At times it is called punishment, at times it is called teaching, at times comfort, at times reproof, at others consolation, at times admonition, at times strengthening — all depending on which specific sweet fruit the miserable children of man need.

6. All human misery originates in sin, which itself is the biggest misery. Because of his sin, man has become the object of divine justice, which punishes the guilty one. One only has to look to the first chapters of the history of humanity to see this. The sinner has always been the object of justice, which avenges transgression. But he has also been the object of divine mercy, which seeks not only to alleviate divine punishments and the consequences of sin, but also to overcome both them and sin itself. Thus, justice and mercy, the two hands of God, work on the same fallen, sinful being. After the one strikes, the other binds up the wounds made by the first. Thus, there is a tension because of God's effects on and in man. Now the question is, "How can man escape from this? "

He will escape it to the extent to which the will of a man bows under the reprimand, recognizes his state and suffering as punishment, and judges himself and his behavior in contrition and repentance. Indeed, to this extent justice yields to mercy and leaves it plenty of room so that it can drip the heavenly blessing of divine redemption and reconciliation into the justly struck wounds. But to the extent to which the will of a man rebels against justice and the pain of the wounds struck by it, ignores the call to repentance and hardens itself in defiance and pride, to this extent mercy yields to justice and eventually hands the haughty, impudent sinner over to a most holy, cruel sword.

Thus the tension of this double divine effect on the sinner does not last forever, but in one way or the other the divine effect becomes just a single one. Men for their part become either children of God's mercy or people of His avenging hand. And certainly the use and abuse of the remains of His free will is what leads man to mercy. Therefore, the bowls of the scales go up and down. But you, however, are the one to tip the scales, for, because of the way you are, you can do no good, and only hinder all the good that your God wants to do to you. Beware, for from your stubborn unwillingness, according to divine decree, even almighty mercy retreats.

How long can you go on resisting God's merciful will? When will mercy turn away from you and leave you to justice? Where are the divisions between justice and mercy? You do not know these answers, but grace is there for everyone that seeks it, even in their last moments.

The Church says that the time of grace lasts as long as life. Yet there is already a judgment before death for living people whose sin is so grievous that St. John does not say that one should pray for them (1 John 5:16). In spite of seeing life as a time of grace, there are warning examples along the path of life, which lead us to conclude that mercy might end its work before we breathe our last. Where there is suffering and pain, a longing and desire for grace, then there certainly is grace and mercy. But where there is a false security and the illusion of self-righteousness, there the gruesome air of death blows across deathbeds. Therefore, joyfully comfort all who cry for grace and mercy, but you yourself watch so that you do not pit any evil resistance of your own will against the merciful powers of the Word, lest mercy leave you.

Second Chapter

How Did the Lord, Your God, Practice Mercy in the Old Testament?

7. The Lord, your God, has miraculously led all humankind since the time of the fall. Indeed, I know of no greater miracle than the combination of justice and mercy as seen in the history of humankind. This miracle takes place in Old Testament times as well as in those of the New, and whoever carefully observes the individual periods and peaks of history before and after Christ will find that there are just as many periods and peaks of this miraculous combination of divine virtues.

Rightly, therefore, the Church paints Moses with the Law and our Lord on the cross in the front of the great history book of God. But history does not merely show us the Law. If it is true that all of history is a continuous testimony to the combination of justice and mercy, then it is obviously also a continuous testimony to mercy alone. During all the periods and peaks of history, mercy clearly is not just combined with justice, but prevails against it with great glory. "Mercy triumphs over judgment" (James 2:13).

8. Through the devil's envy, man falls; there divine justice combines with divine mercy, and both drive him out of paradise together, so that he may be punished for his evil deed (says justice), not eat of the tree of life, and live eternally in his misery (says mercy). Before paradise there is encamped the cherub and the striking swords, and the cherub is the angel of the throne of God. For where the angel is, there God has not yielded yet, for He still wills to dwell mercifully on earth. But the swords, however, still bar the access to the tree of life.

In the same manner also after the fall, the combination between the two great divine virtues of justice and mercy is actively doing the work of the Lord. The justice of God drives the one who committed fratricide out of Eden, but yet his mercy marks the man's forehead lest he be slain by anybody who finds him. Similarly, the justice of God prepared the flood, while the mercy of God allows one hundred twenty years as a time for repentance. When the deluge of water breaks in, justice drowns the whole world, but mercy carries Noah and seven souls safely and peacefully through the awesome waters to Mount Ararat and brings him the olive leaf of forbearance by the means of a dove. There, dear children, you have a catechism of justice and mercy for the first period of the world, an instruction to pursue the matter further and to locate the two divine virtues more often in the same period.

9. Humanity grows in amazing progressions after the flood as a result of divine mercy. That same mercy preserves the little light of godly insight in the growing population. But look! Justice rises to punish humanity because it does not want to follow that

light, but instead wants to clear its own ways and to light its own light for the future. Mercy joins it quickly, and both work together to confuse the languages. As a result, humanity's desire for evil is justly punished by the confusion of the languages, with which the variety of nationalities and religions goes along. Yet the punishment is alleviated by mercy, for disunity is better than unity in that it leaves more doors open for the divine truth than the latter. In this manner also, in the first era of the patriarchs after the flood, justice again goes together with mercy.

10. According to His justice, God lets those who flee from Him go their ways, a gruesome leniency of the Most High toward the corrupt creature! But look! At the same time, mercy enters in and lays in Abraham a seed for that plant that begins like a mustard seed, grows, and becomes the great tree under which all the downtrodden and abandoned peoples can gather again and find Him — He who looked for Adam under the trees in the garden and wills to meet lost humanity at the monument of His love, at the tree of Israel, the cross on Golgotha, to save them. Oh, what a noble and lovely combination of justice and mercy!

11. Abraham moves into Canaan, right into the middle of the cursed children who are dragged along unwillingly rather than walking the way of the curse. Justice is preparing them for eventual extermination. However, first Abraham, Isaac, and Jacob must pilgrimage in the land and preach the name of the Lord who blesses the sinners. To enable them to do this, wise mercy providentially arranges that they bring from Mesopotamia the language spoken in Canaan. Also, mercy restrains the arm of justice for four generations after Abraham, giving Canaan time to repent if it so wishes. After this respite, the fire of the Lord breaks into the land, and mercy rejoices over judgment.

12. From Israel's passing through the Red Sea until the disintegration of the people in the year AD 70, this people had been — willingly or unwillingly, that does not matter — bearers of God's mercy in its holy mission to the Gentiles. On every stage of its development, clear testimonies of the divine Word show that God chose it to be a light for the nations, even a lighthouse and sign for the rest of the saints. This calling of divine mercy is so thorough and so inevitable that it comes to the forefront during the time the people are in exile and during the ensuing period of loss of national independence. The sin of the people and its consequences do not revoke the holy call; indeed, Israel remains the bearer of the Gospel of the single true God and Redeemer of the world whether it believes in Him or not. But because the people as a whole are not good enough for the sacred task God has commanded them, light and power concentrate even more in individual persons, and the strength of the office of the prophet of God casts its rays even more brightly into the farthest regions. In this manner, God shows mercy through Israel, as well as justice. Israel's service for mercy is in vain. So the Almighty enters in with punishments, and chooses for the execution of His judgments the same hand that had to carry the saving light of His grace as it,

for example, took place among the nations of Canaan, who had to be destroyed by the children of the holy patriarchs who had preached them the Gospel. The history of all peoples, especially of the great peoples before Christ, has no other meaning than this: in and by Israel mercy or justice is offered them, peace or punishment.

13. Just as God offers mercy or justice to the peoples of Israel, so Israel itself as the bearer of God's mercy and justice is constantly experiencing divine mercy and justice. The high hand, which justly practiced arrogance against Pharaoh and the gods of Egypt, is for Israel itself a high hand of mercy. It is like eagles' wings and carries the sword of justice, namely, the people of Israel itself against Canaan to exterminate the peoples. This hand mercifully leads the people through the Red Sea to Mount Sinai to Kadesh; the same hand puts the whole people down into the dust of death in just judgment. Mercifully it leads the next generation across the Jordan River after thirty-eight years, and lets the cities and peoples fall because of their cry. Mercy was even seen in the wars that the Lord fought, and Israel's celebration accompanied His victories according to the mercy that happened to them. Yet soon came centuries under the judges, during which times justice, at times mercy, was seen. This depended on whether the people practiced ungodliness and had a longing to be like the peoples of the world, or whether they were tearfully contrite and returned to Jehovah. In a similar manner, this goes on through all history. Yes, mercy and justice change ever more grandly until the just Lord casts the people away.

14. In the times of Samuel, the desire of the people of Israel to have a king like other peoples grew so strong that it demanded an answer. Although Samuel was unwilling (and the Lord did not rebuke him for his unwillingness), he nevertheless gave one king to the people. Moses had already promised them a king, and a monarchy did not directly contradict the theocracy, but rather served as a shadow of the coming kingdom of Christ.

The first king did not persevere according to the mind of God, yet the second one did according to God's heart. Whatever the sinful people demanded, the Lord granted according to His mercy. Yet He also mingled in His justice, for along with their kings the people had to suffer for the sake of their sin. Indeed, it is under these kings that justice and mercy encounter each other again. However, because kingship is, much like the priesthood, easily prone to corruption, it had to become a chastening rod of the Most High and of His justice for the people. In this way justice could rejoice over mercy, the divine mercy instituted the holy office of the prophets, who were directly influenced by the divine Spirit and who became most prominent whenever the people came into the greatest spiritual danger. In this way mercy rejoiced over judgment again, and the people of Israel had a sure antidote against the human, sinful depravation of both the priesthood and the kingship during the long period of its kings. The more the people succumbed to the influence of the surrounding peoples and the demons, the louder the prophets became; the more the people pushed themselves closer to the edge of the abyss, the more powerfully God stretched out the saving arm of His holy Word. Before the floods of divine justice broke in, mercy applied all means to save the hardened people of Israel. Even until the Babylonian Exile, mercy wrestles for the sparing of Israel from exile as she wrestles for a prize.

15. The just hand of the Most High leads first Israel and then also Judah into exile. There the children of the saints sat at the rivers of Babylon and wept (Ps. 137:1). The Lord soon was sorry for the punishment, for He is merciful and gracious, slow to anger, and abounding in mercy (Ps. 103:8). In the midst of the exile, He gives the people the greatest prophets to direct their behaviors, their hearts, and their hopes during the exile. This He did just like a shepherd who can lead his sheep, and in so doing, He keeps alive their sense of the old homeland and the mount of their God and the holy service and the coming Messiah. In this way mercy prevents Israel from passing away in misery, from despairing and assimilating to the Gentiles. And so they remain God's people in the midst of punishment and, like once in the desert, journey toward a better time. Finally, mercy leads the people home as its spoil, while the service of justice is praised at the same time.

16. After coming home into the Promised Land, the Jews still bear the consequences of divine justice; they are seized by one ruler after the other and suffer from different degrees of oppression and tyranny. Even the prophets are muted, and a strange silence from the one who always has been witnessing among His people commences. In turn, however, divine mercy collected the written testimonies of the prophets in a book, and then awakens a widespread zeal to read that Book of books. The whole people paid attention to the Word, and its knowledge spread in all the strata of the congregation of Israel. Satan led them astray so that they did not merely want to be like the peoples anymore, but now wanted to rule over them. They left bloody paths out of their desire for earthly exaltation under the Maccabees and later eventually failed to recognize Him who was to come. But the testimony of mercy was nevertheless burning and shining among them, and the closer to the advent of the Lord, the less they lacked people like Simeon and Hannah, Zechariah and Elizabeth, Mary and Joseph, people who knew the time in which they were visited.

For in the midst of judgment, mercy shows itself, and in the midst of mercy, justice shows itself. Throughout the whole time of the Old Testament one can always find the combination of both, and time and again the mercy we are talking about moves to again rejoice over justice.

THIRD CHAPTER

How Did the Lord, Your Savior, Practice Mercy in the New Testament?

17. The work and suffering of our Savior, Jesus Christ, is simply the culmination of that highly praiseworthy combination of mercy and justice. The purpose of God

the Father, the execution of the same through God the Son, and the application of the accomplished work to men through God the Holy Spirit — all this is the most irrefutable witness to the fact that justice first had to be satisfied before the Lord could turn to us in grace. What did God want besides this — that His Son should suffer the punishments for our sins and become sin in human nature, so that we might become righteousness that avails before the highest judgment seat? What did the Son do besides suffering the just punishments for our sins and thereby proclaiming their justice, and yet still inviting us to Himself in the sure knowledge of success, so that we might inherit an everlasting mercy from His hand? And what does the Holy Spirit through the preaching of His servants deposit in the hearts of men besides precisely this combination of mercy and justice for the good of the otherwise lost world? In these two thoughts — just and merciful — everything the Triune has done and still does is summed up.

18. In the apostolic period, the streams of mercy go out over the whole world, and justice seems to step back. Yet, nevertheless, the thunders of watchful justice roll right into the heavenly harmonies made by the grace of God, which are heard from the mouth of the holy apostles. First, the congregation gathers around the faith, but the mystery of evil still reveals itself. It also makes itself felt and known, and from the first days of the beginning of the Church of Christ, a great apostasy develops, which will provoke the judgment of the King of all kings. The apostles preach clearly and loudly that the Lamb of God is also the Lion from Judah, and that the Redeemer of the world with His bleeding wounds is also a just and pitiless judge, whose heart full of love can just as easily pour out eternal torture on those whom He has redeemed. Thus, it is in Him that justice and mercy are combined.

19. Every subsequent period of Church history is an echo of the first and a prelude to the last era in history. It is an echo of the first because of the activity of mercy and a prelude to the last because of the breaking in of justice. The history of every Christianized people is nothing but proof of the cooperation between the two great divine virtues. Wherever the Gospel is received, there is blessing everywhere; wherever one deviates from it, there blessedness and fortune go away. What happened so many times in the Old Testament after the sermon of the angel at Bochim (Judges 2:1–5) repeats itself in a New Testament fashion. The way a people acts toward the Gospel determines the way the hand of the Lord and its rod (Zech. 11:7) act toward them. The people's fortune changes according to changes in their behavior toward the Gospel. This remains true in the history of all peoples despite the many and extraordinary differences.

20. One of the most remarkable combinations of mercy and justice is seen in the persecution by the Roman emperors, men who came over the Church. The Christians suffered outrageous injustice, and the Lord paid back the tyrants as they deserved it. Books have been written on the different death penalties the persecutors suffered, but the Christians were rightly persecuted. One should not imagine that the people of the

first centuries carried and appreciated the impulses of the Gospel more persistently than other, later generations. Close to the time of the first outpouring of the Holy Spirit, the first examples of the secularization of the Church and of making a covenant between the Church and Belial can be seen. Indeed, there the persecutions come as a punishment of God, as a revelation of His justice. But the very same persecutions are cleansing storms and a blowing of wind, which rekindle the existing sparks and little flames of faith into the desired fire. After a time of deepest corruption, the most beautiful examples of the holy martyrs shine and show us that one should never despair of the power of God and of His Gospel. The Lord knows to fill His judgments with the powers of mercy and to do according to what is written (2 Sam. 22:36; Ps. 18:35), "When you humiliate me, you make me great."

21. A highly remarkable mingling and combining of divine mercy and justice can be learned from the fate of the Arian nations. These must be looked at in comparison to those who fell away from the pure doctrine of the divine Word. The most gifted Germanic nations belonged to the former group, namely the Goths, the Gepidae, the Vandals, and so on. Some of these (e.g., the Ostrogoths under Theodoric) even enjoyed excellent governments and considerable intellectual freedom. Nevertheless, their measure of mercy was used quickly. By God's justice, they were carried off in wars as mushrooms are torn from soil, although they seemed rooted firmly like oaks. Indeed, there is nothing more detestable in history than the story of the Franks and of their abominations, that is, kings. Nevertheless, the Lord was with them and showed mercy, not justice, toward their sins and abominations while they honored the Son and the Father and confessed the Most Holy Trinity. Here one can see not only mercy and justice but also mercy's limits.

22. In earlier days, the Gospel spread over southern Europe. We are not entirely familiar with its successes because a great extermination arose, but there were successes nevertheless, great and remarkable instances of the impact of the divine Word. Sometimes even whole nations bowed in belief. But the swift hand of God soon came over this harvest of the Gospel, and Attila, the king of the Huns, "the scourge of God," as he called himself, blew from east to west like a storm and flattened the plantations of the Gospel.

Even though, like with other storms, a mountain or a forest provided shelter for some congregations, several nations as a whole needed time to recover from the misery caused by Attila's storm across Europe. His path was one of divine justice over the depravity that was prevalent in Europe. Yet even at his time mercy was still active, and even if the impact of the Gospel was not very broad, it was very intense. The Lord made the glory of His Church shine even brighter over the destruction of the kingdoms and caused His saints to lighten the world with divine mercy. The mercy they passed on to others is still alive, but the destructive wars and calamities they experienced are recognized and remembered by but a few.

23. Other than Rome, the most prosperous congregations of the old world were located in Asia and Africa. We have not always understood the amount of mercy that the Lord showed to His saints in those parts of the world. But it bears noting that this time of grace lasted longer than, for example, the time of grace of the European congregations who experience Attila's scourge and were mentioned in the previous paragraph.

Yet here too mercy came to its end, and the Lord brought the terrible rod of justice to Asia and Africa through the deceiver of the nations, Muhammad. It is a great testimony to the corruption of mankind that scores of people in all lands were willing to exchange the religion of the thorn-crowned, almighty, and holy Jesus for the aberration of an epileptic obsessed by lust. And yet it happened, and God quickly used His hand of justice, for the Lord uses it to punish men. But other punishments were added to it, namely, the pressure and barbarism of Muhammadanism, a pressure that fills all of history, a barbarism that was never more obvious than right now. One must have an open and keen eye to perceive traces of mercy in God's judgment that swept across the nations through Muhammad.

24. Even as judgment spread across Asia and Africa, mercy was not idle in those lands and, moreover, won great victories and triumphs for Christ the Lord in other countries, especially those of northern Europe. What a life emerged at the same time in both Ireland and England and then migrated from there into the Frankish kingdom on both sides of the Rhine! Who can reflect upon the missionary journeys of the old monks — who came across the English Channel, built places for the adoration of Jesus and for moral betterment in the midst of the wildernesses, and had the most hallowing influence on Europe north of the Alps — without confessing that mercy was remarkably busy in those times? Again, we see that mercy is mingled with justice. The lack of total devotion to the Word, however, causes justice to manifest itself in the form of hardships in life and shortcomings of strength for the nations. These are merely signs of the same justice that punishes men mostly through their own deeds. It is, nevertheless, always safe to assert that God strikingly revealed Himself through justice in the Orient and through mercy in the Occident.

25. In those times, divine mercy awakened one man in the Occident who is without par in the world ever since. For the Church, he was an abundance of grace, but for the heathen he was a sword of justice. Although he meant only good for the heathen and gave them scores of teachers and preachers, he, against the declared opinion of his advisers, asked that the heathen either accept or reject the Gospel. One has to admit that his actions reflected a divine providence. Yet here it, too, is clear that the combination and mingling of justice and mercy is not, nor should it be, always the same, and specific inner reasons often determine divine permission.

During the long period of the Roman emperors who succeeded Charlemagne, two main topics were continually discussed, namely, the relation of the Church to the pope on the one hand and the relation between Church and state on the other hand. Groups within the Church arose everywhere, criticizing the right of the pope over the Lord's congregations and seeking to establish a more inward and scriptural life instead of the external and ecclesial life of the Roman church.

Between state and church, however, strife over who ought to submit to whom arose. The popes claimed that the state has to submit to the Church; the emperor, conversely, that the Church be subject to the state. The Church, therefore, was engaged in a double contention against both the emperor and the sects. In both relations, the Church applied somewhat just principles in a sinful manner and, therefore, suffered much from both sides. In the end, divine justice punished its sins.

The emperors were certainly no better than the popes, and their discipline for the popes was more questionable than that of the popes for the emperors. This is why the nations generally followed the discipline of the popes more readily than that of the emperors. In this way, divine justice was done not only against the popes, but also against the lords of this world. However, while one side was always punished by the other, the victory was never clearly won by either side, and divine mercy showed itself on both sides. Finally, the two sides evaluated each other, and the Lord showed to all parties involved how they should better themselves. Whoever reads the long stories of the period briefly mentioned here may find again a combination of justice and mercy and a great example of how mercy rejoices over judgment.

26. Immediately preceding the Reformation era was a time of grave justice. Constantinople and the East Roman Empire, or whatever was left of it, fell under the sword of Muhammad. Whatever great and glorious things the Greeks possessed from age-old times, pagan as well as Christian, were carried away into all the world, just like the wind blows into chaff and disperses it into all different directions. The glory of the Greeks flew out of its nest and was carried to Italy and then to the Alps. This glory was a spirit of knowledge and of delight in languages and literature. Divine mercy helped further this movement in the sense that the languages of the New and Old Testaments were studied more carefully and that Holy Scripture as a whole was also read more carefully. However, this same spirit of the Greeks was also a spirit of wantonness and moral depravation that sowed its seeds wherever it went. This seed grows exuberantly, and once again the warning justice of the Lord is seen in a strange way. It allows men to walk on wrong paths and looks on, watching whether they will turn from their ways and seek mercy before it brings the final judgments.

Prior to this, mercy and justice seem to be engaged only in preparatory work during the so-called Renaissance of the arts and sciences; they are busily preparing for the Reformation. The Reformation era itself appears to be a time filled with grace and some of the most blessed evidences of mercy. Yet Martin Luther, the foremost among the reformers, often complained that mercy did not find open windows and that, therefore, punishment would come over the world, especially Germany. And so it happened. At the end of Luther's life the situation changed, and the religious wars began to rage over the world like hurricanes filled with evil and sin. They were especially destructive in Germany and our homeland is suffering from those wounds to this day. Thus, in the Reformation era, God shows Himself as great in justice as in mercy. And yet here again mercy rejoices over justice, especially because His Word and Sacrament remain among us even after gruesome times.

27. From the second half of the seventeenth century until recently, one finds an odd combination of justice and mercy in the Church that was hardly ever heard of in previous time periods. Apostasy awoke in the form of freely promoted freethinking, which refused to be bound to the divine Word, and in licentious lifestyles, which refused to abide by the divine law anymore. The emergence of this liberal spirit planted seeds of religious and moral calamity that sprouted wildly and in whose cancerous expansion consisted the just punishment for the Church, which did not resist the evil with any resolve. As the sin we are talking about did not cease, the punishment, which keeps up with sin as it spreads, did not either.

However, divine mercy was not altogether lacking. The pietists, as well as those who follow Zinzendorf's name, are testimonies of divine grace and pity, even though they have many errors and shortcomings as a result of sin. Nevertheless, they saw times of revival and awakening for thousands. They are like fingers of divine mercy, helping the Church see that it was touched by God's grace, even when men like Ernst Valentin Löscher or Albrecht Bengel opposed them. But the Church did not always understand God's fingers and the awakened communities began to go their own ways. The result of their actions was more punishment, but this does not render the assertion invalid that God's mercy did indeed show itself.

28. Recent times are no more than a continuation of the previous. Apostasy ran rampant, its channel wider, its consequences more visible in the life of the Church, the state, and the family. Upon the shores of mighty sins divine justice broke and still breaks as well as executes and prophesies ever more severe punishments. But it is true that more recent times have seen special outpourings of divine graces. The children of God, who became great in number, have learned how to apply the plunder of the enemies of the Church — the erudite studies that originally had been begun with a different intention — to favor the kingdom of God. The spirit of prophecy has joined the people's faithful study of Holy Scripture and history, and the hope of the Church has begun to shine more truly and beautifully than many centuries before. People have started to discover what is wanting and wrong in the current state of ecclesial affairs, and many hearts have a deep and great longing to live in a better state.

Even in this era, the separation is increasing: justice and mercy go their separate ways, but mercy still rejoices over judgment. Whoever has eyes to see and ears to hear can flee the future wrath and become worthy to stand before the Son of Man.

29. So there you have an overview of the vestiges of mercy and justice in both new and old times. We were unable to separate one from another. However, the intention was always to pursue the thesis that there were never evidences of divine mercy lacking in the Church and not even in the world. Since the fall of humanity, God has remained faithful in His merciful will to save it. And we know that in the end God the Lord will set aside His mercy and exercise pure justice according to our merit. The kingdom of the Lord is a kingdom of mercy. As the temple of Solomon has two pillars, so this kingdom has two foundational pillars, Boaz and Jachin (1 Kings 7:21; 2 Chron. 3:17), that is, justice and mercy. There will never be just one. There will never be either one lacking, and we will always hold to this theme and will always preach: "The Lord is merciful and gracious, slow to anger and abounding in steadfast love" (Ps. 103:8).

FOURTH CHAPTER

How Did the Lord in the Law of the Old Testament Command His People to Practice Mercy?

30. While the Lord separated His people Israel from the other peoples and led them — with their own government and with their own worship — into a land whose borders caused the people to be separated from the others, God did not want this people to interpret this special role in a merciless and selfish manner. On His part this separation took place as an act of divine mercy, and it should be seen by the people in the same sense. Yet by commanding this, that is, by commanding in a very strict way that His people be separate from other peoples, He did not mean to give them a precept and instruction of selfish mercilessness, but rather they were supposed to keep the commandment of separation out of love and mercy. Israel could not accomplish its mission to be a light to the Gentiles if it did not separate from all Gentiles. If Israel became like those who looked to Israel to learn how to worship rightly, Israel might experience what had happened when Balaam set up a snare for them (Numbers 22–24): instead of converting others, they themselves might be perverted. Whoever wants to shoot arrows has to have a good stand neither too far nor too close from the game. Whoever wants to catch birds cannot step on their wings, and the fisherman does not swim with the fish in the water. This had to be understood if Israel was to fulfill its calling to the Gentiles.

31. God does all His works through His servants. Therefore, His works are divine and human at the same time, and wherever He works He soon opens a wide course of mercy for His saints. But they are only to be, as they should, coworkers of the divine worker.

When, therefore, during the time of Samuel, the Lord mercifully poured out the spirit of prophecy on the children of the prophets, He thereby invited the same children of the prophets to prophesy, to witness, and thus to direct the beams of His mercy into the night of their surroundings. When He gave them David, a king according to His own heart, then the chosen king was to spread the holy and great gifts he received from the mercy of the Lord to the whole people like a well of mercy. When a marvelous glory of worship is unfolded under the prophets Samuel and David, when sacrifices, prayers, psalms, and hymns, moreover the sound of all instruments, the sweetness of the aroma, and everything that was pleasant to the eye had to join in to serve the God of Israel worthily, then all this was a revelation of the Lord, an outpouring of His mercy. But the priests, the Levites, the singers, and the king were also bearers and servants of mercy. As each of these in his specific place made contributions to the great harmony of the whole, they all helped to lead the people to the understanding that the Lord is merciful and gracious, and they, in turn, all practiced mercy.

Thus the great institutions of the Old Testament — prophethood, kingship, priesthood — were not merely creations of this merciful God, but at the same time a threefold mighty call for training and knowledge of the mercy of the Lord.

32. In the previous paragraphs we saw human mercy, led by the hand of the Lord, enter vast areas to serve the Gentiles or, at least, the people of Israel. Just as pipes direct the fertilizing water from a well to the different fields and beds, so mercy is poured out over all the holy people according to the direction of the Old Testament. Although the Old Testament legislation is so marvelously just, and although it is, therefore, praised much and recognized by all, one nonetheless can say that the Shepherd's love and mercy permeates the whole, and that all its parts are based upon a tender, divine providence for each individual tribe, yea, for each individual human being. Even where the words sound most severely, they are severe only on the one side, while on the other, one can see the reign of mercy.

33. Let us now examine in detail what the previous paragraph laid out in general. Looking at the persons to which divine providence is extended, we find that neither the citizen nor the foreigner is forgotten, neither the Levite nor the priest nor the layman, neither the old nor the young, neither the healthy nor the sick, neither the blind nor the deaf, yea, not even the murderer and manslayer. Finally, mercy does not even end where humanity ends, for neither the beasts nor the bird in the nest are forgotten. Looking not at the persons, but at the occasions when mercy is to be practiced, we find the will of God expressed mercifully during the harvest, on a feast day, during a love feast, during a sacrificial meal, during a Sabbath year, during a jubilee. Divine grace and mercy crown all these summits of the high life of Israel as a people and Church, and they smell of the rich herbs and alpine flowers of human mercy. Wherever a life reaches a summit, Israel is to prove that it is the merciful son of a merciful God.

And as it is with the persons and occasions, so it is with the different forms and manners of practicing mercy. A famous text in the New Testament locates mercy in giving, forgiving, and not judging (Luke 6:36–38). No one can deny that mercy and giving are commanded in the Old Testament. An attentive eye and a good will will also find, when they look for it, many texts of the Old Testament that reference forgiving and judging and object clearly to absolute justice. Even sparing someone from pain is a form of mercy. If so, who can fail to recognize then that there can be gathered many texts that reflect God's fatherly sparing of us poor sinners. It will be a delightful, sweet, and even happy task for someone to read the Old Testament law with the purpose of finding examples of any kind and form of mercy.

34. There is one thing we do not find in the Old Testament, namely, no institutions or houses of mercy and no distinct office whose purpose is to show mercy. These are fruits of the New Testament. But yet it is also undeniable that the Old Testament commandments give leeway for the care and institutional practice of mercy. Though the poor have always existed, both in the Old and New Testaments, there were never supposed to be beggars. And there lies the principle, yea, command: to care for the poor and to prevent them from becoming beggars. Even if those in the Old Testament attempted to provide for the poor within the family, there were certainly also in that time, and in the Holy Land, individuals and circumstances that pressed toward an institutional care for the poor. It would, therefore, not be surprising if we somehow discover that such a care actually took place. However, whatever we find or could find will, nevertheless, be different from what is seen in the Church of the New Testament already in the initial time right after its birth.

FIFTH CHAPTER

How Did the Lord, Your Redeemer, and His Holy Apostles in the New Testament Command His Saints to Practice Mercy?

35. Out of mercy the Son of God became man; He lived, died, rose, ascended into heaven, and lives forever to practice great mercy. The motive and purpose of all His works is mercy, and mercy is what He desires for those who are His. Because His love and His Father's and the Spirit's love can only be mercy, so our love for the brothers and all men should also include nothing but mercy. The great basic command for our life is: "Be merciful, just as your Father in heaven is merciful" (Luke 6:36).

36. Just as we see that the mercy of God's children to the heathen in the Old Testament is the will of Jehovah, so the New Testament shows that God's will is to show mercy to the heathen. If eyes are necessary to detect God's will to be merciful to the heathen in the Old Testament, it can be said conversely that blind eyes and deaf ears are necessary to miss the King of eternal glory and His majestic orders when He says (Matt. 28:19-20), "Go therefore and make disciples of all nations, baptizing them in the name of the Father and of the Son and of the Holy Spirit, teaching them to observe all that I have commanded you."

Evangelizing to the Gentiles is the great work of mercy in the New Testament. The New Testament's inner circle, not just its appendix but its very center, is the evangelization of the Jews, about which the Lord says to His apostles (Acts 1:8), "You will be my witnesses in Jerusalem and in all Judea and Samaria, and to the end of the earth." There can be no greater mercy in this world than to propagate the Most High's Word and Sacrament, complete with their fullness of grace, to the poor, lost children of man of all ages and in all lands.

However, the Lord not only commands mercy upon all the world, but He also promises His own helping presence to those who will exercise mercy saying, "Behold, I am with you always, to the end of the age" (Matt. 28:20). This, His great Word, is spoken in direct relation to the practice of mercy in His holy mission. He, the King, and behind Him the redeemed throng of His servants journey around the whole world, carrying the holy gifts of Word and Sacrament until Jericho collapses under the sound of the horns of jubilee, and the kingdoms of this world become a spoil of Him who preaches about Himself, "The Lord is merciful and gracious" (Ps. 103:8). His whole Church is outwardly nothing but a priestly, royal institute of mercy.

37. Just as the Church outwardly is a holy institute of mercy, so it is also inwardly. The apostle as well as the evangelist, but likewise also the shepherd, the presbyter, and the bishop are nothing but instruments of divine mercy toward the congregations on earth. The sheep and lambs of Jesus supervise, lead, and feed through the valley of sorrow to deep wells of eternal calm. This mercy is just as great as when the sheep are called and brought in to the fold through God's holy mission.

Think also of the Samaritan, the man who brings to the inn him who has fallen prey to murderers. He is like an evangelist or missionary. The inn is the congregation; the keeper of the inn, to whom the saved is entrusted, is the bishop of the congregation and can make well what the murderers made evil. The whole apostolic order of office and church is, therefore, nothing but an instruction for a shepherd to show merciful love. The highest Shepherd has equipped the office of Word and Sacrament, the office of reconciliation, with obligations and authority to mercifully sacrifice oneself for the salvation of the sheep, just as He sacrificed Himself for the sheep according to the unfathomable gift that He received.

38. Working alongside the office of the Word is the office of bodily mercy. In Holy Scripture, all offices of the Holy Spirit are called diakoniai, or "service," just as all those — beginning with Christ all the way down to the most humble ones — who carry out offices and duties in relation to people in the name of God are called diakonoi or "servants." Nevertheless, however, the words diakonia and diakono were used in the first congregation in Jerusalem and were transferred as specific titles to the office of bodily mercy.

As a result, the word deacony refers to nothing but the holy duty of caring for the poor, and the deacons refer to those seven who first occupied this office and their successors. This office was first one of service at the table, a distribution of the gifts gathered by the congregation for those who ate there publicly, especially the widows.

This, however, was but the first sprout of the whole office that sprang up from the fertile soil. Now when the poor widow did not come to the table because she was sick or had become infirm, was the office of the deacon and his care for the widow to come to an end or did it simply take on a different form? Without any doubt, the latter. After the congregation had eaten, the seven visited those who had not been at the meal — the sick, the infirm, the weak, the aged — and began their holy care for their temporal needs. Or, to investigate the expansion of the office into a different direction, did the holy deacon only care for the widow? Did the widow look at her children, the orphans, with tears of sorrow in her eyes while the needs of her body were met? Or would not the congregation have also directed its love through the holy seven to the children as well? Or when the pilgrims came, hundreds of thousands that used to come to Jerusalem, of which some doubtless turned to the Gospel, would no deacon have cared for them, even if they were poor or sick? Would not a new branch have grown out of the noble plant of deacony, the branch of holy hospitality that through love provides a home to the stranger in a foreign land? Who would even bother to answer these very easy questions?

Everyone sees that the bodily mercy of the Lord was reflected in the office of the seven and that it could be no different according to the holy nature of the matter. An institutional organization of aid and care for every bodily misery developed, and in the splendor of the holiest human love, the deacon, full of blessing, walked alongside the bishop and the elders through the congregation and laid down the earthly gift of mercy alongside the heavenly goods of the divine office. Yet, from the outset, this office was not purely bodily. Those who served the tables in the name of the congregation had to be able to pray at the table, and those who brought the needs to the sick person had to hand it over to him with spiritual hands, offering silver apples in golden bowls. In short, according to the order of the holy apostles, the deacon had to be a man filled with the Holy Spirit in order to know how to administer bodily matters spiritually and to be recognized in many ways as someone who came out of the sanctuary of the New Testament. He had to be permeated by the Holy Spirit to such a degree that the bishop could lay into his faithful hands the earthly gifts with which the body and blood of Christ had joined themselves. Those who brought all temporal gifts to the congregation had to be found worthy to bring also the blessed bread and the blessed cup to those who suffered from a double hunger, the one for daily bread and wine and the one for the heavenly goods, which the hymn of thanksgiving of the elect praises. Thus, the office of holy deacony became a spiritual office, an office of double mercy, which was so deeply rooted in the congregation that it sometimes shone brighter than the splendor of the office of Word and Sacrament. Such glory gives He who on the Last Day will ask His saints about mercy and especially the office of bodily mercy.

39. We have the motivation and the right to give special consideration to the deaconess as a servant of mercy, especially because the goal of this text is to turn the reader's hearts toward the specific service of women to the wretched and needy, an activity that developed in the New Testament. We certainly cannot say that the deaconess is mentioned frequently in the New Testament, especially because one of the most preeminent texts in that regard (St. Paul speaking about widows in 1 Tim. 5:1–15) is not clear enough that it can be persuasively applied to the office of the deaconess.

However, the deaconess stands in the Bible like the humble violet in the garden, known by its smell, pleasant to God and men, in a hiddenness that God Himself wanted. She does not hold the first and greatest office in the kingdom of God, but she leads the choir of widows and virgins and shows the whole female gender the paths that are meant for them. For the deaconess does not have her own specific duties, inaccessible to everyone else. Her duties are those of women in general, and her peculiarity consists only in carrying out those female duties, not in her own family, but for those who are abandoned in the congregation.

The duty of all women for which God created them is to help men; after the fall, this task constitutes nothing but showing mercy to man and his sphere of activity. Thus, all women pursue the same goal of mercy, led by the deaconess as their forerunner, an example to be emulated by all. She, the widow, as she is called in antiquity and obviously already in the New Testament (1 Timothy 5); the virgin, as she is described by St. Paul in 1 Corinthians 7; the unmarried, emancipated from her own worries, for whom it is made easy already by the circumstances to have a free heart — she is to show to all how to do the works of female mercy. Out of a soul that is betrothed to the Lord, she works in holy freedom, teaching women to help all earthly things from a soul that is betrothed to the Lord. Like the whole deacony, the office of the deaconess is a plant entirely grown on Christian soil. She should and could be a friendly sign of the presence of the Lord in His congregation.

40. If, therefore, the Church's constitution as well as its offices can be understood in light of mercy, then this already gives great glory for the Lord of the Church. All His officers, His male and female servants, practice either spiritual or material mercy. However, we are not to see only His officers in light of mercy, but His whole congregation on earth. His most holy teaching is a religion of mercy. Therefore, everything that is His, every soul that belongs to Him, the individual and as well as the whole, is to be merciful.

Bodily mercy is not enough to accomplish this, His purpose. The whole congregation is meant to be merciful in the spiritual realm, that is, in the realm of holy *discipline*. That simple, seminal word, which we read in Matthew 18:15, did not come from the apostles, no matter how noble and great their reputation remains in the Church, but from the mouth of the Lord Himself. The main principle of this word, if not the thesis, is that "No Christian is to remain in sin." It is nothing new that a Christian sins; every moment there are new examples, and this is the way it is going to be until the end. But no one who wants to belong to Christ must persist in sin; every brother and sister in Christ is to stand up after lapsing, is to be raised up out of weakness, is to be brought back from error. This mercy is a command of the Lord.

The mouth of the Lord indicates how this holy command is to be carried out. If anybody lapses, then his neighbor is to raise him. If this does not work, then the call of mercy comes to one or two more. If this does not help, then it says (Matt. 18:17), "Tell it to the church," and thus the whole camp is called up in the interest of one individual with the intention of dragging a single person out of sin and, thereby, out of eternal damnation. Only the King of eternal mercy, who knows all things and to whom everything is clear, could have given such a mandate, so perfect, so sufficient, and yet so full of simplicity and usefulness.

It is sad, though, that His holy Word cannot find its due obedience in Christian congregations because of the sinful way the people act. It is also sad that out of the most blessed acts of love and mercy many caricatures grew in the Church, and these were not the image of that holy, merciful love that the good Shepherd carries to His sheep.

41. The New Testament extends its instructions not only to the congregational and official practice of this virtue, but it is also rich and detailed in regard to individual persons and their different kinds of the blessed practice of mercy.

First of all, one notices that the New Testament upholds all those passages of the Old where mercy is commanded and, subsequently, applies them to its own areas of life. Wherever Old Testament situations come up, there the Old Testament admonitions come to life, even if they are not explicitly repeated and confirmed by words of the New Testament. Thus, all the Old Testament exhortations regarding mercy — beginning with the person that wants even a bird to be spared all the way to those that practice mercy toward the aged and parents — belong also to us, the children of the New Testament. Therefore, when one inquires about mercy, this enhances the horizon.

Additionally, when the Lord indicated what He will say on the Last Day (Matt. 25:31), He did touch on certain classes of misery that could not even be mentioned in the Old Testament in the form given here. He talks about those who were hungry and thirsty and naked and sick because such people obviously existed in the Old and New Testaments. But He also says (Matt. 25:36), "I was in prison." This He applies to His brothers, those Christians who would be in prison for the same reasons as Christ, that is, for the sake of the truth. In saying these words, He points to the New Testament mercy shown the holy confessors and martyrs, and the Church of the first few centuries understood this very well.

Another text, where the general command to be merciful is specified, is that well-known one about the widows (1 Tim. 5:10), which lists a number of persons who need mercy: children who are to be brought up, pilgrims who are to be lodged, saints whose feet are to be washed, and afflicted ones who are to be relieved. Each of these indicates an entire class that has come to such a state and situation where mercy is needed. Indeed, it would be a great delight to look at those texts in the divine Word of the New Testament that open ditches for the spring waters of mercy and direct their ways to flow forth.

While there is no time for this exercise here, we must not forget the triumph of mercy in the New Testament. We look to those people who by the pierced hands were, surprisingly for some souls, admitted to the order of those who are to receive mercy, namely, their enemies. "Love your enemies and pray for those who persecute you" (Matt. 5:44). These are words and orders worthy of the one who even on the cross prayed for His enemies, and who, since He is ascended into heaven, has nothing else to do but to heap fiery coals of holy mercy on the heads of His ungrateful Church (Prov. 25:21ff; Rom. 12:20), and who preaches ceaselessly (Matt. 5:46, 48), "For if you love those who love you, what reward do you have? You therefore must be perfect, as your heavenly Father is perfect." In these words, there is a hint of the merciful ones' merit of grace and of the eternal blessing for those who understand and bestow mercy.

42. By introducing the persons to whom one should show mercy, we have already given an instruction as to how to identify the manifold kinds and manners of mercy. Who, for example, does not realize that mercy is shown to the hungry by food, just as the Lord had mercy upon His people and fed five thousand and four thousand respectively (Matt. 14:15–22; 15:29–39)? And who would not, with some dexterity in locating similar passages, remember the word of the Lord in Luke 14:13, where he says that one is to invite the poor when one gives a feast? Or who could not easily identify the way in which one can have mercy on the thirsty? Who would not remember that passage in Matthew 10:40ff that talks about the cup of cold water, which is to be given to a disciple in a disciple's name? Or, furthermore, who would not know that he is to show mercy to the naked by providing the necessary clothing, just as the highly blessed Merciful pardons the poor, naked world with the clothing of His most holy merit? Or who would not remember upon seeing a sick person that mercy is shown to him when he is healed, just as Jesus Christ healed the many sick in His home country? Who would not realize and find that one has to bring the sick to the Physician and to the medicine of body and soul, to Christ Himself, to practice mercy? Or, finally, what does the prisoner need but either freedom or comfort to strive for a higher freedom, by which one can endure the fetters for a long time?

Everybody sees that the kind and manner of mercy depends on the person it is shown to. Yet it is also seen easily that it is not only defined by the person, but also by the will and the example of the Duke of all mercy. Whoever gave all his possessions to the poor and had his body burned had, thereby, perhaps fed and saved many, but did he also practice mercy, if he does not have love (1 Cor. 13:3)? What is love and mercy without works? And, conversely, what are works without love and mercy? Just as in every body dwells a soul, so in every work dwells merciful love. It is and remains a poor deed that cannot be rewarded. Do not simply focus on the holiest form of appearance of mercy, but also consider that a humbled heart is part of the right way of exercising mercy, which deems it a grace to be allowed to practice mercy, and also a filled heart urged by the saying, "Cursed be he who vainly plays around with the Word of God." Full of love, full of humbleness, full of holy urge, full of fervent mercy — this is, generally speaking, the right way to practice mercy. Regardless of whether it be shown spiritually or bodily or spiritually-bodily, by giving or forgiving, by not-judging or judging, by patience and long-suffering or by the seeming opposite, a sudden outburst of chastisement, it, nevertheless, remains one and the same in its bountiful practice. This it does just as it is the same power of God that brings forth from the soil the manifold plants, and one and the same hearth of light, out of which break forth these myriad beams of the evening sun.

Sixth Chapter

How Did the Church of All Ages Follow Her Lord's Command to Practice Mercy?

43. It is clear from the outset that mercy was practiced the most during the time when the purest desires of the congregation and a right measure of divine grace directly corresponded to the purest and most anointed proclamation of the divine Word. The congregation of the apostolic time was one body and one spirit; thus, the members of the body provided the richest assistance to each other and, thereby, also to the great, holy love itself. There is not just one presbyter Gaius (3 John 1), one Philemon (Philemon 4), one family of Stephanas (1 Cor. 16:15), one Epaphroditus (Philemon 2:25; 4:18), and one Onesiphorus (2 Tim. 1:16) that receive the praise of the high apostles regarding mercy. But there the Holy Spirit, as we can read in Acts 2:44–47 and 4:32–37, praises entire congregations, like that in Jerusalem, because of their mercy, which manifests itself in the form of a respectful, brotherly love that is accompanied by pity and compassion. Let us then give an orderly overview of all that the New Testament tells us about the practice of mercy. There we come to:

(1) the communal breaking of bread and the office of the care of the poor, which first grew out of the apostolic office;

(2) the oft-discussed communism of the church at Jerusalem;

(3) the agapes or love feasts of the later apostolic time;

(4) the collections.

Everything the apostolic Scriptures preserved about the practice of mercy in the first congregations will be included in these four sections.

44. Acts 2:42 attests to the fact that the first congregation's members continually remained in the teaching of the apostles, in Communion, in the breaking of bread, and in prayer. Two of these items actually relate to our subject matter: the Communion and the breaking of bread. The Communion (κοινωνια, *collecta*) is nothing but the Communion of the earthly things, a sharing of goods. Thus, it is nothing but the practice of merciful, brotherly love. However, we will discuss this in depth later and in conjunction with the apostolic collection. But first we will look at the breaking of bread.

In the later times of the Church, the expression "breaking of bread" was used simply as a term for the Holy Supper. This took place in such a consistent manner that there arose an opposition to this usage. Indeed, some would assert that the expression had nothing to do with the Holy Supper. As often happens, the truth lies in the middle: the Holy Supper was united with communal eating, the daily meal of the first Christians, so that the bread actually was broken not only for the Sacrament, but also for daily nourishment. Later, the practice of communal eating fell into disuse, and the expression "breaking of bread" was shifted to the Holy Supper itself. This was used to describe the congregational meal that was handed down throughout the history of the Church by virtue of divine ordinances, and in this sense the term was rightly used. At this point, however, we must stay focused on the perished custom of the communal meal.

According to the testimonies of Holy Scripture, the first congregation at Jerusalem gathered in the temple at Solomon's Porch (Acts 5:12) for the divine services. The services consisted of the teaching of the apostles as well as the commandments of God. The people had all the right to do so because they were mostly Jewish Christians, that is, Jews who could enjoy their share in the temple just as much as others of their nation and who had not yet given up on the temple. The celebration of the Holy Supper could not take place at the open Porch of Solomon; a different location was needed for it. But the congregation was not lacking such a location for they gathered in groups in the houses of individual members.

Since the first celebration of the Supper had followed another, though also holy, meal, the people believed that it would be most faithful to the institution of the Lord if the holy meal of the New Testament would remain connected with a brotherly meal that was used in the Old Testament. I dare not decide whether the bodily meal preceded or followed the sacramental one, for there are reasons for and against both assumptions. In any case, a bodily meal went with it, and it was hallowed because of its connection with the Holy Supper. As poor and rich ate this meal together and the poor were not able to bring anything for it, the breaking of bread and communal eating became even more necessary because any shortage would be bodily, communally, and spiritually disruptive.

The communal meal awakened the need for holy, merciful, and decent care of the poor, and the office of the holy seven was instituted to meet this need. Initially it was the widows of the Hellenists, that is, of the Greek-speaking Jews, who had been overlooked. But provisions were soon made through the diaconate when the whole congregation, in great wisdom, elected men who belonged to the offended party as deacons. One can assume that all the men were Greek Jews by birth, since all the names of the holy seven are Greek. This election was a very honorable one for the entire first congregation, and the election also spoke of a special guidance from the most high Lord, who put the office of mercy in the hands of the more liberal group in the congregation. Thus, there was then at Jerusalem a table service of seven holy men, who because of their Hellenistic origin were also perhaps equipped with some external education and graceful manner of officiating at the table. Likewise, the Holy Spirit worked in them and enabled them to do their duties in a special way, specifically with heavenly decorum and according to the mind of the Lord. After this, we do not read of any further complaints of either Greeks or Palestinians. The great, important, and tender business of table service and mercy was being done according to the heart of the One who became the example of table service for all the holy seven by His works at Cana (John 2:1–12) and at the feeding of the five thousand and four thousand.

45. The most striking feature of mercy in the apostolic congregation at Jerusalem — and at the same time verifiable proof of the fact that in that congregation mercy had transfigured itself into brotherly love — is what we know about the common possession of all goods. In Acts 2:44–45 and 4:32, we read in clear words of the Holy Spirit that no one said his goods were strictly his own, but that all things were held in common. Indeed, the people even sold their goods and possessions and distributed the proceeds among the others according to their needs. Thus, there was no need among them.

Later, this apostolic communism, emerging simply from the exuberance of the Spirit and brotherly love, is no longer found in a whole congregation; even in Jerusalem itself it was no longer seen because the whole congregation was scattered. Those who gathered there later became a new congregation, which, for example, could be treated by James the Just — as far as his letter is applicable to Jerusalem — in a totally different manner than that first springtime congregation. Also, the additional resources of the congregation at Jerusalem dried up fairly soon, and other congregations had to come to its aid in self-sacrificial love because of the scarcity of goods in AD 44 and even up to fifteen years later.

Although this communism was a transitory phenomenon, in its appearance and disappearance it is and remains a very remarkable thing, and very different opinions were voiced about it from time to time. One group is inclined to see this communism as a confusion of the first congregation; yet who can endorse this opinion, since the apostles did nothing to stop this movement? A man like Barnabas himself set the example (Acts 4:36), and the mild light of divine goodwill, not a single shadow of reproof, appears in the narration of this incident.

Did the almighty and holy Lord want to protect and defend the course of the congregation by punishing certain members in the episode of Ananias and Sapphira (Acts 5:1–11)? Others believed that it was necessary to abstain from anything like this in the further governing of the Church, since even in the congregation at Jerusalem, the firstborn in grace and virtues, this movement did not remain totally pure, as Ananias and Sapphira indicate. Yet even if one admits that such fruits rarely grow on earth and no general commandment can be given to produce them — as the Lord Himself opened the way for the rich youth after he had asked, "What do I still lack?" (Matt. 19:20) — one, nevertheless, has to keep the way, which the Lord showed to the rich youth and in which the first congregation walked.

Finally, others in the nineteenth century, the Communists of the day, have tried to cover their damned theories with the divine Word and the example of the first congregation. Yet the mind and intention of the Communists are as far from the famous passages of the Book of Acts as the morning is from midnight. The communism at Jerusalem was an entirely free and by no means commanded matter, which was practiced or left undone by each individual Christian according to his circumstances. If it had been a general matter, based on legislation and systematic implementation, then one cannot understand, for example, why the mother of John Mark could still possess her own house where, according to Acts 12:12, the congregation gathered for prayer. Likewise, one cannot understand why the example of the holy apostle Barnabas is pointed out, who could easily sell his field since he was a Levite and had his share in the Temple. Also, Peter should have rebuked Ananias and Sapphira for embezzling what was meant for the congregation, not for their hypocrisy. The communism at Jerusalem is like a heavenly, miraculous flaring up of love. It was set at the beginning of the Christian era for everyone to see what great things flow out of love, and for what measure of love and mercy everybody has to pray for himself as well as for others. Never again was there seen such a powerful appearance of loving mercy in the world, and yet it would be of the greatest foolishness to take the rareness of the matter as a proof for its being no good.

46. It might seem odd to include a separate paragraph about the love feasts, especially since I certainly had in mind nothing but the love feasts of the first congregation when previously talking about the breaking of bread in the Jerusalem congregation. Yet also in Jerusalem, the joint eating of the congregation ceased to a degree already discussed. But there were also love feasts elsewhere, and the famous chapter 1 Corinthians 11 clearly bears witness to this.

In Jerusalem the believers ate together daily, and their meals were in fact love feasts. This was chiefly due to the life of love that governed them, and it was a manifestation of the new nature or creation that they ate together. But it was different in Corinth and the remaining congregations. There love feasts were held because one wanted to do it, not because one could not but help it. The meal became a matter of purpose; one intentionally gathered to practice love. While in Jerusalem the joint eating was more a hallowed form of daily life, elsewhere it was a purposeful public testimony of the existing brotherly love. In Jerusalem it was care of the poor; in Corinth and elsewhere it was for public recognition of the principle that the rich members of Christ should care for the poor. One could say that the joint eating and the breaking of bread of the Jerusalem congregation is the most beautiful and unique pearl in the crown of the Lord Jesus, the agapes of the later apostolic time but smaller pearls from secondary water. But what we know about these agapes of the later apostolic time is derived mostly from the eleventh chapter of the First Letter to the Corinthians, even though we find traces of the same matter in other passages of the New Testament. The institutions of the later Christian time are also as useful as a ray of the setting sun reflected by the mountains, which can be used to make inferences about the glory of the sun itself.

William Cave (1637–1713), an author who researched the life of the early Church and wrote valuable books, and others with him hold that the love feasts at Corinth were held before the Holy Supper, since all Christians would probably have been gathered for the Holy Supper. The Corinthians, however, were reprimanded in view of their love feasts, namely, that they did not wait for each other. Cave seems to be quite right, since the apostle closely connects the reproach regarding the way the love feast was held to the doctrine and celebration of the Holy Supper itself. This may have been done so that he who does not mercifully wait and provide for his brother during the love feast goes to the Holy Supper unworthily. However, this by no means implies that the love feast had the same relation to the Sacrament in every congregation. In Corinth it was this way, but elsewhere it was different.

The perversion of the matter in Corinth was doubtlessly very loathsome and punishable, and St. Paul speaks against it. Among the Corinthians, the manner in which they, as pagans, held their primitive meals was obvious. They ate together, but each individually, and there was no thought that here was an opportunity to do good. After Paul's reproach, this Greek sin of eating out of selfishness was supposed to be overcome by the customs of the Semitic congregation. For at the love feast preceding the Holy Supper, a beam of heavenly love was brought out, and it illumined the congregation in Zion during the first days of the apostles more beautifully than the sun rising above the Mount of Olives. One can speculate about whether the admonition of St. Paul awakened the merciful brotherly love of the Corinthian congregation anew and resulted in the people eating the Supper in a manner worthy of the Lamb, but we do not have any reports about this.

47. Although Christian mercy can be called the firstborn daughter of the new love with which the Spirit of Jesus filled His believers, its limits could not be set more narrowly than love itself permitted. Just as love did not just cover the members of the individual congregation but embraced all who were born out of God, all who were recognized as believers, so mercy also was not content to drive every kind of misery out of the closest proximity, out of the area of the individual congregation, but it wanted to do good and help those who lived afar off. The Spirit of the Lord assisted it so that its manifestation could bring even more honor to Himself and Jesus.

For instance, through the prophet Agabus He prophesied a great scarcity that would, once it started, hit the poor Jewish-Christian congregations particularly hard. Soon the spirit of the congregations awoke, especially in the Pauline congregations, which, as a precaution even before the calamity started, gathered everything that might bring relief (Acts 11:28–30). And when the Palestinian congregations were hit again by scarcity, famine, and calamity about fifteen years later, the old zeal of Paul and the fervent love of his congregations became fresh and new again, and now the aid of the pagans, who had received the spiritual wealth from the Jews, gratefully flowed back into the old native areas through material benefits (Rom. 15:27). Those lengthy passages, written by the most faithful hand of Paul (2 Corinthians 8) where he urged the Christians with all the power of heart-felt Christian rhetoric to participate in collections for the poor Jewish congregations, are among the most beautiful passages we can possibly read in the apostolic epistles. Rules are given there, not just regarding the ratio between gift and property, but also regarding the time and way of giving. The most diligent and obedient ones are praised as apostles or delegates of the congregations have to be selected to bring the money to Jerusalem to the elders. In view of an extraordinary contribution, the apostle himself does not consider it an interruption of his apostolic work to personally travel to Jerusalem with the delegates just to deliver the offering of the pagan Christians.

Whoever reads all this cannot but consider the collections that are held for other congregations as sacred and be roused to do likewise, but through simple conclusions he must come to realize also that those first Christians must have been exceedingly rich in their giving. A journey from Macedonia to Jerusalem, done by three or four delegates of the congregations, was expensive to say the least. And think of how big the collections had to be, especially if the needy themselves should immediately deem it worthy of their own delegation after deducing all the travel expenses. Here as always when we compare our situation with that of the early Church, we are moved to beat our chest repentantly and confess our sins unto the Lord.

48. As we set about to make a transition into studying the first post-apostolic centuries and their practice of mercy, we must first put before our eyes the content of our discussion, which is arranged in a clear manner. First, we can examine the persons that were treated with mercy, then the principles of mercy that were followed,

then the difference between private and public practices of mercy, and, finally, the zeal of the Christians that can be observed in the practice of mercy.

49. As for the persons who were the objects of mercy, we find at the top of the list some well-known guests at the tables of the congregation, that is, the widows and orphans, the aged, the infirm, the sick, the abandoned children, the virgins, the strangers, the prisoners of war, the slaves, the confessors and their families, and even the dead. This list shows that the objects of mercy started to become more diverse, just as the spread of Christianity brought with it increasing persecutions, the hatred of the world, and other different circumstances of the different congregations.

The poor *widows* older than sixty years, possibly also younger ones, who were trusted not to marry again were taken care of by the congregation according to an apostolic precedent, and they practiced works of mercy in the congregation. They began to form a distinct rank, so to speak. To the *orphans* was applied the principle that the bishop had to vicariously assume the stead of the father for those who had no other caregiver. He had the boys learn a craft and provided them with the necessary tools; the girls were educated until they were either ready to be married or deemed fit to join the ranks of the virgins.

The *aged, infirm,* and *sick* were supported by the offerings of the Church according to their needs. Pains were taken to not support those poor who could work. Love was only to compensate for that which a person was unable to earn by himself. Instead, it was considered mercy to instruct somebody to use his own strength and to earn whatever he needed. The bishop handed *abandoned children* over to the widows and virgins for education; this part of the Christian work of love was seen as missionary work and blessed as such. The *virgins,* that is, the God-betrothed virgins, who had beforehand renounced marriage, formed their own liturgical rank, which was entitled to take its livelihood from the altar.

The *strangers* received great care from the earliest times on, and the bishops earnestly urged others not to overlook them in the practice of mercy. Indeed, the institute of letters to pilgrims was begun specifically in the interest of strangers.2 *Prisoners of war* or Christians abducted by wild hordes were ransomed with a lot of sacrifice, even if objects such as holy vessels had to be sold. Likewise, all care was given to slaves, although one was not by any means ready to set them free or even ransom them.

Special attention and faithfulness were given to the *confessors.* Their escape was facil-itated. They were received into houses, given food and drink in prison, accompanied before court and defended, and after becoming martyrs they were buried with all diligence. The families of those gone home, their widows and orphans, were certainly taken care of. The deacons diligently kept records and lists of the poor, and they were carefully listed according to name, age, sex, trade, and circumstances. Thus, no one was overlooked or forgotten. Neither were the *dead* forgotten. Because the Lord would not forget them but will raise them out of the earth, the Church also could not forget them, but put them reverently and with sacred service into the soil as God's seeds.

Additionally, one did not stop at the *fellow believers* but also served Jews and the heathen. Splendid examples of this were experienced at Alexandria and Carthage. At different times the plague killed an immense number of people at both places. While the heathen mercilessly threw the sick, the dying, and the dead out of their houses, the Christians, regardless of the dead person's religion and state, carried them into their houses, took care of them, buried them, and in scores fell prey to the disease themselves. At those times the glory of the Christian religion shone so brightly that it was also generally praised by the heathen.

50. As we now have to talk about the principles of mercy, we must first distinguish between principles for giving and principles for the use of the gifts.

There is little doubt that the Christian Church unanimously acknowledged the legitimacy of wealth. Although it was known that the Lord had expected the rich youth to sell all his goods and give the proceeds to the poor, and although the first congregation at Jerusalem had sacrificially followed this word of Jesus, no one saw a firm commandment of the Lord regarding giving, only pastoral advice for certain people and circumstances.

The whole Church realized that a rich person, too, could be a Christian and still remain rich. The question of possessing wealth was separated from the other regarding its use, and it was left to the individual to act according to his conscience, his circumstances, and his gifts. It was only expected that, regardless of how one managed his property, he use it for the glory of God and his Christ and for the blessing of mankind. It was seen clearly that he who managed his goods according to mercy served the Lord and his neighbor just as much as he who simply donated them to the Church for its poor or to the poor themselves.

The principle of the legitimacy of wealth was connected with a second one, namely, that of the unrestricted freedom of all giving. Although many agreed that all Christians had the obligation to give, they were still far from using any further force beyond that of admonition to instruct people on giving. Irenaeus says that the Jews had the commandment and the obligation to bring sacrifices, but the Christians offer God sacrifices more pleasing; for they bring everything willingly (*Against Heresies* IV 13:2–4; 18:2).

Here the church father noted an important difference between the Old and New Testament that is worthy of recognition. For a third principle is connected to the first two: the poor have no right to demand a gift. If they had the right, the gift would not flow from mercy and the marvelous love of God. But according to God's will, there are the poor and the rich, and the chasm between both is to be covered by merciful love. In recognizing this, the Church did not tolerate any mumbling poor but instead, for example, taught the slaves not to despair while waiting to be ransomed, but to fulfill the commandment of the apostle, who instructs the slaves to serve their masters well. Thus he taught them not only to serve the good and gentle, but also the harsh (1 Peter 2:18). One might question whether these principles applied by the Church were to be considered economical. But in any case, passages by the church fathers show a concern for the common good, and based on these texts one could perhaps try to ascertain how much truth is in the so-called economical views, for indeed, some truth is also in them.

51. After the preceding paragraph, we must now list the principles that told how gifts were to be used during the second and third centuries. These will coincide with the previously discussed distinction between public and private mercy. Private charity was not restricted by public charity. Every Christian rejoiced in public charity and supported it and participated in it. But he also insisted on the joy of detecting misery with his own eyes, visiting it on his own feet, and alleviating it with his own hands.

Women especially excelled in this holy calling of private charity. Due to their faith they were not tempted to join in worldly entertainment. Instead, they used their time and strength to visit the shanties of the wretched, all the while fulfilling their calling at home and exhorting themselves and others to make sacrifices and show love, even when their own strength proved to be insufficient. It goes without saying that we cannot give any accurate report regarding private charity, for as there are secret sins that must not come to light, so there are also secret ways and settings of mercy that the Father, who sees in secret (Matt. 6:4), wills to reveal on that Great Day.

Conversely, there is still something to be said about the public charity of Christians. The Christians gave offerings in their Divine Services, which were partly used for the poor, especially for the agape meals. These meals, however, like the celebration of the Sacrament, were no longer offered daily, and not always in connection with the Sacrament anymore. Besides the oblations, the Christians used to deposit special weekly and monthly gifts in the congregation's charity chest. On special occasions, such as on the conversion and reception of heathen or heretics, or on the installation into an ecclesial office and so forth, great gifts were given. Many gave the tithe of the Old Testament voluntarily, and this was publicly approved, yet without making a law out of it. When greater calamities appeared nearby and far away, collections were announced. When one foresaw that there was no way for the congregation to give the gifts, a fast was scheduled, and the savings from the food of one day were laid on the altar.

Legally the bishop and his lower clergy, specifically the deacons, were the administrators of all public finances and gifts of mercy. Nothing was saved or invested. Whatever the congregation laid on the altar was transformed into a brook or river of love that could not stand still but that looked for its fall to where the misery lived, and that continually had to be of immediate use in the congregation. One did not seek to establish foundations meant to remain operational for centuries, but one practiced mercy immediately and handed down that understanding to the follow generation. One did not donate one's alms in such a way that the bishop was unable to use it right away if a more urgent need emerged. And indeed it goes without saying that lists were made, and that accounts were kept and rendered. A wise man never tolerated management of money without supervision, and he certainly never led his brother into temptation by releasing him from rendering an account. By no means were these gifts, these sacrifices, left unaccounted for.

52. As for the zeal of the Christians in the second and third centuries, one can already conclude from looking at history that it had to be great and extraordinary. Whenever a great calamity arose, the need for mercy spoke powerfully to the congregations of Jesus, and hearts were prepared, willing, and inclined to follow the call to help those in need. Additionally, not only the congregations but also those in the holy ministry were in full bloom back then. There was no lack of faithful, respected bishops and teachers who knew how to pour fresh oil into the lamps of pious mercy.

For wherever the Word of God meets willing hearts, there is no lack of zealous renderings of good works. One could find enough individual examples as proof, but it is hardly necessary to point to the sacrifice of individuals when such principles governed the entire Church. The public and private practice of Christian love was not only highly recognized among heathen as well as Christians, but it was even turned into an accusation by the former. The sacrifice, the dedication, the love — when it breaks forth with such a force as in both centuries about which we are talking — is too much a stranger in this world to be understood by it. Instead, it is usually misunderstood. In view of those times this has to be even more true, and especially back then, when the world set the abominations of the apostasy from God unabashedly and numerously before everyone's eyes.

53. As we now proceed to the fruits of mercy during the next three centuries, that is, the fourth, fifth, and sixth centuries, it will be by no means superfluous to consider these centuries and their shape in general. In this period, the gruesome end of the western Roman Empire and the deep decay of the eastern Roman Empire take place. The Roman Empire and the Roman population in general were unable to exist without being ruled by foreign governments. The flow of Germanic nations into both halves of the old Roman Empire occurred. General devastation and destruction were wrought on both countries and cities. Nations lost their populations. There was no peace.

Who can look at these events without thinking that these centuries must have offered huge amounts of work for those wanting to show Christian mercy? And yet these events only mark the general external outline of the time and do not answer the question, "Why is this time period so different than earlier years, and why did it turn out this way?" If the whole Roman Empire is covered by a stream of nameless misfortune and misery, then a terrible guilt must have preceded it, for the Lord is a just God.

But then why were the Romans previously lords over the Nordic nations by whom they were now overcome? Why the weakness? What is the cause of all these terrible punishments? One could certainly give many answers here, none of which has to be wrong in and of itself. One could simply say that the Romans had previously overcome, robbed, and plundered all nations, and so now it is their turn, and it is done to them according to the Word: "With the measure you use it will be measured back to you" (Luke 6:38).

The Romans themselves, having become rich and great, were not content with the gifts of a rich and good providence. This is why now all the poor, frugal ones come from the darkness of their woods and prairies and show others how it feels when one comes to experience the bad things he has done to himself. This is why fear from God comes over the beautiful lands of the South, why the inhabitants flee, why the cities become desolate, and why the remains of kindness sink into the dust before the avenging swords of the Germans and later of the Huns. Already this answer would suffice to point out the rich seed of an even richer crop. Yet we want to give one more answer out of the many, as it can be gathered from the research that has been done in recent times.

A general calamity covered the whole territory of the Roman Empire. Rome — from the very outset an agricultural nation and little acquainted with industry and commerce — had come under increasing pressure regarding its fields because of looming warfare. The military duties were incumbent on the masters, and the slaves were supposed to tend the field but were lazy, evil workers. The fields became desolate. Then the small owners sold their land to the bigger ones, and so the individual farms became immeasurably large. So it happened that in that period many a Roman farm's acreage was equal or even superior to that of a German principality. These immense farms were run by crowds of lazy slaves, and yielded so little that they were eventually abandoned, because of which difficulties of a different kind were experienced everywhere. The complaints were many, for the number of slaves and poor became immense, and the hatred against the masters and rich was growing. So when the field of mercy had already been great, now it was altogether overwhelming.

Additionally, the victory of the church over the Roman Empire did not bring about a greater zeal but only indifference. Because there was no longer a threat of persecution, the church grew complacent and sought to prosper as much as possible. While its own fire cooled off, the hundreds of thousands — who according to the example and precept of the emperors joined the church — brought little additional strength and were instead a great burden and icy cold. The church fathers now had to struggle with the violent, the impudent, the ostentatious, the greedy, the avaricious, the wasteful, the usurers, and with all kinds of injustice within the church, as they did formerly with the heathen.

When one reads the speeches of the great church fathers of the fourth, fifth, and sixth centuries, everything is just like today. Depraved masses — loving Christians as an exception — knew no better way to keep from being seduced by a so-called Christian state of affairs than to go into the wilderness, the deserts, and the monasteries.

To such a church the task was assigned to alleviate — I do not say to eliminate — this nameless misery. Misery flowed and now covered the land with its waters because of God's just providence and retaliating hand. The disproportion between agriculture and commerce, between slavery and freedom, the terrible consequences of the Roman conquests, oppression and extortion in all countries, and the like, are to be counted among these sources. The church knew that while it was unable to stop the flow of sadness, it ought to drain off the water. Yet it lacked the necessary hands to do the work. All this causes a very bleak view into the centuries about which we are talking. The church did what it could, but did it really reach the goal of making this misery-filled world, which did not want spiritual help, materially happy?

54. When exercising the care of the poor, the church encountered the same persons we listed in the previous period, but in greater diversity and in incomparably larger numbers. Added to these were some forms of misery we had previously no reason or necessity to note. For example, the church had to work with day laborers and small free landowners, both of which frequently had to languish in the greatest misery. Therefore, the old task was again made more difficult because of the same principles as before. It considered wealth legitimate, the gift voluntary, and the poor by no means being entitled to demand the aid. Yet frequently the call for help from the shepherds or bishops of the congregations became so urgent that one was tempted to forget that love is a matter of freedom.

Yes, the great calamity attributed such a value to the alms that even the greatest church fathers ran the risk of attributing money a value far greater than was legitimate. By taking their starting point from certain passages of Holy Scripture, which have to be seen within the whole picture of salvation or they are easily misunderstood, they come to a point where they frequently emphasize the atoning virtue of the alms and their influence on one's attainment of eternal life. We must not endorse these ideas or use them ourselves, and we must certainly not be like those who attempted to elaborate on these passages and give alms a value, which one cannot do without infringing upon the blood of Jesus. So it is certainly right that the holy Fathers attacked the usurers, assailed the greedy, and challenged the rich and wealthy in their thinking. By wresting the offering from unwilling hearts, they fulfilled a double sacred duty, namely that of Christian care for the poor and for their souls. Yet when the gift is wrested from the rich — not by pointing them to love, not by pointing them to the fact that it will bear witness to faith in eternity, not even by telling them that heaven and eternal blessedness are the gifts they received in return — then such a cry for help might be excused as merely the voice of one despairing.

So it comes as no surprise that people have a hard time proving that, in spite of the exaggeration, the church still held the old apostolic teachings regarding wealth, alms, and the way to eternal life.

55. As for the ways that people showed love to others, many great changes took place in these centuries. The church never wanted to supersede or absorb private charity, not even during these centuries. And so the former remained active alongside the latter for a time, and the public activities continued to be based on the oblations, agapes, and collections, regular and irregular contributions.

But the calamity began to grow bigger and the love colder. The number of those in need made it necessary for the church to be inventive, to assess the means and to think about how to have the greatest success with as little as possible. In the past, every home was used as a poorhouse, a hospital, or a hospice. But as extraordinary as the activity of the church was, only individuals, not groups, were supported. Soon people began to think that perhaps it was cheaper to support ten poor in one house than to give them what they needed individually, and so institutional care emerged and replaced the care for individuals.

The monasteries became the paradigmatic objects of study for this purpose. Christianity was corrupt, perhaps even more corrupt than it is today. People did not know how to protect themselves from the influences of corruption on their souls other than to flee into the wilderness and deserts. The great leaders of the church, far from reproving or hindering such separation of the best members of the orthodox church, protected this idea and personally participated in it as much as possible. They saw this as a good example for the rest of people who had to live in the world. In the settlements of the secluded ones, they saw asylums and places of refuge for all who were tired of the world and sin and longed for the strengthening and restoration of faith.

Wherever the monks settled together, there the principles of frugality and poverty and the interest of others were observed. Plato, Aristotle, Cicero, and the whole pagan world after them deemed bodily work unworthy of a free man. Hence no Roman worked, and slaves did farming and trade. After a time, the words of the apostle Paul finally began to shine fully, where he commands everybody to "labor, and make with his hands something good, that he may have something to give him who has need" (Eph. 4:28). From these words, a different state of public affairs began to emerge, where the spirit of the holy apostles was at work and became influential. This was the case mainly in those monasteries of the Orient and later of the Occident, especially when Benedict of Nursia, the father of all Occidental monks, developed and brought to light his salutary principles of combining prayer, study, and manual labor.

Soon crafts were practiced in the settlements of the monks. In sacred silence and singing praises, one did what only slaves did among the heathen. Through one's frugality one spared the assets of the settlement, and through one's work one increased them, both for the good of the poor. This was carried out mostly by those who had been raised in luxury, who had, like all their peers, brought their property as a dowry when they entered the monastery or the settlement, and who had enough to do to get used to the hardships. However, in return, those quiet settlements far from the world and from worldly congregations brought the greatest blessing not just upon the poor and wretched but also upon the whole church. When charity and mercy began to build their institutions — such as those of Basil of Caesarea in Cappadocia, a man most worthy of his title "the Great," who first fought against but then made the idea of institutional care of the poor his own — then one had nothing better to do than to shape the emerging institutions according to the principles, ways, and manners of the monasteries.

Thus, highly diverse institutions arose. There were hospices (*xenodochia*), institutions for infants (*brephotrophia*), and many others. In short, one sought to meet each person's every need by gathering those with similar needs together. Some of the church fathers mourned that the offerings and the simple deacony of the first centuries did not prevail anymore, were averse to foundations and endowments, and adhered most fervently to the principle that the church should not store or invest any riches but spread all gifts through charity as soon as possible. These men were by necessity the first, richest, and most powerful, and they lived in the era of institutions that still is not past and in which we also still live, to whose principles we, too, by necessity still have to pay tribute, and which might last until the Lord comes.

56. From the very beginning of the Christian church, the agapes are such a lovely phenomenon that some remarks must be made about their disappearance. Already in the previous period, we find that they are not connected with each consumption of the Supper anymore. In this period, however, they appear more and more rarely, mainly only at the celebration of the consecration of a church, at funerals, and on memorial days of revered blood witnesses of Jesus. Yet this was not the last restriction they experienced. The general corruption of the whole church became visible especially in the celebration of the agapes, whose character became more and more worldly, at which the rich Christian paraded his alms and the poor indulged himself as well as possible. This is why the best teachers of the church began to speak against them. Men like St. Ambrose abolished them in their dioceses, and others like Augustine followed suit. After the fifth century, they are found only here and there as an exception or in a rudimentary form. As honorable as the remains are, as much as there was also reason for sparing and cultivating them, one nonetheless realizes of how little use they can be in a sinking, spiritually decaying church.

57. We must now focus on what kind of institution was found most frequently in earlier times and what kind was endowed with the most money. In our age, when every third house in a city or village is usually the shop of a greedy innkeeper, one would not expect that long ago ecclesial institutions, such as hospices or houses for

pilgrims, began to appear. These usually combined all the other smaller institutions and were themselves most richly endowed.

In one of his letters, St. Jerome speaks beautifully of these hospices. A woman named Paulina had died, and her widower, Pammachius, found the deepest consolation for the death of the deceased in emulating her works of love. He, the noble offspring of the great heathen Camillus, was not content with distributing the immeasurable riches he inherited from his wife among the poor in Rome. As a result, he took off the purple gown of the senators and put on the black rugged garb of the monks and founded a hospice near Rome, just like the widow Fabiola in Rome itself. Then Jerome wrote to him from Bethlehem (ep. 66:11, cf. ep. 77:10): "I understand that you have founded a *xenodochium* [hospice] and have transplanted an offspring of the hospitable oak of Abraham to the Ausonic shores; just like Aeneas you set up your camp on the banks of the Tiber and build a Bethlehem [a house of bread] for this shore that has been visited by famine for a long time." That which had been entirely abandoned and that had become the last among us without any good reason had become the best of institutions. Thus, the first has become the last and had patiently waited for becoming the first once more.

Besides this first fruit, I must also list some institutions that the church cherished. These were namely the penitential monasteries for fallen girls, the asylums for women who had become slovenly out of poverty, and the hospitals for incurables.

58. The splintering of the church into different factions, schisms, and sects made a significant influence upon its charity. The church had formerly practiced mercy, though chiefly toward the fellow believers, yet without excluding anybody in the wider circle. The loving hearts, giving hands, and the administration of the assets of the church and institutions were Christian and only Christian, but the recipients could be Christians, Jews, or pagans without any distinction. The honor of the congregation consisted in not applying any difference of religion and confession to the area of charity, although blameless conduct of the Christian poor was required, and slovenly people were banned from the aid of the church.

Yet as the church disintegrated into different factions, every group went its own way and cared only for its own members. One can regret this difference as much as all schisms, although it is good to note that the works of mercy and zeal actually increased through this. It became a matter of honor for each faction not to fall behind the other but to possibly top it in the practice of love and to prove also by this that they had all the right on their side. Indeed, this is how the Lord knew how to turn the disadvantage into blessing. Yet still the vileness of men brought forth different consequences from this new situation, and they were bad ones.

59. Real help consists in two parts: (1) the removal of the calamity, and (2) the stopping of its sources so that it does not come back. Consequently, it has been said that the care of the poor has a double goal of removing or alleviating existing poverty

and then providing for the future so that no calamity might arise again. This double goal of care of the poor may be called praiseworthy and nice, but it is a different question whether it can actually be attained.

If it is attainable, then it is worth all trouble and sacrifice. It may even be that it was once attained here and there in a very limited circle and for a short period of time. But would it be possible to refute someone who asserted that it was, generally speaking, never attained and never will be? Does not the one word of the Lord — "For you always have the poor with you" (Matt. 26:11) — already speak powerfully and forcefully in favor of these assertions?

As there will never be a situation where there is ecclesial unity without purity and ongoing purification, so there will never be general prosperity on earth without calamity and poverty bidding the love and mercy of the children of God to do their old duty. Additionally, we have reasons enough to assert that hunger and poverty and nakedness will be awarded by the Lord of glory as a punishment for great disobedience until the end. This prophecy, this shadow of history pointing forward, shows us what is to come, and history itself as the body will not belie its own shadow. We can, therefore, approve of the double task of the care of the poor mentioned above only insofar as it gives us a goal that is worthwhile. Yet from the outset we have to renounce the hope of ever fulfilling it on earth.

This, however, does not mean that we cannot measure our achievement against this goal. Conversely, the standard is a good one if used rightly. Indeed, it will be vital in pointing out our own shortcomings and will cause humility, for the Church has known for some time that this is its task. When it made a difference between the poor that were supported and those that were not to be supported, when it stimulated the poor to endure evil and the rich to show mercy, when it ransomed the prisoners and thereby returned the workers to their families, when it had the foundlings and orphans reared and instructed them in and made them good at crafts, when it instructed girls in how to manage a household, and so on, what else did it do but to pursue the task of mercy? Who would have ever done more to reach this goal than the Church, giving from its treasure of love?

Nevertheless, there can be no doubt that the calamity was too abundant and the misery too broad and too deep to think of anything beyond what was at hand, namely, the alleviation of the most crying need. There is a rich stream of love flowing from the cross of Christ through the centuries. Filled with admiration, we see its rich, deep waters. But we also realize that He who caused it to stream out of the hearts of men, only after it had come out of His own pierced heart, does not bind Himself only to the modern time. Instead, He provides for His people at all times to do the necessary in the simplest way. Thus they help in their own time and place, and at other times they plan and provide for the future of the poor as the Spirit of God exhorts them to do so.

281

60. So far we have only talked about the ecclesial activities, but an entire mighty realm of life standing beside the Church, that is, the state, has hardly been touched. The alliance into which the Church entered with the state from the days of the first Christian emperor, Constantine the Great, was one of great consequences. When we look at the consequences and take them as a whole, we will find it very difficult to view this association as something at all fortunate for the Church. Yet the overarching spirit of the Church dominated the state in so many ways that one can point to a lot of coincidentally good results.

The ancient Roman legislation was nothing less than Christian. However, one could notice that the pagan emperors could not keep themselves entirely impervious to the teaching of the Lord Jesus, even when persecution raged against the flock of Christ. Everything changed when Constantine fully grasped the cross instead of the scepter. One ancient man holds that the laws of Constantine look as if he had issued them right after hearing a sermon, as if he had been touched by the powers of a world to come, or as if a hero of the desert, like St. Anthony for example, had stood behind and admonished him.

Yet the influence of Christianity emerges even more clearly in the legislation of Justinian. From Constantine onward the mighty victory of the Christian Church over the state becomes visible, and the light of godly wisdom started to be reflected here and there in the emperors' laws and decrees. However, the legislation frequently covered areas of life where it had to be either merciful or merciless. In many cases, merciful care was extended to the debtors, to abandoned children, to the slaves, and so on. The rulers of the Roman Empire often instituted such merciful laws and even extended certain rights and privileges, which they granted the Church and its charitable institutions in their lands, so that they were of utmost importance toward helping the poor.

Because of this, charitable institutions received important corporation rights, as well as the right to accept endowments and testaments. The churches, and indeed all the surroundings and possessions of the churches, received the right of asylum, and the clergy, specifically the bishops, received the right of intervention. One can see from these examples that the Christian state promoted the Church and its works of mercy. For while the state had not yet thought about founding its own institutions of mercy, it still held to the principle that all mercy is to be placed into the hands of the loving Church. It also believed that the wisdom of the state consists in giving the Church support in its sacred efforts, which are rich in blessing. The Christian emperors even felt free to issue regulations to prevent abuses by unworthy members and servants of the Church. The way in which the legislation was used at that time is important for us all and remains worthy of imitation.

61. We now come to the middle period of the history of the Christian Church to point out how mercy was cultivated during this era. Yet just as one cannot fully comprehend a period of history if he is ignorant of the Christian influence during that time, so one cannot fully comprehend the Christian life apart from secular, external events, which are fruits of this life. And so we call back to our memory the notion that during this period the Christian Orient became estranged from the Occident. God's judgment was over in the Occident. A new era dawned, and new beginnings became visible all over. But in the Orient, the night of the half-moon gruesomely covered the lands, and God's judgment and death were increasing.

We have to remember that all life became paralyzed there because of this. Here, however, the supreme bishop of the Occident took the place of the pagan worldly rulers. He began reorganizing new states like a pope and unfolded his authority and might for the blessing of the nations. To be sure, the great might and exalted position over the Occident, which God conceded to the Roman bishops in His holy providence, led them to exaggerate their importance. Because of this, battles between the Roman emperors of the German nation and the leaders of the Occident emerged. These reactions could and had to come, because the Lord lets no transgression go unpunished and because the bowls of His just scales always seek and find the balance.

However, even if the papacy developed in an ungodly manner because of the guilt of the popes and their supporters, the reactions evidently did not remain without reproach. He who has an eye to see will also notice that the Lord makes His way right, that His work never ceases, that no one can hinder Him. We ought to recall this time full of battles, full of deadly convulsions, and yet also full of the hope of life. Let us look at all events from the beginning of the Frankish Kingdom up to the Reformation, and try to answer the question, "How did God's holy mercy, even in the midst of this unrest and travail, still bear its rich fruit? "

62. The number of poor that had to be taken care of during this period was the same, except that there was one more form of misery in the Occident, which we — praise and thanks be to God — do not find in our area anymore. Unfortunately, there were numerous lepers in the Occident, and so one was forced to provide for institutions for lepers nearly everywhere, in every city, in every hamlet. Likewise, the principles regarding the support that was to be given as well as regarding the administration of the endowments and charitable institutions remained the same. One still rightly saw the practice of mercy and the care of the wretched as a churchly matter, and all administration remained under the control of the bishops and their councils. All endowments, regardless of whether they were founded by the laity or the clergy, were in the hands in the hands of the clergy, and even at a time when mercy began to be provided more independently, no one had the intention to challenge the supervision

and direction of the Church or to replace it by something else. However, there were great differences and changes in the ways and means love was shown as compared to previous times, which we will present summarily.

63. In this time, there are no agapes and oblations anymore. Along with this, deacons and deaconesses begin to disappear, first in the Occident and then in the Orient. Therefore, the distinguishing mark of the Christian era — the care of the poor provided by individuals — is now over. Instead of this, the institutional care of the sick and wretched is all that remains. Since there are no congregations left that are able to provide for the poor, believing it to be something to be done by each and every one, and since the care of the poor needs hands and hearts, it becomes absolutely mandatory that like-minded persons associate.

This is why one sees institutions emerging in the bosom of nursehoods. As a rule, for every new institution, some nursehood is formed. These nursehoods are diverse, and one can observe a remarkable development regarding the principles of the same. For at first, these nursehoods are actually monastic orders. Then the chivalric orders emerge and finally the lay brotherhoods. These different organizations of nursehoods follow the same logic as church buildings, where out of the Romanesque style the Gothic evolved and so on. So too, the nursehoods changed through the introduction of more independent, worldly principles.

The longer the monk is a member separated from his congregation, the more he wants to belong to the clergy. The religious knight wants to be a monk and is a monk. But in spite of the vows of poverty, celibacy and obedience, he wants to be a nobleman, and before long he gets bored at the sickbeds. This is why, after becoming a monk and a nurse, he also wants to be a fighter against the unbelievers with the sword. In this manner, the religious orders of knighthood mingle spirit and flesh and thereby plant the seed of their death, which had to take place at some time.

The lay brotherhoods planted their seed of death in a similar manner. They had every reason to come into being at the time in which they did. In general, they had no intention to withdraw from the Church. For they not only tolerated its oversight but also wanted it. Added to this, they had a strong impulse and desire to grow out of ecclesial oversight, not to dedicate themselves to the truth more than the contemporary Church did, even though it would have been the right thing to do, but to worship their own private opinions. Some of these opinions were mystical, some theosophical, some philosophical. And usually the majority of these opinions were no more compatible with the religion of the Lord Jesus than those of the Gnostics of the earlier times.

Despite all this, time marched on toward the Reformation. Progress was only slightly visible in the institutions, such as nursehoods, about which we are talking. For unfortunately, like always in all good and splendid things, there is a progressive mingling of flesh and spirit, of lie and truth. And so eventually, religious organizations do not simply end by giving way to some temporal things, but they generally end in sin and shame and leave a bad name to posterity, so that no one even remembers their better times.

64. The preeminent orders of knighthood were the two orders of the Hospitallers of St. John of Jerusalem and the Teutonic Knights. Both were originally founded for the care of the sick in Jerusalem, and from there they spread over the Occident. Beginning in AD 1048, merchants from Amalfi in southern Italy had prepared a refuge for pilgrims in Jerusalem and had built a hospice and a chapel, Santa Maria Latina, next to it. Two more hospices were soon erected next to the first and then two more after that.

The nursehood grew in such a way that they were able to aid Godfrey of Bouillon significantly during the siege of 1099. Because of this, he rewarded them with the Lordship of Montboire in Flanders. Young noblemen from the army of the crusaders joined them. Consequently, the rector of the hospital, Gérard Tonque, decided to sever the ties between the hospital and the abbey of Santa Maria Latina and to form an independent brotherhood in honor of St. John the Baptist. This caused hot, even bloody disputes. The new Hospitallers prevailed, however, and the new order became rich in goods, so that their beneficial activity spread into the Occident.

Under the guidance of Raymond du Puy, who called himself the "Servant of the Poor of Jesus Christ and Warden of the Hospital at Jerusalem," the order, which had an abundance of means and men at its disposal, added to its works of mercy also the struggle against the unbelievers. In doing so, it took a big step toward gaining worldly power, but it also planted the seed for its estrangement from the original task. Gradually the care of the sick was left to the religious, and the others became more interested in military service.

Around AD 1128, a German man and his wife, living in Jerusalem, founded a *xenodochium* (a hospice) to fulfill the commandment of being hospitable to others. Their goal was to assist fellow Germans who were poor, sick, and ignorant of the local language. Since his venture prospered, the German built a chapel in honor of the Mother of God, and his wife built a second hospital to care for harassed German women. Gradually many forces turned to this noble endeavor and founded the Association of the Brothers of the Hospital of the Holy Virgin Mary at Jerusalem. Before long this association, too, was joined by knights. In this way, here too, people began to want not only to care for the sick but also to fight against the unbelievers.

In 1142, Pope Celestine II placed these Brothers of Mary under the supervision of the Hospitallers, a position that did no damage to their work but, as it is so frequently the case with subordination, upheld the virtue of showing mercy. In lowliness, poverty, and piety, the Brothers of Mary lived for a long time free from pride, greed, and discord. During the siege of Acre in 1199, the Brothers of Mary joined some citizens of Lübeck and Bremen to ease the distress of the sick, and their pious sacrificial work caused Duke Frederick of Swabia to found the Teutonic Order after the pattern of the Templars and Hospitallers, since the members of the Templars and Hospitallers were mostly French and Italian noblemen. Until the fifteenth century, this order of the German knights never totally forgot why it was founded. At that point, their abundance of power and wealth became a cause for impudence and discord, but until then they served faithfully.

There are still Teutonic Knights in Austria, but their possessions became an imperial fief in 1834. In Prussia in 1812, King Frederick William III founded a royal order of St. John, which Frederick William IV tried to resuscitate by designating its entrance and membership fees for the establishment and maintenance of hospitals. But what is all this compared to the old way of doing things? Back then, one would not just simply gather some money, but would make one's body and life, money and goods available to the Lord for His serving of the wretched and poor.

It must be noted that both orders, the Hospitallers and Teutonics, also had female sisterhoods at their side about whose toil and work less can be said, although they might have accomplished more than their male orders. Out of the later nursing associations emerged the Order of the Holy Spirit, which became very active in different lands and still today works for the care of the sick in Austria under the name of Crosiers. Yet this order is different from the two previously mentioned orders of knighthood, and we mention it here simply because of its many beneficial activities.

65. Besides the knighthoods, more independent communities who cared for the sick began to emerge at the end of the twelfth century, and these deserve to be noted. In the first place, the Beguines and Beghardes are to be mentioned. The whole community borrowed its name from a pious priest at Liège, Lambert lè Begue, although many have interpreted it differently.

Upset by the worldly lifestyle of the clergy around him, Lambert desired an association of people who desired a more pious way of living. In a great garden outside the city on the Maas, he erected many individual houses, which were all enclosed by a single wall. This was the first Beguinage, and it became the pattern for the later ones, for fifty years after the death of Lambert, there were already fifteen hundred sisters living on this court. Two to four sisters lived in individual houses, and each took care of her own little household. The individuals lived on the proceeds of their handiwork and teaching, and each had control over her possessions. Some were allowed to live in the city with their relatives, but then they had no permission to wear the dress of the Beguines. For the Beguines wore a distinct dress, which came close to the clerical garb, and they vowed chastity and obedience for their time of residence at the court, but were free to leave and get married at any time.

The center of the court of the Beguines was the hospital, in which the sisterhood practiced the care of the sick for their own members. Yet they also cared for sick people outside the court in private homes. In the course of the rather impure attempts at a reformation before Luther's time, the Beguines were very frequently drawn into heresies and enthusiastic movements, which severely undermined their almost inde-structibly good name. In Germany, the word *Beguines* was not well liked, and so the name *Seelschwestern*, meaning soul sisters, was used instead.

Besides the Beguines there were the Beghardes, a brotherhood of married men that was founded in the Netherlands in 1228. This order originally consisted of poor married weavers, but they later imitated the lifestyle of the Beguines and dug their own grave by affiliating with heretical associations.

Besides the Beguines and Beghardes, one has to mention the Kalands Brethren. Each group was headed by a cleric, and it also had lay members. The actual purpose of this brotherhood was every kind of mutual bodily and spiritual aid. Therefore, they cared for their brothers and sisters in disease, as well as for paying their members the last honors due them and then burying the dead. They gathered on the first day of every month for Mass, and after that for a covenant meal. Gradually these meals became the main thing, and gluttony and lewdness spread. The kaland brothers became known for their excesses, and before the Reformation even took place, the kaland was abolished almost everywhere.

Among the brotherhoods that belong here, we additionally mention the Bridgemakers, which made the crossing of waters easier for pilgrims traveling to Rome and other sites of devotion, as well as erecting hospices at the shores for the pilgrims.

In a time rich in nursehoods, one also notes some associations for the mentally ill. In Germany, one could name the Elizabethians, who bear the name of St. Elizabeth of Thuringia (1207–1231), who, as everybody knows, founded hospitals in Eisenach at the foot of the Wartburg and later at Marburg. This order still exists and usually takes care of female patients only.

Before we proceed to the Reformation era, we note in passing that *xenodochia* and hospitals were separated from each other in the Occident during the period we have just discussed. The hospitals formed a style of their own and divided into various subcategories, not just according to the nature of the disease, but also according to nationality of the person. Later on, individuality and subjectivity become more prevalent, and the dividing continued, which was both a blessing and curse, but which was unavoidable.

66. In the Reformation era, we must speak of merciful love differently because the church split. Therefore, we have to focus on the Roman Catholic church by itself, and likewise the Protestant church societies by themselves. In previous time periods, when there were factions within the Roman church, most of the groups had still encouraged the importance of living the Christian life. Indeed, these branches of the Roman church encouraged active love and mercy.

But during the time of the Reformation, one can see that depraved living took hold of the Roman church, its doctrine, and its hierarchy. As a result, the Roman church does not look at all like those earlier communities that separated from it. One can tell right away that there was a confusion between the pure teaching of the old, traditional principles and the restoration of divinely pure doctrine.

To be sure, there are things that are greater than even human life, namely the order of salvation and the way to life eternal. It may well be then that because of the greater good, the smaller recedes into the shadow even if only for a while. Likewise, until the path to the heavenly Jerusalem is cleared, the paths on which the merciful Samaritan is to walk on earth become somewhat rough and dark.

Because of this, the branches of the Roman Catholic church seem to lag behind it, and the untrained eye, which does not understand what the Reformation is all about, has a hard time determining which side has the greater advantage. Yet one must consider that it is not Christian living or works of mercy but the pure Word and the unadulterated Sacraments that are the marks of the true Church. Nevertheless the Reformation took place, unperturbed by the splendor of the Romans in the centuries before and after it, and it carries on with the intention that the pure doctrine of the true Church may bear fruit. Like the Reformation, we know that when the spring of truth comes, then the earth shall turn green from love, and all trees will bear the fruit of mercy.

67. When focusing on the Roman church in the post-Reformation era, it is undeniable that its zeal for works of mercy has only grown since the Reformation. Generally speaking, the Roman church owes a great deal to the Reformation. It is no mistake to say that the flurry of activity in showing mercy, which began to pop up here and there in its midst, was also caused by the Reformation. Brotherhoods and sisterhoods emerged everywhere in the area of the Roman church, most notably in southern and western Europe. They flourished, and their hopes and ideas for showing mercy have not been exhausted even today.

Among the brotherhoods, the Hospitaller Order of St. John of God ought to be mentioned first. It was founded by the Spaniard John of God at Grenada in 1534. The order's members commit themselves to the care of the suffering. Today they maintain twenty-nine hospitals in Austria alone, and they care for an average of twenty thousand patients each year.

Besides this order, there are many other brotherhoods of Hospitallers. Yet they are surpassed in splendor and activity by the sisterhoods. The order of the Daughters (Sisters) of Charity, founded in 1617 by Vincent de Paul (1580–1660), has to be mentioned, for its different branches spread over all the lands and even into Germany. The most esteemed branch of the Daughters of Charity is that of the Sisters of Mercy of St. Borromeo, founded in 1626 by Pierre de Stainville at Nancy. Besides this, one should mention the Vincentians, who have their motherhouse at Strasbourg. It is not necessary to elaborate on the Daughters of Charity because in our day and age their recognition is exceedingly high even among Protestants, and the famous works by F.

J. Buss, Clemens Brentano, Clemens August Droste von Vischering, Johann Hermann Schmidt, Wulf, and so forth are found everywhere and read by everyone.

68. The church of the Reformation, as sad as its appearance looks when comparing it to institutions and distinguishing works of mercy, nevertheless has shown Christian mercy a great service. It has done this by correctly relating works and faith according to St. Paul's example, by rejecting the foolish idea that human merit is capable of influencing eternal salvation, by holding to the holy doctrine of the merit of grace, and by banishing all erroneous attempts of works righteousness and instead clinging to the scriptural definition of a good work.

It is clear from its church orders that the church had the intention of practicing pure doctrine. In many of these orders, there is a clearly recognizable effort to revive the deaconate, which had ceased to exist in the Roman church. Although the church did not succeed in giving a fresh impetus to mercy, and although neither the deaconate nor the common chests that collected money for the poor amounted to very much, one has to keep in mind that the Reformation era was a period of extreme unrest. The greed of the princes strongly interfered in the movement, and severe sufferings and terrible punishments from God came because of the rejected Word. These sufferings can be seen most clearly in the Thirty Years' War, a war that transformed Germany into a desert. In addition to all this, the church was busy attempting to maintain pure doctrine, and so these reasons justify the fact that the church of the Reformation was doing its best to keep its works of mercy from going down the wrong path.

69. Toward the end of the seventeenth and at the beginning of the eighteenth centuries, there rose within the Lutheran church a strong reproach against this church itself. This was a result of dead orthodoxy and a great lack of living faith and active love. It was a just reproach, even if the men and the party that raised it did not articulate their reproach in an irreproachable manner, were unable to defend the truth worthily, and failed to recognize the good that still remained in the church.

At the helm of the party was the noble Philipp Jacob Spener (1635–1705) and later A. H. Francke (1663–1727), whose orphanage at Halle was a good example of institutional work in the Lutheran church and whose charitable example was beneficial. It was during the time of A. H. Francke that in Germany, in the Lutheran church, and in all Protestant lands many orphanages and institutions emerged. Some are still partly blooming today, but others, after doing their share, have sunk into the dust again. All charities of the nineteenth century doubtlessly follow the impulse of A. H. Francke. All those who have recently advocated the scriptural idea of deacony, such as Amalie Sieveking at Hamburg (1794–1859), Pastor Fliedner (1800–1864) at Kaiserswerth, and Candidate Wichern (1808–1881), are part of the train and stream that began with Spener and that beneficially permeates the Protestant churches.

One must also remember that the ecclesial associations of the Protestants, and the Protestant imitations of the Catholic brotherhoods and sisterhoods, owe their origin only to the impulse of the Pietist party. Because of this, the Protestant communities are making up for what had been neglected, and the Spirit of the Lord is being seen in abundance. All manner of charity has continually become filled with delight and truth, and we pray that the church not succumb to the errors that, because of the devil's envy, so easily attach themselves to movements founded by God. In light of this, one ought to remember to observe everything that the movement of love in the contemporary church brings about, without loftily turning away from the charity that is found among associations of different parties. Indeed, whoever is wise learns from the enemy. Why not learn from those whom one cannot call enemies, although according to God's Word we are different from them? However, one must also remember that it is our sacred duty to remain watchful in view of the activities of the modern time and guard the hearth so that there is no profane fire brought to it (Lev. 10:1).

70. One thing the Church must avoid is joining ranks with those who hold the secular view of charity called the economical. We live in a time in which misery grows in tremendous progressions. There seems to never be enough help for those in need, let alone enough to stop the sources of misery all together. This is why the wise men of the time reflect on misery, and the great men study what needs to be done to prevent it. The situation can be likened to one who works systematically, the way one does his math, calculating the consequences of certain measures one wants to take. And because of his studies, one arrives at an impractical experiment, which in addition to being expensive, eventually increases misery instead of doing away with it.

Because of the way the situation ends, such accusations can be rightfully leveled at the book by Chastel, who wrote about the practice of mercy during the first six centuries. Everyone who is guided and driven simply by economical or scientific considerations regarding the existing need for mercy, and not by Christian love, will be the object of the same accusations. When love counsels and reigns over the leaders of the nation, then they will do whatever is possible to eliminate and even prevent misery. And they will do it quickly, and love, an angel of God on earth, will prove itself as the master of economy, even if it does not want to deal with the secular mind and name.

71. One great question remains, namely, "Who is to take the effort of mercy in his hands and govern it — the state or the church?" The judicious recognize that the state can do nothing without the willing spirit of the church, which holds the key to the treasures that the needs of our time require. Those who have studied the matter the most are convinced about this the most.

Therefore, it is time for every person to let the Spirit of the Church of Jesus stream into himself and to assist the tremendous job that the Lord has given His Church. Although state charity alone is not going to get the job done, we should not entertain the idea of relegating the state to the status of a mere observer of the things that take place under the hands of the church. Even if it is not proper for the hand that holds the sword to bring the oil and wine of the good Samaritan, it nonetheless can make room and defend. Thus, just as one has to award the church the full right and the full duty to do the works the Lord will ask for on the Last Day — the works of mercy — so one has to preach to the lords of the world and the rulers of the states that they are founded and instituted to the glory of God, and are not to hinder His works but to foster them.

SEVENTH CHAPTER

How is a Deaconess to Practice Mercy?

72. For the sake of clarity, we must say first that we are strictly talking about the deaconesses of the nineteenth century and not about all deaconesses in general. That being said, the resuscitation of the biblical office of deacony, and of deaconess in particular, is not due to the Roman church or some other church but to the Reformation. Thanks are due to the Reformation era, and we must be grateful that in more recent times the Protestant church has put its old traditions into practice one again.

But on the other hand, we must also acknowledge that the deaconess of the nineteenth century is different from that of the Early Church. She is not a deaconess emerging out of the congregation, but she is a Protestant duplicate of the Roman Catholic sister of charity. Given the current circumstances, she can be nothing but this. Since there are no longer congregations like those in the past, then there can no longer be congregational deaconesses.

Deaconesses in our day and age are not forced to do their work, but they are set apart as a matter of free will and because they voluntary associate with those who are drawn to, and awakened for, this position by God. Because of this, we know that generally speaking, the brotherhoods and sisterhoods are not marks of a dead church, but of a strong and good will. And yet while the desire to show mercy has not changed, the way in which a brotherhood or sisterhood is organized has changed throughout the course of time. Depending on the changes, that organization may be more or less useful. Every era in history has to accept its specific form of organization, and so the deaconess of the nineteenth century must accept the organization of the deacony's existence and gladly embrace it. She must do this, even if she always keeps her eyes upon the more beautiful perfection of earlier times, grieving after it, longing for it, and, as far as possible, striving for it. In spite of this, she occupies her place in time as well as possible and strives to be better.

73. The deaconess of the nineteenth century lives at a time in which there is a great deal of confusion about everything, especially mercy and charity. She may even be confused as to what is better — congregational care of the poor or institutional care.

She may wonder what is more accurate — to leave the whole sacred matter to the church or to hand it over to the state. More than likely, she has many more questions like these on which, in the end, so much depends.

This is why it befits a deaconess to be a light bearer into this darkness, to implant and advocate sound doctrine wherever she is placed. Yet how can she do this without knowing it for herself? And can she know it without hearing or reading? Out of this emerge the sacred duty of study and the instruction of others who are weaker in intellect and engage less in studying. Every deaconess should know not only the history of mercy, but she should also know and pursue in her studies all the things that are only briefly mentioned in this piece of writing. She should familiarize herself with the charitable systems of different countries and areas, with the organization and reports of the institutions that flourish the most, and with the writings on mercy that have been published back and forth. She also should learn the history of ancient times, of the ancient orders, of the nursehoods, and the biographies of the preeminent male and female champions of mercy. This will help to form her in that branch of human care to which she dedicates her life. But there is more. It is altogether impossible for a deaconess to avoid going into the writings of the confessions, which is why she must be firmly rooted in the divine truth so that she is able to recognize the good of the Church's confessions without being attracted by the errors of others. This will open up an expansive field of knowledge for the deaconess. But above all else she must not forget that the first and most beneficial study is of the Bible, through which the Holy Scripture of the Old and New Testaments is and remains her dearest paradise and the place for holding sacred knowledge. Glancing at what there is to be learned, one sees that there is nothing more miserable than a deaconess who does not want, does not know, does not desire to learn, and who does not somehow find the means to live up to her calling to be a light bearer for others according to her gifts.

74. The formation of a deaconess does not depend solely on knowledge and studies. Commensurate with studying, there must be a formation and sanctification of her heart. Knowledge that does not influence a person's inmost being is nothing more than whitewash on a decaying tomb. If this is the case, she has no roots under herself, and she will bear no fruit. It is then clear that her heart has not been receptive soil.

The Roman church realized this potential problem and instituted a threefold vow for its deacony. But should not this promise instead be made out of a free will and as a result of inner growth? The deaconess should, not because of a vow or law or duress but because of the impulse of the Holy Spirit, be free from and unaffected by sexual matters, not enchanted by earthly possessions, and not subject to any needs that in reality cannot be called needs. In joyous humility and sacrifice of her own will, she ought to dedicate herself to carrying out the sacred thoughts and works that she has come to know and is determined to do. She who desires a strong hand and a faithful, sacrificial will may first of all purify her heart. For she cannot fancy herself to be well-formed for the calling of deaconess as long as her heart and inmost being have not thoroughly and faithfully grasped the goal of learning through will and prayer.

75. When a deaconess has appropriated ideas and knowledge, and when the pure, faithful, strong will to [do] good is there, there is still lacking a third element, which can be called practice or skill. With her male and female instructors, the true deaconess focuses on every aspect of deaconess work. She studies, evaluates, and tries out her talents for each and every one. She seeks to train herself especially in the areas of her gifts, but she also needs holy discipline and sternness to train herself in those matters that she finds difficult. She strengthens her weak sides through the constant diligence of practice, excuses herself from nothing that the Lord commands, and forgives herself nothing that lacks for her calling.

Yet this work of strengthening and training can become absurd. A deaconess might not have any gifts for a given task of a deaconess, might therefore be released from all diligence, and might nevertheless still stoically direct all her yearnings and her diligence to this task. For this she has male and female guardians and instructors, who, tirelessly and without fear of her displeasure, will resist her and push her into an area where her talents might open a great deal of activities for her. But apart from this ignorant absurdity of untalented people, there remains the indispensable duty and sacred rule of every Christian to take care of the deaconess' weaknesses — unpretentiously and modestly but also faithfully and persistently — so that her formation is as well rounded and perfect as possible.

76. It goes without saying that the skill and knowledge of a normal female is to be expected of every deaconess. There will be exceptions until the end of the ages, but it will always remain as a rule that the formation and skill of the deaconess in the matters of the ordinary household should be exemplary. The deaconess shall be able to easily carry out what every maid can and does. By doing everything nobly and gracefully, she can show others that one can transform the humble duties of his or her calling into priestly works. Thus, it is good for every deaconess to at least know something about barn and field, the washtub and kitchen, the teaching and care of souls, and everything in between. She may be in the best or worst of occupations, but her attitude ought to never change. In so doing, everyone will realize that this woman is at home everywhere, that she is very knowledgeable, that she has a big heart, that she spends time in the sanctuary, that she has practical intelligence, and that such a girl has not only accomplished more than the well-known poetess or paintress, but that she has done more than the noble nun, who has become accustomed to fly to the eternal home, but who here on earth is unable to bestow the blessing of her inner life on others through work and deed.

77. What if the most competent deaconess, well trained for her calling, went out alone to live out her calling? What would all those gifts profit her? What if, for all her wisdom, she did not realize that a deaconess without community and connections is actually no

deaconess at all? It is included in the whole calling of the deaconess that she walks her ways, inwardly and outwardly, together with all those who have set their eyes on the same goal and are driven by the same intention. That is why training for deaconesses concentrates both on the individual soul practicing mercy, as well as the group which appears as a sacred force, focusing on the greatest thing women can possibly choose: serving others in love and helping them to be awakened to the same walk.

The church also looks to the deaconess to help the male office of the Holy Spirit in a female manner, to create, if possible, congregations; to kindle old, existing congregations for the love of Christ; to found congregations better than the existing ones on virgin soil wherever necessary. By doing so, she provides for the highest level of her own calling. For if congregations saw her true value, there would be no lack of deaconesses. Indeed, that most noble office of deaconess would rise up again, and the deaconesses would serve the congregations themselves.

To accomplish this task, it requires many and joint forces, but the deaconess has first another task. She must pass on her office to posterity. It was not good that historically the office of the deaconess died out. Thus, it is not to be resuscitated now, just to perish yet again. But what the Lord and His holy apostles thought to hand over to the Church as a permanent institution is now to rise again to perish nevermore.

For what good would it do if deaconesses only worked here and there for a short while, and yet the enthusiasm and mighty love would not lift them up and unite them, which alone can cause others to be ignited by the same mindset? The Lutheran church has already known for three hundred years that deacons and deaconesses are scriptural. One might wonder then why it had neither deacons nor deaconesses. It is probably because the ancient deacony had to appear as a new creation, and every start is so hard. But now it is different, for the start has been made, and the little lamp of the wise virgins is finally burning. He who has lit it wants it to be guarded and fueled. Diligence is to be maintained so that the fire and brightness of the good widows and virgins remain on earth until the Lord comes.

Knowing this, one might also remember that not only individual believers in Jesus but also united bands of followers, who practice the work of mercy, are able to pass the ongoing spirit of kindness on to others. Thus, the calling has to be seen in such a way that one does not simply do every work of a deaconess, that one does not simply accomplish what appears to be most necessary and useful. Rather, the idea of service must become clearer and clearer, that the understanding of each individual work is seen in relation to the whole, and that, so to speak, a tradition of sacred ideas and sacred wisdom can be passed on from one generation of deaconesses to the next.

The widows and virgins of the holy deacony are to keep alive a certain kind of human beings that have an active faith and a faith-filled love and know how to cultivate them. This is why a true deaconess will instinctively perceive the concern for her offspring — future generations of deaconesses — as one of the main purposes of her life. If she does not do it, we know that the Lord will still help His people. But that deaconess will be held accountable for her laxity on His Day. May the Lord grant these deaconesses His Spirit, His power, and His wisdom, to escape judgment on that Day, and to be worthy of standing before the Son of Man.

Amen.

CHRIST TAKING LEAVE OF HIS MOTHER

Mary feels the sword's first piercing as her son Jesus blesses in divine determination in departing to suffer and die. c. 1505

ORDINANCE OF A COMMON CHEST

BY MARTIN LUTHER

TRANSLATED BY WALTER I. BRANDT

TRANSLATED BY ALBERT T. W. STEINHAEUSER

INTRODUCTION BY WALTHER I. BRANDT

PREFACE BY MARTIN LUTHER

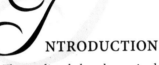

NTRODUCTION

The medieval church required financing at the local level as well as at the top. Church buildings, once erected, had to be kept in repair; clerical and lay personnel connected with them needed to be furnished a livelihood. Funds were required too for the church's efforts to deal, however inadequately, with the problem of widespread poverty among the masses. Normally the bulk of the local revenue for these purposes came from income-producing foundations or properties, endowments of altars at which special masses were celebrated, compulsory tithes, and fees for ministerial acts, especially those performed for the souls of the departed.

Some of these sources were already drying up before the Lutheran movement got under way. Others were condemned in principle by the reformers; private masses, for example, were frowned upon.[1] Secular princes, who had long coveted the wealth of the church, were on the point of confiscating the lands and property of church and monastery. Many laymen used the new "freedom" as a pretext for refusing to pay tithes. The burden of poor relief showed no signs of diminishing; estimates are that from 15 to 30 per cent of the population may have been paupers and vagrants in towns of that period.[2]

---

[1] While at the Wartburg, Luther wrote to Melanchthon on August 1, 1521, that he would never again celebrate a private mass. WA, Br 2, 372; S-J 2, 50. Before his return to Wittenberg, his own monastery had ceased to celebrate mass in the accustomed fashion, according to a letter of unknown authorship dating from about December 4, 1521. S-J 2, 75–78.

[2] Smith, *The Age of the Reformation*, pp. 558–559.

Begging, a common practice during the Middle Ages, one which had become almost respectable through the activities of the several mendicant orders, was condemned by the reformers. As early as 1520, in the *Long Sermon on Usury*, Luther denounced the practice on the basis of Deut. 15:4, 11; Christians were not to let anyone be in want or beg.[3] In his 1521 *Open Letter to the Christian Nobility* he suggested that every city should take care of its own poor, and that an organized system of poor relief be set up to replace the current haphazard system.[4] All these circumstances made imperative a complete reorganization of the parish financial system.

The first attempt in this direction was made by Karlstadt in Wittenberg during Luther's stay at the Wartburg.[5] Other communities quickly followed suit, either on their own initiative or through the Wittenberg influence. Among these may be cited Augsburg, Nürnberg, and Altenburg in 1522; and Kitzingen, Strassburg, Breslau, and Regensburg in 1528.[6]

The Leisnig ordinance of 1523 is therefore by no means unique. It is included in the present volume because it was drawn up on Luther's direct advice, had his hearty approval, and was published by him together with a preface of his own. It was one of the most thoroughgoing of these ordinances, almost a rudimentary congregational constitution, and illustrates a number of the difficulties encountered in the complicated process of reorganizing parish finances in the sixteenth century.

The parish of Leisnig on the Mulde River in electoral Saxony was already in existence when in 1191 the Cistercians founded the monastery of Buch some distance up the river. In the same year Emperor Henry VI granted the parish of Leisnig to the monastery. Later, when a small city[7] grew up about the castle, and the church of St. Matthew was erected there and made the parish church, the bishop of Meissen decreed that the abbot of Buch should have the right to name the parish priest. This right was repeatedly confirmed; in 1419 it was specifically recognized by Pope Martin V. According to contemporary law, Leisnig was at once both a religious and a political community.[8]

---

[3] See pp. 281–282, 286–287.

[4] See PE 2, 134–135.

[5] Karlstadt's ordinance, which has many similarities with the later Leisnig ordinance, is summarized in Herrmann Barge, *Andreas Bodenstein von Karlstadt*, I, 378–382. See the complete text in Aemilius Ludwig Richter, *Die evangelischen Kirchenordnungen des sechzehnten Jahrhunderts* (2 vols. in 1; Weimar: Landes-Industriecomptoirs, 1846), II, 484–485; or in Hans Lietzmann, *Die Wittenberger und Leisniger Kastenordnung*, 1522–23 ("Kleine Texte für theologische Vorlesungen und Uebungen," No. 21 [Bonn: Weber, 1907]), pp. 4–6.

[6] Detailed references to these instances are given in WA 12, 2. See also O. Winkelman, "Die Armenordnungen von Nürnberg (1522), Kitzingen (1523), Regensburg (1523), und Ypern (1525)," Archiv für Reformationsgeschichte, X (1912–1913), 242–280, and XI (1914), 1–18.

[7] In 1523 Leisnig had a population of about 1500. WA 12, 3, n. 1.

[8] MA³ 5, 400.

Abbot Antoninus of Buch (d. 1526) was hostile to the Reformation. Nevertheless, the reform movement spread among the nobility, bourgeoisie, and peasantry of the parish, which then included eleven rural villages, until it seems to have become virtually unanimous.

In response to repeated requests from certain members of the Leisnig parish, Luther paid them a visit on Sept. 25, 1522.[9] Presumably two items were discussed: first, the right of the parish to select its priest and preacher; second, the establishment of a common chest for the parish. It appears that Abbot Antoninus had appointed one of his monks, Heinrich Kind, as parish priest of Leisnig. After assuming the post, Kind embraced the evangelical cause, and was recalled by the abbot.[10] The Leisnig congregation, however, elected him as their priest, and Johann Gruner[11] as their preacher.[12] The two took office about the end of the year 1522.

Naturally, the abbot of Buch resented this usurpation of his well-established right of patronage, and instructed a new appointee to take over the parish. The bishop's appointee was notified by Sebastian von Kötteritzsch,[13] speaking on behalf of the parish, that they wanted Kind and Gruner, that they looked upon him as a stranger not called by the congregation, and that they refused to recognize or accept him as their shepherd of souls. Thereupon the appointee departed.[14]

Official attempts at a compromise between the parish and the abbot failed. Hans von der Planitz[15] and Hans von Minkwitz, acting for the elector, proposed that the abbot name the priest and the citizens name the preacher. This was unsatisfactory to both parties. Next they proposed that the abbot yield up all his rights over the parish in return for an annual stipend. The abbot seems to have been willing, but most of his

---

[9] See Luther's letter to Spalatin dated Sept. 25, 1522. WA, Br 2, 604.

[10] See Paul Kirn, *Friedrich der Weise und die Kirche* (Leipzig: Teubner, 1926), p. 116. Kind served as parish priest at Leisnig from 1523 until he was retired, for reasons of age and other considerations including his own request, by the visitors of 1529. WA 12, 7, n. 1. Cf., however, WA, Br 3, 22, n. 2.

[11] Johann Gruner is probably the "Johannes Gronigerus" or "Groner," former preacher in Oschatz, who in 1524 sought and obtained from Prince Wolfgang of Anhalt the appointment as parish priest in Zerbst, being installed there at Christmas-time, 1524. He was the author of the treatise, *A Booklet to Comfort All Poor Consciences*, published at Wittenberg in 1524. WA 12, 7, n. 1.

[12] Their choice is reported in an undated letter from the Leisnig parish to Elector Frederick, quoted in WA 12, 3–4.

[13] With his brother Hans, Sebastian von Kötteritzsch (d. ca. 1575) held the fiefs of Sitten and Kroptowitz in the Leisnig parish. Having served as a magistrate in Altenburg, he was without office in 1523, but later became a magistrate in Bitterfeld and participated in the visitations of 1528–1530, 1533, 1534. At the Diet of Augsburg (1530) he was among those accompanying the Elector John of Saxony. WA, Br 3, 23, n. 3.

[14] WA 12, 4; Kirn, *op. cit.*, p. 116.

[15] Hans von der Planitz (d. 1535) was probably already in Elector Frederick's service when, together with Hans von Minkwitz, he visited Jerusalem in 1518. In 1521 he became chief magistrate in Grimma, where his work was frequently interrupted when he was sent on diplomatic errands by the elector. He was present at the Leipzig Debate in 1519, and represented the elector on the Council of Regency in 1521 where he worked to block implementation of the Edict of Worms. In 1530 he accompanied Elector John to the Diet at Augsburg. *Allgemeine deutsche Biographie*, XXVI 232–233. His reports from the diets of Nürnberg, an important source, have been edited by Ernst Wülcker and Hans Virck, *Des kursächsischen Rathes Hans von der Planitz Berichte aus dem Reichsregiment in Nürnberg 1521–1523* (Leipzig: Teubner, 1899).

monks refused to accept this.[16] An agreement never was worked out between the parish and the monastery.[17] The independence of the parish never received formal recognition until it was confirmed by the visitation commission of 1529, and thus also by the temporal authority.[18] The Leisnig congregation protested to the elector that they had never granted the right of patronage to the abbot themselves, and that their right of choice was established by Christ fifteen hundred years before, namely, "that the whole congregation through the grace of God and by ordinance of divine Scripture has the right to call, choose, install, and depose one, two, or three persons from within its own company."[19]

The abbot, sensing the trend of the times and fearing more serious conflict, apparently failed to push his claims, or the elector may have intervened on the side of the parish.[20] At any rate, the congregation proceeded with confidence in taking over all church properties within the parish and establishing an organization to administer them, to provide for divine worship and schools, and to assist the poor and needy. Luther's influence in the matter is seen by the fact that the town council and the congregation sent two representatives, Sebastian von Kötteritzsch and Franz Salbach, to Wittenberg with a formal letter dated Jan. 25, 1523,[21] requesting his advice and counsel in the matter of their proposed ordinance, a copy of which they probably presented to him at that time. The ordinance itself may well have been the work of Kind and Gruner.

The delegation also presented two other requests to Luther: first, that he give them a written statement in approval of their procedure in calling Kind and Gruner to serve them; second, that he furnish them with an evangelical order of service. Luther replied promptly and briefly to the council in a letter of Jan. 29, expressing his approval of their ordinance for the parish.[22] In the same letter he also promised to comply with their other two requests, a promise he fulfilled in the spring of that same year with the publication of two treatises: *The Right and Power of a Christian Congregation or Community to Judge All Teaching and to Call, Appoint, and Dismiss Teachers, Established and Proved from Scripture,*[23] and *Concerning the Ordering of*

---

[16] See the letter from Antoninus to Von der Planitz dated October 4, 1524, and the text of the proposed agreement to a stipend in Kirn, *op. cit.*, pp. 189–191.

[17] *Ibid.*, p. 117.

[18] The visitation report stated, "Whereas the parish assembly at Leisnig on their own initiative conducted a common chest for some years according to their written and printed ordinance, it is to remain in force by authority of this visitation, as follows ... ." Emil Sehling, *Die evangelischen Kirchenordnungen des XVI. Jahrhunderts* (6 vols.; Reisland, 1902–1957), I, 608.

[19] *WA* 12, 4.

[20] *WA* 12, 4–5.

[21] See the text of this letter in *WA*, Br 3, 21–22.

[22] *WA*, Br 3, 23.

[23] *WA* 11, (401) 408–416; *PE* 4, (71) 75–85.

Divine Worship in the Congregation.[24] Luther's reply to the congregation came later in the form of a written preface to the ordinance; he had both preface and ordinance printed and published together.

Encouraged by the warm approval expressed in Luther's letter to the council, the Leisnig congregation proceeded to set up their common chest and to reform the order of service. On Feb. 24 they elected the ten directors of the chest; on Sunday, March 8, they set aside the sacrifice of the mass, thereby abolishing the functions of the priests attached to the four side altars.[25] The report of the Saxon visitation of 1529, where it speaks of the changes that had to be undone, shows the thoroughness of their early reform of the service. Clerical vestments were abolished; the clergy consecrated the elements while garbed in lay attire; the three great festival periods of the church year were each reduced to a single day and celebrated in the "forenoon only, the afternoon being regarded as a work day … in order to avoid excessive drinking, carousing, and idleness."[26]

Unhappily, the administrators of the common chest encountered difficulties.[27] The city council was reluctant to transfer to the directors of the chest its existing right to dispose of endowments, bequests, etc., and maintained that it could not take such a step without the elector's express permission. The congregation appealed to the elector, who named the tax commissioner of Kolditz to hear the disputing parties. Negotiations dragged on for weeks.[28] A compromise was finally reached to the extent of having both parties agree to keep the peace and bring their differences to the elector for resolution as they might arise; on April 12 the elector wrote the congregation that he was happy over this agreement.[29]

In August 1523, probably at the elector's request, Luther again visited Leisnig to look into the matter of the common chest. He found that the council was still withholding funds; despite his urging the council remained obdurate. Meanwhile, the congregation was running short of funds with which to pay its officials. On Aug. 11 and again just eight days later, Luther wrote angrily to the elector, requesting confirmation of the Leisnig ordinance,[30] but the elector, as usual, hesitated and delayed. As late as Nov. 24, 1524, Luther complained to Spalatin that the Leisnig preacher, Tilemann Schnabel,[31] might soon have to leave for want of pay and sheer hunger. He deeply

---

[24] WA 12, (31) 35–37; PE 6, 60–64.

[25] WA 12, 6. On the altar priests, see p. 180.

[26] See the text of the 1529 visitation report in Emil Sehling, *op. cit.*, I, 605–606.

[27] For bibliographical references see Enders, *D. Martin Luthers Briefwechsel*, IV, 71, n. 1.

[28] Kawerau (ed.), Köstlin's Martin Luther, I, 551.

[29] WA 12, 6.

[30] See his letters in WA, Br 3, 124–125 and 128–129.

[31] Tilemann Schnabel (d. 1559), an Augustinian monk, received his doctorate in theology at Wittenberg in 1515 and became a provincial of his order in Alsfeld shortly after 1520. There he preached evangelical sermons so eloquently that he

regretted that the Leisnig attempt, the first of its kind, which should have been such an example of success, had turned out to be such a miserable example of failure.[32]

There is no direct evidence to show when the preface with the appended ordinance came from the press. It has been held[33] on the basis of Luther's letters of Aug. 11 and 19 that it did not appear until the time of Luther's second visit to Leisnig in August 1523. Against this may be cited the fact that a copy of the first edition bears a marginal note by its original purchaser that he paid ten pfennig for it on July 6, 1523.[34] Furthermore, Luther was prompt in replying to the Leisnig request for a letter approving their method of choosing a preacher and for an order of service. These two documents came from the press between Easter and Pentecost, 1523; it would be strange if he then withheld the ordinance from the press for several months. Judging by his actions on other occasions, it is quite probable that he rushed the ordinance into print without consulting the elector, in order to give it the widest publicity and confront the elector with an accomplished fact. His very haste may have militated against the success of the Leisnig experiment, for in his sermon of Dec. 26, 1523, where he suggested how a city parish might organize a system of poor relief, he added, "But we do not have the personnel for this, therefore I do not think we can put it into effect until God makes Christians."[35]

The translation of Luther's preface given here is a revision of the one that appeared in PE 4, 92–98. The ordinance itself is here translated for the first time in English. The translation of both documents is based on the first Wittenberg printing by Cranach and Döring: *Ordenung eyns gemeynen kastens. Radschlag wie die geystlichen gutter zu handeln sind* (1523), as that has been reprinted with annotations in WA 12, 11–30.

---

won over the whole town by 1522, only to be forbidden to preach by the Landgrave Philip. Doffing his cowl, he remained for a time with Luther at Wittenberg until he accepted the office of preacher at Leisnig, succeeding Gruner. After Hesse embraced the evangelical cause, Philip granted the citizens of Alsfeld, as a reward for their faithfulness in the Peasants' War, their request to have Schnabel appointed as their priest. He served as superintendent of Alsfeld from 1531 to 1541, resigning on account of poor health. *Allgemeine deutsche Biographie*, XXXII, 81–82.

[32] See the letter to Spalatin in *WA*, Br 3, 390.

[33] This is the position, e.g., of De Wette, *Dr. Martin Luthers Briefe*, II, 382.

[34] *EA* 22, 106.

[35] *WA* 12, 693.

PREFACE

Translated by Albert W. Steinhaeuser

Suggestions on how to deal with ecclesiastical property Martin Luther, Ecclesiastic[36]

To all Christians in the congregation of Leisnig, my dear sirs and brethren in Christ: Grace and peace from God the Father and our Savior Jesus Christ.

Dear sirs and brethren. Since the Father of all mercies has called you as well as others to the fellowship of the gospel, and has caused his Son Jesus Christ to shine into your hearts; and since this richness of the knowledge of Christ is so active and powerful among you that you have set up a new order of service,[37] and a common fund after the example of the apostles [Acts 2:44–45; 4:32–35], I have seen fit to have this ordinance of yours printed, in the hope that God will so add his gracious blessing that it may become a public example to be followed by many other congregations, so that we, too, may boast of you, as St. Paul boasted of the Corinthians that their effort stirred up many others [II Cor. 9:2]. Nevertheless, you will have to expect and take comfort from the fact that if what you are undertaking is of God it will necessarily meet with vigorous opposition, for Satan never rests or takes a holiday.

We cherish the hope that this example of yours will come to be generally followed, and that as a result there will be a great decline in the existing foundations, monastic houses, chapels, and those horrible dregs[38] which have until now battened on the wealth of the whole world under the pretense of serving God. This decline is also being mightily facilitated by the holy gospel which is now bursting forth once more, and which reveals this blasphemous and damnable "service of God" in its true colors. Moreover, the clergy themselves are behaving in such a manner that goodness and integrity have vanished from their midst and will have nothing more to do with them. Things have everywhere come to such a pass that it seems both God and man have grown sick and tired of monkery and clericalism, and there has to be a change. At the same time for this very reason there is need of great care lest there be a mad scramble for the assets of such vacated foundations, and everyone makes off with whatever he can lay his hands on.

I have resolved, therefore, to the extent of my ability and duty to forestall such a catastrophe while there is still time, by offering Christian counsel and admonition. For since I have to take the blame whenever monasteries and foundations are vacated,

---

[36] Ecclesiastes ("the preacher") is the Greek title for one of the Old Testament writings. Luther used it as a self-designation to assert his status as a man of the church after that dignity had been denied him by the papal bull and the Edict of Worms. *MA3* 5, 401, n. 45, 1; *MA3* 3, 374, n. 16, 2. See his defense of this title in his 1522 *Wider den falsch genannten geistlichen Stand des Papsts und der Bischöfe. WA* 10^II, 125–126. Cf. also the title of Emser's rebuttal: *Wider den falschgenannten Ecclesiasten und Wahrhaftigen Erzketzer Martinum Luther* (Leipzig, 1523).

[37] See the Introduction, pp. 165–166.

[38] *Grundsuppen* has reference to the priests who are at the bottom of it all. *MA3* 5, 401, n. 45, 22; *BG* 7, 111, n. 3.

when the number of monks and nuns decreases, and whenever anything else happens to diminish and damage the clerical estate, I refuse to accept any additional responsibility if some greedy bellies should grab these ecclesiastical possessions and claim as an excuse that I was the one who put them up to it.

If it comes to that, I fear that very few will be guided by my advice, for Greed is a disobedient and unbelieving scoundrel. I will nevertheless do my part, clear my own conscience, and place the burden upon theirs, so that no one can accuse me of remaining silent or speaking up too late. Let whoever will, then, follow my well-meant advice or reject it; I am not to blame. But first I want to warn sincerely, and kindly request, that no one heed or follow these suggestions of mine unless he realizes and thoroughly understands from the gospel that monkery and clericalism, as they have been for the past four hundred years, serve no useful purpose and are nothing but harmful error and deception. A weighty matter like this has to be tackled with a good and unshakeable Christian conscience; otherwise, things will go from bad to worse, and on our deathbed we will be overwhelmed by terrible remorse.

First. It would have been a good thing if no rural monasteries,[39] such as those of the Benedictines,[40] Cistercians,[41] Celestines,[42] and the like, had ever appeared on earth. But now that they are here, the best thing is to let them dwindle away, or, where it can properly be done, to assist them to disappear altogether. This can be done in either of two ways: first, by allowing the inmates, if they so desire, to leave of their own free will, as the gospel permits; second, by each governing authority arranging with the monasteries under its jurisdiction to admit no further applicants and, if there are too many inmates, to send the excess elsewhere and let the remainder die out.

Since no one is to be coerced into faith and the gospel, those who because of their age, their bellies, or their consciences elect to remain in the monastery should not be ejected or harshly dealt with, but should be supported for the rest of their days just as before. For the gospel teaches us to do good even to the unworthy, just as the heavenly Father sends rain and sunshine upon the good and the evil alike [Matt. 5:45]. We must remember, too, that these persons have drifted into this estate as a result of the blindness and error which prevailed generally, and have never learned a trade by which they could support themselves.

---

[39] *Fellt kloster* was Luther's name for the monastic settlements which, to enable their monks to retire from the world, grew up outside of the cities and engaged primarily in agriculture. *BG* 7, 112, n. 7.

[40] The term Benedictines applied to a number of autonomous religious orders professing the Rule drawn up by St. Benedict of Nursia (ca. 480–ca. 550) for his monks at Monte Cassino.

[41] The Cistercians were a religious order founded in 1098 at Citeaux as an offshoot of the Benedictine Order, and given new life by the entry of St. Bernard of Clairvaux in 1112. For purposes of seclusion their houses were erected only in remote places, and hence frequently became important centers of pioneering agriculture.

[42] The Celestines were also an offshoot of the Benedictine Order, founded about 1250 by Peter of Murrone, who in 1294 became Pope Celestine V.

I would recommend that the governing authorities take over the property of such monasteries, and from it make provision for those inmates who choose to remain there, until they die. This provision should be even more ample and generous than what they may have had before, so that men may realize that this is not a case of greed opposing clerical possessions, but of Christian faith opposing monasticism. In carrying out this policy the permission of pope or bishop is not to be sought beforehand, neither is their ban or anathema to be feared; for I am writing this solely for those who understand the gospel and who have the authority to take such action in their own lands, cities, and jurisdictions.

Second. The property of those monasteries which are taken over by the governing authorities should be used in the following three ways. First, those inmates who choose to remain should be supported, as has just been said. Second, those who leave should be provided with sufficient funds to find a position and make a fresh start in life, even though they brought nothing with them when they entered the monastery. For when they depart, they are leaving at the same time their lifelong way of making a livelihood; and they have been defrauded, because the time they spent in the monastery might have been employed in learning something else. As for those who brought something with them when they entered, it is no more than right in the sight of God that they should have it returned to them, to each his own portion,[43] for here matters are to be determined by Christian love and not by strict human justice. If anyone is to suffer injury or loss, it should be the monastery and not the individual, for the monastery is the cause of their error. The third way is the best, however, to devote all the remaining property to the common fund of a common chest, out of which gifts and loans could be made in Christian love to all the needy in the land, be they nobles or commoners. In this way, too, the will and testament of the founders would be carried out. For although they erred and were misled when they gave this property to monasteries, their intention certainly was to give it for the glory and service of God; but their purpose was not realized. Now there is no greater service of God than Christian love which helps and serves the needy, as Christ himself will judge and testify at the Last Day, Matthew 25[:31–46]. This is why the possessions of the church were formerly called *bona ecclesiae*, that is, common property, a common chest, as it were, for all who were needy among the Christians.[44]

---

[43] *Yhe eyns teyls* is here taken to mean "*jeden sein Teil*" (*MA*³ 5, n. 47, 15, and *CL* 2, 406, n. 20) rather than "*Jedem ein (gleiches) Thiel*" (BG 7, 114, n. 1 and Lietzmann, op. cit., p. 8, n. 5).

[44] At least from the time of the investiture controversies and throughout the Middle Ages the church's legal rights to acquire, receive, hold, and dispose of property had been largely asserted and defended in terms of the rights of ecclesiastical personages over against persons not of the spiritual estate. The First Lateran Council of 1123, e.g., decided "that laymen ... have no faculty for determining anything concerning ecclesiastical possessions ... let the bishop have the care of all ecclesiastical business." Denzinger, *Sources of Catholic Dogma*, p. 147, No. 361. The Council of Constance of 1414–1418 asserted over against John Huss "that it is permissible for ecclesiastical personages to hold possessions and temporal goods" and that if the laity "lay hold on these ecclesiastical goods [*bona ipsa ecclesiastical*] they are to be punished as sacrilegious persons." *Ibid.*, p. 218, Nos. 684–685. Luther is using the term *ecclesia* in its etymological sense to underscore the communal aspect of such ecclesiastical property — in Greek ekklesia means "the assembly of people" — as belonging to laity as well as

If the heirs of the founder are impoverished and in want, however, it is fair and in harmony with Christian love that the foundation revert to them, at least a large portion of it, or the whole amount if their need be great enough to warrant it. It certainly was not the intention of their fathers — and should not have been — to take the bread out of the mouths of their children and heirs and bestow it elsewhere. And even if that was their intention, it is false and un-Christian, for fathers are in duty bound to provide for their own children first of all; that is the highest service they can render to God with their temporal goods. But if the heirs are not poor and in need of it, they should not take back their father's bequest, but let it go into the common chest.

But you might say, "That is opening the door too wide; on that basis the common chest will receive precious little, for everyone will claim the whole amount and say that his needs are so great, etc." Answer: This is why I said that Christian love must judge and act in this matter; it cannot be handled by laws and regulations. Besides, I am setting down this advice only in accordance with Christian love, and for Christians only. We have to expect that greed will creep in here and there. So what? We cannot just let things slide on that account. After all, it is better to have greed take too much in an orderly way than to have general plundering, as happened in Bohemia.[45] Let each one examine himself to see what he should take for his own needs and what he should leave for the common chest.

Third. The same procedure should be followed in the case of bishoprics, foundations, and chapters which have under their control lands, cities, and other possessions. Such bishops and foundations are neither bishops nor foundations; they are in actual fact secular lords with ecclesiastical titles. Hence, they should be turned into secular lords, or else their possessions should be divided between the impoverished heirs and relatives, and the common chest. As for prebends and benefices, they should be left to their present incumbents; when these die no successors should be appointed, but the properties should be divided between the needy heirs and the common chest.

Fourth. The possessions of monasteries and foundations in part, and the prebends in large measure, are based on usury, which today is everywhere called "repurchase"[46]

---

clergy. In Acts 2:44 and 4:32 the Vulgate term was *Omnia communia*, "all things in common."

[45] Luther is referring to the excesses of the radical Taborites during the Hussite Wars of 1420–1432. One of the "Four Prague Articles" set forth by the Hussites in 1420 demanded that the clergy be divested of all worldly goods. The *Compactata* agreed upon by the Council of Basel in 1433 complied with this demand as regards all clergy bound by vows of poverty, allowing the church itself, however, to acquire and hold temporal goods, but merely as administrator.

[46] *Widderkauff* was known as early as the thirteenth century and was actually a type of sales contract in which the sale was conditional upon the seller's right to repurchase what he had sold. The two sales transactions together were the equivalent of a loan. A merchant would sell an article on credit for a given price, and immediately repurchase it from the buyer for cash in a smaller amount, the cash being then in effect a loan. The difference between the two prices became in effect an interest charge on the outstanding loan. See Herbert Heaton, *Economic History of Europe* (New York: Harper, 1936), p. 203; and Grimm, *Deutsches Wörterbuch*, XIV1, 1063. The scholastics up through the fifteenth century condemned such contracts of sale and resale in the name of the whole medieval prohibition against usury — which was designed to protect the debtor— largely because of the unfair prices involved. The resale clause itself was not condemned, but incorporated into the fifteenth century *zinss* contract (see pp. 234–238) as a redeemability clause. John T. Noonan, *The Scholastic Analysis*

and which has in but a few years swallowed up the whole world.[47] The holdings thus derived would first of all have to be separated, like leprosy, from the property which consists of simple bequests. For the advice I gave above refers only to foundations established by true and honest bequests apart from "repurchase." Foundations established on the basis of "repurchase," however, may rightly be regarded as usury; for I have never yet seen or heard of a proper redeemable *zinss* contract.[48] In this matter, therefore, it is first necessary to make up for the usury by returning to each one what is his own before allowing such assets to go into the common chest, for God says, "I hate robbery with a burnt offering" [Is. 61:8]. If it should prove impossible to find the persons who had suffered loss in the repurchase transaction, the common chest might then receive the property.

But the right and wrong of "repurchase" is too long a story for the present; I have dealt with it sufficiently in the treatise on usury,[49] from which one may learn what portion of such prebends and foundations should be restored to those who have been paying *zinss*. For there is no doubt that a good many prebends have long since received back the principal sum of their loans, yet they do not stop sucking the sweat and blood out of their creditors. Hence, this matter is decidedly one of the most pressing problems for consideration by emperor and kings, princes and lords, and everybody else.

Fifth. Mendicant houses located in cities[50] might be converted into good schools for boys and girls,[51] as they were before.[52] Other monasteries could be converted into dwellings if the city needed them. The fact that they were consecrated by bishops should raise no obstacle, for God knows nothing of such consecration. If this advice of mine were acted upon in a Christian way, many other things would suggest themselves and be found feasible, and much would be learned by experience, more than can now be proposed in words, for various and extraordinary situations would arise where only Christian love can judge aright.

---

of Usury (Cambridge: Harvard University Press, 1957), pp. 95–98. It is the mutually redeemable *zinss* contract—relatively recent (see p. 295. n. 141) — to which Luther here refers.

[47] Living in the "age of discovery," Luther saw in his lifetime a remarkable growth in trade and commerce, cities and the merchant class, and a consequent increase in the demand for capital which was accompanied by a sharp rise in prices and exorbitant "interest" rates. See *BG* 7, 494–513.

[48] *Zinsskauff auff Widderkauff*. For a discussion of the meaning of the mutually redeemable zinss contract, see Noonan, op. cit., pp. 230–235.

[49] See the *Long Sermon on Usury* (1520) in this volume, pp. 273–308, esp. p. 295 ff.

[50] The monasteries of such mendicant orders as the Dominicans, Franciscans, and Augustinian Hermits were built mostly within the cities, in contrast to those rural orders mentioned on p. 171.

[51] Cf. Luther's 1521 *De votis monasticis*. *WA* 8, 615 and 641.

[52] The burden of lay education in the early Middle Ages was borne mainly by the monasteries, which conducted not only "internal" schools for future members of the order but also "external" schools to educate children of various classes for life in the community outside the monastery. The instruction was given gratuitously. *Catholic Encyclopedia*, XIII, 555–556. See in this volume, p. 341.

If God were to grant that these suggestions be carried out, not only would we have a well-filled common chest for every need, but three crying evils would diminish and eventually cease. The first of these is begging,[53] which does so much harm to land and people in soul and property. The second is the terrible misuse of the ban,[54] which serves no other purpose than to torture people in the interest of the possessions of priests and monks. If they had no possessions, there would be no need of this ban. The third is this cursed *zinss* contract,[55] the biggest usury on earth, which up to now has asserted its validity even in the matter of ecclesiastical properties — there above all.

If anyone does not care to follow these suggestions, and in so doing quench his greed, I wash my hands of him. Well do I know that few will accept such advice. I am content if only one or two follow me, or would at least like to follow me. The world must remain the world, and Satan its prince. I have done what I can, and what I am in duty bound to do. God help us all to do what is right and to stand firm. Amen.[56]

---

[53] Luther had previously denounced begging in *An Open Letter to the Christian Nobility* (1520). *PE* 2, 134–135; and in the *Long Sermon on Usury* (1520), in this volume, pp. 281–282, 286–287.

[54] In 1520 Luther had written *A Treatise Concerning the Ban. PE* 2, (33) 37–54.

[55] On the *zinsskauff*, see pp. 295–310; on its use in the churches, see especially p. 306.

[56] Luther's own preface ends here. What follows is the Leisnig Ordinance itself, of which Luther is not the author, though he gave it his hearty approval and himself had it published. See the Introduction, pp 162, 165.

Fraternal Agreement on the Common Chest of the Entire Assembly at Leisnig[57]

TRANSLATED BY WALTHER I. BRANDT

In the Name of the Holy undivided Trinity, Amen.

Since by the grace of the Omnipotent God, through the revelation of the Christian and evangelical Scriptures, we have been given not only firmly to believe but also profoundly to know that, according to the ordinance and precept of divine truth and not according to human opinion, all the internal and external possessions of Christian believers are to serve and contribute to the honor of God and the love of the fellow-Christian neighbor, we the nobility,[58] council, craft supervisors,[59] gentry,[60] and commoners dwelling in the city and villages[61] of the assembly and parish of Leisnig, by these presents confess and make known that we, for ourselves and our posterity, upon the considered and mature counsel of men learned in the divine Scriptures,[62] have drawn up and adopted the following fraternal agreement among ourselves as a community, and that both now and for the future it is to be held true and inviolable, namely:

Filling the pastoral office

In matters which relate to the filling of the pastoral office in our parish, including the calling, choosing, appointing, and dismissing of our pastor for the sole purpose of preaching God's word and administering the sacraments, we solemnly purpose and promise at all times to use, exercise, and employ our Christian liberty solely in conformity with the precept and ordinance of the divine biblical Scriptures; and in such a pre-eminently spiritual undertaking as the care of the poor and needy, to be obedient in true humility to the well-founded and proven instruction and counsel of those learned in the divine Scripture, submitting to it and following it by the grace of God, of which we have a clear token in our midst in the administration given to our parish, which shall be retained intact.[63]

---

[57] Since no title at all appears in the Wittenberg printing at this point, we have supplied the title which appears on the cover of a very early original manuscript still extant at Leisnig, which is designated as "L" in WA 12, 9.

[58] The *Erbar manne* are named specifically in the last paragraph on p. 194.

[59] The *Viertell meister* (literally, "quarter master") exercised a certain supervisory authority in a particular quarter of the city. The term was also applied to the chief of any particular craft since shops of a given sort tended to be concentrated in a given area. Grimm, *Deutsches Wörterbuch*, XII2, 331. The crafts in question are named in the last paragraph on p. 194.

[60] *Eldesten* is the equivalent of *Honoratioren*. CL 2, 408, n. 34.

[61] According to the report of the 1529 visitation, the parish included the eleven villages of Gorschmitz, Röda, Brösen, Tautendorf, Minckwitz, Meinitz, Neudörfchen, Vorwerf Hasenberg, Dölen, Lichtenhain, and Liebgens Mühle, the last three of which subsequently became part of Leisnig itself as the city expanded. WA 12, 3, n. 1; BG 7, 117, n. 3.

[62] This was probably a reference to Luther, who had visited Leisnig on Sept. 25, 1522; see the Introduction, p. 163.

[63] This is probably a reference to Leisnig's priest and preacher, Kind and Gruner, whose appointments had been challenged by the erstwhile patron of the parish but successfully defended by the congregation itself. See the Introduction, pp. 163–164.

On hearing God's word

We solemnly purpose and promise that every master and mistress of a household within the confines of our parish shall be obliged themselves — and out of Christian love shall also hold their children and servants to it — to listen faithfully to God's saving and comforting word at the appointed days and hours and take it to heart for our own improvement, as God grants us grace.

Reverencing God and keeping his commandments

We solemnly purpose and promise that as masters and mistresses we shall diligently see to it — each one for himself and for his children and servants in his own home as God grants us grace — that God is reverenced, and we shall studiously avoid, guard against, and prevent open blasphemy, excessive drinking, fornication, ruinous dice games, and other sins and offenses which are known to be in direct conflict with God's commandments. If any member of our community is found to be negligent or lax in this regard, an assembly of the whole parish shall have the right and power to take up the matter and by proper means, with the aid and co-operation of the authorities, to secure appropriate punishment and salutary improvement.

Property, resources, and receipts for the common chest

In order that our Christian faith — in which all the temporal and eternal blessings won by our Lord and Savior Christ out of pure grace and mercy are granted unto us by the eternal God — may bear fruit in brotherly love, and this love truly express itself in deeds of tender kindness, we, the aforesaid general parish assembly, acting unanimously, for ourselves and our posterity have ordained, established, and set up a common chest, and by these presents we do now ordain, establish, and set up this same chest on the authority of this our fraternal agreement as to purpose, scope, and form, as follows.

The property and resources of the common chest shall consist of the following enumerated items: incomes [*zinsse*], properties, rights, moneys, and goods everywhere amassed, collected, brought, vested, and assigned in perpetuity.

Receipts from parish properties and rights

We, the parish assembly, by virtue of our universal priesthood,[64] have always had and should have had the full right and authority, which we reserve wholly to ourselves and in no way relinquish, to acquire all properties and rights, hereditary lands, quitrents, and supplementary rents,[65] proprietary rights, buildings, manor places, gardens, fields, pastures, stores, and chattels personal without exception, insofar as they were in every case granted and assigned by the original donors, and by those who later

---

[64] Luther had taught the priesthood of all believers three years earlier in *An Open Letter to the Christian Nobility. PE* 2, 66–73; and *The Babylonian Captivity. LW* 36, 112–117; and again in *The Misuse of the Mass* (1521). *LW* 36, 138–146.

[65] *Gatter zinse* were rents which had to be collected in person by the landlord or his agent, and only at the latticed gate (*gatter*) of the debtor. Grimm, *Deutsches Wörterbuch*, IV¹, 1511; 7, 237.

supplemented these bequests to the priestly and pastoral office here in our midst, and have in times past thereto belonged and therein been used — this was the substance of the negotiations and the decision reached between ourselves and the abbot of Buch in the chancellery of our most gracious lord, the Elector of Saxony[66] — which properties and rights are now on deposit in our common chest. Likewise, whatever belonged to the school and the sacristan's place[67] has been turned over to this chest.

Receipts from church property and rights

All property and rights, hereditary lands, quitrents and supplementary rents, bridge tolls,[68] ready cash, silver and jewels,[69] stores, chattels personal, and thus everything that accrues to the church either regularly or from time to time, together with the written documents, lists, and records pertaining thereto, shall be included without exception in the common chest and there remain.

Receipts from the property and rights of the four beneficed altars[70] and other foundations

When the present beneficed altar priests die or the benefices otherwise become vacant,[71] the four benefited altars in our church shall henceforth no longer be provided for. Instead, the four chapels, together with their properties, rents, revenues, usufructs, jewels, stores, and chattels personal, and the written archives, inventories, and records pertaining thereto, shall be put in the common chest. In addition, all their masses for the dead, perpetual memorials, indulgence weeks or octaves, and other onetime foundations[72] and alms for the hospital[73] or other objectives, shall be turned over to the common chest.

---

[66] See the Introduction, pp. 162–165. If the elector, Duke Frederick of Saxony, did intervene, as this sentence seems to suggest, no records of his disposition of the case are extant either at Weimar, Dresden, or Leisnig. WA 12, 5.

[67] *Kusterey* had reference to the office and holdings of the sacristan, who was usually attached to a certain benefice. His task was to care for the church property, particularly its sacred vessels and vestments (see p. 187). The term was also applied to that facility, in or near the church, in which the church's treasures were kept in custody (see p. 184).

[68] The wooden toll bridge over the Moldau was church property until transferred to the state in 1847. WA 12, 18, n. 2.

[69] *Silberwerg, Cleinod* had reference to the costly materials used in decorating, and in such altarware as monstrances and shrines for relics. BG 7, 120, n. 3.

[70] The four side altars in the church at Leisnig, each separately endowed and served, were those of the Cross, the Annunciation of Mary, the Conception of Mary, and the Corpus Christi. WA 12, 18, n. 3. The most heavily endowed of the four according to the 1529 visitation report, the Corpus Christi, had an annual income of 32 gulden, 26 groschen, 6 pfennige, and 1 heller. Lietzmann, op. cit., p. 13, n. 11.

[71] One of the four altar priests died shortly after the ordinance went into effect. The other three continued to receive their stipends, although they had no functions to perform; the congregation had forbidden them to read mass, and they refused to celebrate an evangelical mass. WA 12, 6.

[72] *Begengnus* were "masses for the dead," including vigils and requiems, not the funeral itself. They were distinguished as being either *einlitzige*, "one-time," those held 8, 30, or 365 (the "anniversary" so-called) days after the death or burial, or "perpetual memorials," the *Jahre tage* held annually on the anniversary of the death or burial. The "indulgence week or octave" is a memorial in which mass is held and prayers offered for the deceased over a period of one week, to procure indulgence for him. Each of these expressions can also stand, as here, for the fund endowed for the particular memorial in question. MA³ 5, 403, n. 52, 17. Luther had inveighed against such masses already in his 1520 *Address to the Christian Nobility*. PE 2, 125.

[73] The hospital, besides being a hospice for the lodging of strangers, was a charitable institution for the care of the aged, infirm, poor, sick, and dependent children.

311

Receipts from brotherhoods[74]

Whatever has hitherto been collected and is now available to the famous brotherhoods, the Calends,[75] St. Anne,[76] and the Cobblers,[77] in the way of ready cash, annuities [*tzinsskauffen*], jewels and silver, stores, and chattels personal, together with their written documents, lists, and records, shall without exception be turned over and assigned to the common chest, and there remain.

Receipts of donations to the church[78] by artisans and peasantry

Contributions, craft guild rights,[79] levies, penances, penalties, and fines, which as donations to the church were formerly collected, and in years to come will continue to be collected, within the city from the artisans and in the country villages outside the city from the peasants in our entire parish, into a reserve supply, are and in the future shall be all turned over to and deposited in the common chest.

Receipts of edible foodstuffs and money in the alms chests and coin boxes

It is ordered that in our church there shall at all times be kept two barrels or casks, not to be removed, in which bread, cheese, eggs, meat, and other foodstuffs and provisions may be placed, and a little box or two for coins, both for the maintenance of the common chest. Likewise, whenever our parish assembles in the church, two of our officials shall always be present to solicit each person for support of the poor, and the alms and love gifts thus received shall at once be contributed to and placed in these receptacles. Articles of food, being perishable, shall be distributed by the appointees among the poor as needed without delay, in accordance with their instructions hereinafter specified. Whatever is not perishable is to be kept until the following Sunday and then distributed as may be appropriate and beneficial for the poor.

Receipts of gifts made during days of good health, and by will at the time of death

Other voluntary gifts made during days of good health and by will at the time of death, insofar as they are made with a Christian intention, to the honor of God

---

[74] Brotherhoods were organizations, usually of laymen, formed for the purpose of performing devotional and charitable works for which the whole membership would receive spiritual credit. See Luther's own sharp critique of them dating from 1519 in *The Blessed Sacrament of the Body of Christ*. LW 35, 67–73.

[75] The Calend brotherhoods probably grew out of the priestly conferences held on the first day of each month (calendae). MA3 5, 403, n. 52, 22. Their membership was restricted pretty largely to clergy, whose surfeiting at the common meal was almost proverbial. Albert Hauck (ed.), *Realencyklopädie für protestantische Theologie und Kirche* (3rd ed., 24 vol.; Leipzig: Hinrichs, 1896–1913), IX, 704. The Calends had endowed one of the four beneficed altars in Leisnig, the one to the Annunciation of Mary. Lietzmann, op. cit., p. 14, n. 5.

[76] The patron saint of the St. Anne brotherhood was Anne, according to tradition the mother of the Virgin Mary. Sodalities bearing her name spread "like an epidemic" after the fourteenth century. LW 35, 68, n. 44.

[77] The Cobblers brotherhood was composed of journeymen shoemakers united under church auspices for the purpose of aiding their deceased fellow craftsman through prayers and masses. BG 7, 121, n. 5.

[78] *Gotsgabe* (literally, "a gift to God") was the general term for a contractual endowment of a church institution, usually a benefice, a living, or a foundation involving gifts and benefits in cash or in kind made and administered "for God's sake." Grimm, *Deutsches Wörterbuch*, IV¹, 1240.

[79] *Zunfftgerechtigkeitten* has reference to legal claims of the church against craft guilds. MA³ 5, 403, n. 52, 29.

and love of neighbor, whether they consist of property, ready cash, jewels, stores, or chattels personal, shall be given wholly to this common chest and there remain. Faithful admonition thereto shall also be made by our pastor from the pulpit, and elsewhere in legitimate instances, even at the sickbed if the prospective heirs give their approval and the patient is still in possession of his faculties.

Setting up the administration of the common chest

The administration of the common chest shall be set up in the following manner: annually each year, on the Sunday following the octave of Epiphany,[80] at about eleven o'clock, a general assembly of the parish shall convene here in the town hall. There, by the grace of God united in true Christian faith, they shall elect from the entire assembly ten trustees or directors for the common chest who shall be without exception the best-qualified individuals; namely, two from the nobility; two from the incumbent city council; three from among the common citizens of the town; and three from the rural peasantry. The ten thus duly elected shall immediately assume the burden and responsibility of administration and trusteeship of the common chest. They shall do so voluntarily and with a good Christian conscience, for the sake of God and the general welfare. They shall discharge their duties to the best of their ability, without regard to favor, animosity, personal advantage, fear, or any unseemly consideration, and shall be pledged and bound faithfully and honestly to handle the administration, receipts, and disbursements, according to the terms of our agreement herein described.

Locking the chest with four different keys

This common chest or receptacle shall be kept in that part of our church where it is safest, and shall be provided with four separate and distinct locks, each having its own key, so that the nobility shall have one of the keys, the council another, the town citizenry the third, and the rural peasantry the fourth.

The directors to meet together every Sunday

Every Sunday in the year, from eleven o'clock until two hours before vespers, the ten directors shall meet in the parsonage or in the town hall, there to care for and exercise diligently their trusteeship, making their decisions and acting in concert in order that deeds of honor to God and love to the fellow-Christian may be continued in an unbroken stream and be used for purposes of improvement. These decisions of theirs shall be kept in strictest confidence and not be divulged in unauthorized ways. If any of the directors are from time to time absent for good and sufficient reason, the majority shall have the power to go ahead anyway and transact business.

Three books, in which are recorded all properties, rights, and administrative acts

The ten directors at their regular Sunday meeting shall have on hand three record books, namely:

---

[80] Epiphany falls on January 6; therefore, the meeting was to convene on the first Sunday after January 13.

The primary documents. Herein shall be entered and preserved a transcription of this our fraternal agreement, an exact copy of the sealed original deposited in the chest; also, all written documents, deeds of conveyance, lists, and inheritance records having to do with all properties and rights which have ever been brought in and contributed to the common chest, as specified above, and which may come or be brought to it in the future.

The minutes. Herein shall be properly recorded and indexed all deliberations, conclusions, decisions, inquiries, investigations, and resolutions that have been undertaken, made, and completed, which in any way concern the administration, receipts, and disbursements of the common chest, so that the necessary information may be available at any time.

The annual accounts. Herein shall be transcribed at the outset a complete list or inventory of all items of stores, chattels personal, jewels, silver, and cash monies, each accurately described in terms of weight, quantity, and bulk, as they are handed over, item by item, to the aforementioned ten directors each year when they take office, as a balance and as the starting point for continued accounting. Herein shall also be entered every week on Sunday each and every receipt and disbursement, all in accordance with a customary accounting form agreed upon by the general parish assembly and modified from time to time as the assembly may see fit. From this then a definitive ledger, categorized under the necessary headings, shall always be prepared and drawn up by the outgoing directors, and turned over to the ten new directors on the day of their election, to forestall harmful errors and negligence. When these three books have been used in the manner described they shall at once be locked up again in the common chest.

Collecting all earnings and debts
The ten directors shall exercise all diligence in demanding and collecting for the common chest all rents, incomes, accounts, and obligations, both the recurrent and the occasional, to the fullest possible extent but without oppressing the poor; and in preserving inviolate all such sources of revenue.

The office of two building supervisors
The ten directors shall appoint from among their number two building supervisors. These two, with the advice and knowledge of the other eight, shall have charge of the church buildings, the bridge, the parsonage, the school, the sacristan's place, and the hospitals. Both of these men, equipped with two little bags or collection plates, shall also be on hand in the church whenever our parish is assembled, to solicit alms for the support of the poor. Such contributions shall at once be dumped into the two coin boxes provided for that purpose, the keys to which shall be kept in the common chest. Every Sunday the money shall be taken out of these boxes by the ten directors acting in a body, properly recorded in the annual accounts book, and placed in the

common chest. Alms consisting of edible foodstuffs and other perishable stores shall be distributed daily among the poor whenever the ten directors, acting in concert on any particular Sunday, shall deem it necessary and proper. Nonperishable articles shall be removed from the alms chests and stored in appropriate places in the church until some Sunday when, at the judgment of the ten directors, they shall be distributed to the poor.

The burden of caring for nonresidents not assumed

With respect to the perceptible burden imposed in excessive measure upon the entire parish by nonresident, fictitious poor and idlers who are not really in need, a burden which only aggravates our own distressed condition and which men learned in the divine Scriptures have advised us to exclude and disavow, we, the nobility, council, craft supervisors, gentry, and commoners dwelling in the city and villages of our parish, by virtue of this our agreement have accordingly resolved for us and our posterity that this burden is and shall remain excluded and disavowed, namely:

Begging concessions[81] forbidden

No monks, of whatever order[82] they may be, shall henceforth have any sort of begging concession within our parish, either in the city or in the villages; their three houses,[83] therefore, shall also be absorbed into the common chest, from which they shall be indemnified in accordance with a fair appraisal.

Begging by monks, stationaries,[84] and church beggars[85] abolished

No monk, *stationarius*, or church beggar shall be permitted or allowed to beg or have others beg for him in our parish, either in the city or in the villages.

Begging by students from outside the parish forbidden

No student from outside the parish shall be permitted to beg in our parish, either in the city or in the villages. If anyone wants to attend our school he will have to provide his own board and keep.

Men and women beggars forbidden

No men or women beggars shall be tolerated in our parish, either in the city or in the villages, since anyone not incapacitated by reason of age or illness shall work or, with the aid of the authorities, be expelled from the parish, the city, and the villages. But those among us who are impoverished by force of circumstances, or are unable

---

[81] *Termineyen* were the areas within which a mendicant order had the right to solicit alms. The term was also used to indicate the collection of such alms and the houses from which such begging monks operated as a headquarters away from their home cloister. Grimm, *Deutsches Wörterbuch*, XI[1,] 260. Cf. p. 69, n. 34.

[82] See p. 175, n. 15.

[83] Of the three *Termineyheuser* in the parish of Leisnig at the time, the Frieberg cloister (Dominican) was granted in 1529 to the deacon for a residence, and the Oschatz cloister (Franciscan) became the archdiaconate. WA 12, 23, n. 1. Lietzmann, op. cit., p. 17, n. 6.

[84] On the *stationirer*, see p. 69, n. 34, and p. 318, n. 7.

[85] *Kirchenbitter* were monks who did their begging on behalf of church construction. MA[3] 5, 404, n. 56, 30.

to work because of old age or illness, shall be supported in suitable fashion by the ten officials out of our common chest as follows:

Disbursements and assistance from the common chest

We, the members of this parish and our posterity, therefore solemnly purpose and promise henceforth to provide food, sustenance, and support through our ten elected directors out of our common chest, to the limit of our resources as God grants us grace, and as occasion demands to make the following disbursements, namely:

Disbursements for the pastoral office

To the pastor or priest called and elected by our congregation, and to a preacher similarly called by us and appointed to assist the pastor[86] (though the pastor himself should be able and qualified to preach God's word and perform the other duties of his pastoral office), and also to a chaplain[87] if the need for one arises, the ten directors, on the unified resolution of the entire assembly, are to furnish annually each year a specified sum of money, together with certain consumable stores and lands and properties subject to usufruct, to support them and adequately meet their needs, one-fourth to be paid each quarter at the Ember fast[88] out of the common chest, in return for a proper receipt. They shall be content with such annual salary, stores, and usufruct, and shall by no means seek or accept anything more from the people of the parish, unless it be unsolicited, voluntary, free offerings and gifts. In this respect and in the administration of the pastoral office of the congregation, their conduct shall be in accordance with the ordinance and instructions of the men learned in the divine Scriptures,[89] which ordinance shall be kept in our common chest, and be considered and implemented by the ten directors every Sunday, so that no harm may come to the pastoral office.

Disbursements for the office of sacristan

The sacristan or custodian, to whom the assembly entrusts the locking up of the church and the suitable care of it, shall be given by the ten directors out of the common chest in quarterly installments a specified annual salary and certain usable stores and usufructs, as may be determined by the assembly in accordance with the aforementioned scriptural ordinance for the pastoral office of the congregation, which embraces also the duties of the sacristan.

---

[86] The parish priest at the time was Heinrich Kind; the preacher was Johann Gruner. See the Introduction, p. 165.

[87] The Cappellan was a priest appointed to assist in the pastoral duties of the parish.

[88] *Quatemper*, derived from the Latin for "four times," had reference to the fast days with which each quarter of the church year began, namely, the Wednesday, Friday, and Saturday following December 13 (St. Lucy), Ash Wednesday, Pentecost, and Sept. 14 (Holy Cross). For purposes of quarterly rents and payments the Wednesday in question was considered the terminal date. MA^3 5, 404, n. 57, 30; CL 2, 417, n. 2.

[89] See p. 177, n. 27.

Disbursements for the schools[90]

The ten designated directors, in the name of our general parish assembly, shall have the authority and duty, with the advice and approval of our elected pastor and preacher and others learned in the divine Scriptures,[91] to call, appoint and dismiss a schoolmaster for young boys, whereby a pious, irreproachable, and learned man may be made responsible for the honorable and upright Christian training and instruction of the youth, a most essential function. This schoolmaster shall be required to train, teach, govern, and live at all times in conformity with and hold unswervingly to the mandate of the aforementioned ordinance for the pastoral office of our congregation which is deposited in the coffers of our common chest. In accordance with a determination of the general assembly, the ten directors shall give the schoolmaster as compensation for his services a specified annual salary plus certain stores in quarterly instalments out of the common chest. He shall be content with this, and shall neither seek nor accept anything more from our parish assembly or any of its four groups as classified above.[92] But from pupils from outside the parish, who are permitted here only at their own expense without begging, the schoolmaster may, at the discretion of the priest and preacher, together with the ten directors, accept a suitable recompense, so that Christian training and instruction may be imparted to these outsiders too. Our pastor, preacher, and the ten directors shall maintain a constant and faithful supervision over this office of teaching school and governing the youth; every Sunday as need may arise they shall consider this matter, take action, and implement it with the utmost seriousness.

Likewise the ten directors shall grant to an upright, fully seasoned, irreproachable woman an annual stipend and certain stores out of our common chest for instructing young girls under twelve in true Christian discipline, honor, and virtue and, in accordance with the ordinance for our pastoral office, teaching them to read and write German, this teaching to be done during certain specified hours by the clear light of day and in a respectable place that is above suspicion. Beyond that she is neither to seek nor accept anything further from our assembly. But from girls outside the parish who might be sent hither to the German school this woman may, on recommendation of the ten directors, collect an appropriate fee. The ten directors shall also diligently supervise the training and governing of such German schools and young girls, so that Christian discipline, honor, and virtue may be maintained inviolate.

Disbursements for the poor who are aged and infirm

Those individuals in our parish and assembly who are impoverished by force of circumstances and left without assistance by their relatives, if they have any capable

---

[90] *Zcucht schulen*, literally, "training schools," were so called because they were schools intended not simply for instruction of the mind in certain subjects but for training of the entire person in arts, skills, conduct, and the fear of God. Grimm, *Deutsches Wörterbuch*, XVI, 278; BG 7, 128, n. 6. In 1529 there were forty-five pupils in the Leisnig school. WA 12, 24, n. 1.

[91] In 1529 it was accordingly ordered that when next the post of schoolmaster became vacant, a qualified teacher, a graduate recommended by Melanchthon, should be called from Wittenberg. WA 12, 24, n. 2.

[92] The nobility, councilmen, townspeople, and peasants are categorized on p. 194.

of helping, and those who are unable to work because of illness or old age and are so poor as to suffer real need, shall receive each week on Sunday, and at other times as occasion demands, maintenance and support from our common chest through the ten directors. This is to be done out of Christian love, to the honor and praise of God, so that their lives and health may be preserved from further deterioration, enfeeblement, and foreshortening through lack of shelter, clothing, nourishment, and care, and so that no impoverished person in our assembly need ever publicly cry out, lament,[93] or beg for such items of daily necessity. For this reason the ten directors shall constantly make diligent inquiry and investigation in order to have complete and reliable knowledge of all these poor — as above — in the city and villages within our entire parish, and they shall confer on this matter every Sunday. The names of the poor whom they have discovered and decided to help, together with the action taken, shall be legibly entered in the minutes so that the resources of our common chest are distributed in orderly fashion.

Disbursements for the support of orphans and dependent children

Poor and neglected orphans within the city and villages of our entire parish shall, as occasion arises, be provided with training and physical necessities by the directors out of the common chest until such time as they can work and earn their bread. If there be found among such orphans, or the children of impoverished parents, young boys with an aptitude for schooling and a capacity for arts and letters, the directors should support and provide for them, like the other poor, out of the common chest; the other boys will be trained for labor, handicrafts, and other suitable occupations. The girls among the neglected orphans, and likewise the daughters of impoverished parents, shall be provided by the directors out of the common chest with a suitable dowry for marriage.

Disbursements for home relief[94]

To artisans and others suffering in private, whether married or widowers, who are residents of the city and villages within our parish and who are honestly unable to ply their trade or other urban or rural occupation, and have no other source of help, the directors shall advance an appropriate amount out of the common chest, to be repaid at some future date. In cases where despite honest and diligent toil they are unable to make repayment, the debt shall be forgiven for God's sake as a contribution to their need. Such circumstances shall be carefully investigated by the directors.

Disbursements for the relief of newcomers from without

In the case of newcomers to the parish of whatever estate, be they men or women, if they are in Christian and brotherly harmony with our general assembly and wish to

---

[93] Beggars customarily cried aloud in the streets and movingly pleaded their needs at the door of each home. *BG* 7, 130, n. 5.

[94] *Hawssarmer leutte* were those poor who, in contrast to the beggars, suffered their poverty privately and quietly at home, and also received such aid as came to them in the form of home relief rather than alms on the streets and in public places. *BG* 7, 131, n. 8; Grimm, *Deutsches Wörterbuch*, IV², 652.

seek their livelihood within the city or villages of our parish by their labor, toil, and industry, the ten directors shall encourage them, and even offer them help through loans and gifts out of our common chest, as circumstances dictate, so that the strangers too may not be left without hope, and may be saved from shame and open sin.

Disbursements for the maintenance and construction of buildings

The directors shall provide for the daily maintenance and improvement of buildings, and for new buildings, at the following sites belonging to the common chest: the church, the Moldau bridge, the parsonage, the school, the sacristan's place, and the hospitals. With the advice of people skilled and experienced in construction they shall diligently and prudently arrive at decisions, place orders, and cause them to be executed, providing appropriately for supplies of the necessary materials and making the expenditures out of the common chest. They shall carry on the work through their two building supervisors, securing other hand labor, especially for the bridge, by calling on[95] men of the city and the country, as has been customary in the past.

Disbursements for the purchase of grain for the common stores

For the general welfare of our parish, the ten directors shall employ funds from the common chest, supplemented by grants from the town council out of the town treasury, to buy up and set aside a good quantity of grain and peas in storehouses which belong to the council and the entire parish. Such stores are not to be drawn upon in years when grain is plentiful and cheap, but by all means to be increased and supplemented. In this way the people of the whole parish everywhere in the city and villages may by the grace of God have recourse to these stores for bodily sustenance in times of imminent scarcity, through purchase, loans, or grants as the directors may deem fitting and appropriate. Whatever grain is bequeathed by will or given as gifts of love by farm laborers from the city or peasants in the country for the common good, and remains over after support of the poor as noted above, shall also be added to this common store and, as we have just heard, shall be used for the needs of the whole parish.

Paying an annual tax to the common chest

Wherever the rents, collections, revenues, and contributions to the resources and stores of our common chest, as itemized above, should prove insufficient for the maintenance and support of our pastoral office, office of sacristan, schools, needy poor, and the buildings owned in common, as these have been duly set forth in orderly sequence, we the nobility, council, craft supervisors, gentry, and commoners dwelling in the city and villages of our whole parish, for ourselves and our posterity, and by virtue of this our fraternal agreement, have unitedly resolved and consented that every noble, townsman, and peasant living in the parish shall, according to his ability and means, remit in taxes for himself, his wife, and his children a certain sum

---

[95] *Bethe* referred to the notice given those volunteers who were next in line for the duty to report and take their turn. MA³ 405, n. 61, 16; CL 2, 420, n. 22.

of money to the chest each year, in order that the total amount can be arrived at and procured which the deliberations and decisions of the general parish assembly, on the basis of investigation in and experience with the annual statements, have determined to be necessary and sufficient.

To this end, throughout the entire extent of our parish, every householder, domestic servant, journeyman of the various handicrafts, and other persons who are not home owners but who share in the enjoyment and use of our parish rights shall individually contribute annually one silver groschen; that is, three new pennies, the fourth part of the groschen, every quarter at the Ember fast. Each master or mistress shall diligently collect this money and turn it over to the ten directors at each Ember fast.

The parish assembly solemnly purposes and promises that to the honor of God and the love of our fellow Christians we shall never spare ourselves this trifling annual contribution in view of the fact that hitherto, since time out of mind, both residents and nonresidents throughout our common parish have by many methods and devices been overburdened and fleeced incessantly the year round with exorbitant and intolerable impositions and assessments. By the grace of God these practices have now been restored to the true freedom of the Christian spirit. It is the duty of every Christian to see that such Christian liberty is not misused as a cover for shameful avarice [I Pet. 2:16].

Holding a general assembly three times a year

Three times a year, namely, on the Sunday following the octave of Epiphany,[96] the Sunday following St. Urban's Day,[97] and the Sunday following St. Michael's Day,[98] the whole general parish assembly shall convene at eleven o'clock in the town hall and remain in session there at least until two o'clock in the afternoon. First, this our fraternal agreement shall be read aloud; then our ten elected directors shall present their books of minutes and accounts, and make their report. Growing out of their report, and the ideas of us all, there shall be a discussion of the administration, receipts, and disbursements of our common chest, and of other matters generally which are needful and appropriate. Finally, by the grace of God, decisions shall also be made by which this fraternal agreement, according to the circumstances of the common stores and resources, may be maintained and not fall into decline. If anyone in the parish cannot be present on the three appointed days — and no one should absent himself without a manifestly good reason — the assembly shall nevertheless, as mentioned above,[99] legitimately proceed to transact business.

---

[96] See p. 182, n. 45.

[97] St. Urban's Day falls on May 25. *Catholic Encyclopedia*, XV, 209–210.

[98] September 29 was observed as the Feast of St. Michael. *Ibid.*, X, 276–277.

[99] See p. 183.

Directors to furnish a complete annual statement

Annually each year on the Sunday following the octave of Epiphany and on successive days thereafter, our ten elected directors shall make, deliver, and present their annual statement on the administration, receipts, and disbursements of our common chest, both through their books of minutes and accounts, and also by their oral report. This shall be done publicly, in the presence of our whole assembly or an appreciable number or committee acting on behalf of the whole assembly, as circumstances shall dictate, and according to the form and specifications for such a statement, as determined by action of the assembly and presented and turned over to the directors on the day they took office, as indicated above.[100] When this statement has been executed by the directors and accepted, then with a resolution of profound thanks on behalf of the assembly, the directors shall be declared discharged, freed, and relieved of all responsibility. They shall then immediately entrust and turn over to our newly-elected ten directors the common chest together with all its written documents, lists, and records, as well as the three books, namely, the primary documents, minutes, and annual accounts, as many of them as exist. They shall also turn over all items of inventory which according to their final statement remain on hand and in storage, namely, grain, consumable stores, chattels personal, jewels, silver, cash monies, and all sorts of building supplies, all accurately described in terms of weight, quantity, and bulk. This transfer shall be duly recorded anew in a separate inventory or list which shall be sealed in the name of the whole assembly by the nobles, councilmen, and four craft supervisors, and deposited in the common chest as the starting point for continued accounting.

New directors to get help from their predecessors

The new directors, whenever they feel it necessary, may also consult with former directors. The former directors, for the sake of God and the common weal, shall not shirk this responsibility, but shall furnish reliable guidance and counsel.

In witness whereof, and so that all the articles, items, and provisions of this our fraternal agreement recorded above shall at all times be applied, used, and administered faithfully and without fraud by the parish here in Leisnig for no other purpose than the honor of God, the love of our fellow Christians, and hence for the common good, we the nobility, to wit, Balthasar von Arras, Sebastian von Kötteritzsch,[101] and Sigmund von Lausk, have affixed to this present document our family seals; and we, the council, the privy seal of our city; and we, the duly sworn craft supervisors of the four handicrafts, namely, clothmakers, bakers, cobblers, and coopers, our customary craft seals. This we have done on behalf of and at the request of each and every inhabitant of the city and villages of our parish, under legal public notarization, for ourselves and our future parish assembly. Done and given at Leisnig, in the one thousand five hundred and twenty-third year after the birth of Christ our dear Lord.

---

[100] See p. 184.

[101] See p. 163, n. 13, and the Introduction, p. 165.

CHRIST PRESENTED TO THE PEOPLE
"So Jesus came out, wearing the crown of thorns and the purple robe. Pilate said to them, 'Behold the man!'" John 19:5 c. 1509

On Almsgiving

by Martin Chemnitz

(Chapter 4 of Chemnitz's Locus on Poverty in his Loci Theologici)

Translated by Rev. Dr. James A. Kellerman

[Tr. note: In his locus on poverty, Chemnitz has two groups especially in mind: the monks in Roman Catholicism, who taught that the poverty of the monks merited God's favor, and the Anabaptists, who taught that no one ought to own private property, but everything should be held in common. Before Chemnitz discussed the matter of almsgiving, he established that God has ordained private property and that it is to be managed for His glory rather than to be abandoned. After this, chapter on almsgiving Chemnitz discusses the marketplace and usury.]

Note the most beautiful balance in these portions of the doctrine. The Anabaptists see that there is a certain sharing of wealth and works among people in this life, as both the law of nature prescribes and the doctrine of the Gospel commands. Hence they argue that we ought to abolish entirely all ownership of wealth and any distinctions between individual properties. They have in mind to establish a common ownership of all property, as Plato taught, in which there would be no room for legal transactions. The witness of Scripture rightly and truly opposes them. The Scriptures approve of the distinguishing of properties as something divinely ordained.

As soon as we have established this truth, however, many use it as a pretext to nurture their greed. They think that they are righteous enough and more than righteous, provided that they refrain their hands from taking their neighbor's goods, even if they do not help human society by sharing any of their goods. For they suppose that the distinguishing of property is approved in Scripture as if each one ought to watch over his own wealth nor care one whit about others, just as the rich man in Luke 12:19 is portrayed.

Therefore, it is proper and necessary for balance to append to any discussion about the distinguishing of properties the teaching about the legitimate exchange and sharing of possessions that takes place either through generosity or through other transactions.

One must show that God distributed the ownership of wealth so unequally, not because He chose the wealthy and rejected the poor or so that some could be fattened while others waste away from hunger, but because He wished in this way to spread around opportunities for the human race to be united in the common task of sharing wealth and service. Indeed, He also wants our faith to be seen and charity (love) exercised through that sharing of goods. So a careful notice of the order in this doctrine admonishes us many things.

There are also some elegant thoughts on this matter by the old fathers. Ambrose, commenting on Luke, says:

> "Perhaps someone will say, what injustice is it, if I do not meddle in anyone else's property, but diligently take care of my own? O impudent statement, what are you calling 'your own'? Do you mean those things which you brought down with you in this world when you entered into this light, when you left your mother's womb? With what property and with what provisions were you accompanied when you entered this world? Let no one call 'his own' what is common to all. That which more than suffices for one's expenses has been violently obtained. You do not think, do you, that God is unjust, so that He does not distribute equally the provisions of life so that you are wealthy and in abundance, while others are in want and are needy? Do you not rather think that He wished to confer proofs of His kindness to you and to crown your poor neighbor with the virtue of patience? When you have received the gifts from God and drawn them into your bosom, you do not think that you have done anything wrong, if you are the only one to have obtained the sustenance of so many people's lives? Who then is so unjust and so greedy as he who uses the livelihood of many other people not merely to satisfy his own needs, but to have an abundance and ingratiate his delights?"

Ambrose adds:

> "You should be reproached for nothing less than robbery when you are wealthy and can be of assistance and yet reject the requests of the poor. It is the bread of the hungry that you hold back. It is the widows' covering that you hide away. It is the money to redeem the wretched that you dig up in your treasure chest. Therefore, you know that you can enter these goods as often as you can offer them.

The opinion of Chrysostom is cited in distinction 47: "God wanted us to be dispensers, not lords, of His riches."

Moreover, that sharing does not degenerate into endless confusion and seditious greed, but it has been ordained not only through the establishment of the state but also through the divine voice in the word of God. For the Seventh Commandment of the decalogue hallows the sharing of property in such a way that it does not permit anyone to seize the possessions of another with violent rapacity nor to take away another's property by fraud. For it says, "You shall not steal." Therefore, the commandment wishes that there be a legitimate exchange of property and services, in which an equality is maintained. And 2 Cor. 8:8 states, "I say this not as a command," that is to say, alms ought not to be extortions compelled from people as the Anabaptists contend. Again, "For I do not mean that others should be eased and you burdened," [2 Cor. 8:13] that is, there ought not to be wasteful squandering or prodigality. Indeed, God Himself ordained under Mosaic law certain forms of legitimate exchanging of goods, namely, either through liberality or through contracts. Though the Mosaic law is not binding on us, nonetheless we can rightly ascertain from it what are the legitimate forms of exchanging property, the forms which God approves. In a later section we will explain contracts; in this present section we will explain alms.

It is altogether necessary to go over this doctrine repeatedly as it has been correctly and faithfully passed down. For it is very easy to go astray to one side or the other. The papists made out of almsgiving acts that made satisfaction for sins. Now after that opinion has been withdrawn, the zeal for helping the poor has clearly been restrained and has been all but wiped out. To make the explication of this article easier and more expeditious, we will divide it into a few different headings.

I. The definition of the term must be considered as well as its use in the Scriptures. For the names that are applied in the Scriptures to objects are not only grammatical notations, but they embrace and demonstrate the very foundations of things. Therefore, lawyers call it "a donation;" philosophers call it "liberality" and "magnificence." The Greek orators call it *eranon*, public contributions, from which meals were established for the poorer citizens at public expense.

The apostles used unique names, so that they might show from their very words that the alms given in the church ought to differ from the liberality espoused by the philosophers or a donation imposed by civic duty. Therefore, the writers of the Gospels always use the term *eleemosune* [gift of mercy], a term derived from the Septuagint translation. In Dan. 4:24 [4:27] the Hebrew text has, "Break off your sins by practicing" *bi-tsedakah*," that is, "in righteousness"; the Septuagint translates *bi-tse-dakah* as *eleemosune* [gift of mercy]. And that word is often repeated in the books of Sirach and Tobit.

This demonstrates that this word was used in the speech of the church of that time. And the apostles willingly used this word so well known and commonly accepted, because the name itself admonishes many things. For two things are required in this duty of charity, just as both are joined together in Luke 6:36, 38: "Be merciful," etc. The word *eleemosune* [gift of mercy] beautifully demonstrates that one ought not merely to look at the external largess, but above all one ought to instruct the mind, just as the name indicates. The term also indicates to whom alms ought to be given, namely, not to the wealthy and flourishing, but to those whose fortune is worthy of pity. The term also demonstrates to what purpose charity is bestowed upon the poor.

Therefore, the term itself encompasses and declares many thoughts of the Scripture. The Scripture instructs the mind of the one who gives: "If you pour yourself out for the hungry" (Is. 58:10); "Did I not weep for him whose day was hard? Was not my soul grieved for the needy?" (Job 30:25); "Yet closes his heart against him" (1 John 3:17). The Bible distinctly requires mercy in carrying out one's duty of love toward the poor: "Light dawns in the darkness for the upright" (Ps. 112:5 [112:4]); "Whoever is generous to the poor lends to the Lord" (Pr. 19:17); "Blessed be the man who took notice of you" (Ruth 2:19); "I desire steadfast love and not sacrifice" (Hos. 6:6; Micah 6:8).

The name "gift of mercy" encompasses all these things. And it is recognized that the Greeks took that term from those very statements that make mention of mercy in gift-giving. The Hebrews have two words that are joined together in Daniel 4. The first word is *tsedakah* or righteousness. It means, however, not only such grace as resides in the emotion of the mind, but advances toward the work itself, as in the phrase "In your righteousness free me" and "Do not enter into your righteousness [or judgment]," etc. And in 2 Cor. 9:9 Paul retains the word "righteousness" instead of "righteousness," alluding to Ps. 111:9 [112:9]. Even today the Jews call their gifts of mercy *tsedakah* or "righteousness." The second word used by the Hebrews is CH-S-D. This term without doubt is explicated in those statements such as Is. 58:10; Job 30:25; and 1 John 3:17. It denotes rather tender emotions, such as the *storgai* [affections] of parents. Such a concept is commonly rendered "mercy" or "kindness."

These are the two terms of the Hebrews. The one instructs the emotions of the donor, the other teaches that the act of giving itself ought to be joined with the emotion. That may be the reason that it is called "righteousness," namely, because the righteousness of God has distributed property unequally because of the reasons previously cited. Therefore, whoever closes his heart sins against the righteousness demanded by the Seventh Commandment.

According to Luke, Paul in Acts 24:17 uses the term "gifts of mercy." Paul does not use the noun in his epistles, although he uses the corresponding verb ("The one who does acts of mercy, with cheerfulness," Rom. 12:8). However, he does use other terms that are clearly noteworthy, each of which pronounce something about the teaching of giving alms. In 2 Cor. 8:4 and 9:13, as well as Rom. 15:26, he calls it *koinonia* [fellowship]. That is, he teaches that God ordains and approves of the distinction of proper-ties, while at the same time he embraces the notion of sharing, just as has been said previously. He also calls almsgiving *charis*, that is, a gift advanced by a benevolent mind. He also calls it *diakonia* [service], so that there may not be a contracting or selling of the duty of charity, but that it might be done to help the poverty of the neighbor. He calls it *eulogia* [blessing] or munificence or joy in giving. In 1 Cor. 16:1 he calls the opposite *pleonexia* [greed] and calls the alms logia [collection], since it was being collected publicly as contributions. Heb. 13:16 calls it *eupoiia* [well doing]; cf. Mark 14:7, "You can do good for {the poor}." In 2 Peter 2:13, banquets are called *agapai* [love feasts] because in a public place after the church services these banquets were offered by the wealthier members for the poorer ones. This term was used by the old church fathers, especially Tertullian. In Acts 9:36, alms are called "good works," as a synonym to "gifts of mercy." Cf. Gal. 6:10 ("let us do good to everyone") and 1 Tim. 6:18 ("*agathoergein*" [to do good]). In 2 Cor. 9:6, it is called a seed, because it is cast abroad just as over a field, but the fruit will follow in its own time (Ecc. 11:6).

II. There are many statements in the Scriptures, both in the Old and New Testaments, in which the command concerning the giving of alms is inculcated through earnest repetition. It is very useful to collect these statements and always to have them ready — to have them right in front of the eyes, as it were — because greed, the root of all evil, makes us rather stingy so that we easily grow tired (Gal. 6:9). We should have these statements ready at hand so that by meditating upon them and pondering them, the bowels of mercy might be aroused and opened up by God's help.

Because some statements contain both promises and threats, while others describe the manner in which alms should be given, let us refer to them in their own place. Here we will note only those places which simply contain a commandment: "Open your hand" (Deut. 15:8); "Share your bread with the hungry (Is. 58:7); "Break off … your iniquities by showing mercy to the oppressed" (Dan. 4:24 [4:27]); "Give and it will be given to you" (Luke 6:38); "Give to everyone who asks" (Luke 6:30); "Give as alms" (Luke 11:41); "Sell your possessions and give to the needy" (Luke 12:33); "Give to the one who begs;" (Matt. 5:42); "Honor the Lord with your wealth" (Prov. 3:9); "When you give a feast … " (Luke 14:13); "Make friends for yourselves by means of unrighteous wealth" (Luke 16:9); "Whoever has two tunics … " (Luke 3:11); "If your enemy is hungry … " (Rom. 12:20). See also the following verses: Sirach 3:23; 4:17, 36; 12:2–3; 14:13; 17:18; 18:25; 29:15; Tobit 4:7, 12; 5:8–9.

III. One ought to establish a definition of the matter, as to what is properly almsgiving. The scholastics say that there are two types of almsgiving, corporal and spiritual. They count and describe as corporal almsgiving that which appears in Matt. 25:35–36. They sum it up in this line of verse: "I visit, I give drink, I feed, I redeem (namely, the captives), I clothe (namely, the naked), I gather (guests, wanderers, and exiles), I bury (namely, the dead)." They summarize the spiritual almsgiving in this line of verse: "Counsel, chastise, comfort, forgive, bear, and pray.

But we are not discussing now concerning all the works of mercy and charity that pertain to the Fifth Commandment. For there are rather many of those works than are able to be fit within the narrow confines of these two lines of verse. The question is only about those works of mercy that are called in that peculiar expression "gifts of mercy" and which pertain to the Seventh Commandment.

The scholastics hand down this definition: "almsgiving is the work in which something is given to the poor out of compassion and for God's sake." However, there is a very simple and certain method to establish true definitions, if they are gathered from certain statements of the Scriptures and are distributed into the various parts of the definition. And so let these two sentences be taken: 1 John 3:17 ("If someone has *bion* [the means of supporting life], the world's goods and sees his brother.") and Is. 58:6-7 ("Loose the bonds of wickedness, to undo the straps of the yoke, to let the oppressed go free, and to break every yoke."), and it will be clear what portions pertain to the method of true almsgiving:

(1) The general category to which almsgiving belongs can be taken from the various names applied to it, so that it can be deemed a beneficence, a gift, a work, a gracious act of kindness or a work of mercy.

(2) These statements show to whom largess ought to be given, namely to the needy, oppressed, broken and afflicted, whose condition and circumstances are worthy of commiseration. For these are the words of Scripture (Lev. 25:35): "Cannot maintain himself," that is, not to the lazy. In this rule Scripture does not make any distinction between friends and enemies, but says, "Give to the one who begs from you" (Matt. 5:42; Luke 6:30; Rom. 12:20).

(3) The material cause of almsgiving, concerning what John calls the *bion* [the means of supporting life] of the world, is all things that pertain to the sustenance of this life in this world. The specific types of almsgiving are enumerated in Matt. 25:34-36; Is. 48:6-7; Rom.12:20.

(4) 1 John 3:17 calls the heart the efficient cause. See also Is. 58:10: "Pour yourself out," that is, the commiseration for the calamity of one's neighbor.

(5) John says that the final cause is the charity of God [1 John 4:10].

(6) Isaiah hands down this observation: It is a giving of alms to offer those things that are not owed under one's civic duties and to forego those things that are owed, if a neighbor is oppressed and afflicted by this exaction of debt. So also Moses teaches in Lev.25:35-36; Deut. 24:12; and Ex. 22:25. Therefore, almsgiving is a gracious gift, when the wants of the needy are relieved by the means that pertain to the sustenance of this life; and this takes place from the charity of God and the commiseration of the misfortune of one's neighbor.

IV. To whom do those commandments about almsgiving pertain? For the command concerning loving and fearing God, etc., pertained equally to Lazarus and to the rich man, but the commandment concerning the giving of alms did not apply to them both equally. 1 John 3:17 answers this question with these words: "If anyone has the world's goods ... " Paul says (2 Cor. 8:14), "your abundance ... should supply their need," and two verses earlier, "It is acceptable according to what a person has, not according to what he does not have." Cf. Luke 16:9, "Make friends for yourselves by means of unrighteous wealth"; Luke 3:11, "Whoever has two tunics is to share with him who has none, and whoever has food is to do likewise, "that is, those things that are necessary for the daily sustenance of life. And in Matt. 25:40 there are stationed at our Lord's right hand not only those who gave the alms, but also the hungry, thirsty, naked, etc. So in Acts 3:6 Peter answered the lame man seeking alms, "I have no gold and silver." And in Luke 11:41 we read, "Give as alms, *ta enonta* [the things present], that are within."

For God has distributed the human race into two categories: (1) There are some who possess wealth, to whom the commandment has been delivered concerning the giving of alms. (2) There are some needy people, who are to be helped by alms, as the Scripture says (Deut. 15:11), "There will never cease to be poor in the land." No third category, i.e., those who neither are in need nor give, can be found in the Scripture.

Moreover, that abundance, as Paul calls it, should not be understood as if he were talking about the wealth of Croessus [one of the wealthiest kings of antiquity], as if nobody should be bound to the commandment concerning alms except for those who abound in much overflowing wealth. For Paul (in Eph. 4:28) commands also those who seek their manner of living with the labor of their hands to set aside something out of their wages, that they might share it with the needy. And in Mark 12:43 and Luke 21:3 Christ praises that poor little widow who put her mite into the treasury. She did that out of her own penury, which was barely sufficient for the daily sustenance of her own life, so that she reserved nothing for herself. And Christ prefers her to alms of the rich, who were donating more money by far, but out of their abundance. Our Savior Himself, although He lived by alms (Luke 8:3; John 12:6), nonetheless gave to the poor (John 2:8; 13:29).

Here a statement of Ambrose is relevant, which is cited in the decrees, distinction 86:

"The command of mercy is common to all walks of life, is necessary for people of all ages, and is to be handed down by all. The tax collector is not exempt, nor is the soldier, nor the farmer, nor the city dweller, rich or poor. All are admonished in common to help the one who does not have."

V. To whom should alms be given? John in 1 John 3:17 and Paul in Eph. 4:28 answer simply and in general terms that one ought to give alms to the needy. Elsewhere those who receive alms are enumerated by categories: the hungry, the thirsty, the naked, exiles, the sick, those who are not able to look for work (Matt. 25:35-36, Is. 58:6-7), those who have been bereft of their property because of their confession of faith or because of some misfortune (Rom. 12:20), widows who are alone and who are wearied by old age (1 Tim. 5:16). Moses says in Deut. 15:7 that whoever diligently does the duties of his calling ought to be supported by the giving of a loan, by the remission of debt and by other means, whenever he is deprived of the blessing of God.

Thus, the Scriptures enumerate nearly every kind of beggar. At the same time, Paul does not count the pay of the preachers in the church as alms. Instead, he calls it a debt (Rom. 15:27), something that was in his power to accept (1 Cor. 9:4), something to be transferred from the account of the one giving into the one receiving (Phil. 4:16). Augustine describes it nicely: "It is not a form of beggary, but his right, when a minister of the gospel receives his pay." In the same way Paul calls the money paid to the civil magistrates tribute that is owed (Rom. 13:7). We have spoken in an earlier chapter about those hypocrites, those mendicant monks. Concerning them Christ says (Matt. 23:14): "Woe to you … [who] devour widows' houses and for pretense you make long prayers." Such monastic beggary becomes blasphemy when it was woven into superstitions about satisfaction for sins and merit, such as in the tale told about Alexius, who demanded alms from his own servants from their own goods. Alexius is said to have heard a voice from heaven say that Rome stood because of his own merits. Of Christ's poverty alone has it been written that by His poverty we have been made rich.

Moreover, Paul adds that one ought to see that the alms are able to be sufficient for those who are truly poor. He says (1 Tim. 5:16 and 2 Thess. 3:12) that the able ought not to receive bread free of cost, that is, they should not live off of alms, but they ought to work, so that they may eat their own bread. He then adds in [2 Thess. 3:]10, "If anyone is not willing to work, let him not eat." The civil law, too, imposes the penalty of slavery for those able bodied people who beg. Sirach 122:5 says, "Give to the just and do not give to a sinner." And it is often useful to give due diligence to considering to whom alms should be given, just as that statement of Augustine in his letter to the Donatist Vincent [*Letters* 93.4]:

> "It is better to love with harshness than to deceive with gentleness. For it is more useful for bread to be taken from the hungry, if he neglects righteousness when secure concerning his food, rather than for the bread to be distributed to him, and he be seduced by unrighteousness and acquiesce to it."

Nonetheless, that examination ought not to be excessively rough and prying. For after Paul had reproached the parasites who were abusing the generosity of the Christians, he adds (2 Thess. 3:13), "Brothers, do not grow weary in doing good." For although alms are often deceived, nonetheless Christ says (Matt.10:41), "The one who receives a righteous person because he is a righteous person will receive a righteous person's reward." And in 25:40, He says, "You did it to me." A comment of Chrysostom on Heb.13 exists to this effect and is cited by Gratian under Distinction 42.

In addition, it is relevant to discuss here in what order alms ought to be given. To be sure, the command is universal: "Give to everyone who begs from you" (Luke 6:30). Nonetheless, almsgiving has its own degrees and its own order. For first we are more closely obligated to those of our own household than to those outside of it. When Paul speaks about the maintenance of widows (1 Tim. 5:8), he says, "If anyone does not provide for his relatives ... he has denied the faith." And Christ reproaches those who deprive their aging and ailing parents of their necessary nourishment under the pretext that they had offered gifts or alms in the temple treasury (Matt. 15:5). Secondly, [we are obligated to help fellow Christians.] "Let us do good to everyone, and especially to those who are in the household of faith" (Gal.6:10). Cf. 12 John 3:17, "If he sees his brother in need ... "; Matt. 10:41, to the righteous and the prophet; Matt. 25:40: "one of the least of My brothers"; Luke 16:9: "Make friends for yourselves by means of unrighteous wealth." Thirdly, [we are obligated to help our neighbors.] "If one of your brothers should become poor," (Deut. 15:7). In the same chapter, but in verse 12 [verse 8], he states, "Open your hand to him and lend him sufficient for his need, whatever it may be." Again, "There will be no lack of poor people in the land you will inhabit." Fourthly, strangers, travelers, and exiles ought to be helped. See Matt. 25:35; Is. 58:17 [58:7]; Gen. 18:3; 19:2; Rom. 12:13. And in 3 John 9 Diotrephes is scolded because he had instructed the members of his household not to welcome strangers. Fifthly, "your enemy is hungry" (Prov. 25:21; Rom. 12:20).

Concerning how one ought to select the recipients of alms, the philosophers do not agree with the teaching of the church. Seneca says: "Although you ought to give to everyone who asks, nonetheless when giving alms we ought to investigate the recipients' character, mind, dwelling, known associates, and the deference shown to us." Even Ambrose (Book 1 of *On the Duties of the Clergy* [30.158]) orders us to consider the age, disability, and truthfulness of the recipient, as well as to ask whether it was by pure misfortune that he fell into poverty. Yet the Scripture hands down this rule in the parable of the Samaritan (Luke 10:33): Let us ourselves not pick out those whom we wish to assist, but rather those whom God puts before us on whatever occasion, just as God put the man who had been robbed and beaten in the path of the Samaritan. Thus, Augustine says in book one of *Concerning the Teaching of Christ*, "Although you cannot help everyone, you can be of assistance chiefly to those who are connected to you by the opportunities of place and time or some other matter. They have become joined to you, as it were, by some chance."

VI. How much ought to be given? Paul says that there is not a certain number or a definite measure in the Scriptures, as there is in tributes imposed by the government: "I say this not as a command, but to prove ... that your love is genuine" (2 Cor. 8:8), that is, Scripture indeed commands that alms be given, but it does not command the manner or the measure. It leaves it free to the benevolent will of the godly, just as 1 Cor. 16:2 says, "Each of you is to put something aside and store it up." So, too, 2 Cor. 9:7: "Each one must give as he has decided in his heart." To be sure, the Scripture generally describes the manner of liberality in the church in this way: "I do not mean that others should be eased and you burdened, but that as a matter of fairness, your abundance at the present time should supply their need." (2 Cor. 8:13-14); "Your springs ... ." (Prov. 5:16). John the Baptist preaches the same thing: "Whoever has two tunics" — that is, those things that are not necessary for the sustenance of one's own life and body. Elsewhere indeed Christ Himself had two tunics and Paul even had a cloak in addition to his tunic. "Give as alms those things that are within" (Luke 11:41). "The disciples determined ... to send relief to the brothers" (Acts 11:29). "Give to the poor according to your strength" (Sirach 14:13).

Since avarice easily abuses that Gospel freedom as if it were a pretext, the Scripture adds some other statements: (1) "Honor the Lord with your wealth" (Prov. 3:9), that is, alms should not be given from what is spoiled and is useful to no one. (2) "Sell your possessions and give to the needy" (Luke 12:33), which means in the case of need, just as I explained this statement in an earlier chapter ["On the abandonment of one's goods"]. "He has given to the poor" (Ps. 112:9); cf. what the disciples did in Acts. (3) "Whoever sows sparingly will also reap sparingly, and whoever sows bountifully will also reap bountifully" (2 Cor. 9:6). In verse 8 he says that it is the work of the Holy Spirit to abound in good works. Also 2 Cor. 8:8 states that genuine charity is shown through generous giving of alms. So Paul praises the Macedonian churches because they were inclined to give not only in accordance with their strength, but also beyond their strength, just as that poor little widow. From these foundations one can easily construe a full teaching concerning the manner and measure of alms giving.

VII. How ought alms to be given, or what stipulations ought true, Christian almsgiving to have? An unregenerate man is able to make an outward contribution, as is said in the case of a certain Simon of Athens, who bequeathed all his possessions to the poor. The papists dream up many impious teachings concerning how almsgiving is virtuous by its own power [i.e., apart from the faith of the giver], as in that tale of Peter the tax collector. They imagine that the alms of Cornelius were made acceptable to God without faith and love. However, Paul says, "If I give away all I have ... but have not love, I gain nothing" (1 Cor. 13:3). And Matt. 6:2 says concerning the alms of the Pharisees, "They have received their reward." Therefore, above all else, one ought to consider the differences in the act of giving itself between churchly almsgiving and pagan generosity. Thomas [Aquinas] says, "Alms ought to be an act of three virtues: mercy, justice, and service." Others count the virtues of almsgiving as generosity, affection, and love. There are those who list the following as conditions of almsgiving: (1) willingness, (2) swiftness, love, (4) bounty, (5) kindness, (6) sincerity, (7) liberality, (8) property and (9) opportunity. But if the words are taken from the very statements of Scripture, the chief conditions of true Christian almsgiving seem to be able to be numbered in the following way.

(1) It must be done out of faith, that is, not out of that hypocritical thought of merit, forgiveness of sins, and eternal life. But a person is reconciled by faith through Christ and decides by faith that this work is pleasing to God. See Heb. 11:9; Rom. 14:23.

(2) It must be done out of love (see 1 Cor. 13:3). That is to say, the Holy Spirit must move one's heart and the alms must be given out of consideration of the command and will of God.

(3) Consequently, because He Himself loved us first and demonstrated His love, giving His Son as the most excellent pledge of this love, we too love our brothers for His sake with whatever sort of distribution of alms, so that honor and obedience are offered to God, as 2 Cor. 9:13 and 1 John 3:17 make clear.

(4) There should not be any wastefulness or prodigality, but one ought to have compassion for the common calamities, as it is called. See Is. 58:10; Job 30:25 and 1 John 3:17.

(5) It should be done in sincerity (Rom. 12:8). "Let there be no seeking" — i.e., "after greater advantage or repayment," as Jerome adds. "Let there be no hunting after a little glory" (Luke 14:12), "that they may be praised by others" (Matt. 6:2; 23:5), "but do not let your left hand know what your right hand is doing" (Matt. 6:3). That is to say, you should not reveal to your neighbor nor should you even inform your own mind about it, for we will either render ourselves haughty or put ourselves above others. If you seek applause, it will be given to you, says Christ quite clearly in Matthew 6 and 25. Jerome, writing to Nepotianus [Letters 52.9], says, "There are those who offer a little to the poor that they may receive much. They seek riches under the guise of almsgiving, which really ought to be called legacy-hunting rather than almsgiving. For beasts, birds and fish are caught by putting a little food onto a hook." Lactantius (Institutes 6.12) writes, "Above all, one must be careful that any hope for reward is absent from the act of showing mercy. For if reward is expected by anyone, it will no longer be an act of humanity, but a lending of some benefit." Seneca says, "Nothing is fouler to the venal than a genuine act of mercy." Sirach (29:11) notes, "Do not drag the poor into slavery by your alms."

(6) It should not be done out of sadness or necessity, because God loves a cheerful giver (2 Cor. 9:7). However, that cheerfulness arises when God makes every grace to abound in us so that, being sufficient in all things, we abound in every good work, as Paul says.

(7) It should not be done sparingly or with ill disposition, as if we were controlled by greed, but it should be a generous and kind liberality, for this is what Paul calls "in generosity" (2 Cor. 9:6) and Solomon calls "extending one's hand" (Prov. 31:20) and Moses calls "open wide your hand" (Deut. 15:11). Here the following statements of Scripture are relevant: "Honor the Lord ... with the firstfruits of all your produce" (Prov. 3[:9]); "Make yourself dear to the poor" (Sirach 4:7); "Make your face cheerful every time you give" (Sirach 35:11). "The gift of the foolish will not be useful to you. He will give scantily and he will reproach much" (Sirach 20:14–15).

Gregory writes, "There are some people who, as soon as any needy brothers have requested some necessities, first hurl insulting words at them. Even if later they carry out their service of piety with deeds, nonetheless by their insulting words they lose their grace of humanity, so much so that they seem to be paying an atonement for the injury rendered, when gifts are given after insults."

"Do not say to your neighbor, 'Go, and come again tomorrow I will give it' when you have it with you" warns Prov. 3:28. "Do not afflict the heart of a needy man and do not delay your gift to the poor" (Sirach 4:3). "If I have withheld anything that the poor desired, or have caused the eyes of the widow to fail" (Job 31:16). Saeneca writes, "It is an unpleasant gift which sticks too long to the hands of the giver." He also says [*On Acts of Kindness* 2.1.2], "Nothing is bought at a dearer price than whatever is procured by begging" [*On Acts of Kindness* 2.4.1]. Again: "Most pleasing are those acts of kindness which befall men easily, where there is no delay except for the modesty of the recipient." [*On Acts of Kindness* 2.1.3] Macrobius says, "It is only partly an act of charity, if you quickly say no to what is requested." Augustine says, "He loses both the power and the merit of his donation if he gives not in order to refresh the heart of the needy, but to be rid of the beggar whom he finds disgusting." Again he says, "It is not perfect mercy which has to be extorted by begging."

> (1) Alms ought to be conjoined with justice, so that one's need may not be taken from someone else's property or by robbery. "Share your bread" (Is. 58:7); "I hate robbery and wrong" (Is. 61:8).

> Thus, Zacchaeus gave back four-fold to the one whom he knew he had defrauded; later, however, since he was not able to make restitution to all, he gave half of his estate to the poor.

> (2) We should love not only in word and tongue, but in deed and truth, as 1 John 3:18 and James 2:16 make clear: "[If] one of you says to them, 'Go in peace, be warmed and filled,' without giving them the things needed for the body, what good is that?"

Here a discussion of the manner of distributing alms is relevant, as it has been preserved and written down by the saints. Examples from the Old Testament: (1) A private individual gave money to a private individual (Deut. 15:11). (2) Something was left behind in the field, vineyard and orchards for the poor in general (Ex. 23:11; Lev.19:10; 23:22; Deut. 23:25; 24:19). (3) A public tithe was collected, which was distributed by people in public office. For three tithes had been instituted, one for God (from which the donors themselves could eat; Deut. 14:22), another for the Levites (Num. 18:21), yet another for the poor (Deut.14:28). And there was a public place appointed for them to bring those gifts. It was commonly called the temple treasury (Neh.10:37; Ezek. 40:17; Mark 12:41; Luke 21:1). This was the place where Christ sat and taught (John 8:2). In 2 Kings 12:9 it is called the chest, into which money was thrown for building the temple. Cf. Sirach 29:25 [29:15], "Throw money into the storehouse." Paul seems to have imitated this in 1 Cor. 16:2, "Each of you is to put something aside."

In the New Testament private almsgiving is described in the same way (Mark 10:46; Luke 16:20; Acts 3:2). Also public contributions were gathered, not in the custom of Mosaic law, i.e., through tithes and through gleanings left in the fields, but in Christian freedom, as it seemed most convenient for the circumstances of the times, the people, etc. Sometimes it took place one way, other times a different, as in the sharing of goods mentioned in Acts, the donation of money in 2 Cor. 8:14; 9:7 and 1 Cor. 16:2. See 1 Tim. 5:16; Phil. 4:16. Tertullian in his *Apology* [39.5–6] remembers that alms were accustomed to be given street by street; moreover, he mentions the chest into which the public alms money was gathered for the deacons and the poor. Later, Constantine bestowed revenue to the churches because alms were being collected rather scantily. Chrysostom in sermon 37 remembers that it had been the custom that alms would be offered to the priests so that they themselves might distribute to the poor in accordance with each one's need. But because the deacons were deemed most honorable in this obligation, Chrysostom asked that they themselves dole out the money.

VIII. Finally, one ought to add a consideration concerning the divine promises and threats which have been added to the teaching about alms. This last part, however, has been horribly distorted by the papists, who do not hesitate even today to ascribe to our alms the honor of making satisfaction for our sins and the honor of meriting eternal life. The scholastics ascribe the honor of making satisfaction of sins to three items; the chief and most efficacious way of atoning for sins they ascribe to almsgiving; the others are prayer and fasting.

Indeed, when some of the older fathers of the churches saw the love of their parishioners growing cold, they went a little overboard in ensuring that their exhortations struck home with their audience. Lactantius ([*Institutes*] 6.12) says, "The reward of mercy is great. God has promised that He will forgive all the sins of one who shows mercy." The opinion of Ambrose is quoted in the treatise *Concerning Repentance* (distinction 12, chapter C. "Medicine"): "We have more resources by which we may redeem our sins. You have money; redeem your sins. It is not that the Lord can be bought and sold. No, you yourself are venal and have sold yourself to your sins. Therefore, redeem yourself with your deeds and with your money, for sins are redeemed by almsgiving."

Based on these sayings of the fathers, the papists gave birth to many sacrilegious opinions and legends. For after this godless notion was established, genuine charity clearly lost all its vigor. For no one likes to be good without being rewarded, as the poet says. No doubt God did not wish to put forth the doctrine concerning almsgiving without any explanation, but He impressed it upon us in various ways, viz., by commanding, exhorting and beseeching. He added promises and threats because he knew that the root of evils — greed — sticks very tenaciously to our corrupt flesh. Therefore it is useful always to keep in mind to explain this doctrine correctly in regards to those promises. The promises were not given so that we might attach to this doctrine some ungodly notion about rewards, but so that we might arouse thoughts of mercy by considering those promises.

Indeed, because many different promises have been added to this doctrine, they seem to be able to be conveniently divided into categories for the sake of teaching about them in an orderly fashion, so that the explanation of the promises is not thrown into confusion. Some are general promises; others can be arranged in the following categories: promises of rewards, promises of external blessings (also called temporal or bodily blessings), promises of spiritual blessing which nonetheless are received in this life, promises of reward at the resurrection of the just in the life to come. These distinctions bring a little light to the explanation.

(1) These are the general promises: "He will by no means lose his reward" (Matt. 10:42). "For God is not unjust so as to overlook your work and the love that you have shown for his name in serving the saints" (Heb. 6:10). "His righteousness endures forever" (Ps. 112:9). "Blessed is he who is generous to the poor" (Prov. 14:21). "Whoever is generous to the poor lends to the Lord, and He will repay him for his deed" (Prov. 19:17). "Do good to the just and you will find great reward, if not from him him-self, certainly from the Lord" (Sirach 12:2). "Cast your bread upon the waters, for you will find it after many days" (Eccl. 11:1).

(2) These statements pertain to the category of promises of external blessings: "Give and it will be given to you" (Luke 6:38). "Then your barns will be filled with plenty, and your vats will be bursting with wine" (Prov. 3:10). "One gives freely, yet grows all the richer" (Prov. 11:24). "Whoever gives to the poor will not want" (Prov. 28:27). "In the day of trouble the LORD delivers him" (Ps. 40:1 [41:1]). "Alms will fight more than the shield of the mighty and more than a spear against your enemy" (Sirach 29:18 [29:16-17]). "There is no one who ... will not receive a hundredfold now in this time ... with persecutions" (Mark 10:30). "Alms frees from every evil" (Sirach 29:15). "It is well with the man who deals generously and lends, who conducts his affairs with justice ... his heart is firm , trusting in the LORD" (Ps.112:5, 7[-8]). "Then shall your light break forth like the dawn ... your righteousness shall go before you ... the Lord will guide you continually ... and you shall be like a watered garden" (Is. 58:8, 11) "The father's alms will not be forgotten" (Sirach 3:16).

"In a time of misfortune he will find a solid foundation" (Sirach 3:30 [3:17])
Consequently, bodily rewards are promised: (a) repayment in temporal
goods, (b) relief in times of disaster, (c) bodily health and a long life, (d)
good fortune and success in business, (e) blessings also for one's posterity.
The statement of Jerome is relevant here: "I do not remember ever reading
about anyone dying an evil death who had led a merciful life."

(3) Spiritual promises have also been added to almsgiving. For because
God's mercy is not a number, He does not keep to a mathematical formula
when dispensing punishments and rewards. It is as the scholastics say: He
grants rewards more than we deserve and when he imposes punishments,
He does this less than we deserve. Therefore, He promises even spiritual
rewards to the bodily act of almsgiving. But we must accurately explain what
they are and how they are promised, especially because of the errors of the
papists who ascribe to almsgiving the power to atone for sins, redeem from
eternal death and merit eternal life. To be sure, one ought to increase the
preaching about good works, but it should be done in such a way so that
the chief teaching of the Gospel and the benefits of Christ are not obscured.
The forgiveness of sins, redemption from the devil and death, salvation and
eternal life are the merits of Christ alone and the free gift of God, which are
accepted by faith alone.

Therefore, the following statements have to be interpreted according to the
analogy of faith. "Break off your sins by practicing righteousness, and your
iniquities by showing mercy to the oppressed, that there may perhaps be
lengthening of your prosperity" Dan. 4:24 [4:27]). "Alms frees from every
sin and from death and will not allow one's soul to go into the shadows.
Alms will be a great pledge before God for all who give it" (Tobit 4:11–12).
"The angel said, 'Alms will free from death and it will be the means which
purges your sins and it will make you find mercy and eternal life'" (Tobit
12:9). "Water extinguishes a burning fire and alms will expiate sins" (Sirach
5:33[incorrect reference]). However, one follows the analogy of faith
when the chief and main articles of heavenly teaching, which are certain,
well-founded and clear, are affirmed and an interpretation in accord with
these articles is sought in obscure, or ambiguous passages, as well as those
passages that do not directly treat those doctrines. The interpretation ought
not to disagree with those chief articles, but should agree with them. The
following are the most important, certain, firm and chief articles: (a) It is
Christ's work and His alone as our mediator and high priest to redeem from
sins, free us from death and merit eternal life. (b) These benefits are offered
through the Gospel. (c) They are received through faith, not by works.
Whatever promises are made about alms ought not to contradict this chief
and most fundamental expression of the Gospel.

Therefore, these passages can be harmonized with the analogy of faith along these lines:

(a) The statements of Daniel can be interpreted in this way. Daniel is treating the doctrine of complete repentance, just as is customary in the Old Testament. (Cf. Is. 1:16 "Remove the evil"; Ps. 37:27: "Cease to do evil") The brevity of these statements can make them misunderstood. However, it is certain that true repentance comprises three parts: contrition, faith, and new obedience. Therefore, Daniel urges the king now to show worthy fruits of repentance by his acts of righteousness and kindness, because earlier he had sinned by his unrighteousness and his plunder of his subjects. Then it is also certain that forgiveness of sins, life, and salvation are promised for the converted and repentant. The Gospel indeed adds the noteworthy and clear explanation that these benefits are not given because of the worthiness of any deeds (whether past, present or future), but they are freely given because of Christ. Finally, the Gospel clearly shows that these gifts are received in true repentance, not by contrition nor by the fruits of repentance, but by faith alone. And in this rather obscure and condensed passage, Daniel nevertheless makes explicit mention of faith and the righteousness of faith.

(b) Brentz relates another way in which these passages can be harmonized with the evangelical doctrine. Alms is not what merits forgiveness and eternal life, nor is alms even the instrument by which this is acquired, but rather is the fruit of repentance. Therefore, alms is said to redeem from death and free from sin because they testify to us about faith, just as fruits attest to the goodness of a tree — and by faith we receive the forgiveness of sins and Christ dwells in our hearts, etc. Therefore, alms attests in this way concerning forgiveness of sins, these things have been given and received freely for Christ's sake through faith.

(c) Some explain these statements as pertaining to temporal punishments of sins. It is certain that such punishments can be mitigated by complete repentance.

(d) The following interpretation is related in the *Apology* [*of the Augsburg Confession* 4.263]: Alms do not free from the guilt of past sins (Romans 3) but from future sins. For while good works are being pursued, sins are avoided. Or you could say that God saves His elect so that they do not fall into tragic sin.

(e) The excessive praises of almsgiving, as can be read in Tobit and Sirach, do not exist in the canonical books. Meanwhile, the statement of Daniel can be much more conveniently explained than those in Tobit and Sirach.

The remaining statements in Scripture about spiritual rewards are even clearer. Note the following: "Such sacrifices are pleasing to God" (Heb. 13:16). "Share your bread with the hungry and bring the homeless poor into your house ... then you shall call, and the Lord will answer; you shall cry, and He will say, 'Here I am'" (Is.58:[7,] 9). These statements do not contradict John 16:23 ("Whatever you ask in My name ... ."). Instead, it is the opposite that reveals the true explanation of Hebrews 13 and Isaiah 58. "Whoever closes his ear to the cry of the poor will himself call out and not be answered" (Prov. 21:13). In Acts 10:4, when the angel announced to Cornelius, who already had the beginnings of faith, that he should seek out a fuller explanation from Peter, the angel said, "Your prayers and alms have ascended before God." Thus, an increase of spiritual gifts was given to the widow of Zarephath and to Obadiah, who fed a hundred prophets in the caves. This explains the following passages: "He [who] is a prophet will receive a prophet's reward, and the one who receives a righteous person because he is a righteous person will receive a righteous person's reward" (Matt. 10:41); "for they shall receive mercy" (Matt. 5:7); "Give as alms those things that are within, and behold, everything is clean for you" (Luke 11:41), namely in the enjoyment of one's possessions.

Even the faithful are hardly able to avoid all sin in the acquisition and use of earthly goods (that is why it is called "unrighteous Mammon"). Therefore, he says, "Cleanse yourself inwardly, and outwardly give alms; then all things will be pure," namely, in their use. Cf. 1 Cor. 7:14, where the children [of a believing mother] are called "sanctified," and 2 Cor. 9:8,10 ("And God is able to make all grace abound to you, so that having all sufficiency in all things at all times, you may abound in every good work"). Therefore, these are the spiritual promises: (a) God is pleased. (b) He will hear and show mercy. (c) He will redeem you from sin and free you from death. (d) You will grow in knowing God. (e) You will abound in every good work. (f) God will keep you from future sins. (g) He will give you an antidote against avarice, namely, sufficiency. (h) He will hallow your enjoyment of property.

(4) The pious act of giving alms has the promises not only for this life but also for the future life. "Go, sell what you possess and give to the poor, and you will have treasure in heaven" (Matt. 19:21). "Provide yourselves with moneybags that do not grow old, with a treasure in the heavens that does not fail" (Luke 12:33). "You will be repaid at the resurrection" (Luke 14:14). "Your Father ... will reward you" (Matt. 6:4), just as is described in Matt. 25:34. "Inherit the kingdom" (Luke 16:9). "Your righteousness shall go before you; the glory of the Lord shall be your rear guard" (Is. 58:8). "[You

will] receive a hundredfold now in this time" (Mark 10:30). "Storing up treasure for themselves as a good foundation for the future, so that they may take hold of that which is truly life" (1 Tim. 6:19). For although eternal life is a gift of God for Christ's sake, nonetheless it is at the same time a payment for the works of charity.

Finally, one must add as an antithesis a list of the threats for not giving alms, so that the promises may be understood more correctly. "Whoever gives to the poor will not want" (Prov. 28:27). "Whoever closes his ear to the cry of the poor will himself call out and not be answered" (Prov. 21:13). "Do not turn your eyes away from the poor in anger, for his plea will be heard as he curses you in the bitterness of his soul" (Sirach 4:5-6). "Whoever oppresses a poor man insults his Maker" (Prov. 14:31). "Whoever sows sparingly will also reap sparingly" (2 Cor. 9:6). "The one who sows to his own flesh will from the flesh reap corruption" (Gal. 6:8). "Judgment is without mercy to the one who has shown no mercy" (James 2:13). "How does God's love abide in him?" (1 John 3:17). "I was hungry and you gave me no food" etc. (Matt. 25:42). Cf. the parable of the rich man in Luke 16:19 and the history of Nabal in 1 Sam. 25:2. However, all these threats can be clearly categorized in the same way as the promises.

DEATH OF MARY
c. 1510

On the Duties of Ministers of the Church

Theological Commonplaces
Locus 23, Chapter 6, Section 2
by Johann Gerhard

Translated by Richard Dinda

The priesthood "is not leisure but the task of tasks," Bernard writes somewhere, and "the name 'bishopric' is a word of work, not of honor," according to Augustine (Bk.19, *de civ. Dei*, c.19). Now that we have explained the reasons for the ministry of the church and the necessity thereof, as well as the utility and dignity depending on it, it remains for us to speak about the duties of ministers of the church.

Various writers list those duties in different ways. "Every administration of the church consists in three things: in the sacraments, in the holy orders and in precepts" (Hugh of St. Victor, Bk.2, *de sacr.*, part 2, c.5). "The duties of the priest are to learn something from God, or to teach the people, or to pray for the people, etc." (Jerome, on Leviticus 8). For our list to be quite complete, however, we say that the duties of the ministry are most accurately evaluated on the basis of the end, because the church was divinely instituted and is still being preserved. In earlier sections we said that that end was dual: namely, a principal purpose, the glory of God; and an intermediate goal, the conversion and salvation of people. The intermediate goal holds the rationale of some means through which one reaches the principal and ultimate end. From this it has even received its name. To achieve the intermediate purpose, God uses the duties and activities of ministers for the effective conversion and salvation of people.

First, the people who are to be converted and saved are born in the darkness of ignorance (Is. 9:2, Luke 1:79, John 1:5, Acts 26:18, Eph. 5:8). They are "alienated from the life of God because of the ignorance that is in them" (Eph. 4:18). The Holy Spirit wants to dispel that naive darkness through the light of the heavenly Word (Ps. 19:8, Ps. 119:105, 2 Peter 1:19). Therefore, **the most important duty of ministers of the church is to preach the Word**, through which the Holy Spirit provides an inner illumination of the heart. "I shall appoint you to serve … the gentiles, to whom I am sending you to open their eyes, that they may turn from darkness to light" (Acts 26:17-18).

Second, to the Word are added the Sacraments, the signs of divine grace and of the promise of the Gospel, so that the ancients call them the "*horaton*" or "visible" Word. Therefore, **the second duty of ministers is to administer the Sacraments.** "This is how one should regard us, as servants of Christ and stewards of the mysteries of God" (1 Cor. 4:1). "Go therefore and make disciples of all nations, baptizing them" (Matt. 28:19). Here, preaching the Word and administering Baptism are connected. Third, every effort of ministers is in vain without the blessing of heaven.

"I planted, Apollos watered, but God gave the growth. So neither he who plants nor he who waters is anything, but only God who gives the growth" (1 Cor. 3:6-7). Augustine, sermon 4, on the words of the apostle: "It is we who speak, but God who teaches. He who does the internal teaching has a throne in heaven."

Therefore, **the third duty of ministers is diligently praying for the flock entrusted to them.** "Far be it from me that I should sin against the Lord by ceasing to pray for you; and I will instruct you in the good and right way" (1 Sam. 12:23). Here the instruction of hearers and of praying for the fortification of the Word are connected.

It is proper for ministers to lead their hearers with the example of an excellent life. Those who teach sound material but live shamefully take away with the left hand what they gave with the right. At times, they can hurt more by example than they benefit with the Word. **Their fourth duty, then, is the honest control of their life and behavior.** "Show yourself in all respects to be a model of good works" (Titus 2:7).

Because in addition to the native darkness of ignorance, a corruption of the will and a proclivity toward every evil adhere to people, the bonds of ecclesiastical discipline (which have been entrusted divinely to the ministry) must be used to keep those things from hindering conversion through the Word or from snatching the converted and putting them at a crossroads. Therefore, **the fifth duty of ministers is to administer church discipline.** "If [the member] refuses to listen to them, tell it to the church" (Matt. 18:17).

In the solemn public exercise of divine worship, certain rituals related to decency and good order were introduced by consent of the entire church and should be preserved. Therefore, ministers should protect those rituals approved by serious consideration and give useful advice about many things in the public assemblies. Furthermore, the ministry should not change them because of some private desire of the mind at the offense of the church. Consequently, **the sixth duty of ministers is to preserve the rituals of the church.**

Finally, because among the hearers are orphans, widows, the poor, the homeless, the ill — duties of charity are especially owed to alleviate their poverty and affliction. Therefore, **the seventh duty of the ministry is the care of the poor and the**

visitation of the sick. He should collect and spend faithfully the money destined for use for the poor. If this duty is entrusted to those in charge of the church treasury, he should exhort members diligently to demonstrate their generosity toward the poor. He also should see to it that dispensing the goods is done lawfully and correctly (1 Cor. 16:2; 2 Cor. 9:1).

All told, therefore, there are seven duties of ministers of the church. We can relate all the rest to those seven: *first*, preaching the Word; *second*, dispensing the Sacraments; *third*, praying for the flock entrusted to them; *fourth*, controlling their own life and behavior; *fifth*, administering church discipline; *sixth*, preserving the rituals of the church; *seventh*, caring for and visiting the sick. We shall discuss each in greater detail.

Preaching the Word

We say that the first duty of ministers is preaching the Word. The mandates given to the apostles and their successors in the ministry prove this. "Go, therefore, and make disciples of all nations … teaching them" (Matt. 28:19-20). "Go into all the world and proclaim the gospel" (Mark 16:15). Second, the Holy Spirit has attributed to them both titles and praises. They are called "teachers" (1 Cor. 12:28, Eph. 4:11). Therefore, they should teach the people of God (Acts 20:28). They are called "shepherds" (Is. 63:11, Eph. 4:11), therefore, they should feed the flock entrusted to them with heavenly doctrine. They are called "messengers of the Lord" (Mal. 2:7, Rev. 1:20) and "ambassadors" (2 Cor. 5:20); therefore, they should explain the will of God by preaching His heavenly Word. They are called "laborers" (Matt. 9:38, 2 Tim. 2:15); therefore, they should labor in the Word (1 Tim. 5:18).

Third, we prove this duty by the apostolic rule, according to which we must examine bishops (1 Tim. 3:2, Titus 1:9), which expressly requires that a bishop be "able to teach." Fourth, we prove this from the goal of the ministry as it has been established. Certainly, God established and still preserves the ministry, especially so His Word is preached, and that through the preaching of His Word, the church be gathered from mankind (Eph. 4:11). Fifth, we prove it by the distinction of the ministry of the church from the political regime and from all other orders. After all, it is the minister's job to use the sword of the Spirit, namely, the Word of God, but not the corporal sword, for that belongs to the political magistracy (Eph. 6:17, Rom. 13:4, 2 Cor. 10:4, etc.).

Sixth, we prove it from the practice of Christ, and from the apostles and bishops in the early church. After all, they did not administer or create a political organization, but were busy preaching the Word (Matt. 4:17, Acts 6:2, etc.). Augustine relates (Bk.6, *confess.*, c.3) in regard to Ambrose that Ambrose delivered sermons to his people every Sunday. Seventh, the testimonies of the fathers prove it. Jerome (Bk.1, *adv. Jovin.*, c.20) comments as follows on the apostle's words that a bishop must be a teacher: "To enjoy a consciousness of virtues benefits none at all unless he can instruct a people who believe him, so that he can exhort them in doctrine and confute those who contradict him." Prosper, Bk.1, *de vita contempl.*, c.2: "Those who have charge over the church should each live a holy life in order to set an example, and should teach for the sake of the performance of his administration."

Eighth, the opinion of canon law proves it. "A bishop must be skilled in the sacred writings. In the Old Testament, therefore, the high priest, among his other ornaments, wore on his breast the breastplate on which was written the manifestation and the truth, for on the breast of the high priest there ought to be a manifest knowledge of the truth. Hence, also the poles with which the ark was carried were always inserted into rings so that, when they had to carry the Ark of the Covenant, there was or occurred no delay in putting in the bars; just so, the preachers by whom the church is carried around ought always to stand on the sacred writings so that they then do not ask to learn because, according to their office, they ought to be teaching others" (*C. Qui ecclesiast.*, dist.36, from epistle 1 of Sozimus, to Hesychius).

"If anyone wishes to be the high priest, let him imitate Moses and Aaron not so much in word as in just deserts. For what is said about them? — that they did not depart from the tabernacle of the Lord. Moses, therefore, was always in the tabernacle of the Lord. What need was there for this? — that he either learn something from God by reading Holy Scriptures and be meditating on them very often; or that he teach the people, but he should teach those things that he has learned from God, not from his own heart nor from human reason but what the Holy Spirit teaches" (*C. Si quis*, same dist., from Jerome, from Origen, homily 6 on Lev. 8).

"Every activity of priests should consist of preaching and doctrine. They should edify all people as well with a knowledge of faith as with discipline of activities" (*C. Ignorantia*, from the Fourth Council of Toledo, c.24). At the beginning of dist. 86: "A bishop must be a teacher lest the faults of lesser people be thrown back upon him who has not received the office of teaching, which he does not know how to perform or which he neglects."

"In season and out of season, without interruption, a bishop must teach the church, direct it wisely and love it, so that it avoids sins and can attain eternal salvation" (C. Sicut vir, case 7, q.1, from epistle 2 of Euaristus). In an epistle of Clement, Peter is related to have said to him: "Be free for this alone — to teach the Word of God in season and without interruption, for through it people can attain eternal salvation." We also add the civil law (*Bk. Addictos. In c. de epist. aud. imp.*), where they claim that it is the responsibility of bishops to temper Christian people with the publishing of religious teachings.

Ninth, the types of the Old Testament prove it. Among the ornaments of the high priest was a breastplate, which he wore on his breast and on which had been engraved "Urim" and "Thummim" (doctrine and truth, Ex. 28:30). That signified that ministers should teach the people doctrine and truth. The breast and right thigh from the peace offerings belonged to the priest; this signified that "ministers have to have wisdom to teach and fortitude to endure the defects of their hearers" (*Thomas*, p.1, 2, q.102, art.3). "No one whose testicles are crushed or whose male organ is cut off shall enter the assembly of the Lord" (Deut. 23:1). That is, whoever does not have the seed of the Word through which to sire spiritual children for the church is not to be tolerated in the ministry. To this we must relate from the New Testament that the apostles receive bread from the hand of Christ that they distribute to the multitude (Matt. 14:19). Thus, the duty of ministers is to provide for the hearers the bread of life, that is, the Word of the Gospel, which they have received from the hands of Christ. Also, we include the fact that bishops are called "stars" in the hands of Christ (Rev. 1:20), because it is their function to illumine others with the light of doctrine (Matt. 5:14).

The Pope and his Prelates are not True Bishops

From this we correctly conclude that the pope in Rome, who refrains completely from the office of teaching, and his prelates, who are involved with politics and even with military business at times, and who touch almost no part of the ministry of the church, are not true bishops. The exception that the Jesuits make is not true, that, "even if the pope does not himself teach, he nevertheless teaches through the others to whom he entrusts this duty." We respond.

First, the arguments and testimonies brought out prove that the pope himself ought to be teaching, and that, if he neglects to do this, he is a bishop only in title and word. Second, to preach the Word and to teach begin the definition of the bishop's responsibility. Therefore, that cannot and should not be separated from a properly-called bishop. Third, Christ, whose vicar the pope boasts he is, Peter, as whose successor he wished to be regarded, and the rest of the apostles by no means rejected their responsibility of teaching. Rather, they themselves went out into the churches and fed the people with the heavenly Word. Fourth, both to teach and to ordain others to teach are required for the office of a bishop. Including one should not mean excluding the other. Fifth, in kingdoms of this world, ambassadors of kings have their own subdelegates; in the spiritual kingdom, however, ministers of the church themselves should perform the ambassador's responsibility, which God has committed to them. "Therefore, we are ambassadors for Christ, God making his appeal through us" (2 Cor. 5:20). Sixth, it is not proper for the pope and his bishops to judge as unworthy of their lofty positions the duty of teaching because the entire Holy Trinity performed it: Father (Matt. 3:17 and 17:5), Son (Matt. 4:17, Acts 1:3, etc.) and Holy Spirit (2 Sam. 23:2, 2 Peter 1:21). Thus, the apostle says, "I am not ashamed of the gospel" (Rom 1:16). Seventh, at times, those the pope sends to teach are not skilled in teaching. Almost all of them teach their hearers (in place of the doctrines of the heavenly Word) human superstitions and corruptions.

Sermons

The teaching responsibility is particularly involved with delivering sermons. We explained how these should be organized in great detail in our "Method of Theological Study," part 3, sect.4, c.2. We showed that there are two primary functions of the ecclesiastical orator: "the interpretation of Scripture and the application thereof to the salutary use of the hearers."

The interpretation of Scripture includes both "an investigation of the true and genuine meaning" as well as "a clear explanation" thereof. That application we can relate to five general headings according to the apostle's prescription (Rom. 15:4 and 2 Tim. 3:16): to teaching, to reproof, to correction, to training and to consolation.

To be sure, the application of Scripture, as it is explained legitimately and with sound meaning, is either theoretical or practical. The theoretical involves a knowledge of the truth (from which comes teaching) and a refutation of what is false (from which comes reproof). The practical is involved with doing good (from which comes training); with fleeing the evil of fault (from which comes correction); and with enduring the evil of punishment (from which comes consolation). We have explained in specific canons in the aforementioned treatise what one must be careful to observe in all this.

With similar rationale, we showed that gathering the sheep through teaching and driving the wolves away from the Lord's sheepfold through reproof are related to the office of teaching. In the preface to our "Theological and Theoretical Aphorisms," from the statement of the apostle (Titus 1:7-9), we read: "An overseer ... must hold firm to the trustworthy word as taught, so that he may be able to give instruction in sound doctrine and also to rebuke those who contradict it"; from the type of the rebuilding of Jerusalem and the temple, in which they accomplished the work with one hand while carrying their weapons in the other (Neh. 4:17); from the comparison of teachers of the church with shepherds, who not only led their sheep to healthful pasture but also protected them against ambush and the attack of wolves; from their comparison with doctors for whom a double goal is set: to preserve one's present health and to restore it when it has been lost, etc.

Consequently, to discuss the activity here does not seem worthwhile. To these we can add a comparison drawn from a farmer. Just as it is a farmer's responsibility to properly sow the seed, it is also his job to pull out the bad weeds and sterile grasses. So also it is the theologian's responsibility not only to sow the seed of sound doctrine, but also to weed out the tares of error from the Lord's field.

Origen says it beautifully (*homily 2, on Genesis*, part 1, opera, p.14): "The squared timbers in the ark of Noah denote teachers of the church. It is squared so that it does not shake on any side. Whenever you turn it, it lies there with trustworthy and solid stability. They are timbers which bear on the inside the weight of the animals and on the outside the weight of the waves. These I believe are teachers in the church, schoolmasters and examples in the faith who comfort the people within with the power of the Word. With the wisdom of reason they oppose those who attack from outside or the heathen or heretics who stir up floods of questions and storms of controversies."

Jerome (*epistle 83, to Oceanus*): "The madness of the wolves must be kept off by the barking of dogs and the shepherd's staff." Augustine (*sermon 89, on the Times*): "Through this figure (Num. 16:39) the following seems to be shown. Those censers which Scripture calls 'bronze' hold the figure of Holy Scripture. Upon this Scripture, heretics place an alien fire, namely, introducing a meaning or error and understanding that is foreign to God and contrary to the truth. Thus, they offer up to the Lord not a fragrant but a foul-smelling incense. If we put those bronze censers, that is, the voices of heretics, on the altar of the Lord where the divine fire, the true preaching of the Word, is; then the better will shine with the very truth, over against the false."

Question 1: Whether the Magistracy Can Forbid the Refutation of Heretics

Can the Christian magistracy prohibit ministers of the church from censuring stubborn and demonstrated heretics by name? And, if such a prohibition be published by authority of the magistracy, can ministers of the church obey it with safe and undisturbed consciences? We respond: Absolutely not! First, this conflicts with the calling of the ministers of the church. In fact, not the last of their duties is to resist corruptions of heavenly doctrine. "If you utter what is precious, and not what is worthless, you shall be as my mouth" (Jer. 15:19). "All Scripture is … profitable for teaching, for reproof, for correction, and for training in righteousness, that the man of God may be complete, equipped for every good work" (2 Tim. 3:16-17). A bishop "must hold firm to the trustworthy word as taught, so that he may be able … to rebuke those who contradict it" (Titus 1:9).

Second, it conflicts with the general divine commands by which the genuinely devout are ordered to "beware of false prophets, flee idolatry, prove the spirits," etc. (Matt. 7:15 and 16:11, Rom. 16:17, Eph. 4:14, Phil. 3:2, etc.). But, if ministers of the church do not warn the lambs about the wolves, the lambs cannot recognize and flee from them. It also conflicts with the special divine commands that order teachers of the church to resist the wolves that wish to destroy the Lord's sheepfold. "Catch the foxes for us, the little foxes that spoil the vineyards" (Song of Songs 2:15). Augustine comments on those words as follows, (*sermon 107, on the Times*): "Arrest, censure, rebuke, confute them, lest the vineyard of the church be destroyed. What else does it mean to catch the foxes but to refute heretics by the authority of the divine law and to bind and restrict them by the testimonies of Holy Scripture as by some sort of chains?"

When the apostle foretold that there would rise up "wolves … not sparing the flock and men … speaking perverse things," he adds, "therefore be alert" (Acts 20:31). He shows that a divine command keeps ministers of the church under obligation to keep a vigilant eye, watching out for the snares of the wolves and to resist them with all their might. "And the Lord's servant must … [correct] his opponents with gentleness. God may perhaps grant them repentance leading to a knowledge of the truth" (2 Tim. 2:24-25). "For there are many … deceivers … upsetting whole families by teaching for shameful gain what they ought not to teach" (Titus 1:10-11).

Third, to deny refutation of heretics conflicts with the unique duty of the Holy Spirit in the church, which is to reprove. "He will convict the world concerning sin" (John 16:8), obviously through the ministry of the Word, which office is related not only to the primitive church but in general to the church of all times. This ministry reproves not only sins and sinners but also corruptions and false teachers, as appears from the explanation added (v. 9), where Christ says such that sin is unbelief, which is not only the source of actual sins but also embraces "misplaced belief, the baser unbelief," as Epiphanius warns. Whoever wants that reproving activity removed from the church is doing nothing else but placing a muzzle on the Holy Spirit.

Fourth, it conflicts with the praises given to ministers of the church. They are called "watchmen" and "seers" (Ezek. 3:17 and 33:7). They must watch out, then, lest the church incur any harm from false prophets. They are called "voices crying" (Is. 40:3). They are to lift up their voices, therefore, like a trumpet (Is. 58:1). They are called "shepherds"; therefore, when they see a wolf coming, they should not flee like the hired hand (John 10:12), but raise an outcry against it and drive it away, etc. Augustine, treatise 46 on John: "The wolf grasps the sheep by the throat, the devil persuades a believer into heresy. Do you keep silent? Do you not cry out for fear you will offend? O hired man! You have seen the wolf and run away. Perhaps you answer: 'Look, I am here. I have not run away!' You have run away because you kept silent."

Fifth, it conflicts with the divine threats against those who do not resist false teachers out of negligence or fear of dangers, or because of a perverse desire for the favor of the world. "Cursed is he who does the work of the Lord with slackness" (Jer. 48:10). "His watchmen are blind; they are all without knowledge; they are all silent dogs; they cannot bark" (Is. 56:10). "If I say to the wicked, 'You shall surely die,' and you give him no warning … his blood I will require at your hand" (Ezek. 3:18). "Would that you were either cold or hot! So, because you are lukewarm, and neither hot nor cold, I will spit you out of my mouth" (Rev. 3:15-16).

Sixth, it conflicts with the practical advantages that rise from the refutation of false teachers. However, those cannot be seen better than if those things be considered as disadvantages, which generally come forth if we permit heresies to rage unchecked and create confusion. They are weeds that hinder the growth of the grain (Matt. 13:38). They are the leaven, a tiny bit of which leavens the whole lump (Matt. 16:11-13, 1 Cor. 5:6). They are the gangrene that immediately corrupts the neighboring limbs if it is not checked (2 Tim. 2:17). Jerome says it beautifully in Galatians 5: "As soon as they appear a spark must be extinguished, the leaven removed from near the lump, rotting flesh cut away and an animal with scabies removed from the sheepfold, lest the entire household burn, the lump be spoiled, the body putrefy and the flock perish," etc.

Seventh, it conflicts with the practice of the church of the Old Testament. Philo writes about Abel in his book that, because a meaner thing generally lies in wait for a better, Abel argued with Cain about his sacrifice and religion. Regarding Moses, Augustine writes, epistle 119, to Januarius, that "he resisted the restless hatred of the heretics such as Jannes and Jambres, Korah, Dathan and Abiram." As regards Elijah, Jeremiah, Micah, Amos and the rest of the prophets, we agree that they opposed themselves manfully against the Baalites and other false teachers.

Eighth, it conflicts with the practice of Christ, John the Baptist and the apostles in the New Testament. They reproached by name (with very strong language) the adversaries of divine truth. In Matt. 3:7, Jesus calls the Pharisees and Sadducees "a brood of vipers" in the presence of the entire multitude. In Matt. 16:11, Christ says to the disciples: "Beware of the leaven of the Pharisees and Sadducees." In Matt. 23:13 and several times elsewhere He repeats: "Woe to you, scribes and Pharisees!" In 1 Tim. 1:19b-20, when the apostle had said in general that "some have made shipwreck of their faith," he adds by name: " ... among whom are Hymenaeus and Alexander, whom I have handed over to Satan."

Ninth, it conflicts with the permanent practice of the primitive church and of those who succeeded the apostles in the office of teaching. Polycarp battled against Marcion, Valentinus and other heretics. When Marcion attacked him, Polycarp called him "the firstborn of Satan," according to Irenaeus, Bk.3, c.3. Irenaeus debated against the Valentinians, the Gnostics, the followers of Basil and other emissaries of the devil. Tertullian debated against Praxeas and Marcion; Augustine against the Manichaeans, Pelagians, Donatists, Arians, etc. According to Athanasius, when Antonius was still alive but near death, he addressed his followers: "Avoid the poisons of heretics and schismatics. Follow my hatred against them. You yourselves know that I have had no speech, not even peaceful, with them." The Fifth Council of Constantinople, anathema 11, Vol.2, concil., p.565: "If anyone does not anathematize Arius, Eunomius, the Macedonian, Apollinarius, Nestorius, Eutyches, along with their wicked conscripts and all other heretics whom the church has condemned, as well as those who have a taste for heresies similar to those mentioned above and have remained and do remain in their wickedness, let such a one be anathema."

When Luther left Schmalkalden, he besought his colleagues in the ministry that "they be filled with the Holy Spirit and with a hatred of the pope." Let the devout Christian magistrate be careful, therefore, lest he forbid the condemnation of stubborn and autocratic heretics with violent edicts. Let him beware lest he take away the freedom divinely granted to the ministry to teach and censure. In fact, let him rather listen to that statement of Ambrose, Bk.5, at the beginning of epistle 29, to Theodosius: "It is not characteristic of the emperor to deny the freedom to teach, nor is it characteristic of a priest not to say what he believes. Nothing in kings is so popular and attractive than to love freedom also in those who are subject to them in obedience. In fact, if there is this difference between good and bad princes that the good love liberty while the bad love slavery, then there is nothing in a priest so dangerous before God and so shameful before people than that he not declare freely what he believes." It is written: "I will also speak of your testimonies before kings and shall not be put to shame." Let the ministers of the churches also beware lest because of some perverted desire to please people they agree with those edicts of the magistrates. Nor let them follow the example of Basil Camaterus, who, in order to obtain more easily the patriarchate of Constantinople, bound himself to Emperor Andronicus with a shameful promissory note unworthy of a bishop, saying that he would pursue all things that pleased the emperor and studiously avoid whatever displeased him (Camerinus, part 3, *oper. succis.*, c.6).

For more about this question, see the Calvinist aulicopolitic of Dr. Hutter opposed to Johann von Münster, in which the consultations of Wigand, Chytraeus and Selnecker about this question are set forth. Also see the debate of Dr. Krakevitz on the necessity of reproof of the Calvinist doctrine, published at Greifswald in 1614.

Whether the Formula of Condemnation Conflicts with Christian Love

One asks the second question: Does that formula of condemnation set down in the symbolical books as antithesis to the articles of faith, "We condemn those who believe … "; I say, does that formula conflict with Christian love and modesty? This is the claim of some politicians who secretly favor the Calvinian heresy, for it affects a praise of moderation and covers up their opinion with an interest in peace. The Calvinians and Photinians applaud those who say: "We must not bring legal action against those as heretics who favor false opinions, so long as they confess Christ with us" (Ostorod, preface to his *Instit.*, p.8, and Schmaltz, *Contra Frantz.*, disp.1, p.9). First, we urge the divine commands about being wary of false prophets and keeping the wolves away from the Lord's sheepfold, which we brought out earlier. Second, we urge the examples of Christ and the apostles, who were not afraid to hurl their "Cursed be's" against false teachers. Christ, who has greater love than anyone (John 15:13), and who confesses that He is "gentle and lowly in heart" (Matt. 11:29), denounces the scribes and Pharisees with his "Woe" (Matt. 23:13ff). He also thunders out against the Jews with very serious language (John 8:44): "You are of your father the devil." And "The reason why you do not hear [the words of God] is that you are not of God" (v. 47). With the general lightning bolt of anathema, the apostle strikes all the foes of heavenly doctrine: "If anyone has no love for the Lord, let him be accursed" (1 Cor. 16:22). "Everyone who goes on ahead and does not abide in the teaching of Christ, does not have God" (1 John 1:9).

352

Third, we urge the true nature of true love. You see, because it flows from faith (Gal. 5:6), it therefore does not approve of errors of doctrine, which are repugnant to faith. Because it is a "fruit of the Spirit" (Gal. 5:22), it therefore does not remove the reproving function of the Holy Spirit (John 16:8). It is felt not only for a neighbor, but also and especially for God. Therefore, such love declares that the glory of God is robbed by corruptions of doctrine, and such love avenges that glory. Nevertheless, we must first warn that with those "accurseds," we are by no means condemning those who, because of a sort of naiveté, are in error without stubbornness and blasphemy against the truth. After all, there must be a distinction between misleaders who stubbornly speak against a truth proven to them again and again, whom Luther calls "*duxios*," and misleaders who do not understand the depths of Satan lurking in corruptions of doctrine and have been carried off into an alliance with error out of their weakness, but are prepared to embrace a demonstrated truth. Second, we warn that those anathemas much less condemn whole and entire churches whose pastors have been stained with the poison of papist or Calvinian heresies. In fact, even through their corrupt ministry, God can still gather His church even in the midst of the assemblies of the priests of Baal. He can still save some who do not bow their knees before Baal. Experience shows that at times the ears of hearers are purer than the lips of teachers. But, if there are no others, nevertheless baptized infants belong to the fellowship of the true church even if they are baptized by a heretic, provided that the substantials of this sacrament are observed.

Third, with those anathemas, we do not hand over to the executioners for torture and death those who are struck by an "accursed" because of corruptions of doctrine, nor deny them the blessing of civil peace. You see, we must distinguish between the censures of the church and legal judgments; between the spiritual sword, which cuts off errors but which preserves lives, and the corporal sword; between civil peace and spiritual consensus in doctrine. Note Chrysostom, in his sermon on anathema: "We must argue against and anathematize wicked dogmas that proceed from heretics, but we must spare the people and pray for their salvation."

Chytraeus is thinking of this when he writes as follows in the preface to his pamphlet on eternal life and death:

> Although I disapprove of and repudiate dogmas which we reject in the publicly declared common confession of our churches; nevertheless, heaven forbid that on that account I should claim that we must condemn, or throw out to the flames and punishment, those churches, princes or peoples who at times differ with us. After all, I see that, although Paul himself refuted and condemned certain errors of the Galatians and Corinthians, yet he did not on that account condemn the churches of Galatia and Corinth and hand them over to be destroyed by heathen persecutors. He still embraced and cherished them with all his love.

Fourth, with those anathemas we do not at all hand over to the devil and take away all hope of salvation from those whom false teachers afflict with the rash and sores of errors that we condemn. Rather, those anathemas demonstrate, repudiate and condemn erring doctrines, and the stubborn publishers and defenders thereof, if they are not converted to the demonstrated truth. On the other hand, they forewarn the naive to be careful and wary of errors of that kind lest they attract a divine curse to themselves.

Fifth and finally, we must warn that if we must ever deal orally or in writing with those who are committed to a false religion, we must by no means begin with anathemas. Rather, we must make a distinction between the curable and the incurable and deal with the former in peace and modesty from God's Word. We must be careful of scurrility and levity, jeering and wrangling; we must in reproof apply the words of Scripture. Finally, we must work in every way to make clear to all that in our debate against the erring, we seek the salvation of the soul.

Whether We Should Condemn Those Who Have Not Yet Been Heard in Councils

The third question we hear is whether or not we should condemn heresies that have not been heard and convicted in councils. It is the Calvinists' constant complaint that they are being treated unfairly by having the thunderbolts of anathema brandished against them, because they have not yet been heard, much less convicted, in a council. In the preface of the *orthod. consens.*, among other things, they write: "Up to now we have been convicted of no error; we have been condemned in no legitimate synod. In fact, we have never been able to achieve this, that this controversy be acknowledged in a public assembly." Sturm (*antipap*, 4, p.45 and elsewhere) argues: "We must postpone a condemnation of Calvinian dogma until it be debated in a just council established with select men." Jetzler writes (*de diuturn. bell. euchar.*, case 13, f.107): "The omission of synods is not the least cause of the continuation of the Sacramentarian War. We have condemned the Sacramentarians beyond what is just and fair outside of a council."

Hospinian (*concord. discord.*) cooks up a tragic complaint "about that rash and unproved-by-the-heathen-much-less-by-Christians daring of the authors of the Formula of Concord, by which daring those authors have not been afraid partly to strike with the thunderbolt of anathema, partly to hand over to other nations to be persecuted with fire and sword innocent people who have had no hearing and who have been convicted of either heresy or error." Paraeus, *Irenicum*, urges this very thing on many. This same argument was written and published in Holsatia in 1611.

Pelargus, in his apologetic antitheses against Dr. Baldwin, thesis 31: "Here we easily agree with others that there be numbered with either schismatics or heretics those brethren whom Baldwin attacks and has taught have been condemned and legitimately proscribed either in general council or by the entire church." We freely acknowledge with Augustine (epistle 118) that "the authority of councils is very healthy in the church of God." In fact, provided that they are legitimate and Christian, they are nothing else but sacred and free assemblies of devout teachers and people, where the judgment of Scripture is applied, where the significance of reason is compared and examined. In them something definite is concluded or decreed by the unanimous consent of many in regard to controversies about articles of faith, ceremonies, rituals and even church discipline. All this is done for the sake of the truth and for the tranquility of the church, so that every heterodox teaching is eliminated and condemned.

Thus, what many pious and learned people are seeking they find more easily; errors are brought to a sharper conclusion, which many condemn by unanimous vote according to the norm of Scripture. Things that many decide on the basis of their deliberate consent are considered more carefully and decided more firmly. Nevertheless, we deny that the need for councils is some sort of absolute need, such that one may not at all refute and condemn false doctrines without their previous decision.

In the first place, there is no mandate from Scripture that we must await the decision of a council before we refute heresies. Second, it is the public, perpetual and infallible judgment of Holy Scripture or, what is the same, of the Holy Spirit speaking in and through Scripture, by which heresies are condemned, even if they never are condemned in councils. Heresies have been started in many councils, but Scripture is always in harmony with itself and is never liable to the danger of error. Third, churches and the Christian faith remained unharmed and many heresies were condemned during the first 300 years of the New Testament before Christian emperors held councils. Paul condemned Hymenaeus, Philetus, Alexander and other heretics; Peter condemned Simon Magus; John condemned the Nicolaites, Ebion and Cerinthus; the teachers of the primitive church condemned the Marcionites, the Valentinians and Gnostics, all without any council.

Fourth, councils declare their condemnation of heresies not of themselves and of their own judgment. They seek that only from Scripture. Actually, all heresies have been condemned in Scripture; first, before councils reprove them and, in fact, before they are born. Fifth, to this we must relate statements of the devout ancients opposed to heretics who kept agitating for councils. When the Arians kept asking for a council, Athanasius kept answering them (*epist. de synod. Arimin. et Seleuc.*, p.673): "They run around in vain and pretend that they are asking for councils for the sake of faith, although Holy Scripture is more powerful than all councils." When the Pelagians urged the same thing, Augustine answered them (Bk.4, *contra duas epist. Pelag. ad Bonif.*, c.11, p.182): "Why is it that they say that a subscription has been extorted from naive bishops sitting in their own places of residence without assembling a council? As regards those very blessed and excellent men-of-the-faith, Cyprian and Ambrose, was a subscription ever extorted before them against those Pelagians with such manifestation that we can scarcely find anything more obvious to say? But was there need to assemble a council to condemn an obvious pest? As if no heresy has ever been condemned without assembling a council! Actually, we find those heresies are quite rare that demand a council condemn them. Rather, there are incomparably more heresies that deserve to be censured and condemned right where they have been. Thus, people in other lands have been able to mark them as things to be avoided. However, the Pelagians' pride, which extols itself so much against God that it wishes to glory not in Him but in its own free will, is understood to be trying to capture even this glory that a council of east and west be called because of them. In fact, because they are unable to pervert the Lord, who resists them, they are actually trying to upset the entire world. But, wherever those wolves have appeared, and after sufficient judgment which befits them has been passed, we must with pastoral watchfulness and diligence crush them so that they are either cured and silenced, or are avoided for the salvation and integrity of others."

Sixth, in 1530, when Landgrave Philip of Hesse in the assembly at Augsburg judged that he would have to call a council because of the Zwinglians, Philip Melanchthon and Johann Brenz answered him in this way: "If the emperor were to call a council for these reasons, as it was written it could be acknowledged as a council. But, whether or not he calls a council, certainly no one must be gathered to renounce the true and pious doctrine we profess. Furthermore, one must be very careful that we not hinder the course of true and very certain doctrine with an excessive subtlety which has no certainty. This is something we actually are trying to have done in some way even now."

When the landgrave finally argued, "The Zwinglians have not been convicted of any error in a council," Philip and Brenz later wrote this among other things to him: "We are able to reach no definite decision about asking for and urging a council, not because we consider it necessary to draw and seek the certainty of our faith from the decisions and decrees of a council, but in order that we may be able to crush and wipe away the calumnious lies with which we are being represented and burdened so often. But, if one should occur by the act of God, our consciences will not be overburdened; nor do we believe that a council will be hindered at all by your defense and support of Zwinglian doctrine, which cannot be approved and tolerated anymore than the course of pure doctrine is hindered by the imperial majesty until now." When the theologians of Jena asked for a council in the Interimistic controversy, the same Philip Melanchthon, in letters to his friends, repeats several times that statement of Nazianzen to Procopius (p.329): "In fact, the situation is this, if I must write what is true, that I avoid every meeting of bishops because I have not seen a useful outcome of any council."

Seventh, if one may not condemn false doctrines that conflict with Scripture before a decision of a council, by what right do they themselves condemn the papists, Anabaptists, Schwenkfeldians, etc.?

Eighth, in fact, by what right do they accuse our confession regarding the person of Christ of Eutychianism, Marcionitism, etc., in the false "Thorough Declaration," published at Wittenberg in 1571, and in the *apolog. admonit. of Neustadt* (p.14), because we have never been lawfully convicted in any synod?

Ninth, the Calvinists certainly received a hearing in the conference at Marburg in 1529, at Maulbrunn in 1564, at Mumpelgarten in 1586, in the public assemblies of the empire and in the assemblies of the princes, in the hundreds of books freely published by both sides. Thus, in a booklet published in peaceful Neustadt under the title "*Treuherzige Vermahnung*," they themselves admit that "the controversies which both sides have stirred up so far have been sufficiently distinguished and defined."

Tenth, one must never or surely barely hope for that synod they still seek and await. That is obvious from the words of Sibrand Lubert, commentary on the 99 errors of Vorst (p.43), where he writes: "When *Vorst* says that he is willing to submit to the judgment of all the Reformed churches, this is just as if he were saying that he was unwilling to submit to the judgment of the Reformed churches. After all, the prudent fellow is aware that, whether you take the expression 'Reformed churches' broadly or the word 'reformed' strictly, a council is never going to be called. You see, those princes in whose power the Reformed churches function are occupied with such varied interests that they will never agree upon some one general council." With these words, Sibrand upsets with one blow the demands of Paraeus and his followers. Before the Calvinists demand a synod, there will be a departure from the world.

Whether One Must Approve of Anonymous or Pseudonymous Writings

The fourth question asked is whether, in reproof, we must approve of anonymous or pseudonymous writings. Some of the Jesuits and Calvinists believe this, as their actual practice testifies. To them we oppose, first, Christ's statement: "For everyone who does wicked things hates the light and does not come to the light, lest his works should be exposed. But whoever does what is true comes to the light, so that it may be clearly seen that his works have been carried out in God" (John 3:20-21). Those light-shunners, therefore, show by that very act that they are not the children of light but tools of the devil, who is the spirit of darkness. After all, they either acknowledge and approve the truth, or they confess it with their mouth but deny it in their heart. If the former is true, they should not be afraid to confirm that with the public statement of their name: "That ink which one does not openly admit is dear if a thousand others subscribe to it with their blood." If the latter is true, they become vile hypocrites.

Second, we oppose the inconveniences that arise generally from suppressing or changing the name. The weak are provided with a stumbling block when they note that people publish the truth timidly. Enemies become confirmed in their errors because "the truth fears nothing except to be hidden." It then happens that they deny such a confession of faith is true and sound whose confessors are ashamed to declare it publicly. Anonymous writers are armed with a license to attack, to accuse falsely and to lie. Just as those who wear disguising clothing take for themselves a license to do whatever they please, so also those who take for themselves the posture of a disguising name think they have the license to cook up whatever they wish and to attack it boldly because they have been relieved of the difficulty of proving it.

Third, we note the example of the prophets, evangelists and apostles who prefixed their names to what they wrote. The fathers of the primitive church as well as the sagacious theologians of our time have observed the same practice. See Luther, Vol.1, German edition of Jena, p.477, in the book titled "*Unterricht der Beichkinder*"; Vol. 4, German edition of Jena, p.508, in the book titled "*Christliche Ermahnung an den Churfürst zu Brandenburg.*" Also, Vol. 5, German edition of Jena, p.551: "The Holy Spirit does not sneak but flies openly. Snakes sneak; doves fly. Thus, such sneaking is the moving principle of the devil — a statement that never lacks for truth." Vol. 1, p.425: "When I perceive such movement and flight of light, how can I fear the blind moles who shun the light?" And later: "Surely, it is the devil who sneaks about here secretively and insidiously." Luther says about himself (Vol. 4, p.508): "He may have had to write sharp documents against emperors, kings, popes and other high persons, but each time he has claimed the document and attached his name thereto."

Fourth, we oppose the practice by noting that civil laws subject changing of a name to penalties if it causes damage to another because of wicked deceit. Law *unic., c. de mutat. nominis*: "You are forbidden to change your name, either first or last, legally without some fraud, even if you are a free person." Therefore, from a contrary sense, we must consider that changing a name is forbidden if one makes that change to deceive and harm his neighbor. Law *falsi*, 13ff., on the Cornelian Law about false things: "The declaration of a false first or last name is restrained by the punishment for a falsity." In the decrees of the assembly of Augsburg in 1545, we find the expressed prohibition that "no one may publish writings either without a name or with a changed name." As far as famous satires are concerned, see Law *unic., c. de famos. libel.* and *Peinliche Hals-Gerichts-Ordnung*, art.110. In the imperial decrees, not only defamatory pamphlets but also anonymous and pseudonymous writings are banned. See *Abschied zu Augsb.*, 1548, p.403; *Abschied zu Speier*, 1570, p.666.

Fifth, we oppose the testimony of their own follower. Boquin (*assert. veri et veter. Christian.*, c.1) writes: "They are not sinning insignificantly who in matters of religion take on names that are not their own." Bullinger (*contra lib. Polon.*, published in 1566 at Zurich) says: "The concealing or changing of names in writings of this sort is done for this purpose that those light-shunners may more freely, as if from a dump truck, pour their heaps of attacks and false accusations upon the guiltless. Thus, they can publish common insults as teachings which are heterodox rather than orthodox along with all wicked insulters."

The things they bring up to support the opposite view have an easy explanation, if we distinguish between didactic and refutative writings, between deed and legal right, between political cleverness and theological candor and simplicity.

The Dispensation of the Sacraments

That administering the sacraments ordinarily belongs to the ministers of the church we have shown in our treatises "On the Sacraments" (28) and "On Baptism" (19). However, here we must note that in the sacrament of initiation, as circumcision in the Old Testament and Baptism in the New, when extreme necessity demands, we must entrust its administration to other members of the church. This we showed in detail in our locus "On Baptism" (23). Regarding the dispensation of the sacraments, the minister should first see to it that he admits no unworthy person to participate. "Do not give dogs what is holy, and do not throw your pearls before pigs" (Matt. 7:6). Ambrose (Bk.2, *de poenit.*, c.9): "The command is: 'Do not give dogs what is holy, etc.' That is, the fellowship of Holy Communion must not be shared with those who are befouled with impurities." In this vein we have added more in our commonplace "On the Eucharist" (222ff.).

Second, in the dispensation of the sacraments, the minister should carefully observe Christ's institution and the practice of the apostles. He should reject useless and superfluous ceremonies, and he should administer the sacraments as simply as he can, according to the rule just given.

Praying for the Flock Entrusted to Him

That praying for the flock entrusted to him ought to be recommended to the minister of the church we see, first, from general statements that require all the truly devout to pray for each other and even include the salvation of others in their prayers. "Pray for one another" (James 5:16). The form of prayer Christ prescribed to use included the entire mystical body of the church.

Second, we see it from the example of Christ, who in prayers to God, prays for His apostles and for all who would believe in Him through their words (John 17:20). Third, we see it from the examples of Moses, Samuel, the prophets and apostles who prayed to God for their hearers. "Moses implored the Lord his God and said, 'O Lord, why does your wrath burn hot against your people?'" (Ex. 32:11). "Then I lay prostrate before the Lord as before, forty days and forty nights. I neither ate bread nor drank water, because of all the sin that you had committed, in doing what was evil in the sight of the Lord" (Deut. 9:18). Lev. 5:6 says the priest will pray for the man who has made a rash oath. "This shall be a statute forever for you, that atonement may be made for the people of Israel" (Lev. 16:34). In 1 Sam. 12:23, Samuel says to the Israelites: "Far be it from me that I should sin against the Lord by ceasing to pray for you." (Ministers of the church commit a serious sin, therefore, when they neglect prayers for the flock entrusted to them.) "You, O Lord, are our Father, our Redeemer from of old is your name. O Lord, why do you make us wander from your ways?" (Is. 63:16-17). In Jer. 23:3, the prophet is commanded to pray to the Lord for his people. In Jeremiah, Zedekiah says to the prophet: "Please pray for us to the Lord our God" (37:3). "Now therefore, O our God, listen to the prayer of your servant and to his pleas for mercy, and for your own sake, O Lord, make your face to shine upon your sanctuary" (Dan. 9:17). "We pray to God that you may not do wrong" (2 Cor. 13:7). "Your restoration is what we pray for" (v. 9).

"For this reason, because I have heard of your faith in the Lord Jesus and your love toward all the saints, I do not cease to give thanks for you, remembering you in my prayers, that the God of our Lord Jesus Christ, the Father of glory, may give you the Spirit of wisdom and of revelation in the knowledge of Him" (Eph. 1:15-17). "For this reason I bow my knees before the Father, that according to the riches of his glory he may grant you to be strengthened with power through his Spirit" (Eph. 3:14-16). "Always in every prayer of mine for you all making my prayer with joy" (Phil 1:4). "It is my prayer that your love may abound more and more" (v. 9). "We always thank God ... when we pray for you" (Col. 1:3). "To this end we always pray for you, that our God may make you worthy of his calling and may fulfill every resolve for good and every work of faith by his power" (2 Thess. 1:11). An epistle of the church at Smyrna mentions (Eusebius, Bk.4, *hist.*, c.15) in regard to Polycarp, the disciple of John the Evangelist, that as the time of his martyrdom approached, he did nothing else night and day but continue his prayers in which he humbly asked that all churches throughout the world might have peace.

Fourth, the prayers of the church on behalf of their pastors require that pastors in turn pray for the church entrusted to them. "Earnest prayer for [Peter] was made to God by the church" (Acts 12:5). "Pray also for us, that God may open to us a door for the word, to declare the mystery of Christ" (Col. 4:3). "Brothers, pray for us" (1 Thess. 5:25). (See 2 Thess. 3:1; Heb. 3:18, etc.)

Fifth, the greatest necessity requires that praying be connected to the preaching of the Word. In fact, without the grace of the blessing of heaven, the seed of the Word is not effective in producing fruits in the hearts of its hearers (1 Cor. 3:6). However, the streams of heavenly blessing do not come down to people except through the channels of pious and devout prayers. The devil snatches up the seed of the Word from the hearts of those who hear but do not understand it (Matt. 13:19). However, those birds of hell are driven away by the sound of prayer. "Your adversary the devil prowls around like a roaring lion, seeking someone to devour. Resist him, firm in your faith" (1 Peter 5:8-9). Treating the duties of the ministers of the church the apostle asks (2 Cor. 2:16): "Who is sufficient for these things?" That "sufficiency is from God" (2 Cor. 3:5), from whom one must receive that sufficiency through pious prayers. To those prayers is related also the general blessing of the church, particularly committed to the order of ministers (Num. 6:23), that an assembly should be dismissed with it.

Also related is the special blessing of the newly married, but that blessing (in a certain respect) we shall be able to relate to the rituals of the church about which we shall speak later. Nevertheless, we observe this because of the probity and dignity of marriage so it is a public testimony of a divine institution. We also observe this for the sake of a distinction between divine and illicit unions, for we must think that God has joined together only those whom not senseless passion, but the consent of parents and the minister of the church in the name of God have joined together; and also for the sake of the antiquity of this sanction of the church. According to Platina (*vita pontif.*, f.23, *Soter* I), who administered the bishopric of Rome under the authority of Antoninus Commodus, one did not have a lawful wife unless a priest had blessed her according to that institution. This very ancient custom is mentioned in the Fourth Council of Carthage held in 436 and in the *Novel. Leon.*, 89.

The Honorable Control of Life and Behavior

We see that honorable control of life and behavior is especially required of a minister of the church, first, from the apostolic canons prescribed for bishops and deacons. "This charge I entrust to you, Timothy, my child … that … you may wage the good warfare, holding faith and a good conscience" (1 Tim. 1:18-19). "Therefore an overseer must be above reproach, the husband of one wife, sober-minded, self-controlled, respectable, hospitable, able to teach" (1 Tim. 3:2). "He must manage his own household well, with all dignity keeping his children submissive" (v. 4). "He must not be a recent convert" (v. 6). "Deacons likewise must be dignified, not double-tongued, not addicted to much wine,not greedy for dishonest gain. They must hold the mystery of the faith with a clear conscience" (vv. 8-9). And the apostle adds clearly: "I hope to come to you soon, but I am writing these things to you so that, if I delay, you may know how one ought to behave in the household of God, which is the church" (vv. 14-15). "Train yourself for godliness" (1 Tim. 4:7). "Set the believers an example in speech, in conduct, in love, in faith, in purity" (v. 12). "But as for you, O man of God, flee these things [namely, greed and ambition]. Pursue righteousness, godliness, faith, love, steadfastness, gentleness" (1 Tim. 6:11). "Do your best to present yourself to God as one approved" (2 Tim. 2:15). "So flee youthful passions and pursue righteousness, faith, love, and peace, along with those who call on the Lord from a pure heart" (v. 22). "For an overseer, as God's steward, must be above reproach. He must not be arrogant or quick-tempered or a drunkard or violent or greedy for gain, but hospitable, a lover of good, self-controlled, upright, holy, and disciplined" (Titus 1:7-8). "Show yourself in all respects to be a model of good works, and in your teaching show integrity, dignity" (Titus 2:7).

Second, we see this from the inconveniences and scandals that generally result from ministers' sins. "You then who teach others, do you not teach yourself? While you preach against stealing, do you steal?" (Rom. 2:21). "The name of God is blasphemed among the Gentiles because of you" (v. 24). The efficacy of the Word and Sacraments certainly does not depend on the dignity or lack thereof of the ministers, as we have shown in our treatise "On the Sacraments" (30). Nevertheless, the situation itself makes it obvious that the wickedness of some ministers has thrown not a little delay and hindrance into the course of heavenly doctrine and the fructification of the Word. One destroys the authority of teaching when the minister's works do not support his words. Those who teach uprightly but live wickedly destroy with their bad behavior what they build with sincere doctrine. They build heaven with their words, hell with their life. They consecrate their tongue to God, their soul to the devil. They are like the statues of Mercury that show the way to others — a way they themselves do not follow. They are like the carpenters who offered to help Noah build the ark: They prepared an ark so others could escape the flood, while they themselves perished. Augustine (Bk.4, *de doctr. Christ.*, c.27): "He has to be heard submissively. Whatever may be the majesty of his style, the life of the teacher is of greater significance than that style." Augustine, epistle 112: "The way that a person lives counts more than the way he speaks." Hilary, canon 5 on Matthew: "It is better to teach by example than by talk." Cyprian, *de dupl. Mart.*, p.362: "The witness of one's life is more effective than that of his tongue." Lactantius, Bk.3, *instit.*, c.16, p.159: "It is good to teach upright and honorable things. Unless you also do such things, however, it is a lie. It is out of harmony, and inappropriate, to have goodness on your lips but not in your heart." Lactantius again, Bk.4, *instit.*, c.23: "People prefer examples to words because it is easy to speak but difficult to act as an example. Would that as many as speak well would do well!" On the other hand, as Bernard says (epistle 28): "The ministry is honored because of the seriousness of its behavior, the maturity of its advice and the integrity of its actions."

Third, we see this from the divine warnings published against wicked ministers. "But to the wicked God says: "What right have you to recite my statutes or take my covenant on your lips?" (Ps. 50:16). "But now I rebuke you and lay the charge before you" (v. 21). "Therefore whoever relaxes one of the least of these commandments and teaches others to do the same will be called least [that is, nothing] in the kingdom of heaven, but whoever does them and teaches them will be called great in the kingdom of heaven" (Matt. 5:19). Ignatius comments on these words (epistle 11, *To the Ephesians*, p. 63, Antwerp edition): "It is better to be silent and exist than to speak and not exist. The kingdom of God does not reveal itself in talk but in power. It is worthwhile to teach if the speaker acts, for whoever both acts and teaches is great in the kingdom." Chrysostom (homily 43, on Matthew 23, and also cited in c. *Multi*, dist.40): "He who behaves well on his throne receives the honor of that throne. He who behaves badly does harm to that throne. The wicked priest, therefore, acquires not the dignity of his priesthood but a criminal charge against it, for you are sitting in judgment of yourself. Indeed, if you have lived and taught well, you do instruct your people. But, if you have taught well and lived badly, you will only be your condemner. For by living and teaching well, you instruct your people as to how they should live.

By teaching well and living badly, however, you instruct God as to how He should condemn you." Prosper, *sent. August.*: "For one to speak well but to live corruptly is nothing else than condemning oneself with his own voice."

Fourth, we see this from the absurd discrepancy between life and prayer and status. Nazianzen says (*carmin.*): "It is absurd to see a scout who is lost and a doctor of others who himself is covered with running sores." Ambrose (Bk.10, epistle 82): "Who can bear it if the one who has the responsibility of governing others is unable to control himself? Who can bear it if the one who undertakes the care of another's soul cannot protect his own?" Bernard says: "It is a monstrosity for one to have a lofty position and a low life, a first seat and a last life, an eloquent tongue and lazy hands, much talk and no fruit, a serious face and insignificant action, great authority and no stability." Jerome writes, commentary on Micah 2: "Is it not disgraceful for fat cheeks and full mouths to preach Christ crucified, poor and hungry, and the doctrine of fasting to stuffed bodies?"

Fifth, we see this from the example of Christ, the apostles and the pious teachers of the church, who instructed their hearers not only with words, but also with the examples of their lives. The disciples on the way to Emmaus say Christ was "a prophet mighty in deed and word" (Luke 24:19). Luke says about Him: " ... all that Jesus began to do and teach" (Acts 1:1). Ignatius (op. cit.) applies this to an example of the holy life that he declares all true ministers of the church should follow. About himself Paul says (1 Cor. 9:27): "I discipline my body and keep it under control, lest after preaching to others I myself should be disqualified." As Jerome rightly concludes (*op. cit.*): "If we are in the place of the apostles, therefore, let us imitate not only their speech but also their behavior and self-restraint."

Sixth, we see it from the types of the Old Testament. Gregory (part 1, *pastoral.*, c.4, and cited in c. Sit rector, dist.43): "In Exodus 28 Moses is commanded to enter the tabernacle as the priest and to go around with the tinkling of bells, etc. How else are we to accept these witnesses of the priest than that they are upright works? According to the prophet, he says in Psalms: 'Your priests shall be clothed in righteousness.' So the bells will stay attached to his robe if the actual works of the priest call out the way of life along with the sound of his voice." Gratian, dist.40, at the beginning, from the ancients: "A bishop must be dignified. We take that to refer to the virtues of a bishop, which the Lord continues to promise them when He says: 'My priests will be clothed with salvation.' In the Old Testament, consequently, we read that, in accord with God's command, the priests were dignified with various robes. The life of a priest ought to be resplendent with many kinds of virtues. Thus, that life confers upon his office a comeliness which it does not receive from the person." Berthor, *allegor.*: "The chief priest had an ephod and a breastplate. That is, ministers of the church ought to have good behavior and teaching. The breastplate had to be attached to the ephod (Ex. 28:22); that is, life should not be out of harmony with doctrine." Camerarius, part

1, *meditat. succisiv.*, c.22, *ex. veter.*: "In the artwork of the temple of Solomon were engraved not only lions but also oxen and cherubim that he who rules the people may be vigilant and brave in protecting the laws of justice like a lion, that he may be bound carefully to the laws of humility like an ox, and finally that he may be endowed with the light of knowledge like the cherubim." Isidore of Pelusium, Bk.1, epistle 151, p.39: "Because God's priest comes close to God, he ought to have in his behavior an eye on every side, knowing everything, like those animals endowed with many eyes of Ezek.1 and 10." The face of the lion denotes an unbroken spirit against any peril at all; the face of an ox denotes a patience for hardships, whence Paul applies to ministers of the church the Mosaic law: "You shall not muzzle the ox when he is treading out the grain" (1 Tim. 5:18). The face of a person denotes humanity, because people take care of the weak. The face of an eagle denotes a spirit that is to be carried aloft from earthly to heavenly things.

The Twofold Virtues of Ministers

Furthermore, the virtues that the apostle requires in the minister of the church (1 Timothy 3, Titus 1) we divided earlier into two classes. Some virtues he has in common with all other devout people, but some he has as his own special virtues. The former especially concern his person, the latter his office; the former his life and behavior; the latter the doctrine of his ministry. We can subdivide the common virtues in this way: we relate some to the First Table and some to the Second Table of the Decalog.

To the First Table of the Decalog is related that a bishop should be devout and holy (Titus 1:8). Because he must encourage others to piety and holiness as much as possible, he is absolutely required to have a zeal for holy devotion toward God. In this area, Christ shines forth for ministers of the church as the chief Shepherd who is Himself called "uncorrupted" (Acts 2:27, 13:35; Heb. 7:26). The apostles too, as Paul says, behaved as "holy and righteous and blameless" (1 Thess. 2:10).

Earlier we expressed the virtues that relate to the Second Table of the Decalog: first, by thesis; second, by negation. Here we shall use a different division. Some are expressed with general names that usually involve obedience to the Second Table of the Decalog. This then, is by negation that a bishop must be "above reproach" and blameless (1 Tim. 3:2, Titus 1:6). By these he must be "upright" (Titus 1:8), "sober-minded" (1 Tim. 3:2) and "dignified" (1 Tim. 3:8). On the other hand, some demand obedience to some specific command in particular.

He must be "ανεπιληπτος" **(above reproach)**.

First, a bishop should be "ανεπιληπτος" (above reproach). Those who suffer from epilepsy are called "επιληπτοι." They are so convulsed by epilepsy that they cannot move their limbs; and who are liable to a just charge and accusation. "Επιλαμβανεσθαι" is both to grasp and put in place, and to restrain and hold up. Thus, an ανεπιληπτος is a person who cannot be reasonably restrained and who is not subject to arrest. In Thucydides, Bk.5, p.170, we have "καὶ αὐτὸς τοῖς ἐχθροῖς ἀνεπίληπτος εἶναι," which the scholiast explains as "not liable to provide material for a criminal charge. "

"Ἀνεγκλητος" (blameless)

The same denotation is given by the word "ἀνεγκλητος" (blameless, without blame). He is a person against whom one can throw up no just charge. "Ἐγκαλεισωσαι" is to be accused, to be blamed. "Τὰ ἐγκεκλημενα" are the objects in trials in place of the reproach or the criminal charge. "Ἀνεγκλητος" is used in general about all those who are truly devout (1 Cor. 1:8, Col. 1:22). Neither word appears in the Septuagint translation of the Old Testament. Thus, a bishop is required to live a guiltless and blameless life and not make himself liable to serious criminal charges. Gregory (part 1, *pastoral.*, c.11, and cited in c. *Ecce*, dist. 49): "One must be concerned and fearful that he who is believed to be capable of placating the wrath of God not earn the same thing for himself because of his own guilt. After all, we are well aware that when a person is displeasing, the spirit of the angered person is provoked to worse things. Each should evaluate himself carefully, therefore, and not dare assume a position of command, if sin still holds damning sway in him, lest he whom his own guilt corrupts seek to become the intercessor for the faults of others."

Furthermore, there is a question whether those who slip into some serious sin can be placed in charge of or called back to the offices of the church after they have done penance. There are many decrees about this and contrary ones in canon law, dist. 50. Gregory (Bk.7, epistle 53) correctly urges the example of Peter. He says: "Which is more serious: to commit a sin of the flesh without which few are found or to deny by oath the Son of God, into which sin we know Peter himself fell? Repentance followed his denial and after repentance, mercy was given him. For He who foretold that he would deny Him, did not expel him from apostleship." Jerome, on Micah 3, brings up the example of David, who, after committing adultery and murder, says: "I will teach transgressors Your ways" (Psalm 51). Augustine (epistle 150, to Boniface) distinguishes between the rigidity of the law and its fairness. He says: "That it is established in the church that no one receive a priestly office or return thereto or remain therein after repenting of some legal accusation occurs, not because of a lack of hope of forgiveness but because of the rigidity of the discipline. Otherwise, they will debate against the keys of the church about which it is said: 'Whatever you loose on earth will also be loosed in heaven.' Lest a spirit, swollen with pride by the hope of ecclesiastical office repent of other charges, it is the very severe pleasure of the law that no one may be a priest after repenting of a damnable sin so that out of desperation over temporal promotion, the medication of humility may be greater and more genuine, etc."

Isidore, *ad Massanus*, distinguished between the penitent and impenitent: "The canons command to return to their former positions those who have first made the satisfaction of repentance or a worthy confession of sins. Against those, however, who are not freed of the fault of their corruption and who try by some superstitious rashness to make amends for that very carnal sin they commit, certainly do not receive a grade of honor nor the grace of communion. An opinion must be determined, therefore, so that it may be necessary for those to be restored to their position of honor who through repentance deserve the reconciliation of divine pity. For those who are known to have received a cure for life through the correction of repentance do not undeservedly achieve again the state of dignity which they had lost."

Hrabanus, *ad Heribaldum*, distinguishes between public and hidden sins: "Those who have been publicly apprehended in perjury, theft, fornication and other crimes of this sort should fall down from their position according to the institutions of the sacred canons. It is a scandal for the people of God to have such persons placed over them, persons who, we agree, are sinful above measure. Those who admit secretly to the aforementioned sins, who confess their sins by secret confession before the angels of God or even with a priest present who will exact penance for such sins, and who bewail the fact that they indeed have sinned greatly; I say, for these we must preserve their position and promise them the hope of forgiveness from the mercy of God." A careful and diligent consideration of the circumstances will make clear what we must do in cases like this. Especially, must we distinguish the case of necessity from the ordinary rule? If we can find other suitable ministers of the church, we must by no means select or call back those who have fallen into some quite serious sin, even after they have repented. If there are no others, however, it is agreed that we do admit such people rather than have the church deprived of necessary ministers.

"Δικαιος" (upright)

These are the virtues related to the Second Table of the Decalog and expressed with general names, which generally require obedience to the Law according to the thesis: a bishop ought to be upright, dignified and serious. First, this uprightness of Titus 1:8 could be taken to mean specifically a particular righteousness, which is the virtue of the Seventh Commandment to be opposed to the "greediness for gain" mentioned in the preceding verse. Because it is connected with the word "holy," which is general and expresses an obedience to the First Table of the Law; we, therefore, seem to take it more correctly for a universal righteousness, just as elsewhere "holy and righteous" are connected (Luke 1:75, Eph. 4:24, 1 Thess. 2:10). A bishop, therefore, is required to behave uprightly toward his neighbor, just as he ought to conduct himself with reverence and holiness toward God.

"Κοσμιος" (well-ordered)

Second, "κοσμιος" signifies the man of settled behavior, one who does all things decently and in order. Luther translates it *"sittig"* (well-bred) and also *"ornatus"* (equipped). The Vulgate edition has *"ornatum"* (equipped). That is not an absurd choice, because settled behavior is a person's greatest equipment. Thus, in canon law, bishops and churchmen are required to be equipped within and without. C. *Nos qui*, dist. 40, from Gregory: "We who are charged should be renowned not for the dignity of our positions or kind but for the nobility of our behavior." Dist. 41, at the beginning: "A bishop must be equipped on the outside also, namely, in garb and walk; in garb, that he not wear flashy or dirty clothes." As Jerome says: "Neither the affectation of dirt nor exquisite style will bring praise." This we must take to mean clothes as much as foods. C *Episcopus*, same dist., from the Fourth Council of Carthage, canon 17: "A bishop should have inexpensive furniture and table as well as the food of the poor. He should seek the authority of his dignity in the merits of his faith and life." Here a gloss adds: "We do not have this today."

"σεμνος" (serious)

Third, "σεμνος "(serious) is sometimes taken negatively so that it means puffed up, hateful, overly serious. Here, however, it is praiseworthy and refers to one who is serious with authority and modesty, a man who behaves himself in his words, deeds, life and behavior in such a way that he gains a sort of reverence toward himself in the minds of those who listen to and watch him. Luther renders it "*ehrbar*" (sober). The Septuagint uses it for "na`em — he was pleasing or acceptable" (Prov. 15:27). You see, seriousness coupled in a sort of union with very gentle modesty and friendliness makes a person pleasing and acceptable. The Vulgate translates this as "*pudicus*" (modest).

" ... Who Manages Well His Own Houshold"

We can distinguish the virtues relating to the Second Table of the Law and which specifically require obedience to some specific Commandment as follows: We relate some to each of the Fourth, Fifth, Sixth, Seventh and Eighth Commandments. To the Fourth Commandment of the Decalog, we relate that a bishop should "manage his own household well, with all dignity keeping his children submissive" (1 Tim. 3:4) and be one whose "children are believers and not open to the charge of debauchery or insubordination" (Titus 1:6). This very thing is also required of deacons, that they should manage "their children and their own households well" (1 Tim. 3:12).

We must consider as a man who is rightly in charge of his own household and children, not someone who sits inside his house and rakes together his riches and looks out for the liberal support of his own family, but someone who brings up his children and servants "in the discipline and instruction of the Lord," as the apostle explains (Eph. 6:4). This is a man who has children who are not insubordinate wastrels but who are subject in all integrity, as the apostle explains in these passages.

On the other hand, the apostle explains parenthetically why a bishop is required to rule his household well and reasonably: For "how will he care for God's church?" (1 Tim. 3:5). This is an argument from the lesser to the greater. If a person does not know how to manage his own household, how will he be able to manage the church, which is "the household of God"?(1 Tim. 3:15 and 5:17). If a man does not know how to keep his children and servants in their places, how will he keep the entire assembly of the church in its place?

Chrysostom, homily 10, on 1 Timothy 3: "It is necessary that a bishop provide evidences of his virtue, both from his neighborhood and from his household. After all, who would believe that a man who has not kept his children subject is going to keep some strangers subject? This is something that even worldly authors say, that the man who manages his own household well also can manage the business of the state well. You see, the church is like a certain household, etc."

The sins of children and servants argue the negligence of parents and householders in the correct controlling of their stewardship. If a man is negligent in the management of his private stewardship, how will he be concerned over the right management of the church? Consider the example of the priest Eli, about whom the Lord says (1 Sam. 3:13): "I declare to [Eli] that I am about to punish his house forever, for the iniquity that he knew, because his sons were blaspheming God, and he did not restrain them."

"Μη πληκτης" **(not violent)**

To the Fifth Commandment of the Decalog is related that a bishop should be "not violent" (1 Tim. 3:3), "not arrogant or quick-tempered" (Titus 1:7); but "hospitable" (1 Tim. 3:2); "gentle, not quarrelsome" (v. 3); "a lover of good" (Titus 1:8). First, a man is called "violent" who is quick to give a beating. Plutarch, *Fab.*, calls it "being quick from the hand" from "πληττειν" (to strike, to beat).

Chrysostom (commentary on 1 Timothy 3) relates this to tongue-lashing or to censuring. For he writes (homily 10): "As he speaks here he does not mean a man who hits with his hands. What then does 'not violent' mean? Now that there are some who are beating the consciences of their brothers at the wrong time, I believe that he is hinting at these." He also writes, commentary on Titus 1, homily 2: "'Not violent' here refers to a violent person, for it is necessary that everyone who admonishes or rebukes does not mistreat." Jerome has the same opinion. He relates this to a sharpness of tongue, namely, that "a bishop should not be a savage and wicked rebuker," as it says in 1 Tim. 5:1: "Do not rebuke an older man."

However, it is taken more accurately in regard to striking the body. "Πληκτιζεσθαι," which comes from our word, means to contend all the way to blows, to come to blows in an altercation. Eustathius, *Iliad*, φθτ, notes that πληκτιζεσθαι is used for "μαχεσθαι" (do battle) or for "εριχειν εως πληγης" (to quarrel to the point of blows).

This is the way Chrysostom himself takes it when he adds etiologically that beautiful statement: "A doctor is a teacher of souls. Certainly, a doctor does not strike a person; but, even if he happens to have struck a sick person, he is correcting, improving and curing him." Luther says: "Ein Bischof soll nicht pochen" (A bishop should not beat another person).

"Μη αυθαδης" (not arrogant)

Second, "αυθαδης" is self-pleasing, arrogant, proud; a person who pleases himself in such a way that he holds others in contempt before himself. It comes from "αυτος" (self) and "αδειν," which is "to please," as Aristotle explains (Bk.1, magn. ethic). We commonly explain it as unyielding and stubborn, because pertinacity generally stems from haughtiness. Cicero translates "αυθαδειαν" as "obstinate."

Consider this: Luther here translates it as "*eigensinnig*" (capricious). In the margin Luther writes this note: "A person who is his own man yields only if it is absolutely necessary, and plunges headlong into anything."

In 2 Peter 2:1, "αυθαδες" (willful) is connected with "bold." There the Vulgate translates it as "self-pleasing," but here as "arrogant." The Septuagint translators use "obstinate" or "stubborn" for "a`z" in Gen. 49:7. The sense then is that a bishop should not please himself in such a way that he clings stubbornly to his own opinion, listens to no one with opposing ideas and forces all people to be obedient to his own ideas.

"Οργιλος" (quick-tempered)

Third, "οργιλος" is "quick to anger," a person who allows himself to be angered. Aristotle (Bk.4, *ethic.*, c.5): "Hot-tempered people get angry quickly and with the wrong persons and at the wrong times and more than is right, but their anger ceases quickly."

Elsewhere they are called "οξυχολοι" or "πικροχολοι," quick to anger and bitter-tongued, "people easily rubbed the wrong way." Luther translates it "*zornig*" (wrathful). Instead of the "hasty in his words" of Prov. 29:20, the Septuagint translators use "a man of the nostrils," that is, a man who is prone to anger, which causes his nostrils to swell. They also translate "'*ish hemah*" (Prov. 29:24) as "a man of heat" and irascibility.

The sense, then, is that a bishop should not be prone to anger, become angry for insignificant reason, etc. Chrysostom adds an excellent reason in his commentary on Titus 1: "By what logic will he who has not first taught himself teach others to control this sin of wrath? Leadership of that sort every day produces more criminal activities and creates a displeasing bother. For even if it is very modest, its quickness to anger produces countless and daily crises. If each person does not meditate long over this and does not attain it, he will become very upsetting, he will corrupt many things and will destroy much of what his responsibility includes."

"Φιλοξενος" (hospitable)

Fourth, "φιλοξενος" is hospitable, a person who is happy to receive others as their host. Luther calls it "*gastfrei*" (hospitable). In 1 Peter 4:9 Peter requires that all Christians "show hospitality to one another without grumbling." Here it is specifically and especially required of bishops. Because of persecutions at that time, there were more frequent banishments and public hospices had not yet been established. Therefore, the apostle requires hospitality from a bishop so that his home becomes a refuge and receiving place for exiles.

Dist. 42, at the beginning: "A priest must be hospitable lest he belong to the number of those to whom it will be said in judgment: 'I was a stranger, and you did not take me in.' He who follows the apostle should invite others into his hospitality. If he closes his own home to guests, how will he be able to be an encourager of hospitality? You see, if a priest should demand first from himself and from his own domestic church what he later demands of his own people and if in imitation of Christ he himself should first do what he later teaches his people; then he must receive the poor into his hospitality so that he thereby may attract his subjects more easily to hospitality by his own examples. One who is about to be ordained as a priest, therefore, ought to remember how Abraham and Lot pleased God with their works of hospitality and deserved to receive angels into their hospitality; how the angels who entered a hospitable household of Sodom freed Lot and his family; how fire touched off and destroyed closed homes along with the residents therein; and how a person who is proved to keep more than the necessities for himself is guilty of stealing another's property, etc., according to Jerome, *regul. monarch.*"

If we forbid from being received by the church a widow who does not receive the poor into her hospitality, who does not wash the feet of the saints, who does not perform every good work; all the more must we keep from the priesthood those who prove to be strangers to the works of piety. Ministers of the church must not be hospitable in a passive way, happy to live by the arrangement of others nor to let their hospitality degenerate into frequent feasts.

In this regard we have a precept in the church constitution of the Elector of Saxony, art. general.16, p.337: "Pastors should avoid taverns and bars. Even in their parsonages they should not do much partying nor often have guests, etc." Jerome, epistle to Demetrius: "You are praised by the stomachs of the hungry who are not vomiting up rich foods."

"Επιεικης" **(gentle)**

He is called "επιεικης" who prefers justness to the strict law, who yields or concedes by his own right for the sake of peace. Aristotle, Bk.5, *ethic.*, c.10: "The man who is no stickler for his rights in a bad sense but tends to take less than his share although he has the law on his side is 'επιεικης' (equitable)."

Also: "We say that a gentle man is especially a man who makes concessions, for gentleness concedes some things. Here Budaeus says a gentle man is a "kind grantor of forgiveness." In lexicons "επιεικης" is defined as "gentle, mild, modest," and this is the way the Vulgate translates it here. Luther renders it "*gelinde*" (gentle).

In 1 Peter 2:18 they are called "gentle masters," masters who are mild-mannered and moderate, to whom are opposed the overbearing. In 2 Cor. 10:1 "meekness and gentleness" are paired. The Septuagint translators render the "sallach" of Ps. 85:4 as "kindly-disposed, giving way." The sense, then, is that a bishop, after the example of

Christ the chief Shepherd, ought to be "gentle" (Matt. 11:29). He should not demand his strict due in all things. Rather he should pursue equity and moderation.

Consequently, it is added that he ought to be sixth:

"Αμαχος" (not quarrelsome)

A person who is "αμαχος" is a stranger to fighting. You see, those who rigidly pursue their own legal right frequently fall into brawls and fights. Those who pursue gentleness cannot be quarrelsome. Thus, in James 3:17 "peaceable" and "gentle" are paired. In Suidas those who "are not quarrelsome" are those who abstain from fighting, coming from "α" and "μαχομαι" (to fight). In Titus 3:2, the not-quarrelsome and gentle are said to be those who "show perfect courtesy toward all men." Luther gives consideration to fighting with words and translates it here as "*nicht haderhaftig*" (not inclined to chopping).

"Φιλαγαθος" (a lover of good)

Seventh, "φιλαγαθος" is a person who loves good people and goodness. We could take it generally to mean a zeal for virtue; but, because it is connected with the word "hospitable," we seem to take it more accurately as meaning especially the person who willingly does good for others. Luther translates it "gütig" (good). For the Greeks "αγαθα ποειν" is to do kindnesses toward someone. For the Greeks "αγαθαποιοι" are those who are generous and open-handed. The Septuagint translators use it only once in the Wisdom of Solomon 7:22, where they say that in wisdom there is a "πνευμα φλαγαθον" (a spirit that loves the good). The sense, then, is that a bishop should be obliging, happy to be generous to another.

"The Husband of one Wife"

To the Sixth Commandment of the Decalog is related that a bishop should be, first, "the husband of one wife" (1 Tim. 3:2, Titus 1:6). About what these words mean, we gave information earlier. We shall say more later about the marriage of ministers.

"Εγκρατης" (self-controlled)

Second, a bishop should be "εγκρατης" (self-controlled) (Titus 1:8). Someone who cannot control himself is said to be "ακρατης." Thus, "ακρατης αφροδισιων" is one who is uncontrolled in regard to venereal pleasure, lustful; and "ακρατης τιμης" is a man who cannot control and bridle his desire for glory.

Aristotle, Bk.7, *ethic.*, c.1, writes that "ακρατης" and "ακολαστον" (incontinent) are used interchangeably. To that we oppose the "εγκρατης," the person who knows how to bridle his desires, especially in regard to food, drink and sex. Budaeus translates these three: controlled in regard to food, drink and sexual intercourse with one word: "continent." Luther rendered it "*keusch*" (chaste), giving consideration to the most important kind of self-control. However, the word is a general one, that a bishop should control himself in food, drink, emotions, sex, etc.

Erasmus, notes on Titus 1: "As Jerome indicates, some people by no means accurately relate 'εγκρατη' to lust alone because it refers to all emotions: anger, greed, ambition, envy, fear."

Chrysostom, homily 2 on Titus 1: "Εγκρατη: 'Here he did not mean one who fasts but instead one who takes control of his emotion, tongue, hand and wandering eyes, for self-control consists in not being dragged down by passion." Athanasius and Oecumenius take this word to mean a person "who commands his tongue, eyes, hands," etc. Furthermore, as is virginal and conjugal chastity, so also is "εγκρατεια" when it is taken in a special sense so that it is attributed only to virgins living chastely without being married. "If they cannot exercise self-control, they should marry" (1 Cor. 7:9).

On the other hand, it is sometimes taken generally so that it also befits devout married people (Gal. 5:23). In 2 Peter 1:6 self-control is listed among the fruits and virtues of the Spirit required in all the devout. In Ecclus 26:15 self-control is especially attributed to married people: "A self-controlled spirit no scales can weigh." Here it is apparently speaking of a married woman, as we see from v. 16: "The favor of a wife delights her husband." However, we shall say more about this in the question about the marriage of ministers.

"Μη παροινος" (no drunkard)

"Μη παροινος" means "not a drunkard" (1 Tim. 3:3, Titus 1:7). The apostle himself explains what he means by παροινος, namely, "one who is given to wine" (1 Tim. 3:8). In the *Athenaeum*, Bk.10, he is called an "ανθρωπος παροινος," whom the Latins call "*vinosus*," that is to say, sitting down to drink wine heavily or to "play the Greek" with wine.

The "παροινια" is the petulance, harm, insulting behavior, etc., that accompanies drunkenness, from which Chrysostom's statement undoubtedly started. He takes the "drunkard" to mean a wanton person, homily 10, on 1 Timothy 3: "It does not say here 'the drunkard,' but the wanton, the stubborn." In canon law there are some very clear canons about this. At the beginning of dist. 35: "That bishops should not be given over to wine was introduced on the basis of the authority of the Old Testament. Ministers of the church are forbidden to drink wine and liquor so that drunkenness does not burden their hearts, so that their good sense always flourishes, or because a belly bloated with wine easily foams up into lust."

C. *Episcopus*, etc., same dist., from the *Apostolic Canons*: "A bishop or elder or deacon who is in service to dice and drunkenness either should cease or certainly must be condemned." C. *Ante omnia*, same dist., from the Council of Agatha: "Above all, drunkenness is forbidden to clergymen. It is the nurse and kindler of all sins. He who is established to have been intoxicated should be removed from the communion for thirty days or should undergo physical punishment." At the beginning of dist. 44: "When a bishop is forbidden to be a drunkard, he is not permitted to have an intem perance of the throat. It is not that drunkenness is forbidden and gluttony allowed, for the apostle lists both among the works of darkness" (Rom. 13:13).

> "The insatiable belly easily provokes one to luxurious living and dissolves every good work. That is why Jerome writes to Amandus: 'The stomach and genitals are chains for themselves, so that because of the proximity of these parts of the body they are known as an alliance for sins.' Hence, Nabuzarda, prince of cooks, is said to have destroyed the walls of Jerusalem because the stomach, which the multitude of cooks serves, reduced the structures of virtues to dust. A priest, therefore, should seek to live about the altar, not luxuriate therein."

V. *Non oportet*, same dist, from the Council of Laodicea, c.24: "Serving clerics from elders to deacons and, in fact, all members of the order of the church, etc., should not enter taverns except in the case of necessity."

This same constitution is repeated in the church constitutions of Saxony, (gen. art.16, p.337). C. *Clerici*, same dist., from the Third Council of Carthage, c.27: "Clergymen should not enter taverns to eat or drink unless compelled by the necessity of their travels." C. Pro *reverentia*, same dist., from the Fourth Council of Toledo, c.7: "On behalf of reverence to God and to priests, the whole council establishes this, that (because useless tales generally come up with frequency at the tables) the reading of Holy Scripture be interspersed at every meal of priests. Through this, souls are edified for good, and unnecessary tales are forbidden."

"Νηφαλιος" (sober)

Fourth, a bishop must be "νηφαλιος" (sober) (1 Tim. 3:2). Among Latin speakers *sobrius* is used to refer not only to sobriety of body but also to sobriety of the mind, namely, to vigilance, prudence and attention. So also among the Greeks this word is used in both senses. Just as "νηφειν" is opposed to "μεθυειν," so also that is said about him who is watchful, prudent and circumspect.

Epicharmus, in Lucian and Cicero: "Be sober and watchful for unbelief, for the sober and prudent soul dwells in temperance." Thus, it is coupled with "being wakeful" (1 Thess. 5:6; 1 Peter 5:8). Thinking of this, Chrysostom, homily 10, on 1 Timothy 3, and in *de sacerd.* takes "sober" to mean prudent and circumspect. He says: "The sober person has been endowed with a very keen edge of mind and has countless eyes looking in every direction and with those he sees all things very sharply." And later: "He must be wakeful who not only has the care of himself but also the care of the rest. It befits him to be very vigilant who is of such a type that he glows with enthusiasm and shows the fire of his emotion with his works and surpasses all his leaders with his concerned industry. Day and night he will review his army and camp; he will work and fulfill very diligently the responsibility of his office; he will manage a care and concern for everyone." According to this explanation, "sober" should have to do with the office of the ministry, but because "prudent" is added, it is taken more conveniently about sobriety of body. Luther too renders it *"nüchtern"* (sober). For this reason it is a virtue of the Sixth Commandment and is opposed to the fault of drunkenness.

"Σωφρων" (prudent)

Fifth, he must be "σωφρων" or, as it were, "σοφρων." That is, he must be a prudent person. The Vulgate renders it as "prudent, sober." It is used to describe a person of moderation and temperance. Demosthenes and Aeschines have paired "prudent" and "restrained." Luther translates it here as *"mäszig"* (moderate). "Σωφροσυνη" is not only prudence but also temperance and moderation, according to Aristotle, Bk.6, ethic., c.5, as if it came from "σωζουα την φπονησιν" (maintaining judgment). Stephanus does not approve of this etymology.

Aristotle, Bk.1, *rhetor.*, writes: "Prudence is a virtue because of which people hold firm against the pleasures of the body as the law commands." To this he opposes "intemperance." Jerome renders it as *"castus"* (chaste), and Euripides also uses it in this sense. Erasmus, *annot.*, remarks that "σωφρων" to the Greeks sounds not so much like "prudent" as "sober" and "of a sound mind," so we may take it to mean a spirit that is collected and intoxicated with no desire.

Furthermore, from the fact that a bishop is forbidden to be given to wine, the constitution of the church of the Elector of Saxony rightly concludes, gen. art.16, p.338: "Pastors should refrain from selling wine and beer so that they do not retail, put out signs, or seat paying guests in their home. From such activity comes great scandal to the church, and to them, the pastors, comes often great rebuke, scorn, danger, inconvenience and injury. For this reason such selling is to be allowed to no official of the church. They should all diligently refrain from that."

This constitution is in harmony with the decree of the Sixth Synod cited in c. *Nulli*, dist. 44: "No clergyman is allowed to have a tavern or brewery of this sort, so much the more does he minister to others in it. On the other hand, if any clergyman has been doing this, he should stop it or be removed from his ministry."

This is supported with very good reason. First, "ζυθεψησις" that is, the business of cooking up and brewing beer, ill befits the authority of the ministry. It is not proper for a preacher of the Word and teacher of the church to be a wine seller and brewer of beer. "No soldier on service gets tangled in civilian pursuits" (2 Tim. 2:4). Second, it erodes his freedom to rebuke the wastefulness of his hearers. In fact, for the sake of his own profit, he will invite them to drink. Third, it provides an opportunity for excess to the children and servants of ministers (although the apostle quite clearly commands [Titus 1:6] that a bishop should keep his children "not open to the charge of debauchery or insubordination "), for experience is the witness that the children of such brewers very often degenerate into prodigals and drunkards.

Fourth, it draws the interest of the pastor into many areas foreign to his ministry and gives him an effective reason to be forced to hear, see and endure many things that are much more worthy of rebuke. Fifth, it is repugnant to the honor of the parish buildings and, secondarily, even to the sanctity of the church, to which the buildings of the church generally are quite close. After all, what can be more shameful than to erect a tavern close to a temple? Surely we read that Christ twice drove the buyers and sellers from the courtyard of the temple (John 2:15 and Luke 19:45).

Sixth, it is opposed to the apostle's faithfulness to the responsibility of teaching. However, their imitators ought to be sincere pastors. In Acts 6:2 they say: "It is not right that we should give up preaching the word of God to serve tables." Because by municipal law with respect for one's own buildings, it seems that we must allow such "cooking of beer" to some pastors, the church constitution therefore in the aforementioned paragraph applies this gentle restraint:

> "Church officials might produce their own wine or might be given the tithe in wine. They could brew beer in the parish, or they had other rights to brew beer. All this they could do for more than their own needs. Or they had their own homes where they had the right to brew beer. Thus, what we say about selling wine and beer one should understand to mean that they should be allowed to sell to others in barrels, buckets and kegs."

"Μη αισχροκερδης" (not greedy for gain)

For the Seventh Commandment of the Decalog is related that a bishop should be, first, "not greedy of filthy lucre, no pursuer of disgraceful gain" (1 Tim. 3:3, Titus 1:7). "αισχροκερδης" comes from "αισχρος και κερδος." To some this means given over to greedy gain, making a filthy profit. To others it means not given over shamefully to profit. We must prefer the first explanation, for one could be said to be given over shamefully to profit who is zealous and eager for profit above the normal, although the profit itself may not be filthy. The word "αισχροκερδεια" occurs in Demosthenes, *adv. Aeschin.*: "They preferred private profit and shame to that of the public good." Budaeus warns that "greediness for gain" denotes a sin related to "avarice," for the avaricious generally are "greedy for gain." In fact, to them the fragrance of profit from anything at all is good. Peter also advises elders that they should carry out the areas of their duty "not for shameful gain, but eagerly" (1 Peter 5:2).

Chrysostom, homily 2, on Titus 1: "'Not greedy for filthy lucre,' that is to say, showing great disdain for property." Luther translates it: "*der nicht unehrliche Handthirung treibt.*" From this apostolic canon is taken that statement of the church constitution of the Elector of Saxony, in the aforementioned place: "Ministers should abstain completely from all dishonorable work like selling wine and beer, merchandising, selling at excessive profit and similar commercial ventures."

Examples of "greediness for gain" we shall occasionally meet if we wish to consider the marketing of masses and indulgences, jubilees, the Roman curia's assessment of penance in which they demand a certain price for each and every sin. Thus, we take that statement of 2 Peter 2:3 to refer to papal clergymen: "And in their greed they will exploit you with false words." Would that examples of "greediness for gain" would be totally banished from the pastors of our churches! About some we must use the words of the poet: "They sin within and without the walls of Troy."

"Ἀφιλαργυρος" (no lover of money)

Second, he must be "αφιλαργυρος" (a stranger to greed) (1 Tim. 3:3). "Φιλαργυρια" is a lover of silver, a desire for money. Hesychius explains it as "a love of property, the acquisition of which is worth good silver." The apostle says that this is "the root of all evil" (1 Tim. 6:10). Therefore, "no lover of money" is a person who is not liable to this fault, who is not a lover of money. Luther translates it "*nichts geizig*" (not covetous). "Keep your life free from love of money, and be content with what you have" (Heb. 13:5). Here, "being a money-lover" is opposed to "αυταρκεια" (self-sufficiency) with which one is content with his lot and present circumstances.

Μη διλογος (not double-tongued)

To the Eighth Commandment of the Law is related that ministers of the church should not be "διλογοι" (double-tongued) (1 Tim. 3:8). This is required especially in deacons, but in general we relate it correctly to all ministers of the church. They are said to be "double-tongued" who declare one thing with their mouth and hide another beneath their breast. Elsewhere, Scripture says they "speak by and with their heart." Luther translates it "*zweizüngig*" (double-tongued).

Chrysostom, homily 11 on 1 Timothy: "Not 'double-tongued,' that is to say, not false nor deceitful." This hypocritical fault concealed by the disguise of political prudence is common to many people today, but it ought to be as far away as possible from ministers of the church. Chrysostom adds the reason, *ibid.*: "For nothing is so base a habit to practice as treachery; nothing is so useless in the church as deception." The minister who in civilian society is double-tongued or deceitful loses his people's confidence in him when he preaches the Word.

These now are the virtues of a bishop that concern his person, life and behavior. In these virtues, he should try very hard to surpass the others by as great a distance as the summit of the dignity of his office is from them. The characteristic virtues of a bishop that concern his office and doctrine are these: he should be apt to teach, "able to give instruction in sound doctrine and also to confute those who contradict it" (Titus 1:9). We discussed this in greater detail in another section.

The Administration of Church Discipline

Up to this point we have addressed ourselves to the fourth duty of ministers, which is the honorable control of life and behavior. We now go on with the fifth: the administration of discipline within the church. Just as in the political and economic spheres, so also in the church we must have discipline. Without it, subjects and servants on one hand and hearers on the other cannot be restrained in their duty. The object of church discipline are the people received into the household of God and family of Christ who have sinned (Matt. 18:15 "If your brother sins against you"); those who have been preoccupied with falling away (Gal. 5:1); and those who are to be rebuked, reproved and corrected so they return to the way and perform their duty according to the prescription of the Word.

Such falls are twofold, having to do with doctrine and behavior. A fall in doctrine is an error in dogmas, which arises out of simple ignorance and has no stubbornness connected with it. It also may begin from malice and wickedness and is defended stubbornly as it holds the judgment of the church, as taken from the Scripture, in contempt. For this reason it degenerates into heresy.

A fall in behavior is a sin committed either by words or actions and is either public or private. A public sin is either committed openly or is known publicly; it is paired with obvious scandal. A private one is committed in secret. Only one person or a few are conscious of it. It is not paired with public or infamous scandal. One commits both out of ignorance, weakness or wickedness. Correction is arranged either publicly before all or privately. It is related either to one person who sins or in general to the common assembly of hearers or to correction.

There are three levels of correction: first, "νουθεσια" (admonition) and "επιτινμια" or "επιτιμησις" (censuring or rebuking); second, lesser excommunication, which is a temporary suspension from partaking of the Lord's Supper; third, greater excommunication, by which a person is rejected from the fellowship of the church.

Just as lepers and the unclean were ordered to be removed from the Israelites' camp (Num. 5:2), so also those who were infected with notorious public sins (as with leprosy and persevere in those sins without repenting) should be rejected from the fellowship of the church by excommunication. There are some who add a fourth level, anathema, the Hebrew "*cherem*" by which the incorrigible person is cursed with eternal damnation (Gal. 1:8, 1 Cor. 16:22). However, this is not so much a part of the discipline of the church as it is a terrible curse made in accordance with the prophetic spirit. In the primitive church, especially presbyters or elders were in charge of this church discipline (church consistories have succeeded them today).

The Rules Relating to Church Discipline
Here are the rules relating to the administration of church discipline.

First, with private sins, one must begin with a private admonition before progressing to public censure. "If your brother sins against you, go and tell him his fault, between you and him alone ... But if he does not listen, take one or two others along with you If he refuses to listen to them, tell it to the church" (Matt. 18:15-17).

Here you should not think that Christ speaks only about those private offenses with which we plague each other in our daily life. Note that the Greek phrase "εἰς σε" (against you) can be translated "before you, in your presence" or "and you are aware of it." Thus, we understand that Christ is speaking in general of any sins committed that are known to one's neighbor. Second, in this private admonition, one must use prudence. You see, if a person has sinned because of ignorance or weakness, it is enough to admonish him gently and to encourage him to be careful about slipping in the future.

On the other hand, if the person sinned out of wickedness, we must have a more severe rebuke. Ambrose, Bk.8, on Luke: "A friendly reproof is more beneficial than a stormy accusation. The former indicates a sense of shame; the latter arouses indignation. In this administration of church discipline, one must not indulge his personal emotions (1 Tim. 5:21), but must rather direct all things to the single target of the conversion and salvation of the erring brother. Third, those who sin publicly and provide a public scandal because of their fall we must also correct publicly. "As for those who persist in sin (clearly along with public scandal), rebuke them in the presence of all so that the rest may attend in fear" (1 Tim. 5:20).

In Gal. 2:14, when Paul saw that Peter was sinning in public, he rebuked him "before them all." Therefore, when rebuking sins, we should not always use the same method. Some we must show openly so that they encourage no one to imitate them. Some we must deal with gently; others more sharply. We can scarcely place all of this within definite rules. Rather, we must leave them to the prudence of the faithful pastor as to a doctor of souls. He should know which procedure fits in each situation. As a prudent builder and faithful steward (1 Cor. 3:10 and 4:1), he ought to know how to apply that with urgency in and out of season (2 Tim. 4:2).

Fourth, in a public admonition, he must also use prudence lest the cure exceed bounds. Augustine, epistle 64, to Aurelius, urges him "to use severity towards the sin of a few, but in the case of sins which have swept over the entire multitude and have gone off to nearly become customs," he writes as follows: "As far as I can opine, we must not remove those things harshly, not roughly, not imperiously but rather by teaching than by commanding, rather by warning than by threatening. In mercy a man should reprove what he can; but what he cannot, he should bear patiently and bemoan and weep over it with love."

Fifth, the clemency of gentleness should always temper the severity of the discipline and correction. The Third Council of Bracar, canon 6: "A person who has been chastised with gentleness has respect for the one who has chastised him. A rebuke of excessive severity brings neither a rebuke nor salvation." Gregory, Bk.1, epistle 25: "Let the ark, that is, the church and the state, and its leader, have the Tables of the Law as the rod of discipline and correction and the sweetness of manna in ruling. Hence, the Samaritan pours wine and oil upon the wounded man so that the wine stings the wounds and the oil soothes them. Therefore, let there be love but not a softening love;

let there be strength, but not the strength that makes things worse." See also Gregory, part 2, *pastoral.*, c.6, and Bk.20, *moral.*, c.6.

Ambrose, Bk.20, *moral.*, c.6: "Discipline and mercy lack much if one be applied without the other. As regards their subjects rulers ought to have mercy, which offers just advice and discipline, which provides a pious service. Thus it is that wine and oil are applied to the wounds of the half-dead man whom the Samaritan took to the inn. In this way the wine stings the wounds and the oil soothes them. In the same way each person who is responsible for healing wounds should apply the bite of restraint in the wine and the soothing quality of pity in the oil. Wine cleanses rotting wounds; oil soothes them for healing. We must, therefore, mix gentleness with harshness and must take a proper measure of both so that we might not exacerbate our subjects with excessive severity nor let them off with excessive gentleness. In fact, this is what that ark of the tabernacle signifies, in which ark, along with the tables of the Law were the rod and manna because if, along with a knowledge of Holy Scripture, a good ruler has the rod of restraint in his breast, let him also have the sweetness of manna. Hence also David says: 'Your rod and Your staff, they comfort me.' Certainly, the rod strikes us, and the staff supports us. Therefore, there should be the restraining force of justice to strike and the comfort of the staff to support one. Let there be love, then, but not love too soft; let there be harshness, but not an exacerbating harshness; let there be zeal, but not a zeal that rages unduly; let there be pity but not a pity that spares more than it helps."

Sixth, we should not resort to excommunication, especially to major excommunication, without first having tried everything without success on the sinner, for, as that is the greatest and ultimate judgment of the church, so also it is the most terrifying judgment.

Seventh, a minister of the church should undertake neither major nor minor excommunication without the judgment of a senate or consistory of the church. The power to excommunicate does not belong to any one bishop, but to the presbytery that represents the entire church. "Tell it to the church. And if he refuses to listen even to the church [that is, to the presbytery and the assembly of elders], let him be to you as a Gentile and a tax collector" (Matt. 18:17), separated from the fellowship of the church. In fact, major excommunication of the church ought to occur only with the knowledge and approval of the entire church. "When you are assembled in the name of the Lord Jesus and my spirit is present, with the power of our Lord Jesus, you are to deliver this man to Satan" (1 Cor. 5:4-5). "For such a one, this punishment by the majority is enough" (2 Cor. 2:6).

The most serious responsibilities of the church ought not be undertaken without the consent of the entire body of the church. As Pope Leo writes: "That which has to do with all the people ought to be done with the consent of all the people." But what can be more serious and what relates more to the body of the church than to cut off some member from that body? If the entire church should refrain from familiar and ordinary association with the excommunicated person, it certainly is necessary that the excommunication take place in the assembly of the entire congregation and with the tacit approval of the same.

Eighth and finally, the minister must be very careful in his use of the keys that he not loose what must be bound and not bind what must be loosed, because God, as Jerome says on Matthew 16, "does not ask for the opinion of the priests but for the life of the accused, and because the key of power accomplishes nothing without the key of knowledge and discretion."

Rebuking the Prince

The first question asked here is whether we must give or grant permission to bring suit against a minister who is too vehement in censuring his hearers' sins. We can set up two parts of such a suit. The first is preparatory, the accusation contained in the complaint and the citation thereof; the second is the inquiry into the case and its adjudication. Here, the question concerns not the latter, but the former as it applies to the citation of the accusation. Must we allow to be called into court without discrimination any ministers at all, that is, those whose zeal has become known and investigated according to factual knowledge (Phil. 2:22), as well as those who lack such a zeal (Rom. 10:2)?

As far as the first class is concerned, we prove the negative first from the apostle's statement (1 Tim. 5:19): "Do not admit a charge against an elder except on the evidence of two or three witnesses"; second, from the case of law. Those who want only to behave well in regard to the eternal salvation of others and to the entire church, but who are responsible for deceiving and perverting many, against such we must admit no accusation except under the aforementioned condition. The antecedent is true about good elders and people like them.

Third, we prove it from the unfortunate consequences. The true church is offended by this procedure; the church that takes pleasure only in being called "church" is confirmed in its perversity and is encouraged to make greater advances in this process. See Tarn., de minist., q.6.

The second question asked here is whether ministers of the church can publicly censure a magistrate who sins. Some public officials think that such rebukes are repugnant to the honor due the magistracy and detract from its esteem. In fact, they believe it offers an opportunity for seditious behavior. Also, some counselors of the court notice that such rebukes do not please great men, but are dangerous to them. (Very often they are compelled to hear what King Amaziah told the prophet who accused him of idolatry: "Have we made you a royal counselor? Stop! Why should you be struck down?" [2 Chron. 25:16] and "O seer, go, flee away to the land of Judah, and eat bread there, and prophesy there, but never again prophesy at Bethel, for it is the king's sanctuary, and it is a temple of the kingdom" [Amos 7:12-13].) Then they become negligent in their duty.

However, to them we respond that there is the general command that orders ministers of the church to rebuke sins with no discrimination of individuals (Is. 58:1, 1 Tim. 5:20). Nowhere do we find the addition of the limitation that they must reprove the sins of private citizens but not those of public officials.

Second, we note the particular command that orders ministers of the church to censure even a magistrate. God tells Moses: "Go in, tell Pharaoh king of Egypt to let the people of Israel go out of his land" (Ex. 6:11). "Say to the king and the queen mother: 'Take a lowly seat'" (Jer. 13:18). "The word of the Lord came to me: 'Son of man, say to Pharaoh king of Egypt and to his multitude … '" (Ezek. 31:1-2).

Third, there are the examples of the prophets, the apostles and even Christ Himself. They placed the sins not only of private citizens and commoners but also of public officials and persons who were of the magistracy before their eyes. Obedient to a divine command, Moses and Aaron rebuke the Pharaoh of Egypt because he refused to let the people of Israel go (Exodus 7-9). Samuel reproved King Saul (1 Sam. 15:19); Nathan did the same to David (2 Sam. 12:19); Elijah to Ahab (1 Kings 18:17); Isaiah to Hezekiah (Is. 39:6); and Jeremiah (32:4), foretells to the king the king's abduction into captivity. The prophet Micah says (3:1): "Hear, you heads of Jacob and rulers of the house of Israel! Is it not for you to know justice?" "Hear, you mountains, the indictment of the Lord, and you enduring foundations of the earth" (Micah 6:2). John the Baptist told Herod: "It is not lawful for you to have [your brother's wife]." He said this, as Chrysostom noted, within the hearing of everyone (Matt. 14:4).

Ambrose censured Theodosius for excessive cruelty against the citizens of Thessalonika. Gregory, a Dominican monk, was an ecclesiastical advisor of Duke Frederick of Saxony whom Luther and others recently approved. When Gregory wanted to rebuke the sins of the princes before the congregations, but didn't dare do it openly, he spread it among the people by a trick, using this comparison: "A preacher is not unlike the man who skins a rabbit. You see, even though he draws the pelt from the entire body easily, yet he experiences some difficulty when he comes to the head. Thus, when the preacher censures the sins of the people, it is not that he fears the difficulty. But when he comes to the head (and right here he points to the prince who is standing nearby), 'So streif dich einander!' (That's the way you skin each other!) The prince gave the monk a new cap of honor." See Wolff, cent.16, p.140.

Fourth, we note the dignity of the ecclesiastical office. You see, however much of the individual and property of ministers are under the magistracy, it still is their duty to know no other lord than Christ alone, whose ambassadorship they are performing (2 Cor. 5:20). Therefore, with respect for that relating to the doctrine and ministry of reproof, they know they are subject not to the magistracy, but to God alone.

Luther, Vol.6, German edition of Jena, f.384: "The office of the ministry is the job of neither a court servant nor of a hired hand. He is a servant and laborer of God, and his responsibility surpasses master and servant." To rebuke sins is the work of the Holy Spirit (John 16:8); it is He who speaks through ministers (Matt. 10:20). Therefore, when ministers rebuke the magistrate who sins, God is holding judgment "in the midst of gods" (Ps. 82:1).

Fifth, we note the usefulness of this reproof. It brings good to a magistrate so he is called away from the course of his sins to repentance and brings him to an inheritance of eternal life. Whatever occurs by God's command and for the good of a magistrate, we must not consider as detracting from his esteem nor as offering an opportunity for sedition.

Sixth, we note the necessity of this censure. That censure is necessary with respect to God's command that ministers of the church are bound to obey. "for to all to whom I send you, you shall go, and whatever I command you, you shall speak" (Jer. 1:7). It is also necessary with respect for those very ministers who will be forced to give an accounting at the last judgment for the souls not only of their subjects but even of the magistracy itself (Ezek. 3:17 and 33:7, Heb. 13:17). In addition, upon these, by reason of their office, necessity imposes the preaching of repentance and the remission of sins to all people (Luke 24:47), and certainly then also to the magistrate. That censure finally is necessary with respect to the magistrate himself who must be rebuked and instructed if he is to be led to a knowledge of his sins, to conversion and to salvation.

In fact, the sins of public officials seriously harm the state by example (for whatever they do, their subjects think they have license to do also and "the whole world is arranged after the example of the king"). Therefore, it is especially essential to reprove the sins of magistrates, even as the healing of the body begins with medicine for the head. Furthermore, we add that just as in rebuking other people, so also in the censuring of a public official, we must use prudence, an example of which we have in the case of Nathan (2 Sam. 12:1ff.) and with the anonymous prophet (1 Kings 20:39). By outstanding cleverness, both of these elicited from the mouths of David and Ahab statements that condemned those monarchs.

Second, we must distinguish lesser peccadilloes from great and notorious sins, and secret sins from public disgraces, lest we censure publicly and immediately a magistrate because of minor or secret sins.

Third, we must be extra careful that the censuring office of the Holy Spirit not degenerate into popular outcries raised to incite seditious behavior against the magistrate. Devout ministers are heralds of conversion, not trumpets for rebellion.

Fourth, we must distinguish correctly the office of magistrate from the faults of individuals administering that office. The minister of the church can and should censure the faults of the magistrate no less than those of subjects. However, the dignity of that public office should be sacrosanct to both ministers and subjects.

The third question is whether anyone can confess to a pastor other than his own ordinary one and ask him for absolution. We deny this, first, on the basis of Scripture. "Let none of you suffer ... as a meddler" (1 Peter 4:15, cf. Acts 20:28, 1 Peter 5:2, Heb. 10:25 and 13:17). Secondly, we deny it on the basis of the sacred canons. In c. *Ut dominic.*, etc., in the decretals of Gregory, title *de paroec.*, it is established that on Sundays or festival days, before the priests celebrate the mass, they should ask the people if there is a member of another parish who wants to hear the mass there because he holds his own priest in contempt. If they should find such a one, they should immediately remove him from the church.

Third, we deny it on the basis of a decree of the Council of Carthage that decreed no bishop should be in charge of another's people nor should any bishop be over his colleague in a diocese.

Fourth, we deny it by the authority of Cyprian, Bk.1, epistle 3, q.55, in the Goulartian codex. Part of the flock is ascribed to individual pastors, which each is to control and guide as one who will give an accounting of his activity to the Lord. See also Luther, Vol.5, German edition of Jena, f.76, explanation of Psalm 82; and Bidembach, *decad.2, concil.4* (which belongs to Jerome Mencel, p.99) and *decad.3, cons.6* (which is part of Tilem. Hesshus, p.128).

Fifth, we deny it on the basis of a pairing. No one is allowed to preach in another's parish if that pastor is unwilling, nor may he baptize or marry anyone there. Therefore, he is not allowed to absolve or give the Lord's Supper to anyone from another parish, even if he has a house or an estate there but still is a member of another parish.

Sixth, we deny it because of the inconvenient results. If a person wants to go off to another pastor, he upsets the divinely established order and disdains the ministry of his own pastor.

The Preservation of the Rites of the Church

The sixth duty of ministers of the church involves the preservation of the rites of the church. To be sure, the institution of those rituals relates not only to ministers of the church but also to the Christian magistrate. Such institutions ought to occur with the consent of the entire church, but the preservation thereof is correctly assigned to ministers that they neither change nor abrogate on the basis of personal judgment rituals accepted by the public authority of the church. Instead, they should preserve them to protect harmony and promote good order.

By nature, church rituals are adiaphora because God's Word neither commands nor forbids them, and they do not of themselves constitute some portion of divine worship. Nevertheless, their cessation ought not occur merely because of one party in the church. By such an arbitrary and rash abrogation, one may sin against Christian liberty whose function is moderated by a love that is very careful not to cause a neighbor to stumble by the preposterous use of adiaphora (Rom. 14:15 and 1 Cor. 8:9).

Second, a minister may violate the good order and authority of the church. Third and finally, he may hold in contempt the apostle's command that in either the institution or abrogation of rituals in the church all things ought to be done "to build up" (1 Cor. 14:12). The consequence of this canon is that ministers of the church should not yield even for an hour to enemies of the truth who argue for the introduction or abrogation of some church ritual. This they should not yield lest they subject their Christian liberty to the whim of their adversaries and be taken captive under the yoke of people. "For freedom Christ has set us free; stand firm therefore, and do not submit again to a yoke of slavery" (Gal. 5:1). "You were bought with a price; do not become bondservants of men" (1 Cor. 7:23).

Thus, to the false brothers who argued for circumcision (which at that time was an adiaphoron), the apostle was unwilling even for an hour to yield that he admit this in Titus, for they "slipped in to spy out our freedom that we have in Christ Jesus, so that they might bring us into slavery" (Gal. 2:4). Second, they should not yield, lest by such a yielding to their adversaries they cause them to become more bold in their mental tyranny and provide them with an opportunity to bring false accusations.

Third, they might appear to be in collusion with their adversaries in confession, the symbols of which are considered as rituals in the church. Instead, in this case they should give witness to the truth of their confession by word and deed. "To them we did not yield in submission even for a moment, so that the truth of the gospel might be preserved for you" (Gal. 2:5). "Do not be unequally yoked with unbelievers" (2 Cor. 6:14). "Abstain from every form of evil" (1 Thess. 5:22). They might offer a stumbling block to the weak.

You see, if the weak see such changes being undertaken in favor of the adversaries, they are easily thrown into doubt about the confession's truth and sincerity. This is not being used as an excuse by the very adiaphoric character of rituals, for that ceases in the case of confession; nor by the harmony of the church, for we must not seek that at the cost of the truth, scandal for the weak, or the violation of liberty; nor by the example of the apostle, who testified that he "became all things to all people" (1 Cor. 9:22), for we must distinguish between the weak brothers and the stubborn opponents of the truth of the Gospel.

The Care of the Poor and the Visitation of the Sick

Finally, the seventh duty of ministers is taking care of the poor and visiting the sick. Ministers of the church should not think that anything related to caring for the poor is foreign to them. First, in His own ministry, Christ had the diligent care of the poor (John 13:29).

Second, Paul gave orders about collections for use by the saints in the churches of Galatia and the Corinthians (1 Cor. 16:1; Gal. 2:9-10): "James and Cephas and John … gave the right hand of fellowship to Barnabas and me … Only, they asked us to remember the poor, the very thing I was eager to do."

Third, in the primitive church, "αγαπαι" or public feasts were instituted to help the poor. In the Council of Gangres, c.11 reads: "If anyone despises those who conduct the *agapae*, that is, feasts for the poor, and summon together the brothers for the sake of the honor of the Lord; and if anyone is unwilling to share in assemblies of this sort, believing that what is happening there is of little value; let such a one be accursed."

On the other hand, in the apostolic church, caring for the sick was not connected with church ministry and was committed to some special persons who, because of this diaconate, were called "deacons" (Acts 6:5). To emulate them, today we have church treasurers who are responsible for collecting and distributing the goods of the church.

However, on this account, ministers of the church should not judge that taking care of the poor has nothing to do with them. Rather, with the frequent exhortation of their hearers to exercise generosity toward the poor, by their own example of hospitality and generosity, and by watching over the church treasury, they should support help for the poor. We must commend the visitation of the sick to the minister of the church with this idea: The sick especially must be lifted up by the comfort of the Gospel and armed against the terror of death.

The church constitution of the Elector of Saxony makes the following command about this topic, *art. gen*.14, f.332: "Pastors and church officials are to visit and comfort the sick, oppressed and troubled Christians often, especially when they are near death. They should at the request of such Christians administer to them the sacred Sacrament of Christ's body and blood. They should do this willingly and without vexation, nor should they neglect any such service out of carelessness or revenge and hostility against anyone. They should be just as ready to serve the poor in such cases as the rich. If they notice among the ill great poverty, hunger and other lack of the necessities, they should advise the officials of the treasury of the church about this. In this way such unknown poor people — unknown because out of shame they dare not lament their poverty to anyone — may receive advice and aid. They should address the well-to-do especially and admonish them in a Christian way to be helpful and comforting to such helpless and comfortless ones with their money, food, refreshment, linens and the like. Pastors and church officials, however, should consider carefully the difference and opportunity of each person. They should not depress the ill with vexing words but strengthen, teach and comfort them with a few short, sweet, comforting verses of Holy Scripture, especially if the ill are very weak. When a new member among his hearers falls seriously ill, and if the pastor has something to say to the good for the salvation of that sick person's soul, the pastor should not wait too long. Instead (note this!), uncalled, he should make himself available to that sick person. He should provide all proper encouragement, comfort and admonition with all Christian gentleness and modesty. You see, that ill person can still grasp such assistance and go to his death as a Christian."

What ought to be the chief points of that admonition and consolation we have explained in detail in the church constitution to be published by his illustrious highness and prince, His Highness John Casimir the Elder, Duke of Saxony, etc.

These are the seven most important duties of ministers of the church to which we can relate the rest conveniently. The apostle embraces them all with one word: "This is how one should regard us, as servants of Christ and stewards of the mysteries of God. Moreover, it is required of stewards that they be found faithful" (1 Cor. 4:1-2).

In fact, faithfulness includes not only those duties of the office we explained in the preceding paragraphs but two others: first, steadfastness in one's legitimate calling, so the minister of the church does not change his ecclesiastical duties with a sort of superficial levity but remains firm in the calling to which he believes he was divinely called; and second, the selection of other ministers.

You see, because ministers of the church have mortality in common with all other people, and thus, because ministerial functions begin to go undone because of the blessed death of faithful ministers; they must give thought to ordaining others in place of the dead not only out of the situation itself but also out of the church's need. We have spoken earlier as much as is sufficient about this latter duty, namely, about ordination being attributed by constitutions of the church to bishops alone. Therefore, in regard to the former, let us ask first whether a minister of the church may run away during a time of plague. First, we say no because that is when his hearers need his work and ministry so they may be admonished about true and sincere repentance and may be correctly instructed in regard to a blessed and easy death.

Although a divinely sent disaster or plague suddenly raged and in its swift progress killed 14,700 people, Aaron "stood between the dead and the living" and placated God with his incense (Num. 16:48). Thus, it befits ministers at a time of plague to light the incense of prayer and to fear no peril from closeness to the sick and dead. By order of the Lord, Aaron received no harm from this.

Third, excessive timidity on the part of ministers who run away presents a stumbling block to the weak and argues for a lack of confidence in regard to the divine promises. "A thousand may fall at your side, ten thousand at your right hand, but it will not come near you" (Ps. 91:7). "But even the hairs of your head are all numbered" (Matt. 10:30). "For he has said: 'I shall never leave you nor forsake you'" (Heb. 13:5). For examples that prove the truth of these promises, examples occurring at the time of a very dangerous pestilence, see Exodus 8 and 6; Eusebius, Bk.7, *hist. eccles.*, c.21; Evagrius, Bk.4, *hist.*, c.28.

Some add the limitation that ministers (during a time of plague) may ask for a recess if in their place they substitute others who perform the parts of their duty to the church with no less diligence, dexterity and confidence as they themselves have. However, they must be very careful that they do not cause the weak to stumble. They can hardly be so careful if, when plague comes, those run away whom it befits to outshine the rest with their example and to exhort others to faith, love, long-suffering and generosity, even if they substitute others in their place.

It does not appear to be altogether unseemly that, if a church has several ministers, they could agree among themselves to commit to one or more the duty of visiting the sick or even to send away to safe places one or more whose work could be extraordinarily useful to the church. Others proceed as follows: "A pastor is not permitted to interrupt all or some parts of his responsibility at a time of plague and to surrender the care thereof by committing them to another pastor whom they call 'pastor of the plague.'"

We approve of this idea, first, on the basis of passages of Scripture (Ezek. 3:17, Acts 20:28, Heb. 13:17). Those who were established without condition of perilous times as shepherds of the flock must, without any condition or exception whatsoever, watch for the souls of all their hearers in such a way that they are able to render to God an account of their office which they have administered in this way, just as they have received that office. All pastors have been established without condition of perilous time for the church, etc.

Ergo, second we approve on the basis of authorities: Luther, Vol.3, German edition of Jena, f.426; treatise *Ob man vor Sterben fliehen möge; Wigand, de persec. et exsil.*, p.270; Binder, aitiolog., *theol. de causas pest.*, p.96; Winckelman, Vol.5, *disp. Gissens.*, disp.14, thesis 23. We also add the testimonies of Calvin, *epistol.*, 362; of Beza, treatise *de peste*, p.30; of Ursinus, part 2, *exerc.*, p.514; of Sohn, Vol.1, in the theses regarding this argument, p.195.

Third, we approve for several reasons. First, the reason for such a flight is not legitimate, for it depends on no definite rule with respect either for the asker or the grantor. The asker is the minister, but he has no just reason to flee but is driven partly by lack of faith in God and partly by confidence in his own wisdom in seeking measures outside the Word of God. He is the one who ought to look back in faith to the divine promises of Psalm 91, etc. The grantor is the church, which also lacks a legitimate call and can arrange nothing beyond the word of its Bridegroom, especially to her own disadvantage.

Second, if at this very dangerous time the church can do without the work of its pastor and the pastor in this same condition of peril is allowed to surrender his duties by committing them to another; the same thing can happen, and all the more, at a not-so-dangerous time, and thus he can indulge in a complete cessation from his office.

However, the latter is not so, which we see partly from reason that shows each and every function consists in carrying out the parts or works of each function; partly from the judgment and statement of our own people about the lazy bishops of the papists. The former, therefore, is not so.

Third, every one of Christ's common soldiers and sheep ought to lay down their lives for their brothers (1 John 3:16). All the more then are the standard-bearers and leaders bound to do this. Tarn, *de minist.*, q.3.

Whether He May Flee at a Time of Imminent Danger or Persecution

The second question is whether a minister is allowed to flee at a time of imminent danger or persecution. Here we are not speaking about the flight of courage. A minister experiences this when he sees errors of doctrine and sins of behavior growing stronger among his hearers and when he fears the hatred of more powerful or other perils, but winks at all this and does not stand like a wall against them by censuring and rebuking them.

In regard to this flight, Augustine says very clearly, treatise 46, on John: "Because you said nothing, you ran away. You said nothing because you were afraid," although no one argues that this is forbidden and condemned. Instead, the question here is about the flight of the body that occurs at a time of imminent danger or persecution. Lactantius, Bk.4, c.18: "Christ withdrew not to avoid what He had to suffer and endure but to show what one had to do in every persecution lest anyone appear to have fallen because of His fault."

Augustine, on Psalm 142: "One may flee physically. The Lord has conceded and permitted this as he says: 'If you are persecuted in one city, flee to another.'" With statements and examples Athanasius confirms the same thing in his defense of his own flight. Augustine does the same in treatise 15, on John:

"Any servant of God does not sin if he withdraws to another place when he sees the fury of those who persecute him or of those who are seeking evil for his soul. Furthermore, a servant of God would appear to sin if he were to do this, if the Lord had not preceded him in doing this. This, that good Master did to teach, not because He was afraid."

Treatise 28, on John: "It was going to happen that some faithful person would hide lest his persecutors find him and not in order to find himself in hiding because of his criminal activity. What was confirmed in a member preceded in the case of the Head. Athanasius also defends the affirmative in the defense of his own flight. To Tertullian is simply attributed the negative by Perkins, Bk.2, *de casib. consc.*, c.12, and others, who cite his book about his flight. However, Martyr, clas.3, *loc. comm.*, locus 12, ¶27, and Aretius, part 1, *problem.*, locus 2, p.26, excuse him. Augustine, epistle 180, to Honoratus, uses a distinction.

Indeed, Christ's advice does show that at times, flight is allowed: "When they persecute you in one town, flee to the next" (Matt. 10:23). So does the example of Christ (Matt. 2:13 and 12:15, John 8:59, Luke 4:30, etc.) and the example of Paul (Acts 9:25, 2 Cor. 11:33) and of Polycarp, in Eusebius, Bk.4, *hist.* eccles., c.15; and of Athanasius, in Socrates, Bk.2, *hist.*, c.11. See Theodoret, Bk.2, c.4; Rufinus, Bk.1, c.18, etc. Add also Socrates, Bk.3, *hist.*, c.6; Nicephorus, Bk.10, c.16; *Tripart.*, Bk.4, c.22. "So, be as wise as serpents" (Matt. 10:16).

But serpents look for places to hide when they feel traps are being set against their life. Elijah "ran for his life" (1 Kings 19:3). Basil the Great approved of flight in a homily on the martyr Gordius, as does Augustine, treatise 15, on John. Here are the reasons. First, whatever work whose beginning, object, method of performing it and goal are legitimate is itself licit. Flights of ministers of the Word circumscribed by certain conditions fit all these things. Ergo, second, it is illicit to remain in a church that freely dismisses you to spread the glory of God, to free your conscience and to not aggravate the judgment of your enemies. Therefore, to leave such a church under the enumerated circumstances is licit. Athanasius, argues in the same way, Socrates, Bk.3, c.6. To pursue to kill a person who does not deserve that is a sin. To go away and seek one's safety in flight, therefore, is not a sin.

However, we must distinguish between singular persecutions that seek one minister and persecutions that are common to the entire church. In the former we say that it is allowed; and, in the case of the latter, it is not except in a certain respect. We must further distinguish between states of the church. You see, sometimes the minister of a church flees with the consent and, in fact, at the behest of his hearers so that meanwhile the church, which was his responsibility, does not lack other suitable teachers. This we believe is allowable. (In addition to the consent of the church about which there should be agreement as concerns the one who is fleeing, the one who flees should investigate carefully and examine his courage and the reason for his flight. He ought to have been so prepared that, if his flight has not succeeded in remedying the situation, but God is calling back to death and martyrdom that man who wished to advise himself to flee, then he should be prepared also to follow Him. Here, by seeking out the enjoyment of a longer life, one ought to consider especially and most importantly the glory of God and the welfare of the church or neighbor rather than his own glory and welfare, which come from an excessive love for a long life and a too great care for one's own property. Tarn, *de minist.*, q.4.)

However, when he flees in a way that gives his hearers (who are not asking him to flee and who do not agree with his flight) a stumbling block and gives his foes an opportunity to make false accusations and to set traps for the lambs, that we believe is not permissible.

C. *Adversitas*, case 7, q.1, *Gregor.*: "Adversity which is placed in the way of good men is a test of virtue, not an indication of censure. After all, who is there who does not know how fortunate it was that Paul was going to Italy to preach and on the way suffered shipwreck, but the hull of his ship remained whole in the waves of the sea? We understand then that this must be observed: when among the subjects are found some to whom the life of prelates is beneficial, and when a prelate is not especially requested to flee nor to care that the health of the church be safe through others, let it not be said of him if he begins to desert those to whom he can be useful: 'He is a hired hand, and not the shepherd. The sheep do not belong to him. He sees the wolf approach and he deserts the sheep and flees.' But, when they especially request the prelate to flee, let him flee according to Christ's example, who fled from the face of Herod to Egypt. Let him flee according to the example of Paul, whom his brothers let down from the wall in a basket. Whence Augustine says, epistle 180, to Honoratus: 'Let Christ's minister flee as Christ fled into Egypt. Let him flee who has a special request to flee, while the health of the church remains solid through the care of others, etc.' But, when the safety not only of prelates but of the entire church is at stake and faith itself is attacked, then it is necessary to make a frontal approach and to set themselves upon the day of battle as a wall on behalf of the Lord's house and to risk their lives for their sheep. This they should do in order to kindle by the example of their suffering those whom they can no longer strengthen with a sermon of doctrine."

See Luther, Vol.3, German edition of Jena, f.392. Augustine, op. cit., declares that, when serious persecution arises, "ministers of the church should not all flee nor should all place themselves in the peril of death." Rather, he orders some to stay who seem to be of greater use in the present calamity of the church, but others he believes should be sent away. But, if they cannot agree as they make the choice among them because they all seem equal, then he thinks they must decide by lot.

CHRIST APPEARING TO HIS DISCIPLES

"Then he said to Thomas, 'Put your finger here, and see my hands; and put out your hand, and place it in my side. Do not disbelieve, but believe.'" John 20:27 c. 1510

Sanctification and Charitable Works in Lutheran Theology

by Matthew C. Harrison

I must confess. I have never had the slightest interest in greatly, or even marginally, expanding my understanding of "sanctification" as a locus of Lutheran theology. Surely such absence of desire is the strongest indication of the lack of the presence of the topic of this series of lectures within my own life. It's sort of the inverse of Walther's famous answer to the worried inquirer who frets, "I believe I've committed the sin against the Holy Ghost and that I shall be eternally damned, without any hope!" Walther suggests the reply, "Well, it's obvious you haven't committed the sin against the Holy Ghost, because if you had, you wouldn't be worried that you might have done so!" The implication for Harrison: "You don't care about sanctification because you don't in fact possess the Holy Ghost!"

Schleiermacher on Sanctification: Me and Jesus. And We're Getting Better Every Day!

But alas, such a statement does trouble me. Perhaps there is hope yet … or maybe not. I for one would have been most happy if the locus of "sanctification" in Lutheran dogmatics had never been sanctified (sanctioned). "Sanctification" is but a logically consequent but temporally coterminous part of the doctrine of justification. Early Lutheran dogmatics considered justification, regeneration, renewal, and sanctification all within the locus of justification (e.g. Melanchthon's *Loci Praecipui*; Chemnitz's *Loci Theologici*). After justification came the locus on good works. But it happened sometime between Quenstedt's *Systema* (1690) (where the locus *De Bonis Operibus* follows *De Fide Justificante* — at least in the "didactic" or last section of the great work), and Buddeus's *Institutiones* (1724), where *De Justificatione* is followed by *De Sanctificatione seu Renovatione*. Even Hollaz's *Examen* (1707), with its burgeoning interest in the *ordo salutis* simply follows the locus on justification with that on "good works." Thus Schleiermacher is running in an already very well-worn, century-old track when he sets aside pages for the locus of "sanctification" in *The Christian Faith*. Late orthodoxy had a penchant toward psychologization of the *ordo salutis*, which was intricately expanded in the period of pietism. This led to a temporal disintegration of what are really coterminous realities in the life of the believer. Justification became a "rear-view mirror" doctrine (Scaer) of the Christian life. With this also came the drift toward understanding sanctification in purely individualistic and especially psychological terms (via pietism and rationalism). And thus we have the definition of sanctification in Schleiermacher:

> In living fellowship with Christ the natural powers of the regenerate are put at His disposal, whereby there is produced a life akin to His perfection and blessedness; and this is the state of Sanctification.[1]

Now *that's* the definition of sanctification I grew up with! Justification a mere speck and fading in the rear-view mirror: purely individual! Nicely appreciative of my "natural" capabilities! Of course, with a "living" fellowship with Jesus (we wouldn't want a "dead" fellowship, for goodness sake!). More like Jesus every day! Magnanimously putting myself and my natural powers at Jesus' "disposal." Have you "surrendered" yourself to Jesus? That's a long way from Melanchthon and the old dogmatics locus of "good works" following justification, which led them to think of the Ten Commandments in the context of vocation. "Me and Jesus." "Jesus and me." Maybe, just maybe — with enough time — I'll find out Jesus is me! Hear Schleiermacher:

> Sanctification, then, being understood to be progressive — so that the content of time-experience becomes from the turning-point of regeneration ever further removed from what preceded that crisis, and ever approximates more to pure harmony with the impulse issuing from Christ and therefore to indistinguishability from Christ Himself.[2]

Justification happened to me a long time ago. I'm making progress. In fact, I'm Jesus! Schleiermacher is so edifying; let me quote him again:

> [S]in cannot be perfectly blotted out, but remains always something in process of disappearance. In so far as it has not yet disappeared, it may [sic!] make itself visible, and acts will occur within the state of sanctification similar [sic!] to those common before regeneration, where what emerges is the power of the sinful common life, whereas the traces of preparatory grace lie deeply hidden.

> Even if these intermittent evidences [sic!] of the continued presence of sin make particular instants, as compared with others, seem [sic!] relapses, none the less a settled consciousness remains that the longer the series of such

---

[1] Friedrich Schleiermacher, *The Christian Faith* (Edinburgh: T&T Clark, 1956), 505. See also Werner Elert, *Der Christliche Glaube* (Hamburg: Furche-Verlage, 1956), 486–87. "An diesem Punkt ist die orthdoxe Dogmatik für den damals anheben-den Pietismus, anstatt sein theologisches Gewissen zu sein, zum theologischen Ruhekissen geworden. Das Leben des Wie-dergeborenen ist hier von der Rechtfertigung so weit getrennt, hauptsächlich durch allerlei psychologische Zwischenüber-legungen, dass es nur noch einer geringen Akzentverschiebung bedurfte, um das cooperari das Wiedergeborenen zur Hauptsache zu machen. Und am Ende steht die rationalistische Dogmatik, die dann das Verhältnis von Rechtfertigung und Heiligung vollends auf den Kopf stellt. 'Das Streben nach Heiligkeit' heisst es bei Wesegscheider, 'ist das sicherst Fundament des wahren Glaubens.'"

[2] Schleiermacher, *The Christian Faith*, 506.

fluctuations [sic!] is observed, the greater is the advance seen to be on the whole. … So that in the powers put at Christ's disposal [note who is doing the verbs!] sin can never win fresh ground.[3]

And since with Schleiermacher, too, all theology is Christology, we should not be surprised to find his definition of sanctification rooted in his view of Christ:

If now … we consider how this condition approximates to likeness to Christ, there has above been drawn a boundary line which it is not given to us to overstep. From the beginning of His incarnation onwards Christ developed in every way naturally yet constantly and uninterruptedly in organic union with the indwelling principle of His life, and in its service. … [R]egeneration may be regarded as the divine act of union with human nature and sanctification as the state constituted by that union.[4]

Translation: You wanna be holy like Jesus? Develop in every way naturally yet constantly and uninterruptedly in organic union with the indwelling principle of your Christian life, Jesus.

We might respond to Scheiermacher with an Augustine-esque line: Friedrich, you have not yet considered how light a matter sin is for your *Tauf* Patten, pietism and rationalism! We see here, as we would expect, no serious dogma of incarnation. No requisite serious dogma of sin. There is here no serious sacramentology. There is here no trace of Luther's and Paul's inexorable dialectic of sin and grace, law and gospel, total condemnation under law, and total forgiveness under grace. There is no dogma of the church. Sanctification is an individual — no, individualistic — matter. It's all measurable approximation — the sure indicator that sanctification has fallen completely away from justification, the proper context of its locus. I'd prefer the medieval dogmatic paradigm of the *gratia infusa*, so similar in many respects to Schleiermacher here. At least there was a place for a crucifix in that religion, even if inconsistently so.

Sanctification as a Corporate, Ecclesial Reality

Of the many lines we might pursue here, I wish to consider directly only one (though other concerns will arise). That is, sanctification as a corporate reality in the church's life, in contradistinction from a doctrine of sanctification drawn merely along individualistic lines. This view of sanctification is what rivets my attention these days as I ponder and practice *diakonia* at the level of the national church. Theodosius Harnack complained that "diakonia was not of interest as a constituent part of ecclesiology, but was seen only as an expression of Christian groups and societies alongside the church."[5] That precisely describes the theological/practical reality I see daily expressed

---

[3] Ibid., 508–9.

[4] Ibid., 509.

[5] See Carter Lindberg, "Luther's Concept of Offering," in *Dialogue* 35/4 (1996): 252.

in The Lutheran Church—Missouri Synod and all her related "social ministry" organizations. All this is but a perfect reflection of the fact that dogmatics in our circles relegates all matters of sanctification to the individual. And the locus on sanctification as traditionally explicated in Lutheranism deals only with the individual (e.g., Pieper). Thus, among us there is simply no dogmatic exposition — or biblical exposition — of the reality of the holiness of the church as it lives out in this life its justified, christological, and sacramental reality, particularly as it relates to *diakonia*. The church's life of mercy, then, precisely as a communal, corporate life of mercy, has become an adiaphoron. I am asserting that "sanctification" is above all a communal, corporate reality. Individual holiness flows from communal realities. I am asserting that in the words "Sanctification and the Church's Charitable Works," "sanctification" is corporate. After all, they are the church's charitable works! And I will suggest that these facts best reflect the New Testament (and Luther), which demands diakonia as a "constituent element of ecclesiology."

The New Testament

In what follows I shall begin (and only begin) to trace the New Testament evidence for a corporate understanding of sanctification. To do so I shall, in part, climb on the back of Sasse's great Erlangen colleague Ott Procksch, who wrote the entry for the word *hagiazo* and its cognates for Kittel's *Theological Dictionary of the New Testament*.[6] The entry has little concern for the communal reality of holiness in the New Testament, but the article nonetheless does offer much furtive material when considered from this perspective.

The Communality of the Triune God, Father, Son, and Holy Spirit

It is no unique or profound discovery that according to the New Testament the church's reality is communal and corporate. Here we wish to pursue this New Testament teaching particularly in view of holiness, or "sanctification." The communality of the church is a reflection of God. But this is more than mere metaphor, in the same way that "body of Christ" is no mere metaphor to describe the church. From the Trinitarian trisagion of Isaiah 6 to its repetition in Rev. 4:8, the Bible teaches the corporate, communal nature of the blessed and Holy Trinity. Jesus calls the Father "Holy Father" (John 17:11). "The one who has called you is holy," says Peter (1 Peter 1:15f). The Lord's Prayer calls upon the church to sanctify God's "name." The name can be none other than that one "name" of Father, Son, and Holy Spirit (Matt. 28:19). This communality, based upon the essential unity of Father and Son, is reflected starkly in John's gospel and its use of Old Testament themes, for instance.

Yahweh had shown Himself "holy" to His Old Testament people (Lev. 10:3). His holiness was communicated via His "glory" or holy presence for forgiveness, most strikingly seen in His very "Holy of Holies" or in the pillar of cloud by day, fire by

---

[6] *Theological Dictionary of the New Testament*, ed. Gerhard Kittel (Grand Rapids, MI: Eerdmans, 1983), 1: 88ff.

night. Note what happened when Solomon brought the ark to the temple: "When the priest withdrew from the Holy Place, the cloud filled the temple of Yahweh. And the priests could not perform their service because of the cloud, for the glory of the Lord filled his temple" (1 Kings 8:10). We see clearly in the rest of Solomon's prayer at the completion of the first temple that though Yahweh fills the earth, and no temple can be built to contain Him, nevertheless Yahweh has promised to dwell there with His "Name" (1 Kings 8:29), so that forgiveness may be found at that place. To borrow and adapt a famous political phrase from Tip O'Neill, "All forgiveness, according to the Bible, is local." God's glory, name, and holiness are inseparable and always located for forgiveness. Located glory and holiness without Name and forgiveness leave only a dangerous *deus nudas*. "The glory of Yahweh filled his temple" (1 Kings 8:11). *Doxa* is the Septuagint rendering of the Hebrew word *kabod*. "The Word became flesh and tabernacled among us. We have seen his *doxa*, the *doxa* of the only begotten of the Father" (John 1:14). Jesus is the New Testament Holy of Holies, and beyond His Palestinian days, the Holy of Holies remains His body and blood in Holy Communion (Hebrews 10). "Destroy this temple, and in three days I will raise it up" (John 2:20). Thus Jesus is called the "Holy One" (Mark 1:24; Luke 1:35; 4:34: John 6:69; 1 John 2:20; Rev. 3:7; Acts 3:14; 4:27, 30). In Luke it is based upon His being begotten of the Holy Ghost (1:35), but John has given us the ultimate reason: Jesus is Yahweh.

The communality of Father and Son in the divine attribute of holiness could be pursued at length, as could the nature of the Spirit as "Holy Spirit." But we will forego further investigation of this point. It is this essential communality which indeed makes the Spirit the very Holy Spirit. "But the Helper, the Holy Spirit, whom the Father will send in my name, he will teach you all things … " (John 14:26). The Holy Father sends the Holy Spirit in the name of the Holy One, Christ. The Athanasian Creed might have expressed it beautifully like this: "The Father is holy. The Son is holy. The Spirit is holy. And yet there are not three holies, but one holy."

Sanctification: Going It Alone?

It is clear that the holiness of the Blessed Holy Trinity is corporate and communal and essential. The old dogmatic adage *opera ad extra indivisa sunt* expresses this communal and essential unity. So what happens when this holiness is apprehended by the church *sola fide, sola gratia*? To be sure, each individual apprehends or lays hold of Christ and His righteousness and holiness for himself. But even here, I'm afraid our radically individualistic era has caused us to think of conversion and justification (and also sanctification) merely individualistically. Don't we think of conversion and evangelism today almost exclusively in terms of "personal witness"? Don't we think of them happening individual to individual? And if this "coming to Jesus" is viewed as normally occurring quite outside the confines of "church," does it surprise us that in the minds of many Lutherans "the church" is not essential to salvation?

After all, the largest "Lutheran Church in America" is indeed the "ILC" or "Invisible Lutheran Church." For census data show us that the number of people who describe themselves as "Lutheran" is far larger than the membership of the Lutheran church bodies combined. Baptism and preaching are, however, corporate acts. Walther states somewhere in a thesis that "conversion happens ordinarily [*ordentlicherweise*] through the preaching of called ministers, but extra-ordinarily through the witness of laymen." Where in our church would anyone view conversion in such a communal way today? In view of Rome's success with Rites of Christian Initiation of Adults (RCIA) — which requires no "conversion," faith, or commitment in its initial stages — it is clear (to me at least) that this individualism has really hampered us missiologically. But that is another matter.

Back to the New Testament. "Sanctification" is communal. "To the saints ... " is the plural salutation of the apostolic epistles. Whether holiness is described as imputed (*extra nos*) or inchoate, its communal, corporate connections are striking. In 1 Peter we read, "As obedient children, do not be conformed to the passions of your former ignorance, but as he who called you is holy, you also be holy in all your conduct, since it is written, 'You shall be holy, for I am holy.'" (1 Peter 1:14ff). Communal aspects mark the Petrine paranesis throughout. "Having purified your souls by your obedience to the truth for a sincere brotherly love, love one another earnestly from a pure heart. ... you yourselves like living stones are being built up as a spiritual house, to be a holy priesthood, to offer spiritual sacrifices acceptable to God through Jesus Christ. ... You are a chosen race, a royal priesthood, a holy nation" (1 Peter 1–2).

Paul's letters are filled with the corporate nature of sanctification. "Christ Jesus ... *to us* wisdom from God, righteousness and sanctification and redemption" (1 Cor. 1:30). "Do you not know that *you* [plural] are God's temple and that God's Spirit dwells in you [among *you* — plural!]? If anyone destroys God's temple, God will destroy him. For God's temple is holy, and *you* [plural] are that temple" (1 Cor. 3:16–17). The Corinthians are "holy" precisely as a unified body. The temple suffering destruction is not the individual here, but the church as a body, torn by disagreement or by individuals "going it alone." Each Christian is a temple of the Holy Spirit (1 Corinthians 7), but only because the Holy Spirit dwells in His church. Sexual immorality defiles not merely the one engaged in such activity (1 Cor. 6:18ff), but is a defilement of Christ's body (1 Cor. 6:15ff), the church.

The Communality of Pauline Sacramentology

Sacramental references throughout Paul's letters are communal, particularly as they express aspects of holiness, both with respect to the reception of the gift and the ethical consequences of the same. "Christ loved the church and gave himself up for her, that he might sanctify her, having cleansed her by the washing of water with the word, so that he might present the church to himself in splendor, without spot or wrinkle or any such thing, that she might be holy and without blemish ... For no one ever hated his own flesh, but nourishes and cherishes it, just as Christ does the church, because we are members of his body" (Eph. 5:25–30). In Romans 6 Paul asserts that the myriad individual baptisms across time and space are baptisms into one Christ. His resurrection brings resurrection for all the baptized. The significance of Christ's death and resurrection are described completely in communal terms. "For the death he died he died to sin, once for all, but the life he lives he lives to God" (Rom. 6:10). In Romans 12 — really an extension of the baptismal theology of chapter 6 — where Paul urges the Roman Christians to present their bodies as a "living sacrifice, holy and acceptable to God," this prefaces directly the communal nature of such sacrifices: "For as in one body we have many members, and the members do not all have the same function, so we, though many, are one body in Christ, and individually members one of another" (Rom. 12:4-5). Similar language, of course, peppers 1 Corinthians. Because the Lord's body and blood produce "one body" (1 Cor. 10:16–17), individual freedom has limits: whether to avoid outright idolatry or for the sake of the brother's weak conscience. The instruction on the Corinthian problem regarding the Lord's Supper offers Paul an extensive opportunity to define the consequences for the community created by communion. I, for one, believe that 1 Cor. 11:29 ("For anyone who eats and drinks without discerning the body eats and drinks judgment on himself") is at the very least a reference to the sacramental body of the Lord, but very likely is double entendre: failing to recognize Christ's sacramental body caused the Corinthians to despise the manifestation of Christ's body, the church. This and Holy Baptism gave Paul the opportunity to denounce Corinthian individualism. "For in one Spirit we were all baptized into one body" (1 Cor. 12:13). One Spirit via Baptism and Supper, into one body, bringing many and various gifts "for the common good" (v. 7).

Christology and the Corporate Life of Mercy

At this point, let me make something perfectly clear. I do not wish in any way to deny or undervalue the importance of both imputed (justification) and inchoate (sanctification) righteousness in the life of the individual believer. But in our dogmatic tradition (particularly the recent tradition), "sanctification" has been viewed as a purely individualistic matter. Much as I am struggling for clarity in this, I would like to assert that there is a corporate life of sanctification, if you will. As a body, we the church have been justified and sanctified. And as such a body, the New Testament would have us live out this justification and sanctification as a body, precisely in the practice of churchly, corporate works of charity and mercy.

The church's corporate life of mercy is first of all an extension of Christology. The corporate life of mercy of the church is driven primarily by Christology. Most significant is the fact that the very sending of the Son in mercy, through His incarnation, mandates the life of mercy of the church. Regardless of the referents of "the least of these my brethren" in Matthew 25, we see clearly that Christ expects charity of His followers. We see in the very life of Christ Himself a self-sacrificing love of the neighbor, be he believer or not. Saul's persecution of the church was viewed by Christ as an attack upon Himself, His very body ("Saul, Saul, why are you persecuting me?"). Surely the work of mercy of the church is the very extension, the very expression today of Christ's love demonstrated so readily during His days of humiliation on this earth. I do not wish to go so far as to call what Christians do today for the sick a "continuation of the healing ministry of Christ." That terminology tends to obscure the radically unique nature of Christ's three-year ministry as an unparalleled eschatological event. And the kingdom of God does not advance per se by care for the needy. The kingdom comes via the proclamation of the Gospel. Sanctification as good works, or much less the assistance of the needy, and much less so the transformation of the world into a just society, cannot be the goal of the church's life. The goal of the church's life is simply in being what she has been declared and ever more made in Christ: a people born and sustained of mercy, and therefore a merciful people (1 John 3:15ff).

I do assert that if we are faithful to our own Christology and ecclesiology, the sanctified life of the church must express itself in a corporate, communal life of mercy in the church. Dealing with "sanctification" merely as an individual phenomenon, and then leaving the church's life of mercy out of the locus of the church, has kept us from properly understanding, wrestling with, and defining theologically the church's diakonic life. It is simply not adequate to relegate Jesus' (and the New Testament's) continually demonstrated and proclaimed concern for physical well-being to the realm of the eschatological, such that it need be no concern of the church today.

Christ proclaimed His Gospel, and aided those in need. What does the church as His body continue to do in this world? Indeed, what does *Christ* continue to do in the world? I would love to take a close look at Acts 6, and at Paul's collections for the poor in Jerusalem, which shed great light on the nature of the church as a corporate and merciful body. But that task will have to be postponed so that we have time and space to learn something from the Reformer.

Luther on the Sacrament and the Communal Nature of the Church

In 1519 Luther produced the first longer presentation of his dogma of the Sacrament: *A Treatise Concerning the Blessed Sacrament of the Holy and True Body of Christ and Concerning the Brotherhoods*. The sacrifice of the mass, a topic which would soon consume a great deal of his time and effort, is not discussed positively or negatively. What is significant about this treatise is Luther's elaboration of Pauline themes regarding the nature of the church as the body of Christ as a result of the Sacrament. The Supper is a *synaxis* or *communio*, says Luther. To communicate is to take part in Christ and all His saints.[7] "All the saints, therefore, are members of Christ and of the Church, which is a spiritual and eternal city of God, and whoever is taken into this city is said to be received into the community of saints, and to be incorporated

---

[7] *Luther's Works*, American Edition, ed. Jaroslav Pelikan (St. Louis; Concordia, 1957), 22:10.

into Christ's spiritual body and made a member of him."[8] All the spiritual blessings of Christ and His saints are imparted in the Sacrament, says Luther, and so all the sufferings and sins of the one who partakes are imparted to Christ and the saints. "And thus love engenders love, and unites all." As Paul asserts in 1 Corinthians 12, because of this sacrament, "whether one member suffer, all members suffer with it ... even the smallest toe." Whoever does injury to the one who partakes of the Sacrament, does injury to Christ and all His saints. Likewise, whoever does him a kindness does it to Christ and His saints. "Whatsoever you have done to the least of My brethren, that you have done to Me" (Matt. 25:40). Luther proceeds to draw a clearer picture of the spiritual blessings of the Sacrament: "If any one be in despair, if he be distressed by his sinful conscience ... or have any other burden ... let him go joyfully to the sacrament of the altar and lay down his grief in the midst of the congregation and seek help from the entire company of the spiritual body ... " The Christian goes to the Sacrament to receive the sign (the unfortunate legacy of Augustinian language!) that "I have on my side Christ's righteousness, life and sufferings, with all holy angels and all the blessed in heaven, and all pious men on earth."

This view of the Sacrament has ethical ramifications: "you must in turn also share the misfortunes of the congregation ... "[9]

> There your heart must go out in love and devotion and learn that this sacrament is a sacrament of love, and that love and service are given you and you again must render love and service to Christ and His needy ones. You must feel with sorrow all the dishonor done to Christ in His holy Word, all the misery of Christendom, all the unjust suffering of the innocent, with which the world is everywhere filled to overflowing: You must fight, work, pray and, if you cannot do more, have heartfelt sympathy. That is bearing in your turn the misfortune and adversity of Christ and His saints. ... He said "This is my body ..." As though he said: I am the head, I will first give myself for you, will make your suffering and misfortune Mine own and bear it for you, that you in your turn may do the same for Me and for one another, have all things in common in Me and with Me and let this sacrament be unto you a sure token of this all, that you may not forget Me, but daily call to mind and admonish one another by what I have done for you and still am doing, that you may be strengthened thereby and also bear with one another.[10]

All afflictions, Luther contends, are to be "laid down in the midst of the congregation." Christ's blessings and our misfortunes are "one bread and loaf." Christ and the church are "one flesh and bone." Just as the bread is "changed into his true natural body and wine into his true natural blood, so truly are we also drawn and changed

---

[8] Ibid.

[9] Ibid., 13.

[10] Ibid., 14.

into the spiritual body, that is, into the fellowship of Christ and all saints, and put by this sacrament in possession of all the virtues and mercies of Christ and His saints."[11]

Luther laments the loss in his day of this meaning of the Sacrament:

> But in times past this sacrament was so properly used, and the people were taught to understand this fellowship so well, that they even gathered material food and goods in the church and there distributed them among those who were in need, as St. Paul writes. Of this we have a relic in the word "collect" which still remains in the mass, and means a general collection, just as a common fund is gathered to be given to the poor. That was the time when so many became martyrs and saints. There were few masses, but much strength and blessing resulted from the masses; Christians cared for one another, assisted one another, sympathized with one another, bore one another's burden and affliction. This has all disappeared, and there remain only the many masses and the many who receive this sacrament without in the least understanding or practicing what it signifies.[12]

> No, we must on our part make others' evil our own, if we desire Christ and His saints to make our evil their own; then will the fellowship be complete and justice be done to the Sacrament. For the Sacrament has no blessing and significance unless love grows daily and so changes a man that he is made one with all others.[13]

Conclusion

Sanctification is the living out of the life of justification every day. The doctrine of God, Christology, ecclesiology, and sacramentology of the New Testament portray this life of holiness as corporate, communal, and churchly. Luther's doctrine of the Supper in 1519 provides a powerful interpretation of the sacramental and communal nature of the church, and the church's life of love and mercy for the needy. According to the New Testament, and according to Luther, sanctification as the life of the Christian individual is only a part of the New Testament dogma of sanctification, and it is a distortion if its communal aspects are lost. The dogma of sanctification must embrace the corporate nature of the church as the body of Christ, and thus embrace, or rather be embraced by, ecclesiology. Just as there is a church because there is Christ, and just as she is one body, so also she has works of charity.

---

[11] Ibid., 19.

[12] Ibid., 16–17.

[13] Ibid., 17.

RESURRECTION
"His appearance was like lightning, and his clothing white as snow. And for fear of him the guards trembled and became like dead men." Matt. 28:3–4 c. 1510

One Loving God: Two Hands — Saving and Caring

A PAPER OF THE COMMISSION ON THEOLOGY AND INTER-CHURCH RELATIONS OF THE LUTHERAN CHURCH OF AUSTRALIA

1. The Mandate for Mercy

1.1. The God who is revealed in the Old Testament is a God who saves out of mercy. The Mosaic Law expects that the Israelites who have been rescued from slavery in Egypt will in turn show mercy to all who are in need: the poor and homeless, unprotected people like widows and orphans, all victims of injustice, those who cannot defend themselves. To come to the rescue of people in need and to advocate for them is a sign of belonging to God's people who have received mercy. To deny mercy is to place oneself outside of God's mercy.

See Ex. 23:1–9; 34:6–7; Deut. 10:18.

1.2. Because they were once aliens in Egypt, the Israelites are expected to show mercy also to strangers or foreigners who live among them. The law of Moses repeatedly insists that these outsiders be treated kindly and their rights protected. Strangers who are poor are to be shown the same compassion as the Hebrew poor. God's people are not free to choose those to whom they will show compassion. Animals, too, are to be shown due care.

See Ex. 22:21; 23:9; Lev. 19:33–34; Deut. 10:18–19; 24:19–20.

1.3. The Old Testament prophets repeatedly condemn those who exploit the needy instead of coming to their rescue. They speak hard words against the powerful and the rich who revel in injustice. The lack of mercy and justice in Israel eventually becomes a sign of its total unfaithfulness to God and a reason for God's judgment on the nation in the form of foreign occupation and exile.

See Is. 3:14–15; Jer. 5:26–28; Hos. 6:6; Amos 8:1–7.

1.4. Jesus of Nazareth teaches his disciples that to show mercy on those in need is to reflect the very nature of the heavenly Father. So, "Blessed are the merciful." It is natural to show special care to one's relatives, friends and fellow believers, but true compassion reaches out to anyone who is in need. It asks no questions and expects nothing in return. It requires no means test and crosses all ethnic, social and religious barriers.

See Luke 6:36; Matt. 5:7; Gal. 6:10; Luke 10:29–37.

1.5. Jesus not only teaches the kingdom of God's gracious rule. He also acts out the merciful claim of God on all people as He heals the sick, casts out demons, sides with those who are excluded or marginalised, and eats with outcasts. His is an inclusive ministry of mercy. He includes all who are in need and addresses all their needs: spiritual, material and physical. The standard cry of the needy in Jesus' presence is: "Lord, have mercy!" and He never fails to respond in compassion. He expects His followers to show equal compassion.

See Matt. 4:23–25; 9:27; 15:22; 17:15; 20:30; 25:31–40.

1.6. The Christian church is the fellowship of all who believe in Jesus as God's crucified and raised Messiah and who see in Him the long-awaited final sign of God's mercy on sinful humanity. Christians continually experience God's mercy in being forgiven and renewed for a life of service to others. The church exists not only to care for its members but also for the world. It exists to spread the good news of God's mercy in Jesus Christ through its proclamation and witness as well as through its acts of love and mercy.

See Luke 1:50, 54, 58, 72, 78; Eph. 2:4– 5; Titus 3; 5–1 Peter 1:3–4.

1.7. Following Jesus' teaching, writers of the New Testament repeatedly show that religious profession is without meaning if unaccompanied by acts of love and mercy. So the earliest believers shared their possessions and looked after their own needy, including widows and orphans. They appointed deacons to supervise this ministry of mercy. Mutual care and hospitality among Christians were especially important in the age of persecution, when believers were imprisoned and their property was confiscated. Yet believers were expected to "do good to all people."

See Matt. 9:13; 12:7; James 1:27; Acts 2:44; 4:32; 6:1–4; Heb. 10:32–34; Gal. 6:10; 1 John 3:17; Rom. 12:6–8.

1.8. The apostle Paul spent much time and effort collecting money for the poor Christians in Jerusalem. But every local assembly of Christians took up collections in worship to meet the needs of the poor. The Early Church could take up the challenge of extending its charity to the wider community once the threat of persecution was gone. So the church has a long tradition of serving the needy through direct gifts and through establishing institutions like hospitals and orphanages, and through its monasteries. In former centuries where no social services existed, the needy were often totally dependent on the church. Martin Luther also urged local Christian communities to set up "God's chest" (*Gotteskasten*) out of which material help could be given to the poor and needy.

See 2 Cor. 8; 9.

1.9. The church's ministry of mercy is a vital part of its existence. It cannot exist without worship (*leitourgia*) in which God speaks and acts in mercy and God's people respond in praise. It exists for witness to the Gospel (Greek, *martyria*). But the genuineness of both worship and witness must be called into question were there is no ministry of mercy (*diakonia*), where faith is without works. The *diaconic* work of the church is tangible evidence of its servant role in the world (*diakonos* is Greek for servant or waiter). Worship, witness and service belong together as functions of the church.

See James 2:26; Gal. 5:6b.

1.10. The triune God rules over all our entire world and entire universe but in doing so operates in two different ways. Lutherans speak of the kingdom of the right hand, the kingdom of grace or the realm of the church where God operates through the means of grace, through Word and Sacrament. We speak also of the kingdom of the left hand, the kingdom of law that is the realm of the state. On the one hand, the two kingdoms or ways in which God operates in this world have different purposes, carry out different functions and operate in different spheres and with different kinds of power. For this reason they need to be distinguished.

1.11. On the other hand, the kingdoms are connected and related to each other since God is the one ruler in both kingdoms. Though dealing with the world in different ways — with two different hands — there is one loving and caring God. A holistic approach to care ministry honours God as it points to the fullness of his own glory and of the life he offers to all, as well as reflecting the nature of Christ's own ministry. Programs of Christian care grow out of the right hand work of God in the church, but they exist in the world in partnership with governments and other charitable organisations.

1.12. It is important to stress that also non-Christians participate in God's ministry of mercy. The Lutheran teaching on vocation reminds us that we are all "masks" of God, God's agents in the world as we function as parents, people in government, citizens, workers, carers, entertainers or whatever. God runs the world through us; we are God's hands. In this we are asked to act justly and for the good of all. Non-Christians who have compassionate hearts can participate in the church's ministry of mercy as much as non-Christians can be recipients of its care.

1.13. Our affluent and materialistic Australian society creates its own needy who are easily forgotten in the rush for wealth and the good life. Every human being has value by virtue of being made in and reflecting the image of God the Creator. Meeting human need requires no justification, for to be compassionate is to be truly human. Christians know this because they know Jesus Christ, God's mercy in human form.

1.14. The church's ministry to all people must be holistic. To minister only to the spiritual needs of people or to seek to save their souls only is to deny the created unity of the human person and to fail to draw conclusions from the reality of the incarnation of Christ and His ministry in human history. It is to deny the importance of the body in God's plan from its creation to its resurrection. Spiritual needs cannot be divorced from physical, psychological and material needs. What is spiritual is not immaterial.

See Rom. 12:1; 1 Cor. 6:15,19; 15:42–49.

1.15. The church's ministry of mercy is truly Christian if it is inspired, motivated and empowered by the mercy of God in Christ, is inclusive, asks for nothing in return but the joy of serving those in need and thus brings glory to God who is the source of all "grace, mercy and truth." God calls the church to bring good news to the poor, to stand in solidarity with them, to give a voice to the voiceless and to pursue liberation for those who are oppressed. Like its Lord, the church ministers to the poor and needy.

See 1 Tim. 1:2; 2 Tim. 1:2; Titus 1:4; 2 John 3; Luke 4:18–19.

2. The Ministry of Mercy — Communal and Individual

2.1. The church's provision of care flows from its ministry of Word and Sacrament. Communal worship is the fundamental source from which Christian charity flows. The Gospel announces God's mercy in Christ on the whole of humanity and calls all believers to practice mercy. The sacraments of Baptism and the Eucharist further enact that mercy. The Post-Communion thanksgiving prayer expresses the close connection between faith and love when it asks "almighty God to strengthen us through this healing gift, in faith toward him and in love toward one another."

2.2. By showing love and support to those in need, through acts of caring, we make incarnate God's message of love in Christ. Such activity is to be seen as having its own integrity, as being a legitimate end in itself in the sense that it is offered graciously and unconditionally, that is, without strings attached or ulterior motives. It is offered simply because the neighbor is in need of the service and support.

2.3. Christians continue to live in the kingdom of the left hand, that is, in the world where God orders life according to laws of nature, reason, natural law and coercion. Clearly, most expressions of Christian care will come from individual Christians in their daily lives, as their faith is active in love while carrying out the specific duties of their various vocations. While the individual's ministry of mercy is carried out within the structures of society, it remains otherwise unstructured, responding to human need as it arises.

2.4. Christ's ministry serves as pattern for the Christian's life of service that grows out of love in response to God's love in Christ. It includes evangelism and welfare. Christians are called to use their God-given gifts to provide evangelistic witness and service. Since these are both legitimate ways of showing love and care, having their own integrity and purpose, they should be seen as complementing each other, not as standing in competition or isolation.

For Further Reading

Henry P. Hamann, *The Church's Responsibility for the World: A Study in Law and Gospel, in Theologia Crucis: Studies in Honour of Hermann Sasse*, ed H. P. Hamann, Lutheran Publishing House, Adelaide, 1975, 71–87.

Ian Rentsch, *The Servant Congregation*, resource material prepared for the LCA Board for Welfare Ministry, LCA Board for Congregational Life, December 1991.

Peter F. Lockwood, *By His Hands*, unpublished paper, March 1993.

Communion and Mission, a report from the Australian Lutheran-Roman Catholic Dialogue on the Theology of the Church, Openbook Publishers, Adelaide, 1995.

Reflection on the Two Kingdoms and Social Ethics, unpublished paper offered at the Commission on Theology and Inter-Church Relations, LCA, February 1996.

Lance G. Steicke, *The LCA and Social Justice. From the President*, in The Lutheran, 2 June 1997.

Ian Rentsch, *The Two Kingdoms and Lutheran Community Care*, in Lutheran *Theological Journal* 34:2, August 2000, 82–93.

Lutheran Community Care (Qld), Strategic Plan, 8 September 2000.

Noel E. Weiss, *Evangelism and Servant Ministry*, unpublished paper, March 2001.

Brian H. Schwarz, *Theological Foundations for Justice*, unpublished paper [n.d.].

David G. Stolz, *Comments on the Theology of the Two Kingdoms*, in Report to Victorian District Church Council. 2001.

M. E. Schild, *What's Lutheran in Lutheran Community Care?*, unpublished paper, 2001.

Ern T. Sabel, *What is the unique Lutheran Approach to Aged Care?* Paper presented at the National Aged Care Conference, May 2001.

Neal J. Nuske, *Doing Theology in the Marketplace of Lutheran Schooling, Lutheran Theological Journal* 35:2, August 2001, 51–64.

Constitution of Lutheran Community Care Australia.

Strategic Plan for Lutheran Community Care in Victoria and Tasmania, February 2001.

Friedemann H. Hebart, *Justification, personal identity and human dignity*, keynote address to SA District Convention of the Lutheran Church of Australia, 2001.

Dean Zweck, *Serving after the Service* (Inaugural Lecture, LS 2003), LTJ 2003.

Matthew C. Harrison, *The Church's Role of Mercy in the Community*, LTJ 2003.

Other Sources

Faith Active in Love: Human Care in the Church's Life. A report of the Commission on Theology and Church Relations of the Lutheran Church—Missouri Synod, February 1999.

Carter Lindberg, *Luther and Social Welfare*, in The Canada Lutheran, October 4 1993, 16–18.

Edmund Schlink, Civil and *Ecclesiastical Government*, in T*heology of the Lutheran Confessions*, tr. Paul F. Koehneke and Herbert J. A. Bouman, Muhlenberg, Philadelphia, 1961, 226–269.

(Edited by VCP for CTICR, 28 April 2003. Version two, edited January 2015)

Ref: VCP/CTICR/LCCA revised statement

CHRIST BEFORE PILATE
"And they bound him and led him away and delivered him over to Pilate the governor." Matt. 27:2 c.
1508–1509

WHAT DOES IT MEAN TO BE A LUTHERAN IN SOCIAL MINISTRY?

BY MATTHEW C. HARRISON

his paper was prepared for a think tank on Lutheran identity
In preparing for this event we were asked to reflect on two questions:

1. What are the unique Lutheran accents in Christian theology that inform our ministry of caring for the needs of our neighbors?

2. What are some of the issues and concerns that boards of Recognized Service Organizations (RSOs*) ought to pay attention to if they are to ensure that the ministry of the agency is faithful to the Gospel, the Lutheran tradition and their church?

These questions are indeed vital, as you well know. Jim Schlie of Lutheran Services in America's OASIS lists these traits of RSOs at risk:

1 . Limited guidance

2. Financial pressures

3. Isolation

4. Poor media interaction

5. Breakdown of extended entities

6. Board/staff conflict

7. Limited intra-staff communication

8. Lack of commitment to be a team

9. Loss of spiritual identity

---

*In the original writings, the author used Service Ministry Organization (SMO) to describe what is now called, Recognized Service Organization (RSO). The editor replaced all references to SMO with RSO.

By contrast, healthy RSO traits include:

1. Communicate/listen

2. Affirm and support

3. Respect and trust

4. Balanced interaction

5. Shared vision of ministry

6. Seek help with problems

7. Priority of service

8. Staff interaction valued

9. Knowledge of right/wrong

10. Integrate humor

11. Shared responsibilities

12. Honor traditions and rituals

As I examine these lists, I note that most indicators are in the ethical/relational/ managerial realm. While it is certainly possible for social service agencies to be successful in these left-hand kingdom matters quite without spiritual identity, I think we would all agree that clarity and health in Lutheran spiritual identity is in every way an advantage, indeed a catalyst toward all the healthy RSO traits. Thus there is a very fundamental and mainly pragmatic advantage for Lutheran RSOs to claim happily their Lutheran identity. However, beyond the pragmatic level and much more fundamental to the very being of the church and our agencies, is the divine vocation of the church to be in the world, serving the needy, bringing the balm of the Gospel for healing body and soul. Why does the Lutheran Church create and retain such agencies? Is there something deeper than command that propels the church in this area particularly when the church and RSO are healthy? Is there something more to the uniqueness of Lutheran social ministry than ethics, even uniquely Lutheran ethics? I believe there is.

I've decided to do something fairly radical in this paper. I have turned to a document Luther wrote in 1539. In "On the Councils and the Church," Luther laid out the fruit of his extensive study of the ecumenical councils of the early centuries of the church. He had given his hope of a "free, general" council to address the religious problems of the western church. Meanwhile, the Council of Trent (with its radical rejection of the Lutheran Reformation) was looming and indeed would begin in 1545, the year before his death. What attracted me to this document was the last section where Luther presented seven "marks" that enable a "poor confused person [to] tell where such Christian holy people are to be found in this world."[1] In his brief introductory excursus to this section of the document, the words of the "children's creed" (*sancta ecclesia catholica* — "holy catholic church") propel Luther into a discussion of Christian holiness.

> Because God sanctifies them, theygive and help wherever they can. Thus they do not lie, deceive, and backbite, but are kind, truthful, and trustworthy, and do whatever else the commandments of God prescribe. That is the work of the Holy Spirit, who sanctifies and also awakens the body to such a new life until it is perfected in the life beyond. That is what is called "Christian holiness."[2]

Yet precisely this lived holiness of Christians is not included by Luther among the marks of the church's existence. This is certainly consistent with the Augsburg Confession.[3] Ethics, then, are not uniquely fundamental to the Lutheran Church's being, nor, I would add, to the being of our social ministry organizations or more precisely to their being Lutheran RSOs. As undeniably important as all the managerial/ethical/relational aspects are for healthy Lutheran RSOs, it is not, cannot be, these that finally identify our institutions as Lutheran and Christian.

Our agencies are Lutheran and Christian to the extent that that which makes the church the church has free course in their midst. I do not assert that these institutions are simply "church." They are not. But I do believe our institutions of mercy are and must be "churchly." Thus, what defines the Lutheran church as such must have free course with these institutions. This is a very vital point. For there is widespread confusion within the Lutheran institution community on precisely what "Lutheran" or "Christian" identity means. Some argue that our institutions must cease to be concerned about being "Lutheran" (for that battle — allegedly — was fought and lost long ago). Now the task, so it is asserted, is for them to simply be "Christian." Yet, unfortunately, it would appear that those who would make this argument most intensely define "Christian" more in terms of ethics than anything else. But let me state something rather radical: Ethics are not what constitute, define or mark something as Christian. In fact, you may be surprised to learn that not one of Jesus' ethical assertions was unique to Him. Not "Love your enemy as yourself," not the idea of self-sacrifice, not "judge not lest ye be judged." None of it. All these ethical prescriptions are found in other ancient sources. Thus a Lutheran institution may well emphasize, advertise, enshrine in its mission statements ethical assertions about caring for all, equal value of all who receive care, etc. But these assertions (true as they

---

[1] *Martin Luther's Basic Theological Writings*, ed. Timothy Lull (Minneapolis: Fortress) 1999, p. 545. The treatise is also found in Luther's Works vol. 41.

[2] Op. cit. p. 543.

[3] Augsburg Confession Article VII, "The church is the assembly of saints in which the Gospel is taught purely and the sacraments are administered rightly." *The Book of Concord: The Confessions of the Evangelical Lutheran Church*, ed. Theodore G. Tappert (Philadelphia: Fortress), p. 32.

may or need be) are not what defines the institution as Lutheran or even Christian. What is "Lutheran" must be defined most simply and clearly by the Small Catechism. And what does the catechism purport to be? Luther simply defined it as a summary of the basics every Christian needed to know to be a Christian. The six chief parts are very simple: 1. Ten Commandments; 2. Creed; 3. Lord's Prayer; 4. Baptism; 5. Confession and Absolution; 6. Lord's Supper. An institution is Lutheran to the extent that these simple truths of the Christian faith are acknowledged and venerated.

Now some will retort that this is a ridiculous level of complexity. Really? All that is being requested is that we view our task from the perspectives of the very basics of the Christian faith! If an individual is unable or unwilling to consider what these basics mean for the church's life of mercy, then that individual is not qualified for leadership in a churchly institution. And if an institution is not concerned with these divine verities, it simply has no right to claim association with the Lutheran Church.

Others will retort that an attempt to evaluate churchly institutions on the basis of the catechism is a hopelessly sectarian endeavor in a day and age when many of our institutions do not employ a majority of Lutheran workers, may not have a Lutheran CEO, and certainly don't limit service to Lutheran clients. Yet I should like to respond: What precisely does "ecumenical" mean? If ecumenical means simply that the religious content and context of the institution's life is defined by tolerance, or a "lowest common denominator" approach to religious issues, then perhaps the argument of ecumenism would somehow justify such an approach. But I suggest something different. We might do well to define "ecumenical" as precisely what is clearly confessed as fundamental to the faith in the New Testament and what is most commonly shared throughout the Christian world. In this sense, nothing could be more ecumenical than the Small Catechism's six chief parts! Furthermore, it is the fundamental assertion of Lutheranism that salvation is found where Jesus' Word and His means of grace are present, or more precisely, to the very extent that these are present. Thus Lutheranism never asserted that salvation was to be found only within Lutheranism. And NO conservative Lutheran church body ever asserted anything different in this country. But Lutheranism has always asserted that the Lutheran confession of the faith is simply Christianity in the best sense of the word! Again, if a Lutheran cannot make this basic assertion, then I cannot conceive of how such an individual is capable of leading a Lutheran institution that takes the issue of its churchly identity seriously.

It is not only possible, but it is required, that convinced Lutherans lead agencies that serve the broad spectrum of humanity (far beyond the bounds of the Lutheran faith) with kindness, grace, love and conviction. Such conviction does not mean coercion. It does not mean forcing religious views upon others. It does not mean failing to respect the convictions of others, though they may be quite different from our own; people of conviction respect people of conviction. It does mean proudly bearing the name Lutheran. It does mean struggling constantly with the line between church and state and all the issues related to government funding. It does mean making difficult decisions about the faith life of the community of care and taking concrete steps to see that the basic truths of the catechism are not only not diminished in the life of the community, but promoted. This little paper is a work to consider these things.

What is "Lutheran?" We turn to Luther. After the previous diatribe about the catechism, I should perhaps have used the six chief parts to begin this section. But that part of this paper was written at a stage in the revisions where I had already completed much of what follows. In "On the Councils and the Church" Luther really provides us with the content of the catechism in a form perhaps even more helpful for the topic of this paper. It is, after all, a paper about Lutheran identity. Luther provides seven "marks" of the church in the document under consideration:

1. The Word of God

2. Baptism

3. Sacrament of the Altar

4. Office of the Keys

5. Office of the Ministry

6. Prayer and Worship

7. The Holy Cross

Regarding each of these we shall take note of a few furtive comments by Luther, and then make a few observations directly pertinent to our topic.

1. First, the holy Christian people are recognized by their possession of the Holy Word of God. To be sure, not all have it in equal measure, as St. Paul says [1 Cor. 3:12-14]. Some possess the Word in its complete purity, others do not. Those who have the pure Word are called those who "build on the foundation with gold, silver, and precious stones." Those who do not have it in its purity are the ones who "build on the foundation with wood, hay, and straw" and yet will be saved through fire. This is the principal item, and the holiest of holy possessions [Heiligthum, i.e., relic], by reason of which the Christian people are called holy; for God's Word is holy and sanctifies everything it touches; it is indeed the very holiness of God [Rom. 1:16]. This holy possession is the true holy possession, the true ointment that anoints unto life eternal. We are speaking of the external Word, preached orally by men like you and me, for this is what Christ left behind as an external sign, by which his church or his Christian people in the world should be recognized. It is sincerely believed and openly professed before the world, as Christ says, "Every one who acknowledges me before men, I also will acknowledge before my Father and his angels" [Matt. 10:32]. There are

417

many who know it in their hearts but do not profess it openly. The number of those who believe in and act by it is small. Wherever you hear or see this Word preached, believed, professed and lived, do not doubt that the true ecclesia sancta catholica, "A Christian holy people" must be there, even though their number is very small. For God's Word shall not return void [Is. 55]. For God's Word cannot be without God's people, and conversely, God's people cannot be without God's Word.

In Lutheran institutions, the Word of God has full sway. And this Word "sanctifies everything it touches." In Lutheran institutions, Lutheran Christianity and the Word of God are more than mere suppositions, quietly acted upon. Where the Word of God is, it is "preached, believed, professed and lived." This means that there is an intimate connection between pulpit/ congregation and RSO. Lutheran RSOs will take advantage of every opportunity to have Lutheran pastors proclaim the Word of God in their midst and provide every opportunity for the Word of God to influence every aspect of its program. Lutheran RSOs are very cautious about entering into funding arrangements that limit the free course of the Word of God and its ability to "sanctify" the entire program. Lutheran institutions will be at once ecumenical and confessional. While clearly and joyfully acknowledging the comforting truth that wherever the Word of God is found, it creates "a Christian holy people," Lutheran RSOs must clearly acknowledge the fact that the Word does not have full sway everywhere. Within reasonable bounds, often prescribed by law and respecting the rights of the individuals served, Lutheran institutions will expose clients to the clear balm of the precious and healing Gospel, as proclaimed and taught by Lutherans based upon the Bible as interpreted by the Small Catechism. Lutheran RSOs will be very selective and discerning regarding who is invited to provide religious counsel, instruction, worship and education to clients served. A Lutheran nursing home, for instance, may allow an evangelical or fundamentalist or Roman Catholic priest to conduct services. However, these will serve clients of that conviction, rather than being opportunities for "activity or entertainment" wheeling everyone available and unable to resist to "chapel." Respecting the rights of individual clients and their families, un-churched individuals will be exposed to the blessed Word of God whenever possible.

Among the staff, the Word of God must have full sway. This means that employing pious Lutherans as RSO leaders is critically important. This is crucial if an institution is going to have any real Lutheran ethos. By "Lutheran ethos" I mean a reality permeated with the Gospel and the doctrine of justification by grace through faith (not legalism or moralism, nor merely a post-modern-pseudodoctrine of justification, namely, absolute tolerance). A Lutheran ethos is baptismal (sins are confessed and forgiven). A Lutheran ethos is incarnational. Christ comes as a man in the flesh, speaking and acting for mercy, and we look toward the needs of our neighbor as the hands, feet and mouth of Christ. A Lutheran ethos delights in vocation. That is, each staff member is appreciated as a vital part of the whole, with a holy task, wholly sanctified by the Gospel. A Lutheran ethos respects the authority of the state and the legal rights of clients (particularly children). A CEO may have all the requisite abilities, board members may have all the necessary diversity of experience and insight, but to the extent they are not regularly exposed to Lutheran altars and pulpits and to the Word of God publicly and privately, to that extent the RSO jeopardizes its sacred mandate and task as a Lutheran Christian leaven for mercy in this world.

To the extent legally possible, Lutheran institutions will hire Lutheran professional and non-professional individuals. To the extent that is not possible, they will hire pious Christians, particularly those least prone to be uncomfortable with the larger Lutheran ethos. All staff will be encouraged to develop personal piety, and occasional time will be provided, before, during or after the workday, for serious meditation on the Word of God.

Lutheran RSOs will invite pastors and theologians to reflect upon crucial issues. Such people will be invited into the institutions to provide "in service" opportunities for growth, so that all employees (Lutheran and non-) may better understand the ethos of the institution and their role in that reality.

Lutheran RSOs will respect and use the array of medical, psychological and social professions as good First Article gifts of God. However, they will have clear ideas of the limits of such professions and professionals within the bounds of what is acceptable according to the Word of God (Holy Scripture).

> 2. God's people or the Christian holy people are recognized by the Holy Sacrament of baptism, whether it is taught, believed and administered correctly according to Christ's ordinance. That too is a public sign and a precious, holy possession by which God's people are sanctified. Wherever you see this sign you may know that the church, or the holy Christian people, must surely be present. Indeed, you should not even pay attention to who baptizes, for baptism does not belong to the baptizer, nor is it given to him, but it belongs to the baptized. It was ordained for him by God, and given to him by God.

Lutheran institutions of mercy will give Holy Baptism and its significance a place of high honor. Holy Baptism teaches us that all people are sinners and the sins of all have been paid for on Calvary. Because Christ died for all, all people (Christian or not) are valued as precious — worth the very blood of Christ. Holy Baptism connects believers with Christ, and by virtue of that, with one another (Lutheran or not). In Holy Baptism, we are in fact clothed with Christ, made one with Him (Romans 6) and made partakers of His death and resurrection. How we live with and treat one another now either reflects or denies this reality.

Baptism is the sacred foundation for the valuation of the myriad vocations at work within our RSOs. It is the basis for much of our workplace ethics. Management will go the extra mile to help Christian workers find their productive niche before terminating employment. Management will treat non-Christian employees with dignity, honor and love, as a witness to the blessed love of Christ, and to their own value as God's own creation. Clients will be treated with the value due Christ himself (by virtue of Baptism: "Whatsoever you have done ... " Matthew 25). Management will lead in exemplifying the cycle of the baptized life by participating in confession and absolution in their respective parishes, but they will also be examples to the staff of being willing to admit mistakes and to seek forgiveness from those wronged (so far as the wretched reality of potential litigation allows). Conflict management and resolution plans will employ explicitly Christian elements, and as far as possible, be based upon the reality of Holy Baptism, and return to it confession and absolution.

Lutheran institutions will acknowledge and respect the necessity of Holy Baptism for eternal life ("Unless one is born of water and the Spirit, he cannot enter the kingdom of God." John 5), and its unsurpassed consolation for children, the downtrodden and the needy. Lutheran institutions of mercy will provide every opportunity and encouragement (within the reasonable bounds of civil law) for individuals to be baptized, remembering always that people follow conviction, not coercion. Where appropriate, all staff (particularly health and critical care staff) will be familiar with the rite of emergency Baptism provided in the hymnal and catechism, as well as procedure to contact appropriate clergy. Lutheran RSOs will develop and maintain open and cordial professional relationships with area Lutheran and non-Lutheran clergy, happy to respond to patient/client inquiry regarding baptism and/or instruction in the faith. Priority will be given to Lutheranism in cases where the individual has no preferred church membership.

Insofar as the "priesthood of the baptized" flows from the font, and insofar as is allowable by circumstance, type of care, etc., those served will be encouraged to exercise this spiritual priesthood in service to each other — however that service may look. ("Present your bodies as a living sacrifice" Rom. 12:1) Every effort will be made to connect local Christians, especially local Lutheran Christians, with the work of mercy and care and its recipients, as a reflection of the reality of the body of Christ brought about in Holy Baptism.

> 3. God's people, or Christian holy people, are recognized by the holy sacrament of the altar, wherever it is rightly administered, believed and received, according to Christ's institution. This too is a pubic sign and a precious, holy possession left behind by Christ by which His people are sanctified so that they also exercise themselves in faith and openly confess that they are Christian, just as they do with the Word and with baptism. In addition, the question of whether you are male or female, young or old, need not be argued — just as it matters little in baptism and the preached Word. It is enough that you are consecrated and anointed with the sublime

and holy chrism of God, with the Word of God, with baptism, and also this sacrament; then you are anointed highly and gloriously enough and sufficiently vested with priestly garments. Wherever you see this sacrament properly administered there you may be assured of the presence of God's people. For, as was said above of the Word, wherever God's Word is, there the church must be; likewise, wherever baptism and the sacrament are, God's people must be, and vice versa. No others have, give, practice, use and confess these holy possessions save God's people alone.

There is no more powerful source and motivation for Lutheran churches to be involved in the work of mercy and care than the Sacrament of the Altar. Thus Luther writes:

> This fellowship is of such a nature that all the spiritual possessions of Christ and His saints are imparted and communicated to him who receives this sacrament; again, all his sufferings and sins are communicated to them, and thus love engenders love and unites all ... the members have a care for one another; whether one member suffer, all the members suffer with it (Treatise on the Blessed Sac., Phil. Ed. II, p. 1).

> In this sacrament, therefore, God Himself gives through the priest a sure sign to man, to show that, in like manner, he shall be united with Christ and His saints and have all things in common with them; that Christ's sufferings and life shall be his own, together with the lives and sufferings of all the saints, so that whoever does him an injury does injury to Christ and all the saints, as he says by the prophet, "He that toucheth you toucheth the apple of My eye"; and on the other hand, whoever does a kindness does it to Christ and all His Saints, as He says, "What you have done unto one of the least of these My brethren, that ye have done unto Me" (Treatise on the Blessed Sac., p. 12).

Lutheran congregations will be encouraged and taught to view their respective RSOs as extensions of the life drawn from their altars. Lutheran RSOs will view themselves as such extensions of Christ's love. Parishes will be regularly invited to remember the RSOs in prayer at the celebration of Eucharist and to remember the weak, the downtrodden, the needy, the addicted, etc. Wherever possible, Lutheran RSOs will be located near a Lutheran congregation, and staff be invited for weekday Eucharist before or after work hours. Lutheran institutions will respect the boundaries of altar fellowship with respect to those communions that place limits upon participation in the Eucharist.

Like Holy Baptism, Lutheran theology finds in the Holy Supper the greatest motivation for merciful service of the fellow Lutheran Christian, Christian in general, and non-Christian. The Lord's very body and blood unites the participant with all who receive the same body and blood at altars where this reality is confessed and

421

believed. Thus partaking, such Christians become ever more what they have received, the Body of Christ. The forgiveness, grace and mercy received at the altar is the sweetest Gospel motivation to live toward others in forgiveness, grace and mercy.

4. God's people or holy Christians are recognized by the office of the keys exercised publicly. That is, as Christ decrees in Matthew 18 [15-20], if a Christian sins, he should be reproved; and if he does not mend his ways, he should be bound in his sin and cast out. That is the office of the keys. Now the use of the keys is twofold, public and private. There are some people with consciences so tender and despairing that even if they have not been publicly condemned, they cannot find comfort until they have been individually absolved by the pastor. On the other hand, there are also some who are so obdurate that they neither recant in their heart and want their sins forgiven individually by the pastor, nor desist from their sins. Therefore the keys must be used differently publicly and privately. Now where you see sins forgiven or reproved in some persons, be it publicly or privately, you may know that God's people are there. If God's people are not there, the keys are not there either; and if the keys are not present for Christ, God's people are not present.

In Lutheran RSOs, despite the mountains of regulation, legal concerns, etc., the Gospel must reign. Amid the myriad lefthand responsibilities, the Gospel and Christ's forgiveness must not be suppressed. Lutheran RSO leaders and staff will have a deep sense of their own sinfulness and find great consolation in confession and absolution, participating in it weekly in their own parishes. To the extent that our institutions are in fact Lutheran and Christian, they will make use of confession and absolution in periods of interpersonal difficulty. As much as possible, they will use confession and absolution even in cases where separation has been necessary. Because sin is a reality in all of our lives and thus in our institutional lives, the remedy for sin must also be turned loose and found within these institutions and among those they serve. Medical and psychological experts, physical therapists, indeed all who deal with individual and family matters, will realize that while the assistance they provide is of fundamental benefit to those in need, the crown of such assistance is to provide hurting individuals with the opportunity for self evaluation, recognition of sin and absolution, whether spoken privately by a staff professional, and/or in directing such individuals to pastoral care. If our concern for individuals is indeed holistic, we must return, where it has waned, to a concern for spiritual wholeness.

5. The church is recognized externally by the fact that it consecrates or calls ministers, or has offices that it is to administer. There must be bishops, pastors or preachers who publicly and privately give, administer and use the aforementioned four things that are holy possessions in behalf of and in the name of the church, or rather by reason of their institution by Christ,

as St. Paul states in Eph. 4:8, "He received gifts among men." The people as a whole cannot do these things, but must entrust or have them entrusted to one person. Otherwise, what would happen if everyone wanted to speak or administer, and no one wanted to give way to the other? Wherever you see this done, be assured that God's people, the holy Christian people, are present.

In Lutheran institutions, clergy are highly respected and valued. The proper and natural love and respect that so often develops over the period of service must always be seen in light of the office that the clergy bear. That office is a Gospel office, given to dispense the gifts that bring eternal life. Lutheran clergy will be expected to celebrate the sacrament often in the institution. Clergy are integral to the institution's mission to the extent that the aforementioned "marks" are integral to the institution. Institutions will make every effort to employ Lutheran clergy who have additional expertise in spiritual care or the myriad of possible diakonic vocations. Not unlike the seven "deacons" who were ordained to care for the need of the widows in Acts 6, so also it is quite appropriate for clergy to be called to administrative and diakonic tasks within an institution. Such tasks (like the deacons of Acts 6) may well combine aspects of the standard office of the ministry (preaching the Word, administering the means of grace) with diakonic tasks. Lutheran institutions will value theological training and insight, and make every effort to employ clergy with particular diakonic gifts. They will provide every opportunity for clergy to gain such training and skills that would allow for leadership in the diakonic realm. It concerns me that the number of clergy who are currently leading Lutheran RSOs is ever declining. The complexities — particularly financial, legal and regulatory — have driven many institutions to hire business experts for CEO positions. Where this is the case, the organization structure needs to be adjusted so that clear guidance can be had regarding the issues of Lutheran ethos. As a church body, we must make every effort to provide opportunities for business professionals to acquire a theological education and for clergy to be prepared to administer complex institutions.

> 6. The holy Christian people are externally recognized by prayer, public praise and thanksgiving to God. Where you see and hear the Lord's Prayer prayed and taught; or psalms or other spiritual songs sung, in accordance with the Word of God and the true faith; also the creed, the Ten Commandments, and the Catechism used in public, you may rest assured that a holy Christian people of God are present. For prayer too is one of the precious holy possessions whereby everything is sanctified, as St. Paul says [1 Tim. 4:5].

Lutheran institutions will have vibrant connections to, or be in and of themselves, worshiping communities. A very unfortunate byproduct of our currently boomer-driven society is that traditional forms and institutions tend to be rejected by boomers (I'm one of them!), who are quite certain that such forms are of little value. I served a parish in Indiana's poorest census tract for six years. That parish enjoyed daily chapel in its sanctuary. Matins was chanted four days a week, and the Lord's Supper was celebrated every Wednesday by the entire community. The parochial school of 100-plus children and teachers gathered every morning. The regular pattern of worship followed the Church Year closely. The appropriate texts were always used. The children had memorized dozens of hymns, Psalms, introits, etc. The catechism was recited every Tuesday and a homily given on the catechism of the day. The Bible story explaining that bit of the catechism was the text for Tuesdays. The children later learned to sing morning prayer. They knew two different versions of the "*Te Deum*" by heart. The pastors vested daily. A visit by a Synod official on one occasion brought pointed derision. He was an older boomer. By comparison, the chapel life of the Synod headquarters is stark. These 100 or so inner-city black children, more than half from broken homes, thrived on a daily spiritual fare with a good 10 times the complexity, depth and substance of that of the headquarters.

Why do I make this point? Much of the benefit of the churchly rhythm of prayer, liturgy and worship, including traditional texts, is missed by the generation that demographics currently put in most institutional leadership positions. By contrast, many of those who are weak and suffering and need the services of Lutheran institutions do not share this aversion (particularly the elderly and many others suffering the chaos of urban existence, etc.). Our institutions must become places of rich reliance on Christian texts.

Not long ago I visited a state-of-the-art preschool operated by a Lutheran RSO. It was impressive in every way, except one. There was not a single Christian book or piece of art in the entire facility. I could not "rest assured that a holy Christian people of God were present."

> 7. The Holy Christian people are externally recognized by the holy possession of the sacred cross. They must endure every misfortune and persecution, all kinds of trials and evil from the devil, the world and the flesh (as the Lord's Prayer indicates) by inward sadness, timidity, fear, outward poverty, contempt, illness and weakness in order to become like their head, Christ. And the only reason they must suffer is that they steadfastly adhere to Christ and God's Word, enduring this for the sake of Christ, Matthew 5, "Blessed are you when men persecute you on my account." They must be pious, quiet, obedient and prepared to serve the government and everybody with life and goods, doing no one any harm. No people on earth have to endure such bitter hate. This too is a holy possession whereby the Holy Spirit not only sanctifies His people, but also blesses them.

In short, being Lutheran in social ministry means bearing the cross. This is particularly so in the current budget climate. Yet as Lutheran institutions do their best to act in faith (with wisdom and care), they can be assured that indeed, "all things work together for good." More than that, as RSOs struggle with funding, state regulations, grantors, constituents, congregations, denominational requirements and a myriad of other challenges, which often bring "inward sadness, timidity, fear, outward poverty, contempt, illness and weakness," these all — when suffered in faith in Christ — drive us to Christ and His Word for consolation and strength. And in this very struggle RSOs find that they become much more like, and able to identify with, the weak whom they serve, and even more importantly, with Christ, whom they serve in and through the weak (Matthew 25).

I pray these thoughts are of some value. There are many generalizations. I fully realize the vast array of circumstances our RSOs face is enormous. There is no "one size fits all" approach. But what I desire is that, by thinking about such things, the RSO leaders will give more penetrating thought to, and consideration of, just what it means to be a Lutheran Recognized Service Organization.

BIRTH OF MARY
A mother in labor, typical of a sixteenth century Nuremberg household, surrounded by willing gossips. c. 1503

426

DISASTER RESPONSE HYMN RESOURCES

BY MICHAEL MEYER

"If one member suffers, all suffer together" (1 Cor. 12:26). Think for a moment of a stubbed toe. The entire body feels the pain and springs into action in order to alleviate the condition. The other foot quickly bears the weight, while the back stoops over and the hands reach down to grasp and protect from further pain. Ears twitch and the face contorts itself in ways previously not thought possible. All the while, the mouth breaks forth in glorious song, singing the praises of a God who gives and takes away, who is good in spite of such pain and suffering. Maybe not that last part.

And yet this is precisely the struggle of every Christian who endures some kind of suffering. "No human being can tame the tongue" (James 3:8) because it is led to vocalize the doubts of the heart, as the Old Adam seeks to usurp the voice and declare God as 'not good.' The entire body suffers at the smallest pinprick, and the mouth is tempted to curse and swear rather than bless and praise. Yet the author of James says "these things ought not to be so" (3:10). Instead, he alludes to the bit and bridle of a horse, and the rudder of a boat. They serve to guide the horse and the boat in the right direction.

In a similar manner, the liturgy and hymns of the Church serve as bit and bridle for the tongue. Of course, there are countless other (and better!) reasons for the regular use of the liturgy and the singing of good hymns. But in time of suffering and disaster, when our mouths would rather question, blame and curse, the Church's liturgy and hymns give words of consolation, comfort, and (yes!) even praise. The Church may not have all the answers as to why this particular suffering is taking place (according to the hidden will of God), but she knows that the love of God in Christ Jesus our Lord cannot be taken away by fire or flood, wind or rain, or even death itself.

Thus, in the midst of disaster, the voice of the Church speaks the one thing she's certain of: true comfort and healing come through Christ. Dietrich Bonhoeffer writes that this voice of the Church is heard in singing together. "It is not you that sings, it is the Church that is singing, and you, as a member of the Church, may share in its

427

song. Thus all singing together … see[s] our little company as a member of the great Christian Church on earth" (Life Together, 61).

Certainly, there are a number of wonderful hymns in our Lutheran heritage that are accessible to congregations and well suited for a time of suffering. Luther writes "In the very midst of life snares of death surround us; who shall help us in the strife lest the foe confound us? Thou only Lord, Thou only" (LSB #755). In a similar fashion, Gerhardt adds to the conversation, "Why should cross and trial grieve me? Christ is near with His cheer; never will He leave me" (LSB #756). These are poignant words that point suffering people, not to the despair of disaster, but to Christ. These hymns, and others like them, bridle the tongue and give the very words that the New Adam longs to speak.

Yet when given the opportunity, the Church continues to search for new expressions of the same faith, even as she seeks to raise up new musicians and hymn writers for the next generation — for the edification of Christ's holy people, giving them faithful and clear words to speak in the midst of the muddled circumstances of this life. One example of this is "There Is a Time for Everything"(LSB #762). It was written in the context of a culture that would forever remember the terrorist attacks of September 11th, 2001. It is a beautiful hymn that can be sung at any time of the year, in spite of its being formed in response to such a terrible event.

Likewise, in the summer of 2014, LCMS Disaster Response commissioned a 'Disaster Response Hymn-Writing Contest.' The intent was to broaden the resources available to the church in a time of suffering — not just for those who are immediately enduring the suffering, but also for those who may be thousands of miles away, and yet suffer with them in the Body of Christ.

The result of the 'contest' surprised everyone involved in the process. Nearly 130 entries were received, six of which were seen as 'commendable.' They are presented here (and elsewhere) for the good of the church, to be used in season, and out of season, free of charge to the LCMS.

JOACHIM AND ANNA EMBRACING UNDER THE GOLDEN GATE

The Immaculate Conception, which according to legend took place at the Golden Gate, teaches that Mary was conceived sinless. This is the only woodcut in the series with Dürer's monogram and date. c.1509.

Lord and Savior, Do You Hear Us

1 Lord and Sav - ior, do You hear us? Have You turned Your
2 Then, Your Fa - ther's will ac - com-plished, And Your blood for
3 When dis - tress and trou - ble grieve us, Bring-ing ill - ness,
4 In the world, Lord, You have told us There is trou - ble

face a - way? Do You know the pain we suf - fer And the
sin - ners shed, To Your Fa - ther's hands com - mit - ted, You, dear
storm, or loss, May we, pa - tient - ly en - dur - ing, Bear with
to en - dure. Fill our doubt-ing hearts with cour - age, For in

fear we face each day? Yet You, Lord, have known our sor - row;
Sav - ior, bowed Your head. Dy - ing, trust - ing in Your Fa - ther,
faith - ful - ness the cross. As we, Lord, re - ceive Your mer - cy,
You our hope is sure. As with Your dis - ci - ples sail - ing

You have shared our grief and pain. As the Lamb for
Know-ing You would con - quer death, You gave up Your
May we then Your mer - cy share, Giv - ing com - fort,
On the wind - y, storm-tossed sea, You a - woke and

Text: Carol Geisler, b. 1953. Copyright ©2015 Carol Geisler.
    All rights reserved. Permission is given to LCMS
    congregations to duplicate these pages for congregational use.
Tune: Georg G. Boltze, 18th cent. Public domain.
Setting: *The Lutheran Hymnal*, 1941. Public domain.

LASSET UNS MIT JESU ZIEHEN
87 87 877 877

sin - ners slain, You cried out in si - lent dark-ness, Hang-ing
fi - nal breath. May we al - so, though un - see - ing, Trust our
hope, and care. For this work may we be nour-ished, As our
heard their plea, Still - ing storm and wind and wa - ter, Bid our

from the dread-ful tree: "Why have You for - sak - en Me?"
Fa - ther to ful - fill Ev - 'ry pur - pose of His will.
hearts to love are stirred, By Your Sup - per and Your Word.
fear and sor - row cease With Your qui - et Word of peace.

"Lord and Savior, Do You Hear Us"

"Have You turned Your face away?" These are the thoughts of many who suffer. How could God have let something so terrible happen? The presumed, yet erroneous, answer is that He does not care about us. The truth is that Christ intimately knows all about abandonment and suffering. "Yet You, Lord, have known our sorrow; You have shared our grief and pain. As the Lamb for sinners slain, You cried out in silent darkness."

At the same time, our Lord not only suffers with us, but He has the power to save and give peace to our troubled hearts. "As with Your disciples sailing on the windy, storm-tossed sea, You awoke and heard their plea, stilling storm and wind and water, bid our fear and sorrow cease with Your quiet Word of peace." This close connection to Jesus calming the storm also makes this hymn a particularly good selection for Proper 7 (Series B), Epiphany 4 (One-Year Series), when this Gospel reading is used, or throughout the season of Lent.

In Piercing Grief and Deep Distress

Alternate tune: LORD OF LIFE

Text: Wilfred L. Karsten, b. 1957. Copyright ©2015 Wilfred L. Karsten.
   All rights reserved. Permission is given to LCMS
   congregations to duplicate these pages for congregational use.
Music: English; adapt. and harm. Ralph Vaughan Williams, 1872-1958.
Public domain.

KINGSFOLD
C M D

Does He de - light in pain? De - feat - ed, is there
Close by our side He stands, For - giv - ing doubts and
The fi - nal foe to slay; So our life's strug - gle
Our test - ed faith is fed: A liv - ing hope re -

vic - to - ry? In loss is there yet gain?
quell - ing fears. Our times are in His hands.
we can name A vic - tim of the fray.
newed with zeal, For Je - sus is our Head.

5 In piercing grief and deep distress
   God's people see the need.
While serving neighbors they profess
   Their faith in word and deed.
In life together they will share
   A fellowship divine.
Each other's burdens they will bear,
   God's light of mercy shine.

△ 6 In piercing grief and deep distress
   The song will still be sung.
The melody of bitterness
   Is absent from our tongue.
To Father, Son, and Spirit raise
   A joyous, thankful strain,
For even in the darkest days
   Our God will ever reign.

"In Piercing Grief and Deep Distress"

"Fierce doubts and questions rise." Yet in all things, we know that God is working in the midst of disaster to bring about His good and gracious will. Joseph confessed this truth in regards to his brothers who sold him into slavery: "As for you, you meant evil against me, but God meant it for good" (Gen. 50:20a). And while we may never see or understand these things, that doesn't make them less true. Some things, however, can be seen, such as the many acts of mercy (διακονια) that the church often engages in after a disaster. "Each other's burdens they will bear, God's light of mercy shine."

Possible liturgical uses for this hymn include Proper 3 (Series C), Proper 19 (Series A) or Trinity 4 (One-Year Series) when the account of Joseph and his brothers is heard. It could also be substituted for a hymn in the "Society" section of *LSB* or the "Hope and Comfort" section.

God of Mercy, God of Comfort

1 God of mer - cy, God of com - fort, An - swer now Your
2 May com - pas - sion from Christ's Bod - y Now en - cir - cle
3 When one hurts, we hurt to - geth - er; Lord, u - nite our
4 Help them, Lord, to face the fu - ture Know-ing that Your

chil-dren's cries Who are reel - ing from dis - as - ter And can
all who grieve. May our pres-ence soothe and strength-en All who
hearts in prayer. Keep all vic - tims whol - ly trust - ing, Con - fi -
love sur - vives. Walk be - side them, give them cour - age, Help them

scarce-ly raise their eyes. Lift their bur - dens, ease their pain;
strug - gle to be - lieve That Your wis - dom will not end,
dent that You are there. May Your heal - ing touch be sent
to re - build their lives. On - ly strong foun - da - tions last

Tune: Johann Balthasar König, 1691-1758. Public domain.   DER AM KREUZ
Setting: *The Lutheran Hymnal*, 1941. Public domain.   87 87 77 88

Be their sun - shine af - ter rain. Let their trust be
Though their hearts with doubt con - tend. Dry their tears, O
Through Your Word and Sac - ra - ment. Move our hands and
When de - struc - tive storms are past. Je - sus Christ, be

not for - sak - en, That their faith re - mains un - shak - en.
Man of sor - rows, Grant them hope for bright to - mor - rows.
feet for car - ing, For the love of Je - sus shar - ing.
their foun - da - tion, Life and health and res - to - ra - tion.

"God of Mercy, God of Comfort"

A common prayer during a time of suffering is one which asks for comfort. Related to this request is the prayer for strength and endurance. This hymn is a prayer for the suffering, that God would "lift their burdens, [and] ease their pain." It also illustrates nicely the understanding that we are all one in Christ's Body, and when one part suffers, we all suffer with it. Furthermore, our Lord, the "man of sorrows" (Is. 53:3) walks with us all the way. Our future is in His hands, and all those who put their trust in Him will not be ashamed, for He is the cornerstone.

This hymn can be appropriately used on days when Matt. 11:25-30 is read, such as Proper 9 (Series A), or the Feast of St. Matthias on Feb. 24th.

Your Church on Earth Is Crying

1 Your Church on earth is cry - ing, "How long, O Lord, how long?"
2 *Insert appropriate stanza.*
3 Yet Je - sus Christ, a - noint - ed, En - dured our ag - o - ny
4 The Church as one is serv - ing With each new bur - den shared.

Your pre-cious ones are dy - ing; The en - e - my is strong.

The mo-ment God ap - point - ed To end sins's tyr - an - ny.
For love with-out re - serv - ing, The hands and feet pre - pared.

Re - deem-er, we are yearn - ing To see Your ho - ly face.

The prom-ise long a - wait - ed: Ful - filled by God's own Son,
Through al - tar, font, and Spir - it, We join the an - cient song.

We trust in Your re - turn - ing And Your un - fail - ing grace.

His chil - dren re - in - stat - ed The vic - to - ry is won.
The crown we will in - her - it, No more to cry, "How long?"

Text: Lisa M. Clark, b. 1982. Copyright ©2015 Concordia Publishing House.
Tune: Alexander C. Ewing, 1830-95. Public domain.
Setting: *Hymns Ancient and Modern*, 1861. Public domain.

EWING
76 76 D

Natural Disaster

5 The mountains break and crumble;
    The wind and waves rage on.
 In darkened fear we stumble;
    Security is gone.
 O Father of creation,
    Who set in place each stone,
 Provide the consolation
    We find in You alone.

Violence

6 Our treasures left to plunder,
    We face the fearsome sword.
 Our walls are torn asunder;
    Our dwelling place abhorred.
 Restore our sure foundation;
    Come bare Your mighty arm.
 O Rock of our salvation,
    Give peace from dread alarm.

Loss of Life

7 Our spirits ache with sorrow,
    Belovèd life is lost.
 Bereft of new tomorrow,
    We stagger at the cost.
 Speak to our souls, O Savior,
    "Take heart; I give you life.
 I won the Father's favor
    And rescued you from strife."

Persecution

8 The saints beneath the altar
    Cry out, "O Lord, how long?"
 In faith, they did not falter
    And joined the martyr throng.
 The number ever growing—
    O Father, grant us rest!
 When sainted blood is flowing,
    Give strength to stand the test.

"Your Church on Earth Is Crying"

The strength of the enemy is frightening to contemplate. Left alone, we would crumble under the weight of oppression, and fear would completely overtake us. Yet we are not alone, and have not been sent out without being fitted for war. The armor of God clothes us and the sword of the Spirit is in our hands. We stand in His truth and are protected by His grace. The battle cry, that ancient song of old, is borne on the lips of the faithful once more as we sing the praise of Him who died, and we await His return to put an end to all discord and strife. Come quickly, Lord Jesus.

This hymn is particularly suited for a number of disasters and conveniently has verses that can be used for times of 1)natural disaster, 2) violence, 3) loss of life, and 4) persecution. It may also be appropriate for All Saints' Day, or Proper 17 (Series B — Epistle) when the armor of God is described. It could also be substituted for a hymn in the "Church Militant" section of *LSB*.

In Days of Grief or Storm and Loss

1 In days of grief or storm and loss, Help us, dear
2 Your Bod - y giv'n and Blood once shed, By these our
3 As once our suf - f'ring, Lord, You shared And by the
4 Though sor - row's end we can - not see, Yet by Your

Lord, look to Your cross That, shield - ed by Your
wea - ry faith is fed; In faint - ing hearts Your
cross Your love de - clared, Move us, Your Bod - y,
Spir - it, Lord, may we En - dure with pa - tience

nail - marked hand, We in Your grace will safe - ly stand.
Word takes root, With hope and peace its liv - ing fruit.
that we may In word and deed Your love dis - play.
troub - led days And of - fer hum - ble trust as praise.

Text: Carol Geisler, b. 1953. Copyright ©2015 Carol Geisler.
 All rights reserved. Permission is given to LCMS
 congregations to duplicate these pages for congregational use.
Tune: Thomas Tallis, c. 1505-85. Public domain.
Setting: *The Lutheran Hymnal*, 1941. Public domain.

TALLIS' CANON
L M

"In Days of Grief or Storm and Loss"

This is perhaps the simplest of the six hymns here presented. In all things, O Lord, help us to look to Your cross, and "Give to us, Your Servants, that peach which the world cannot give … [and we,] being defended from the fear of our enemies, may live in peace and quietness" (Collect for Peace, Vespers and Evening Prayer). How does God give this peace? Through Word and Sacrament: "Your Body giv'n and Blood once shed, by these our weary faith is fed; in fainting hearts Your Word takes root, with hope and peace its living fruit."

This hymn is particularly suited for use by the entire congregation, including young children. Liturgically, it could be used on Lent 4 (Series B — Gospel), Holy Cross Day (Old Testament), or the Sixth Sunday of Easter (One-Year Series — Old Testament).

Scourging
"Then Pilate took Jesus and flogged him." John 19:1 c. 1509

The Cross of Christ Gives Light and Life

1 The cross of Christ gives light and life Mid tu - mult,
2 From depths of woe we cry to You; Our bro - ken
3 When doubt and dark - ness dim our world, And clouds of
4 Up - on the cross You bore the weight Of sin and

tem - pest, stress, and strife. Though heav - y cross - es
hearts, O Lord, re - new. You know our pain, our
cha - os round us swirl, When life is torn by
death, of shame and hate. You take our grief and

now we bear, In Je - sus' cross we glad - ly share.
bleak de - spair; Lord, quick - ly come, Lord, hear our prayer.
sin and hell, By Your own cross You make us well.
deep - est fear; Your cross gives hope and heal - ing here.

5 Come now with grace and peace divine,
In water, Word, in bread and wine.
Into our midst Your Spirit send;
Give faith and comfort to the end.

6 Lord, fix our eyes on Your dear Son,
Who, by the cross, the vict'ry won;
At last, then bring us by Your grace
Where we may see you face to face.

ROCKINGHAM OLD
L M

"The Cross of Christ Gives Light and Life"

"When life is torn by sin and hell, by Your own cross You make us well." Our sin and the visible results of the fall are great in this world. Yet our Lord and His mercy are greater still, for His power is made known in weakness. "For the sake of Christ, then, I am content with weaknesses, insults, hardships, persecutions, and calamities. For when I am weak, then I am strong" (2 Cor. 12:10). This 'strength' is the result of trusting in someone outside of ourselves, for it is "No longer I who live, but Christ who lives in me" (Gal. 2:20). So: "Come now with grace and peace divine, in water, Word, in bread and wine. Into our midst Your Spirit send; give faith and comfort to the end."

This hymn is appropriate for use during the reception of the Lord's Supper. It could also be used on Proper 9 (Series B — Epistle), Proper 6 (Series C — Epistle), or Sexagesima (One-Year Series — Epistle).

Conclusion

It is our hope that these hymns provide another way for the Church to remember our brothers and sisters in Christ who are suffering; to pray for them in our corporate worship life, and, Lord willing, to stir us up to works of love and mercy.

In the end, the entire Church can (and should) sing these wonderful new hymns, confessing the truth that God is at work in the midst of disaster to bring about His good will of forgiving sins and bringing comfort to terrified consciences. To Him alone be all glory, honor, and praise. Amen.